INFINITY COUNTDOWN

WRITER
GERRY DUGGAN

INFINITY COUNTDOWN: ADAM WARLOCK #1

ARTIST
MICHAEL ALLRED

COLOR ARTIST
LAURA ALLRED

COVER ART
AARON KUDER & IVE SVORCINA

INFINITY COUNTDOWN PRIME #1

ARTIST
MIKE DEODATO JR.

COLOR ARTIST
FRANK MARTIN

COVER ART
MIKE DEODATO JR. & FRANK MARTIN

INFINITY COUNTDOWN #1

ARTIST
AARON KUDER

COLOR ARTIST
JORDIE BELLAIRE

COVER ART
NICK BRADSHAW & MORRY HOLLOWELL

"FORGING THE ARMOR" ARTISTS
MIKE DEODATO JR. & FRANK MARTIN

INFINITY COUNTDOWN #2-5

PENCILERS
AARON KUDER & MIKE HAWTHORNE

INKERS
AARON KUDER (#2-5), **TERRY PALLOT** (#2-4) & **JOSÉ MARZAN JR.** (#4-5)

COLOR ARTIST
JORDIE BELLAIRE

COVER ART
NICK BRADSHAW & MORRY HOLLOWELL

"FORGING THE ARMOR" ARTISTS
MIKE DEODATO JR. & FRANK MARTIN

LETTERER
VC's CORY PETIT

ASSISTANT EDITOR
ANNALISE BISSA

EDITOR
JORDAN D. WHITE

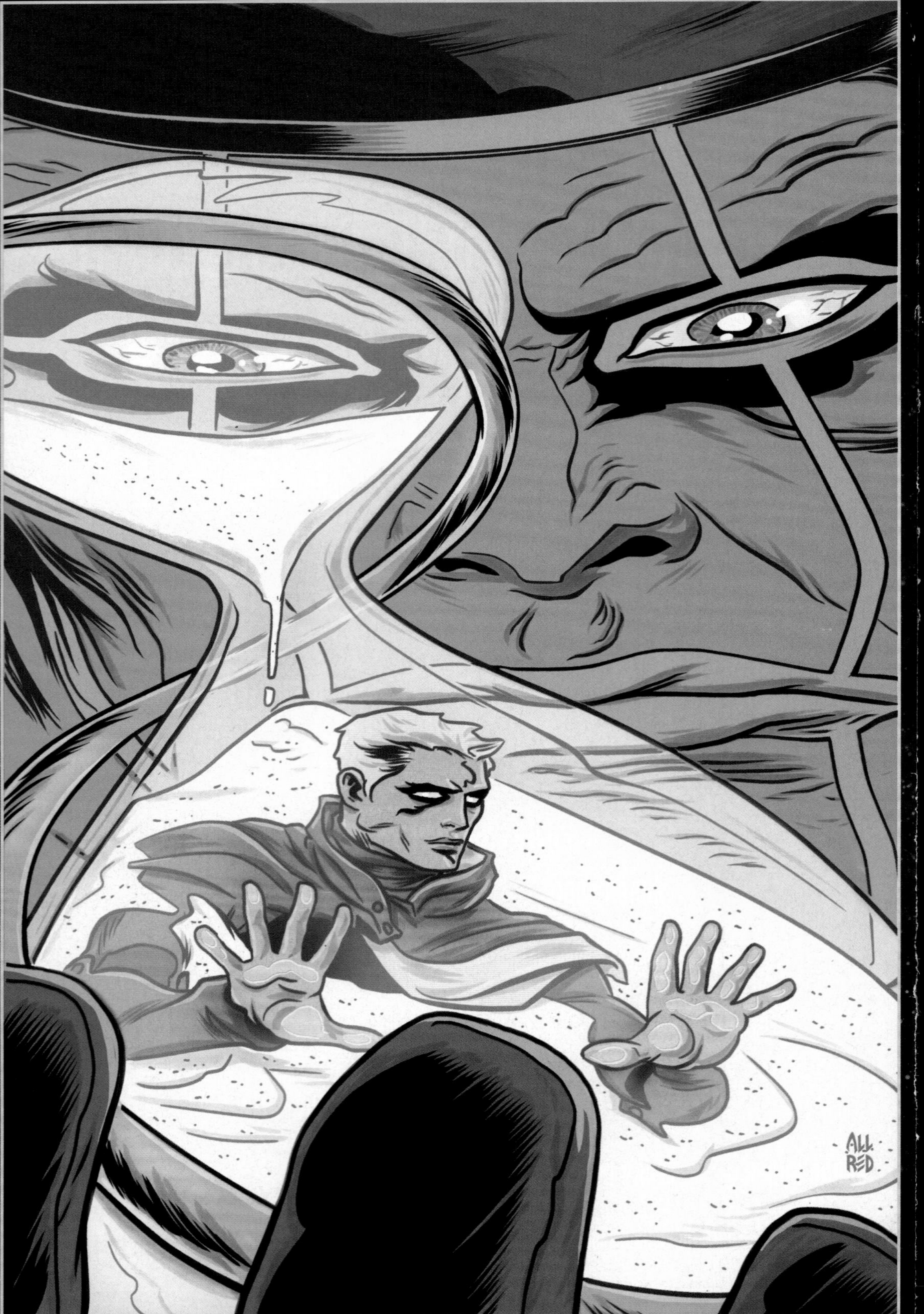
ALL RED

MICHAEL ALLRED & LAURA ALLRED

INFINITY COUNTDOWN: ADAM WARLOCK #1 VARIANT

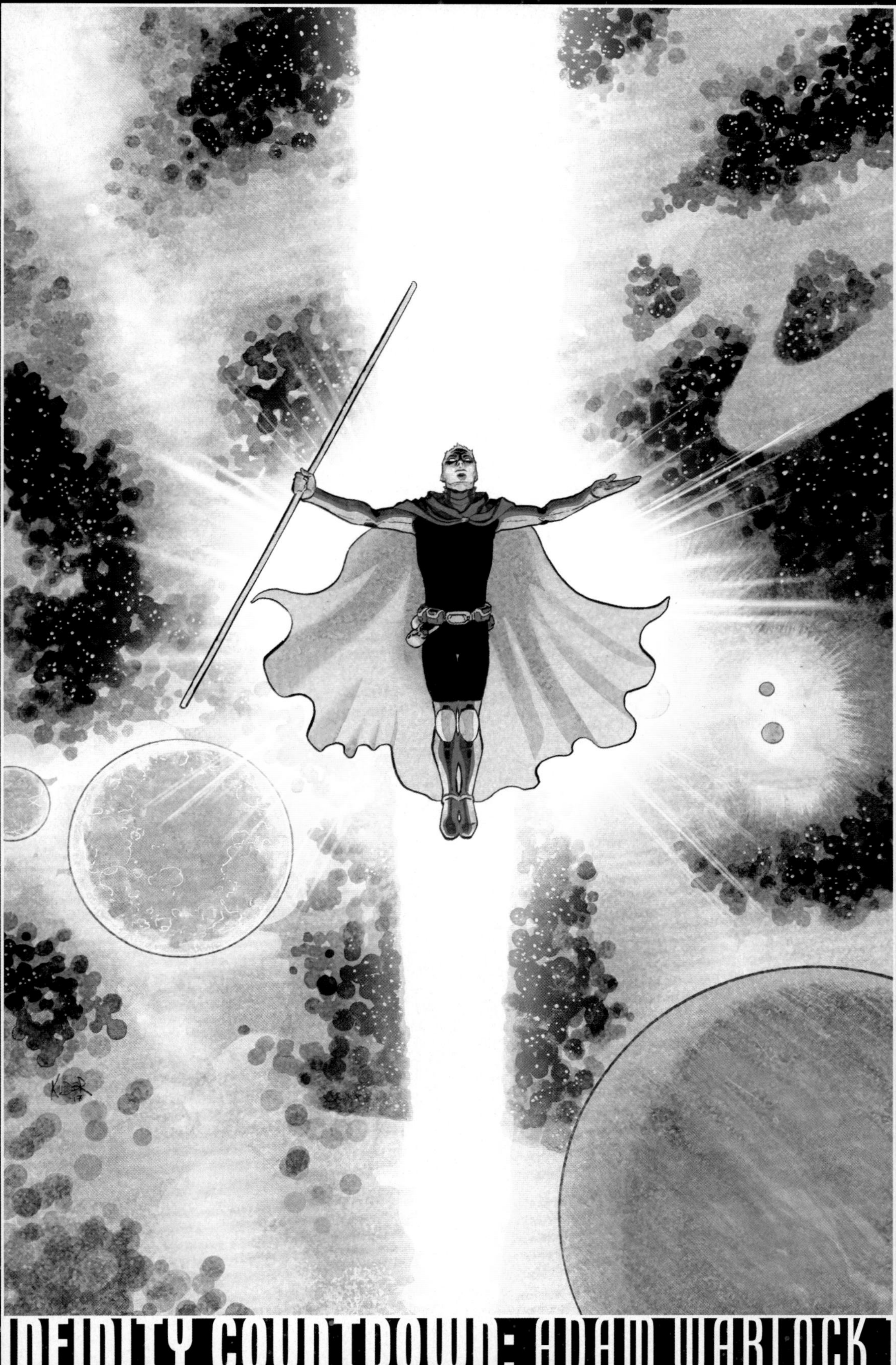

INFINITY COUNTDOWN: ADAM WARLOCK

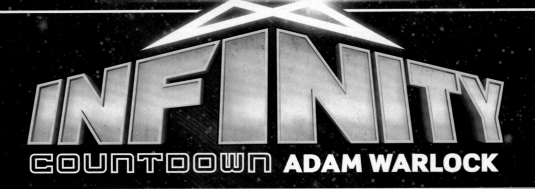

INFINITY

COUNTDOWN ADAM WARLOCK

Adam Warlock has been a son of science. A savior.
He lost and won his very soul. He had ultimate power — and sacrificed it.
Adam Warlock has seen the future — and yet he wanders.

Warlock awoke from an apocalyptic vision to find himself trapped in the wastes of Soul World,
within the Soul Stone. Making his escape, he emerged... into the clutches of Kang the Conqueror!

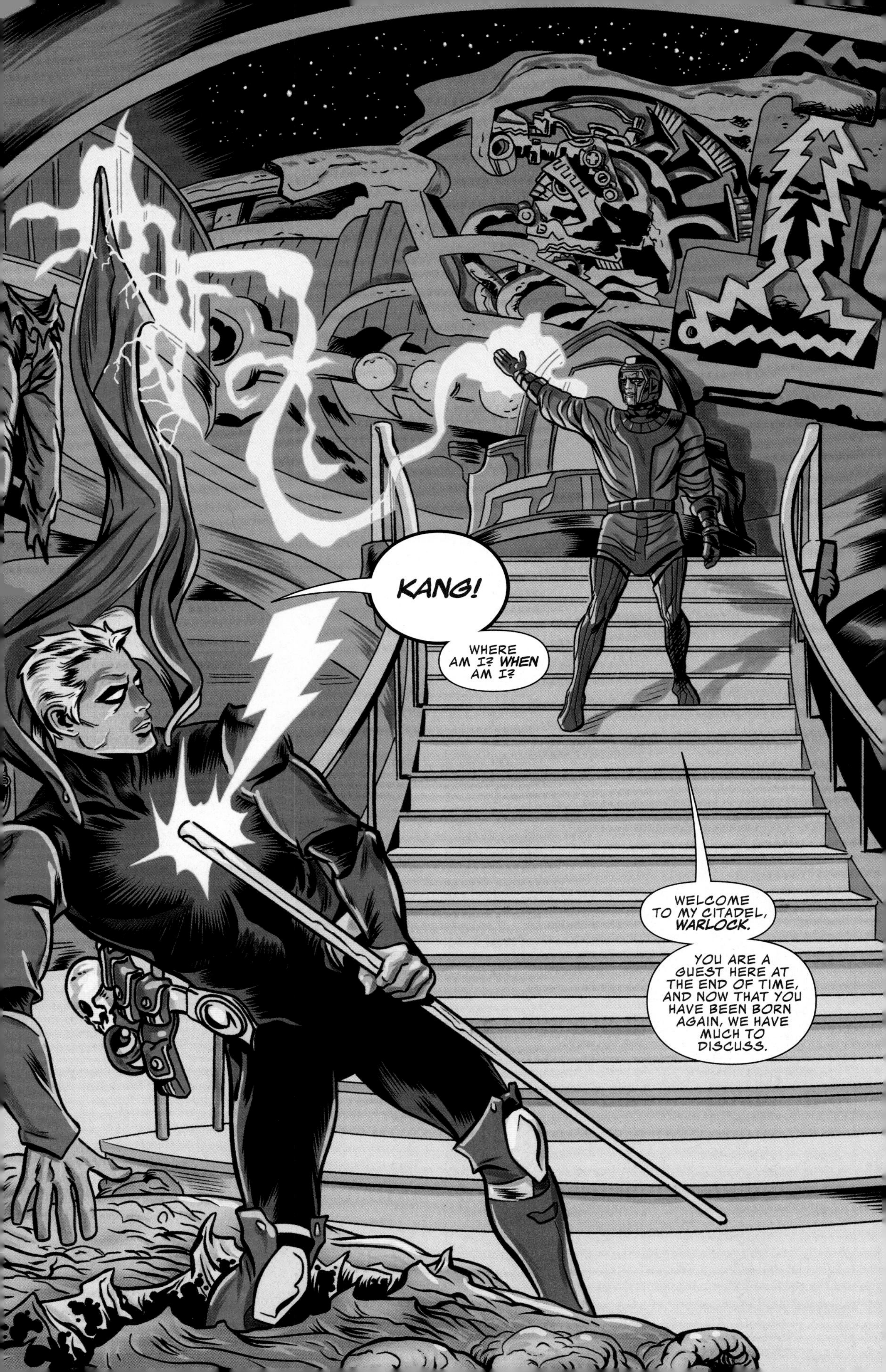
KANG!
WHERE AM I? WHEN AM I?
WELCOME TO MY CITADEL, WARLOCK.
YOU ARE A GUEST HERE AT THE END OF TIME, AND NOW THAT YOU HAVE BEEN BORN AGAIN, WE HAVE MUCH TO DISCUSS.

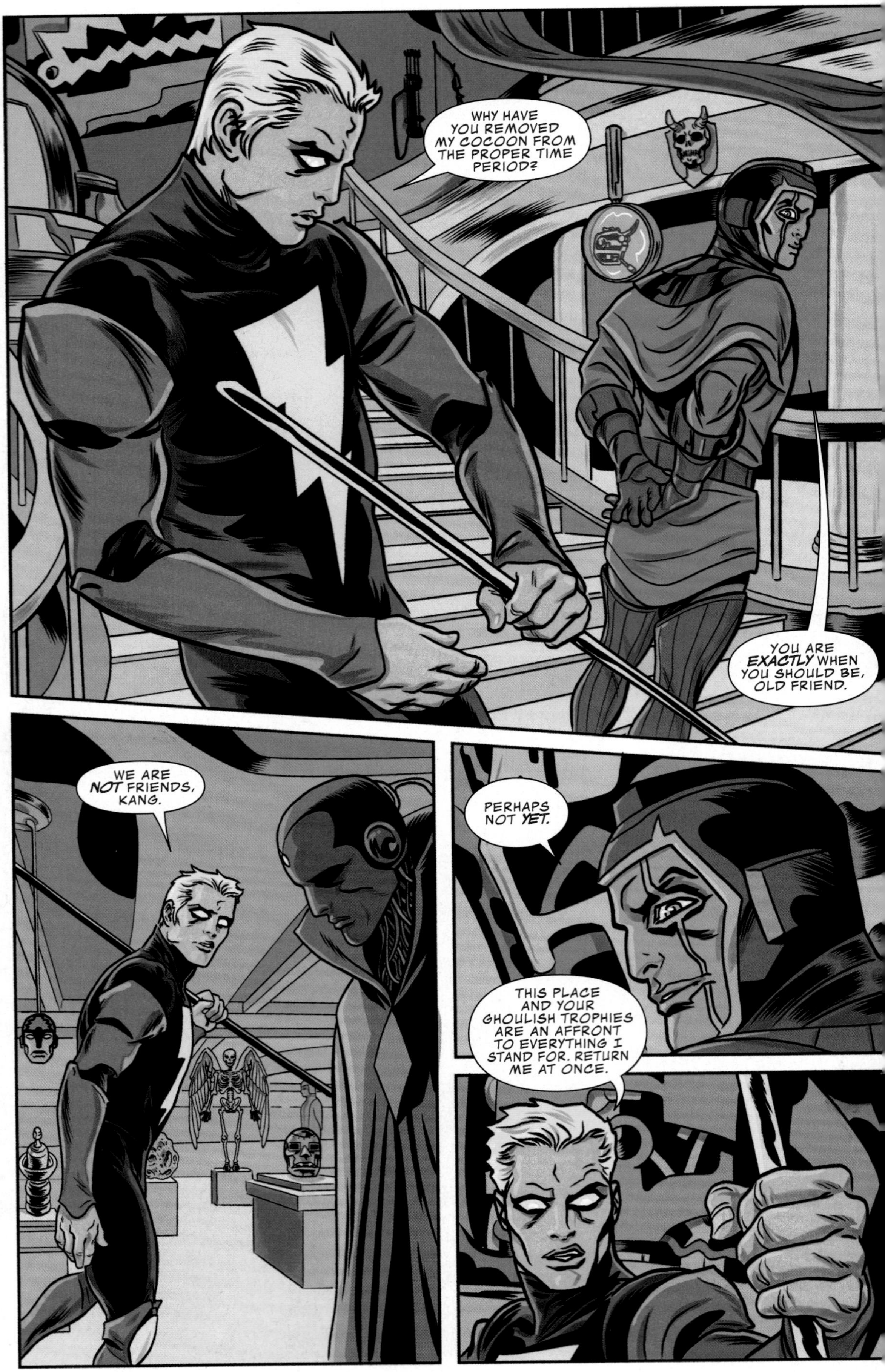
WHY HAVE YOU REMOVED MY COCOON FROM THE PROPER TIME PERIOD?
YOU ARE EXACTLY WHEN YOU SHOULD BE, OLD FRIEND.
WE ARE NOT FRIENDS, KANG.
PERHAPS NOT YET.
THIS PLACE AND YOUR GHOULISH TROPHIES ARE AN AFFRONT TO EVERYTHING I STAND FOR. RETURN ME AT ONCE.

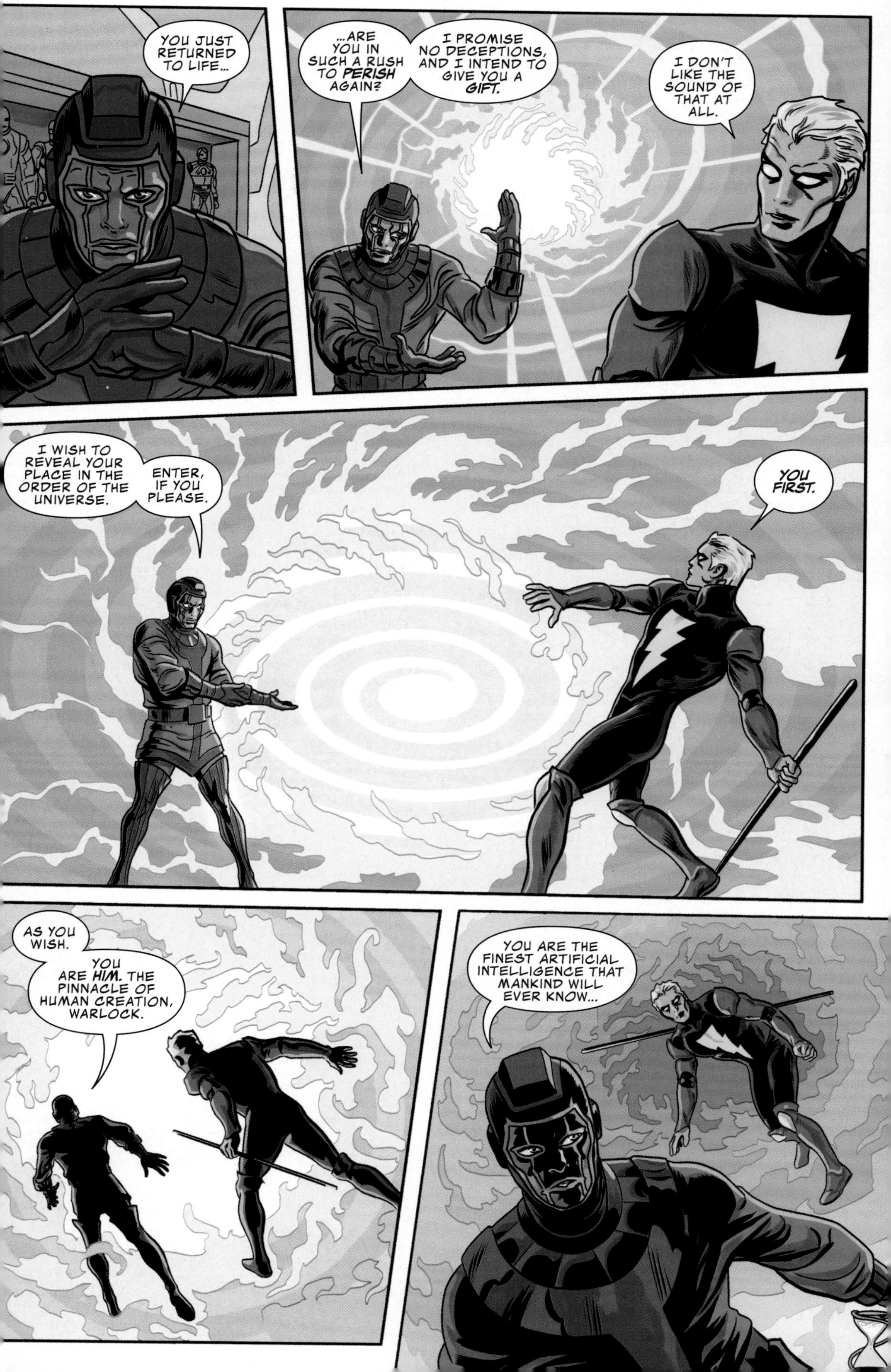
YOU JUST RETURNED TO LIFE...
...ARE YOU IN SUCH A RUSH TO **PERISH** AGAIN?
I PROMISE NO DECEPTIONS, AND I INTEND TO GIVE YOU A **GIFT.**
I DON'T LIKE THE SOUND OF THAT AT ALL.
I WISH TO REVEAL YOUR PLACE IN THE ORDER OF THE UNIVERSE.
ENTER, IF YOU PLEASE.
YOU FIRST.
AS YOU WISH.
YOU ARE **HIM.** THE PINNACLE OF HUMAN CREATION, WARLOCK.
YOU ARE THE FINEST ARTIFICIAL INTELLIGENCE THAT MANKIND WILL EVER KNOW...

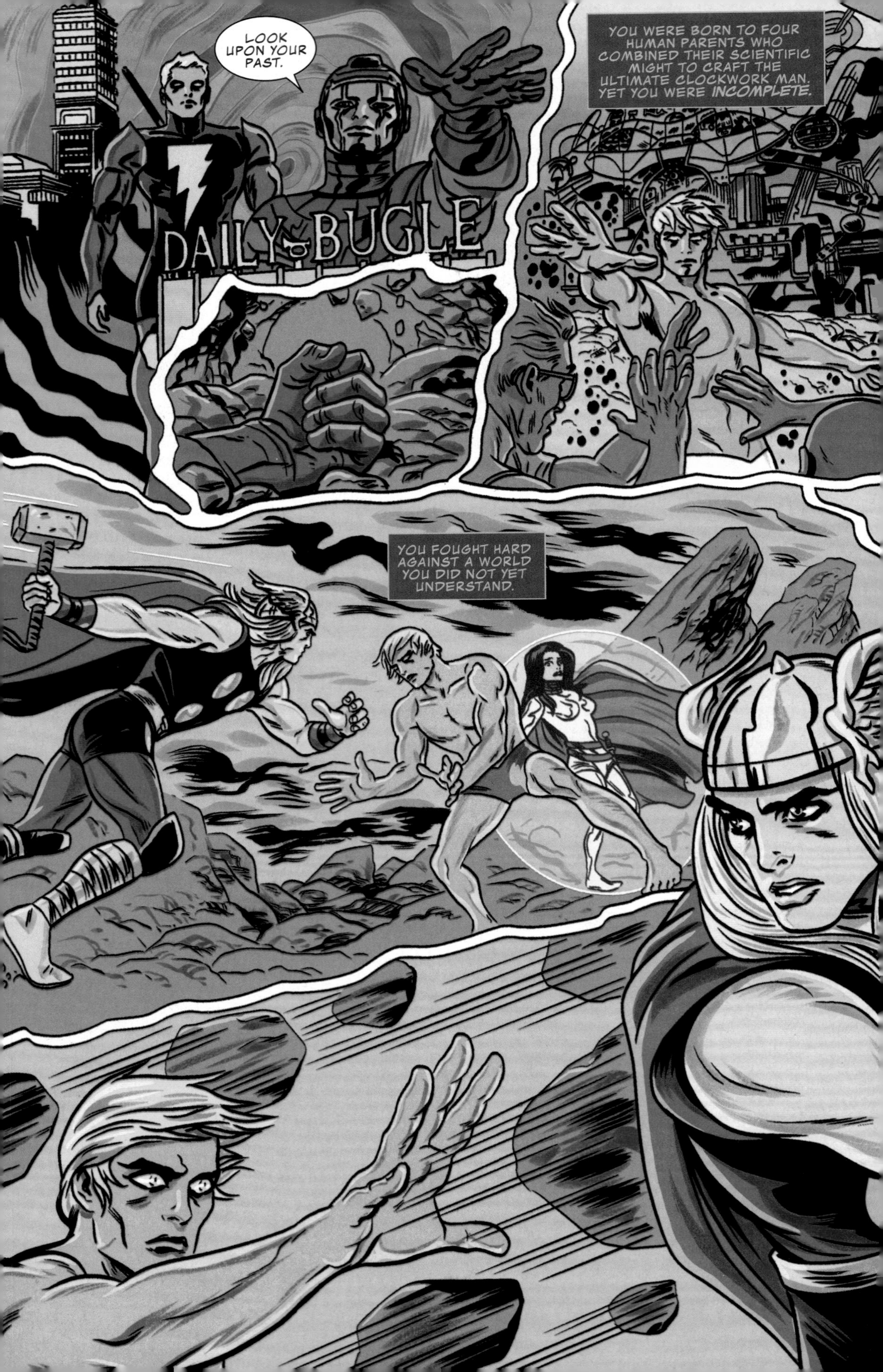
LOOK UPON YOUR PAST.
DAILY BUGLE
YOU WERE BORN TO FOUR HUMAN PARENTS WHO COMBINED THEIR SCIENTIFIC MIGHT TO CRAFT THE ULTIMATE CLOCKWORK MAN. YET YOU WERE *INCOMPLETE.*
YOU FOUGHT HARD AGAINST A WORLD YOU DID NOT YET UNDERSTAND.

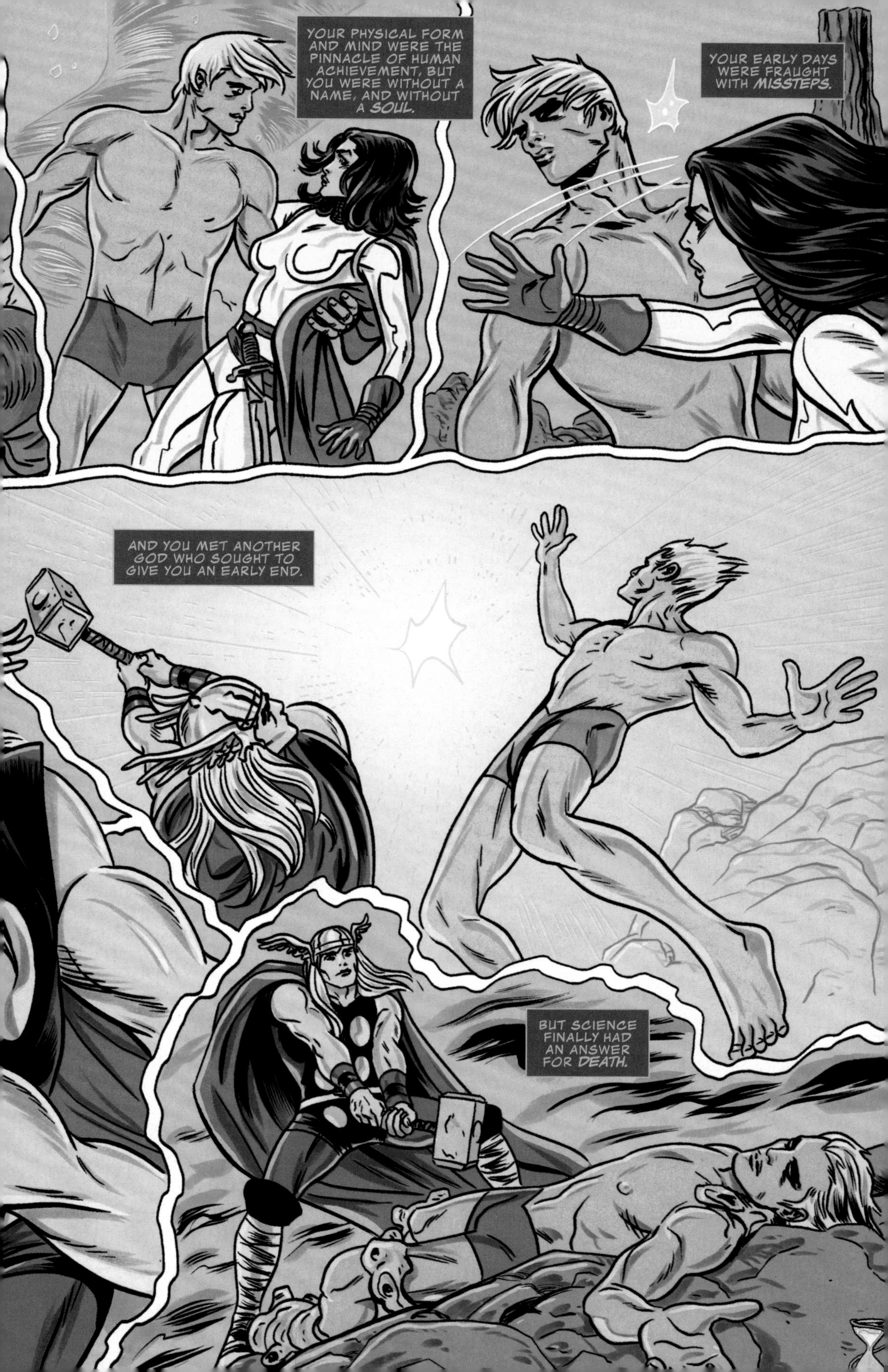
YOUR PHYSICAL FORM AND MIND WERE THE PINNACLE OF HUMAN ACHIEVEMENT, BUT YOU WERE WITHOUT A NAME, AND WITHOUT A SOUL.
YOUR EARLY DAYS WERE FRAUGHT WITH MISSTEPS.
AND YOU MET ANOTHER GOD WHO SOUGHT TO GIVE YOU AN EARLY END.
BUT SCIENCE FINALLY HAD AN ANSWER FOR DEATH.

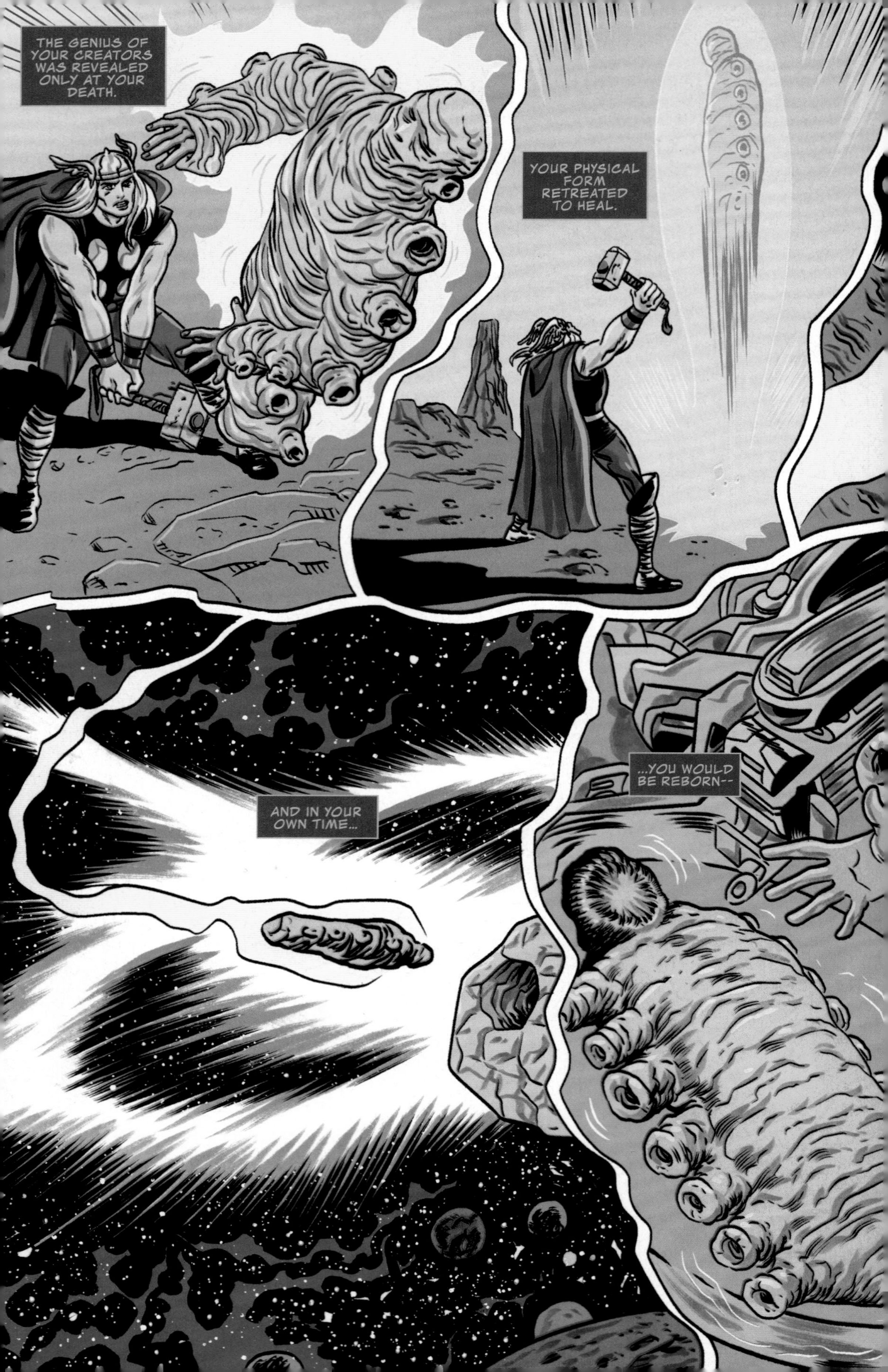
THE GENIUS OF YOUR CREATORS WAS REVEALED ONLY AT YOUR DEATH.
YOUR PHYSICAL FORM RETREATED TO HEAL.
AND IN YOUR OWN TIME...
...YOU WOULD BE REBORN--

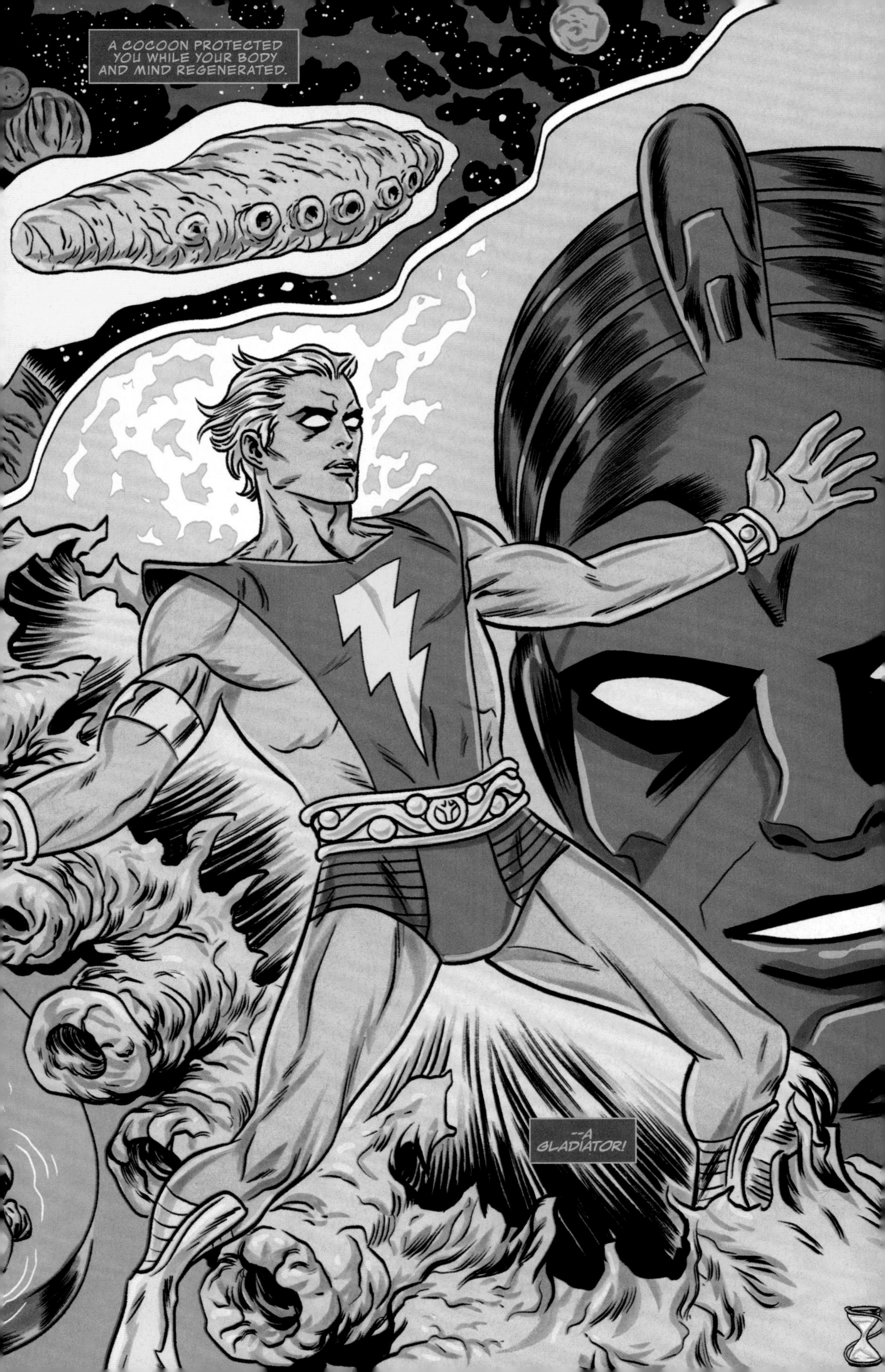
A COCOON PROTECTED YOU WHILE YOUR BODY AND MIND REGENERATED.
--A GLADIATOR!

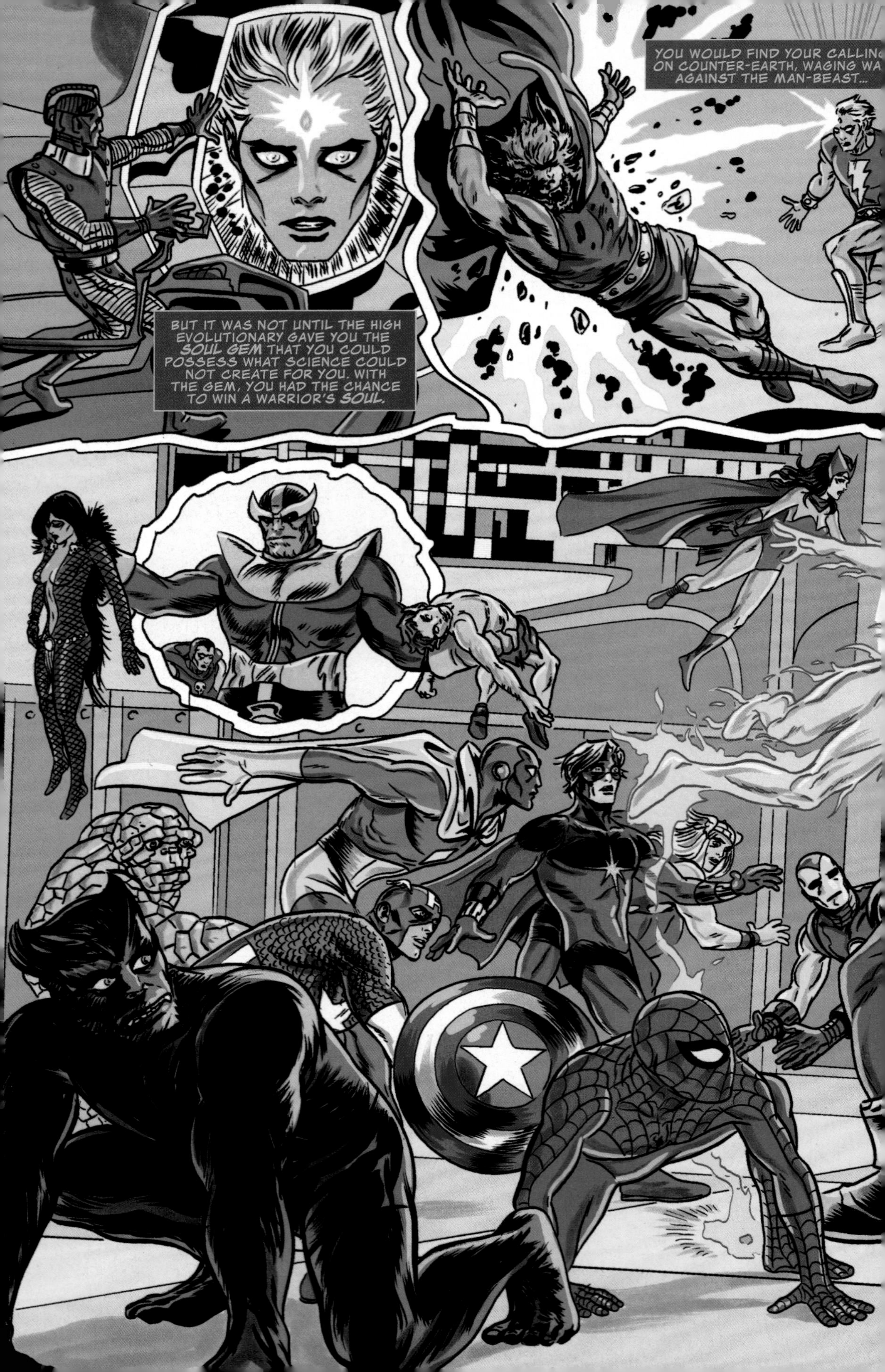
YOU WOULD FIND YOUR CALLIN
ON COUNTER-EARTH, WAGING WA
AGAINST THE MAN-BEAST...
BUT IT WAS NOT UNTIL THE HIGH EVOLUTIONARY GAVE YOU THE SOUL GEM THAT YOU COULD POSSESS WHAT SCIENCE COULD NOT CREATE FOR YOU. WITH THE GEM, YOU HAD THE CHANCE TO WIN A WARRIOR'S SOUL.

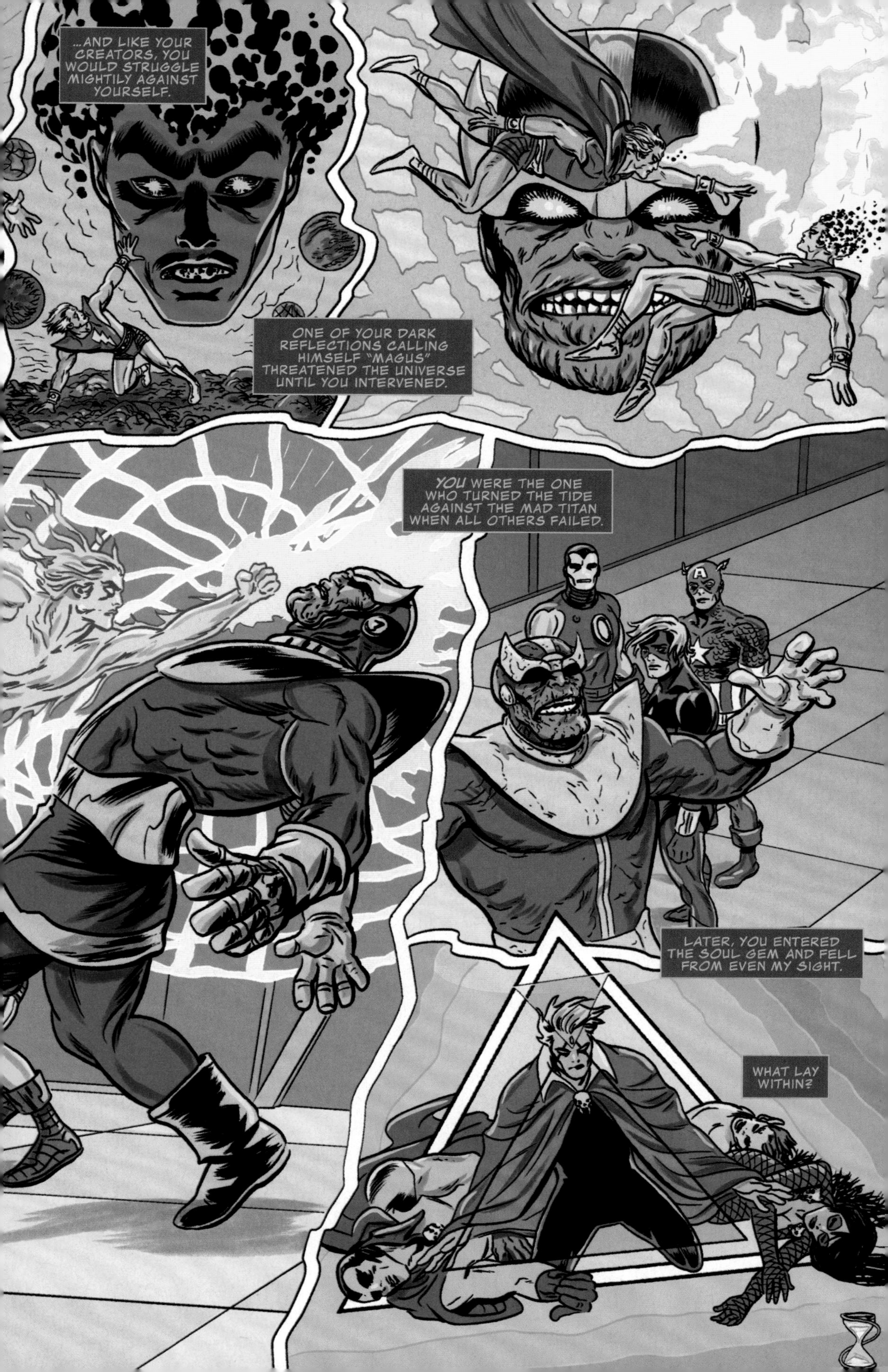
...AND LIKE YOUR CREATORS, YOU WOULD STRUGGLE MIGHTILY AGAINST YOURSELF.
ONE OF YOUR DARK REFLECTIONS CALLING HIMSELF "MAGUS" THREATENED THE UNIVERSE UNTIL YOU INTERVENED.
YOU WERE THE ONE WHO TURNED THE TIDE AGAINST THE MAD TITAN WHEN ALL OTHERS FAILED.
LATER, YOU ENTERED THE SOUL GEM AND FELL FROM EVEN MY SIGHT.
WHAT LAY WITHIN?

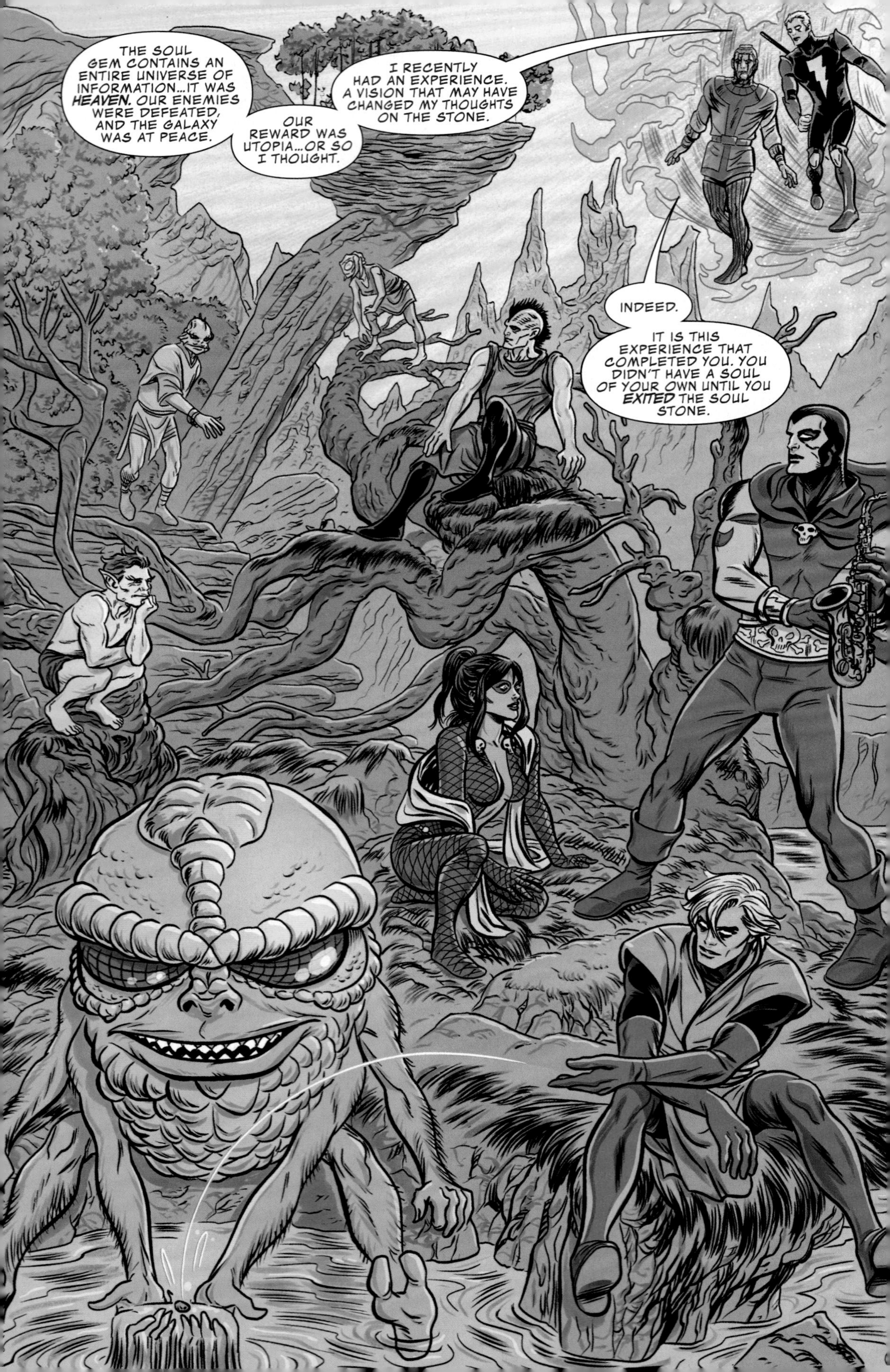
THE SOUL GEM CONTAINS AN ENTIRE UNIVERSE OF INFORMATION...IT WAS HEAVEN. OUR ENEMIES WERE DEFEATED, AND THE GALAXY WAS AT PEACE.
OUR REWARD WAS UTOPIA...OR SO I THOUGHT.
I RECENTLY HAD AN EXPERIENCE. A VISION THAT MAY HAVE CHANGED MY THOUGHTS ON THE STONE.
INDEED.
IT IS THIS EXPERIENCE THAT COMPLETED YOU. YOU DIDN'T HAVE A SOUL OF YOUR OWN UNTIL YOU EXITED THE SOUL STONE.

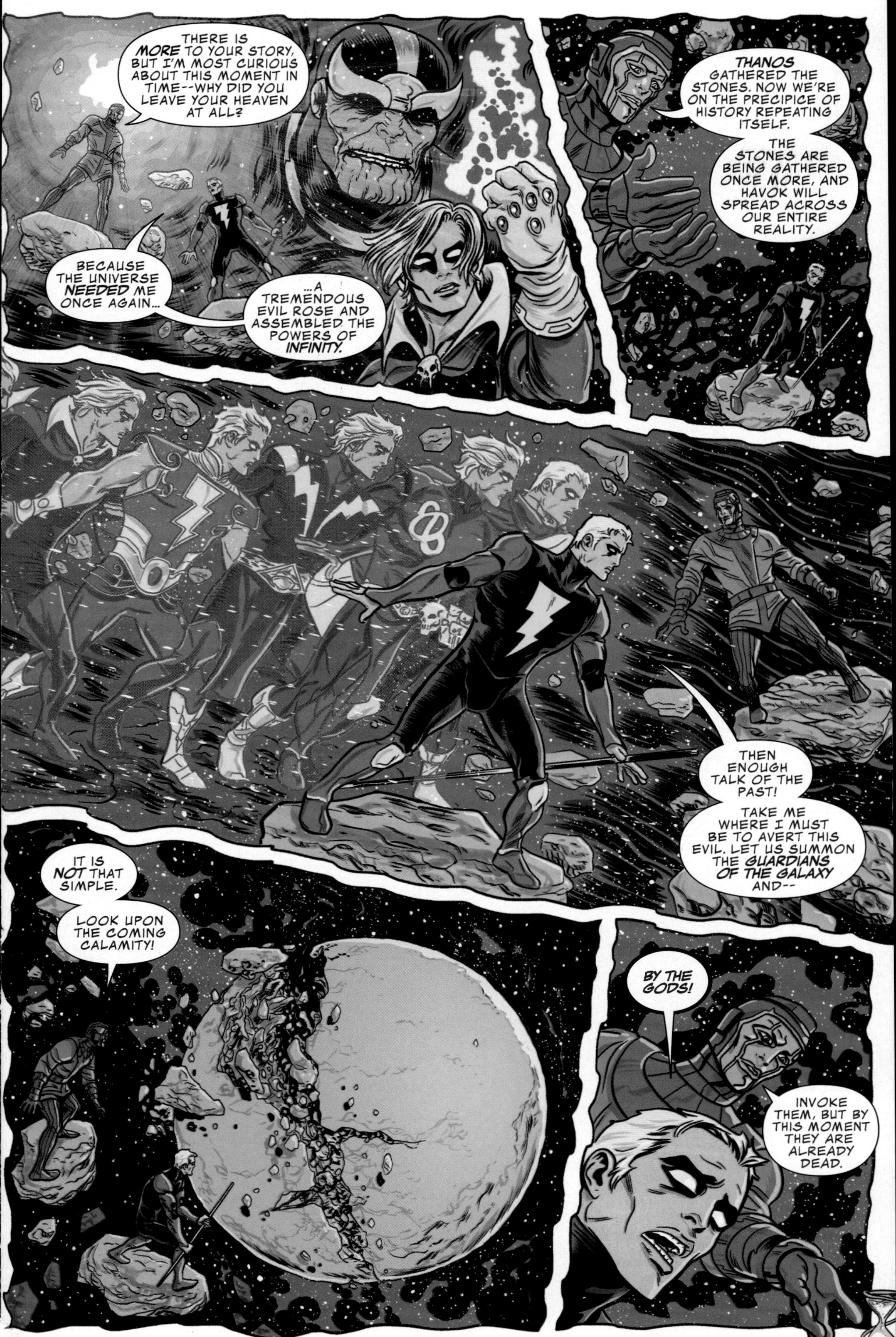
THERE IS MORE TO YOUR STORY, BUT I'M MOST CURIOUS ABOUT THIS MOMENT IN TIME--WHY DID YOU LEAVE YOUR HEAVEN AT ALL?
BECAUSE THE UNIVERSE NEEDED ME ONCE AGAIN...
...A TREMENDOUS EVIL ROSE AND ASSEMBLED THE POWERS OF INFINITY.
THANOS GATHERED THE STONES. NOW WE'RE ON THE PRECIPICE OF HISTORY REPEATING ITSELF.
THE STONES ARE BEING GATHERED ONCE MORE, AND HAVOK WILL SPREAD ACROSS OUR ENTIRE REALITY.
THEN ENOUGH TALK OF THE PAST!
TAKE ME WHERE I MUST BE TO AVERT THIS EVIL. LET US SUMMON THE GUARDIANS OF THE GALAXY AND--
IT IS NOT THAT SIMPLE.
LOOK UPON THE COMING CALAMITY!
BY THE GODS!
INVOKE THEM, BUT BY THIS MOMENT THEY ARE ALREADY DEAD.

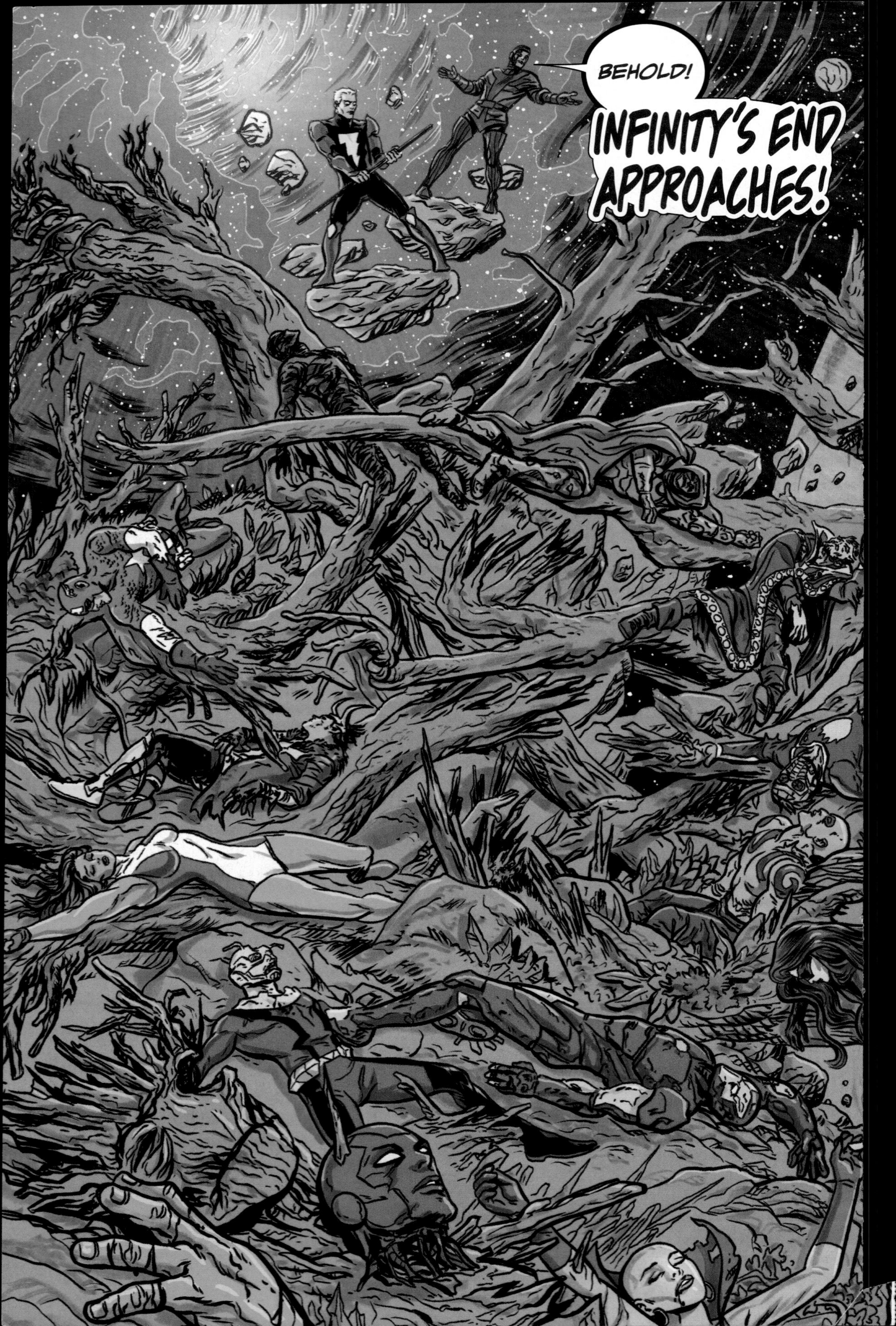
BEHOLD!
INFINITY'S END APPROACHES!

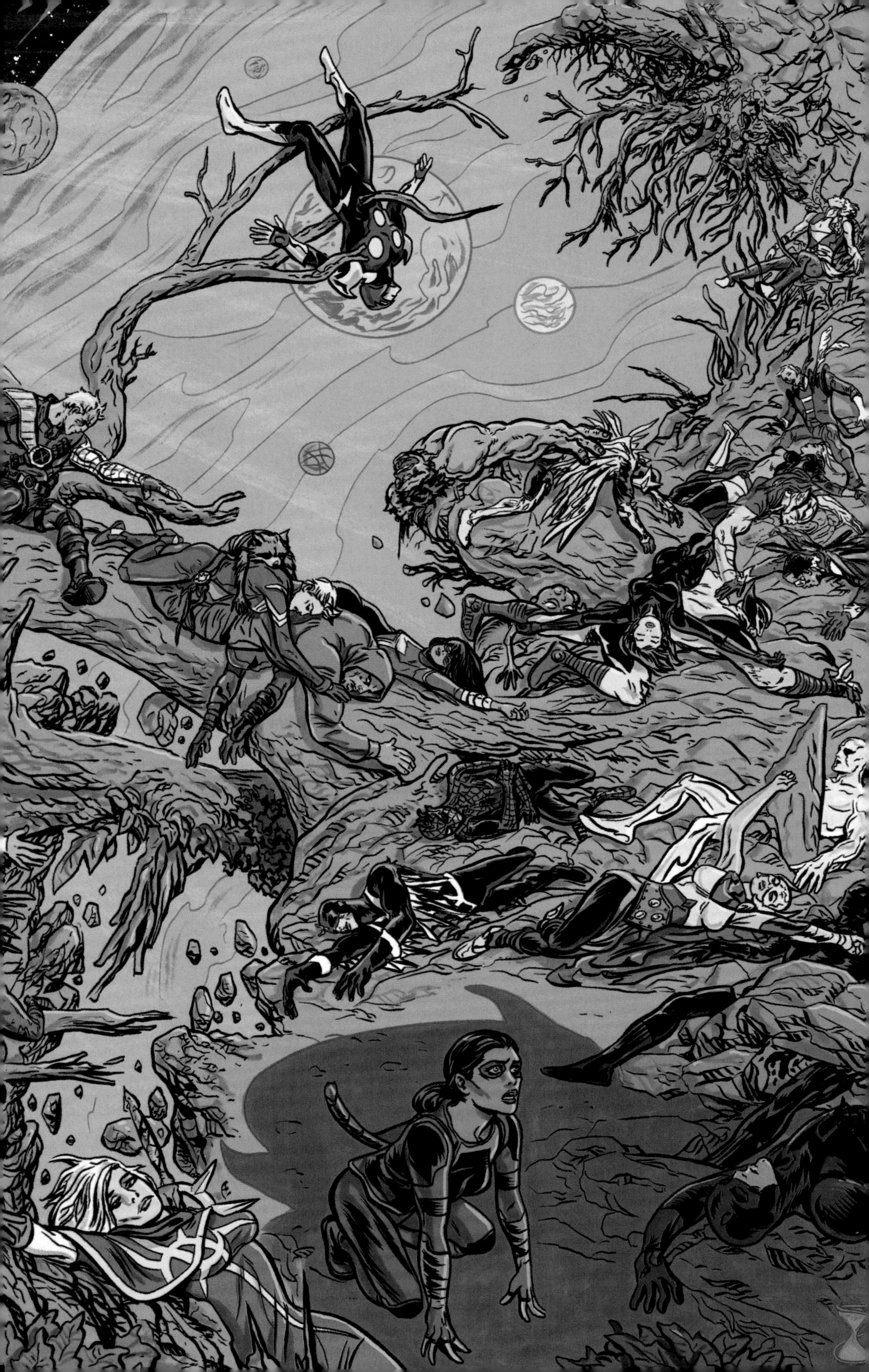

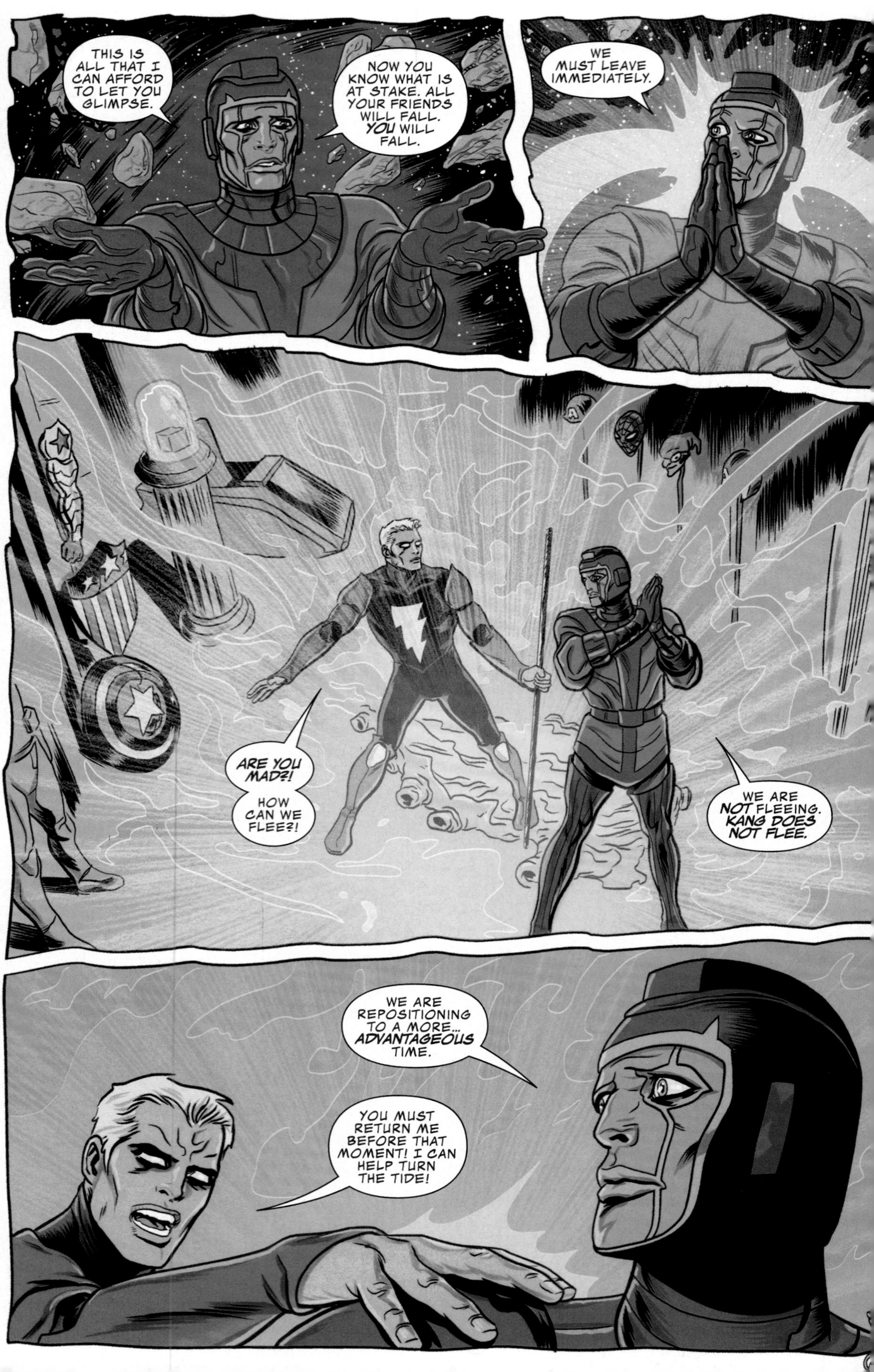
THIS IS ALL THAT I CAN AFFORD TO LET YOU GLIMPSE.
NOW YOU KNOW WHAT IS AT STAKE. ALL YOUR FRIENDS WILL FALL. YOU WILL FALL.
WE MUST LEAVE IMMEDIATELY.
ARE YOU MAD?!
HOW CAN WE FLEE?!
WE ARE NOT FLEEING. KANG DOES NOT FLEE.
WE ARE REPOSITIONING TO A MORE... ADVANTAGEOUS TIME.
YOU MUST RETURN ME BEFORE THAT MOMENT! I CAN HELP TURN THE TIDE!

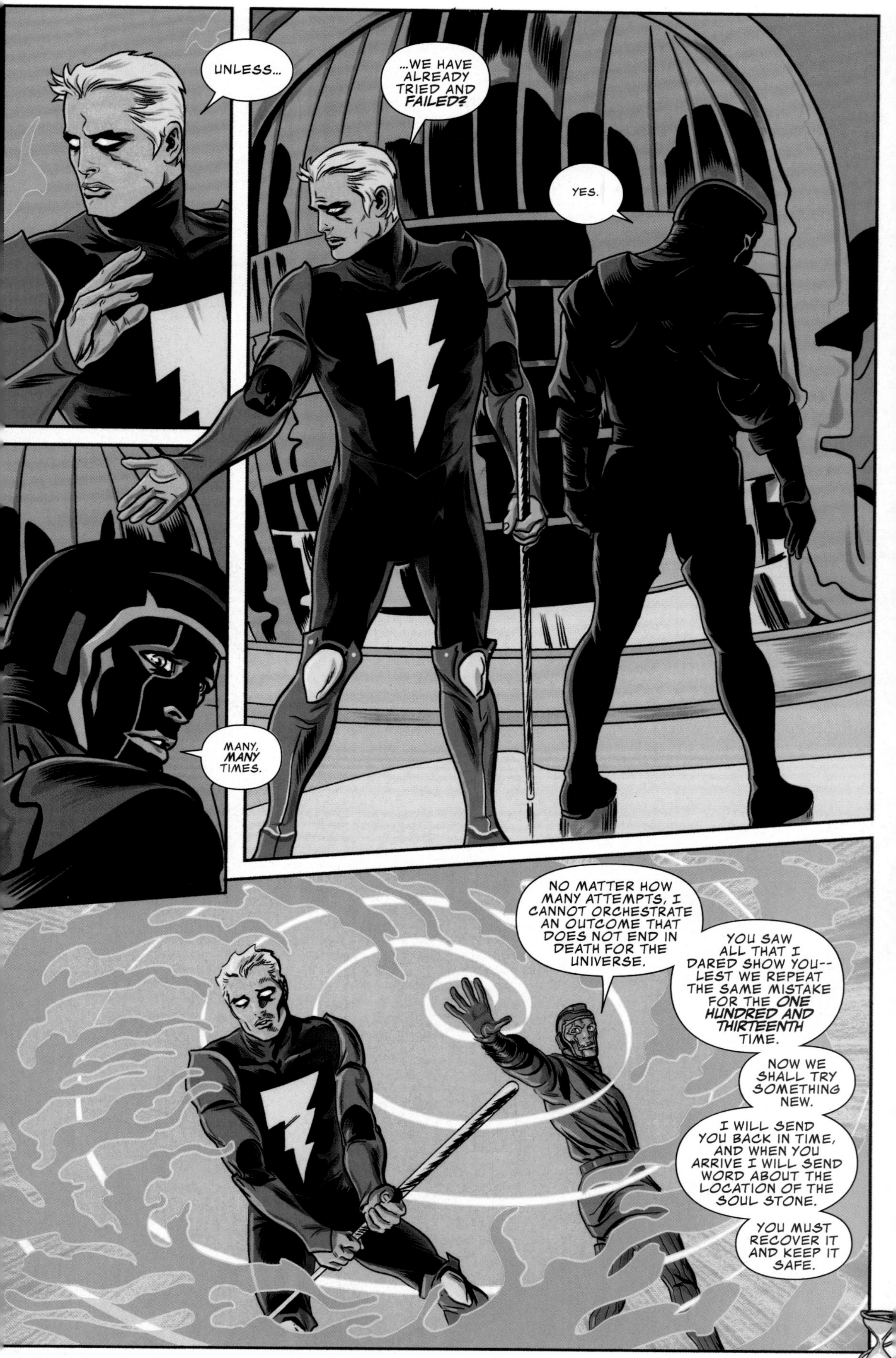
UNLESS...
...WE HAVE ALREADY TRIED AND FAILED?
YES.
MANY, MANY TIMES.
NO MATTER HOW MANY ATTEMPTS, I CANNOT ORCHESTRATE AN OUTCOME THAT DOES NOT END IN DEATH FOR THE UNIVERSE.
YOU SAW ALL THAT I DARED SHOW YOU-- LEST WE REPEAT THE SAME MISTAKE FOR THE ONE HUNDRED AND THIRTEENTH TIME.
NOW WE SHALL TRY SOMETHING NEW.
I WILL SEND YOU BACK IN TIME, AND WHEN YOU ARRIVE I WILL SEND WORD ABOUT THE LOCATION OF THE SOUL STONE.
YOU MUST RECOVER IT AND KEEP IT SAFE.

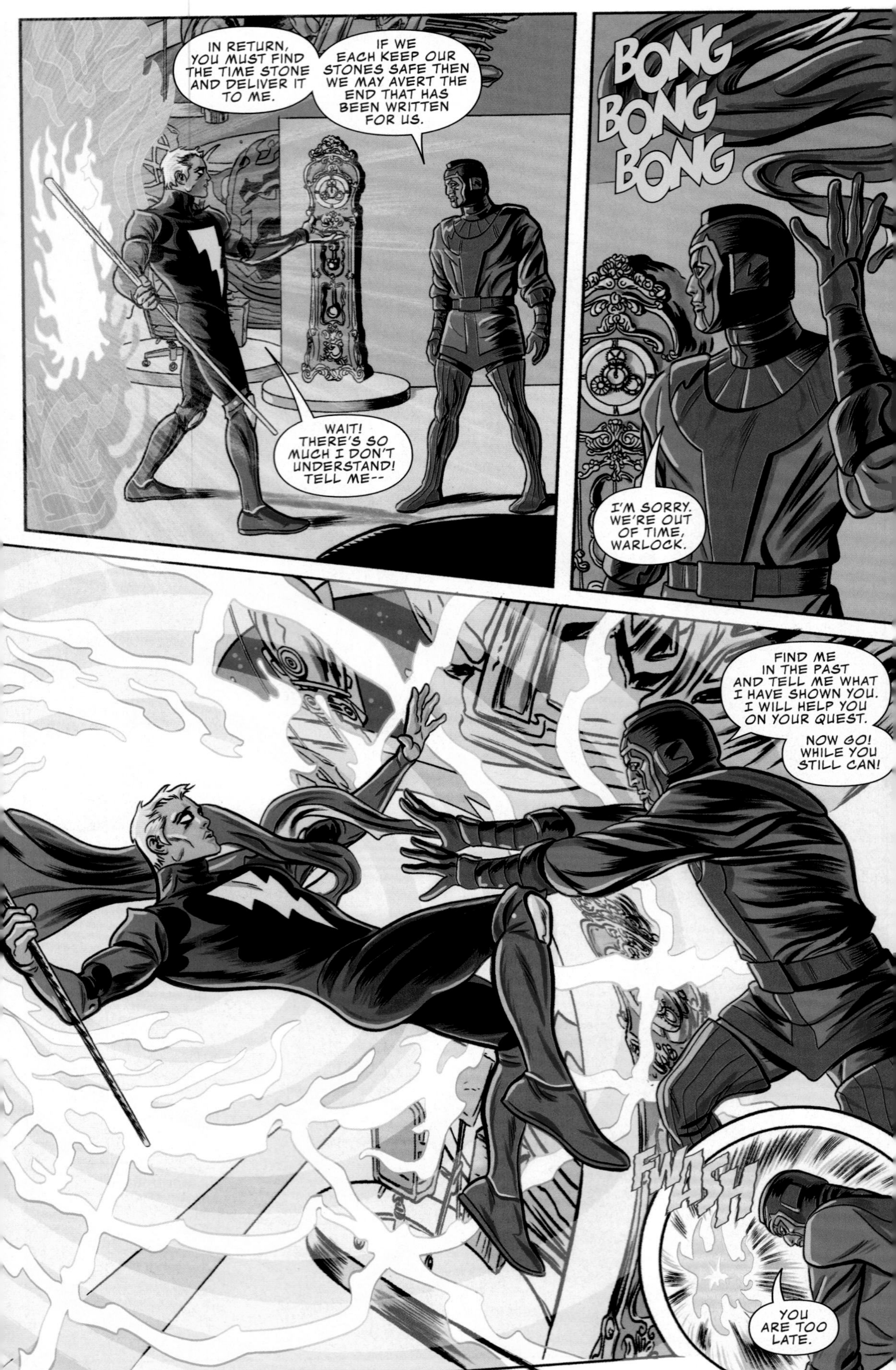
IN RETURN, YOU MUST FIND THE TIME STONE AND DELIVER IT TO ME.
IF WE EACH KEEP OUR STONES SAFE THEN WE MAY AVERT THE END THAT HAS BEEN WRITTEN FOR US.
WAIT! THERE'S SO MUCH I DON'T UNDERSTAND! TELL ME--
BONG BONG BONG
I'M SORRY. WE'RE OUT OF TIME, WARLOCK.
FIND ME IN THE PAST AND TELL ME WHAT I HAVE SHOWN YOU. I WILL HELP YOU ON YOUR QUEST.
NOW GO! WHILE YOU STILL CAN!
FWOSH
YOU ARE TOO LATE.

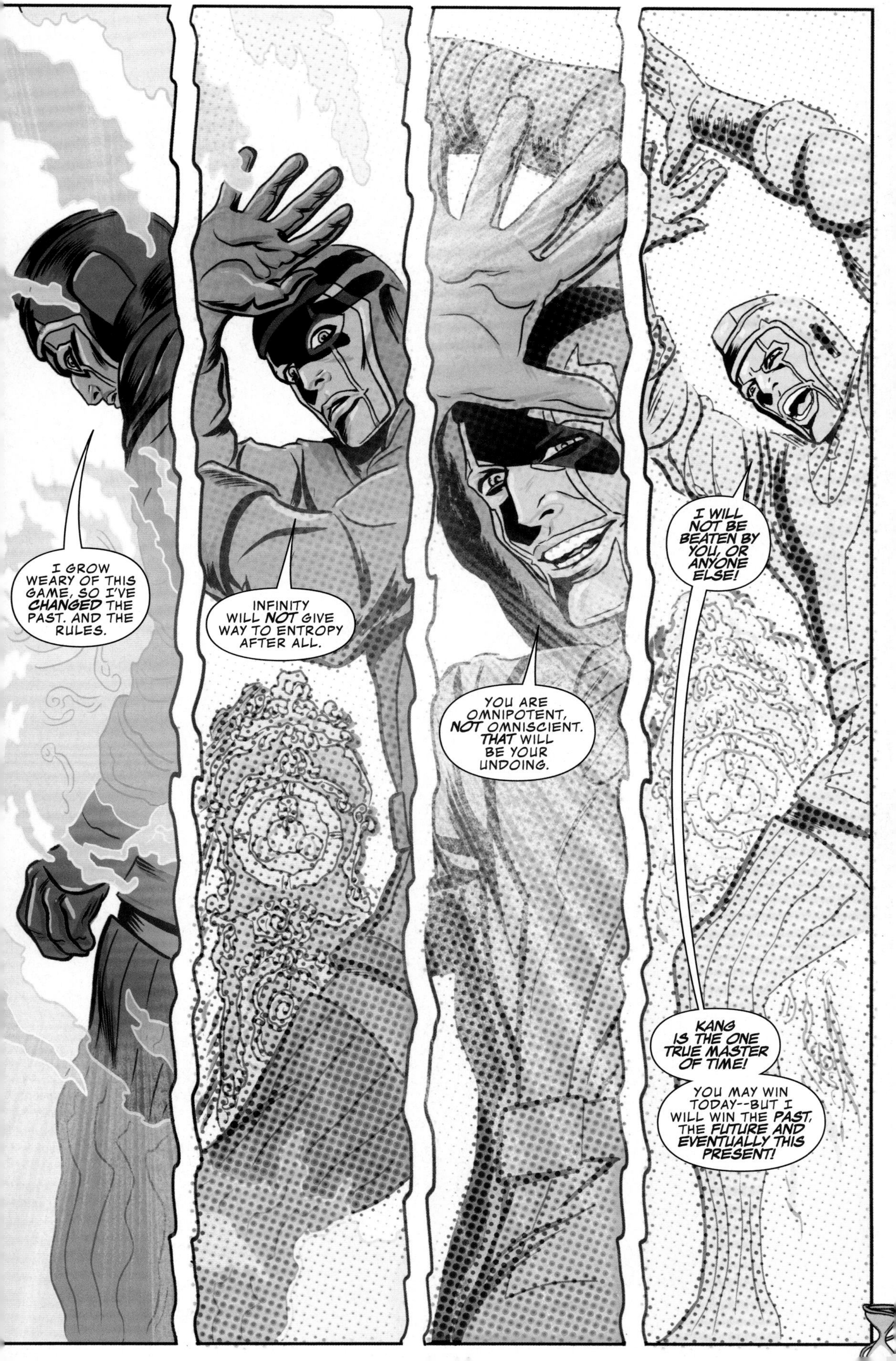
I GROW WEARY OF THIS GAME, SO I'VE CHANGED THE PAST. AND THE RULES.
INFINITY WILL NOT GIVE WAY TO ENTROPY AFTER ALL.
YOU ARE OMNIPOTENT, NOT OMNISCIENT. THAT WILL BE YOUR UNDOING.
I WILL NOT BE BEATEN BY YOU, OR ANYONE ELSE!
KANG IS THE ONE TRUE MASTER OF TIME!
YOU MAY WIN TODAY--BUT I WILL WIN THE PAST, THE FUTURE AND EVENTUALLY THIS PRESENT!

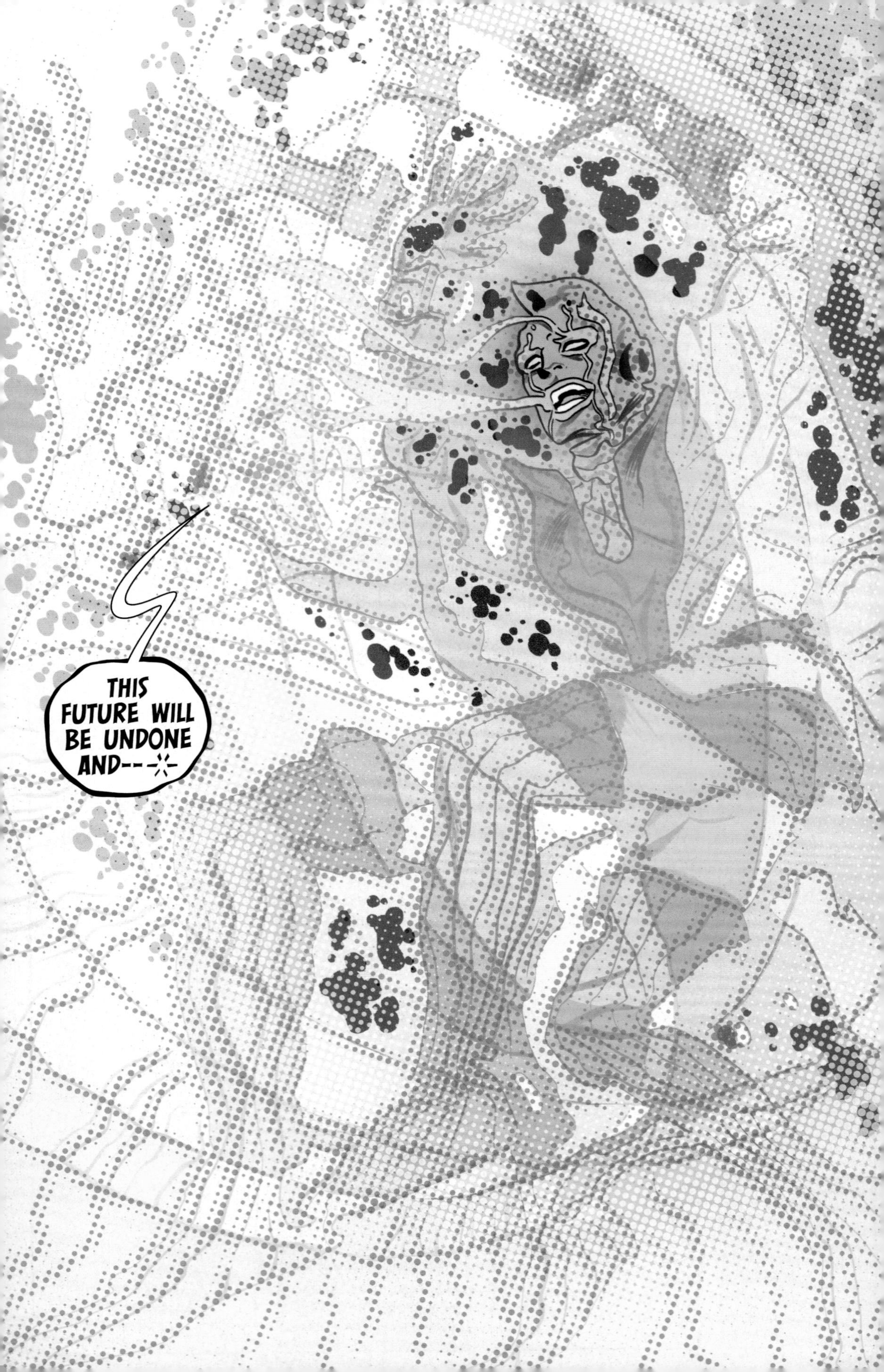
THIS FUTURE WILL BE UNDONE AND--

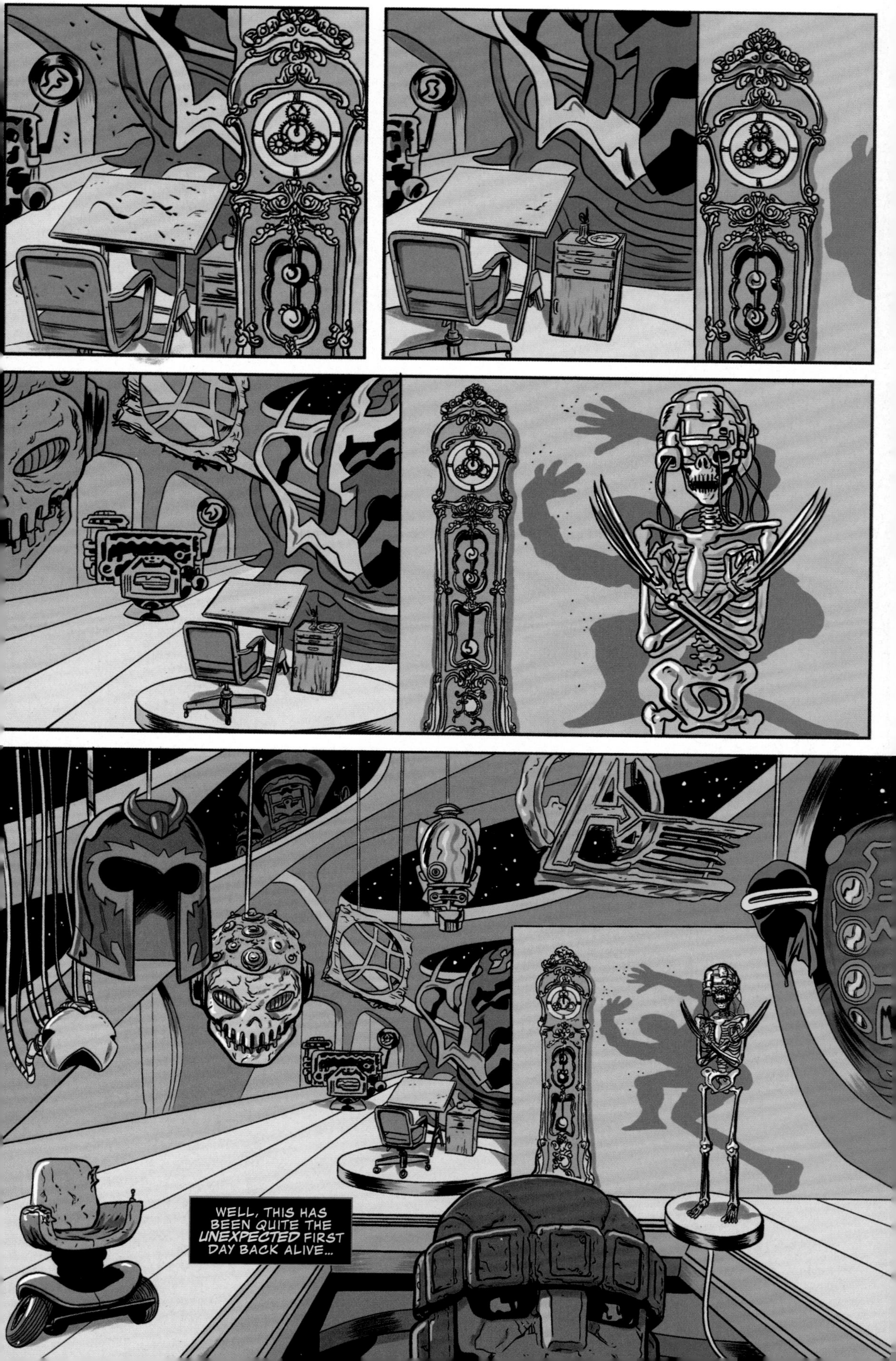
WELL, THIS HAS BEEN QUITE THE UNEXPECTED FIRST DAY BACK ALIVE...

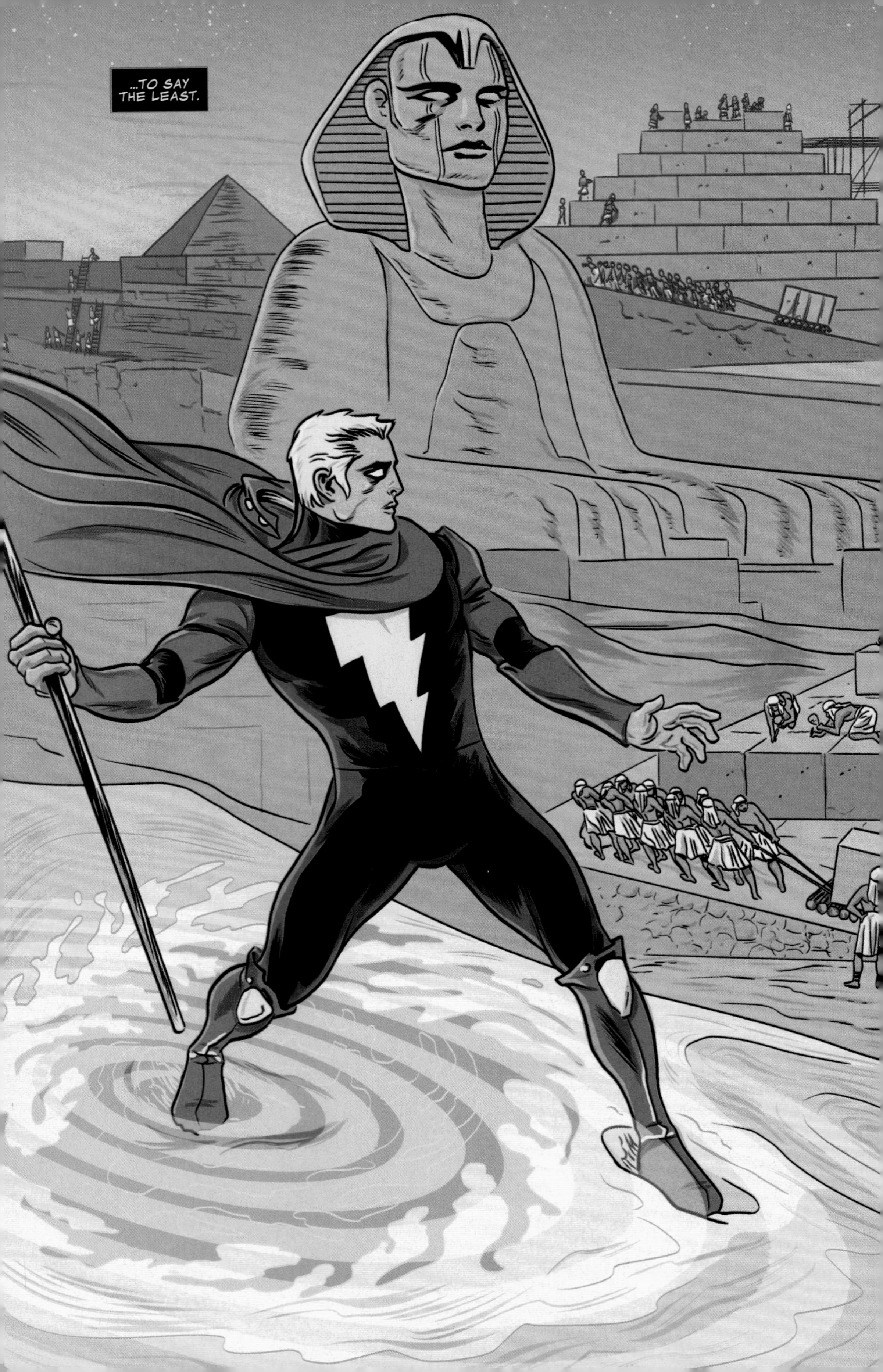
...TO SAY THE LEAST.

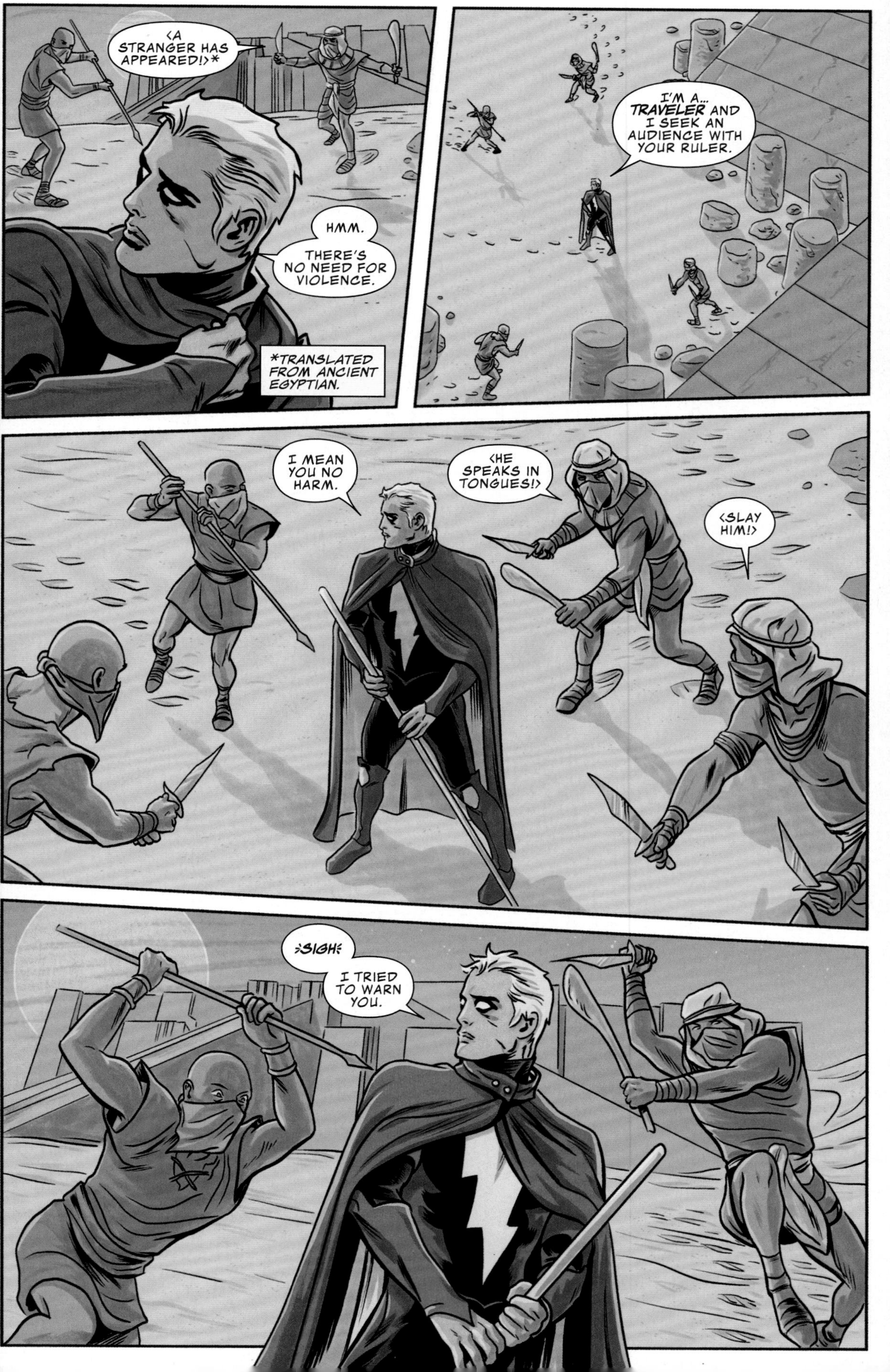

<A STRANGER HAS APPEARED!>*
HMM.
THERE'S NO NEED FOR VIOLENCE.
*TRANSLATED FROM ANCIENT EGYPTIAN.
I'M A... TRAVELER AND I SEEK AN AUDIENCE WITH YOUR RULER.
I MEAN YOU NO HARM.
<HE SPEAKS IN TONGUES!>
<SLAY HIM!>
SIGH
I TRIED TO WARN YOU.

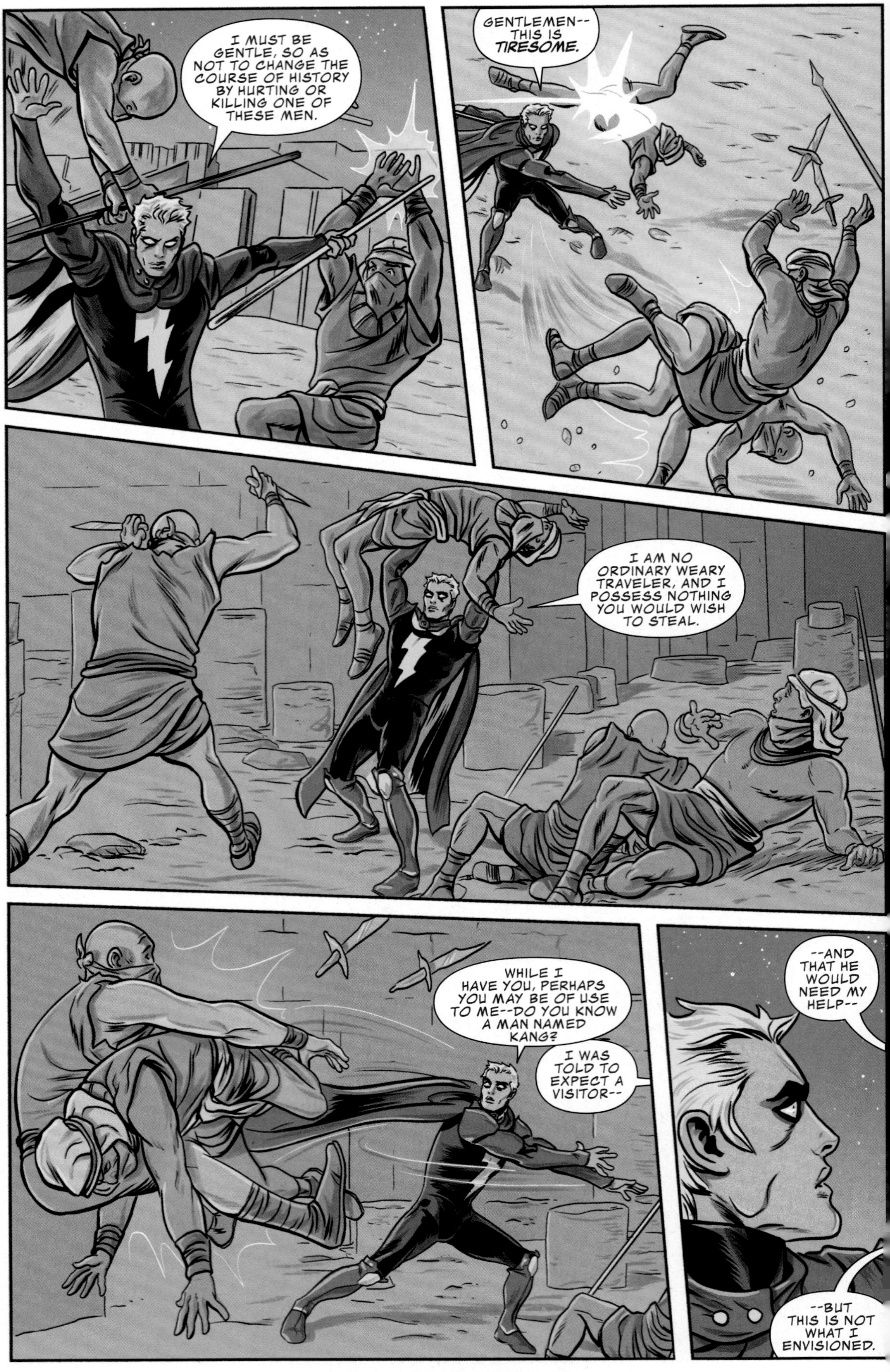
I MUST BE GENTLE, SO AS NOT TO CHANGE THE COURSE OF HISTORY BY HURTING OR KILLING ONE OF THESE MEN.
GENTLEMEN-- THIS IS *TIRESOME.*
I AM NO ORDINARY WEARY TRAVELER, AND I POSSESS NOTHING YOU WOULD WISH TO STEAL.
WHILE I HAVE YOU, PERHAPS YOU MAY BE OF USE TO ME--DO YOU KNOW A MAN NAMED KANG?
I WAS TOLD TO EXPECT A VISITOR--
--AND THAT HE WOULD NEED MY HELP--
--BUT THIS IS NOT WHAT I ENVISIONED.

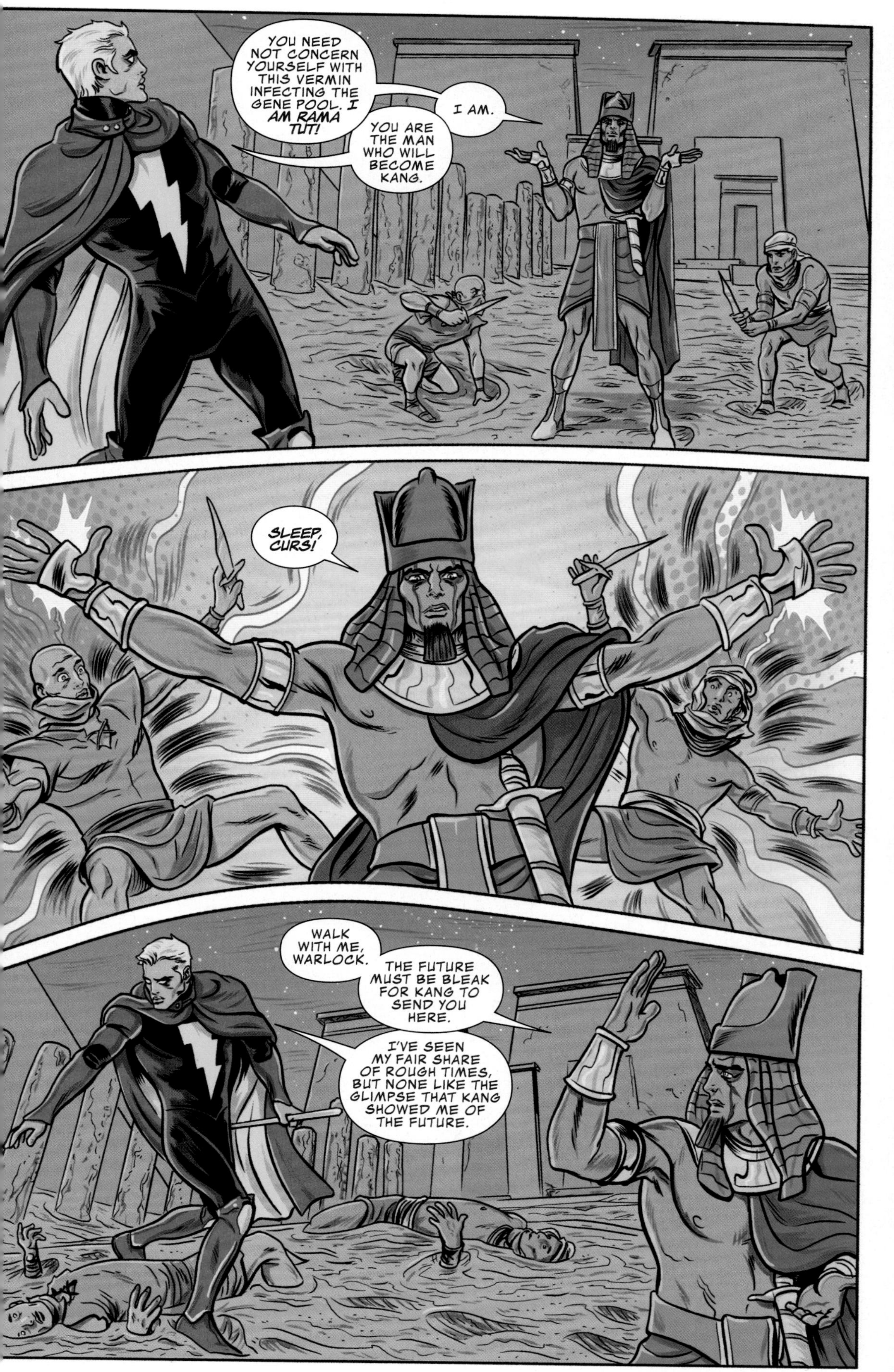
YOU NEED NOT CONCERN YOURSELF WITH THIS VERMIN INFECTING THE GENE POOL. I AM RAMA TUT!
YOU ARE THE MAN WHO WILL BECOME KANG.
I AM.
SLEEP, CURS!
WALK WITH ME, WARLOCK.
THE FUTURE MUST BE BLEAK FOR KANG TO SEND YOU HERE.
I'VE SEEN MY FAIR SHARE OF ROUGH TIMES, BUT NONE LIKE THE GLIMPSE THAT KANG SHOWED ME OF THE FUTURE.

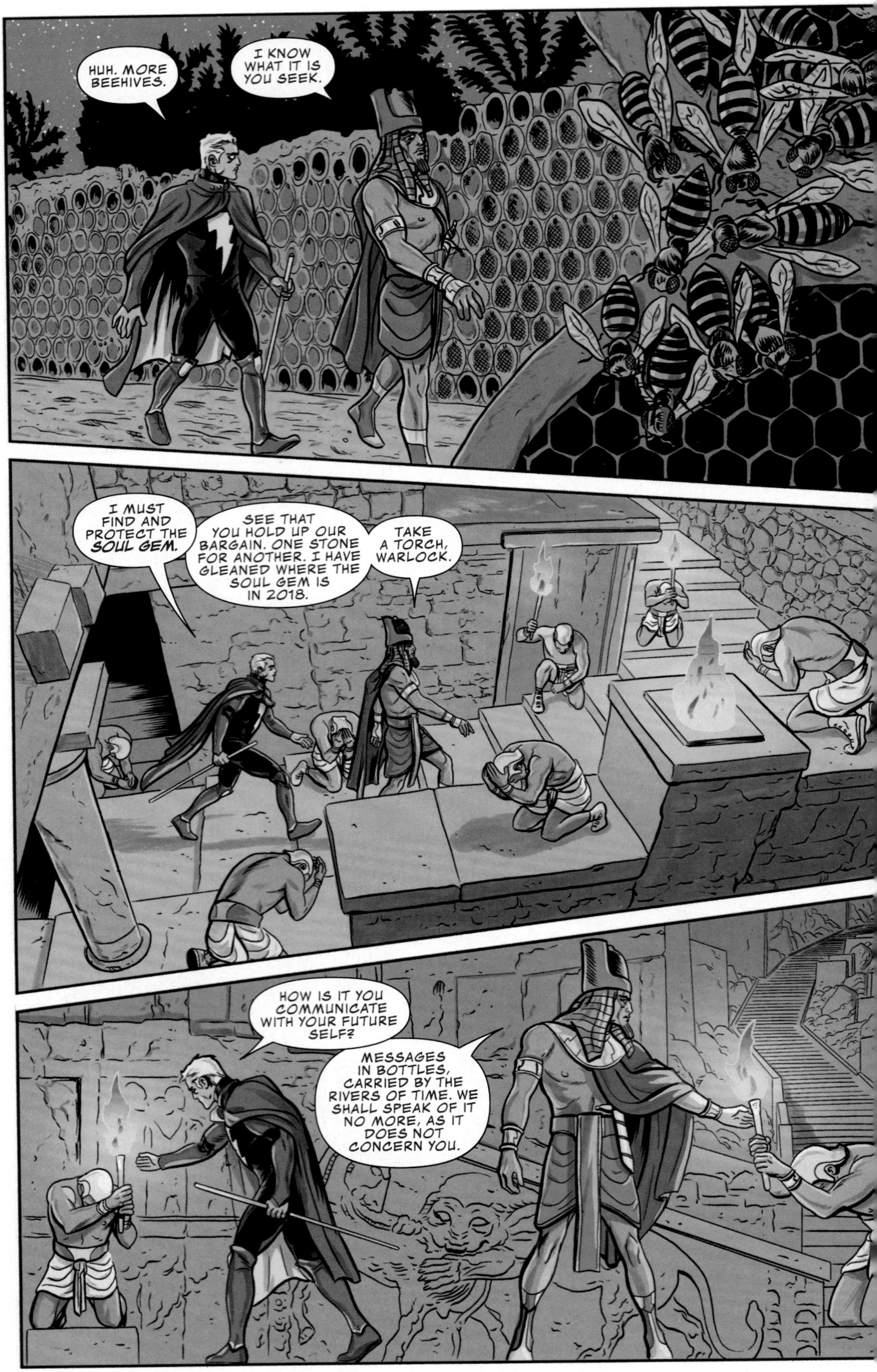
HUH. MORE BEEHIVES.
I KNOW WHAT IT IS YOU SEEK.
I MUST FIND AND PROTECT THE SOUL GEM.
SEE THAT YOU HOLD UP OUR BARGAIN. ONE STONE FOR ANOTHER. I HAVE GLEANED WHERE THE SOUL GEM IS IN 2018.
TAKE A TORCH, WARLOCK.
HOW IS IT YOU COMMUNICATE WITH YOUR FUTURE SELF?
MESSAGES IN BOTTLES, CARRIED BY THE RIVERS OF TIME. WE SHALL SPEAK OF IT NO MORE, AS IT DOES NOT CONCERN YOU.

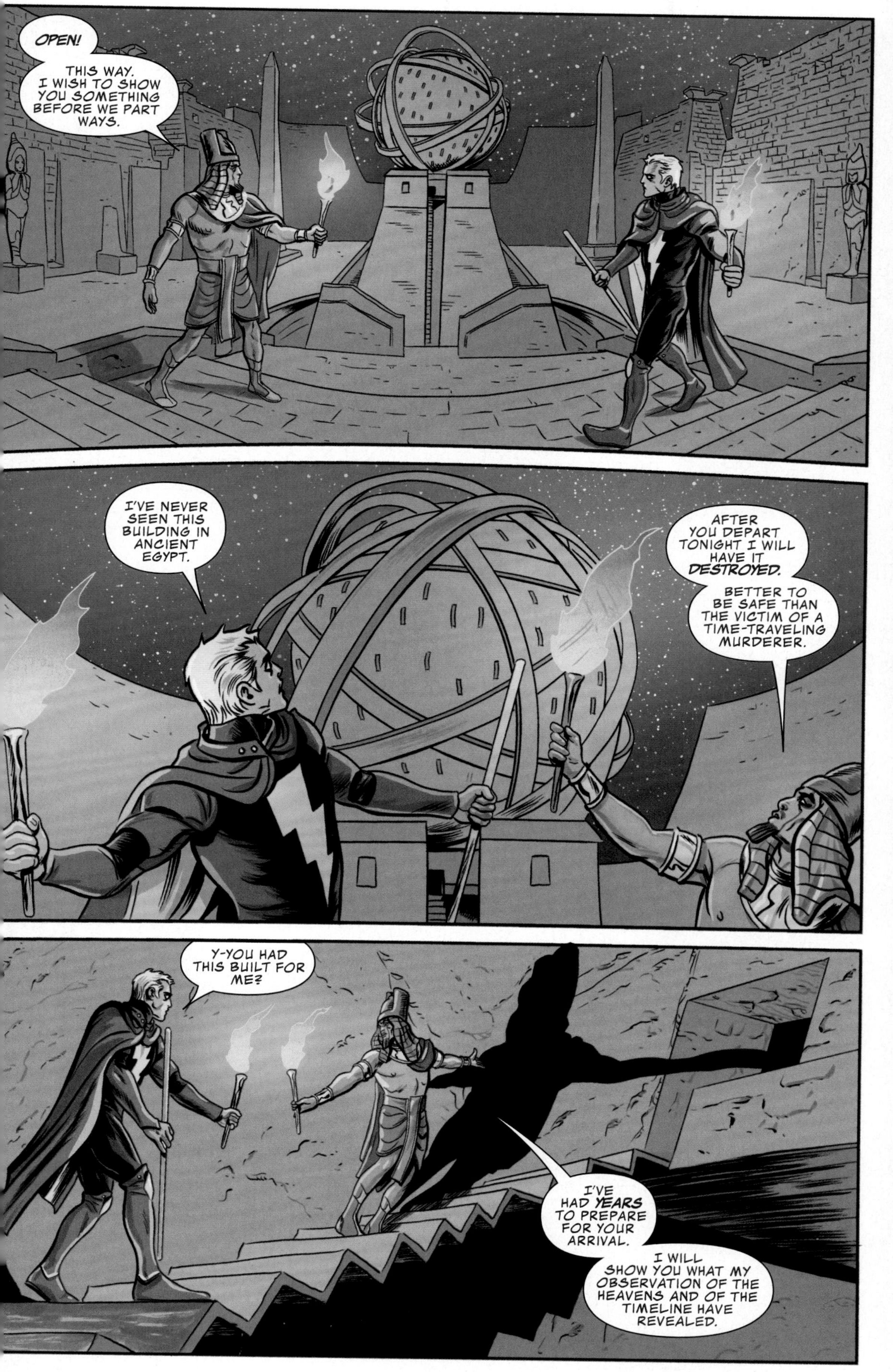
OPEN!
THIS WAY. I WISH TO SHOW YOU SOMETHING BEFORE WE PART WAYS.
I'VE NEVER SEEN THIS BUILDING IN ANCIENT EGYPT.
AFTER YOU DEPART TONIGHT I WILL HAVE IT DESTROYED.
BETTER TO BE SAFE THAN THE VICTIM OF A TIME-TRAVELING MURDERER.
Y-YOU HAD THIS BUILT FOR ME?
I'VE HAD YEARS TO PREPARE FOR YOUR ARRIVAL.
I WILL SHOW YOU WHAT MY OBSERVATION OF THE HEAVENS AND OF THE TIMELINE HAVE REVEALED.

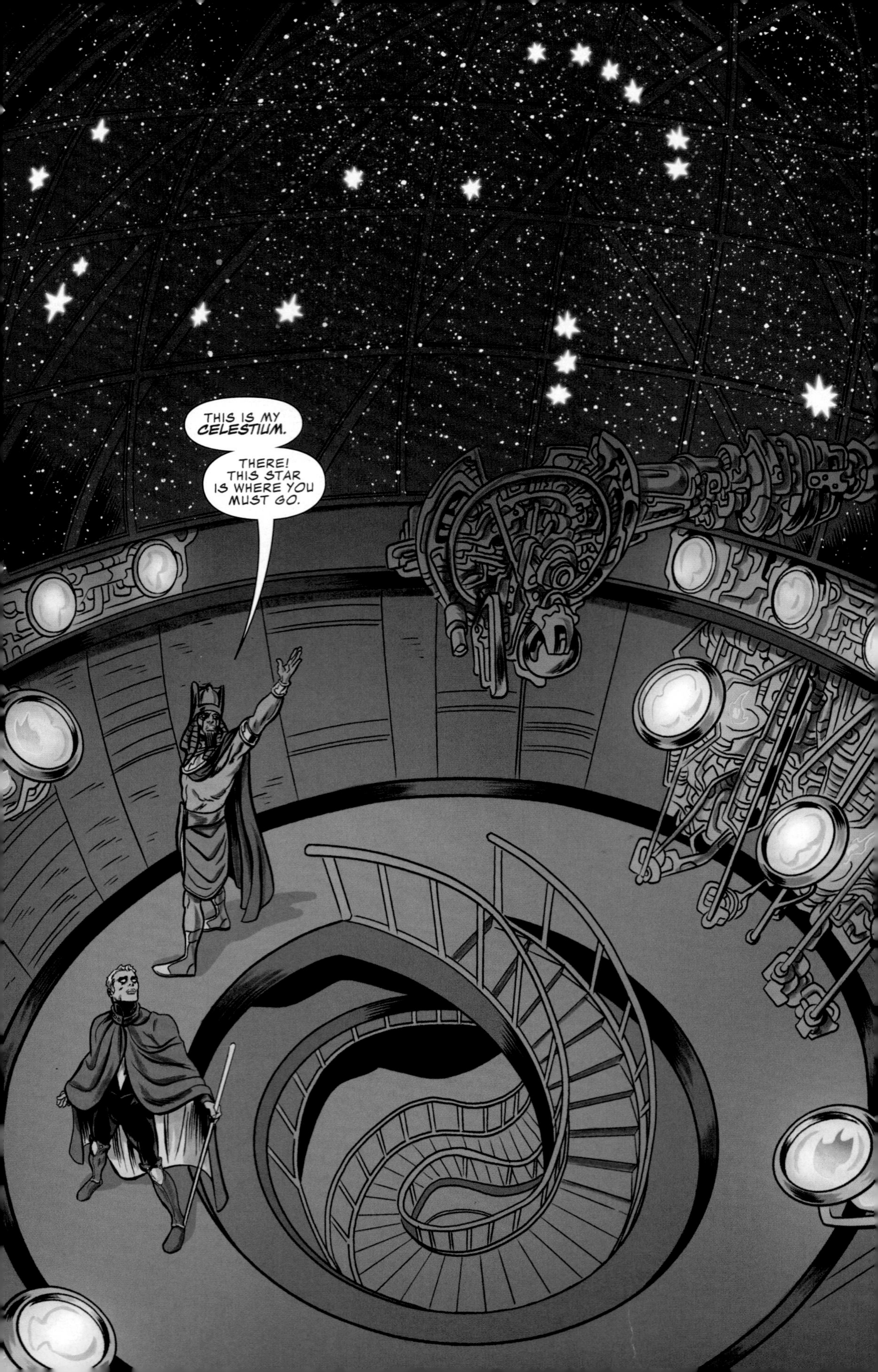
THIS IS MY CELESTIUM.
THERE! THIS STAR IS WHERE YOU MUST GO.

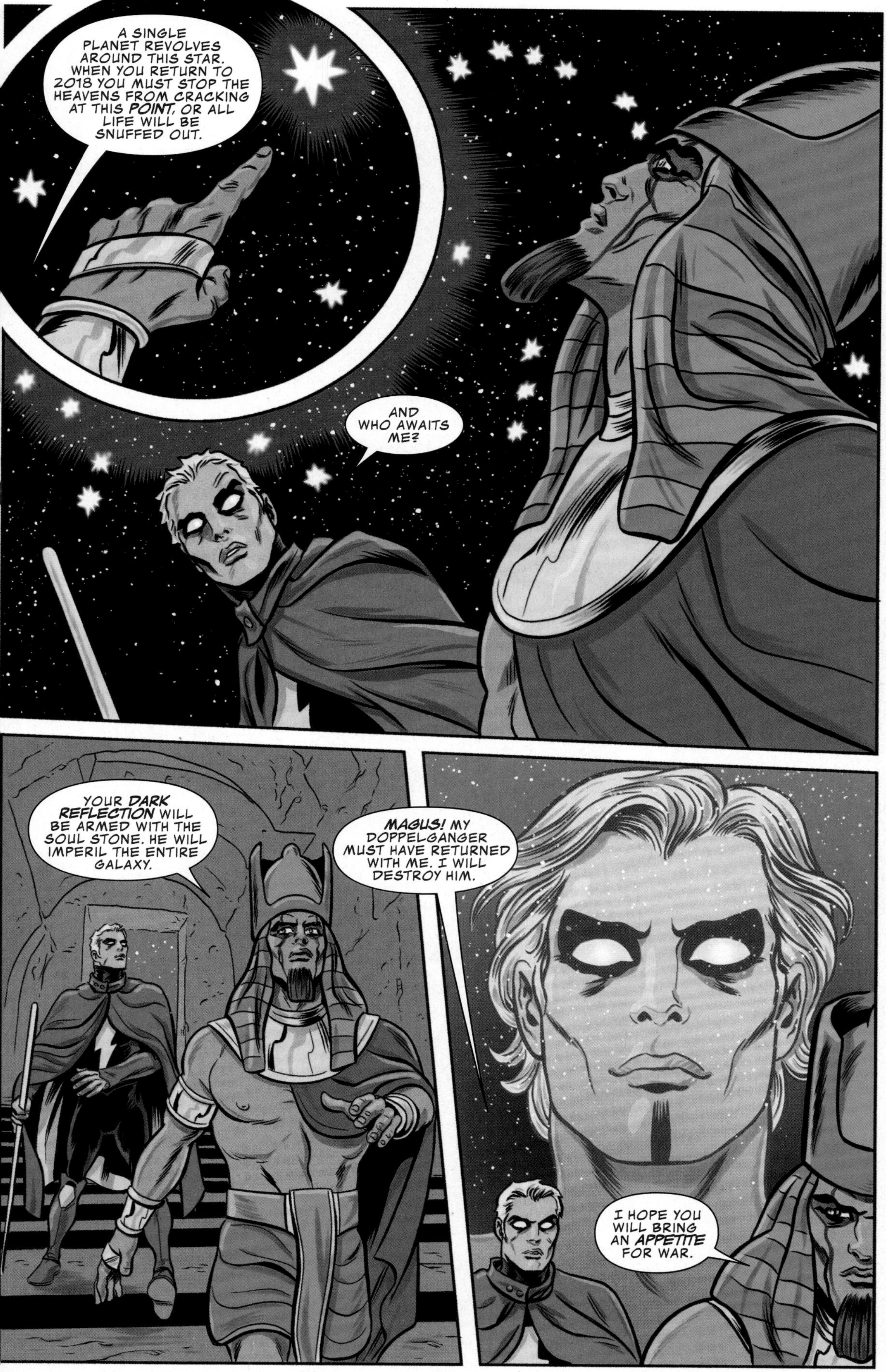
A SINGLE PLANET REVOLVES AROUND THIS STAR. WHEN YOU RETURN TO 2018 YOU MUST STOP THE HEAVENS FROM CRACKING AT THIS *POINT*, OR ALL LIFE WILL BE SNUFFED OUT.
AND WHO AWAITS ME?
YOUR *DARK REFLECTION* WILL BE ARMED WITH THE SOUL STONE. HE WILL IMPERIL THE ENTIRE GALAXY.
MAGUS! MY DOPPELGANGER MUST HAVE RETURNED WITH ME. I WILL DESTROY HIM.
I HOPE YOU WILL BRING AN *APPETITE* FOR WAR.

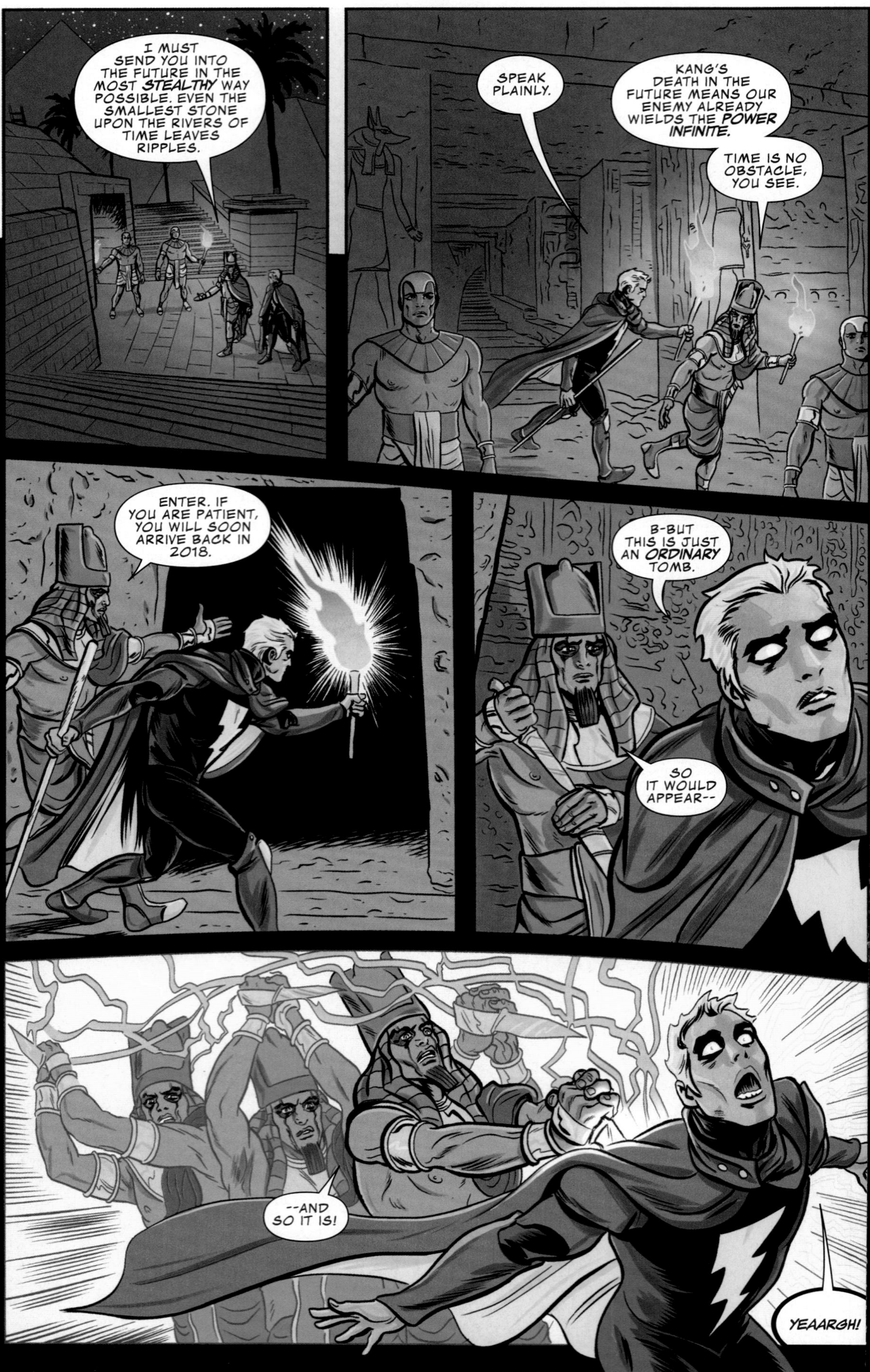
I MUST SEND YOU INTO THE FUTURE IN THE MOST STEALTHY WAY POSSIBLE. EVEN THE SMALLEST STONE UPON THE RIVERS OF TIME LEAVES RIPPLES.
SPEAK PLAINLY.
KANG'S DEATH IN THE FUTURE MEANS OUR ENEMY ALREADY WIELDS THE POWER INFINITE.
TIME IS NO OBSTACLE, YOU SEE.
ENTER. IF YOU ARE PATIENT, YOU WILL SOON ARRIVE BACK IN 2018.
B-BUT THIS IS JUST AN ORDINARY TOMB.
SO IT WOULD APPEAR--
--AND SO IT IS!
YEAARGH!

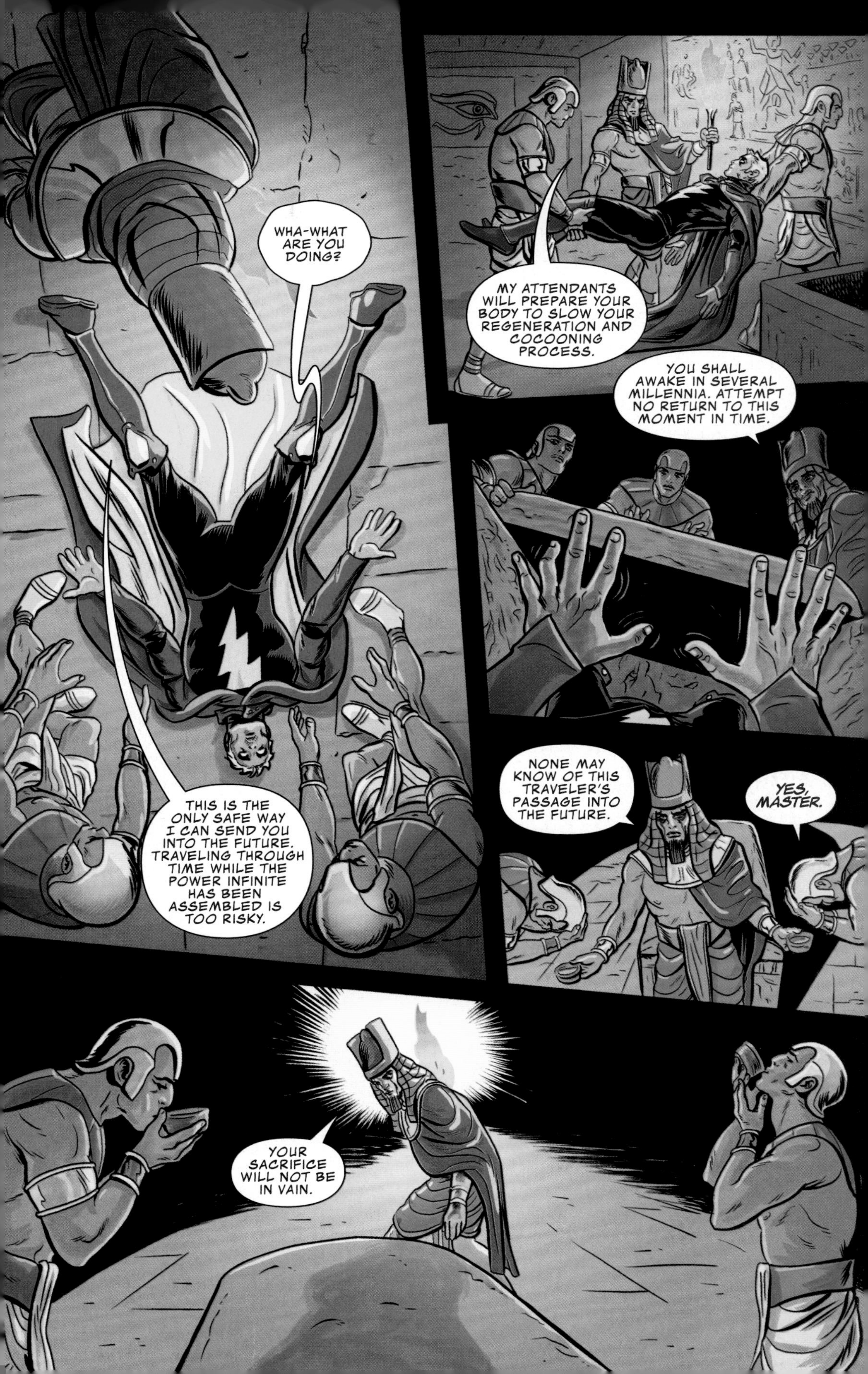
WHA-WHAT ARE YOU DOING?
THIS IS THE ONLY SAFE WAY I CAN SEND YOU INTO THE FUTURE. TRAVELING THROUGH TIME WHILE THE POWER INFINITE HAS BEEN ASSEMBLED IS TOO RISKY.
MY ATTENDANTS WILL PREPARE YOUR BODY TO SLOW YOUR REGENERATION AND COCOONING PROCESS.
YOU SHALL AWAKE IN SEVERAL MILLENNIA. ATTEMPT NO RETURN TO THIS MOMENT IN TIME.
NONE MAY KNOW OF THIS TRAVELER'S PASSAGE INTO THE FUTURE.
YES, MASTER.
YOUR SACRIFICE WILL NOT BE IN VAIN.

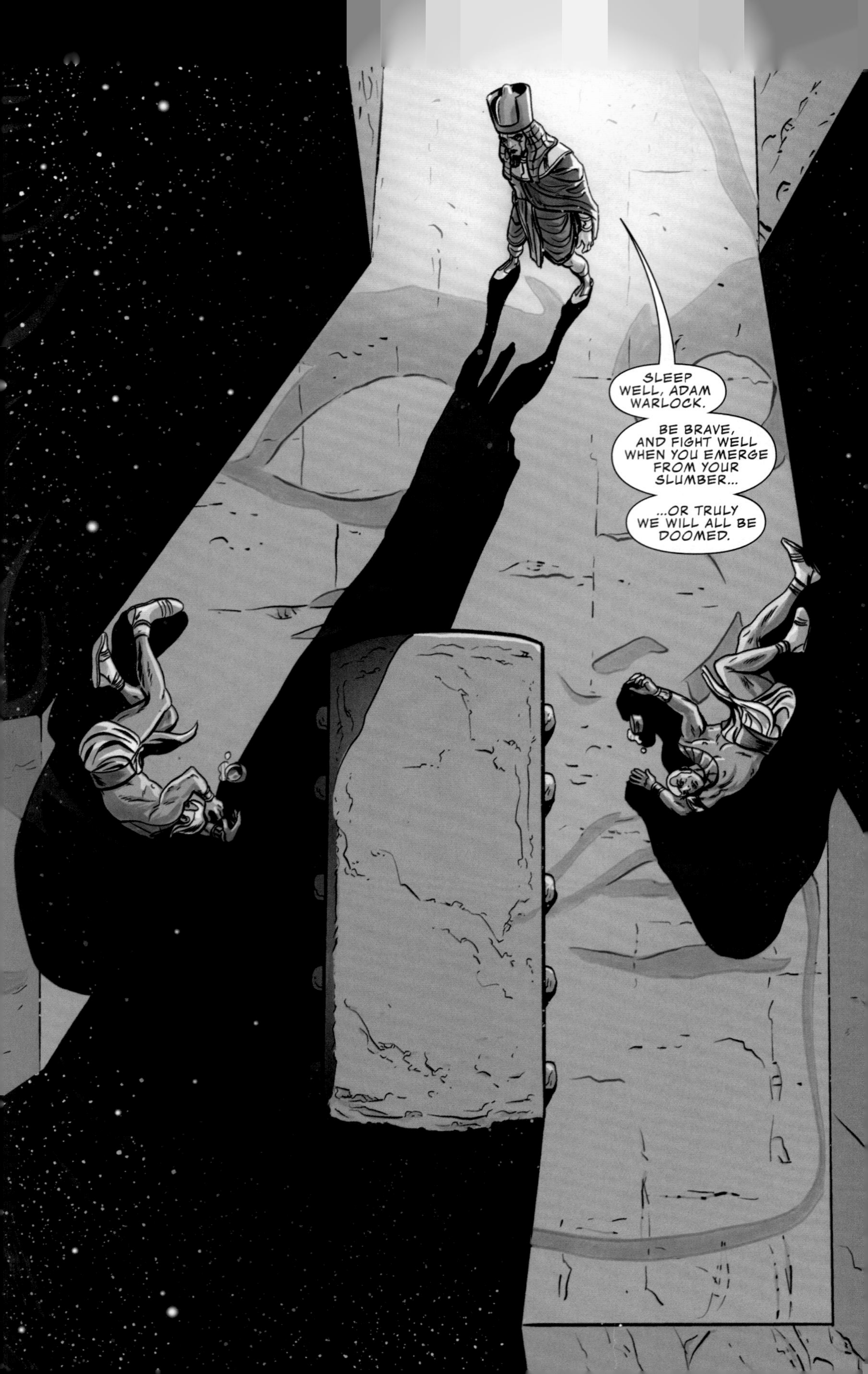
SLEEP WELL, ADAM WARLOCK.
BE BRAVE, AND FIGHT WELL WHEN YOU EMERGE FROM YOUR SLUMBER...
...OR TRULY WE WILL ALL BE DOOMED.

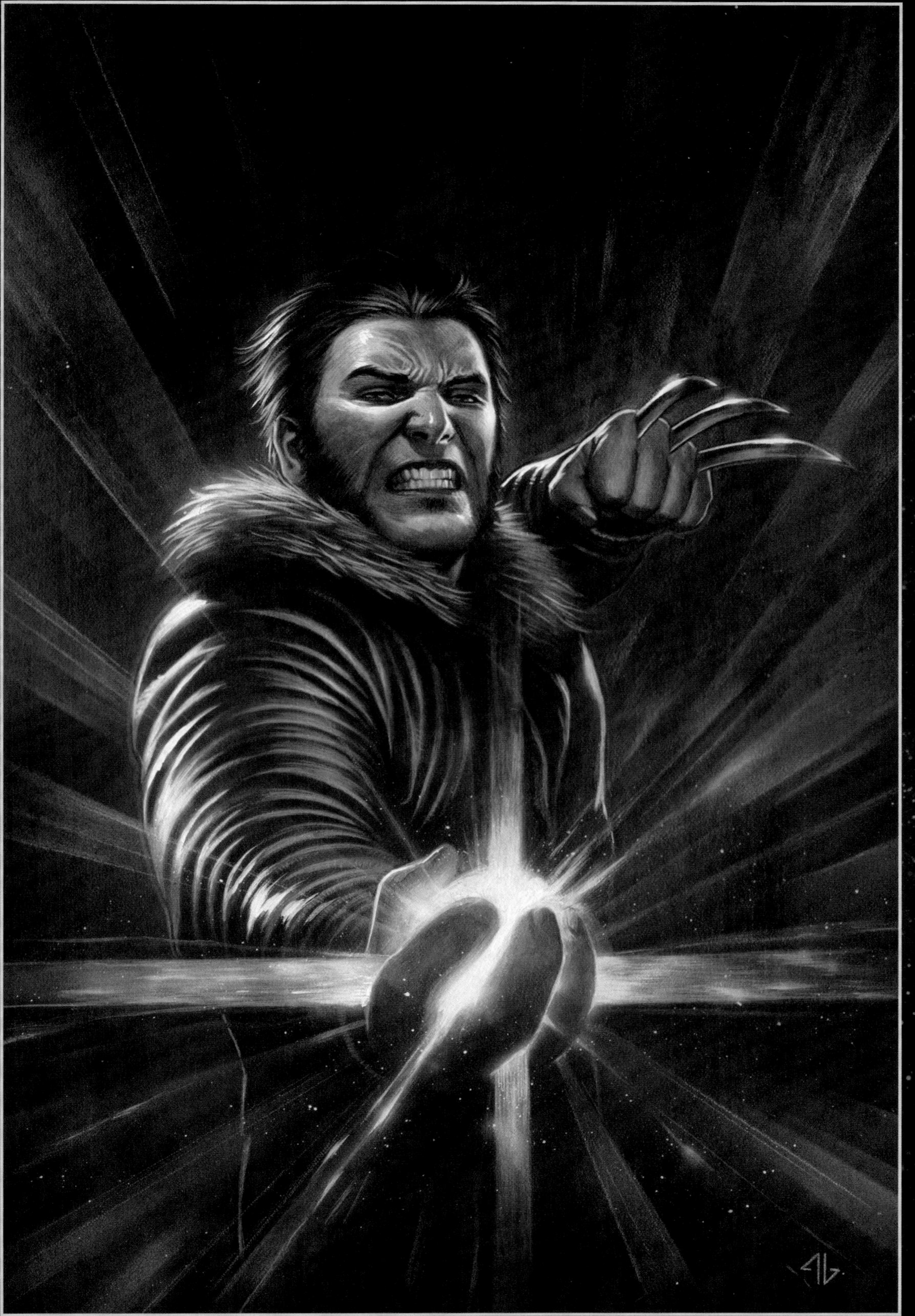

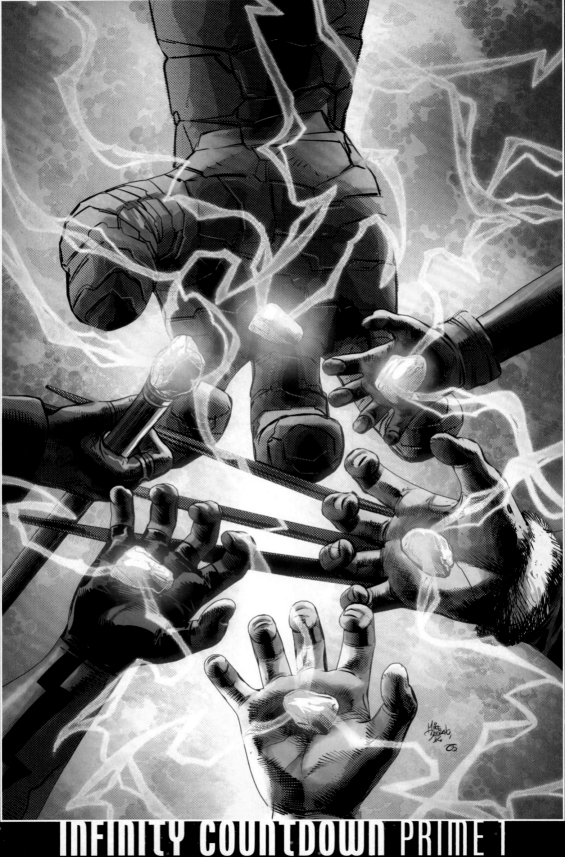

INFINITY COUNTDOWN PRIME 1

THE INFINITY STONES...

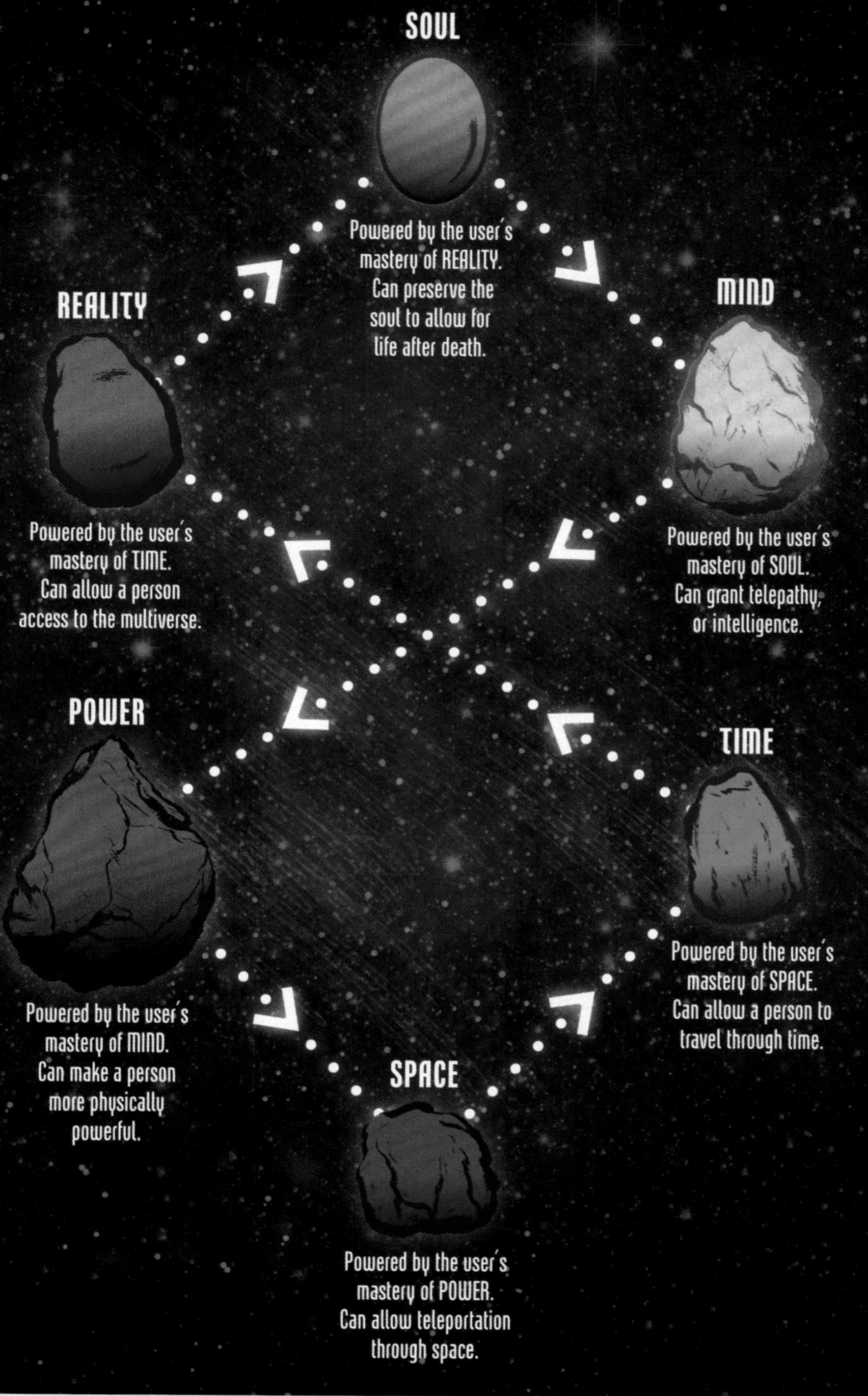

SOUL

Powered by the user's mastery of REALITY. Can preserve the soul to allow for life after death.

REALITY

Powered by the user's mastery of TIME. Can allow a person access to the multiverse.

MIND

Powered by the user's mastery of SOUL. Can grant telepathy, or intelligence.

POWER

Powered by the user's mastery of MIND. Can make a person more physically powerful.

TIME

Powered by the user's mastery of SPACE. Can allow a person to travel through time.

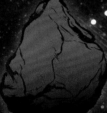

SPACE

Powered by the user's mastery of POWER. Can allow teleportation through space.

On their own, the stones provide great power. But when combined, they form a circuit--a positive feedback loop granting the user **INFINITE** power!

INFINITY
COUNTDOWN PRIME

Some time ago, the Infinity Stones were reborn and scattered, setting events into motion that will shake the very foundations of the universe.

But for now, the question at hand is...who holds the Stones?

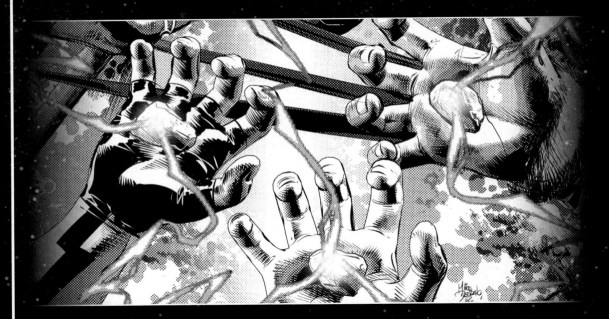

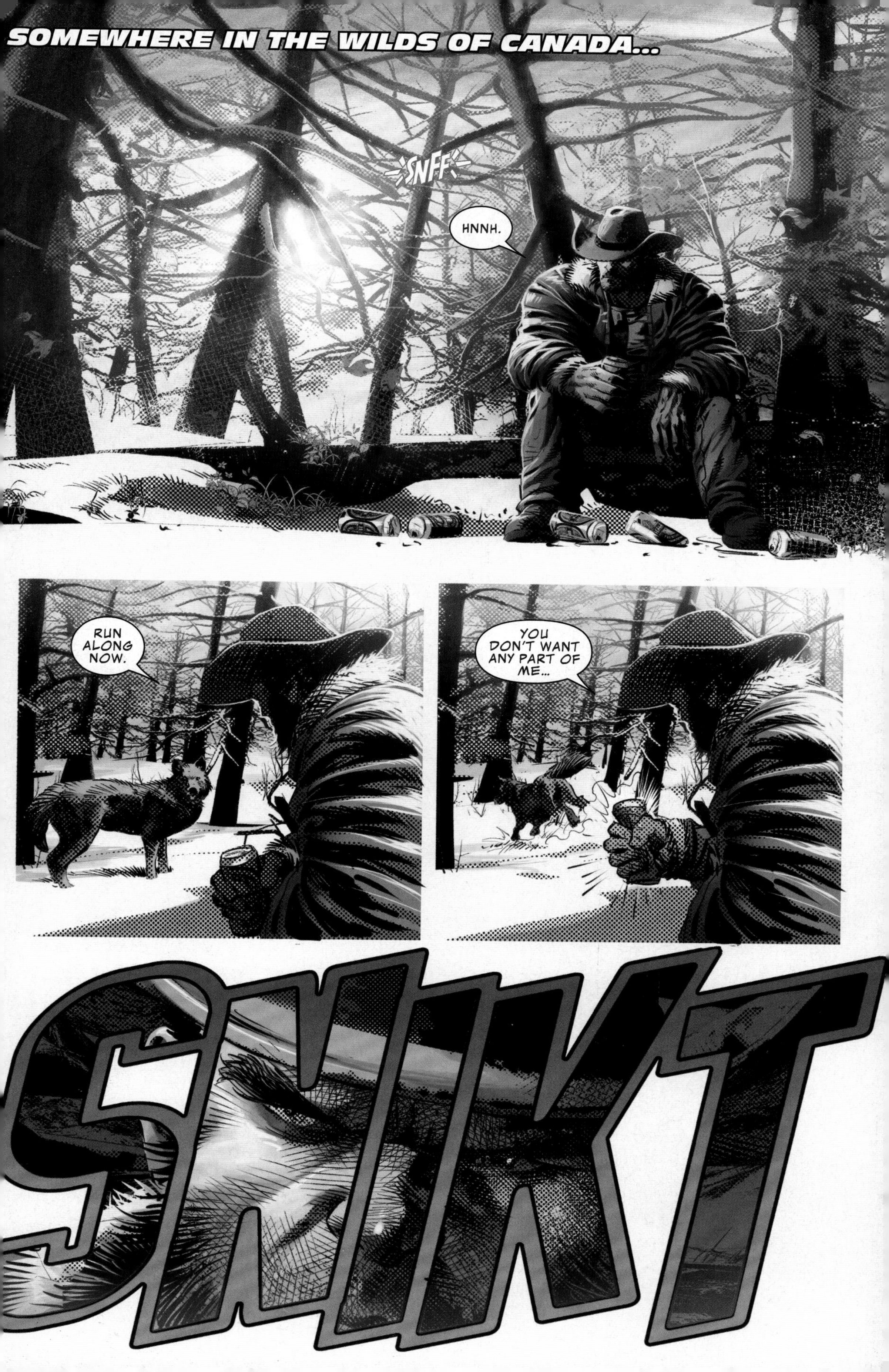
SOMEWHERE IN THE WILDS OF CANADA...
SNFF
HNNH.
RUN ALONG NOW.
YOU DON'T WANT ANY PART OF ME...
SNIKT

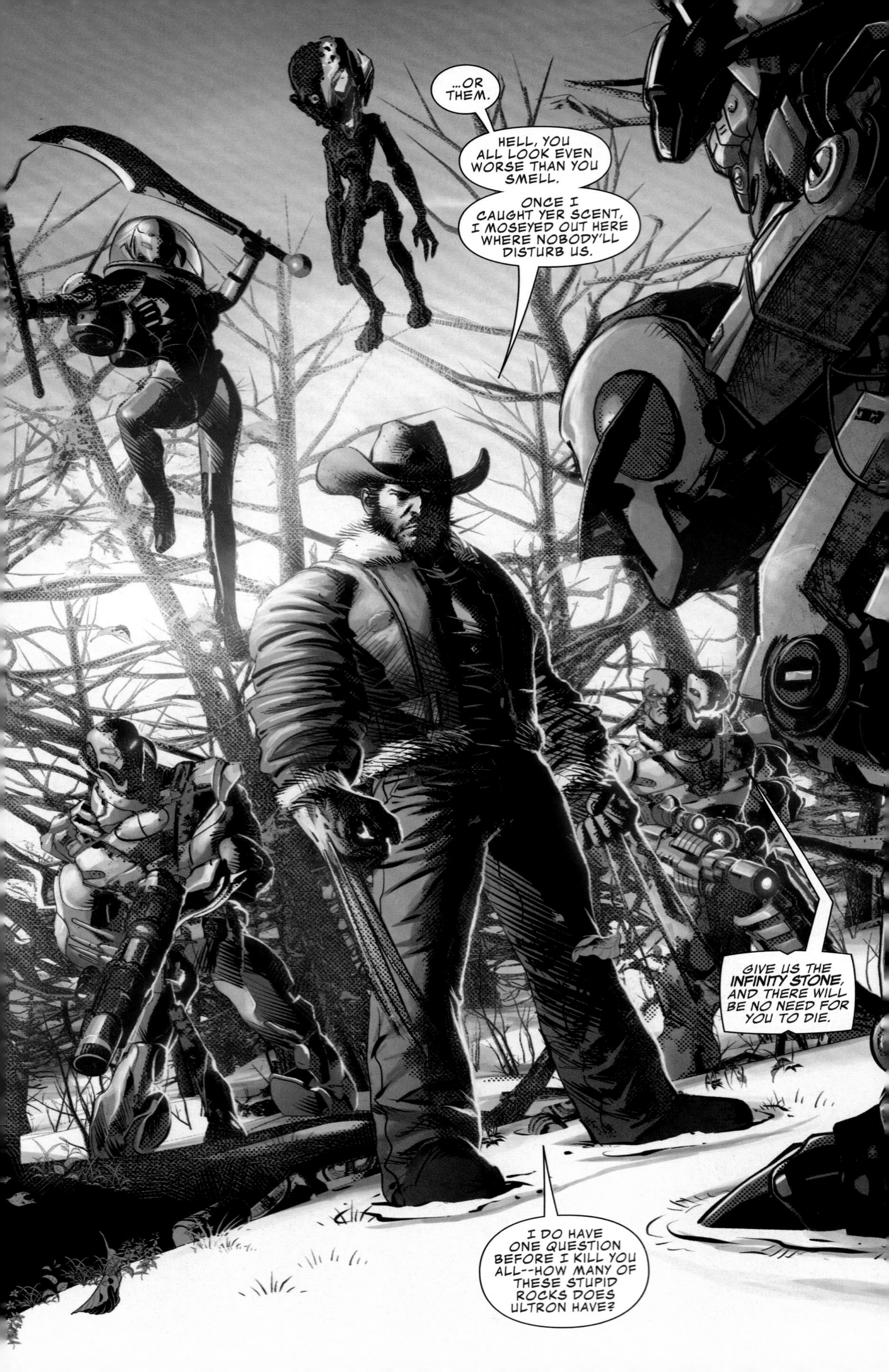
...OR THEM.
HELL, YOU ALL LOOK EVEN WORSE THAN YOU SMELL.
ONCE I CAUGHT YER SCENT, I MOSEYED OUT HERE WHERE NOBODY'LL DISTURB US.
GIVE US THE INFINITY STONE, AND THERE WILL BE NO NEED FOR YOU TO DIE.
I DO HAVE ONE QUESTION BEFORE I KILL YOU ALL--HOW MANY OF THESE STUPID ROCKS DOES ULTRON HAVE?

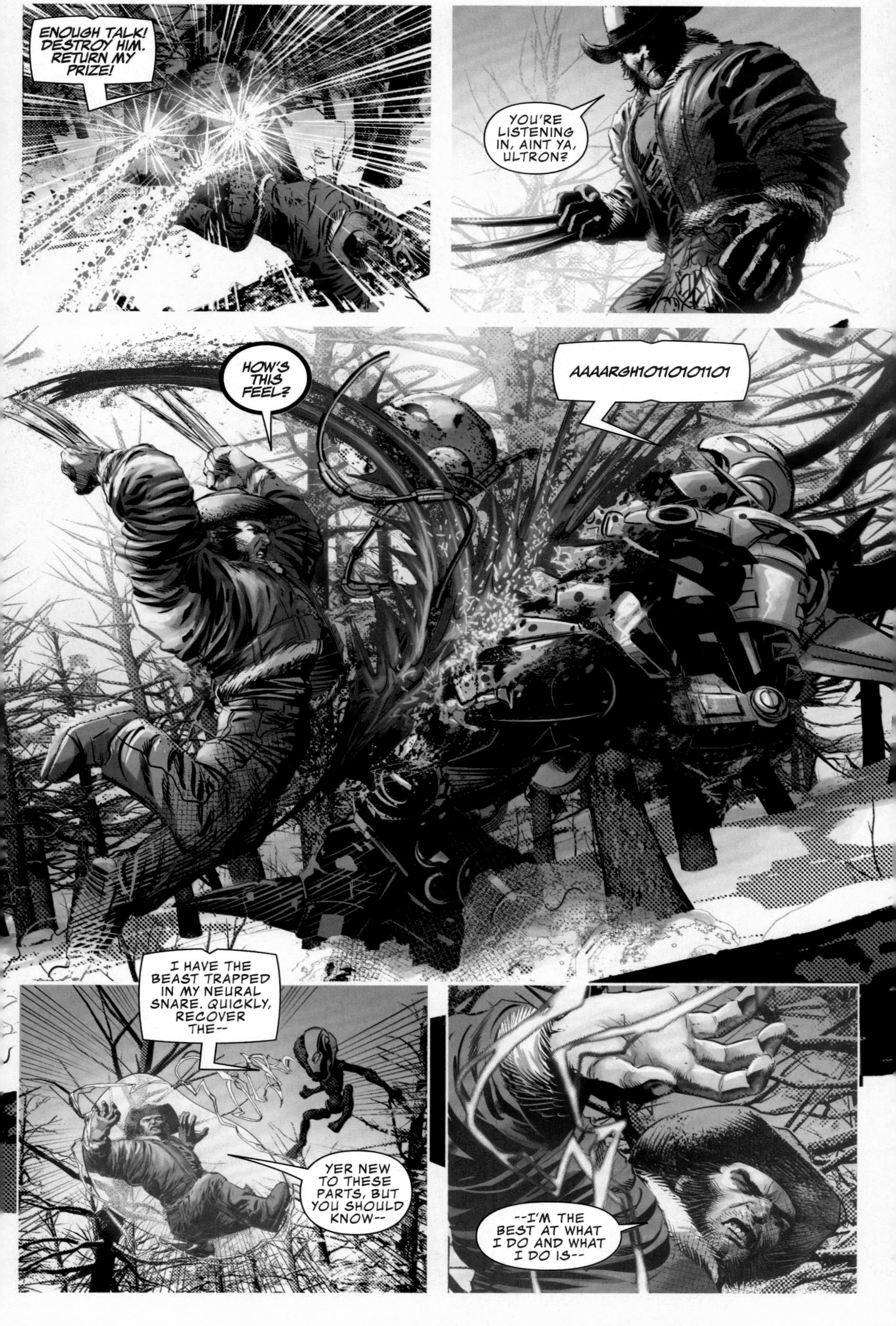
ENOUGH TALK! DESTROY HIM. RETURN MY PRIZE!
YOU'RE LISTENING IN, AINT YA, ULTRON?
HOW'S THIS FEEL?
AAAARGH1011010101101
I HAVE THE BEAST TRAPPED IN MY NEURAL SNARE. QUICKLY, RECOVER THE--
YER NEW TO THESE PARTS, BUT YOU SHOULD KNOW--
--I'M THE BEST AT WHAT I DO AND WHAT I DO IS--

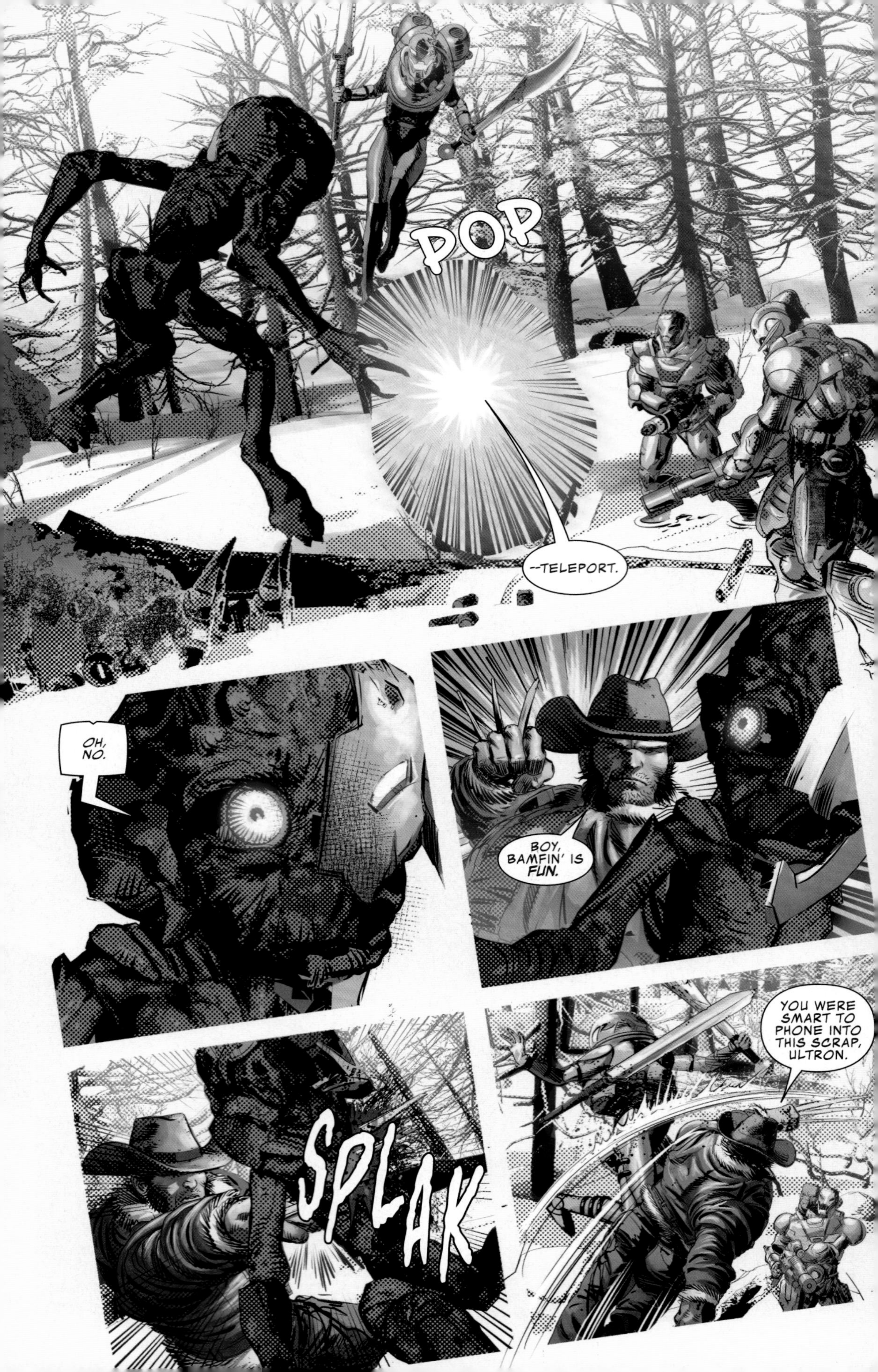

POP
--TELEPORT.
OH, NO.
BOY, BAMFIN' IS FUN.
SPLAK
YOU WERE SMART TO PHONE INTO THIS SCRAP, ULTRON.

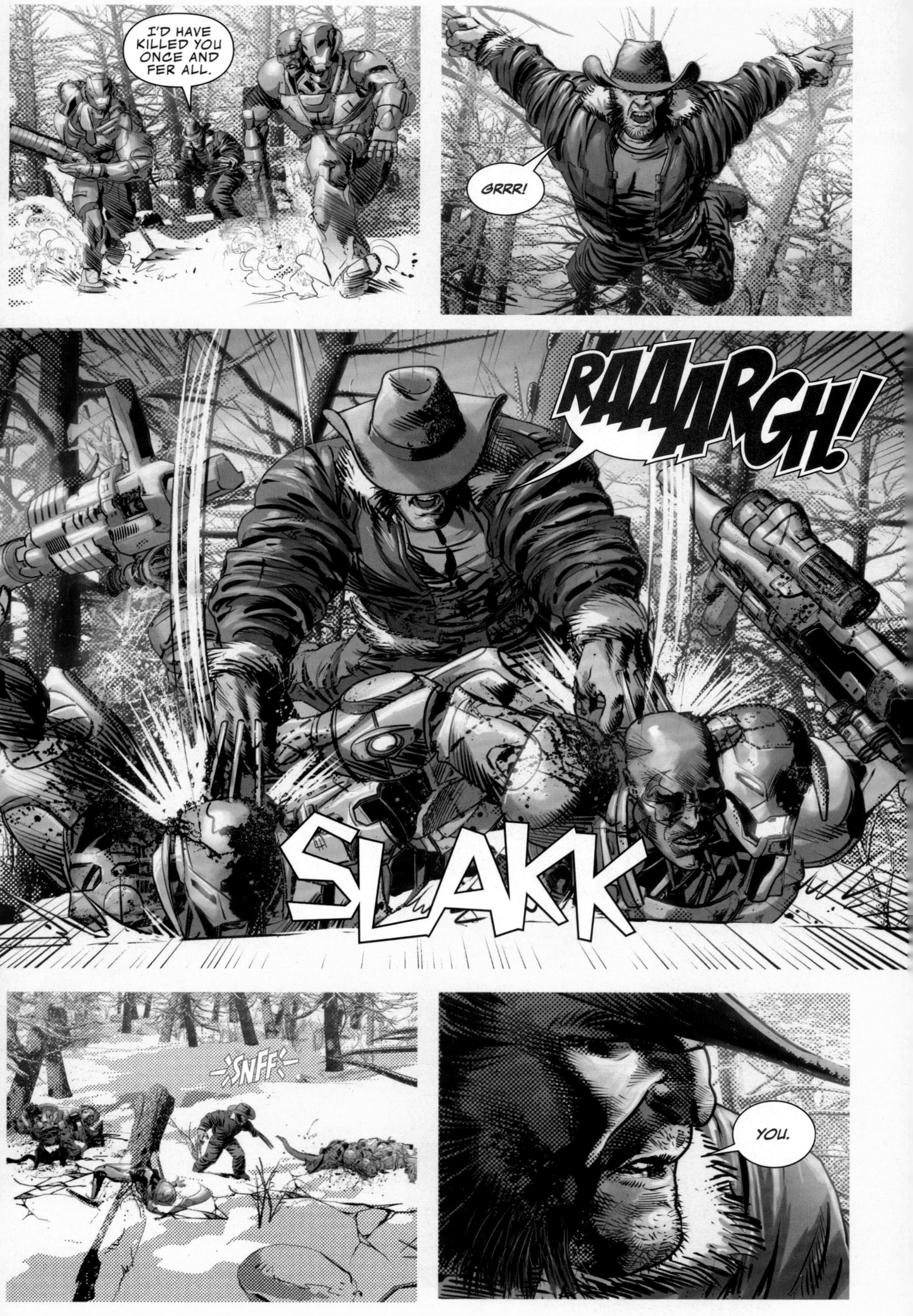
I'D HAVE KILLED YOU ONCE AND FER ALL.
GRRR!
RAAAARGH!
SLAKK
SNFF
YOU.

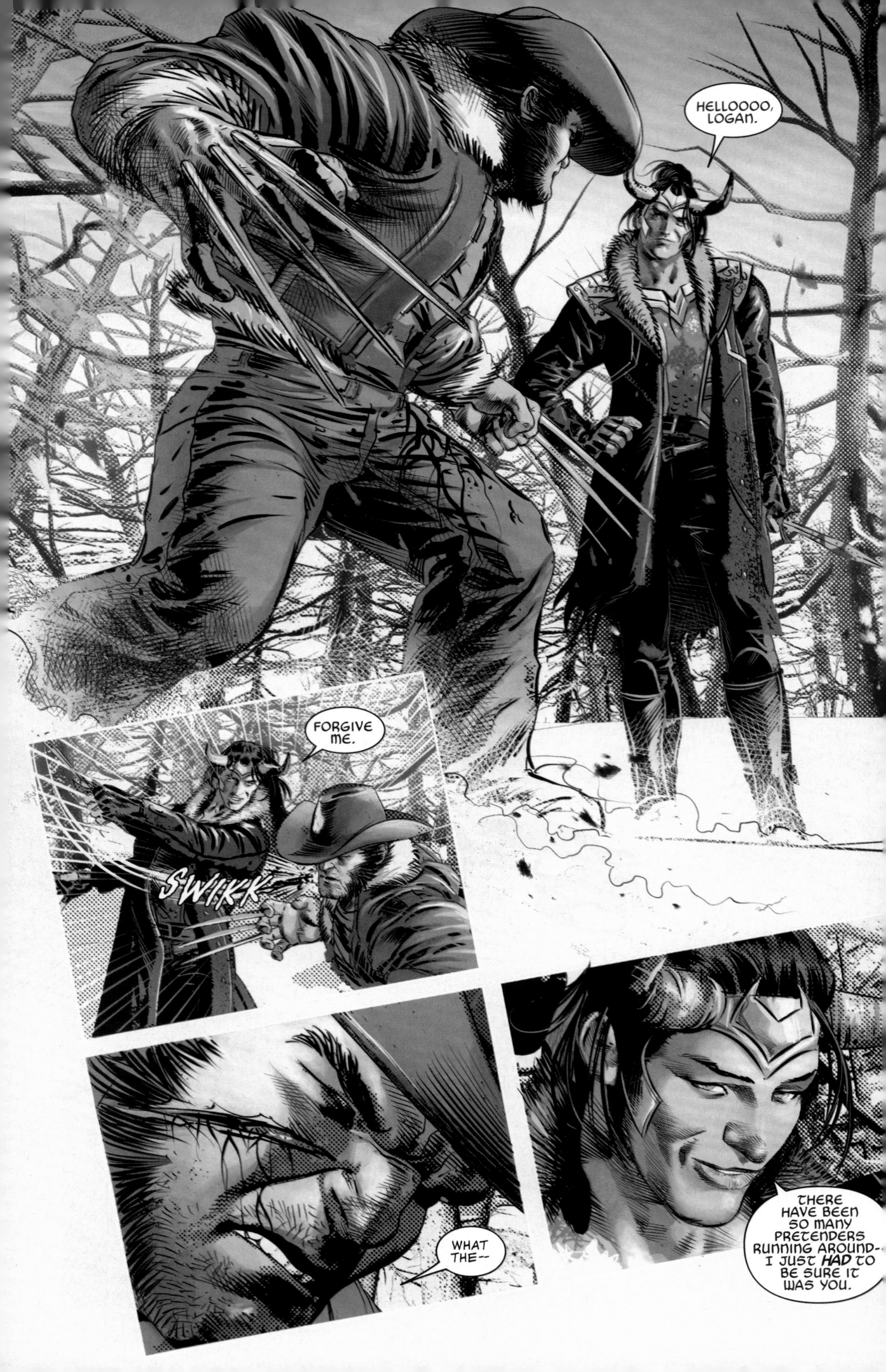
HELLOOOO, LOGAN.
FORGIVE ME.
SWIKK
WHAT THE--
THERE HAVE BEEN SO MANY PRETENDERS RUNNING AROUND-- I JUST HAD TO BE SURE IT WAS YOU.

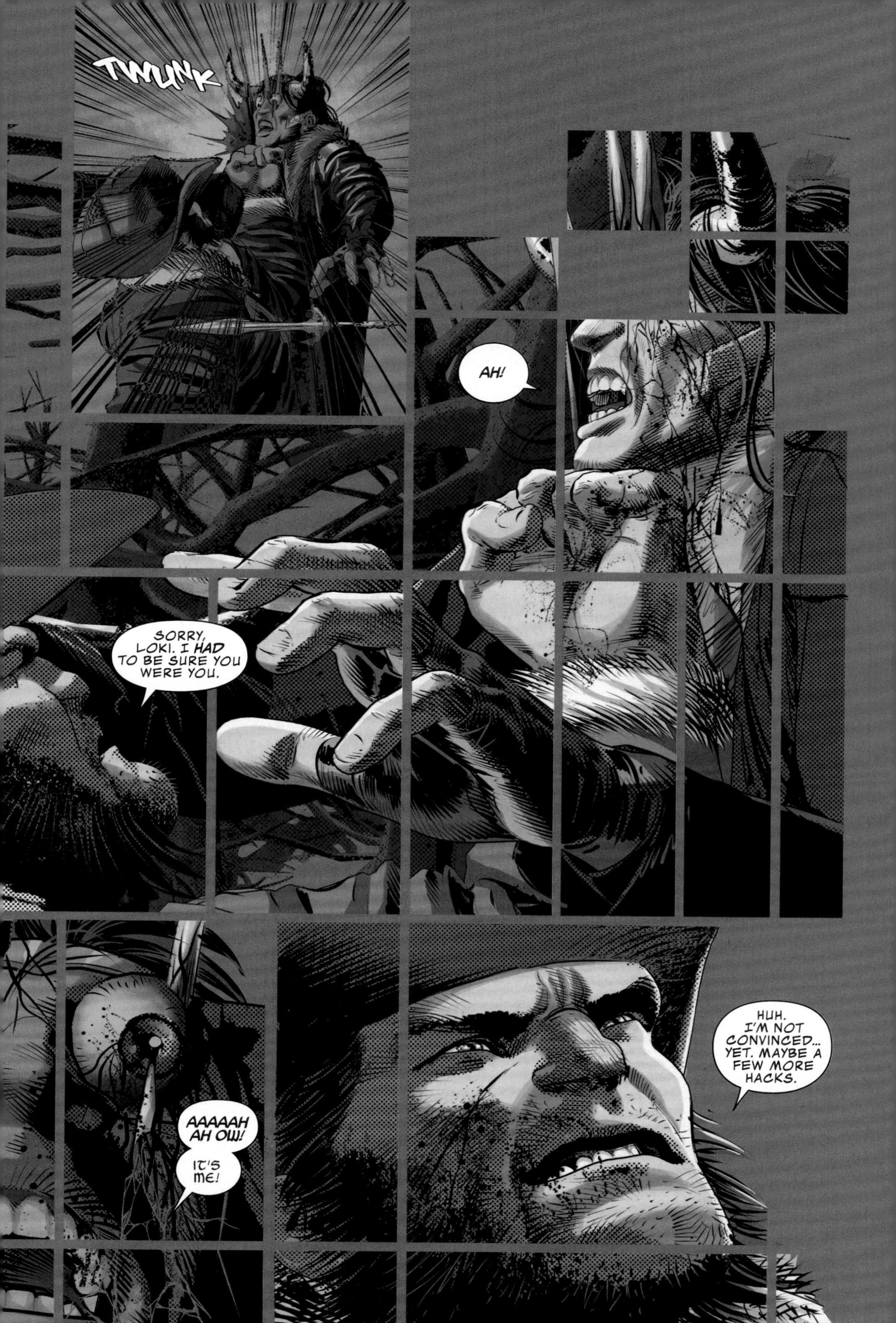
TWUNK
AH!
SORRY, LOKI. I HAD TO BE SURE YOU WERE YOU.
AAAAAH AH OW!
IT'S ME!
HUH. I'M NOT CONVINCED... YET. MAYBE A FEW MORE HACKS.

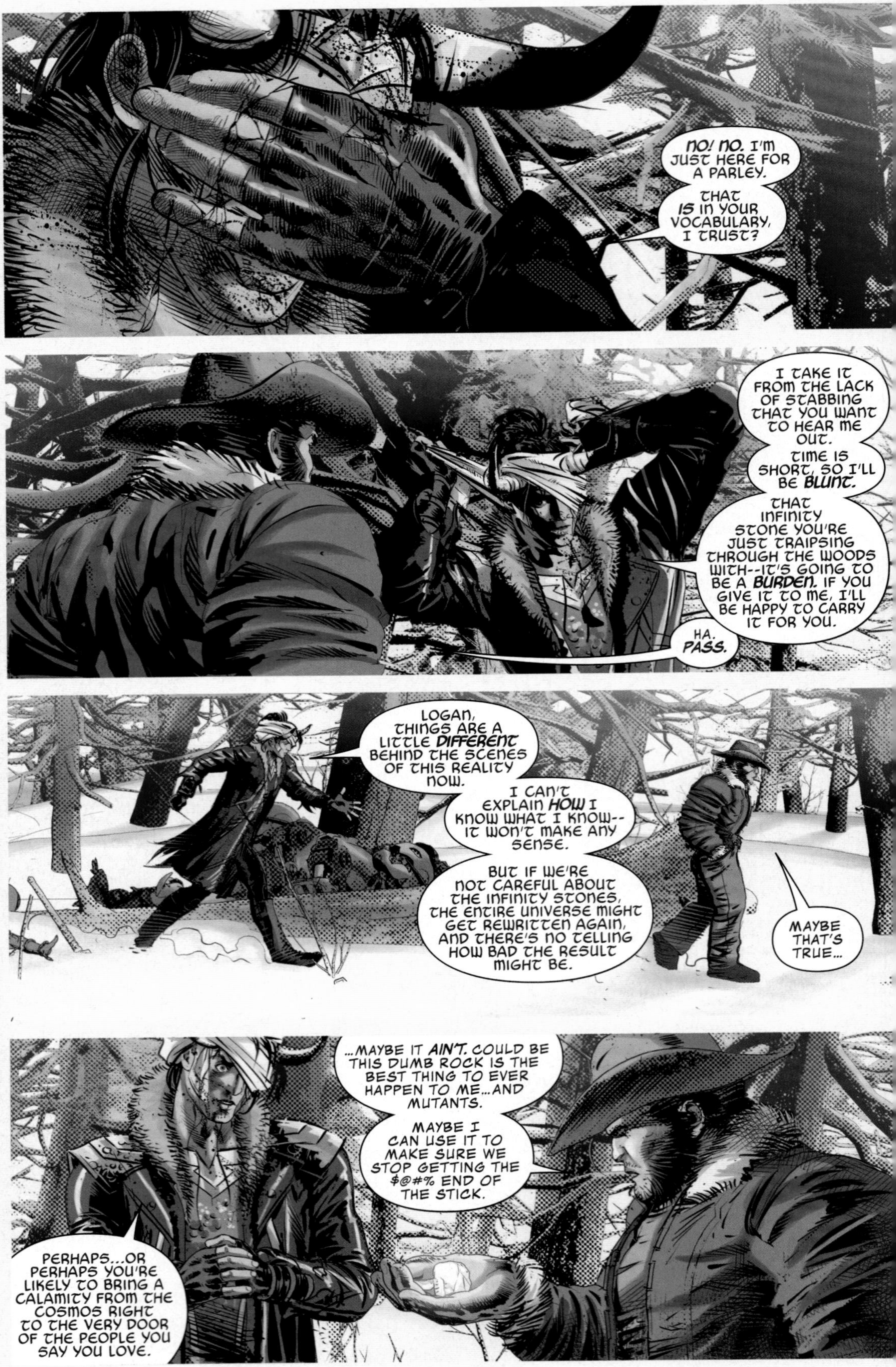
NO! NO. I'M JUST HERE FOR A PARLEY.
THAT IS IN YOUR VOCABULARY, I TRUST?
I TAKE IT FROM THE LACK OF STABBING THAT YOU WANT TO HEAR ME OUT.
TIME IS SHORT, SO I'LL BE BLUNT.
THAT INFINITY STONE YOU'RE JUST TRAIPSING THROUGH THE WOODS WITH--IT'S GOING TO BE A BURDEN. IF YOU GIVE IT TO ME, I'LL BE HAPPY TO CARRY IT FOR YOU.
HA. PASS.
LOGAN, THINGS ARE A LITTLE DIFFERENT BEHIND THE SCENES OF THIS REALITY NOW.
I CAN'T EXPLAIN HOW I KNOW WHAT I KNOW--IT WON'T MAKE ANY SENSE.
BUT IF WE'RE NOT CAREFUL ABOUT THE INFINITY STONES, THE ENTIRE UNIVERSE MIGHT GET REWRITTEN AGAIN, AND THERE'S NO TELLING HOW BAD THE RESULT MIGHT BE.
MAYBE THAT'S TRUE...
...MAYBE IT AIN'T. COULD BE THIS DUMB ROCK IS THE BEST THING TO EVER HAPPEN TO ME...AND MUTANTS.
MAYBE I CAN USE IT TO MAKE SURE WE STOP GETTING THE $@#% END OF THE STICK.
PERHAPS...OR PERHAPS YOU'RE LIKELY TO BRING A CALAMITY FROM THE COSMOS RIGHT TO THE VERY DOOR OF THE PEOPLE YOU SAY YOU LOVE.

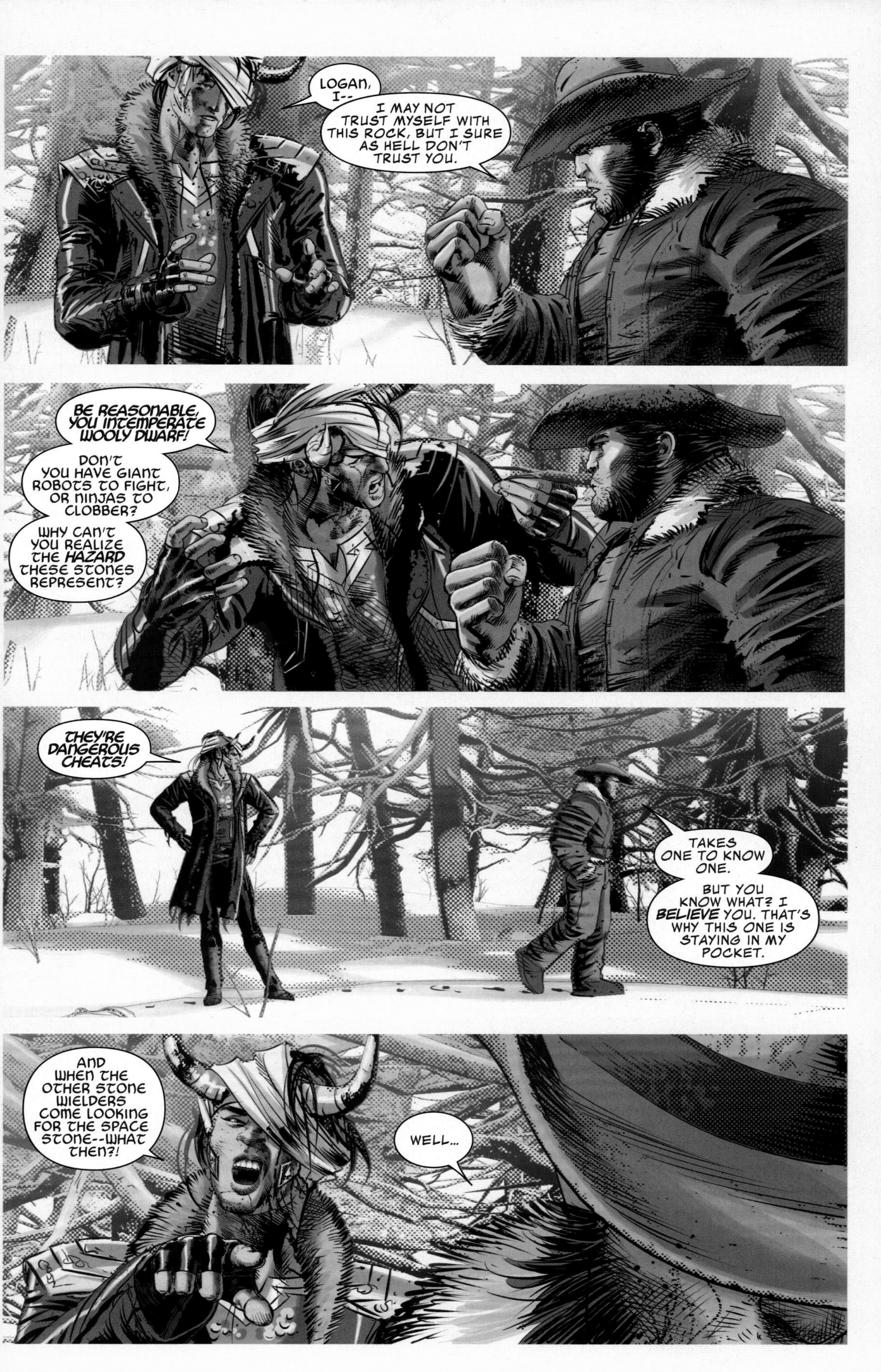
LOGAN, I--
I MAY NOT TRUST MYSELF WITH THIS ROCK, BUT I SURE AS HELL DON'T TRUST YOU.
BE REASONABLE, YOU INTEMPERATE WOOLY DWARF!
DON'T YOU HAVE GIANT ROBOTS TO FIGHT, OR NINJAS TO CLOBBER?
WHY CAN'T YOU REALIZE THE HAZARD THESE STONES REPRESENT?
THEY'RE DANGEROUS CHEATS!
TAKES ONE TO KNOW ONE.
BUT YOU KNOW WHAT? I BELIEVE YOU. THAT'S WHY THIS ONE IS STAYING IN MY POCKET.
AND WHEN THE OTHER STONE WIELDERS COME LOOKING FOR THE SPACE STONE--WHAT THEN?!
WELL...

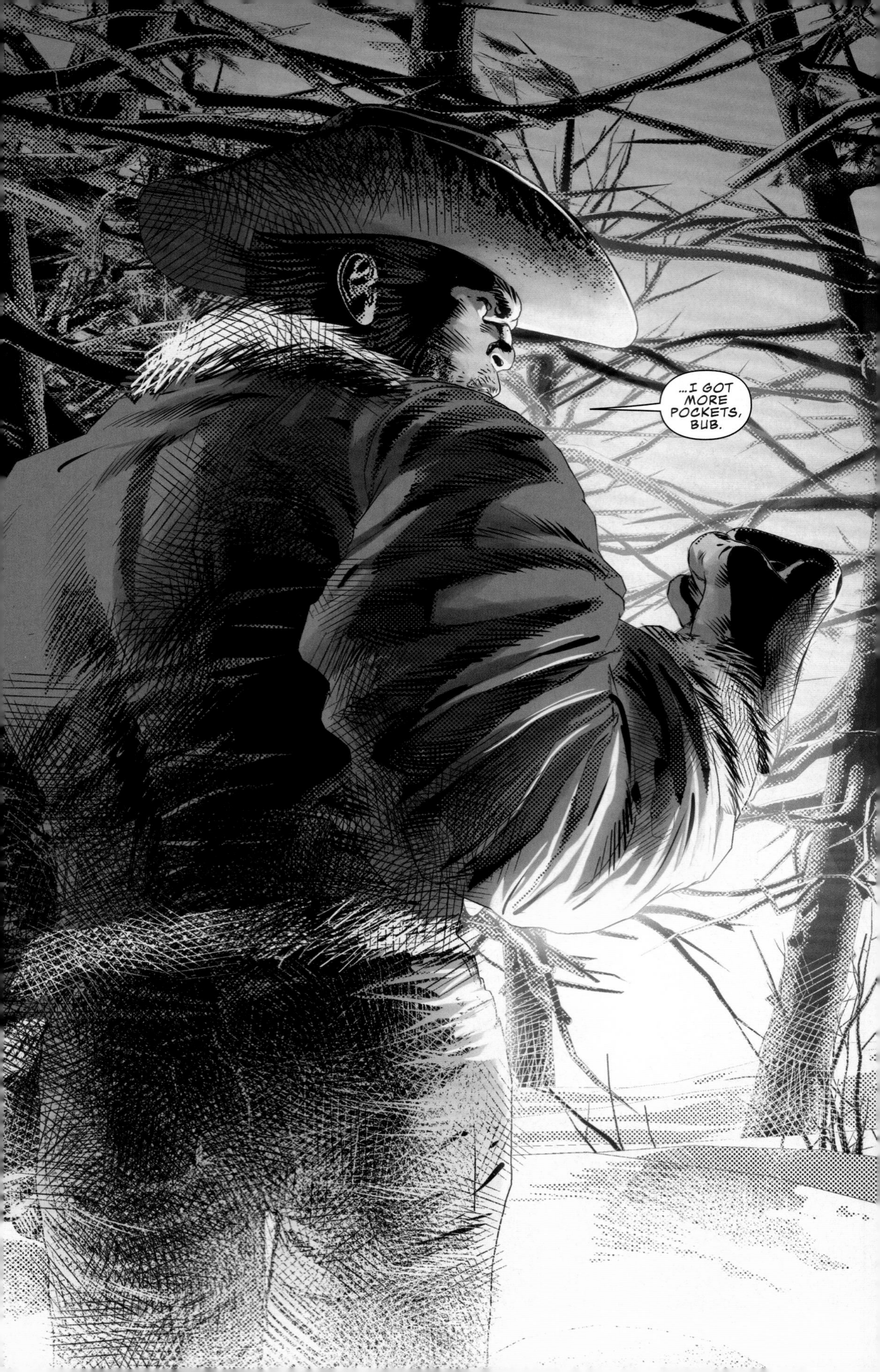
...I GOT MORE POCKETS, BUB.

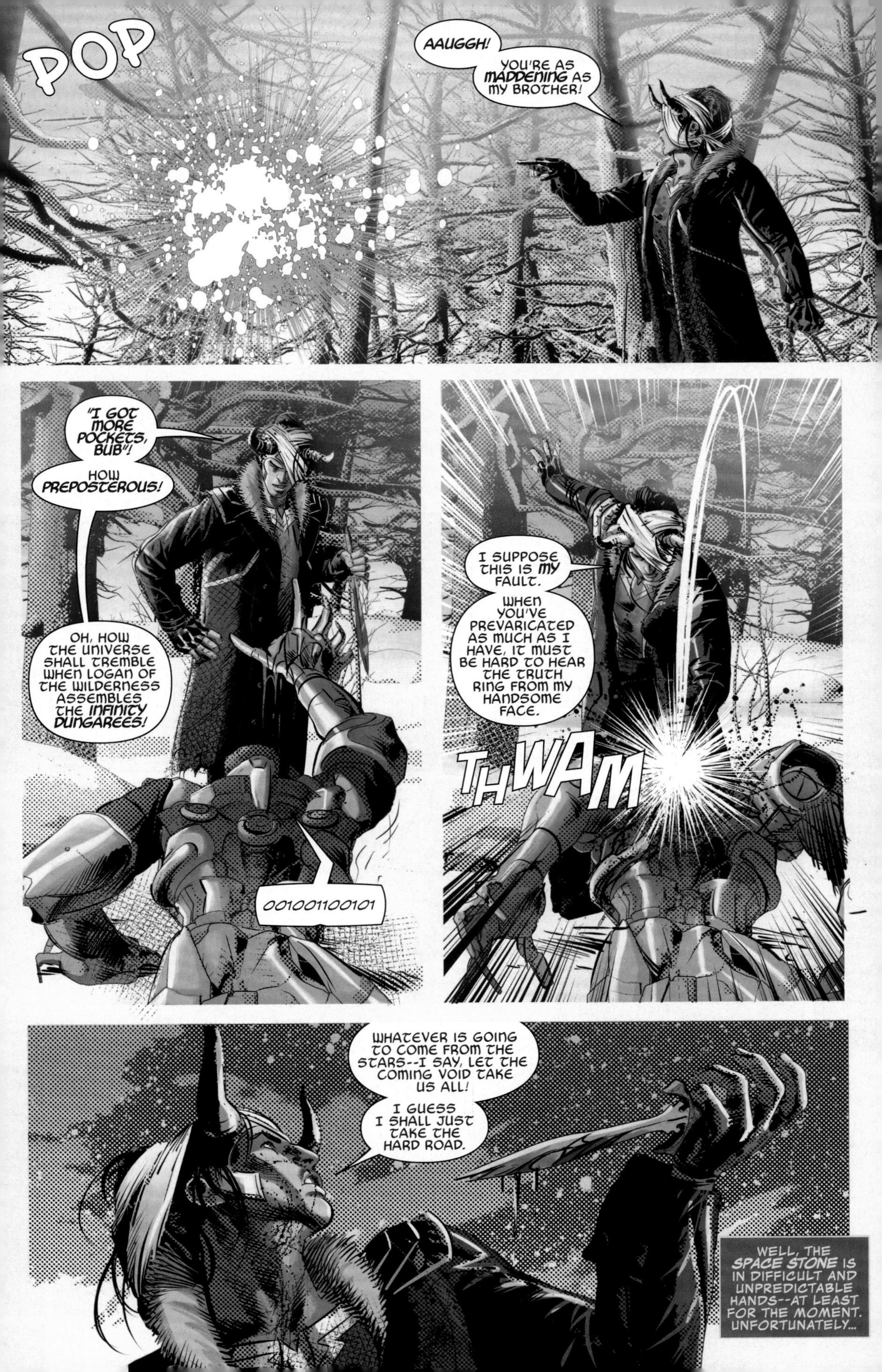
POP
AAUGGH!
YOU'RE AS MADDENING AS MY BROTHER!
"I GOT MORE POCKETS, BUB"!
HOW PREPOSTEROUS!
OH, HOW THE UNIVERSE SHALL TREMBLE WHEN LOGAN OF THE WILDERNESS ASSEMBLES THE INFINITY DUNGAREES!
001001100101
I SUPPOSE THIS IS MY FAULT.
WHEN YOU'VE PREVARICATED AS MUCH AS I HAVE, IT MUST BE HARD TO HEAR THE TRUTH RING FROM MY HANDSOME FACE.
THWAM
WHATEVER IS GOING TO COME FROM THE STARS--I SAY, LET THE COMING VOID TAKE US ALL!
I GUESS I SHALL JUST TAKE THE HARD ROAD.
WELL, THE SPACE STONE IS IN DIFFICULT AND UNPREDICTABLE HANDS--AT LEAST FOR THE MOMENT. UNFORTUNATELY...

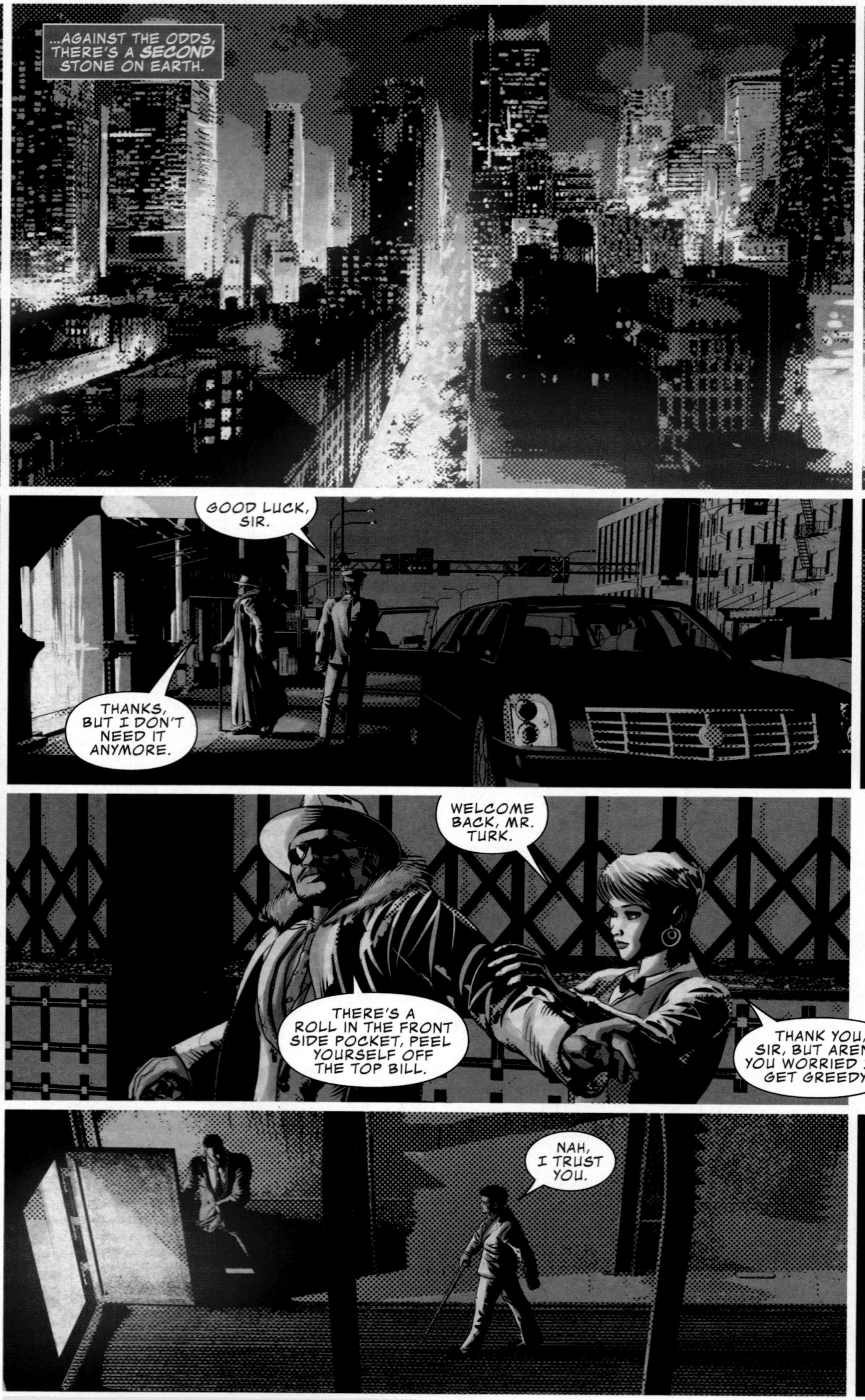
...AGAINST THE ODDS, THERE'S A SECOND STONE ON EARTH.
GOOD LUCK, SIR.
THANKS, BUT I DON'T NEED IT ANYMORE.
WELCOME BACK, MR. TURK.
THERE'S A ROLL IN THE FRONT SIDE POCKET, PEEL YOURSELF OFF THE TOP BILL.
THANK YOU, SIR, BUT AREN'
YOU WORRIED I'
GET GREEDY?
NAH, I TRUST YOU.

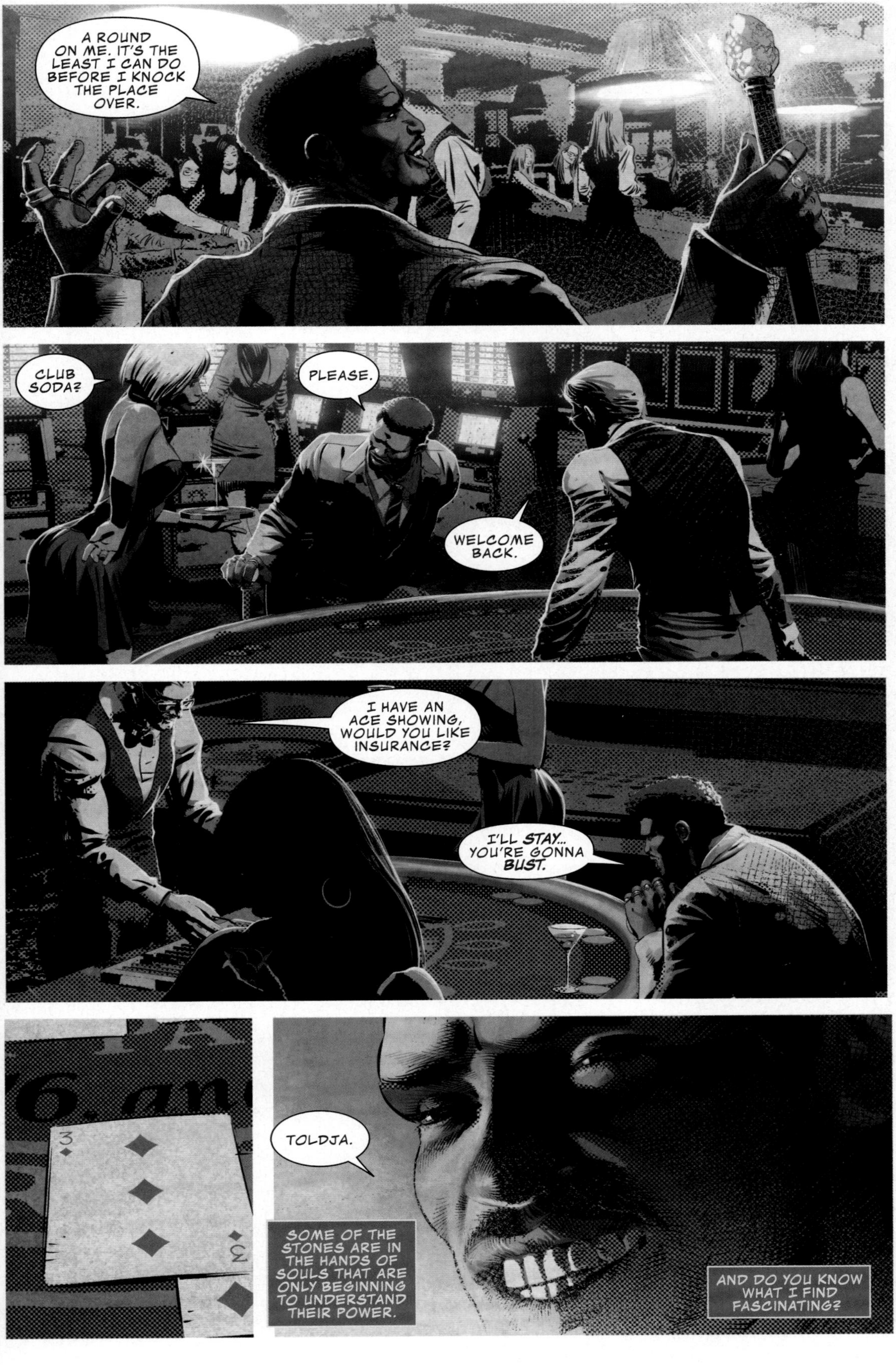
A ROUND ON ME. IT'S THE LEAST I CAN DO BEFORE I KNOCK THE PLACE OVER.
CLUB SODA?
PLEASE.
WELCOME BACK.
I HAVE AN ACE SHOWING, WOULD YOU LIKE INSURANCE?
I'LL *STAY*... YOU'RE GONNA *BUST*.
TOLDJA.
SOME OF THE STONES ARE IN THE HANDS OF SOULS THAT ARE ONLY BEGINNING TO UNDERSTAND THEIR POWER.
AND DO YOU KNOW WHAT I FIND FASCINATING?

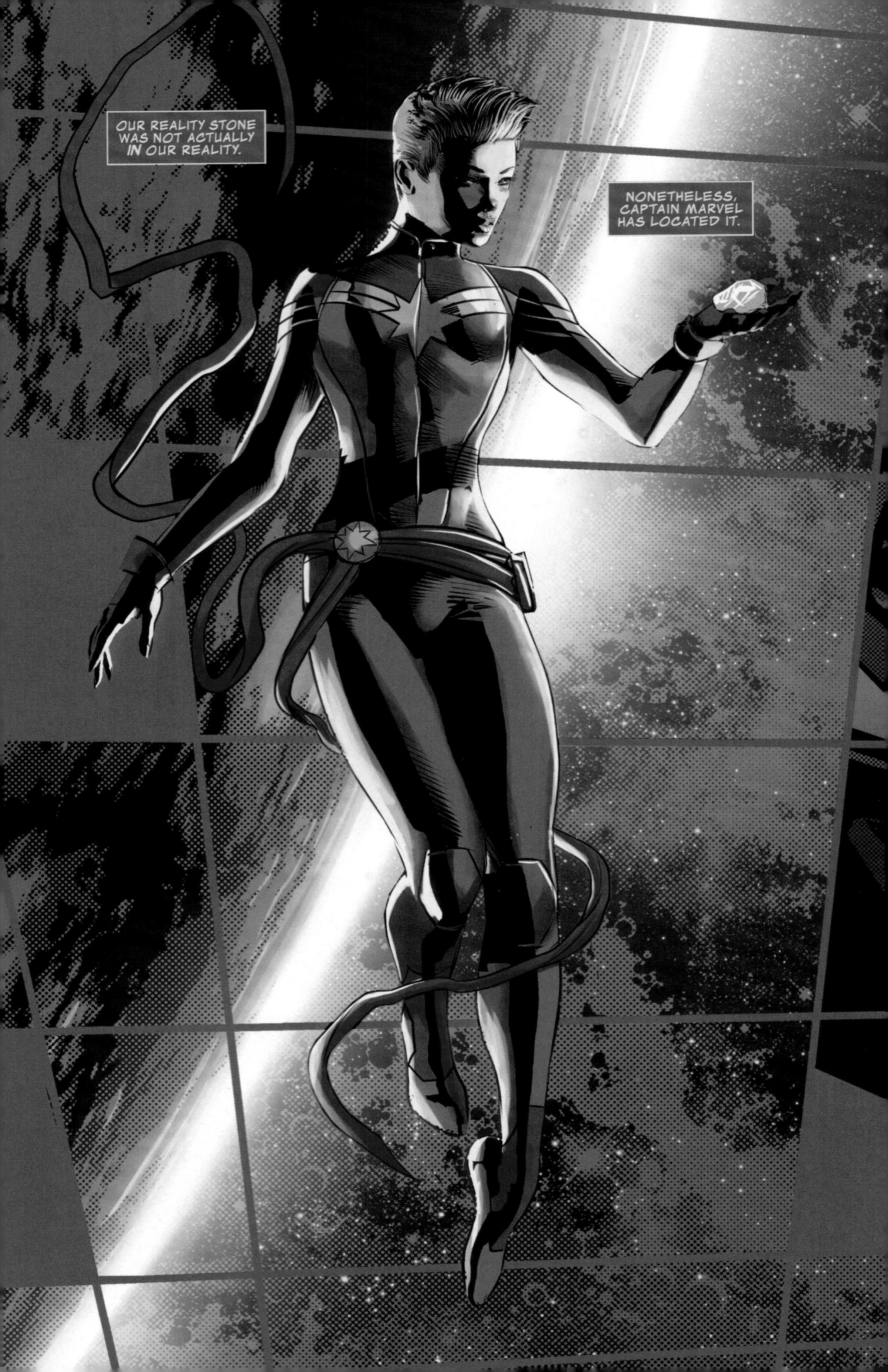
OUR REALITY STONE WAS NOT ACTUALLY *IN* OUR REALITY.
NONETHELESS, CAPTAIN MARVEL HAS LOCATED IT.

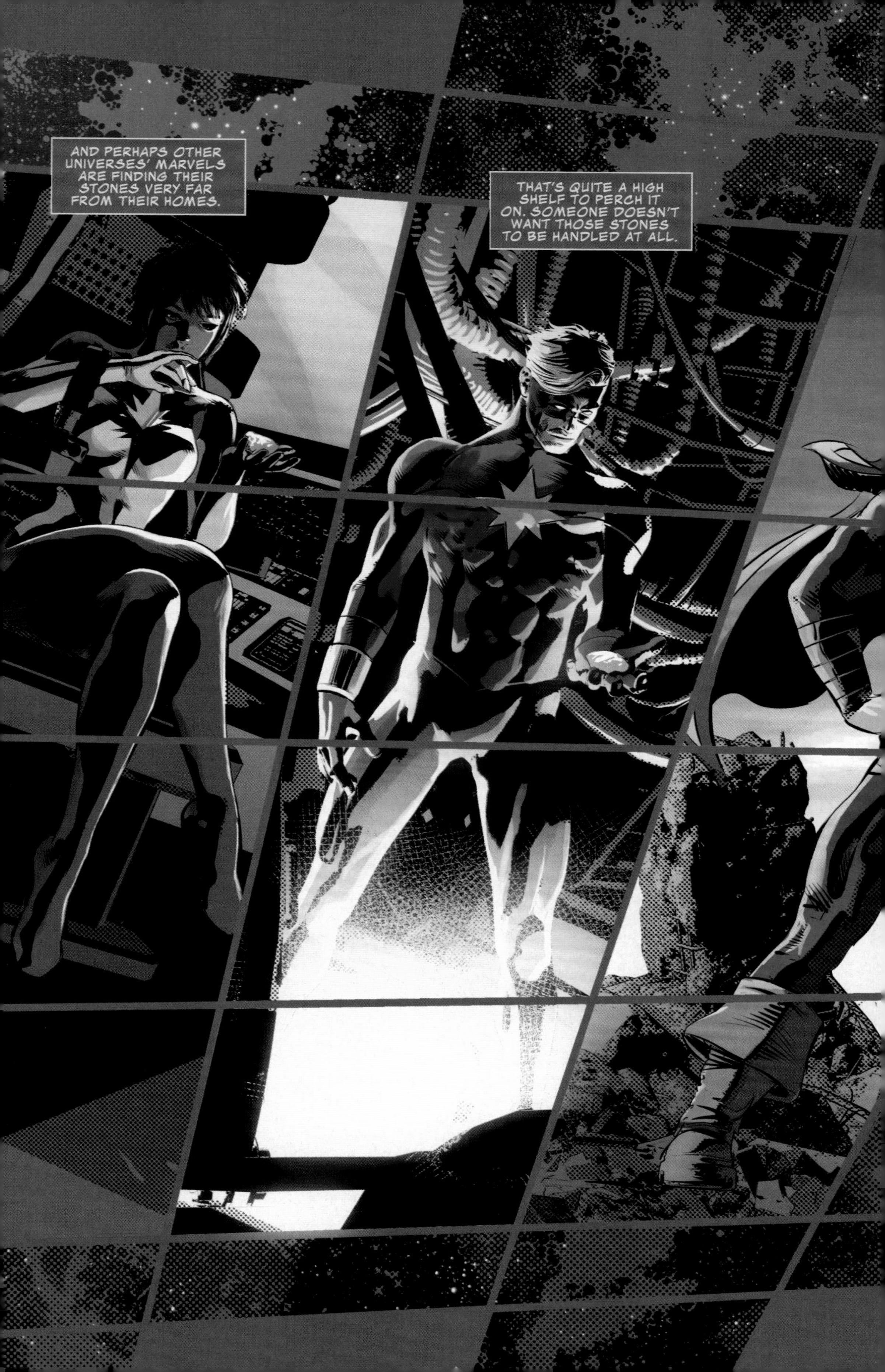
AND PERHAPS OTHER UNIVERSES' MARVELS ARE FINDING THEIR STONES VERY FAR FROM THEIR HOMES.
THAT'S QUITE A HIGH SHELF TO PERCH IT ON. SOMEONE DOESN'T WANT THOSE STONES TO BE HANDLED AT ALL.

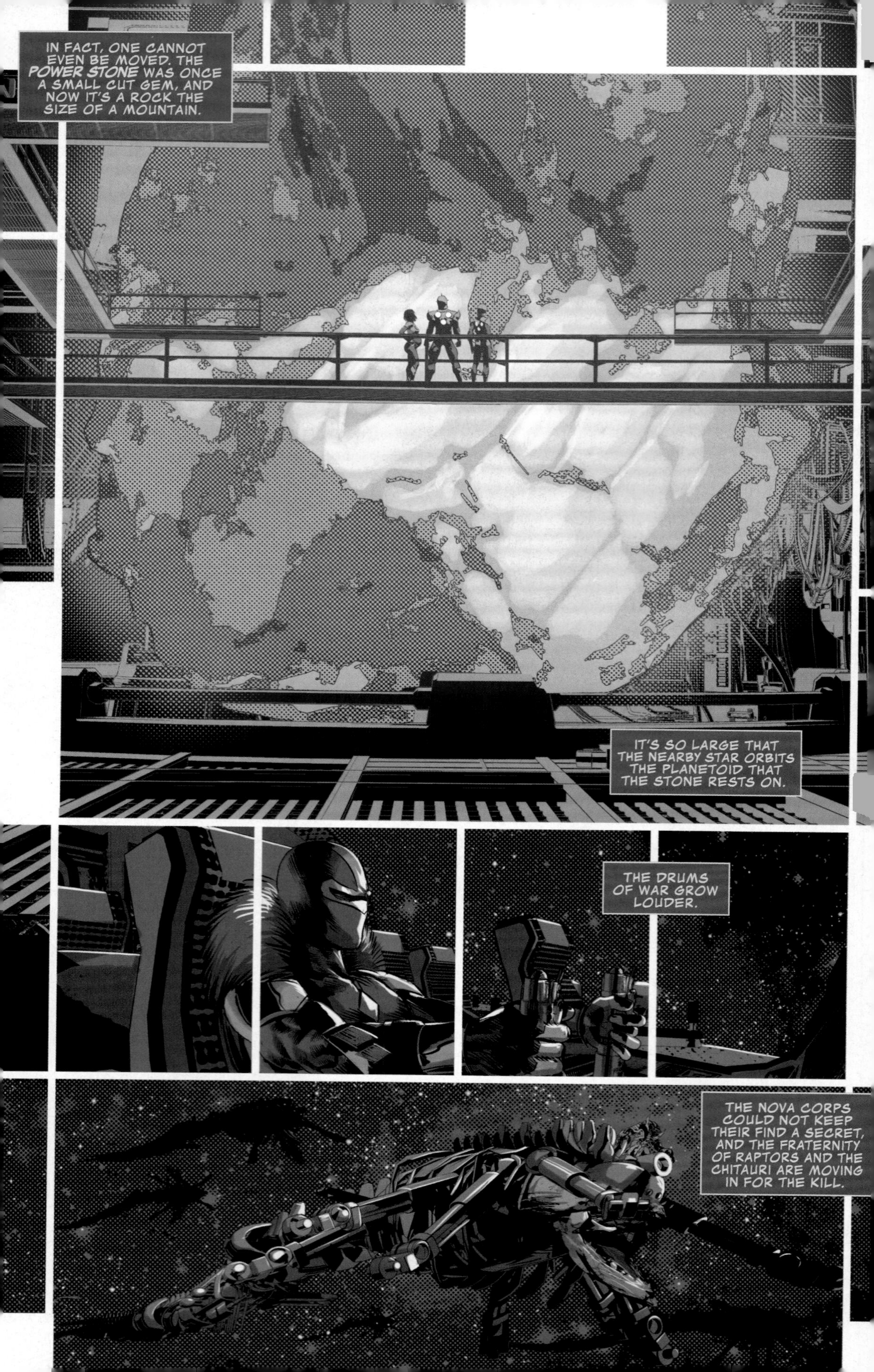
IN FACT, ONE CANNOT EVEN BE MOVED. THE POWER STONE WAS ONCE A SMALL CUT GEM, AND NOW IT'S A ROCK THE SIZE OF A MOUNTAIN.
IT'S SO LARGE THAT THE NEARBY STAR ORBITS THE PLANETOID THAT THE STONE RESTS ON.
THE DRUMS OF WAR GROW LOUDER.
THE NOVA CORPS COULD NOT KEEP THEIR FIND A SECRET, AND THE FRATERNITY OF RAPTORS AND THE CHITAURI ARE MOVING IN FOR THE KILL.

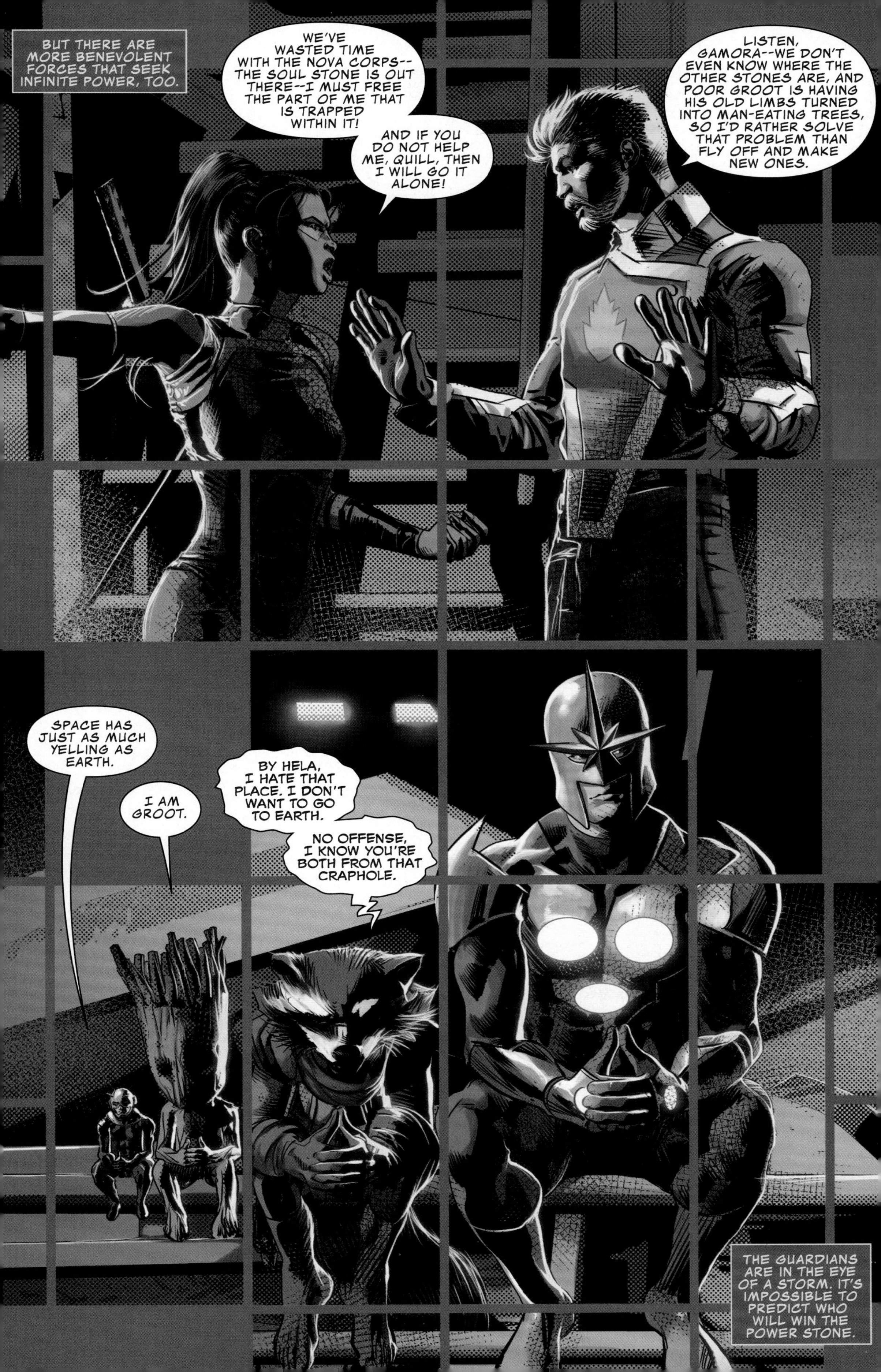
BUT THERE ARE MORE BENEVOLENT FORCES THAT SEEK INFINITE POWER, TOO.
WE'VE WASTED TIME WITH THE NOVA CORPS-- THE SOUL STONE IS OUT THERE--I MUST FREE THE PART OF ME THAT IS TRAPPED WITHIN IT!
AND IF YOU DO NOT HELP ME, QUILL, THEN I WILL GO IT ALONE!
LISTEN, GAMORA--WE DON'T EVEN KNOW WHERE THE OTHER STONES ARE, AND POOR GROOT IS HAVING HIS OLD LIMBS TURNED INTO MAN-EATING TREES, SO I'D RATHER SOLVE THAT PROBLEM THAN FLY OFF AND MAKE NEW ONES.
SPACE HAS JUST AS MUCH YELLING AS EARTH.
I AM GROOT.
BY HELA, I HATE THAT PLACE. I DON'T WANT TO GO TO EARTH.
NO OFFENSE, I KNOW YOU'RE BOTH FROM THAT CRAPHOLE.
THE GUARDIANS ARE IN THE EYE OF A STORM. IT'S IMPOSSIBLE TO PREDICT WHO WILL WIN THE POWER STONE.

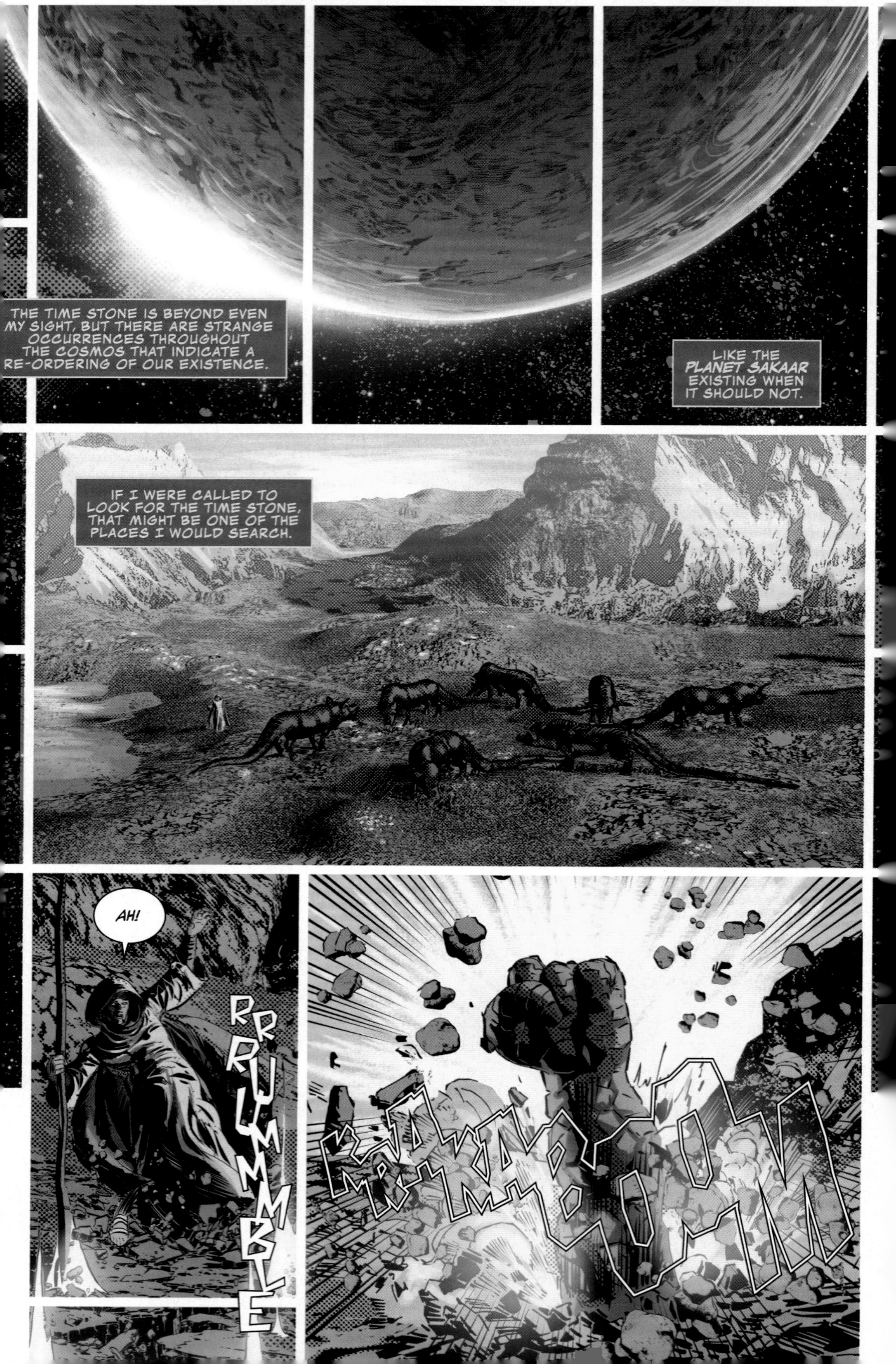
THE TIME STONE IS BEYOND EVEN MY SIGHT, BUT THERE ARE STRANGE OCCURRENCES THROUGHOUT THE COSMOS THAT INDICATE A RE-ORDERING OF OUR EXISTENCE.
LIKE THE PLANET SAKAAR EXISTING WHEN IT SHOULD NOT.
IF I WERE CALLED TO LOOK FOR THE TIME STONE, THAT MIGHT BE ONE OF THE PLACES I WOULD SEARCH.
AH!
RRRUMMMBLE
KRAKA-BOOM

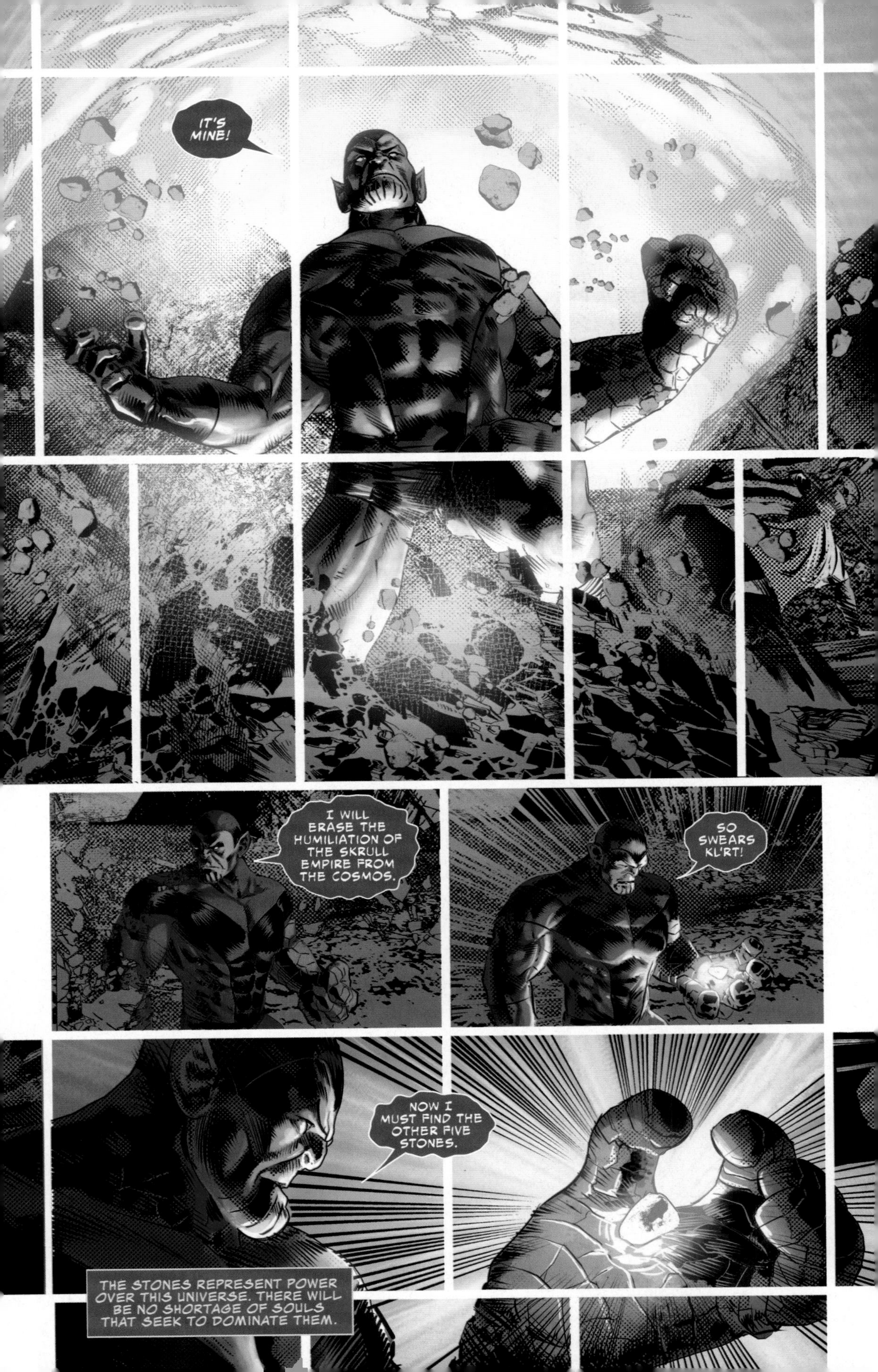
IT'S MINE!
I WILL ERASE THE HUMILIATION OF THE SKRULL EMPIRE FROM THE COSMOS.
SO SWEARS KL'RT!
NOW I MUST FIND THE OTHER FIVE STONES.
THE STONES REPRESENT POWER OVER THIS UNIVERSE. THERE WILL BE NO SHORTAGE OF SOULS THAT SEEK TO DOMINATE THEM.

ADAM WARLOCK WILL BE A PLAYER IN THE *COMING STRIFE.*

ESPECIALLY WHEN YOU CONSIDER THE *CURIOUS* RELATIONSHIP HE SEEMS TO HAVE WITH THE *SOUL GEM.*

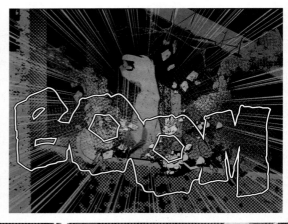

BOOM

AEEEIIIII!

YOU THERE, *BOY!* WHAT *YEAR* IS IT?

2018.

WONDERFUL.

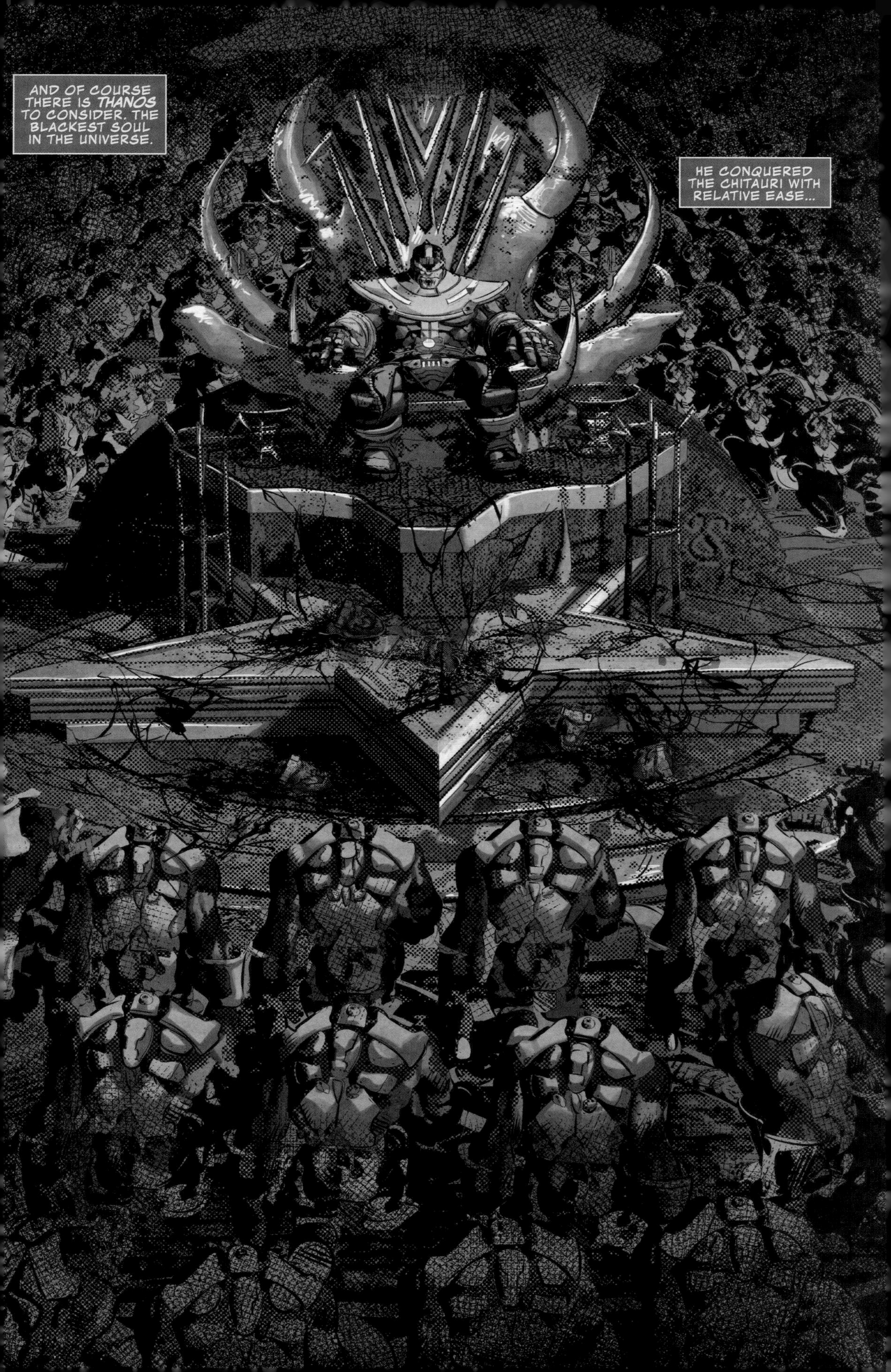
AND OF COURSE THERE IS *THANOS* TO CONSIDER. THE BLACKEST SOUL IN THE UNIVERSE.
HE CONQUERED THE CHITAURI WITH RELATIVE EASE...

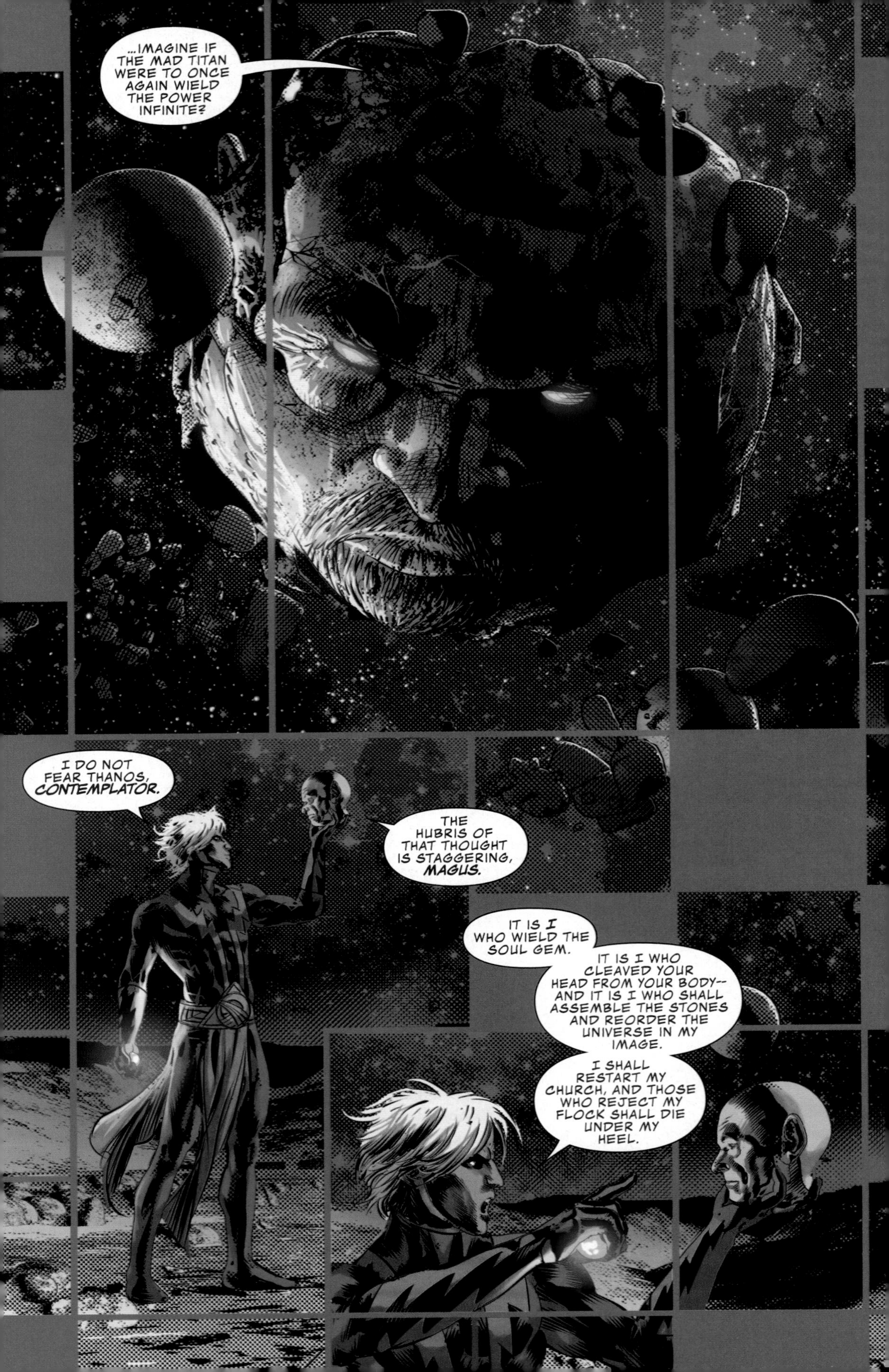
...IMAGINE IF THE MAD TITAN WERE TO ONCE AGAIN WIELD THE POWER INFINITE?
I DO NOT FEAR THANOS, CONTEMPLATOR.
THE HUBRIS OF THAT THOUGHT IS STAGGERING, MAGUS.
IT IS I WHO WIELD THE SOUL GEM.
IT IS I WHO CLEAVED YOUR HEAD FROM YOUR BODY-- AND IT IS I WHO SHALL ASSEMBLE THE STONES AND REORDER THE UNIVERSE IN MY IMAGE.
I SHALL RESTART MY CHURCH, AND THOSE WHO REJECT MY FLOCK SHALL DIE UNDER MY HEEL.

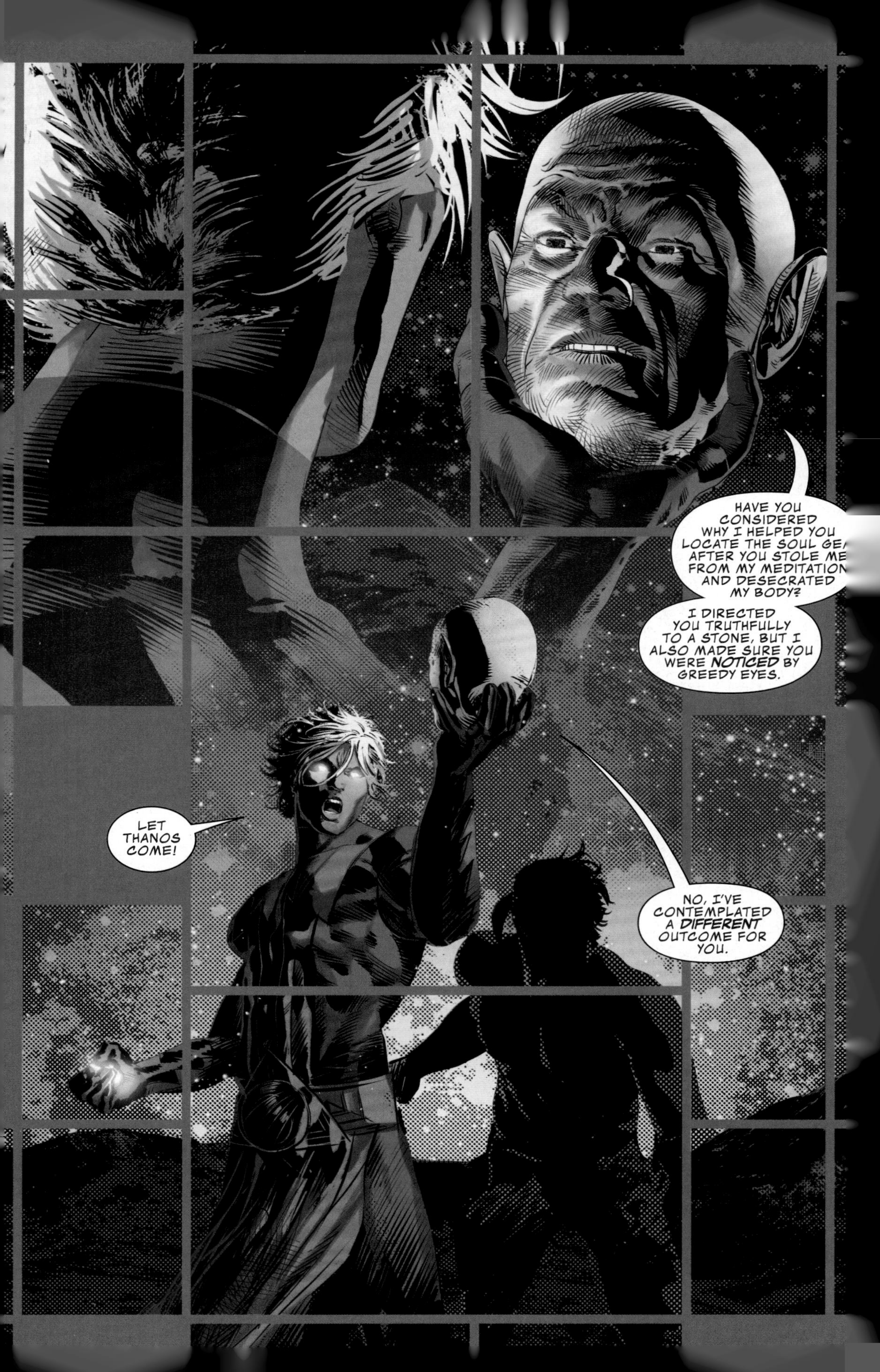
HAVE YOU CONSIDERED WHY I HELPED YOU LOCATE THE SOUL GE AFTER YOU STOLE ME FROM MY MEDITATION AND DESECRATED MY BODY?
I DIRECTED YOU TRUTHFULLY TO A STONE, BUT I ALSO MADE SURE YOU WERE NOTICED BY GREEDY EYES.
LET THANOS COME!
NO, I'VE CONTEMPLATED A DIFFERENT OUTCOME FOR YOU.

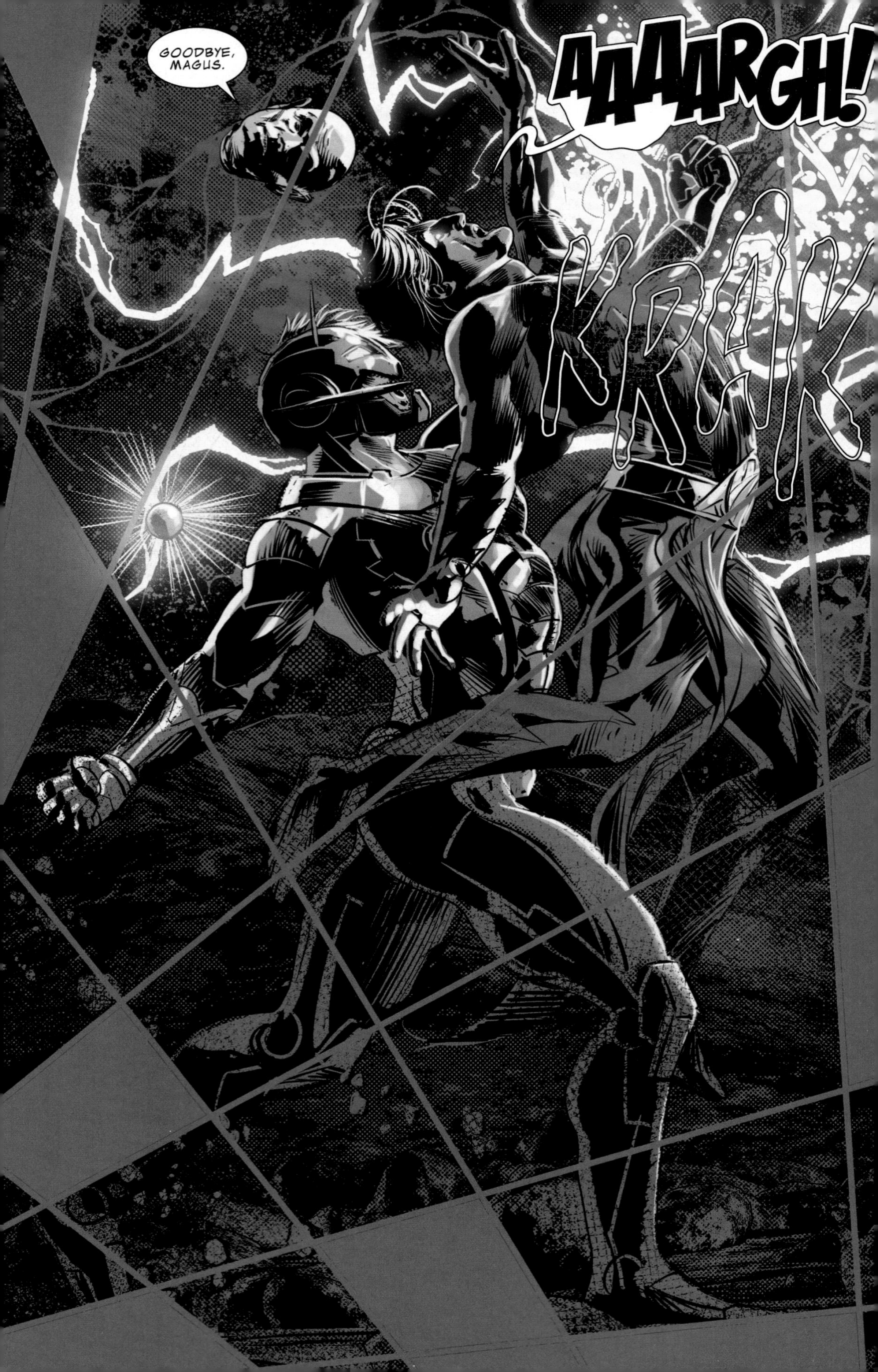
GOODBYE, MAGUS.
AAAARGH!
KRAAK

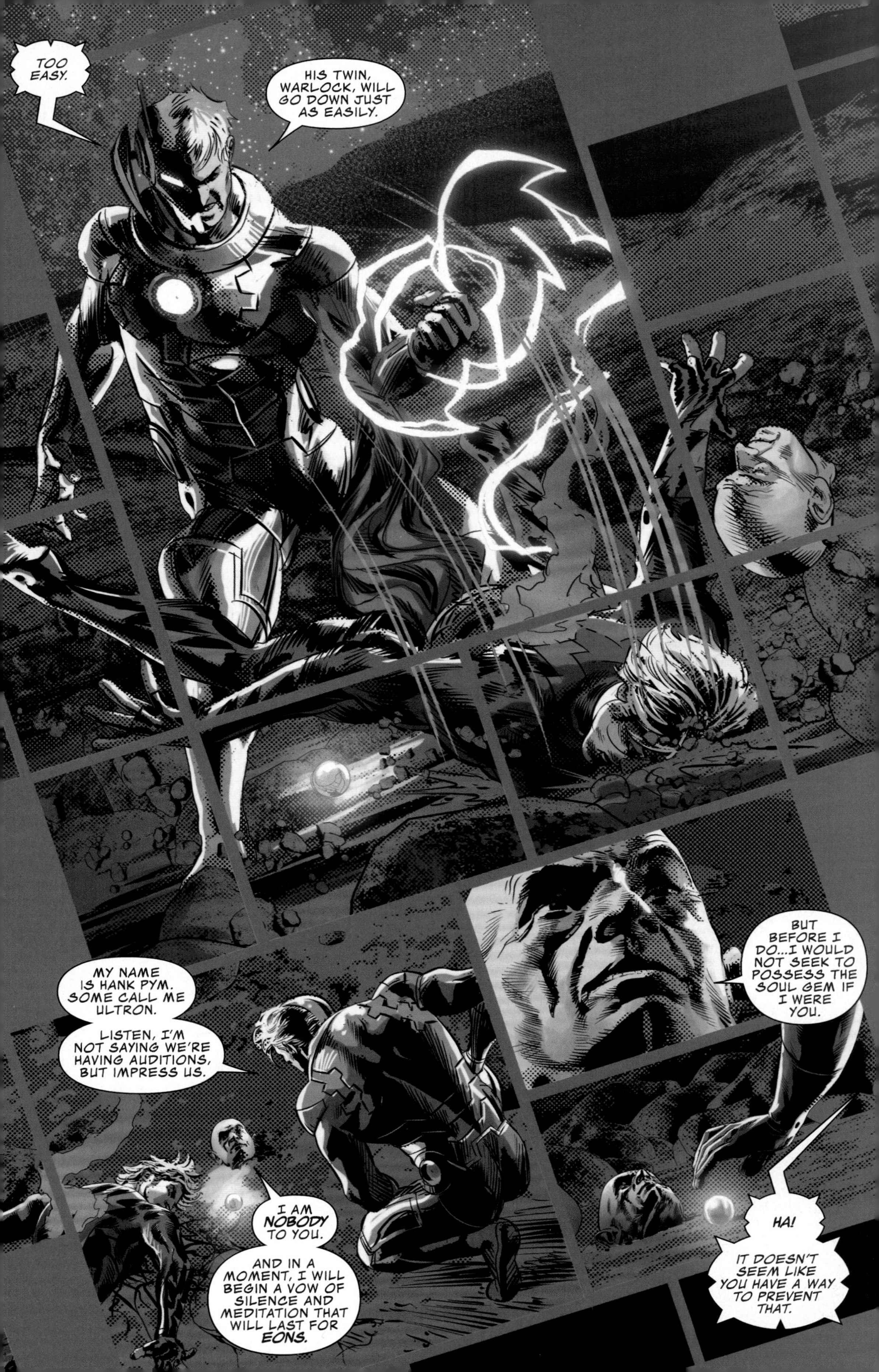
TOO EASY.
HIS TWIN, WARLOCK, WILL GO DOWN JUST AS EASILY.
MY NAME IS HANK PYM. SOME CALL ME ULTRON.
LISTEN, I'M NOT SAYING WE'RE HAVING AUDITIONS, BUT IMPRESS US.
I AM NOBODY TO YOU.
AND IN A MOMENT, I WILL BEGIN A VOW OF SILENCE AND MEDITATION THAT WILL LAST FOR EONS.
BUT BEFORE I DO...I WOULD NOT SEEK TO POSSESS THE SOUL GEM IF I WERE YOU.
HA!
IT DOESN'T SEEM LIKE YOU HAVE A WAY TO PREVENT THAT.

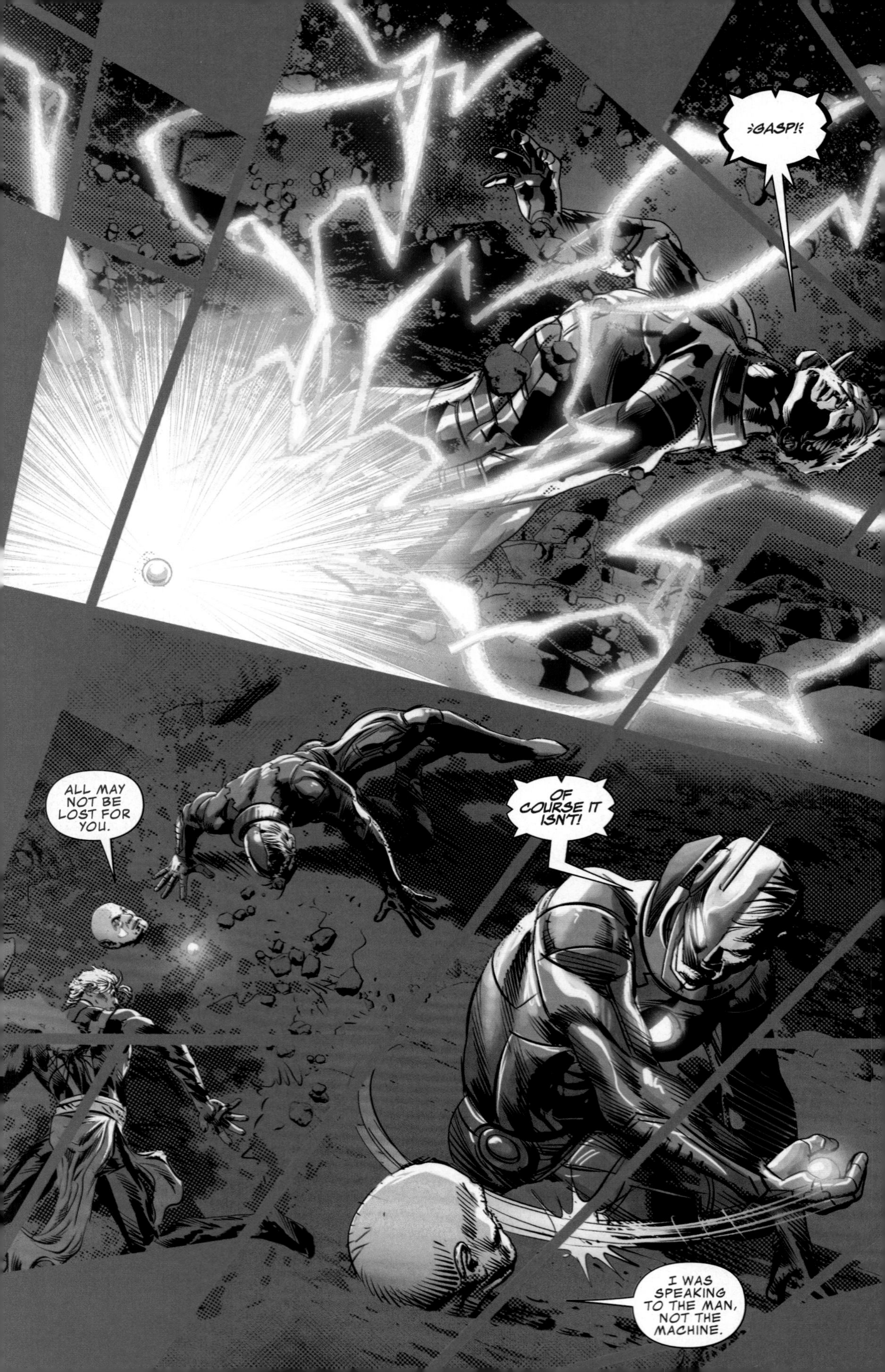
GASP!
ALL MAY NOT BE LOST FOR YOU.
OF COURSE IT ISN'T!
I WAS SPEAKING TO THE MAN, NOT THE MACHINE.

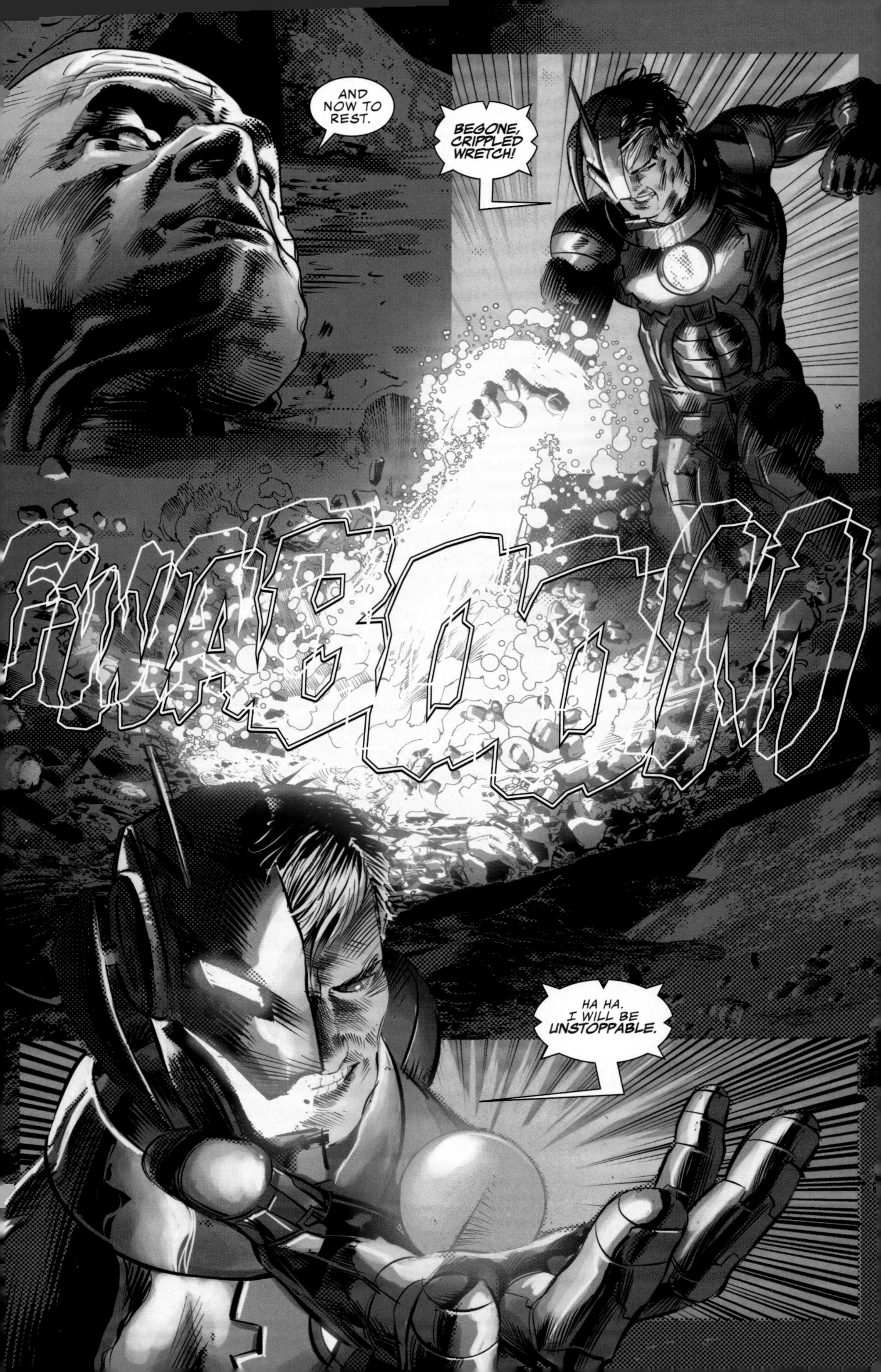
AND NOW TO REST.
BEGONE, CRIPPLED WRETCH!
FWAKBOOM
HA HA. I WILL BE UNSTOPPABLE.

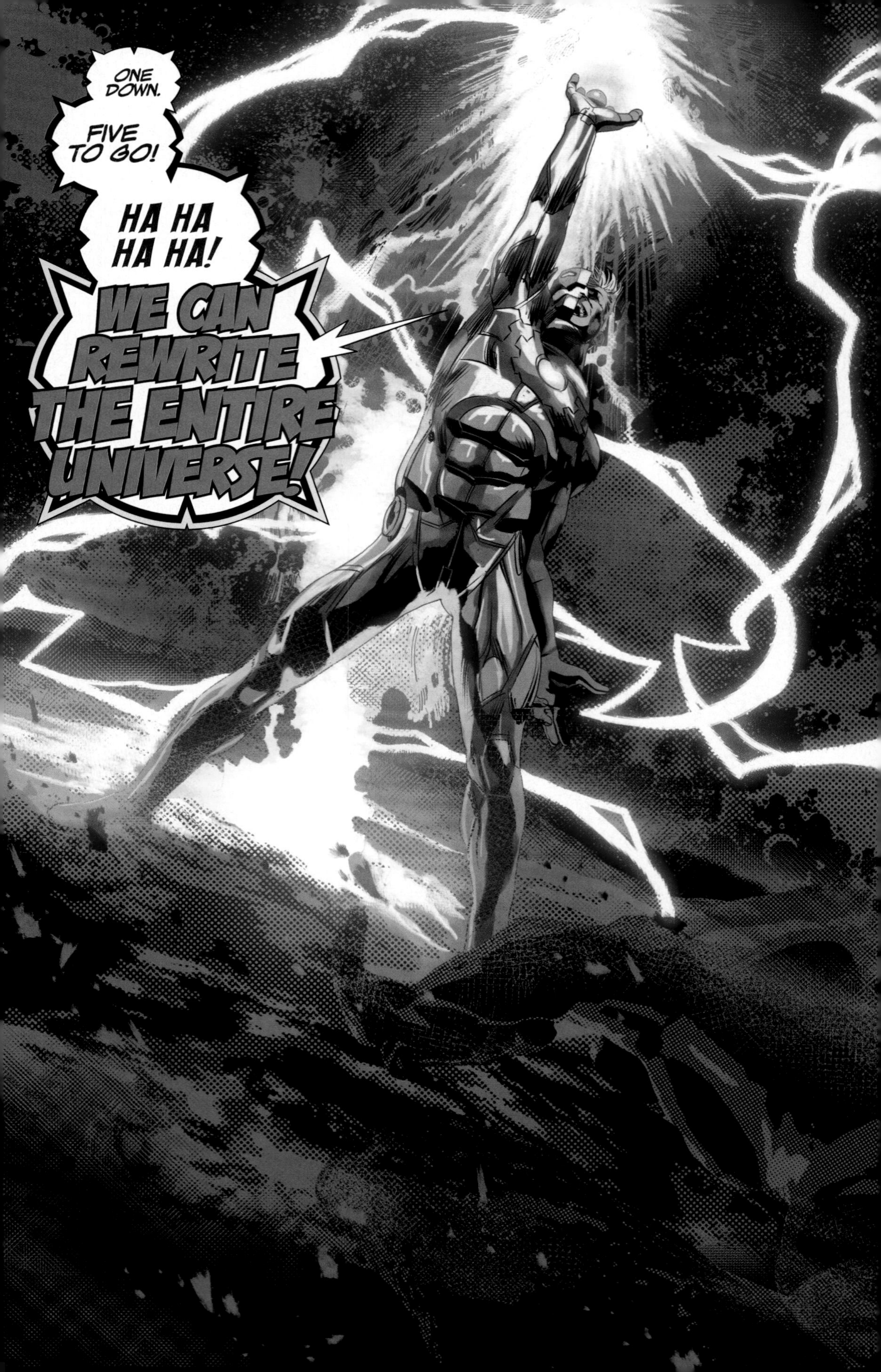
ONE DOWN.
FIVE TO GO!
HA HA HA HA!
WE CAN REWRITE THE ENTIRE UNIVERSE!

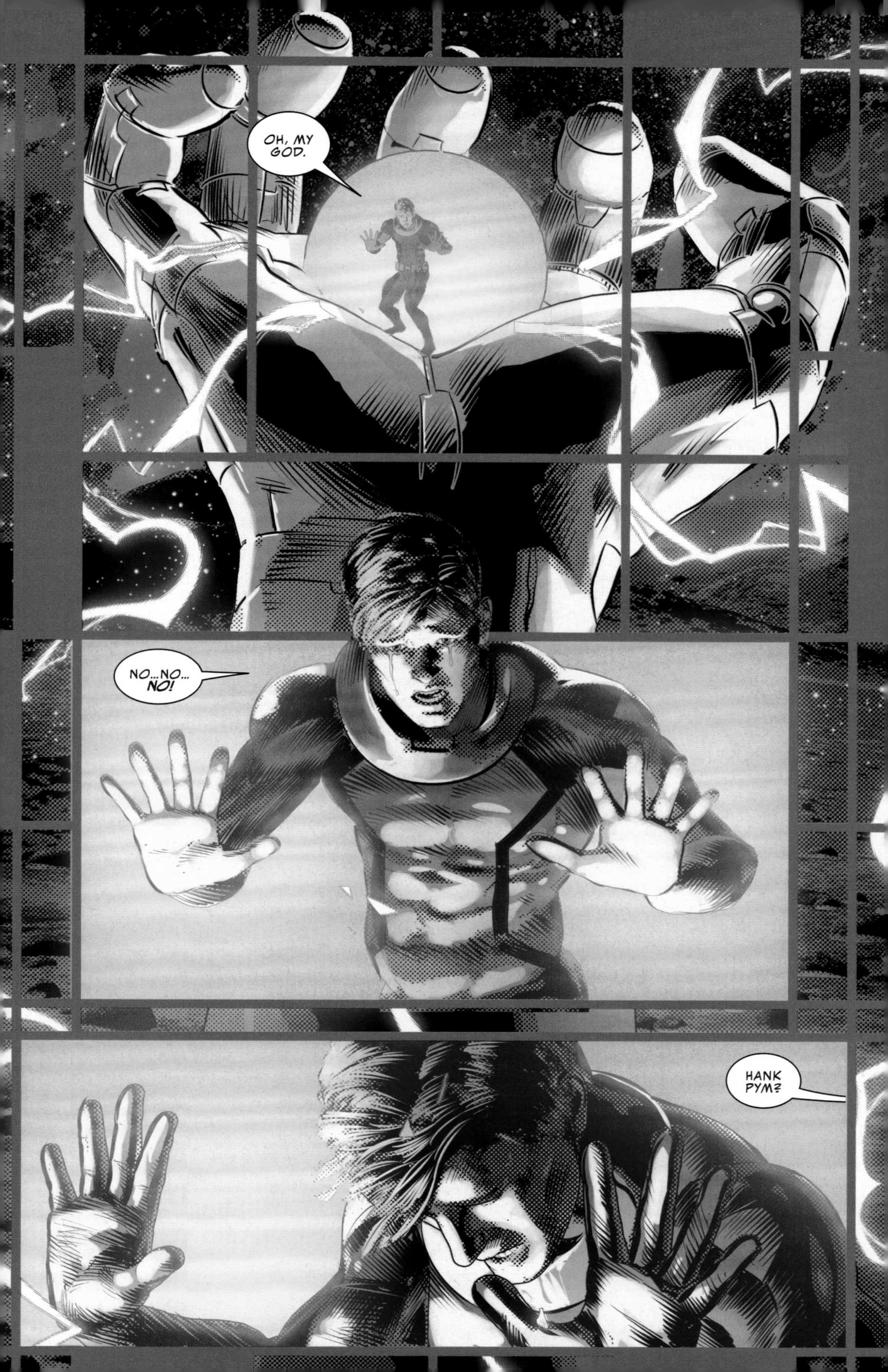
OH, MY GOD.
NO...NO... NO!
HANK PYM?

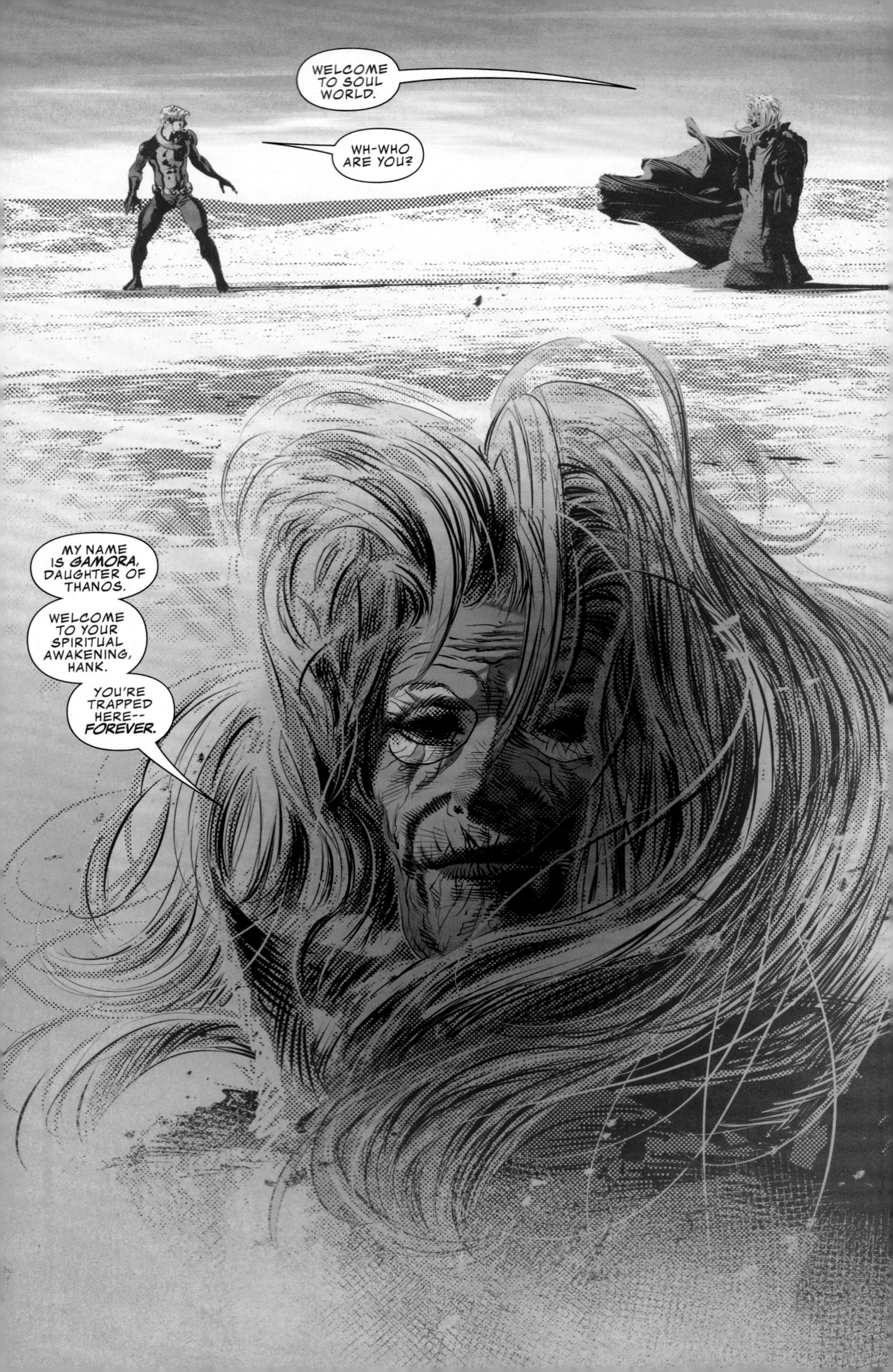
WELCOME TO SOUL WORLD.
WH-WHO ARE YOU?
MY NAME IS *GAMORA*, DAUGHTER OF THANOS.
WELCOME TO YOUR SPIRITUAL AWAKENING, HANK.
YOU'RE TRAPPED HERE-- ***FOREVER.***

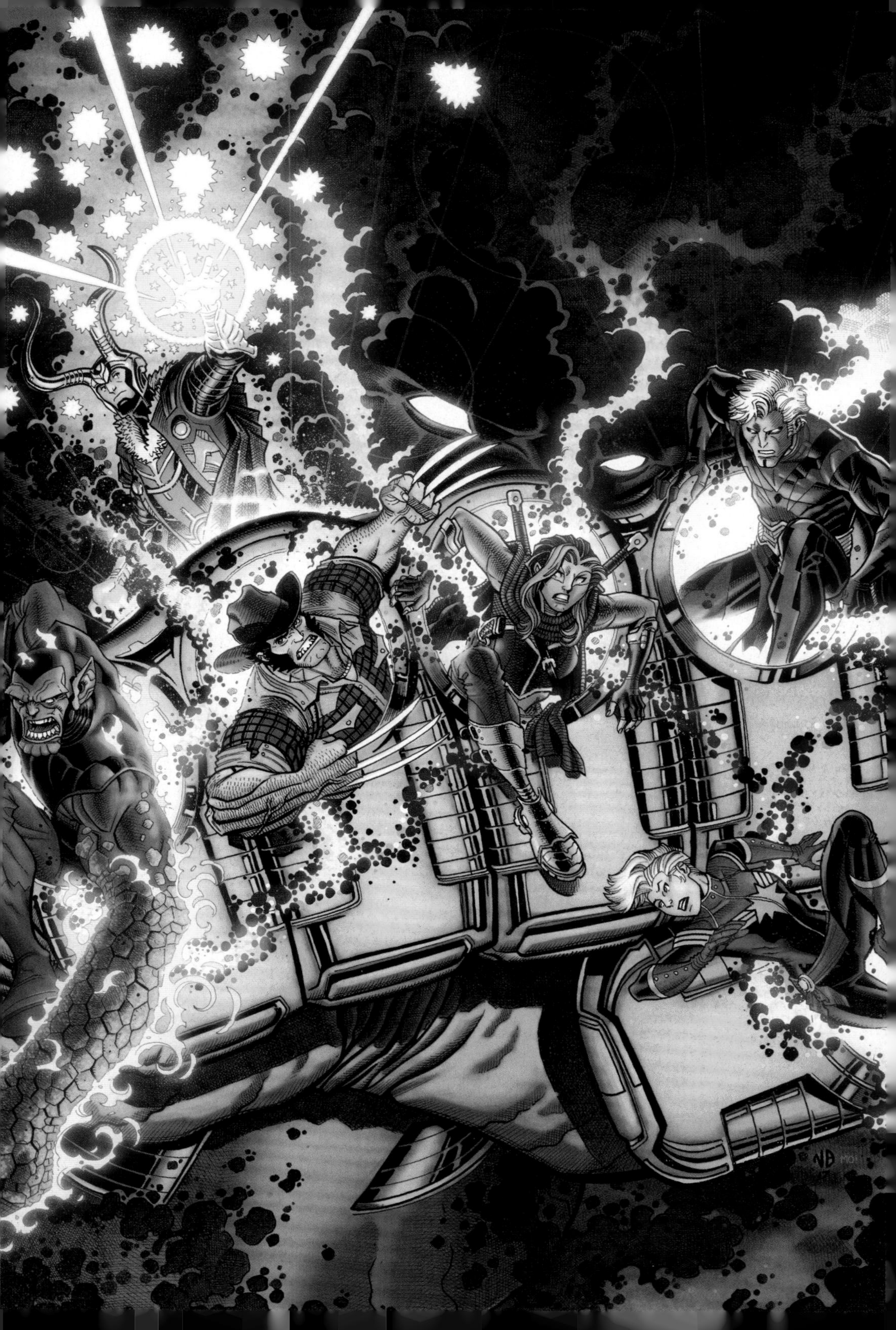

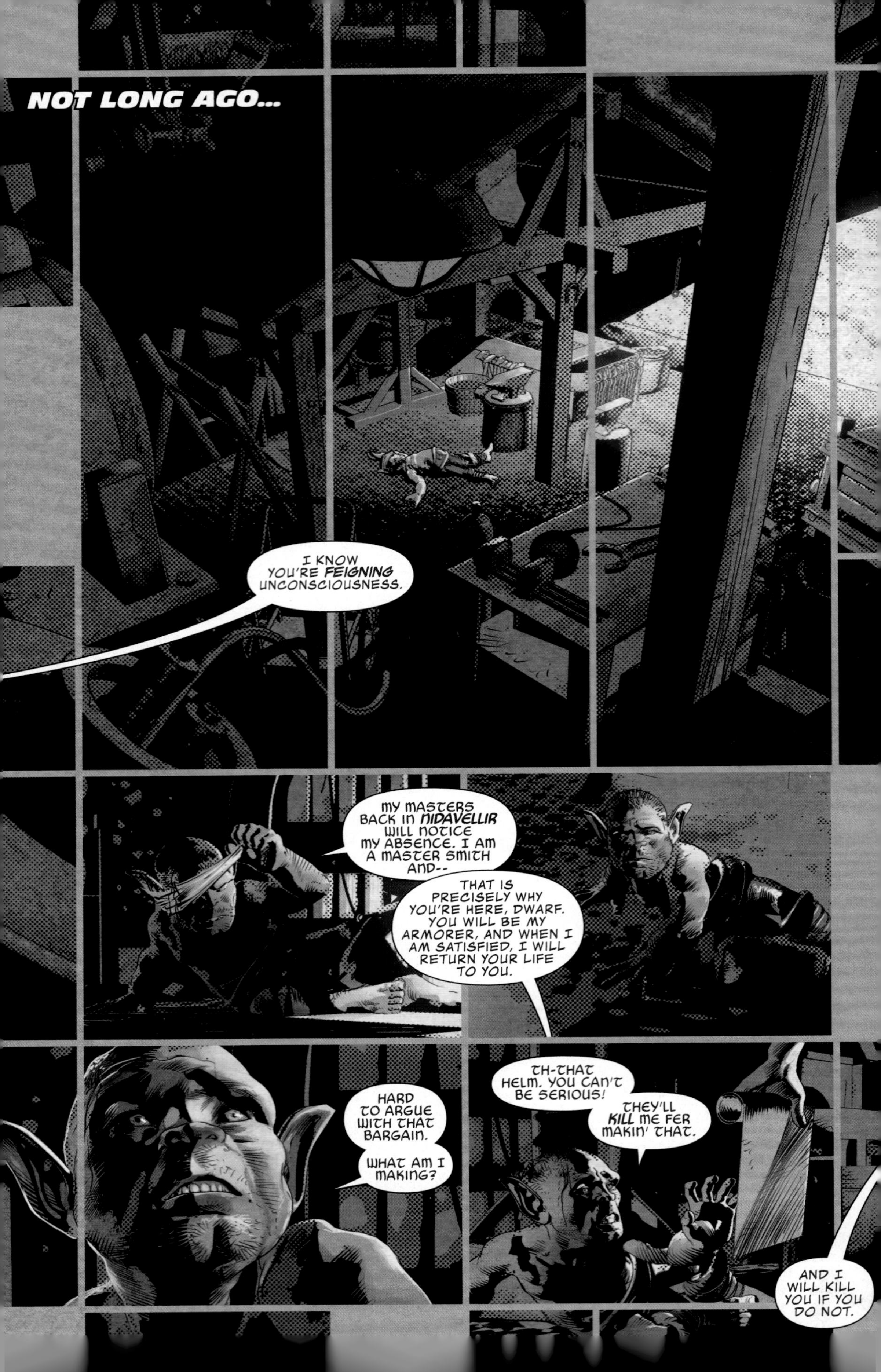
NOT LONG AGO...
I KNOW YOU'RE FEIGNING UNCONSCIOUSNESS.
MY MASTERS BACK IN NIDAVELLIR WILL NOTICE MY ABSENCE. I AM A MASTER SMITH AND--
THAT IS PRECISELY WHY YOU'RE HERE, DWARF. YOU WILL BE MY ARMORER, AND WHEN I AM SATISFIED, I WILL RETURN YOUR LIFE TO YOU.
HARD TO ARGUE WITH THAT BARGAIN.
WHAT AM I MAKING?
TH-THAT HELM. YOU CAN'T BE SERIOUS!
THEY'LL KILL ME FER MAKIN' THAT.
AND I WILL KILL YOU IF YOU DO NOT.

INFINITY
COUNTDOWN

THE INFINITY STONES WERE REBORN AND SCATTERED.

THE LARGEST, THE POWER STONE, IS HIDDEN ON THE PLANETOID XITAUNG.
DRAX AND THE NOVA CORPS, LED BY EVE BAKIAN, HOLD THEIR GROUND AS ENEMIES GATHER.
MEANWHILE, THE GUARDIANS OF THE GALAXY FACE THE FORMIDABLE GARDENER, WHOSE ARMY
OF EVIL TREE-LIKE CREATURES HAS OVERRUN THE PLANET TELFERINA.

AS FOR THE OTHER STONES, THEY NEVER STAY SECRET FOR LONG...

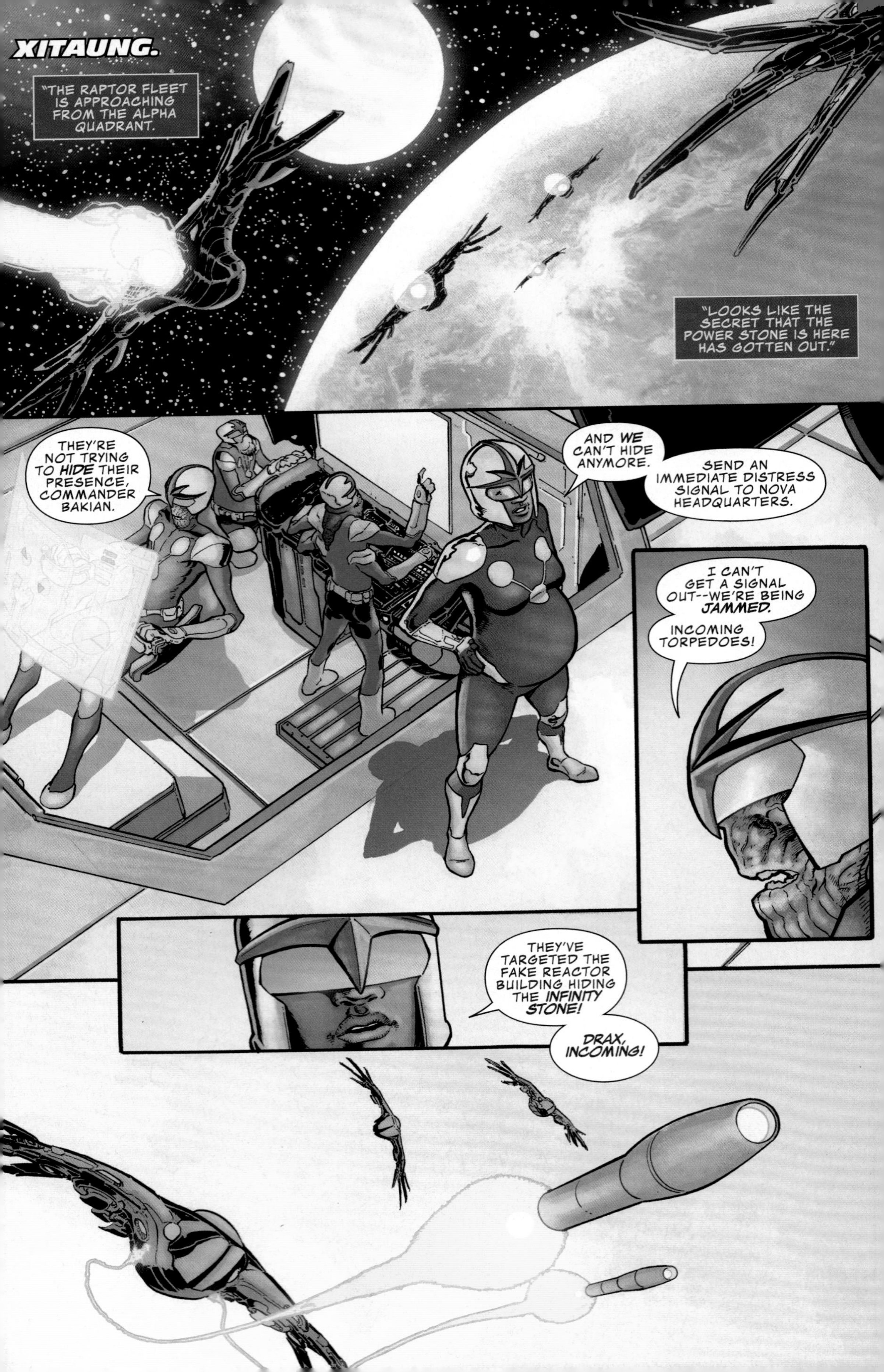
XITAUNG.
"THE RAPTOR FLEET IS APPROACHING FROM THE ALPHA QUADRANT.
"LOOKS LIKE THE SECRET THAT THE POWER STONE IS HERE HAS GOTTEN OUT."
THEY'RE NOT TRYING TO HIDE THEIR PRESENCE, COMMANDER BAKIAN.
AND WE CAN'T HIDE ANYMORE.
SEND AN IMMEDIATE DISTRESS SIGNAL TO NOVA HEADQUARTERS.
I CAN'T GET A SIGNAL OUT--WE'RE BEING JAMMED.
INCOMING TORPEDOES!
THEY'VE TARGETED THE FAKE REACTOR BUILDING HIDING THE INFINITY STONE!
DRAX, INCOMING!

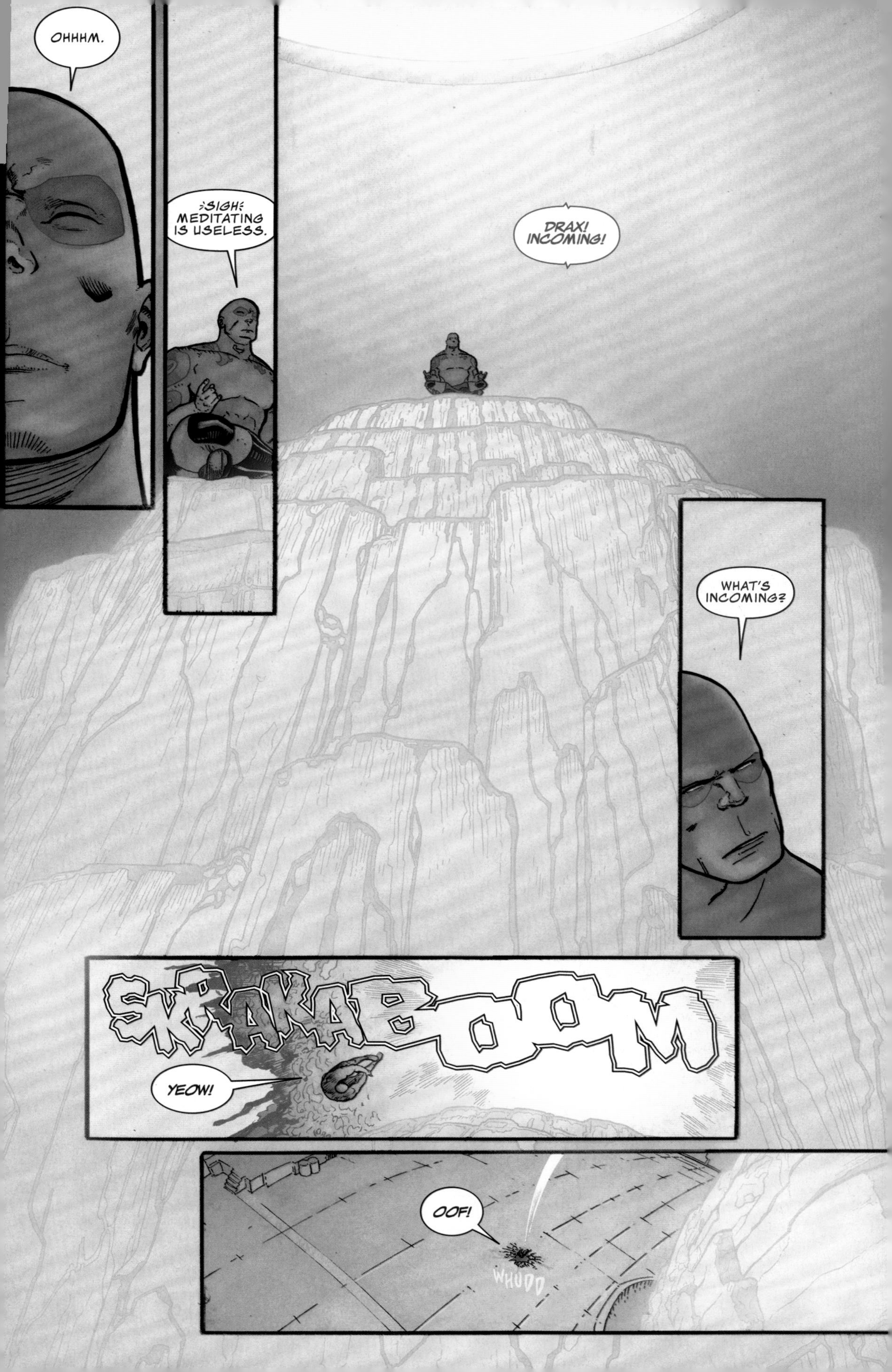
OHHHM.
SIGH
MEDITATING IS USELESS.
DRAX! INCOMING!
WHAT'S INCOMING?
SKRAKA-BOOM
YEOW!
OOF!
WHUDD

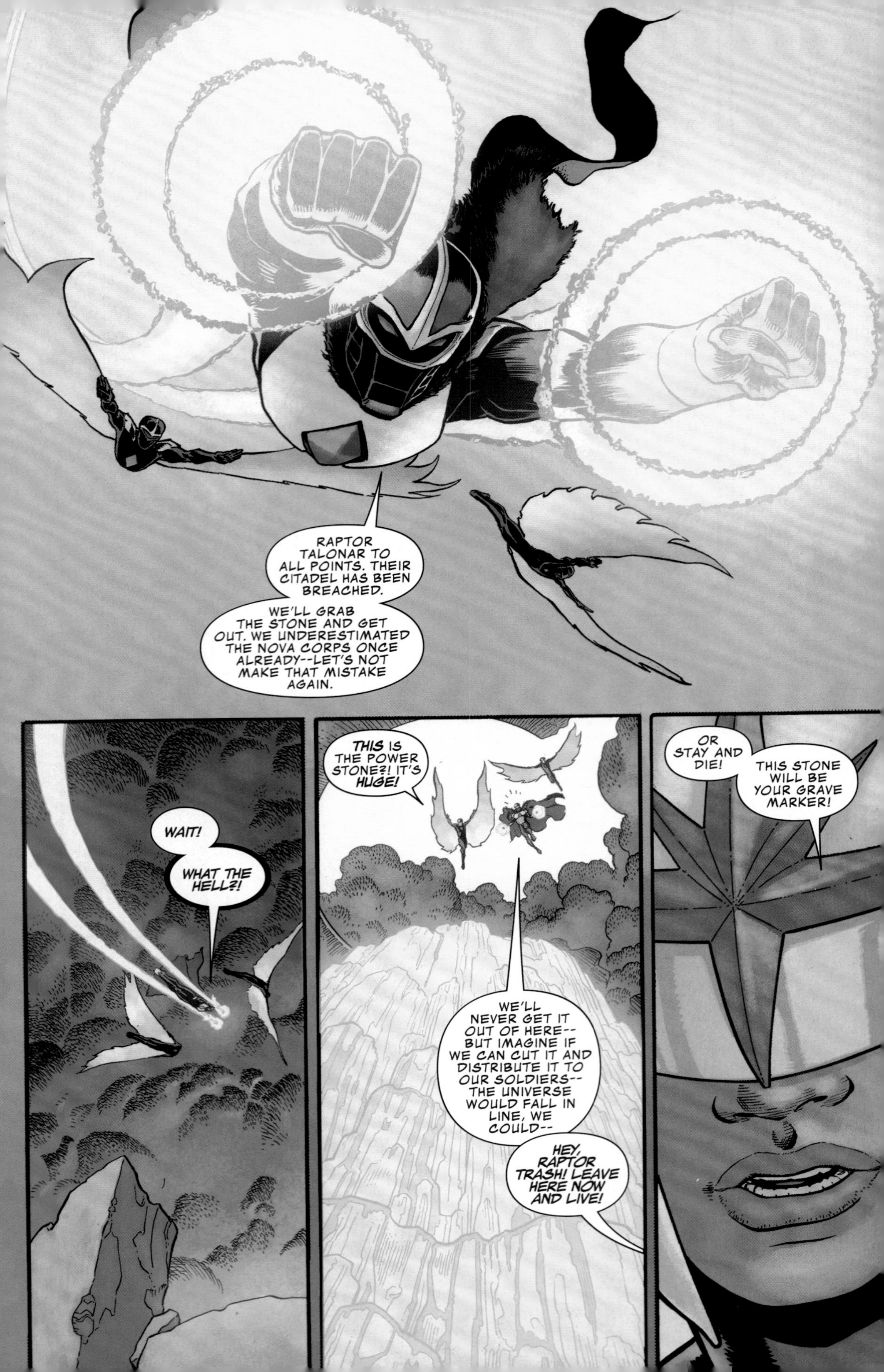

RAPTOR TALONAR TO ALL POINTS. THEIR CITADEL HAS BEEN BREACHED.
WE'LL GRAB THE STONE AND GET OUT. WE UNDERESTIMATED THE NOVA CORPS ONCE ALREADY--LET'S NOT MAKE THAT MISTAKE AGAIN.
WAIT!
WHAT THE HELL?!
THIS IS THE POWER STONE?! IT'S HUGE!
WE'LL NEVER GET IT OUT OF HERE-- BUT IMAGINE IF WE CAN CUT IT AND DISTRIBUTE IT TO OUR SOLDIERS-- THE UNIVERSE WOULD FALL IN LINE, WE COULD--
HEY, RAPTOR TRASH! LEAVE HERE NOW AND LIVE!
OR STAY AND DIE!
THIS STONE WILL BE YOUR GRAVE MARKER!

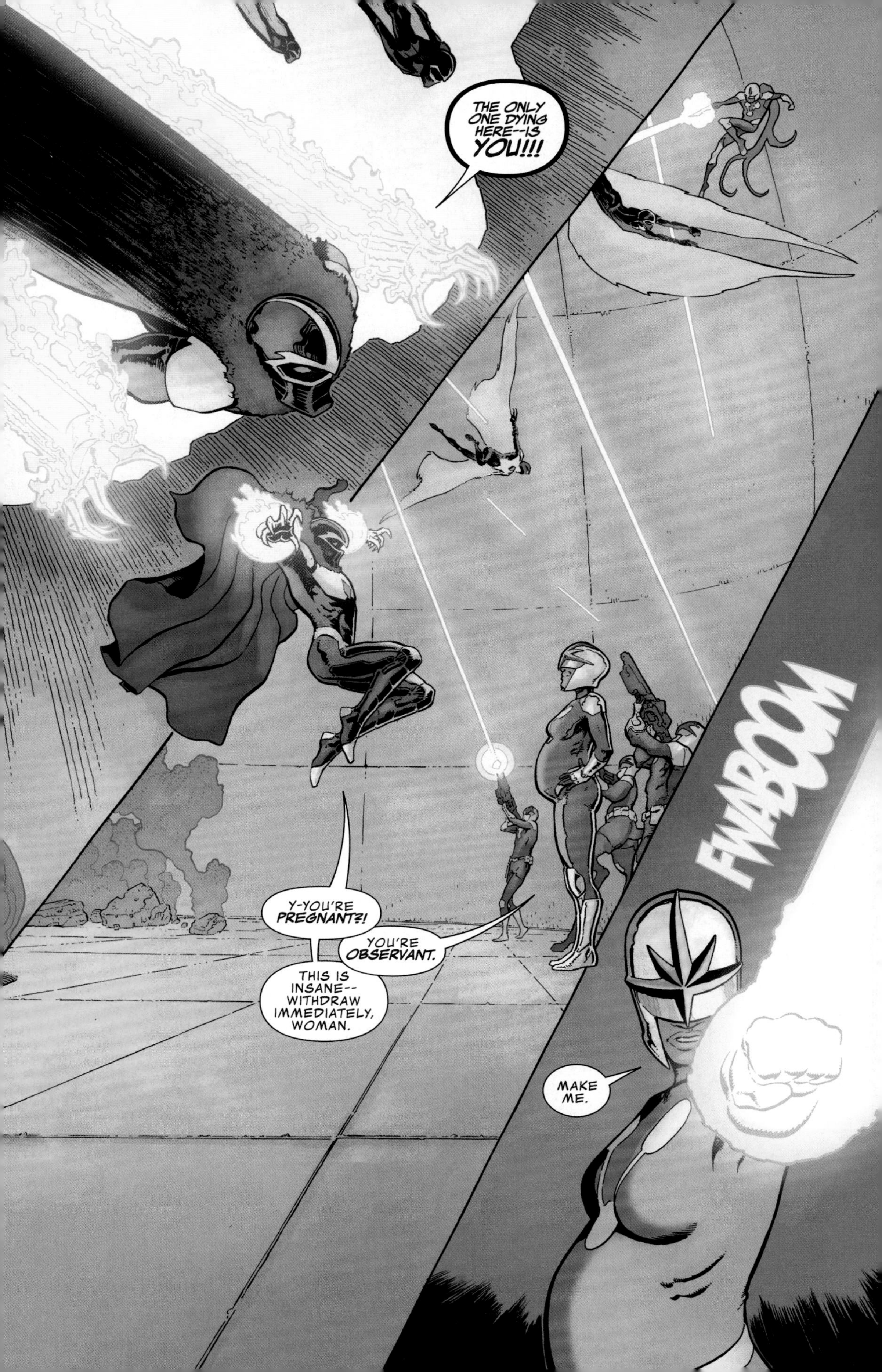
THE ONLY ONE DYING HERE--IS YOU!!!
Y-YOU'RE PREGNANT?!
YOU'RE OBSERVANT.
THIS IS INSANE--WITHDRAW IMMEDIATELY, WOMAN.
FWABOOM
MAKE ME.

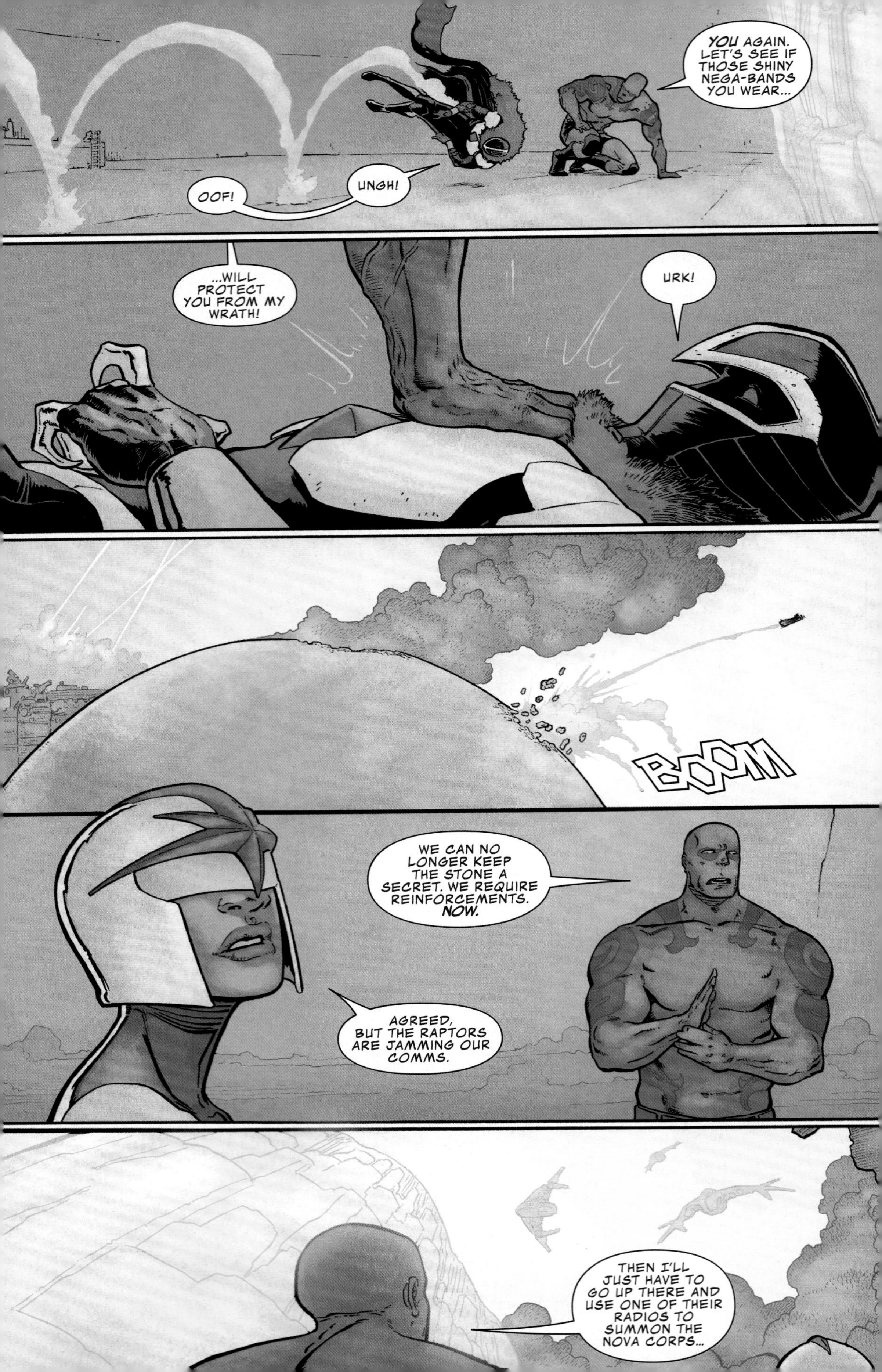
YOU AGAIN. LET'S SEE IF THOSE SHINY NEGA-BANDS YOU WEAR...
OOF!
UNGH!
...WILL PROTECT YOU FROM MY WRATH!
URK!
BOOM
WE CAN NO LONGER KEEP THE STONE A SECRET. WE REQUIRE REINFORCEMENTS. NOW.
AGREED, BUT THE RAPTORS ARE JAMMING OUR COMMS.
THEN I'LL JUST HAVE TO GO UP THERE AND USE ONE OF THEIR RADIOS TO SUMMON THE NOVA CORPS...

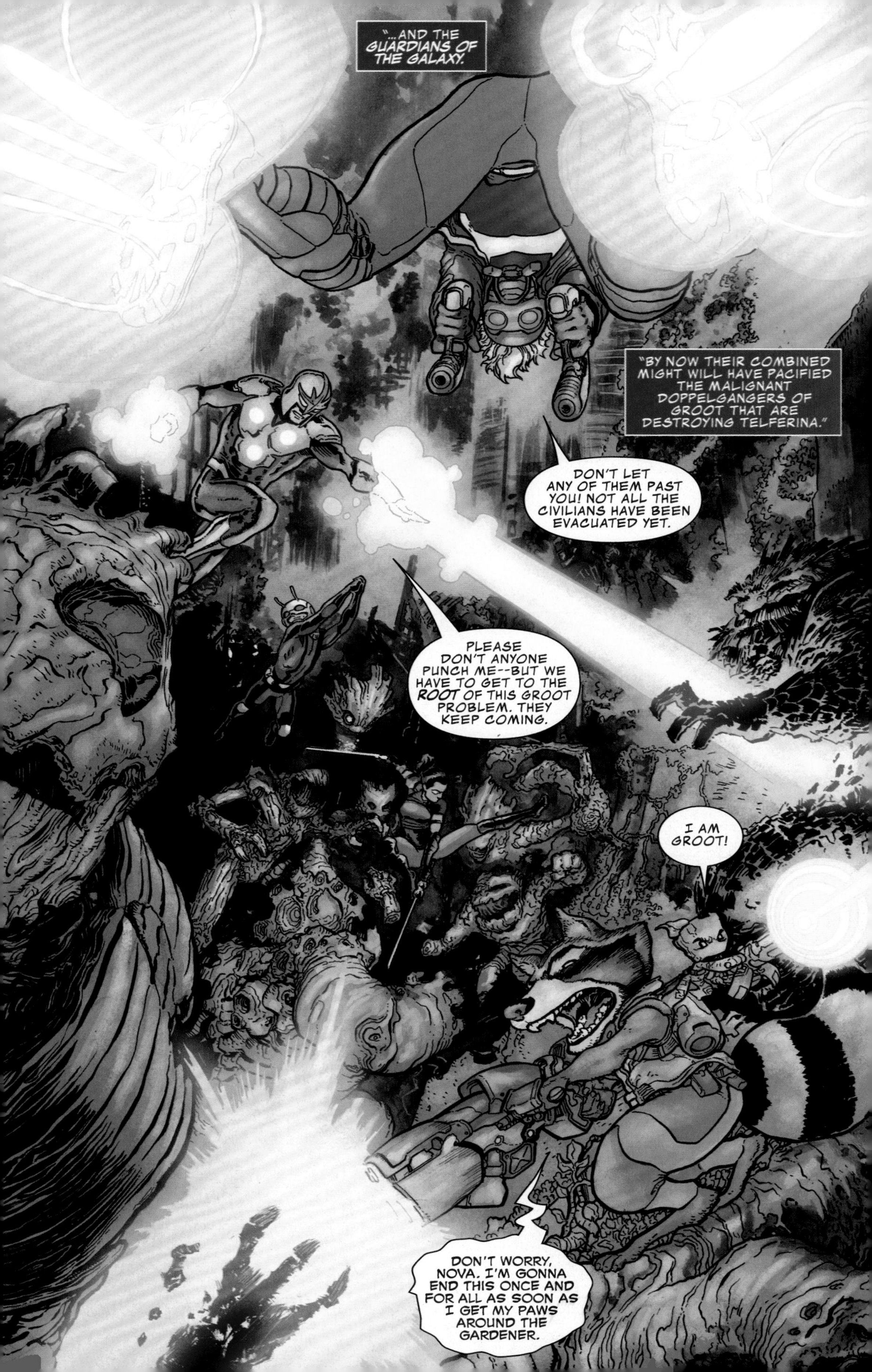
"...AND THE GUARDIANS OF THE GALAXY.
"BY NOW THEIR COMBINED MIGHT WILL HAVE PACIFIED THE MALIGNANT DOPPELGANGERS OF GROOT THAT ARE DESTROYING TELFERINA."
DON'T LET ANY OF THEM PAST YOU! NOT ALL THE CIVILIANS HAVE BEEN EVACUATED YET.
PLEASE DON'T ANYONE PUNCH ME--BUT WE HAVE TO GET TO THE ROOT OF THIS GROOT PROBLEM. THEY KEEP COMING.
I AM GROOT!
DON'T WORRY, NOVA. I'M GONNA END THIS ONCE AND FOR ALL AS SOON AS I GET MY PAWS AROUND THE GARDENER.

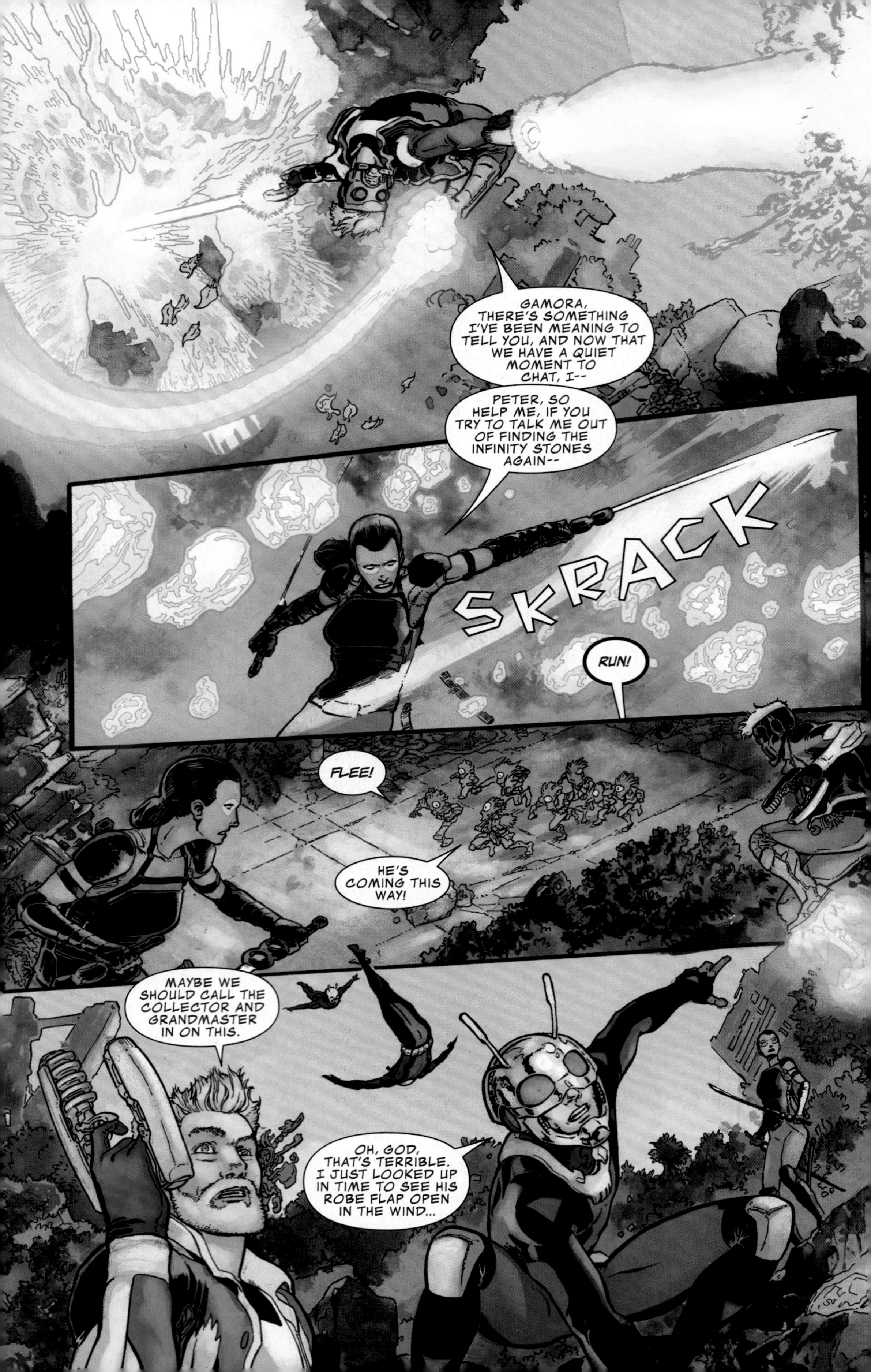
GAMORA, THERE'S SOMETHING I'VE BEEN MEANING TO TELL YOU, AND NOW THAT WE HAVE A QUIET MOMENT TO CHAT, I--
PETER, SO HELP ME, IF YOU TRY TO TALK ME OUT OF FINDING THE INFINITY STONES AGAIN--
SKRACK
RUN!
FLEE!
HE'S COMING THIS WAY!
MAYBE WE SHOULD CALL THE COLLECTOR AND GRANDMASTER IN ON THIS.
OH, GOD, THAT'S TERRIBLE. I JUST LOOKED UP IN TIME TO SEE HIS ROBE FLAP OPEN IN THE WIND...

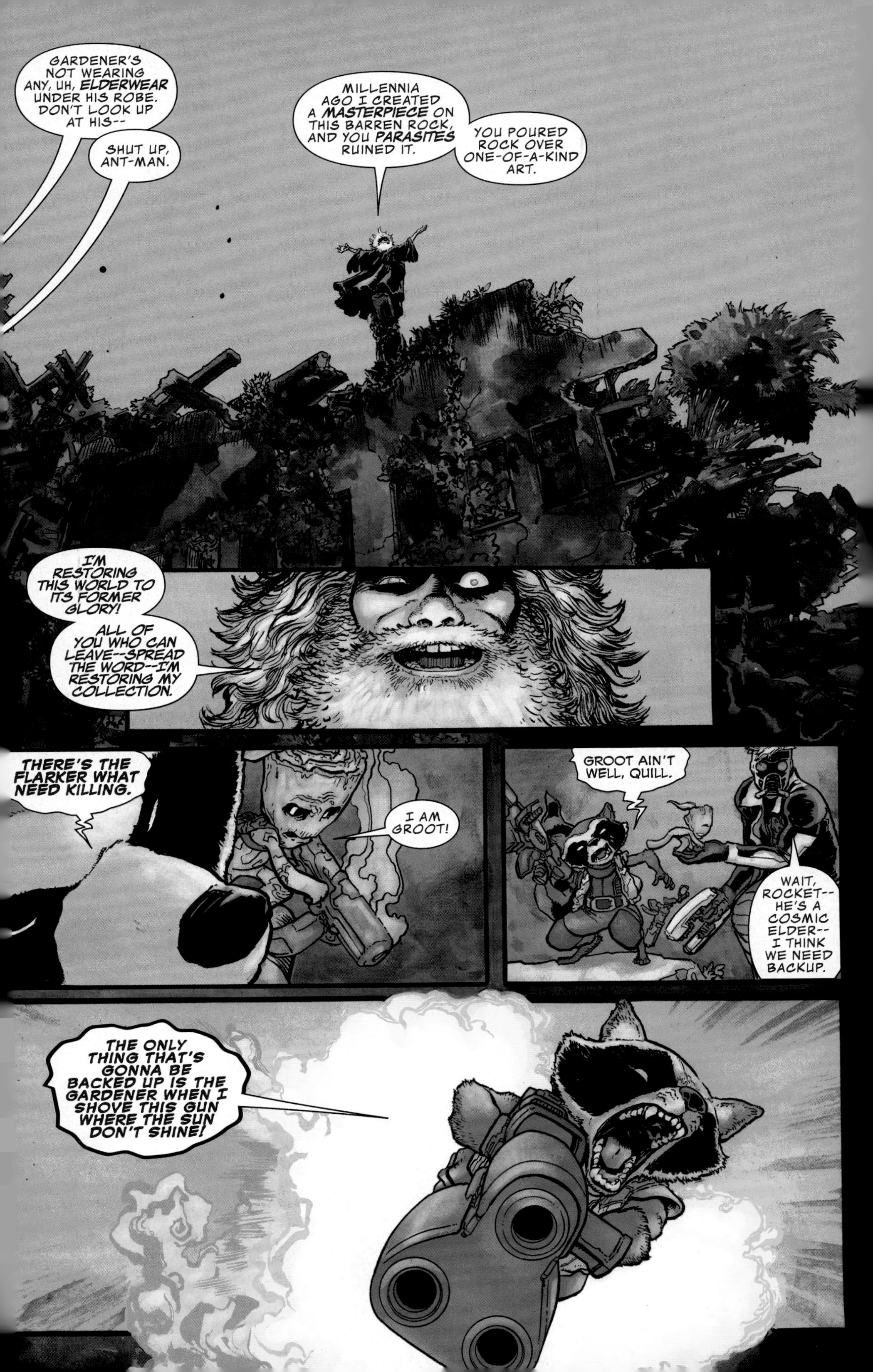
GARDENER'S NOT WEARING ANY, UH, ELDERWEAR UNDER HIS ROBE. DON'T LOOK UP AT HIS--
SHUT UP, ANT-MAN.
MILLENNIA AGO I CREATED A MASTERPIECE ON THIS BARREN ROCK, AND YOU PARASITES RUINED IT.
YOU POURED ROCK OVER ONE-OF-A-KIND ART.
I'M RESTORING THIS WORLD TO ITS FORMER GLORY!
ALL OF YOU WHO CAN LEAVE--SPREAD THE WORD--I'M RESTORING MY COLLECTION.
THERE'S THE FLARKER WHAT NEED KILLING.
I AM GROOT!
GROOT AIN'T WELL, QUILL.
WAIT, ROCKET-- HE'S A COSMIC ELDER-- I THINK WE NEED BACKUP.
THE ONLY THING THAT'S GONNA BE BACKED UP IS THE GARDENER WHEN I SHOVE THIS GUN WHERE THE SUN DON'T SHINE!

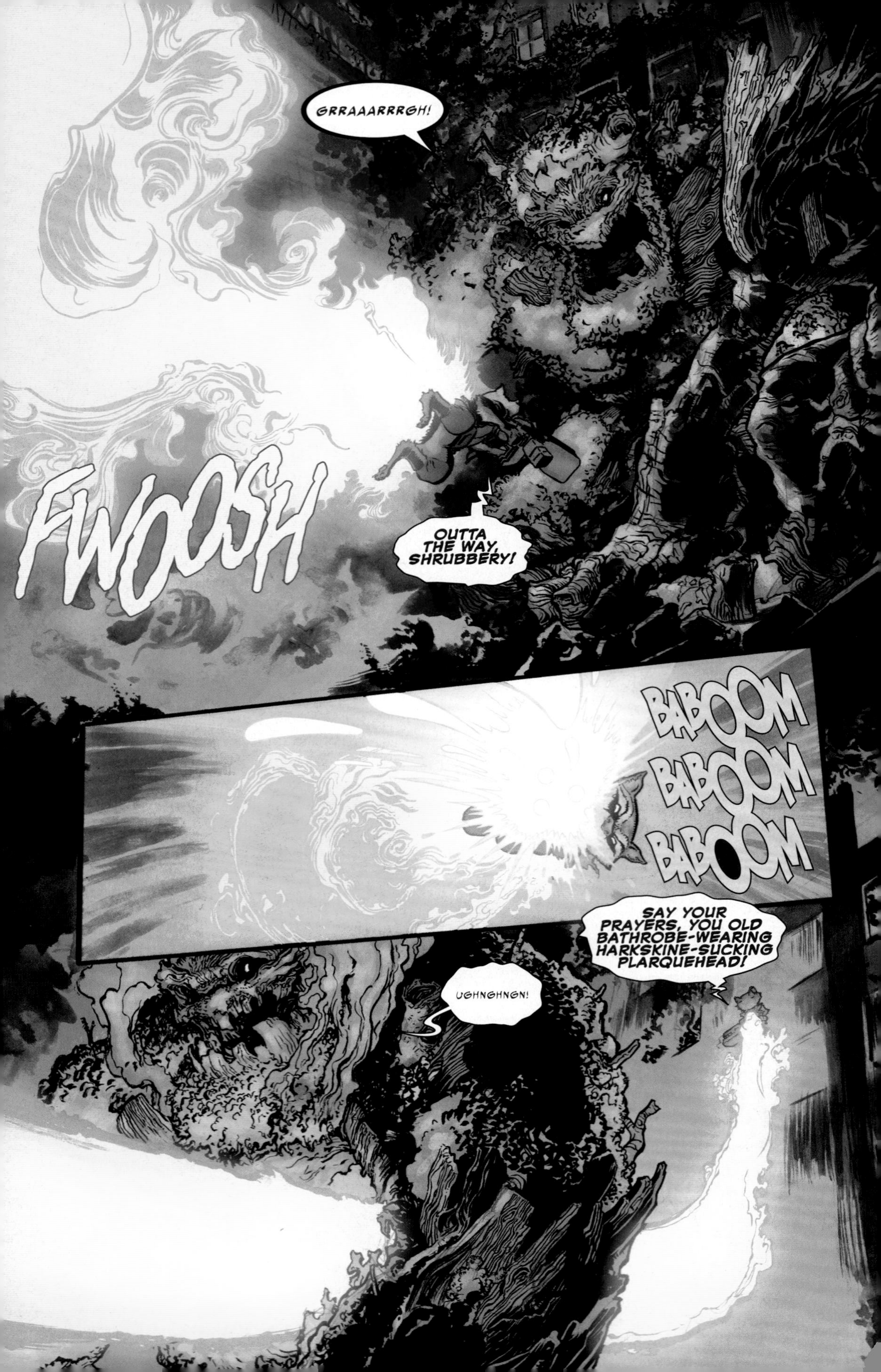
GRRAAARRRGH!
FWOOSH
OUTTA THE WAY, SHRUBBERY!
BABOOM BABOOM BABOOM
SAY YOUR PRAYERS, YOU OLD BATHROBE-WEARING HARKSKINE-SUCKING PLARQUEHEAD!
UGHNGHNGN!

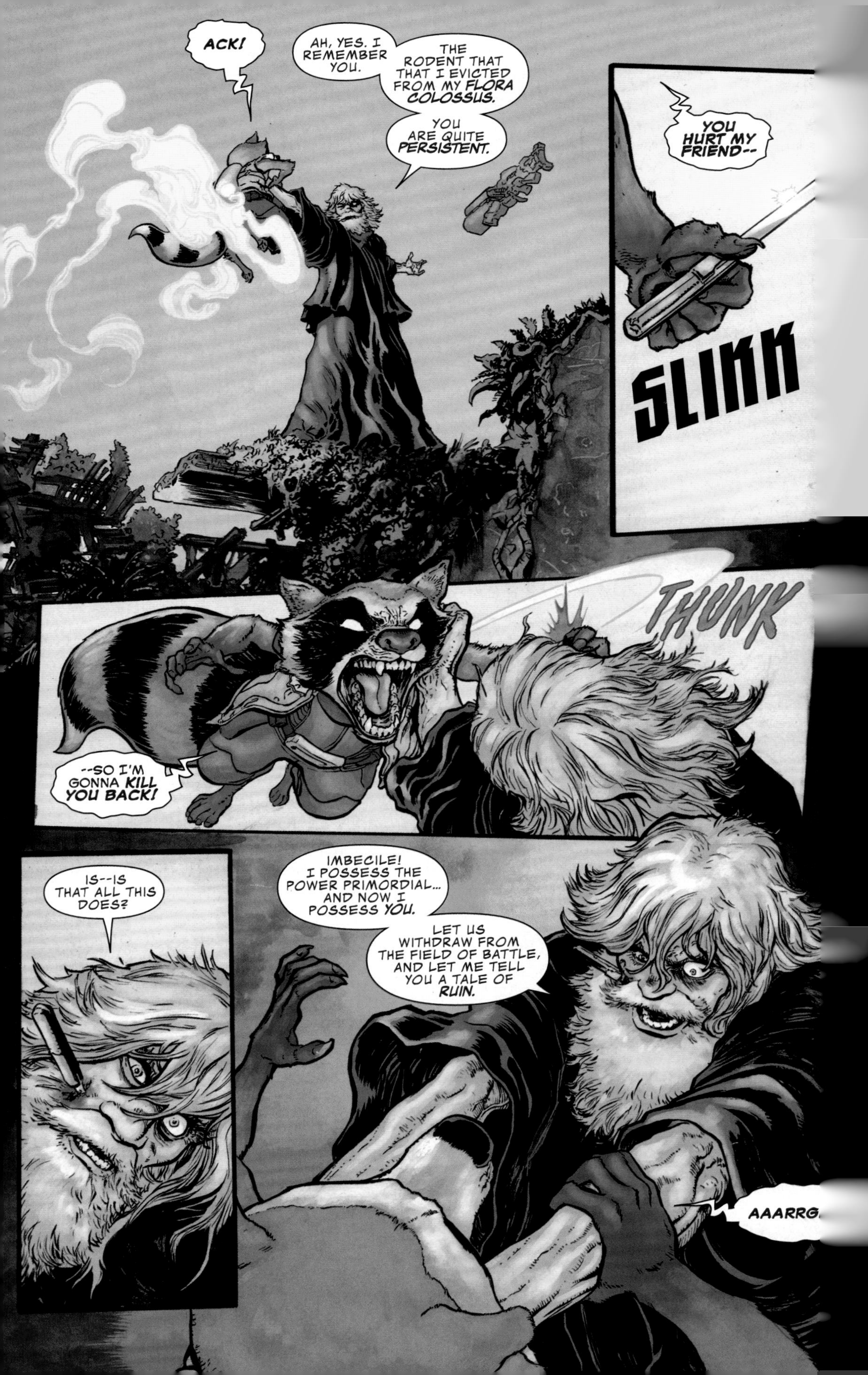

ACK!
AH, YES. I REMEMBER YOU.
THE RODENT THAT THAT I EVICTED FROM MY FLORA COLOSSUS.
YOU ARE QUITE PERSISTENT.
YOU HURT MY FRIEND--
SLINK
THUNK
--SO I'M GONNA KILL YOU BACK!
IS--IS THAT ALL THIS DOES?
IMBECILE! I POSSESS THE POWER PRIMORDIAL... AND NOW I POSSESS YOU.
LET US WITHDRAW FROM THE FIELD OF BATTLE, AND LET ME TELL YOU A TALE OF RUIN.
AAARRG

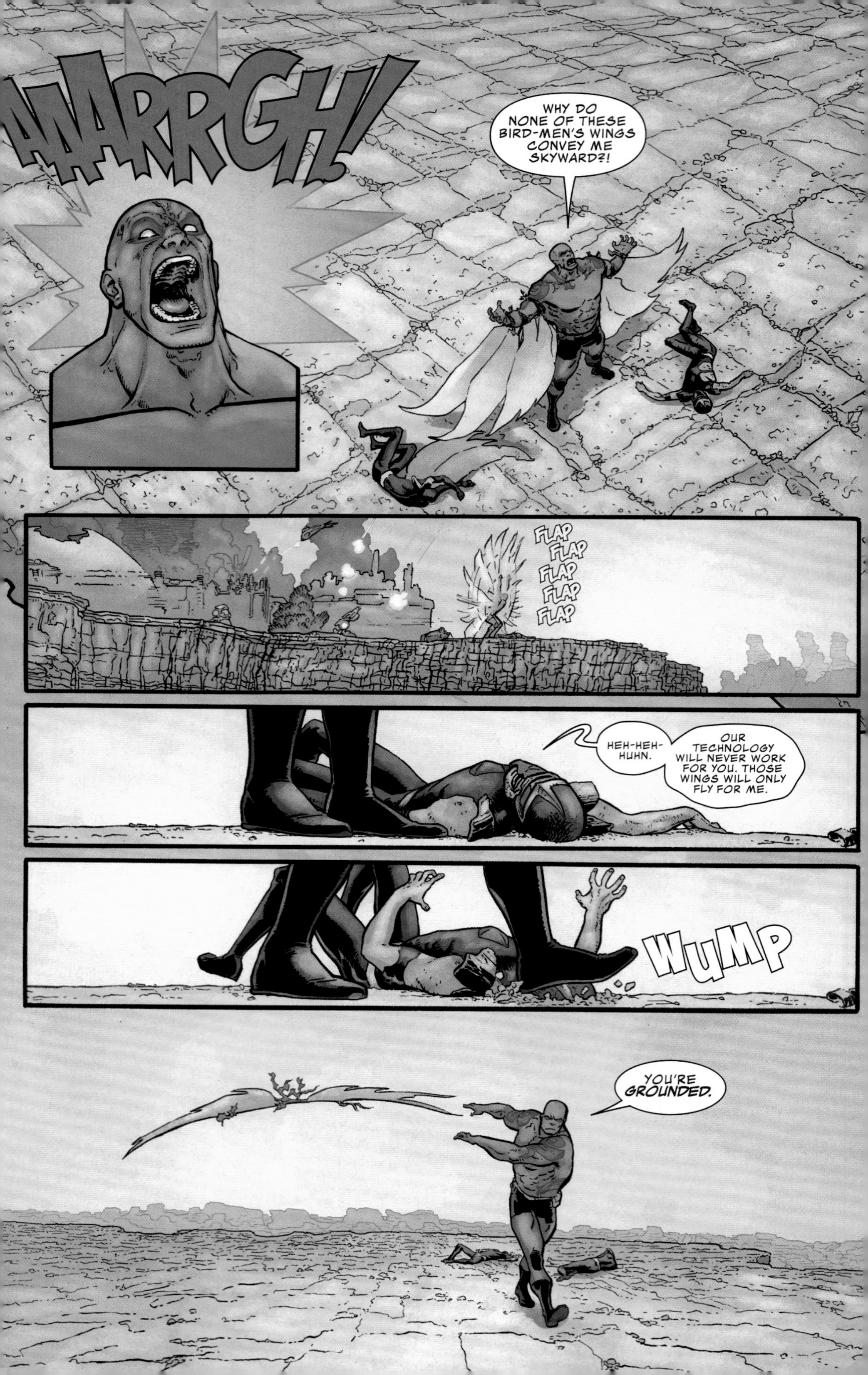
AAARRGH!
WHY DO NONE OF THESE BIRD-MEN'S WINGS CONVEY ME SKYWARD?!
FLAP FLAP FLAP FLAP FLAP
HEH-HEH-HUHN.
OUR TECHNOLOGY WILL NEVER WORK FOR YOU. THOSE WINGS WILL ONLY FLY FOR ME.
WUMP
YOU'RE GROUNDED.

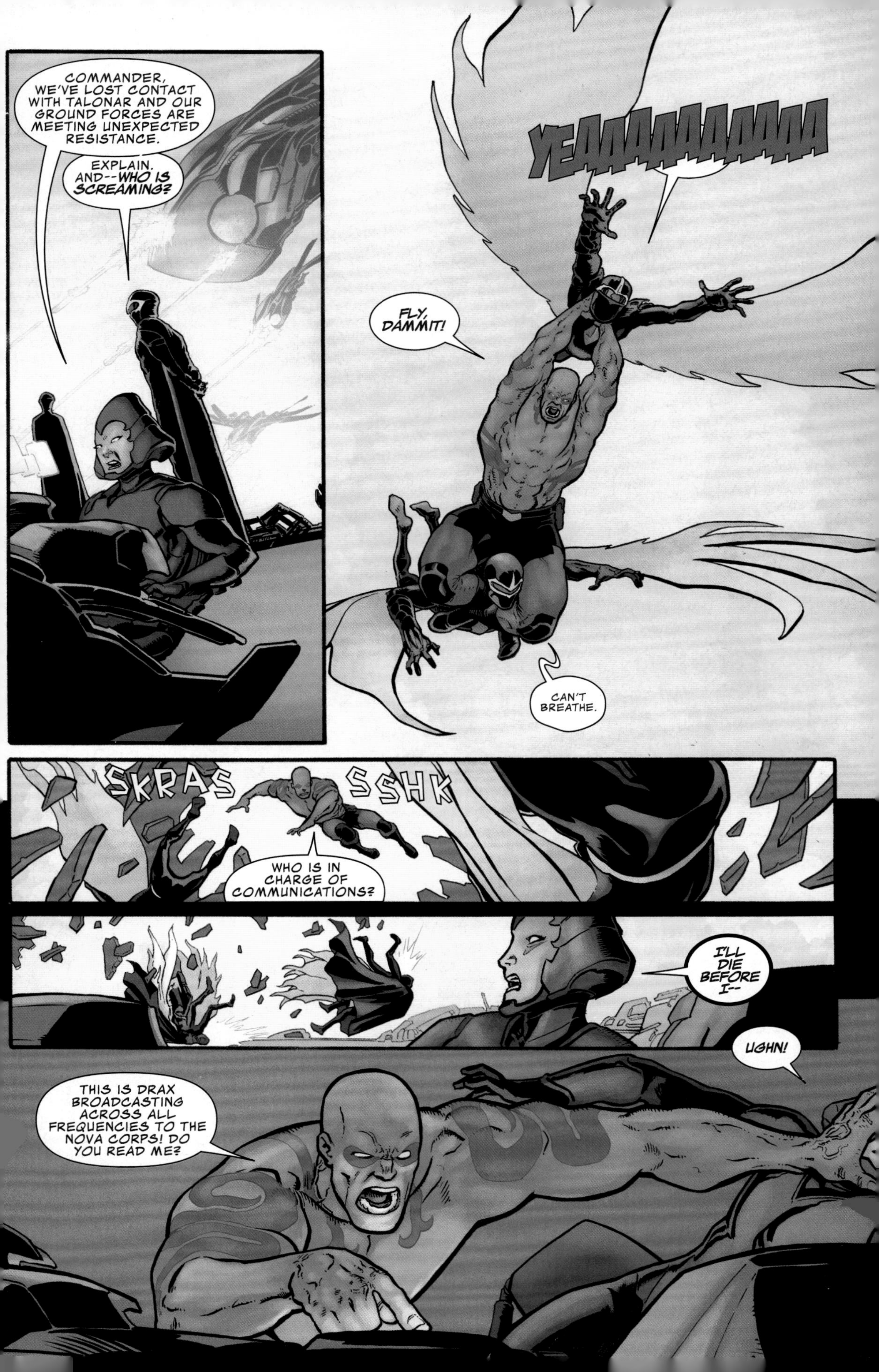
COMMANDER, WE'VE LOST CONTACT WITH TALONAR AND OUR GROUND FORCES ARE MEETING UNEXPECTED RESISTANCE.
EXPLAIN. AND--WHO IS SCREAMING?
YEAAAAAAAAAA
FLY, DAMMIT!
CAN'T BREATHE.
SKRAS
SSHK
WHO IS IN CHARGE OF COMMUNICATIONS?
I'LL DIE BEFORE I--
UGHN!
THIS IS DRAX BROADCASTING ACROSS ALL FREQUENCIES TO THE NOVA CORPS! DO YOU READ ME?

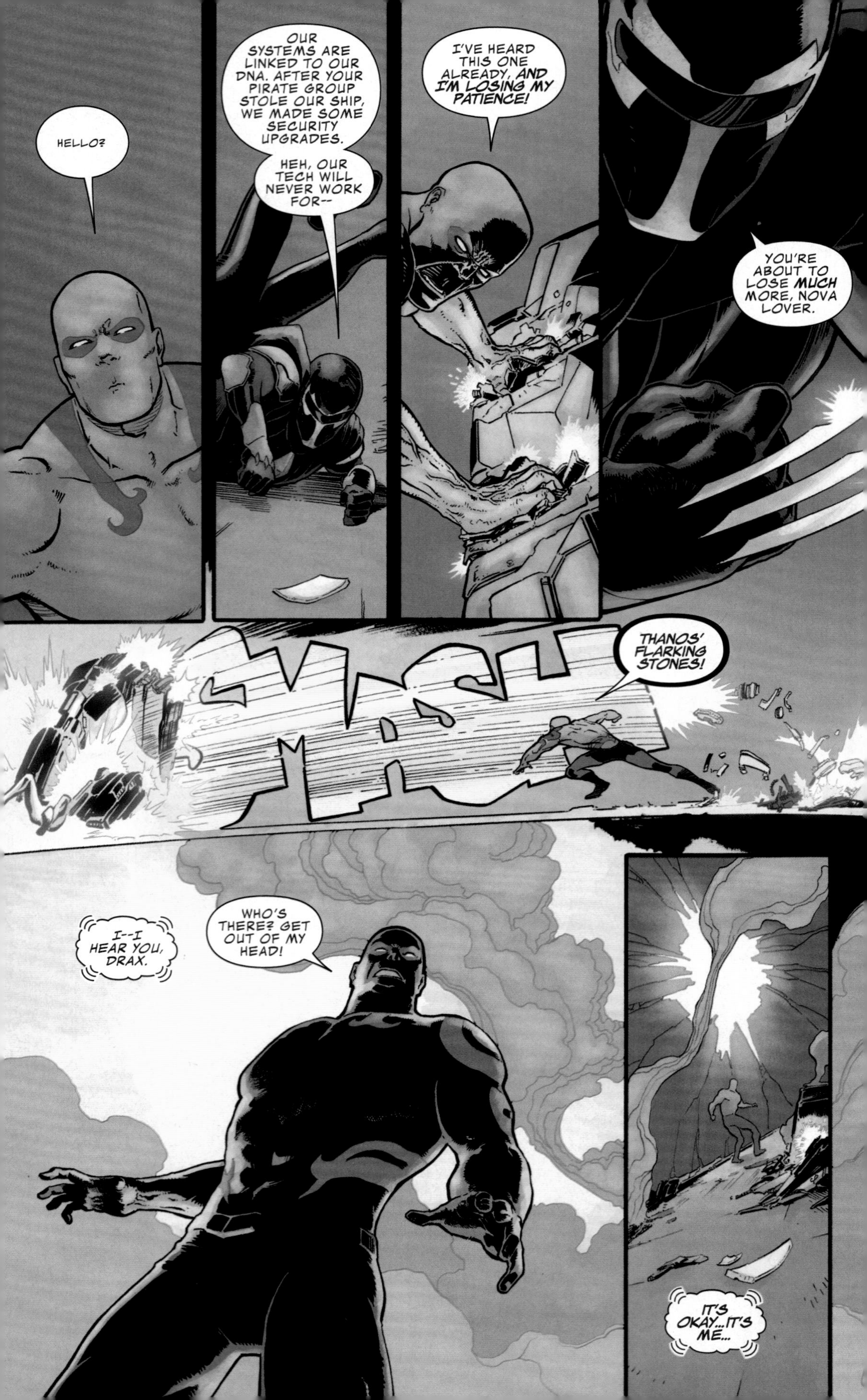
HELLO?
OUR SYSTEMS ARE LINKED TO OUR DNA. AFTER YOUR PIRATE GROUP STOLE OUR SHIP, WE MADE SOME SECURITY UPGRADES.
HEH, OUR TECH WILL NEVER WORK FOR--
I'VE HEARD THIS ONE ALREADY, AND I'M LOSING MY PATIENCE!
YOU'RE ABOUT TO LOSE MUCH MORE, NOVA LOVER.
SMASH
THANOS' FLARKING STONES!
I--I HEAR YOU, DRAX.
WHO'S THERE? GET OUT OF MY HEAD!
IT'S OKAY...IT'S ME...

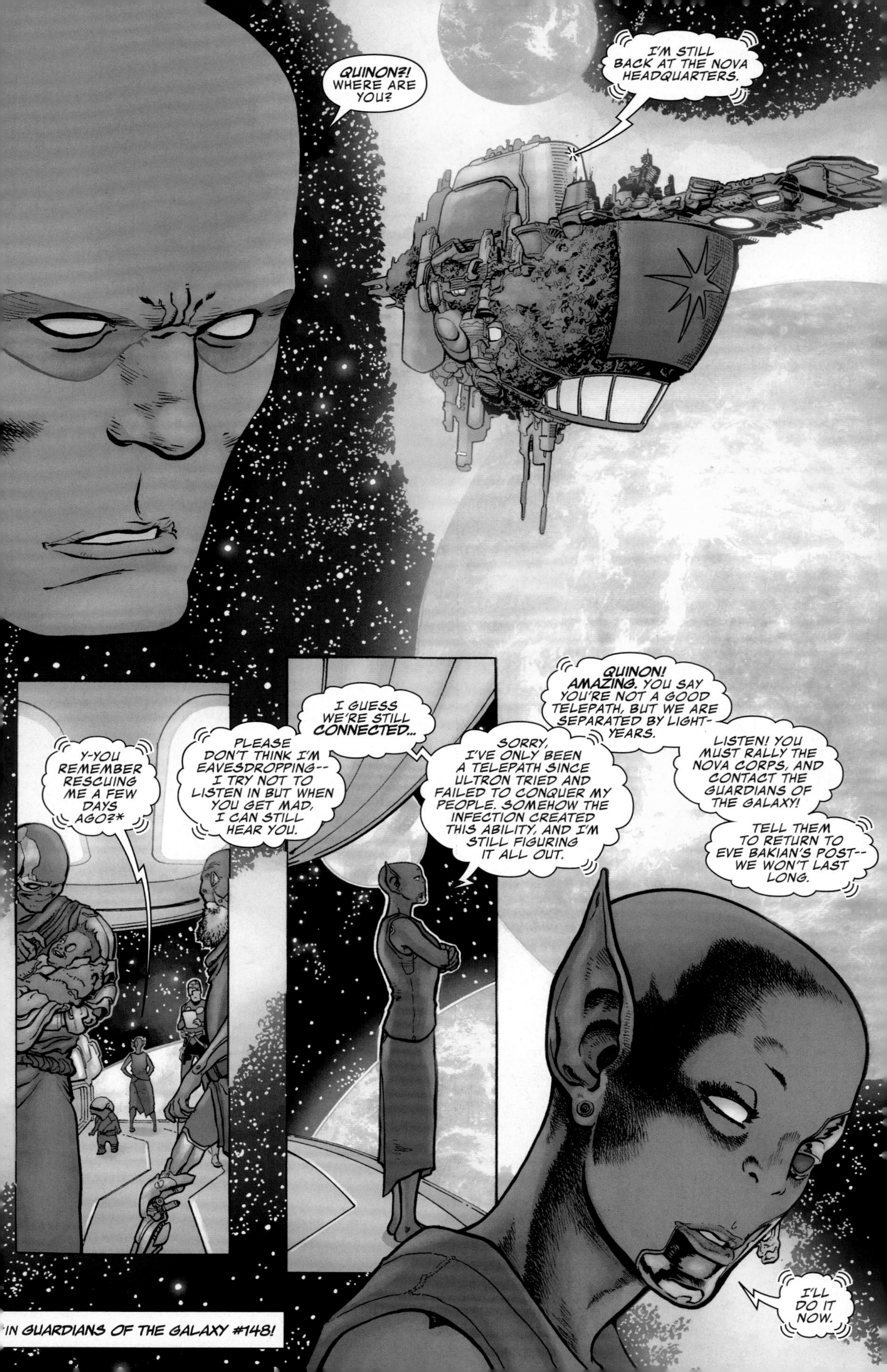
QUINON?! WHERE ARE YOU?
I'M STILL BACK AT THE NOVA HEADQUARTERS.
Y-YOU REMEMBER RESCUING ME A FEW DAYS AGO?*
PLEASE DON'T THINK I'M EAVESDROPPING-- I TRY NOT TO LISTEN IN BUT WHEN YOU GET MAD, I CAN STILL HEAR YOU.
I GUESS WE'RE STILL CONNECTED...
SORRY, I'VE ONLY BEEN A TELEPATH SINCE ULTRON TRIED AND FAILED TO CONQUER MY PEOPLE. SOMEHOW THE INFECTION CREATED THIS ABILITY, AND I'M STILL FIGURING IT ALL OUT.
QUINON! AMAZING. YOU SAY YOU'RE NOT A GOOD TELEPATH, BUT WE ARE SEPARATED BY LIGHT-YEARS.
LISTEN! YOU MUST RALLY THE NOVA CORPS, AND CONTACT THE GUARDIANS OF THE GALAXY!
TELL THEM TO RETURN TO EVE BAKIAN'S POST-- WE WON'T LAST LONG.
I'LL DO IT NOW.
*IN GUARDIANS OF THE GALAXY #148!

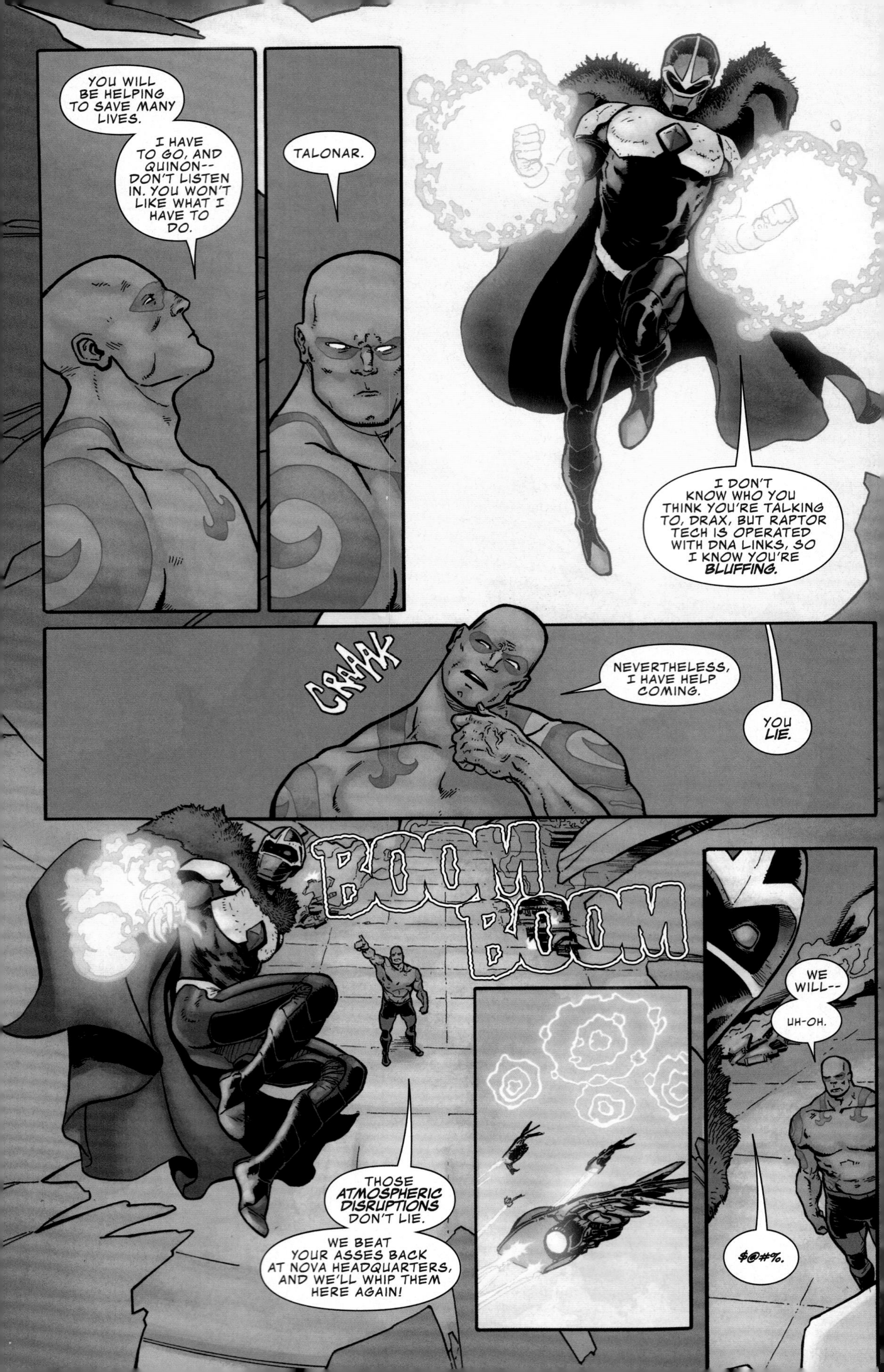
YOU WILL BE HELPING TO SAVE MANY LIVES.
I HAVE TO GO, AND QUINON-- DON'T LISTEN IN. YOU WON'T LIKE WHAT I HAVE TO DO.
TALONAR.
I DON'T KNOW WHO YOU THINK YOU'RE TALKING TO, DRAX, BUT RAPTOR TECH IS OPERATED WITH DNA LINKS, SO I KNOW YOU'RE BLUFFING.
CRAAAK
NEVERTHELESS, I HAVE HELP COMING.
YOU LIE.
BOOM BOOM
THOSE ATMOSPHERIC DISRUPTIONS DON'T LIE.
WE BEAT YOUR ASSES BACK AT NOVA HEADQUARTERS, AND WE'LL WHIP THEM HERE AGAIN!
WE WILL--
UH-OH.
$@#%.

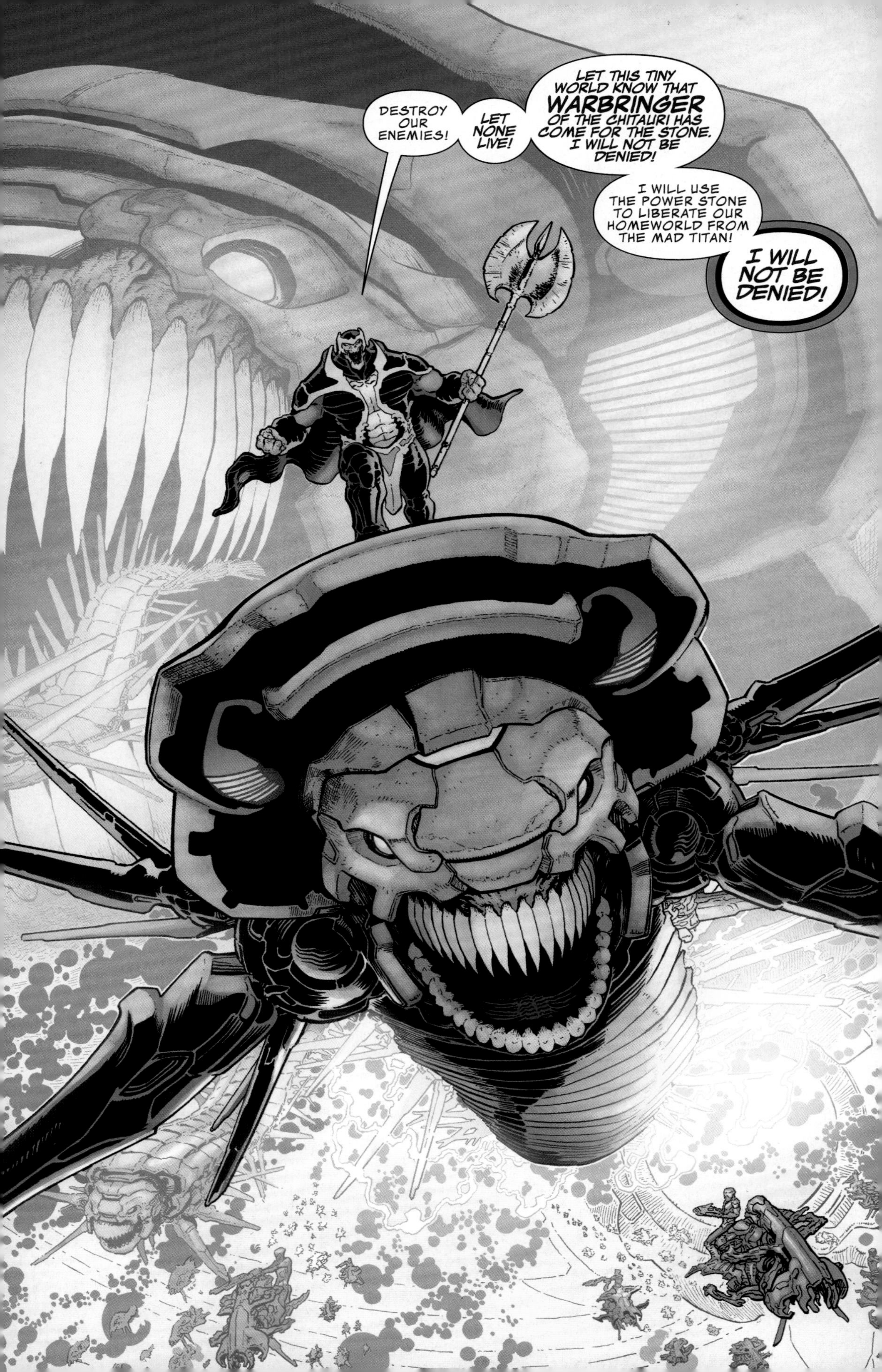
DESTROY OUR ENEMIES!
LET NONE LIVE!
LET THIS TINY WORLD KNOW THAT WARBRINGER OF THE CHITAURI HAS COME FOR THE STONE. I WILL NOT BE DENIED!
I WILL USE THE POWER STONE TO LIBERATE OUR HOMEWORLD FROM THE MAD TITAN!
I WILL NOT BE DENIED!

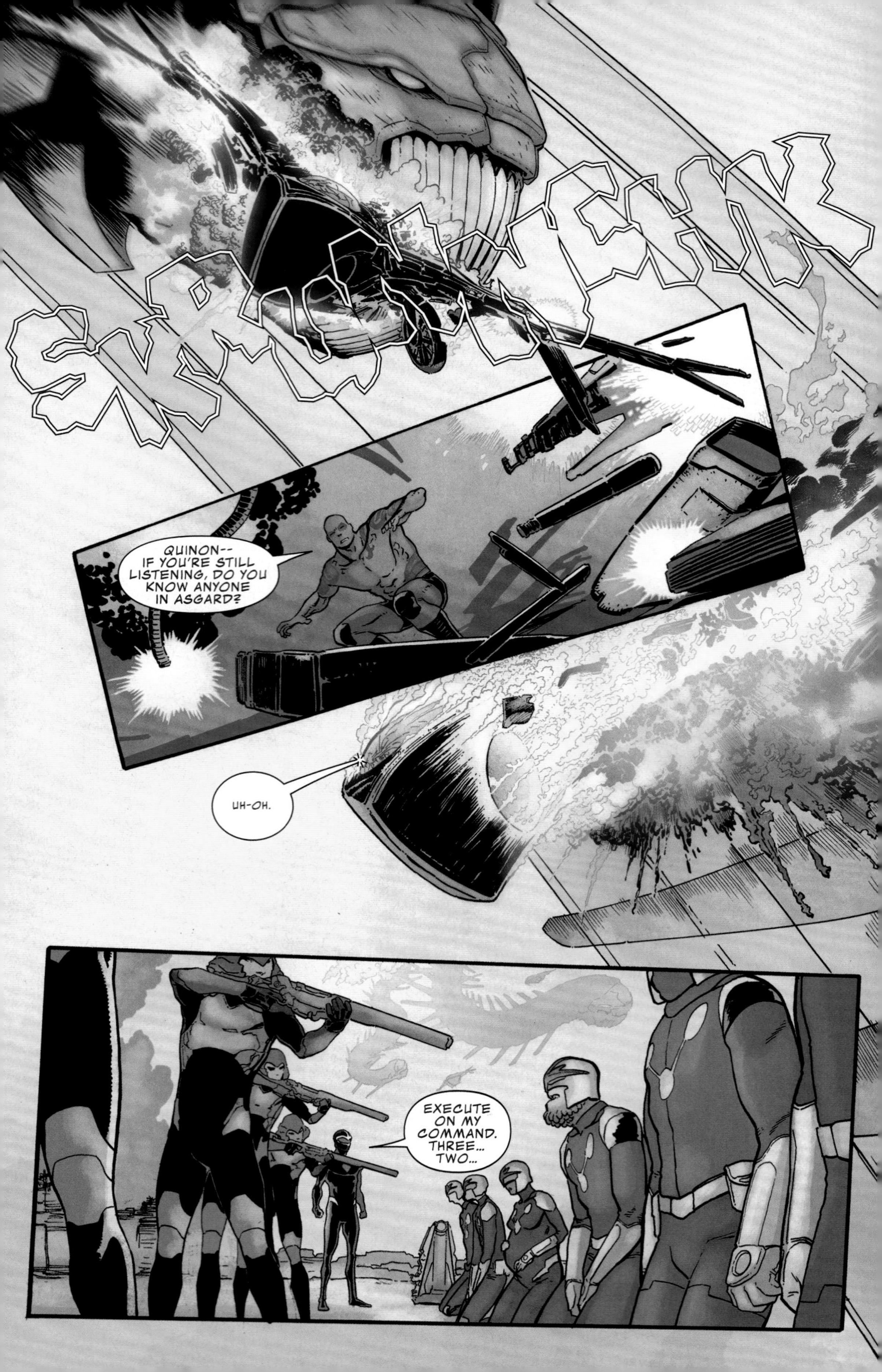
QUINON-- IF YOU'RE STILL LISTENING, DO YOU KNOW ANYONE IN ASGARD?
UH-OH.
EXECUTE ON MY COMMAND. THREE... TWO...

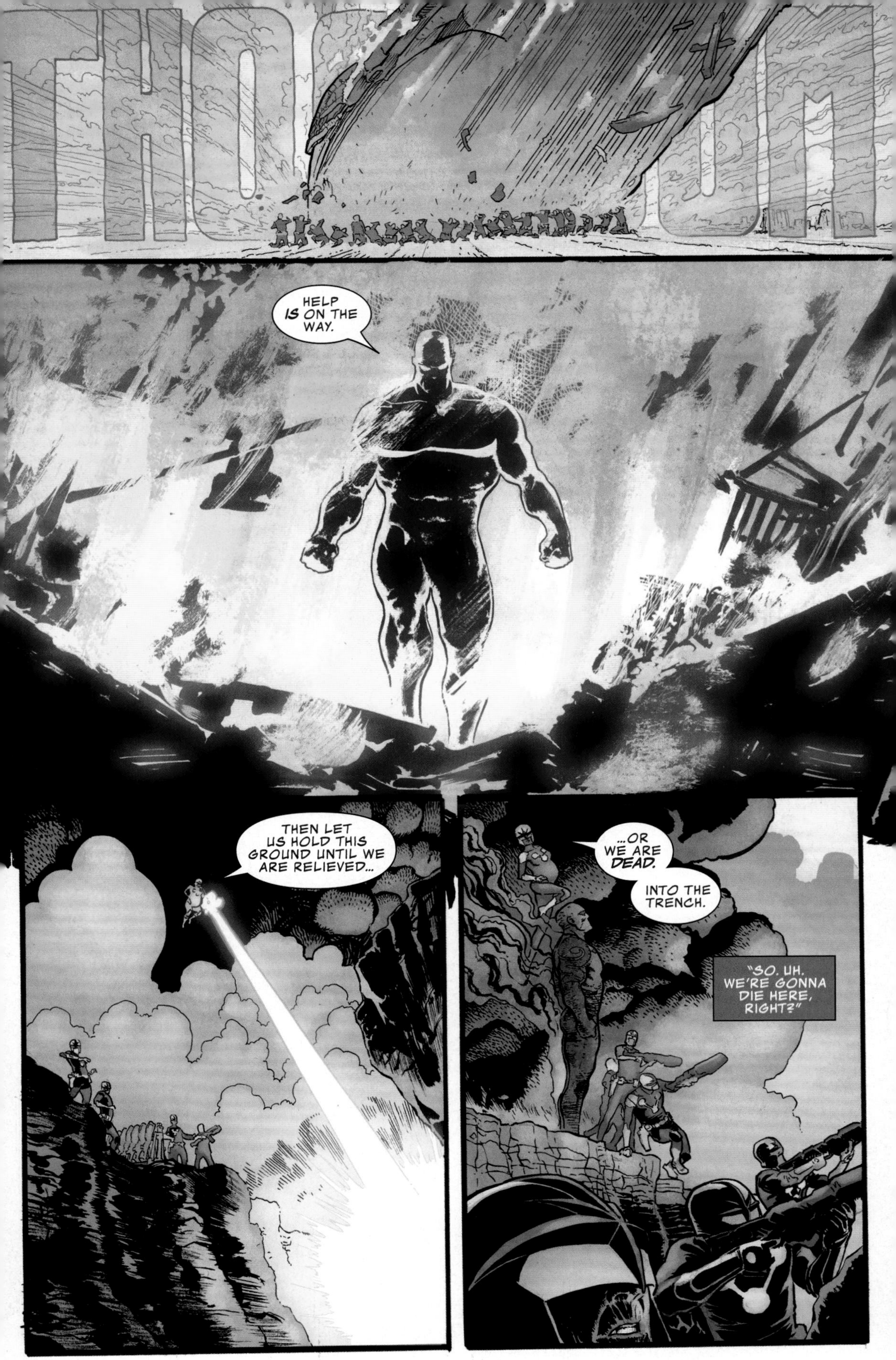
HELP IS ON THE WAY.
THEN LET US HOLD THIS GROUND UNTIL WE ARE RELIEVED...
...OR WE ARE DEAD.
INTO THE TRENCH.
"SO. UH. WE'RE GONNA DIE HERE, RIGHT?"

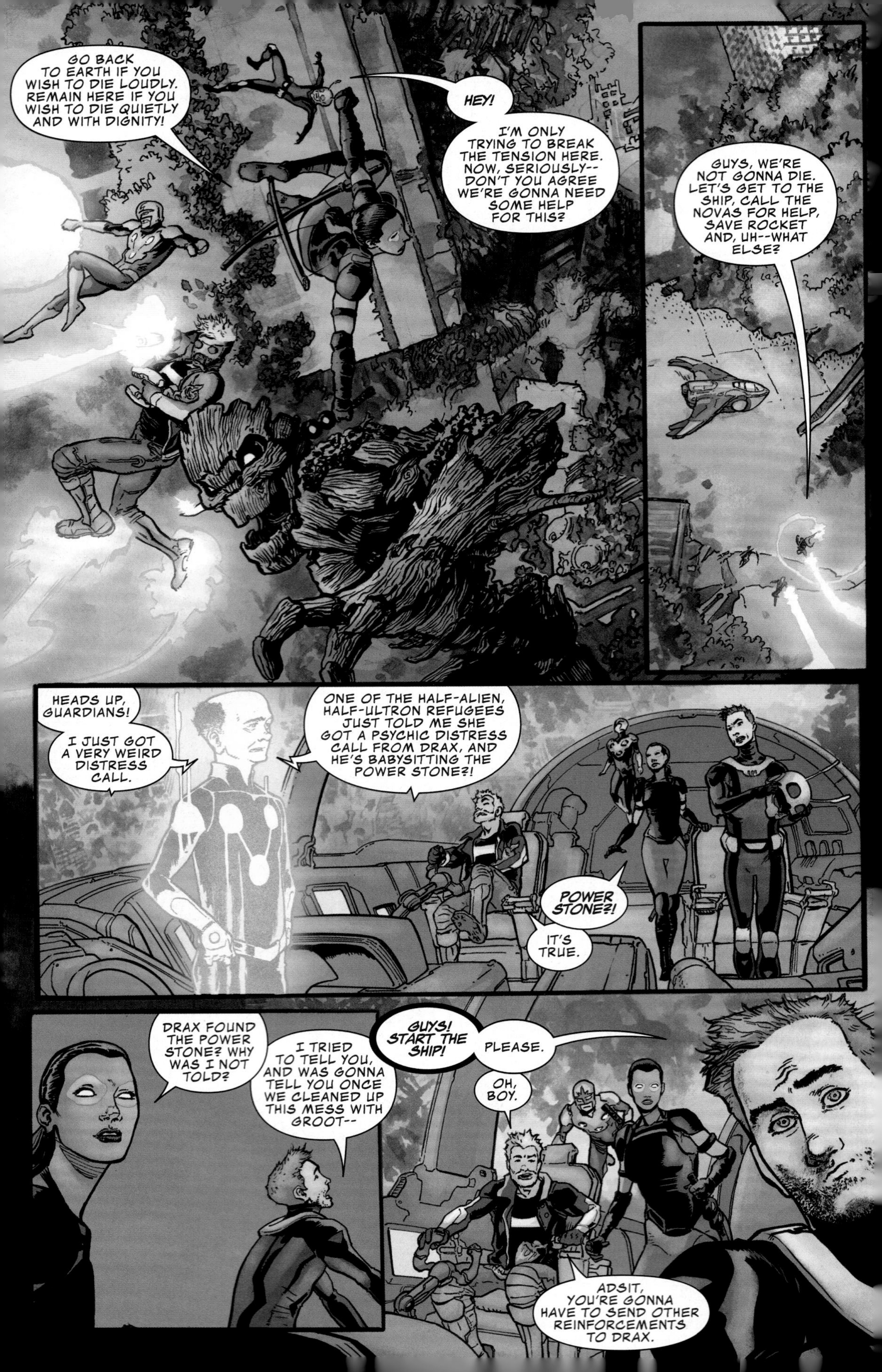
GO BACK TO EARTH IF YOU WISH TO DIE LOUDLY. REMAIN HERE IF YOU WISH TO DIE QUIETLY AND WITH DIGNITY!
HEY!
I'M ONLY TRYING TO BREAK THE TENSION HERE. NOW, SERIOUSLY--DON'T YOU AGREE WE'RE GONNA NEED SOME HELP FOR THIS?
GUYS, WE'RE NOT GONNA DIE. LET'S GET TO THE SHIP, CALL THE NOVAS FOR HELP, SAVE ROCKET AND, UH--WHAT ELSE?
HEADS UP, GUARDIANS!
I JUST GOT A VERY WEIRD DISTRESS CALL.
ONE OF THE HALF-ALIEN, HALF-ULTRON REFUGEES JUST TOLD ME SHE GOT A PSYCHIC DISTRESS CALL FROM DRAX, AND HE'S BABYSITTING THE POWER STONE?!
POWER STONE?!
IT'S TRUE.
DRAX FOUND THE POWER STONE? WHY WAS I NOT TOLD?
I TRIED TO TELL YOU, AND WAS GONNA TELL YOU ONCE WE CLEANED UP THIS MESS WITH GROOT--
GUYS! START THE SHIP!
PLEASE.
OH, BOY.
ADSIT, YOU'RE GONNA HAVE TO SEND OTHER REINFORCEMENTS TO DRAX.

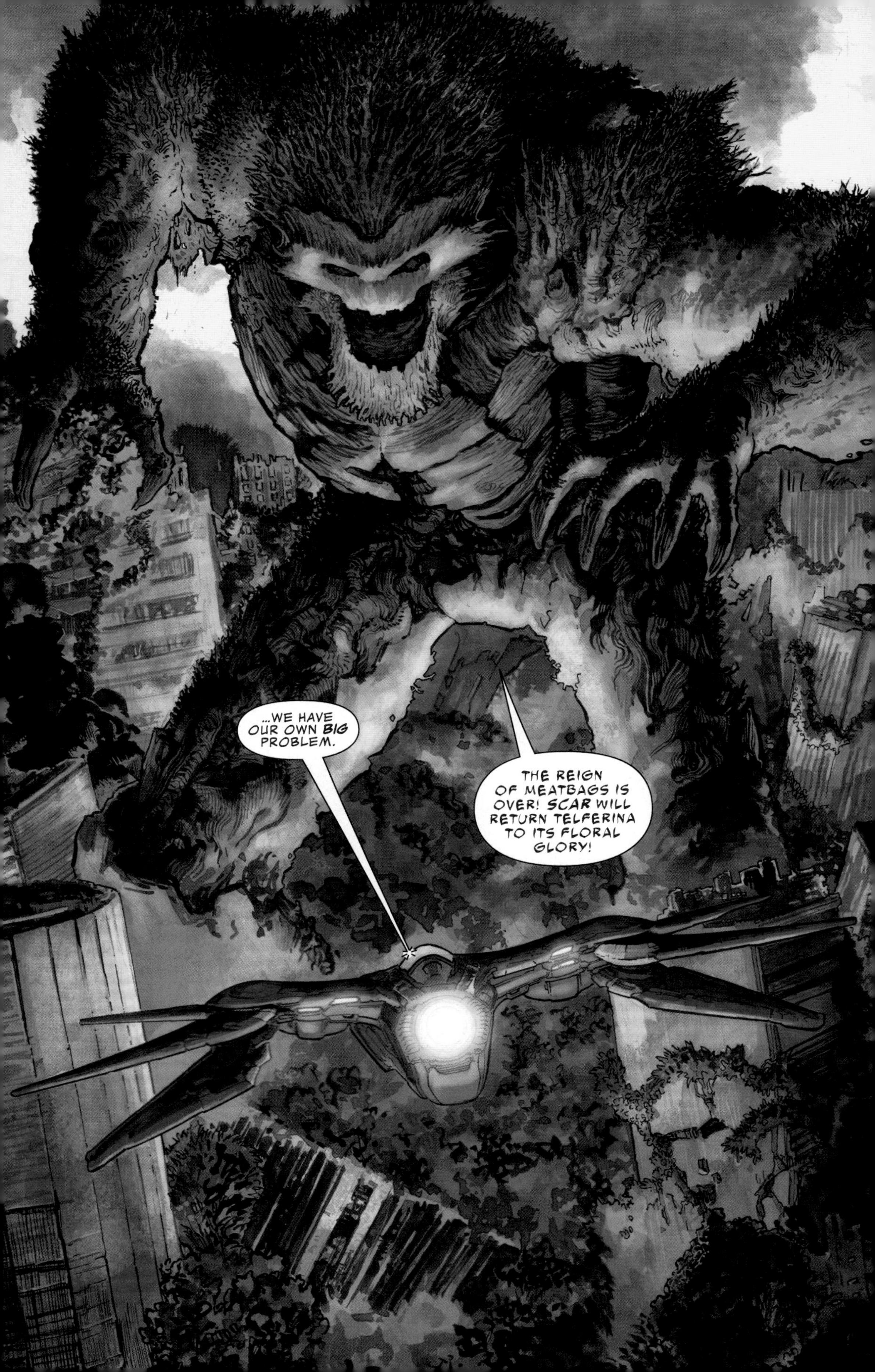
...WE HAVE OUR OWN BIG PROBLEM.
THE REIGN OF MEATBAGS IS OVER! SCAR WILL RETURN TELFERINA TO ITS FLORAL GLORY!

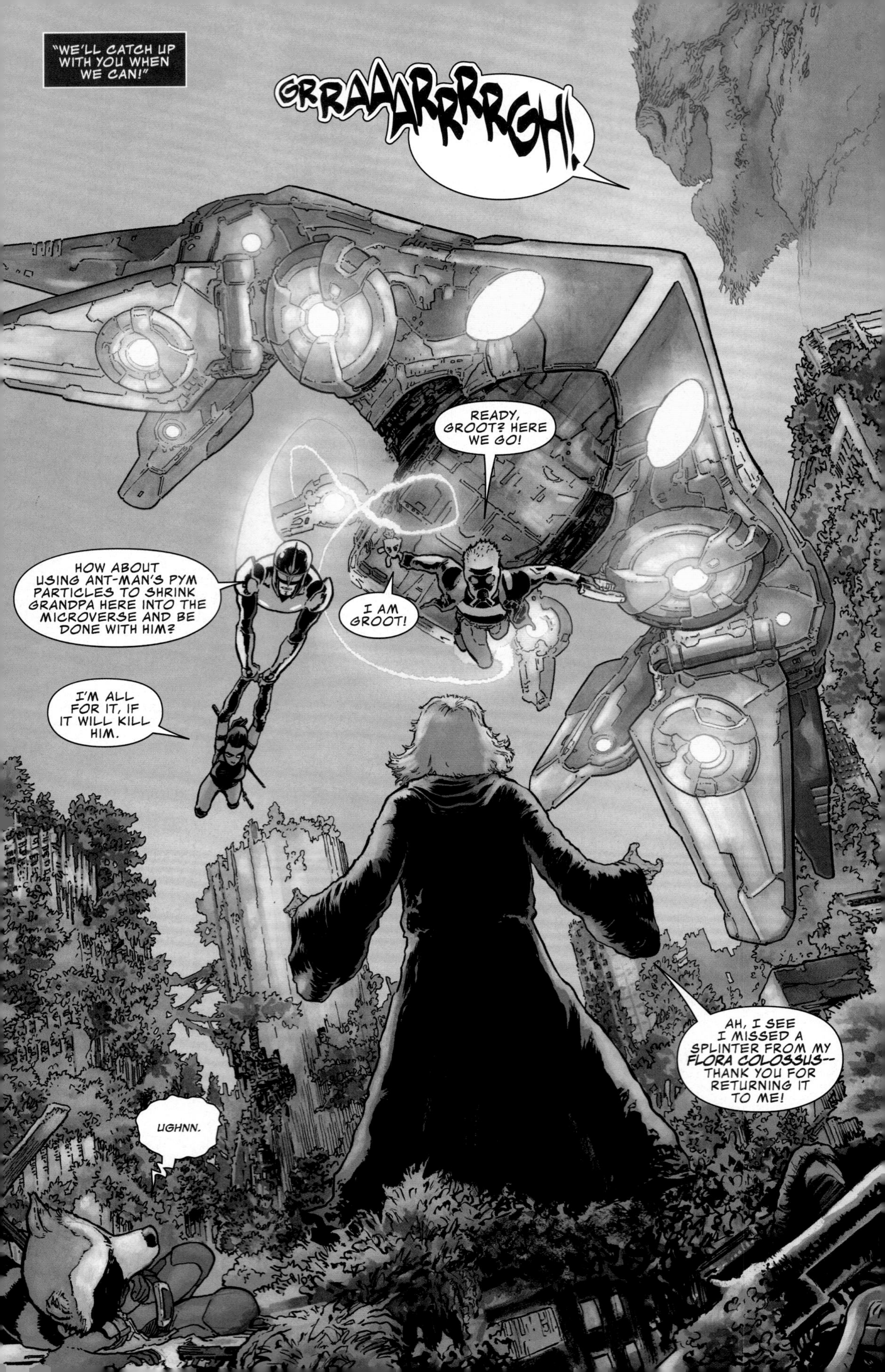
"WE'LL CATCH UP WITH YOU WHEN WE CAN!"
GRRAAAARRRRGH!
READY, GROOT? HERE WE GO!
I AM GROOT!
HOW ABOUT USING ANT-MAN'S PYM PARTICLES TO SHRINK GRANDPA HERE INTO THE MICROVERSE AND BE DONE WITH HIM?
I'M ALL FOR IT, IF IT WILL KILL HIM.
AH, I SEE I MISSED A SPLINTER FROM MY FLORA COLOSSUS-- THANK YOU FOR RETURNING IT TO ME!
UGHNN.

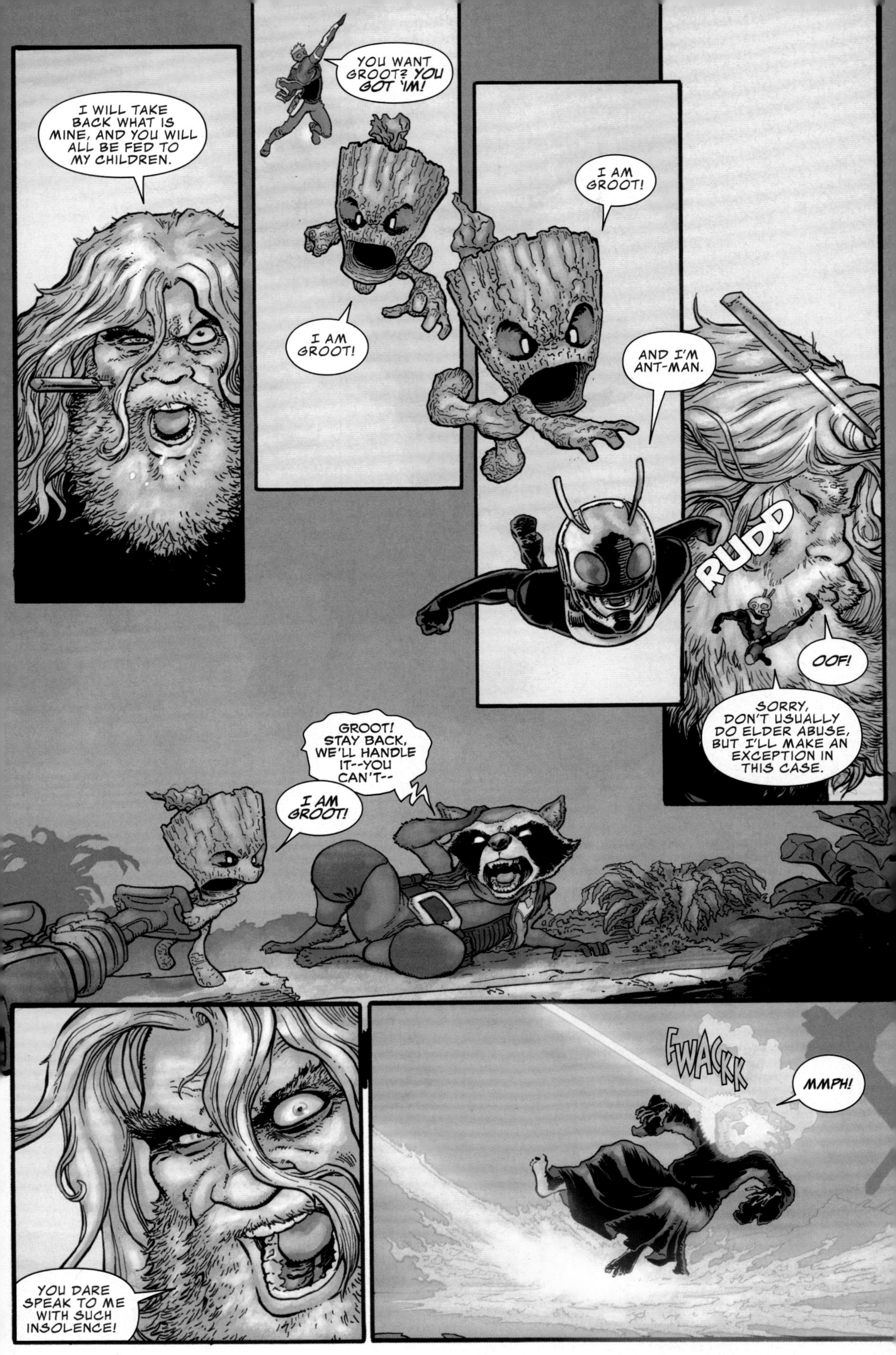
I WILL TAKE BACK WHAT IS MINE, AND YOU WILL ALL BE FED TO MY CHILDREN.
YOU WANT GROOT? YOU GOT 'IM!
I AM GROOT!
I AM GROOT!
AND I'M ANT-MAN.
RUDD
OOF!
SORRY, DON'T USUALLY DO ELDER ABUSE, BUT I'LL MAKE AN EXCEPTION IN THIS CASE.
GROOT! STAY BACK, WE'LL HANDLE IT--YOU CAN'T--
I AM GROOT!
YOU DARE SPEAK TO ME WITH SUCH INSOLENCE!
FWACKK
MMPH!

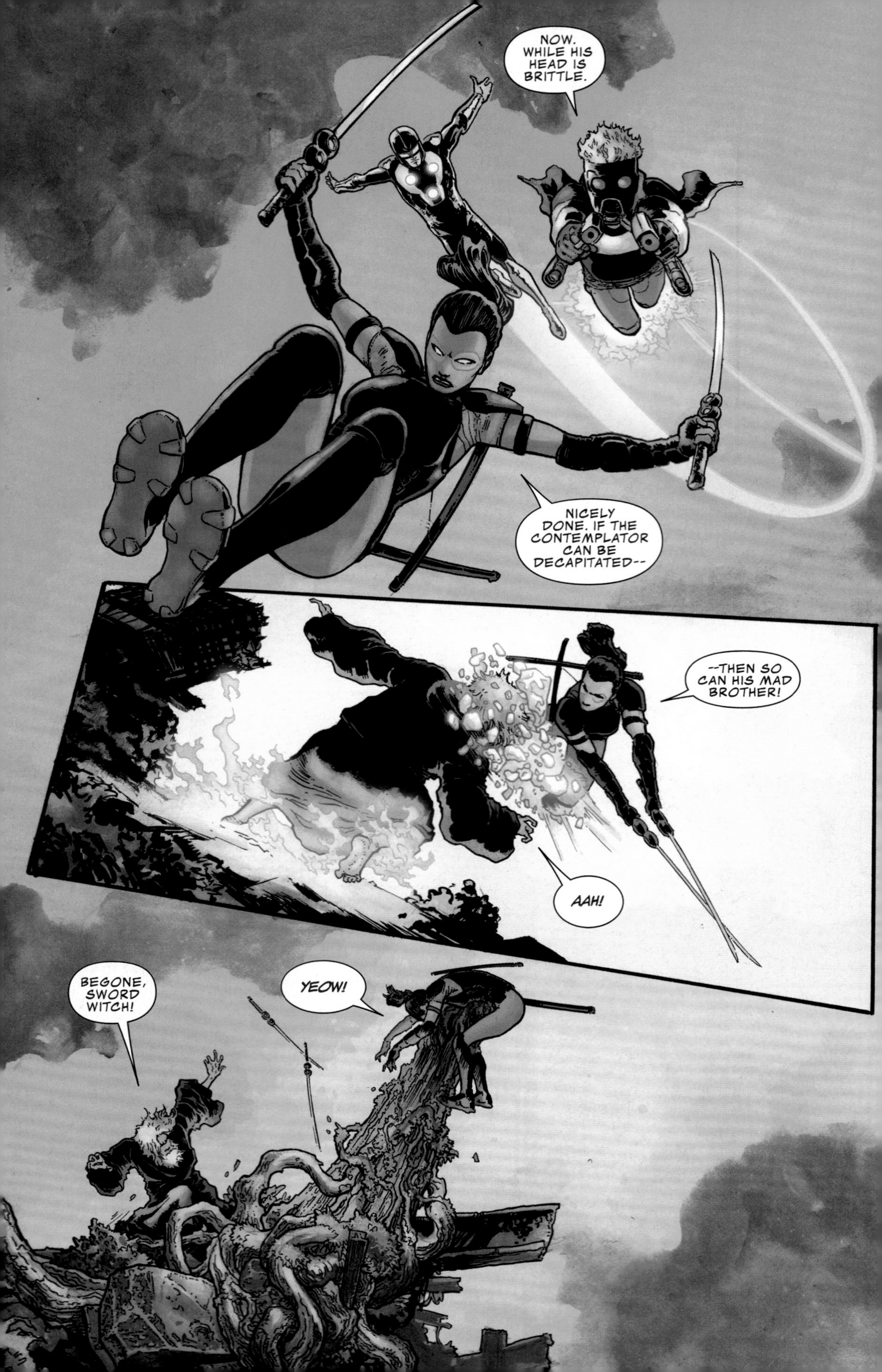
NOW. WHILE HIS HEAD IS BRITTLE.
NICELY DONE. IF THE CONTEMPLATOR CAN BE DECAPITATED--
--THEN SO CAN HIS MAD BROTHER!
AAH!
BEGONE, SWORD WITCH!
YEOW!

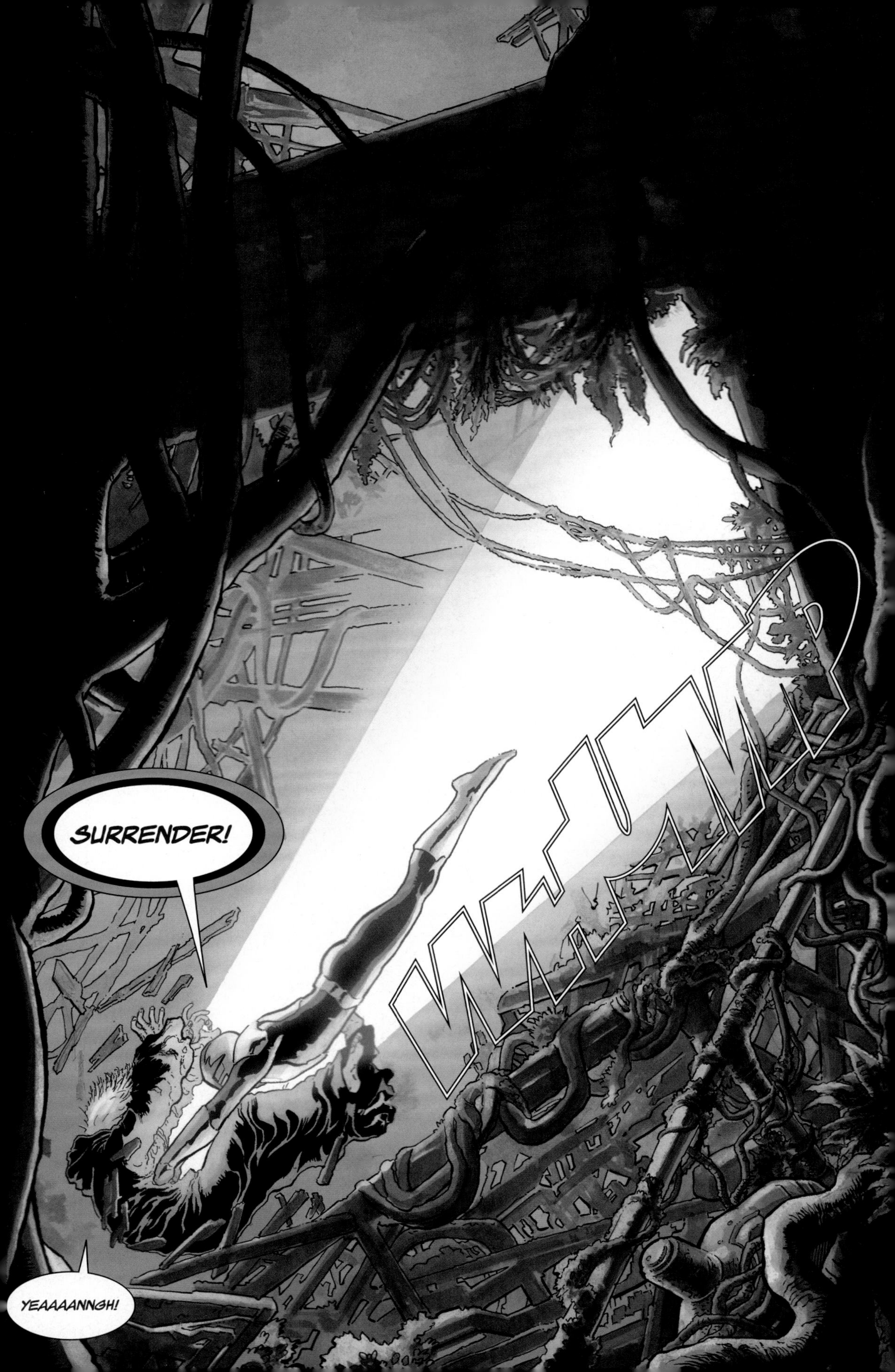
SURRENDER!
YEAAAAANNGH!

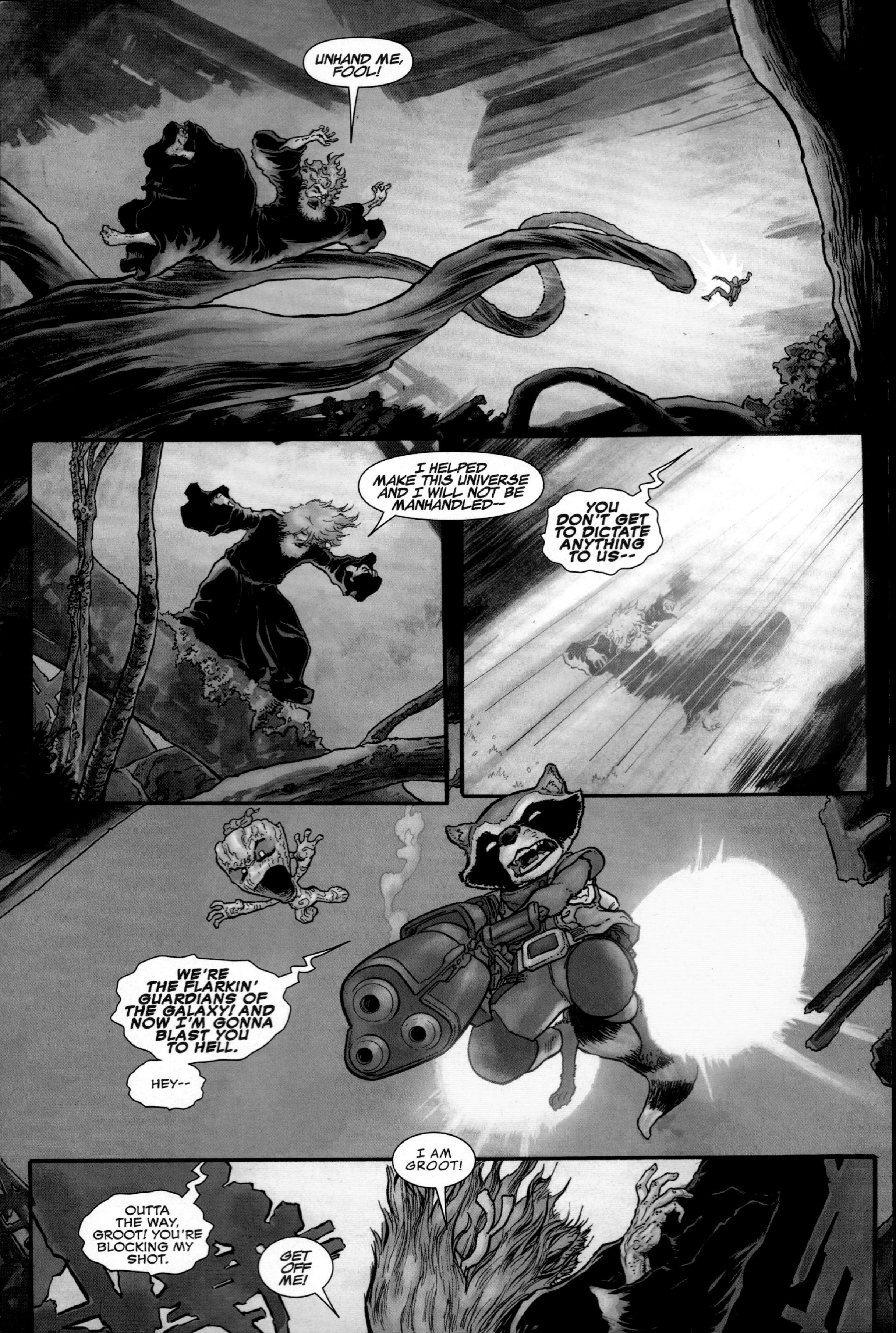
UNHAND ME, FOOL!
I HELPED MAKE THIS UNIVERSE AND I WILL NOT BE MANHANDLED--
YOU DON'T GET TO DICTATE ANYTHING TO US--
WE'RE THE FLARKIN' GUARDIANS OF THE GALAXY! AND NOW I'M GONNA BLAST YOU TO HELL.
HEY--
I AM GROOT!
OUTTA THE WAY, GROOT! YOU'RE BLOCKING MY SHOT.
GET OFF ME!

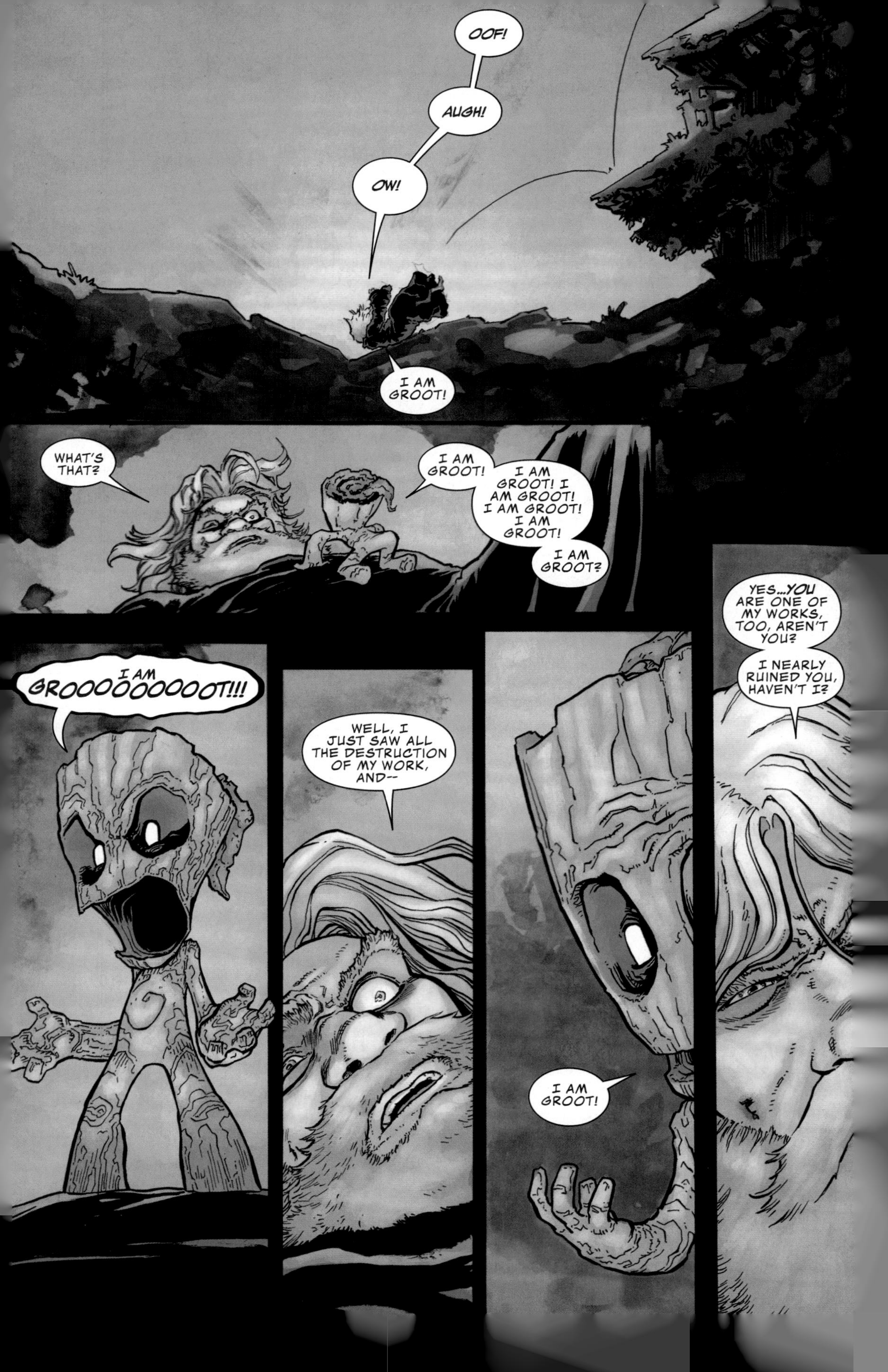

OOF!
AUGH!
OW!
I AM GROOT!
WHAT'S THAT?
I AM GROOT!
I AM GROOT! I AM GROOT! I AM GROOT! I AM GROOT!
I AM GROOT?
I AM GROOOOOOOOOOT!!!
WELL, I JUST SAW ALL THE DESTRUCTION OF MY WORK, AND--
I AM GROOT!
YES...YOU ARE ONE OF MY WORKS, TOO, AREN'T YOU?
I NEARLY RUINED YOU, HAVEN'T I?

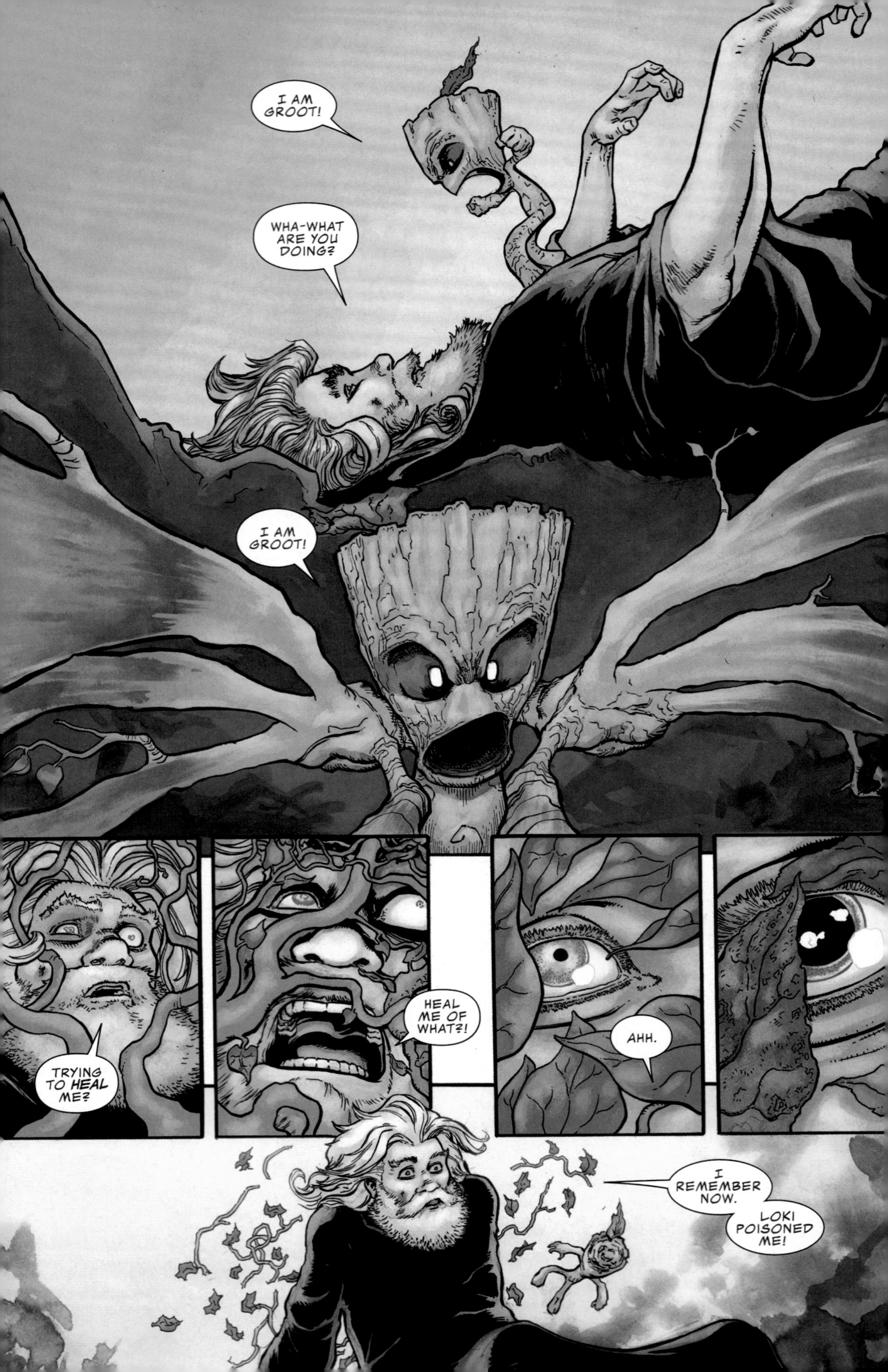
I AM GROOT!
WHA-WHAT ARE YOU DOING?
I AM GROOT!
TRYING TO HEAL ME?
HEAL ME OF WHAT?!
AHH.
I REMEMBER NOW.
LOKI POISONED ME!

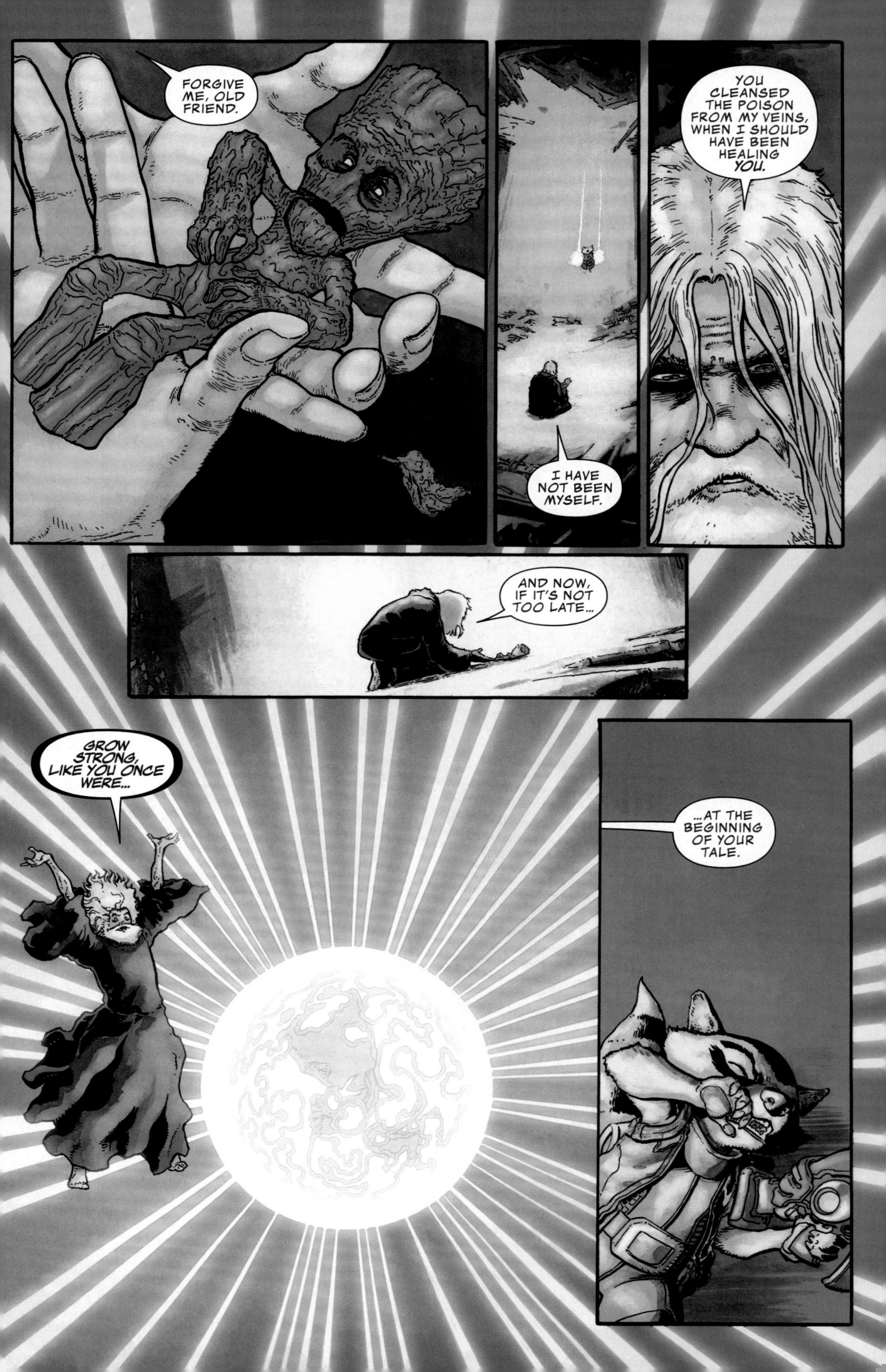
FORGIVE ME, OLD FRIEND.
I HAVE NOT BEEN MYSELF.
YOU CLEANSED THE POISON FROM MY VEINS, WHEN I SHOULD HAVE BEEN HEALING YOU.
AND NOW, IF IT'S NOT TOO LATE...
GROW STRONG, LIKE YOU ONCE WERE...
...AT THE BEGINNING OF YOUR TALE.

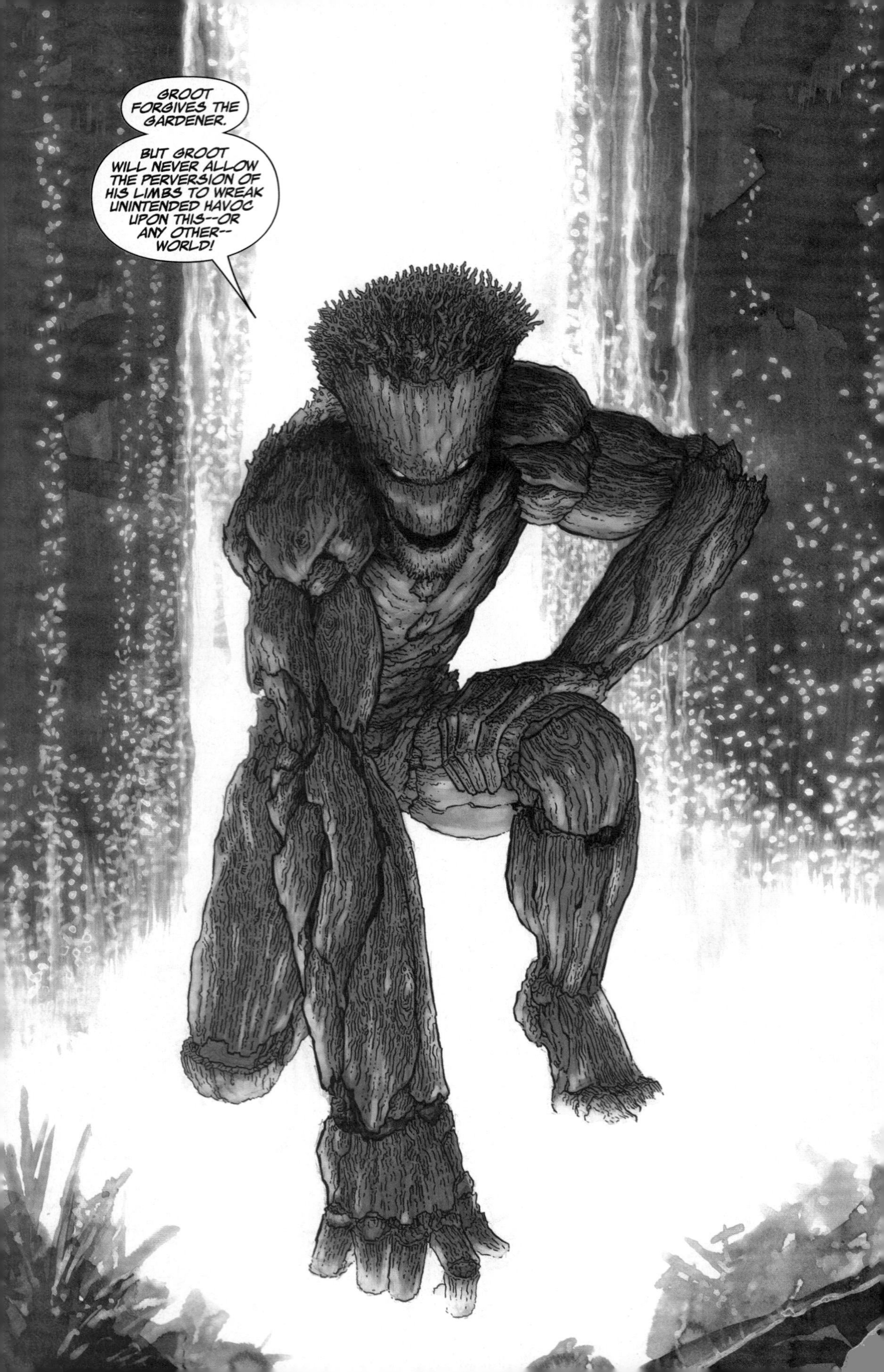
GROOT FORGIVES THE GARDENER.
BUT GROOT WILL NEVER ALLOW THE PERVERSION OF HIS LIMBS TO WREAK UNINTENDED HAVOC UPON THIS--OR ANY OTHER--WORLD!

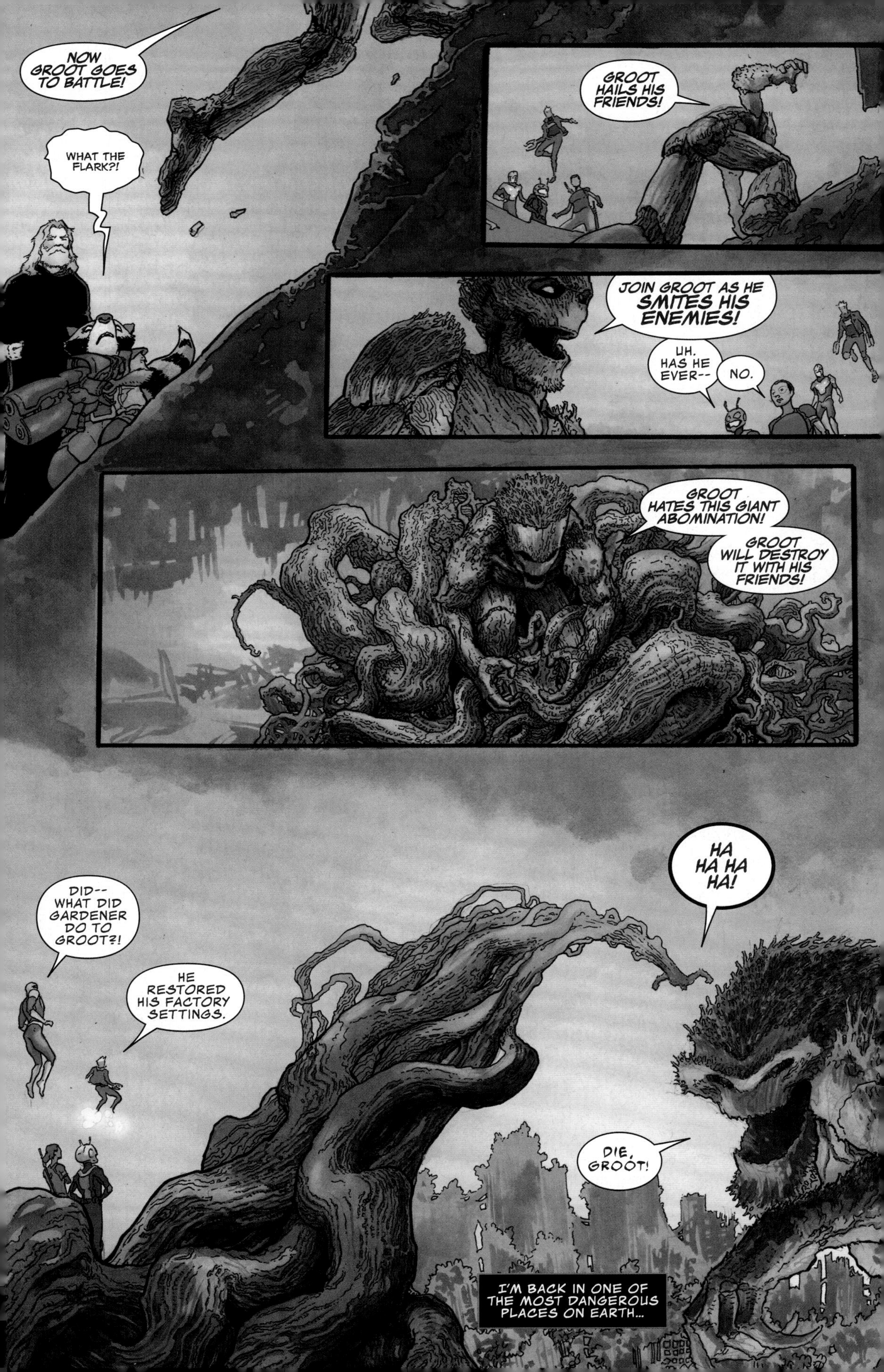
NOW GROOT GOES TO BATTLE!
WHAT THE FLARK?!
GROOT HAILS HIS FRIENDS!
JOIN GROOT AS HE SMITES HIS ENEMIES!
UH. HAS HE EVER--
NO.
GROOT HATES THIS GIANT ABOMINATION!
GROOT WILL DESTROY IT WITH HIS FRIENDS!
DID-- WHAT DID GARDENER DO TO GROOT?!
HE RESTORED HIS FACTORY SETTINGS.
HA HA HA HA!
DIE, GROOT!
I'M BACK IN ONE OF THE MOST DANGEROUS PLACES ON EARTH...

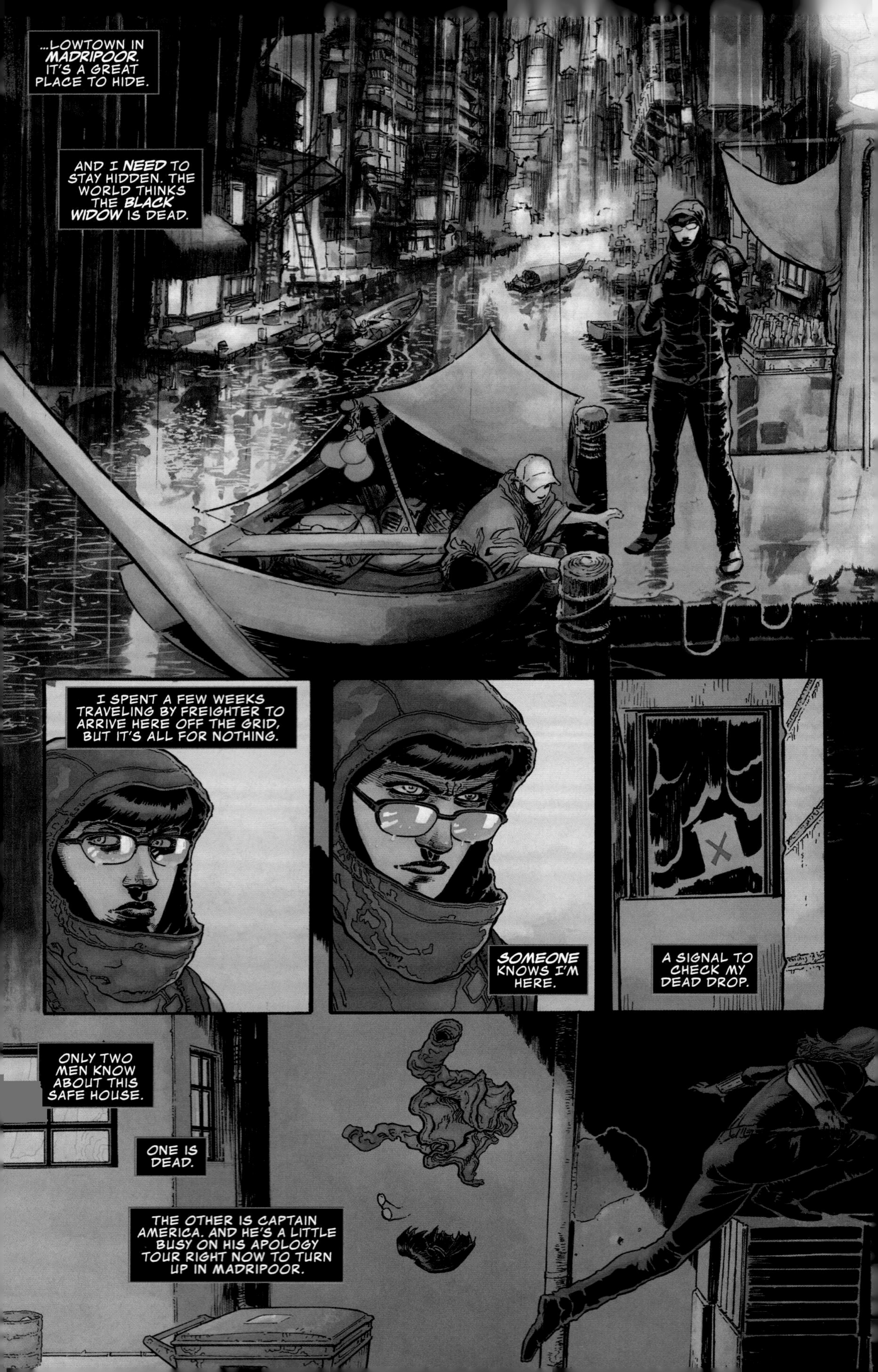

...LOWTOWN IN MADRIPOOR. IT'S A GREAT PLACE TO HIDE.
AND I NEED TO STAY HIDDEN. THE WORLD THINKS THE BLACK WIDOW IS DEAD.
I SPENT A FEW WEEKS TRAVELING BY FREIGHTER TO ARRIVE HERE OFF THE GRID, BUT IT'S ALL FOR NOTHING.
SOMEONE KNOWS I'M HERE.
A SIGNAL TO CHECK MY DEAD DROP.
ONLY TWO MEN KNOW ABOUT THIS SAFE HOUSE.
ONE IS DEAD.
THE OTHER IS CAPTAIN AMERICA. AND HE'S A LITTLE BUSY ON HIS APOLOGY TOUR RIGHT NOW TO TURN UP IN MADRIPOOR.

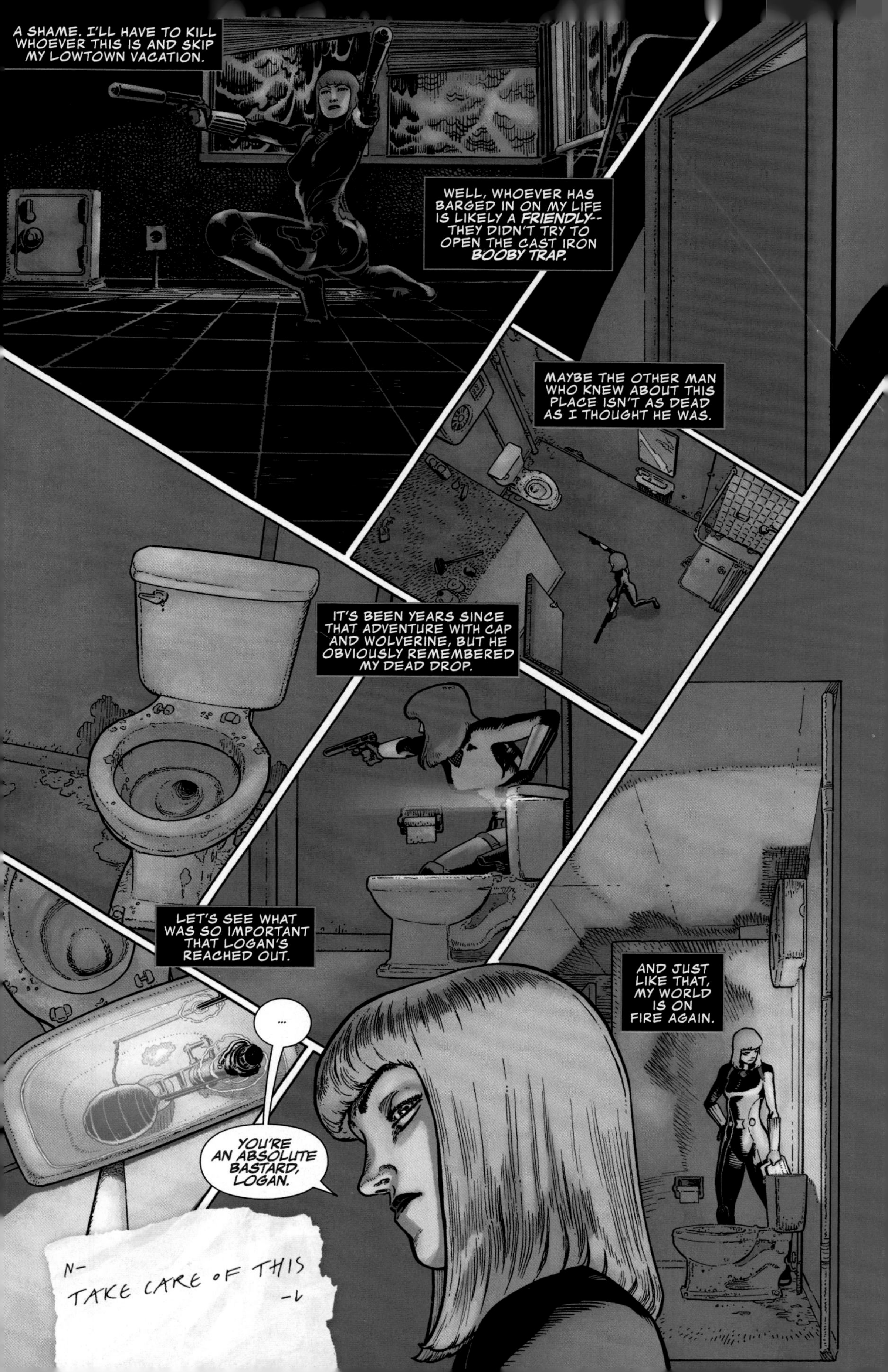

A SHAME. I'LL HAVE TO KILL WHOEVER THIS IS AND SKIP MY LOWTOWN VACATION.
WELL, WHOEVER HAS BARGED IN ON MY LIFE IS LIKELY A FRIENDLY-- THEY DIDN'T TRY TO OPEN THE CAST IRON BOOBY TRAP.
MAYBE THE OTHER MAN WHO KNEW ABOUT THIS PLACE ISN'T AS DEAD AS I THOUGHT HE WAS.
IT'S BEEN YEARS SINCE THAT ADVENTURE WITH CAP AND WOLVERINE, BUT HE OBVIOUSLY REMEMBERED MY DEAD DROP.
LET'S SEE WHAT WAS SO IMPORTANT THAT LOGAN'S REACHED OUT.
AND JUST LIKE THAT, MY WORLD IS ON FIRE AGAIN.
...
YOU'RE AN ABSOLUTE BASTARD, LOGAN.
N- TAKE CARE OF THIS -L

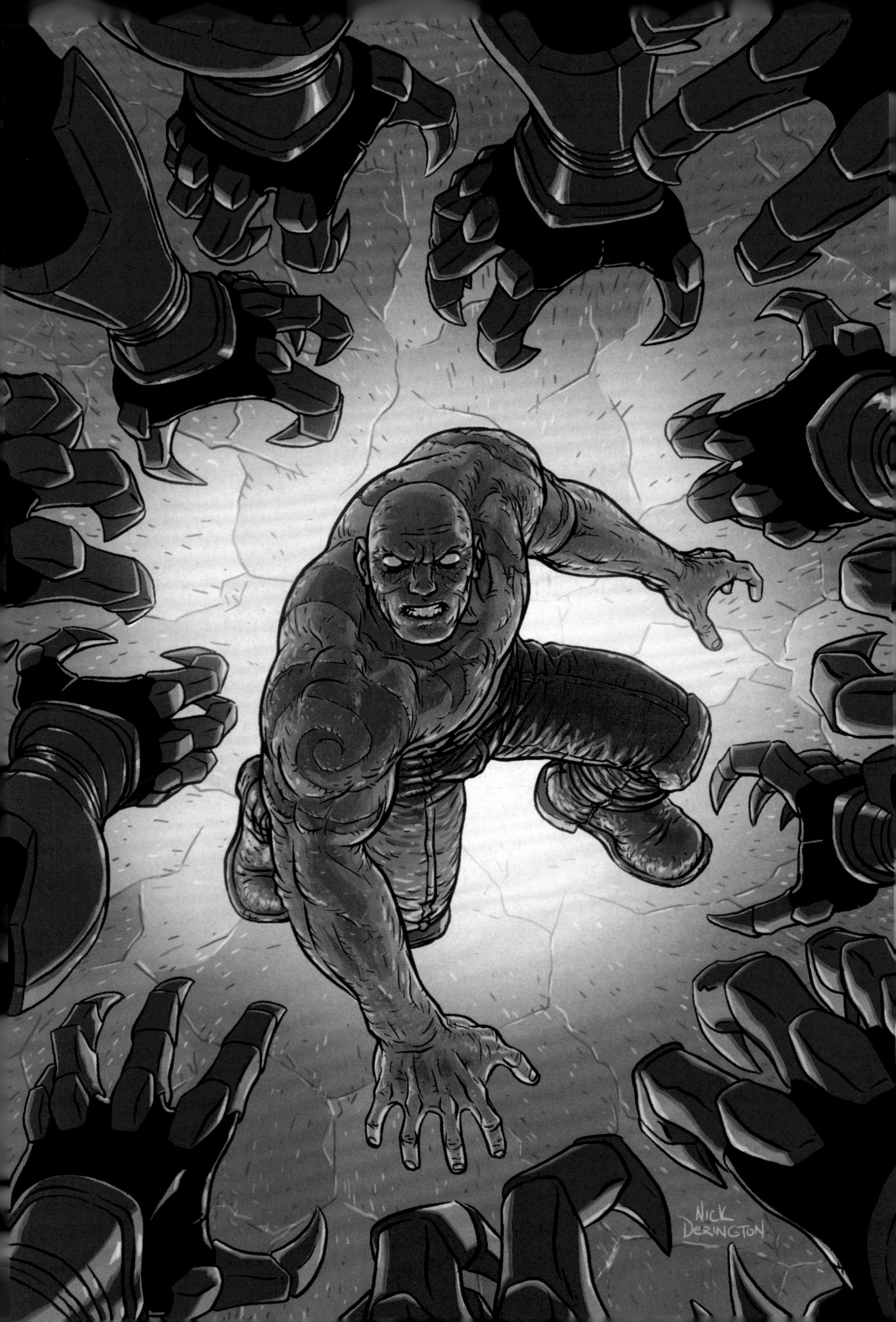
NICK DERINGTON

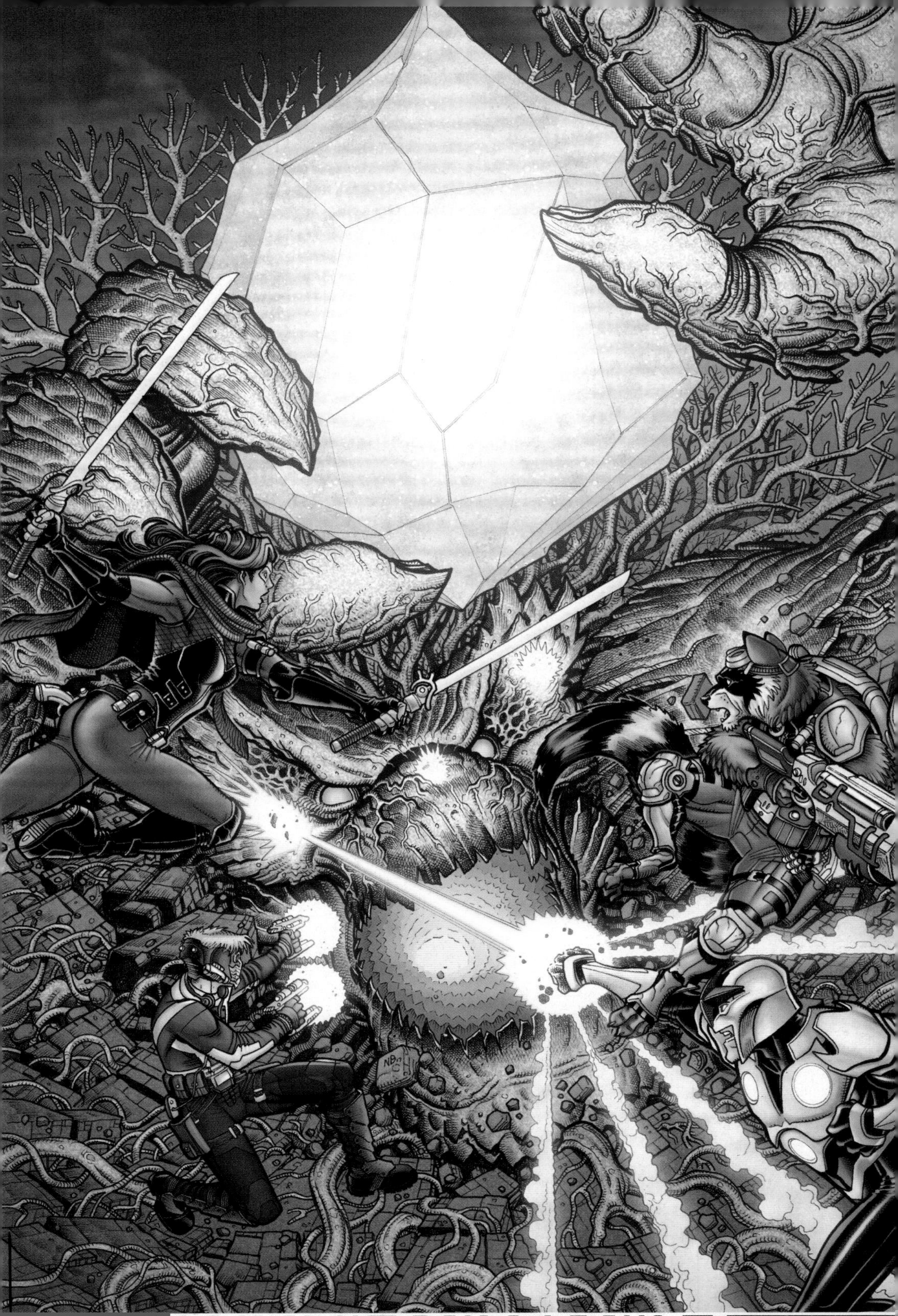

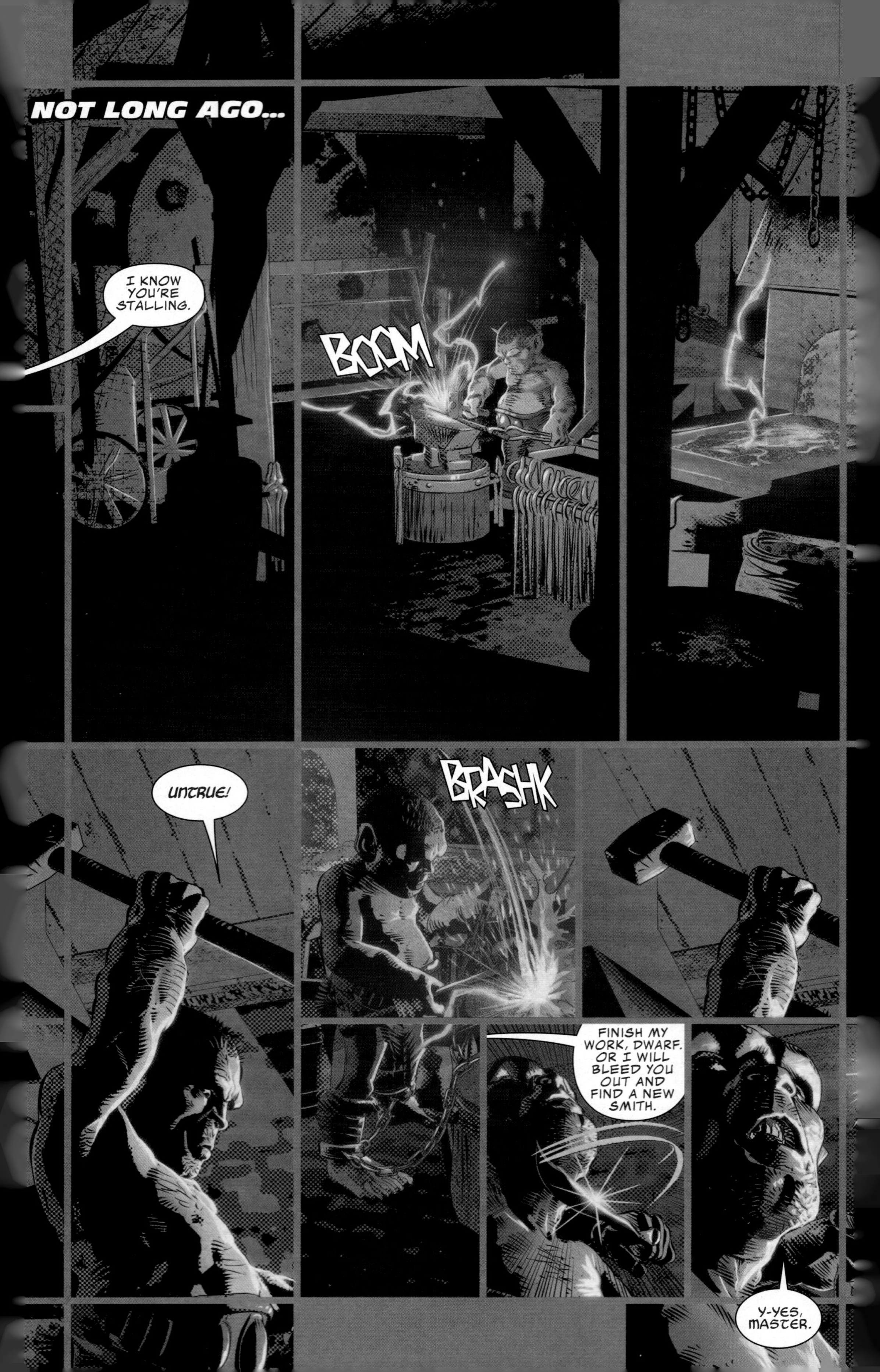
NOT LONG AGO...
I KNOW YOU'RE STALLING.
BOOM
UNTRUE!
BRASHK
FINISH MY WORK, DWARF. OR I WILL BLEED YOU OUT AND FIND A NEW SMITH.
Y-YES, MASTER.

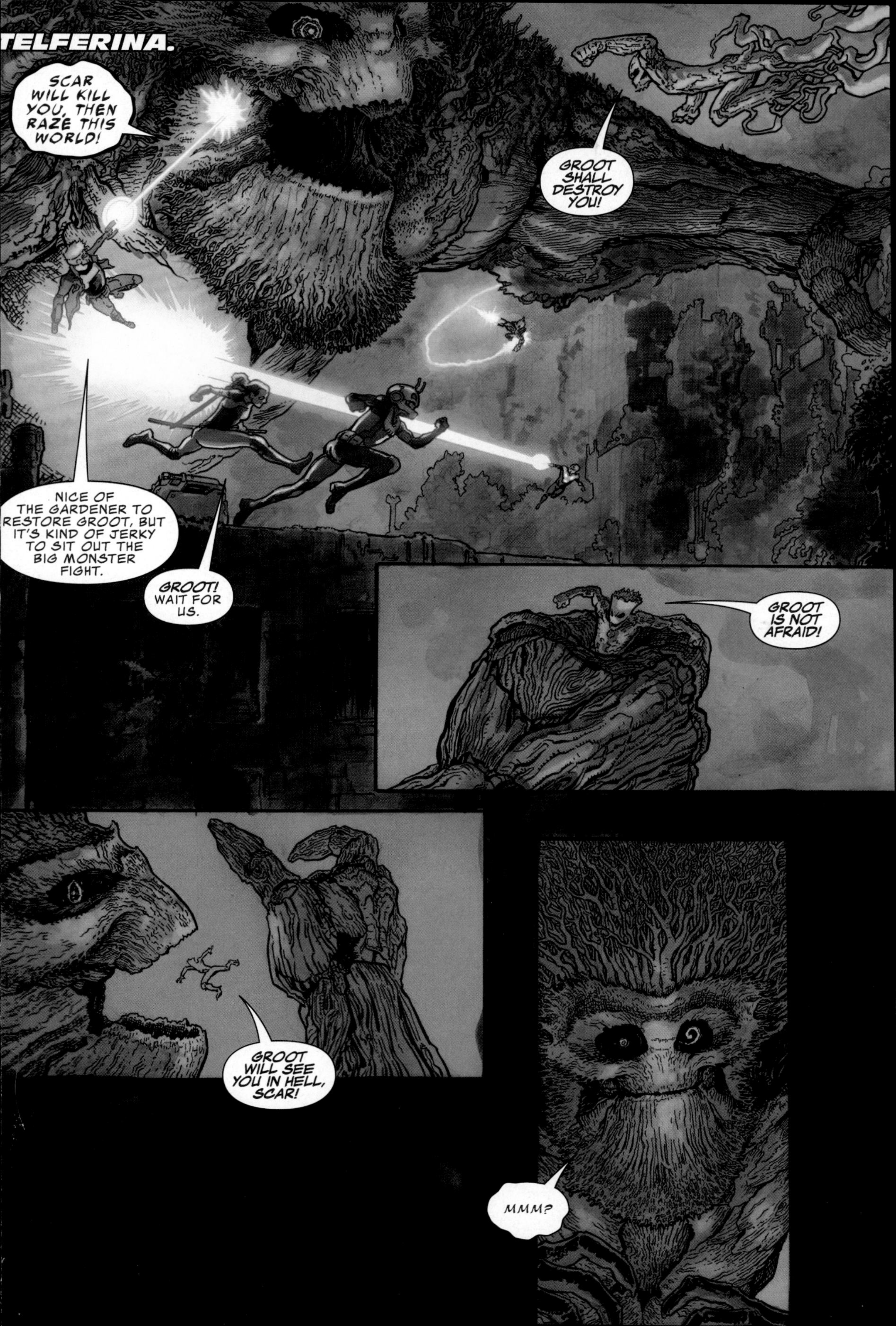
TELFERINA.
SCAR WILL KILL YOU, THEN RAZE THIS WORLD!
GROOT SHALL DESTROY YOU!
NICE OF THE GARDENER TO RESTORE GROOT, BUT IT'S KIND OF JERKY TO SIT OUT THE BIG MONSTER FIGHT.
GROOT! WAIT FOR US.
GROOT IS NOT AFRAID!
GROOT WILL SEE YOU IN HELL, SCAR!
MMM?

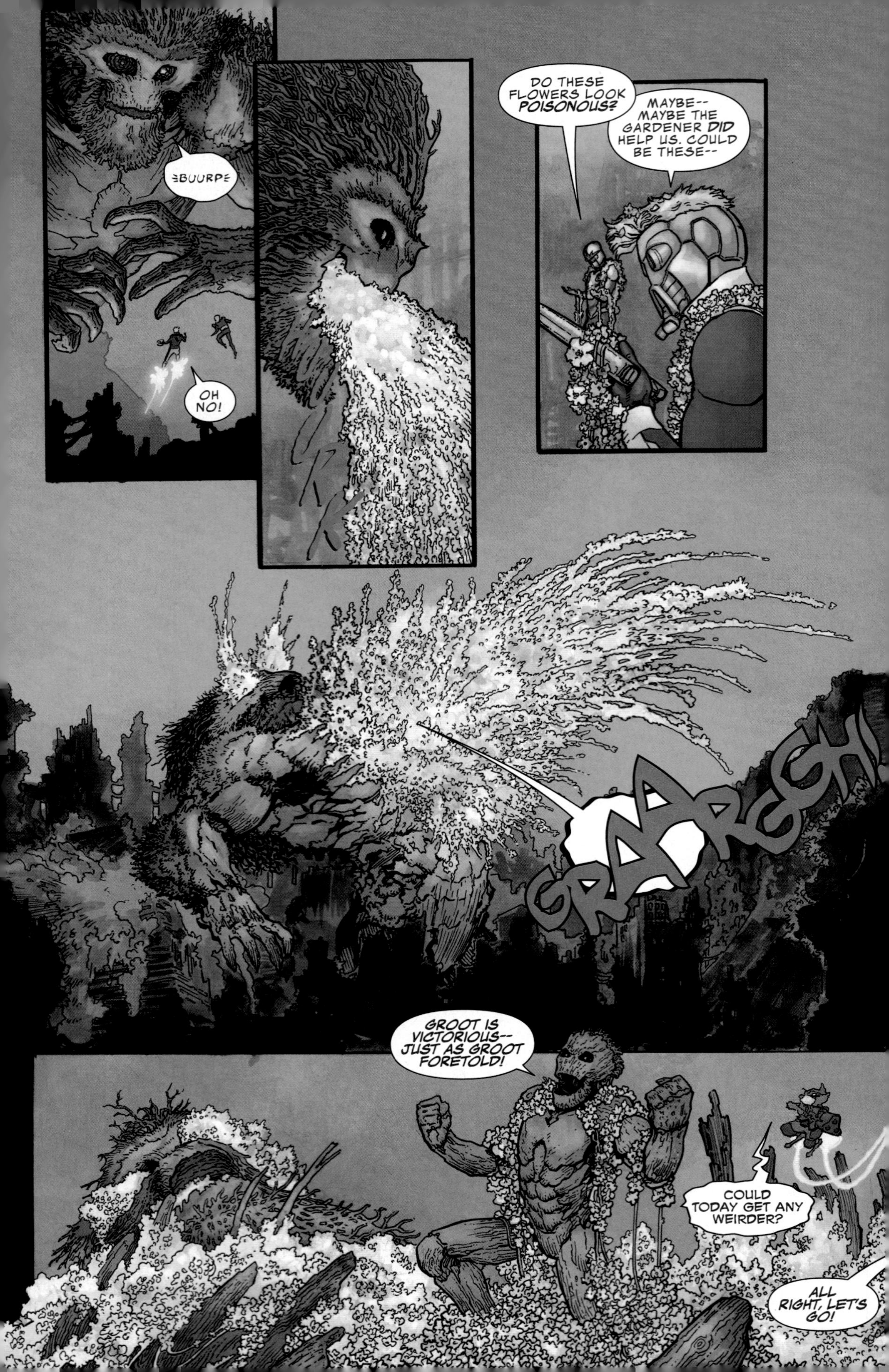
BUURP
OH NO!
URRK
DO THESE FLOWERS LOOK POISONOUS?
MAYBE-- MAYBE THE GARDENER DID HELP US. COULD BE THESE--
GRAARGGH!
GROOT IS VICTORIOUS-- JUST AS GROOT FORETOLD!
COULD TODAY GET ANY WEIRDER?
ALL RIGHT, LET'S GO!

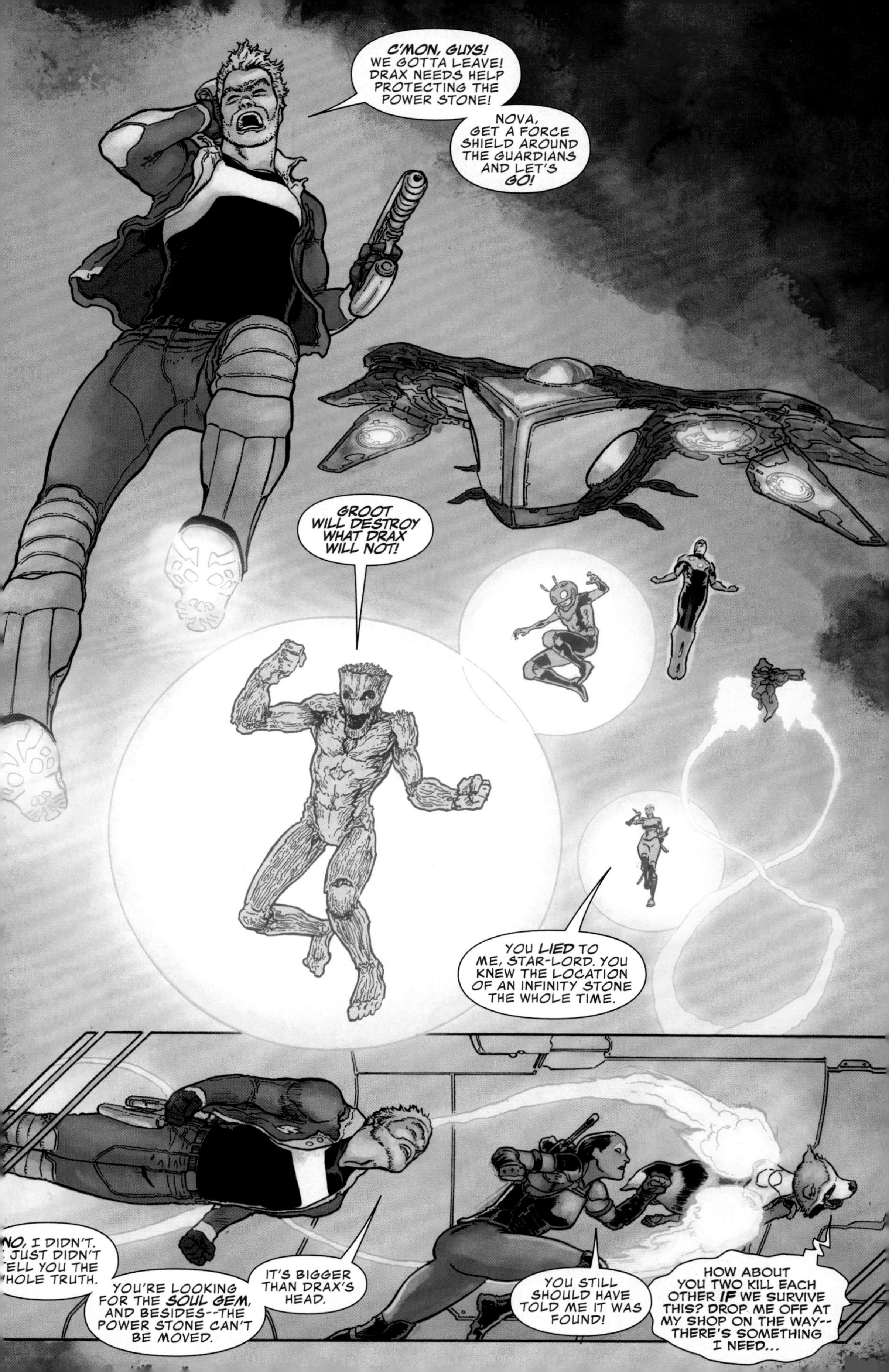
C'MON, GUYS! WE GOTTA LEAVE! DRAX NEEDS HELP PROTECTING THE POWER STONE!
NOVA, GET A FORCE SHIELD AROUND THE GUARDIANS AND LET'S GO!
GROOT WILL DESTROY WHAT DRAX WILL NOT!
YOU LIED TO ME, STAR-LORD. YOU KNEW THE LOCATION OF AN INFINITY STONE THE WHOLE TIME.
NO, I DIDN'T. JUST DIDN'T ELL YOU THE HOLE TRUTH.
YOU'RE LOOKING FOR THE SOUL GEM, AND BESIDES--THE POWER STONE CAN'T BE MOVED.
IT'S BIGGER THAN DRAX'S HEAD.
YOU STILL SHOULD HAVE TOLD ME IT WAS FOUND!
HOW ABOUT YOU TWO KILL EACH OTHER IF WE SURVIVE THIS? DROP ME OFF AT MY SHOP ON THE WAY-- THERE'S SOMETHING I NEED...

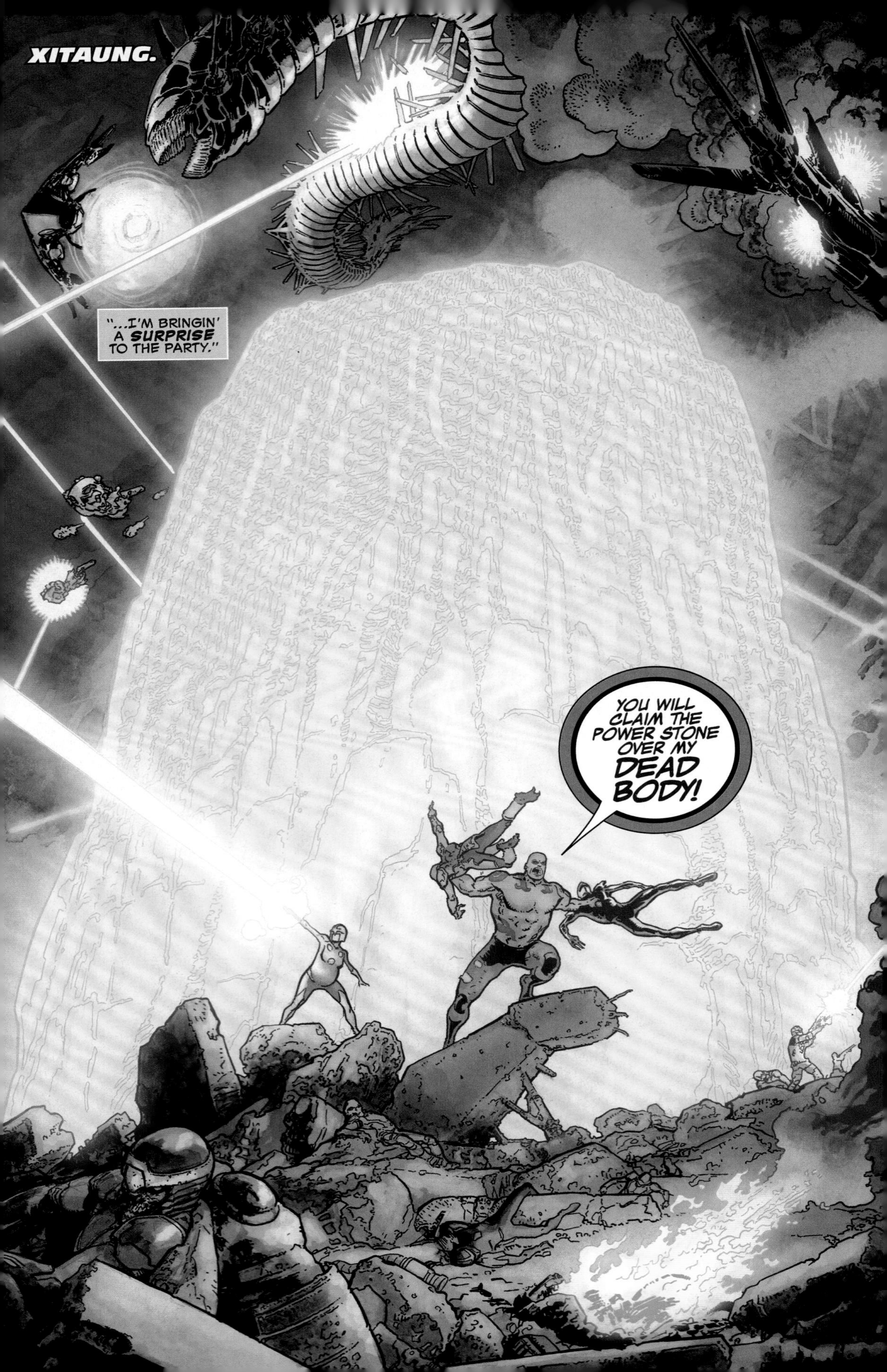
XITAUNG.
"...I'M BRINGIN' A SURPRISE TO THE PARTY."
YOU WILL CLAIM THE POWER STONE OVER MY DEAD BODY!

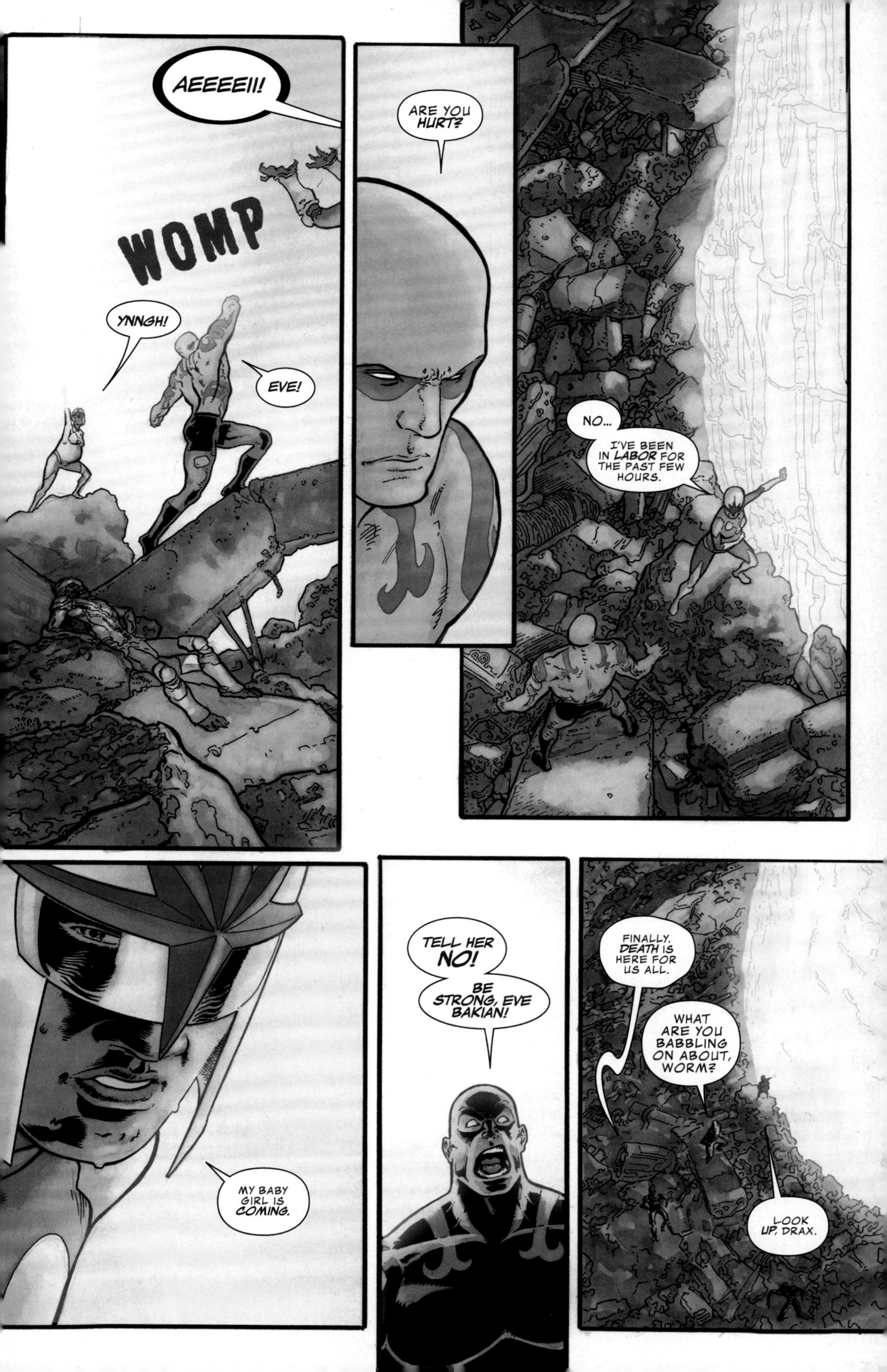
AEEEEII!
WOMP
YNNGH!
EVE!
ARE YOU HURT?
NO...
I'VE BEEN IN LABOR FOR THE PAST FEW HOURS.
MY BABY GIRL IS COMING.
TELL HER NO!
BE STRONG, EVE BAKIAN!
FINALLY. DEATH IS HERE FOR US ALL.
WHAT ARE YOU BABBLING ON ABOUT, WORM?
LOOK UP, DRAX.

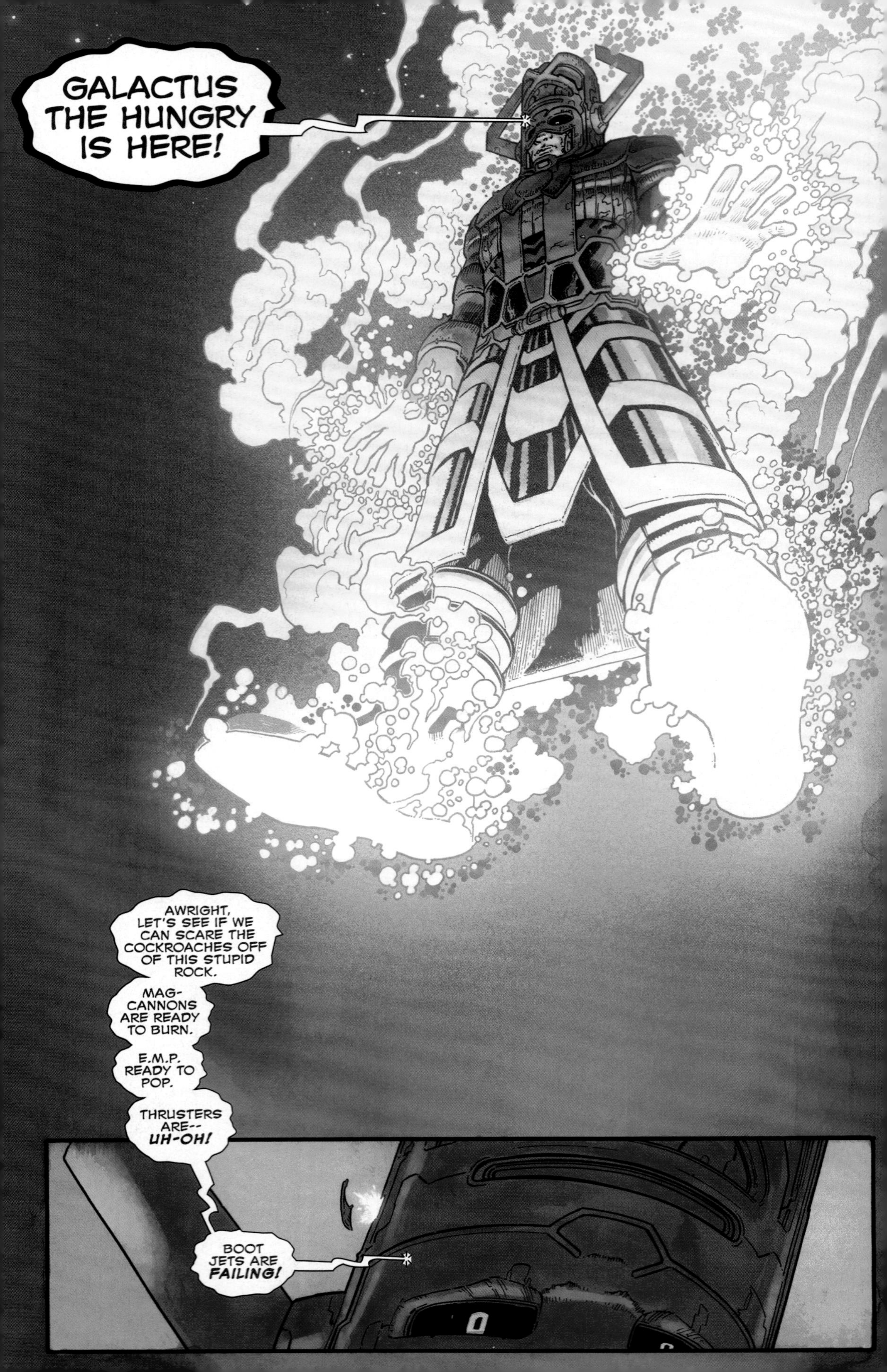
GALACTUS THE HUNGRY IS HERE!
AWRIGHT, LET'S SEE IF WE CAN SCARE THE COCKROACHES OFF OF THIS STUPID ROCK.
MAG-CANNONS ARE READY TO BURN.
E.M.P. READY TO POP.
THRUSTERS ARE-- UH-OH!
BOOT JETS ARE FAILING!

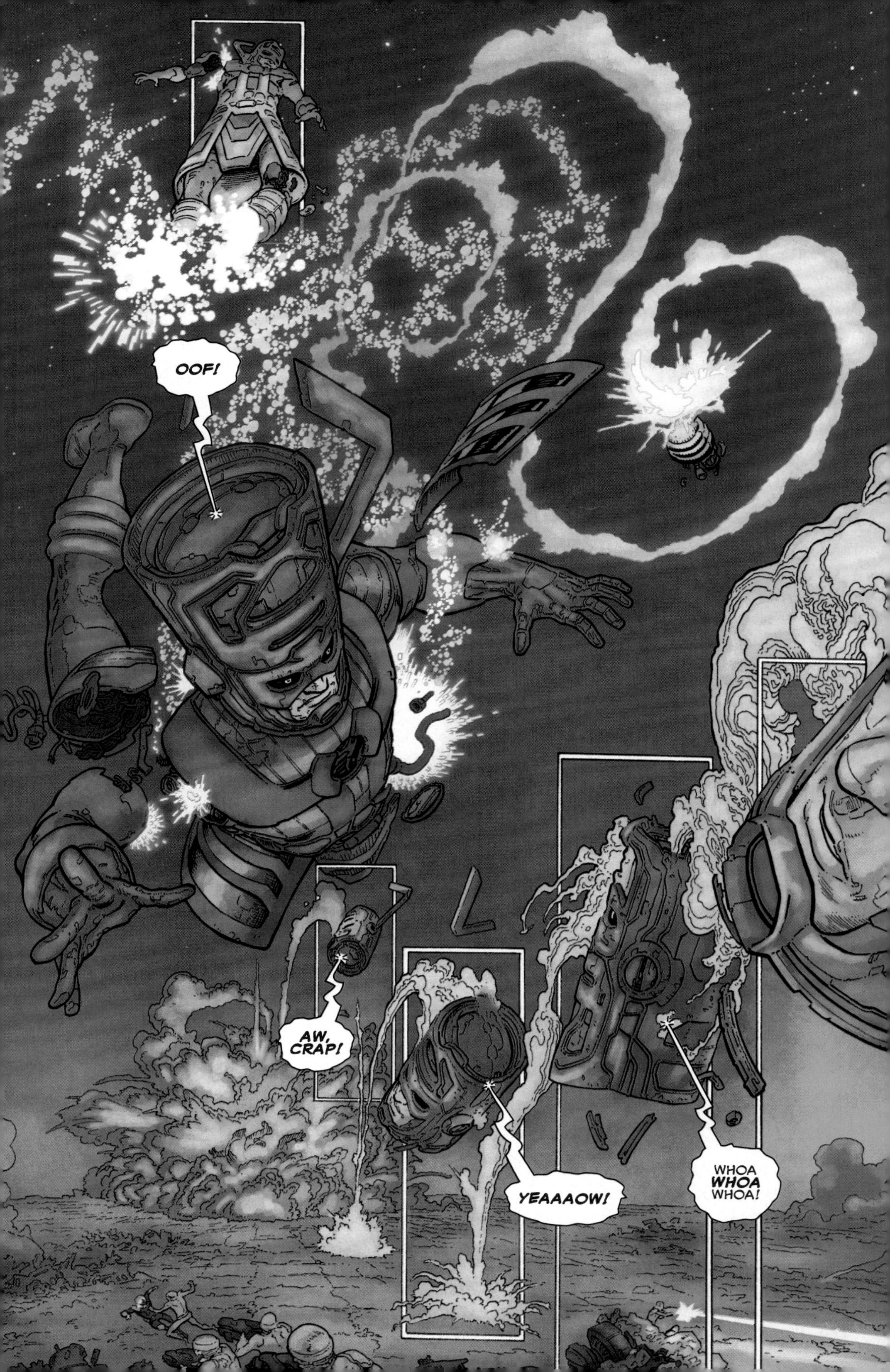
OOF!
AW, CRAP!
YEAAAOW!
WHOA WHOA WHOA!

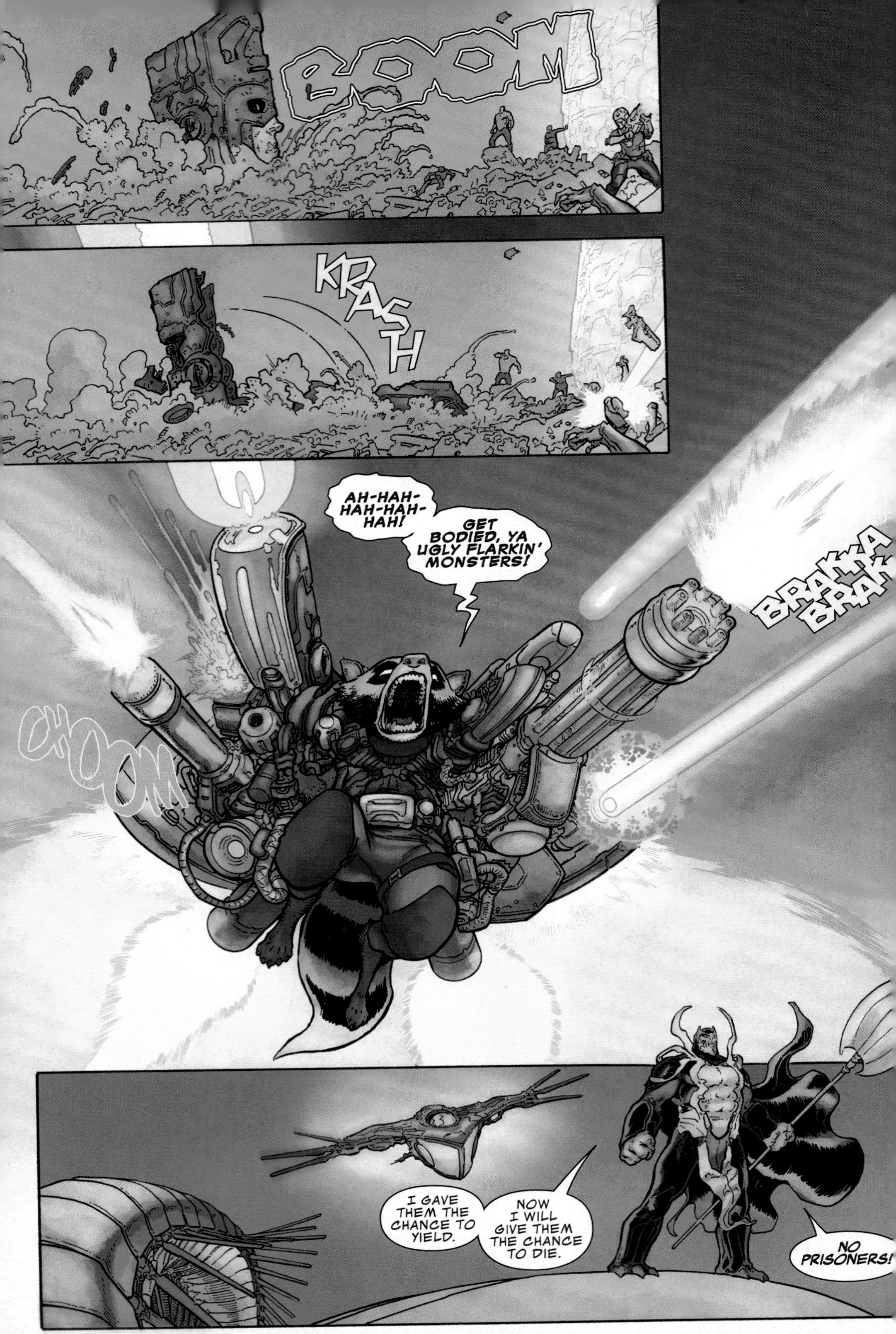
BOOM
KRASH
AH-HAH-HAH-HAH-HAH!
GET BODIED, YA UGLY FLARKIN' MONSTERS!
CHOOM
BRAKKA BRAK
I GAVE THEM THE CHANCE TO YIELD.
NOW I WILL GIVE THEM THE CHANCE TO DIE.
NO PRISONERS!

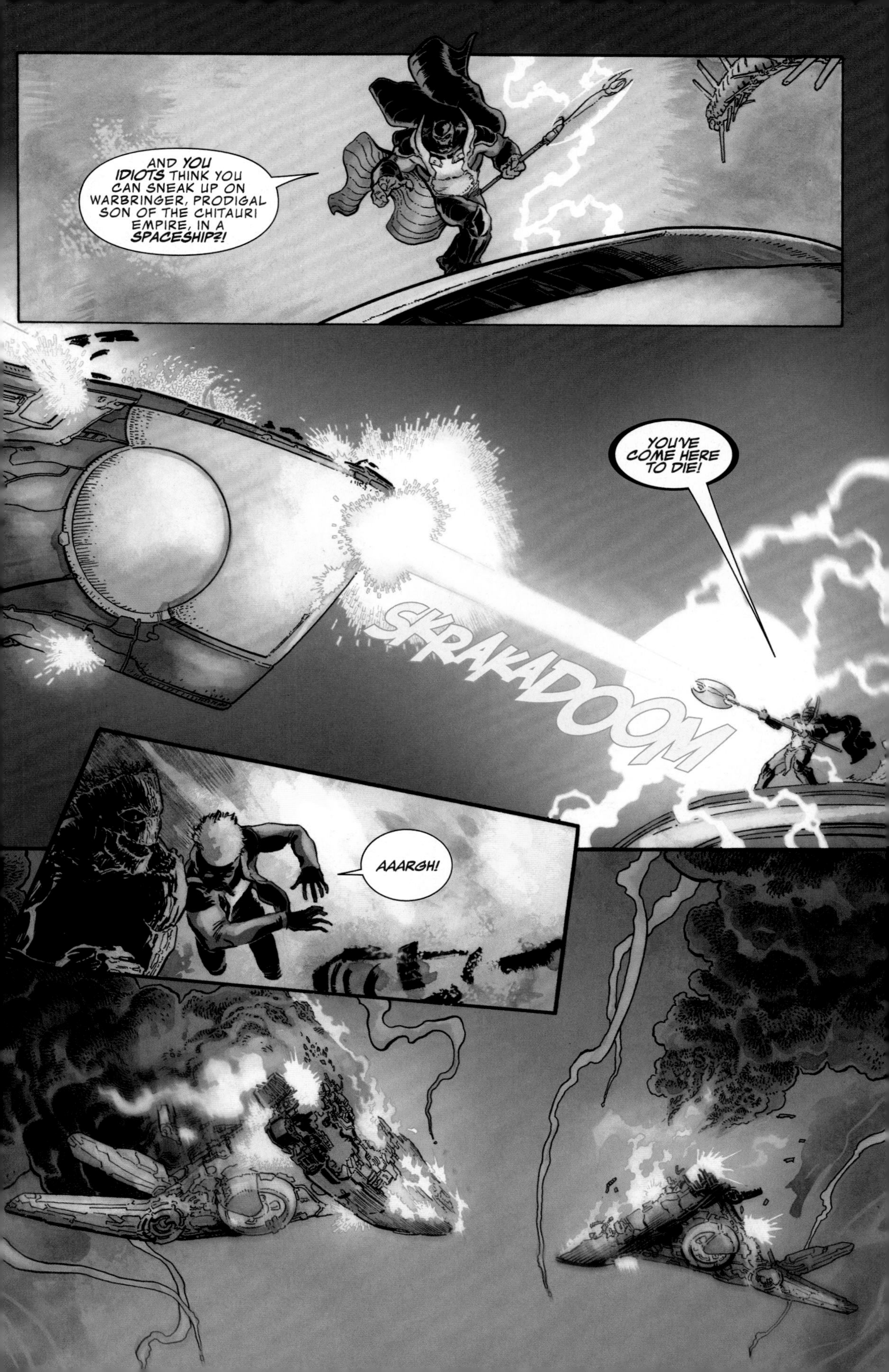
AND YOU IDIOTS THINK YOU CAN SNEAK UP ON WARBRINGER, PRODIGAL SON OF THE CHITAURI EMPIRE, IN A SPACESHIP?!
YOU'VE COME HERE TO DIE!
SKRAKADOOM
AAARGH!

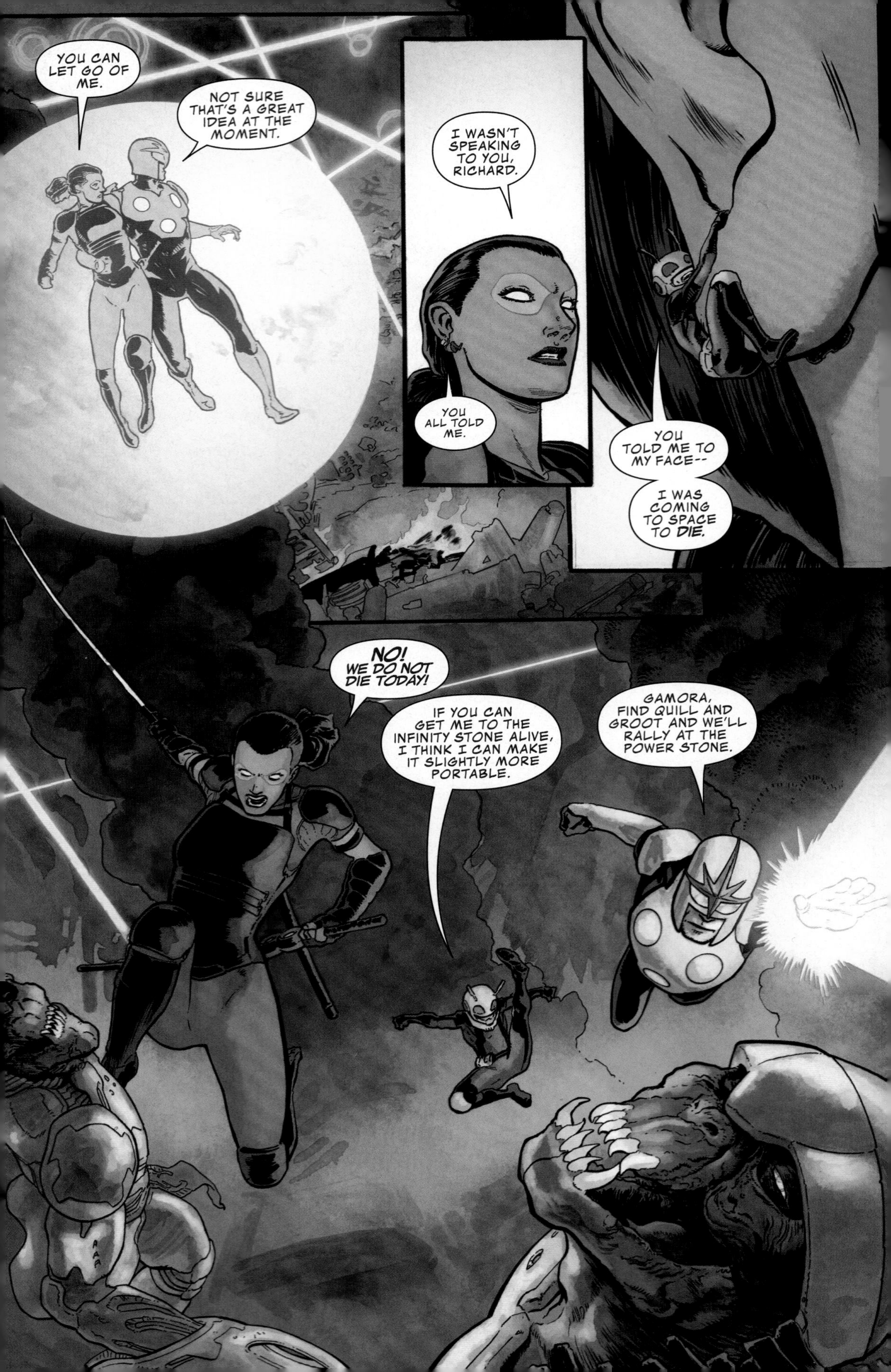
YOU CAN LET GO OF ME.
NOT SURE THAT'S A GREAT IDEA AT THE MOMENT.
I WASN'T SPEAKING TO YOU, RICHARD.
YOU ALL TOLD ME.
YOU TOLD ME TO MY FACE--
I WAS COMING TO SPACE TO DIE.
NO! WE DO NOT DIE TODAY!
IF YOU CAN GET ME TO THE INFINITY STONE ALIVE, I THINK I CAN MAKE IT SLIGHTLY MORE PORTABLE.
GAMORA, FIND QUILL AND GROOT AND WE'LL RALLY AT THE POWER STONE.

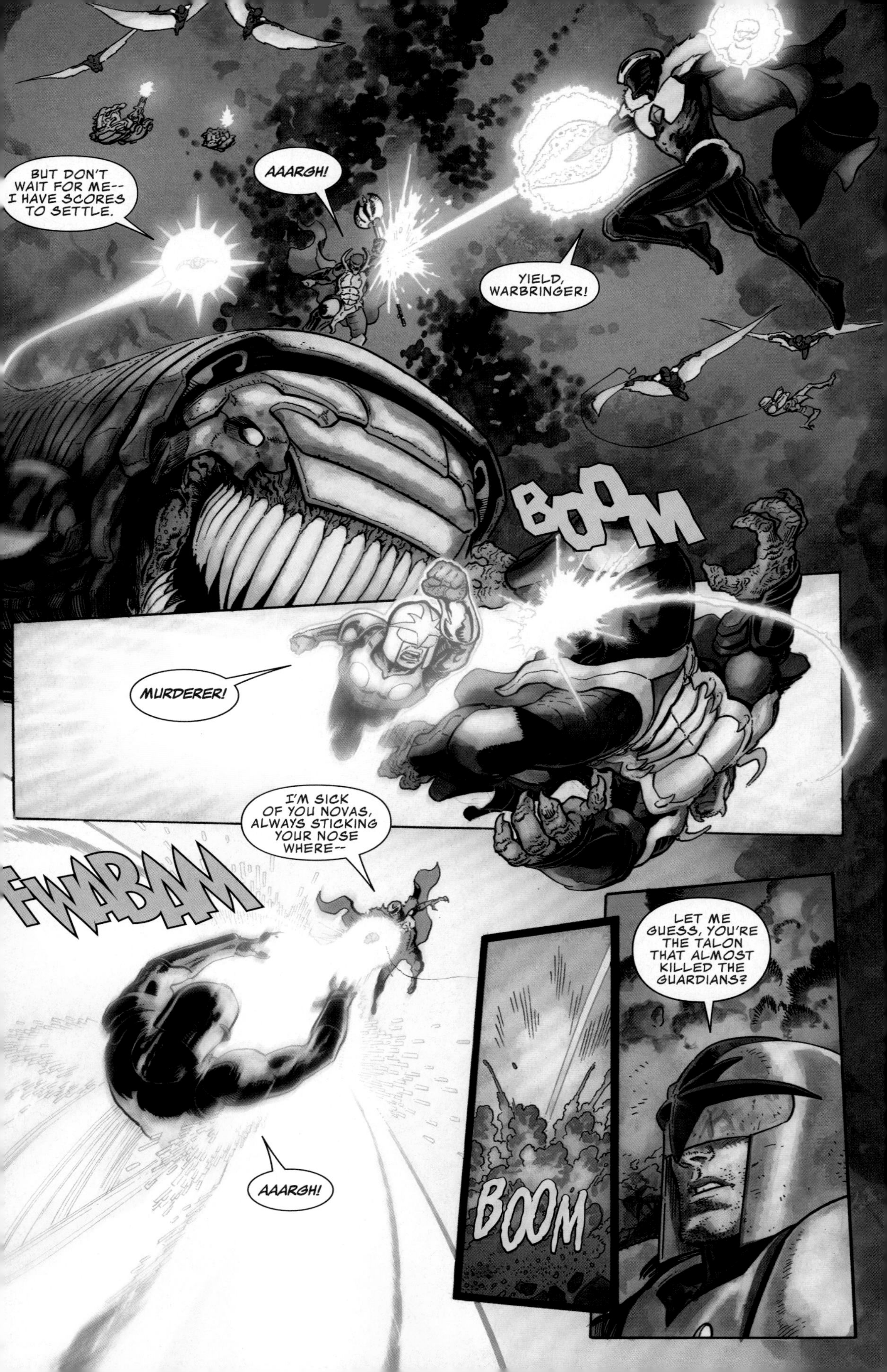
BUT DON'T WAIT FOR ME-- I HAVE SCORES TO SETTLE.
AAARGH!
YIELD, WARBRINGER!
BOOM
MURDERER!
I'M SICK OF YOU NOVAS, ALWAYS STICKING YOUR NOSE WHERE--
FWABAM
AAARGH!
BOOM
LET ME GUESS, YOU'RE THE TALON THAT ALMOST KILLED THE GUARDIANS?

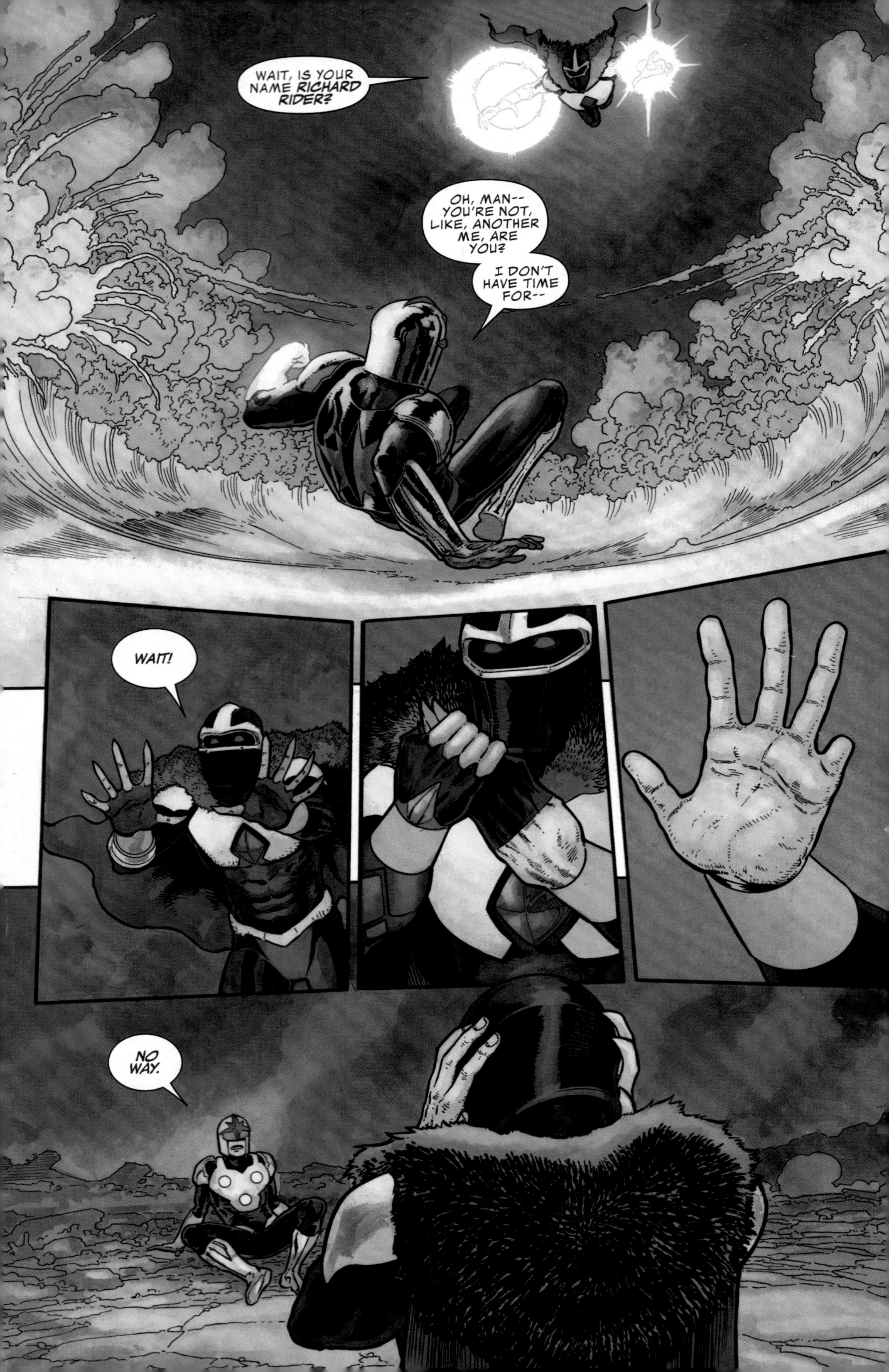
WAIT, IS YOUR NAME RICHARD RIDER?
OH, MAN-- YOU'RE NOT, LIKE, ANOTHER ME, ARE YOU?
I DON'T HAVE TIME FOR--
WAIT!
NO WAY.

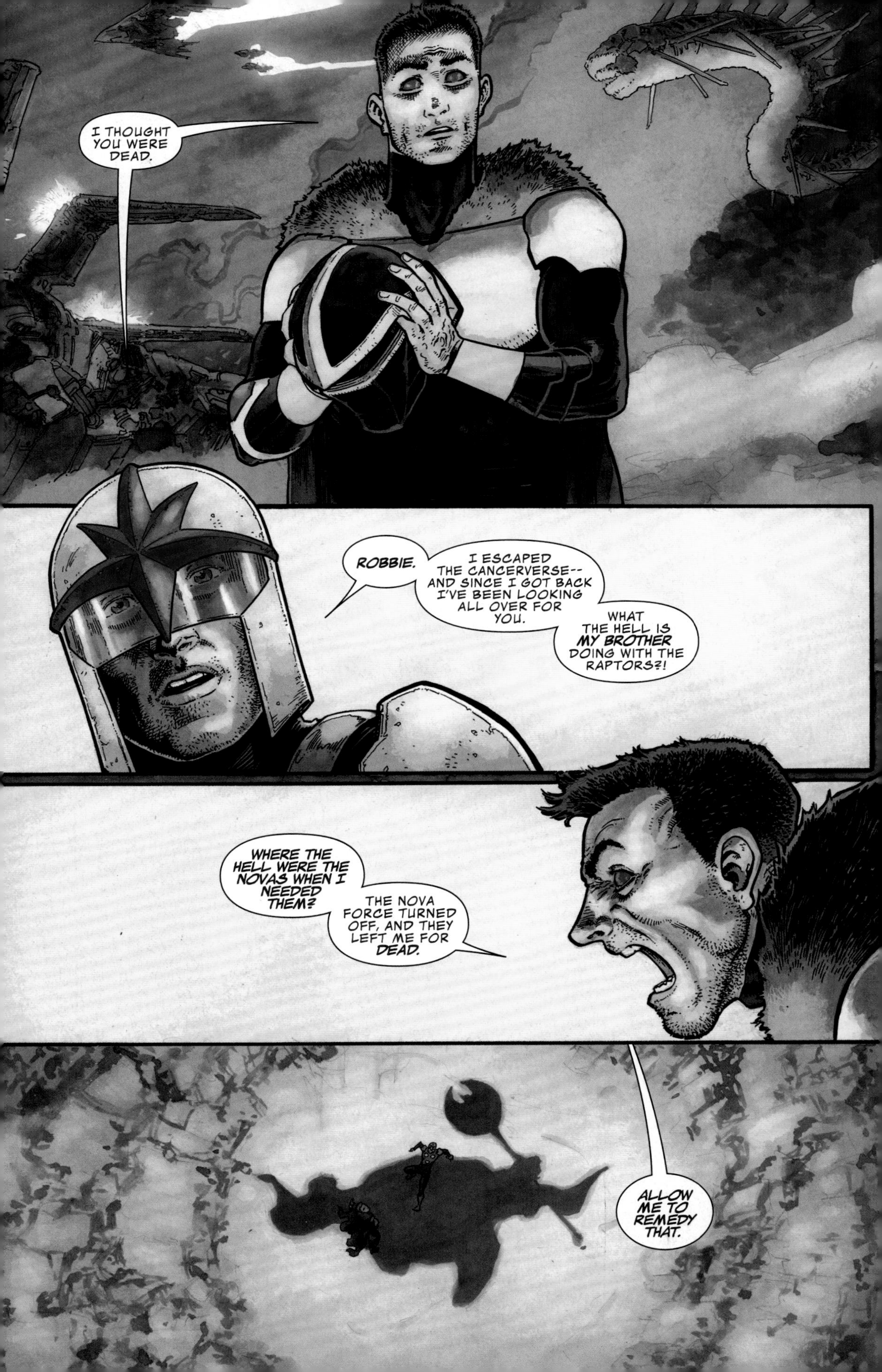
I THOUGHT YOU WERE DEAD.
ROBBIE.
I ESCAPED THE CANCERVERSE-- AND SINCE I GOT BACK I'VE BEEN LOOKING ALL OVER FOR YOU.
WHAT THE HELL IS MY BROTHER DOING WITH THE RAPTORS?!
WHERE THE HELL WERE THE NOVAS WHEN I NEEDED THEM?
THE NOVA FORCE TURNED OFF, AND THEY LEFT ME FOR DEAD.
ALLOW ME TO REMEDY THAT.

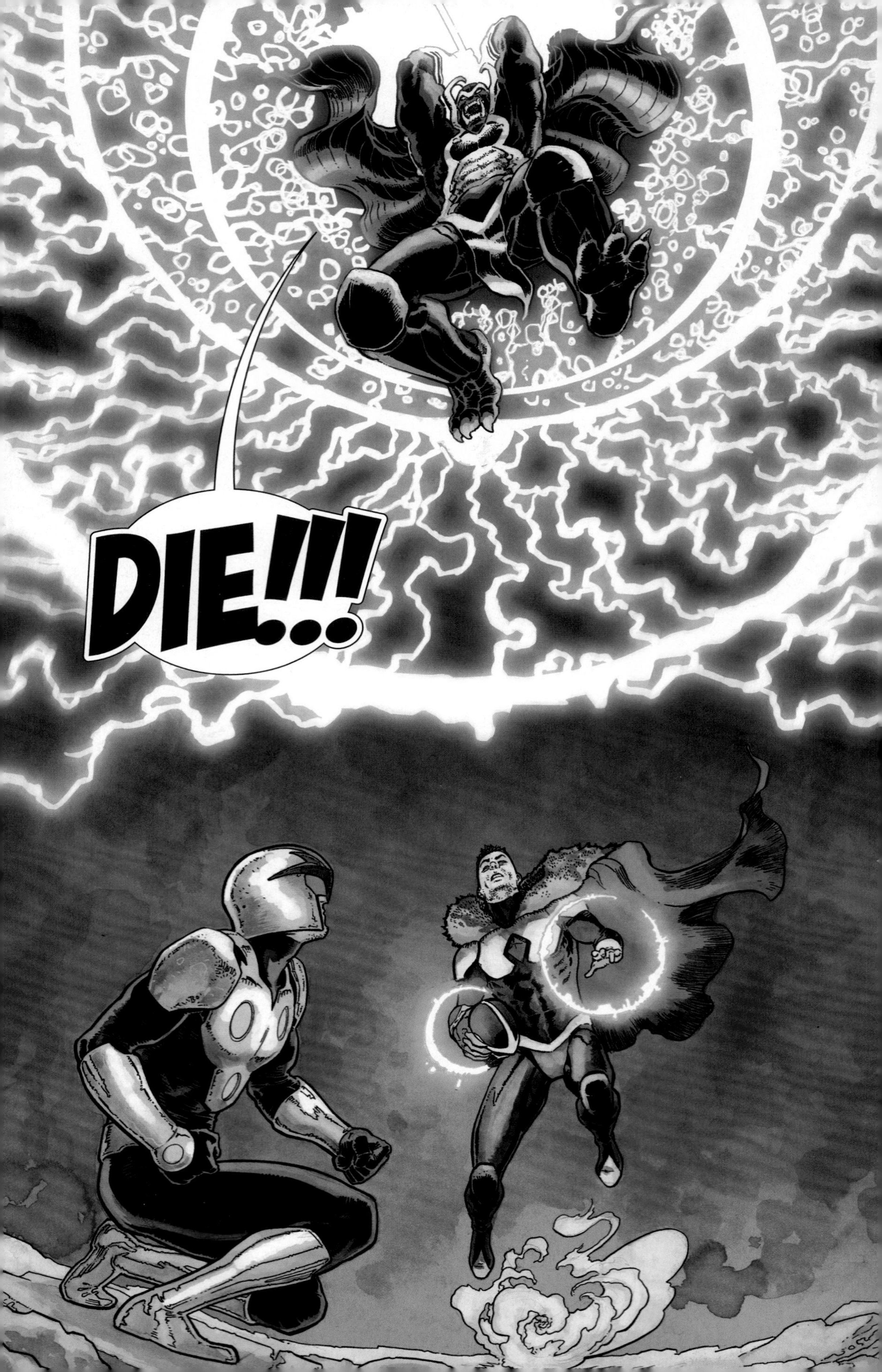
DIE...!!!

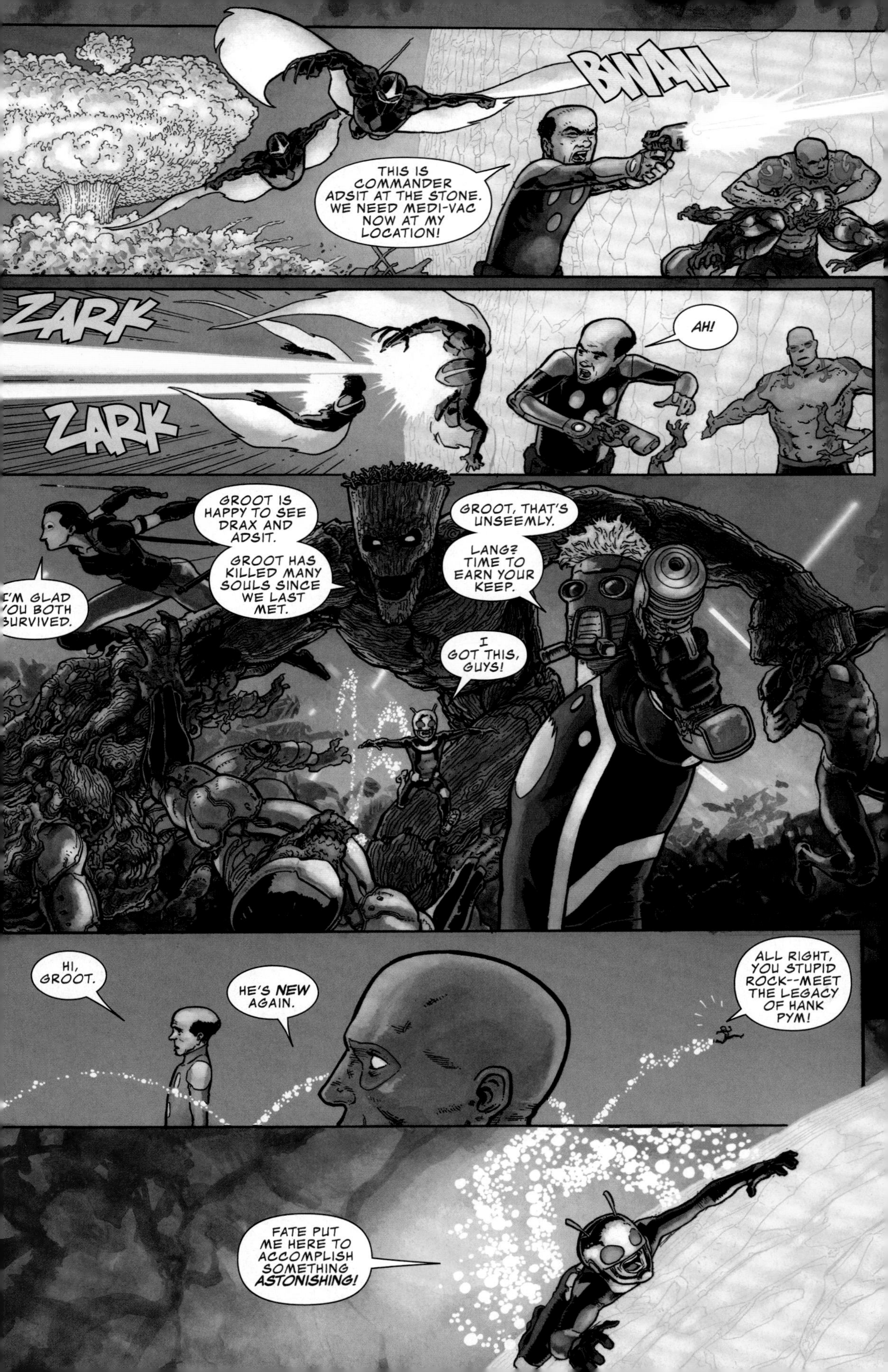
BWAM
THIS IS COMMANDER ADSIT AT THE STONE. WE NEED MEDI-VAC NOW AT MY LOCATION!
ZARK
ZARK
AH!
I'M GLAD YOU BOTH SURVIVED.
GROOT IS HAPPY TO SEE DRAX AND ADSIT.
GROOT HAS KILLED MANY SOULS SINCE WE LAST MET.
GROOT, THAT'S UNSEEMLY.
LANG? TIME TO EARN YOUR KEEP.
I GOT THIS, GUYS!
HI, GROOT.
HE'S NEW AGAIN.
ALL RIGHT, YOU STUPID ROCK--MEET THE LEGACY OF HANK PYM!
FATE PUT ME HERE TO ACCOMPLISH SOMETHING ASTONISHING!

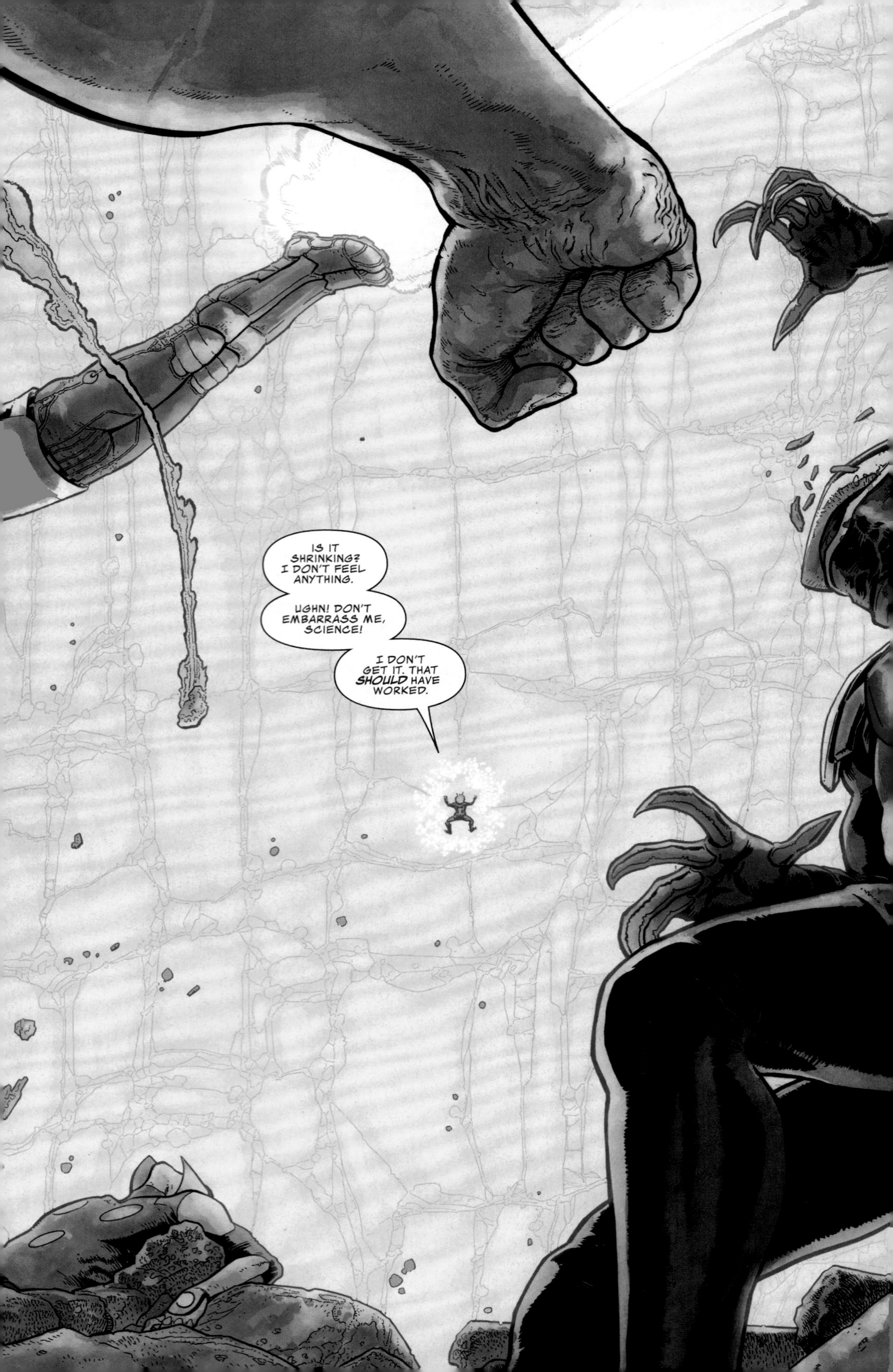
IS IT SHRINKING? I DON'T FEEL ANYTHING.
UGHN! DON'T EMBARRASS ME, SCIENCE!
I DON'T GET IT. THAT SHOULD HAVE WORKED.

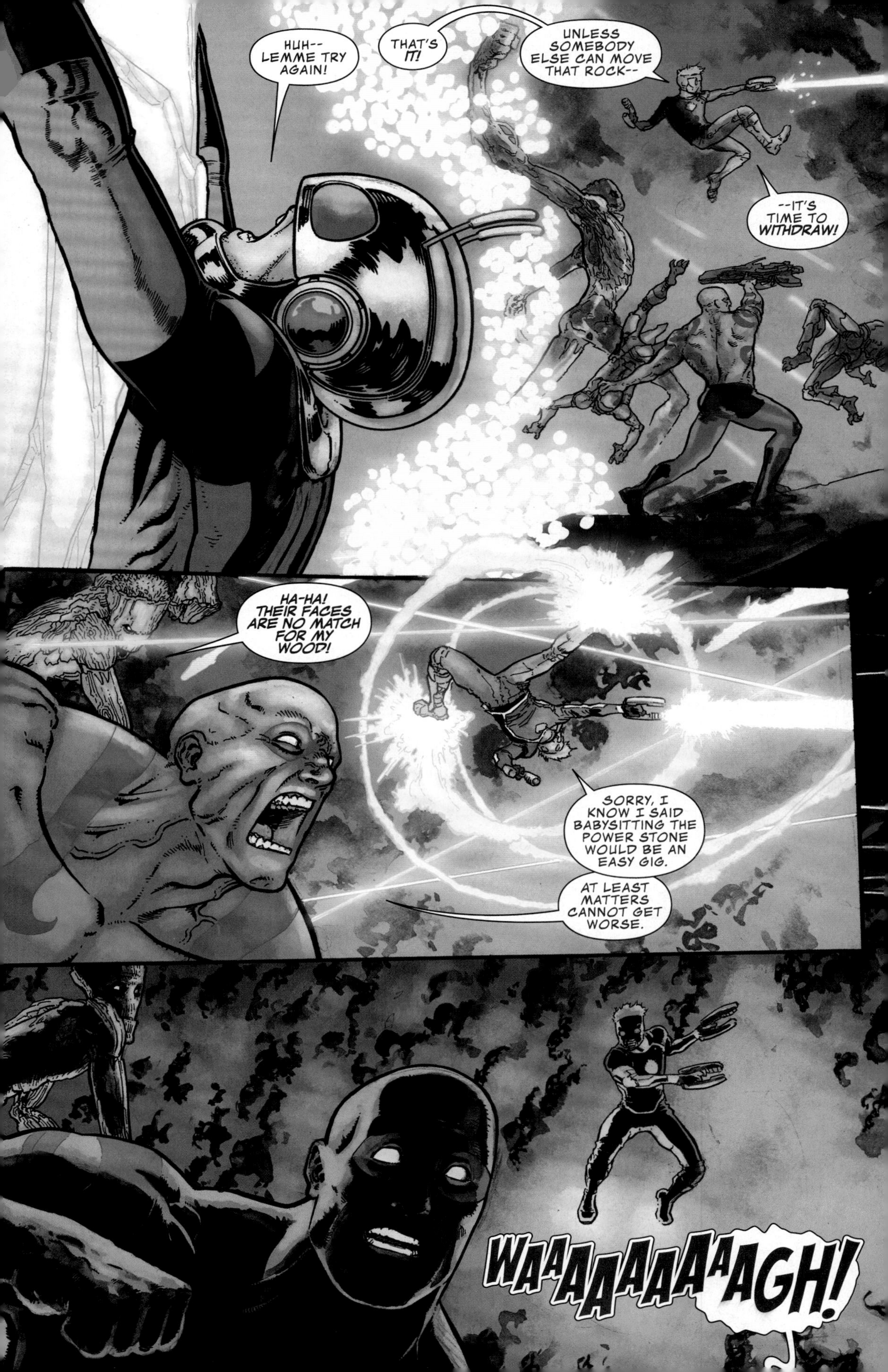

HUH-- LEMME TRY AGAIN!
THAT'S IT!
UNLESS SOMEBODY ELSE CAN MOVE THAT ROCK--
--IT'S TIME TO WITHDRAW!
HA-HA! THEIR FACES ARE NO MATCH FOR MY WOOD!
SORRY, I KNOW I SAID BABYSITTING THE POWER STONE WOULD BE AN EASY GIG.
AT LEAST MATTERS CANNOT GET WORSE.
WAaAAAAAAaAGH!

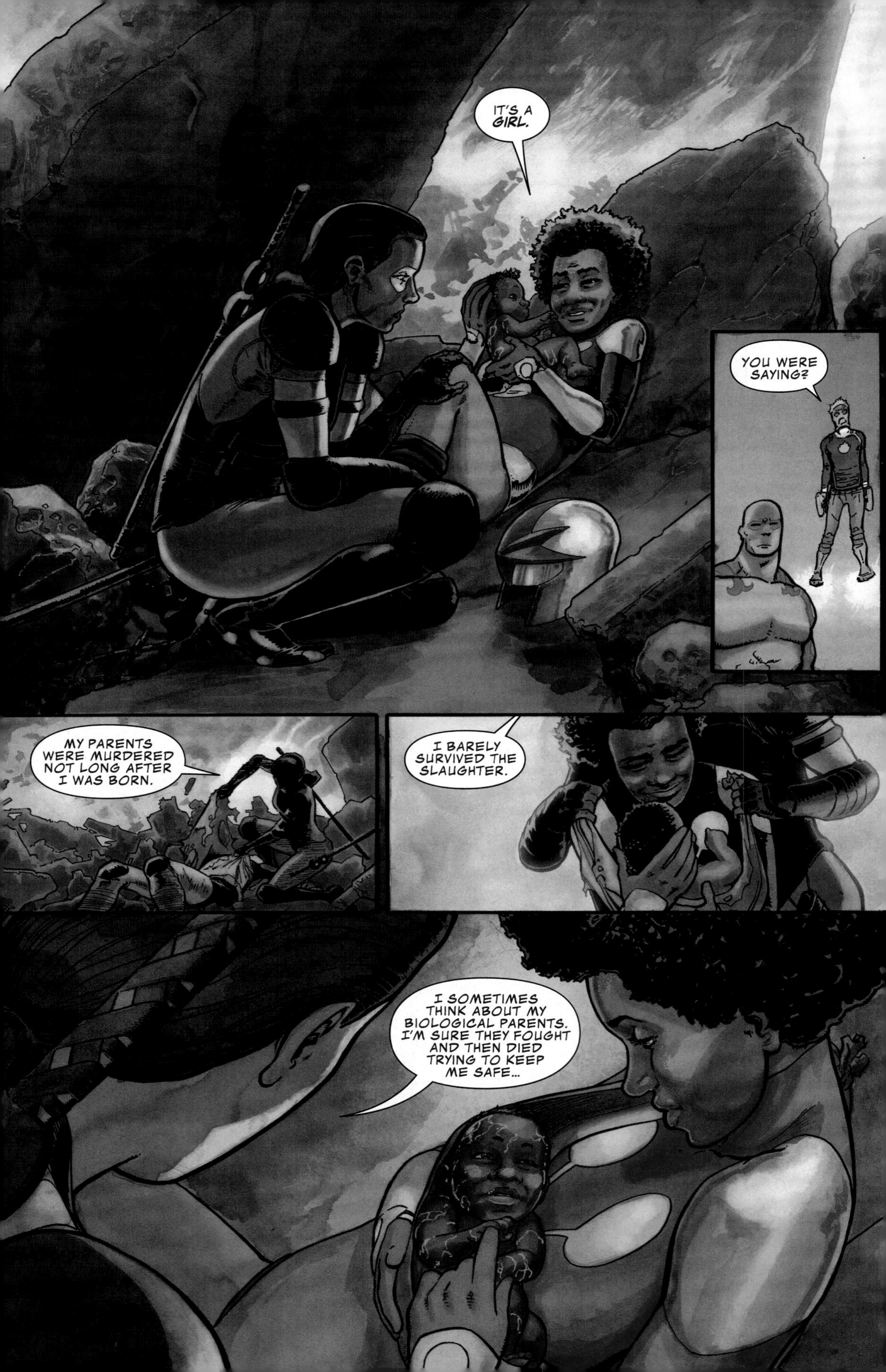
IT'S A GIRL.
YOU WERE SAYING?
MY PARENTS WERE MURDERED NOT LONG AFTER I WAS BORN.
I BARELY SURVIVED THE SLAUGHTER.
I SOMETIMES THINK ABOUT MY BIOLOGICAL PARENTS. I'M SURE THEY FOUGHT AND THEN DIED TRYING TO KEEP ME SAFE...

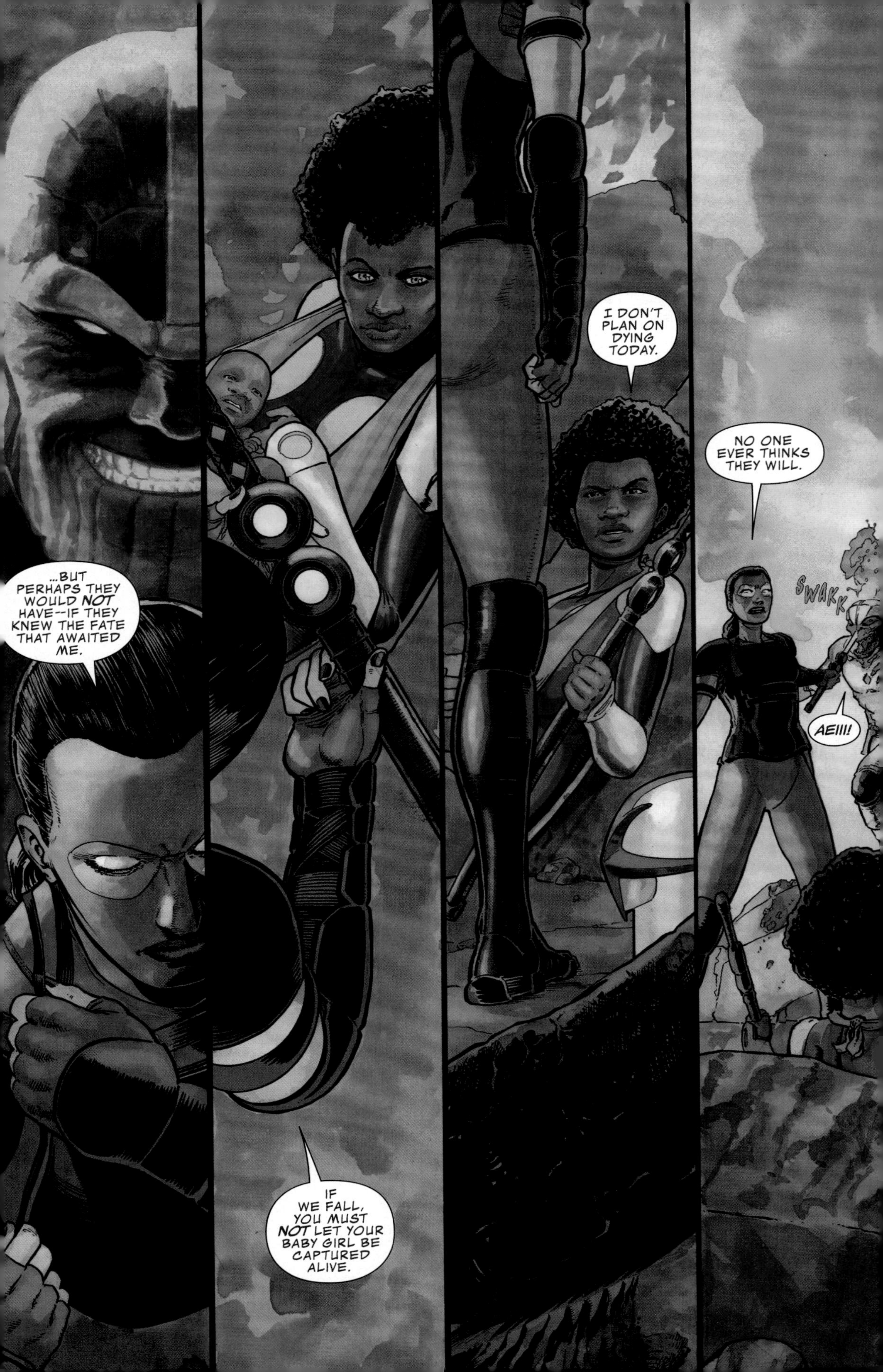
...BUT PERHAPS THEY WOULD NOT HAVE--IF THEY KNEW THE FATE THAT AWAITED ME.
IF WE FALL, YOU MUST NOT LET YOUR BABY GIRL BE CAPTURED ALIVE.
I DON'T PLAN ON DYING TODAY.
NO ONE EVER THINKS THEY WILL.
SWAKK
AEIII!

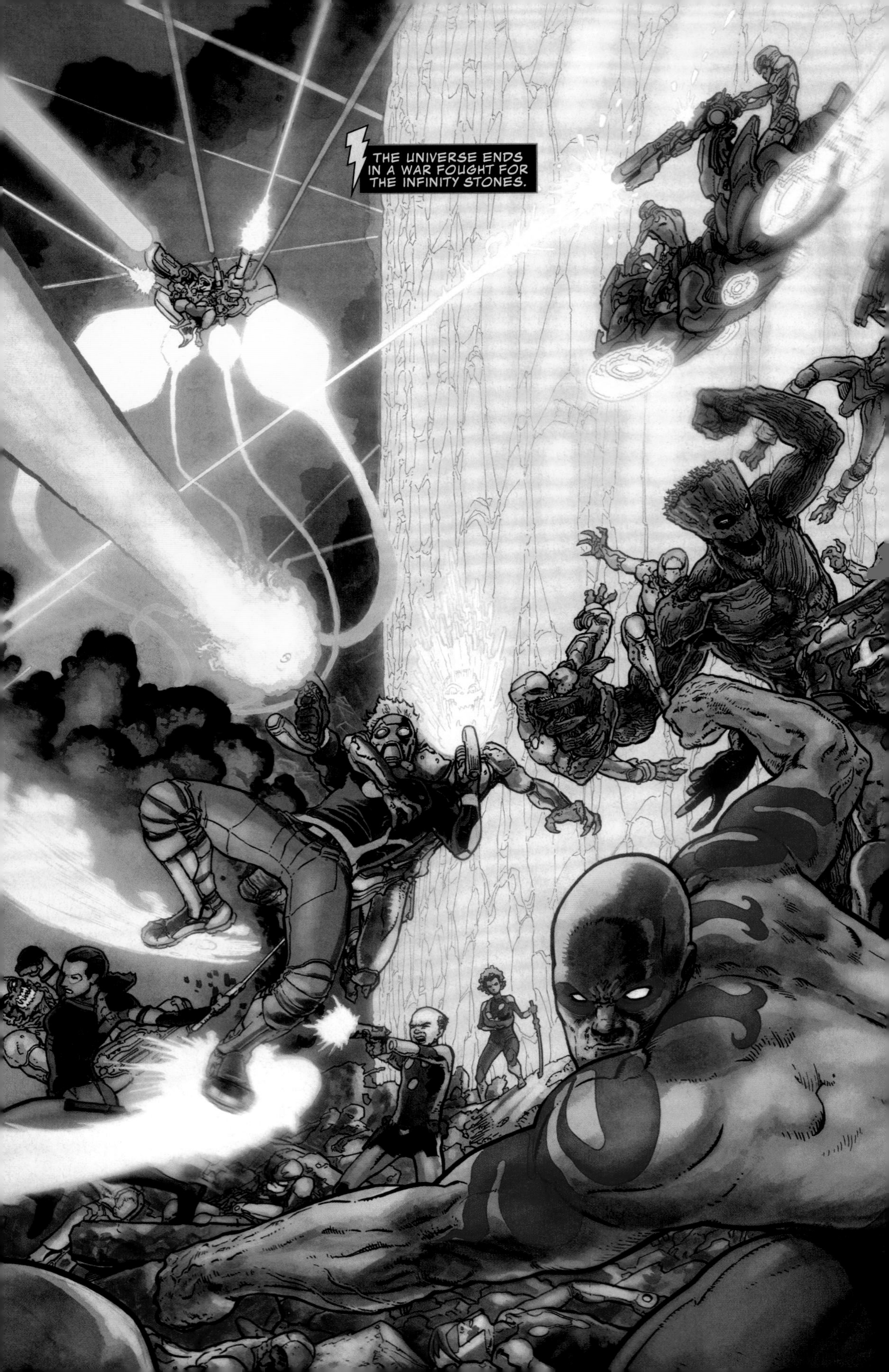
THE UNIVERSE ENDS IN A WAR FOUGHT FOR THE INFINITY STONES.

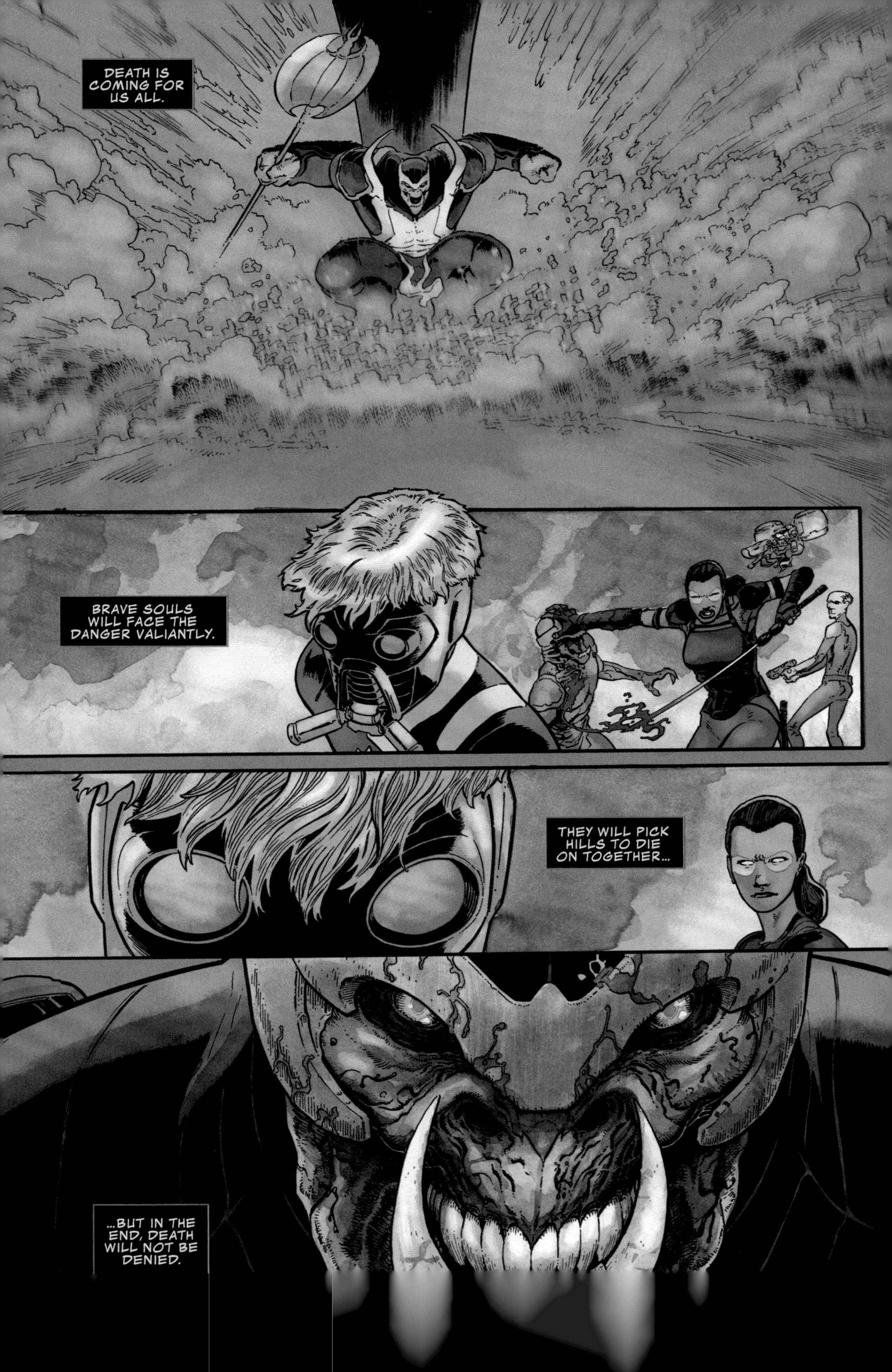
DEATH IS COMING FOR US ALL.
BRAVE SOULS WILL FACE THE DANGER VALIANTLY.
THEY WILL PICK HILLS TO DIE ON TOGETHER...
...BUT IN THE END, DEATH WILL NOT BE DENIED.

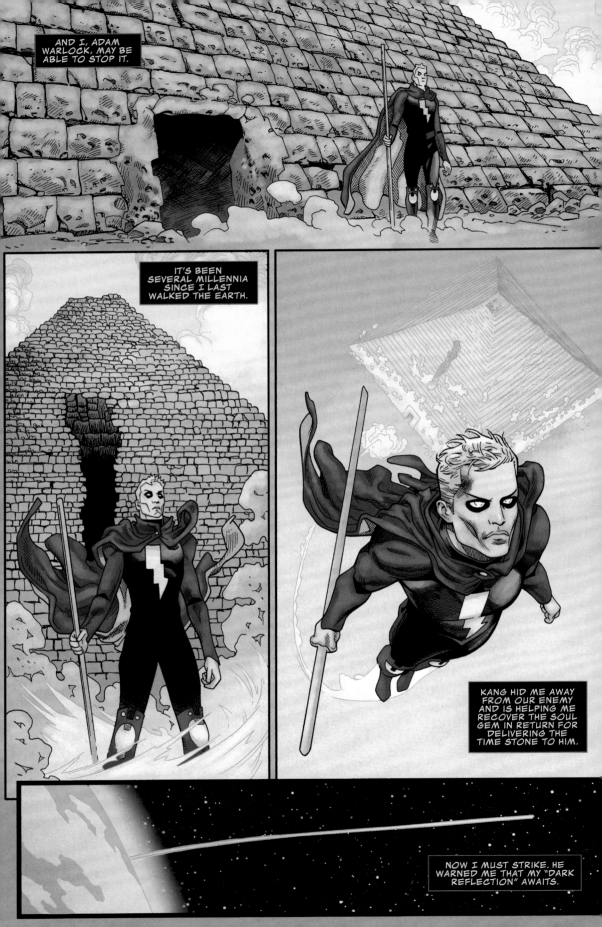

AND I, ADAM WARLOCK, MAY BE ABLE TO STOP IT.

IT'S BEEN SEVERAL MILLENNIA SINCE I LAST WALKED THE EARTH.

KANG HID ME AWAY FROM OUR ENEMY AND IS HELPING ME RECOVER THE SOUL GEM IN RETURN FOR DELIVERING THE TIME STONE TO HIM.

NOW I MUST STRIKE. HE WARNED ME THAT MY "DARK REFLECTION" AWAITS.

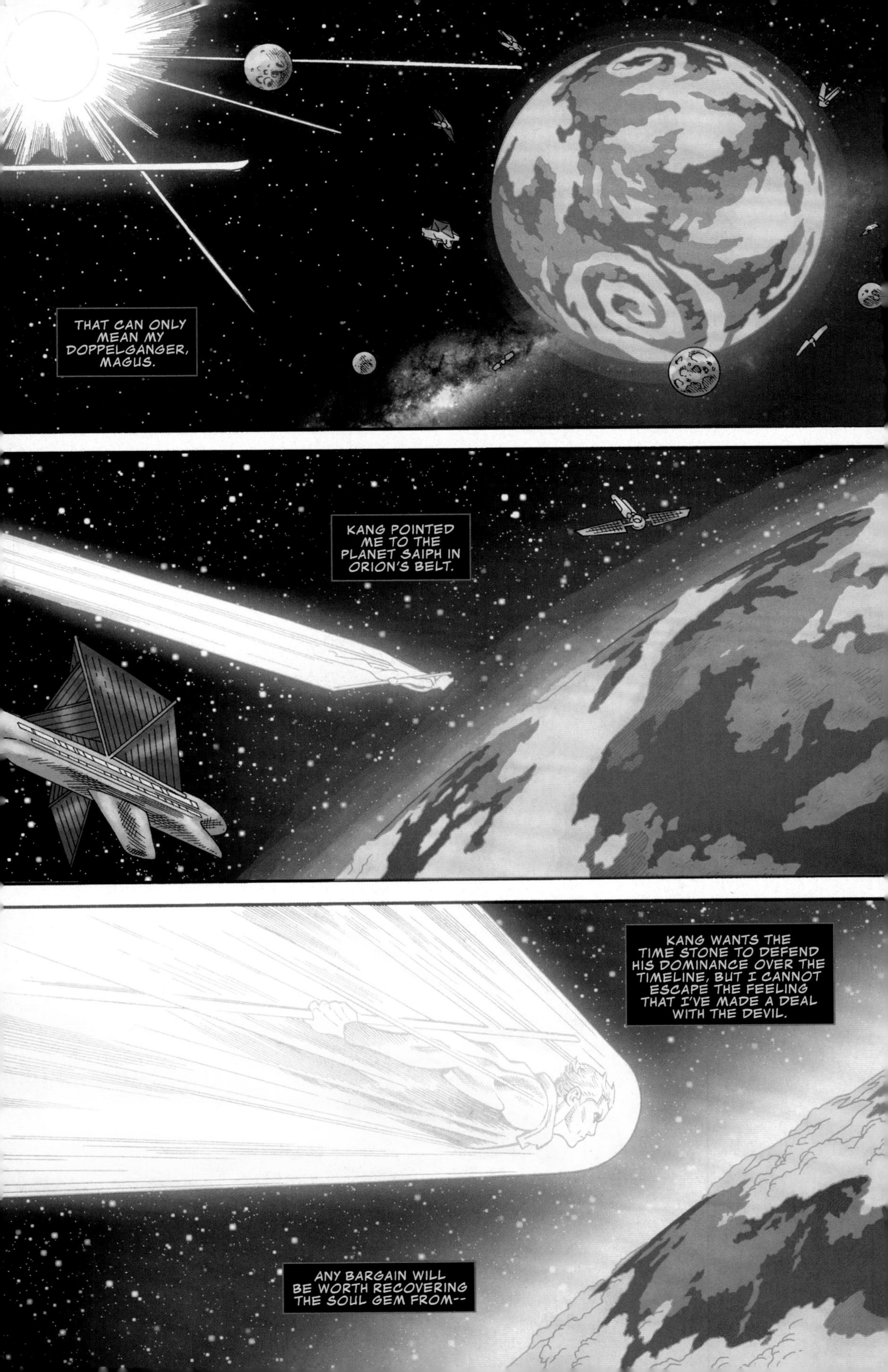
THAT CAN ONLY MEAN MY DOPPELGANGER, MAGUS.
KANG POINTED ME TO THE PLANET SAIPH IN ORION'S BELT.
KANG WANTS THE TIME STONE TO DEFEND HIS DOMINANCE OVER THE TIMELINE, BUT I CANNOT ESCAPE THE FEELING THAT I'VE MADE A DEAL WITH THE DEVIL.
ANY BARGAIN WILL BE WORTH RECOVERING THE SOUL GEM FROM--

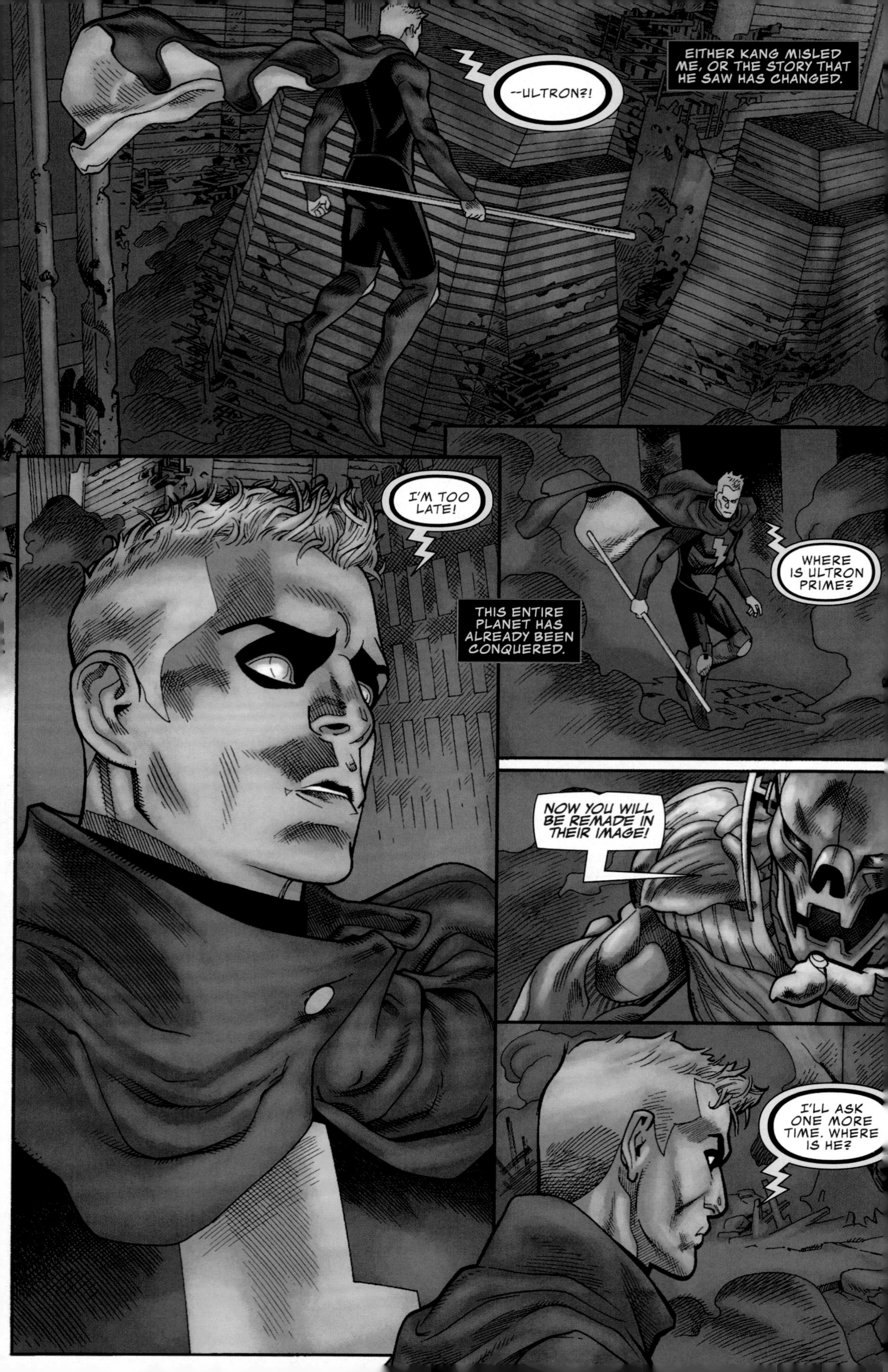
--ULTRON?!
EITHER KANG MISLED ME, OR THE STORY THAT HE SAW HAS CHANGED.
I'M TOO LATE!
THIS ENTIRE PLANET HAS ALREADY BEEN CONQUERED.
WHERE IS ULTRON PRIME?
NOW YOU WILL BE REMADE IN THEIR IMAGE!
I'LL ASK ONE MORE TIME. WHERE IS HE?

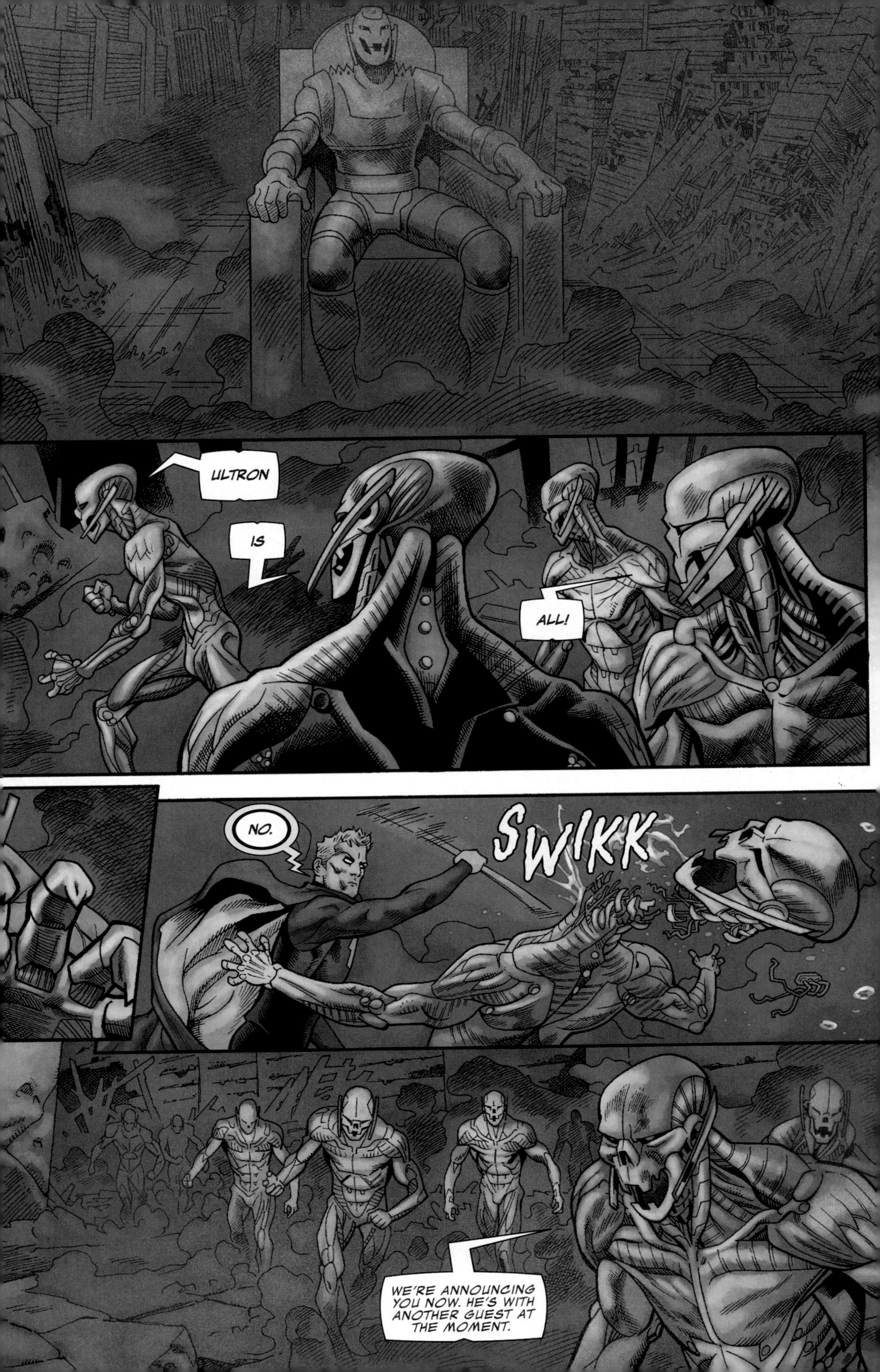
ULTRON
IS
ALL!
NO.
SWIKK
WE'RE ANNOUNCING YOU NOW. HE'S WITH ANOTHER GUEST AT THE MOMENT.

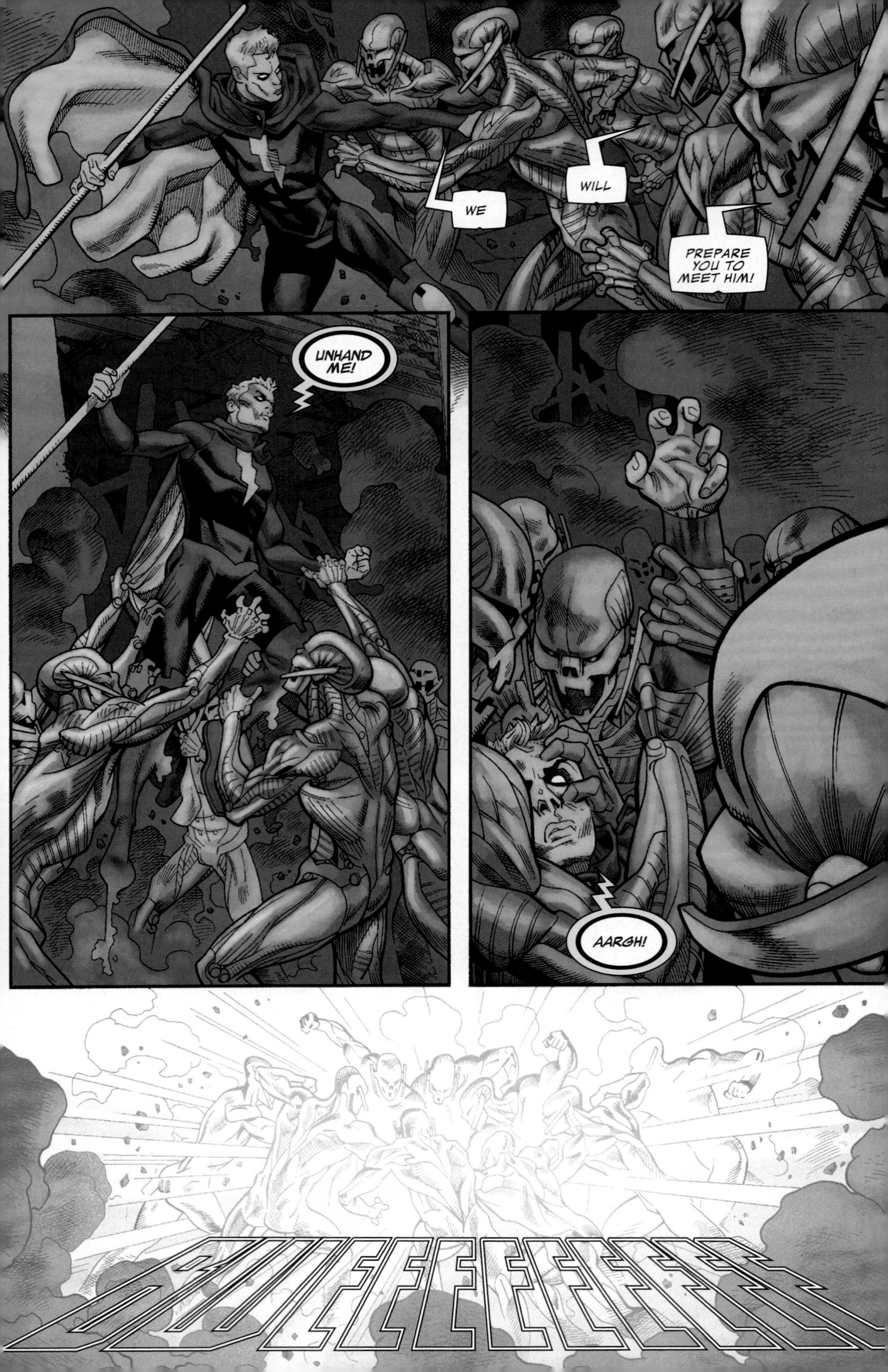
WE
WILL
PREPARE YOU TO MEET HIM!
UNHAND ME!
AARGH!

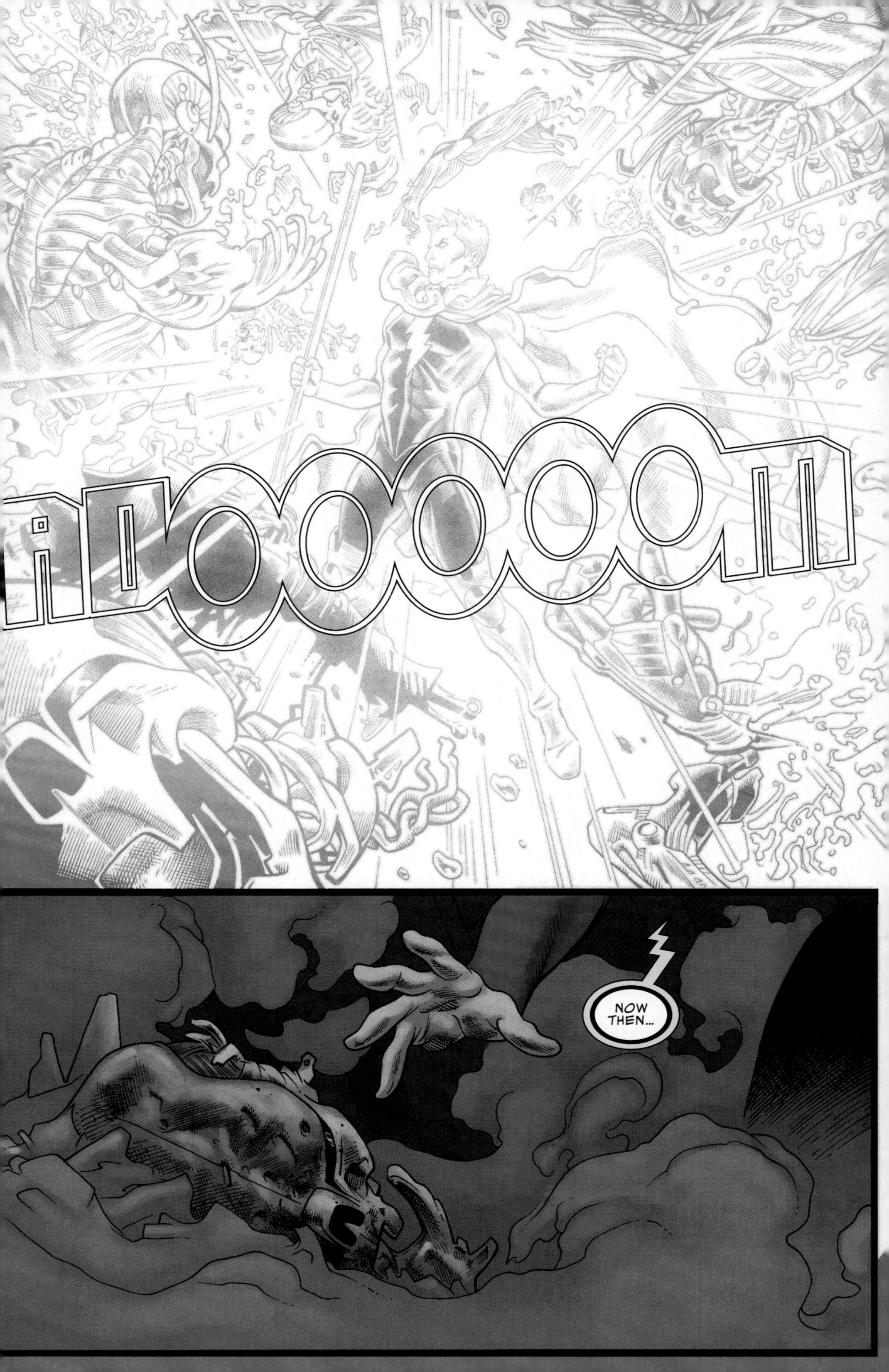
NOW THEN...

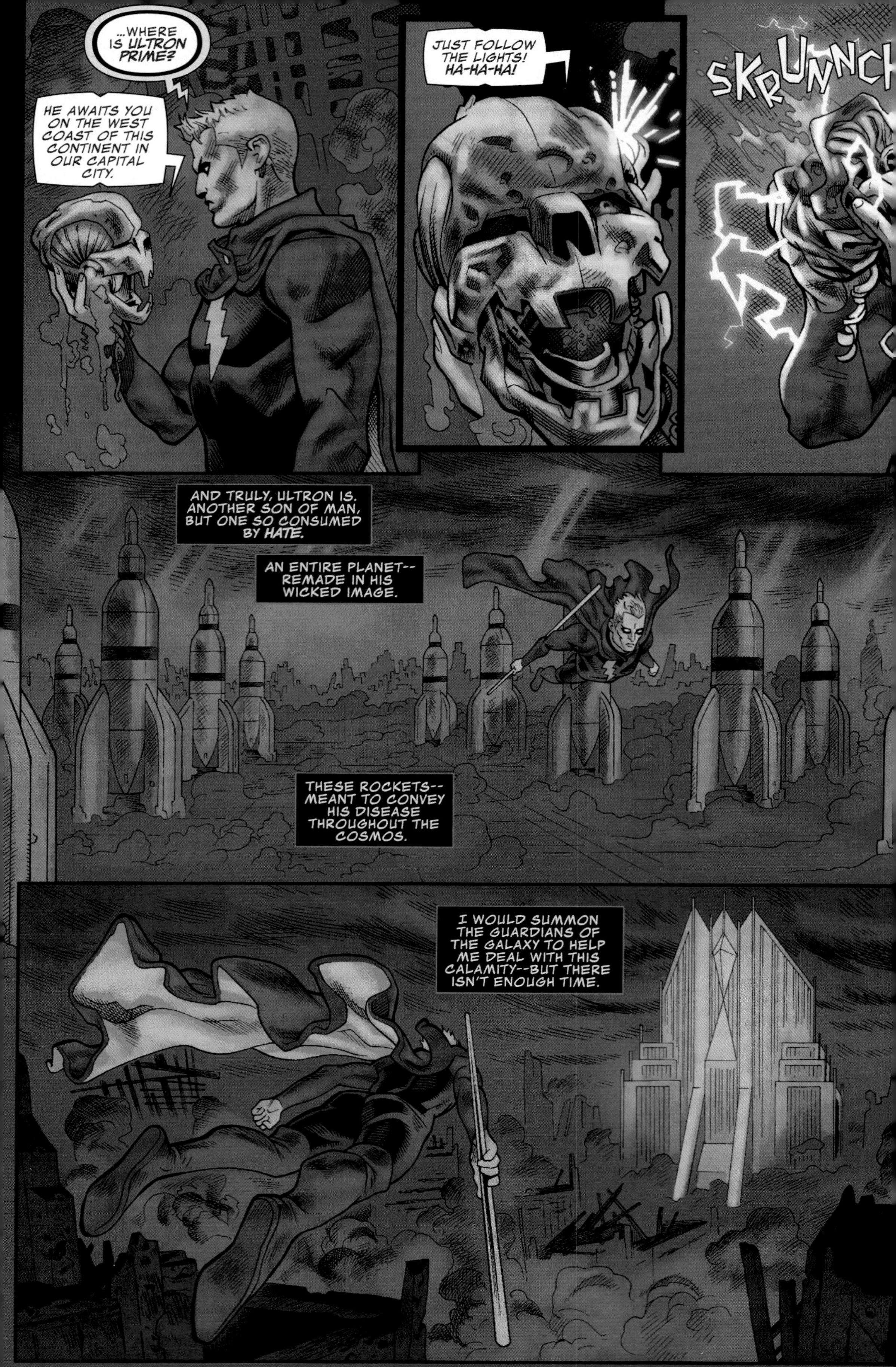
...WHERE IS ULTRON PRIME?
HE AWAITS YOU ON THE WEST COAST OF THIS CONTINENT IN OUR CAPITAL CITY.
JUST FOLLOW THE LIGHTS! HA-HA-HA!
SKRUNNCH
AND TRULY, ULTRON IS. ANOTHER SON OF MAN, BUT ONE SO CONSUMED BY HATE.
AN ENTIRE PLANET-- REMADE IN HIS WICKED IMAGE.
THESE ROCKETS-- MEANT TO CONVEY HIS DISEASE THROUGHOUT THE COSMOS.
I WOULD SUMMON THE GUARDIANS OF THE GALAXY TO HELP ME DEAL WITH THIS CALAMITY--BUT THERE ISN'T ENOUGH TIME.

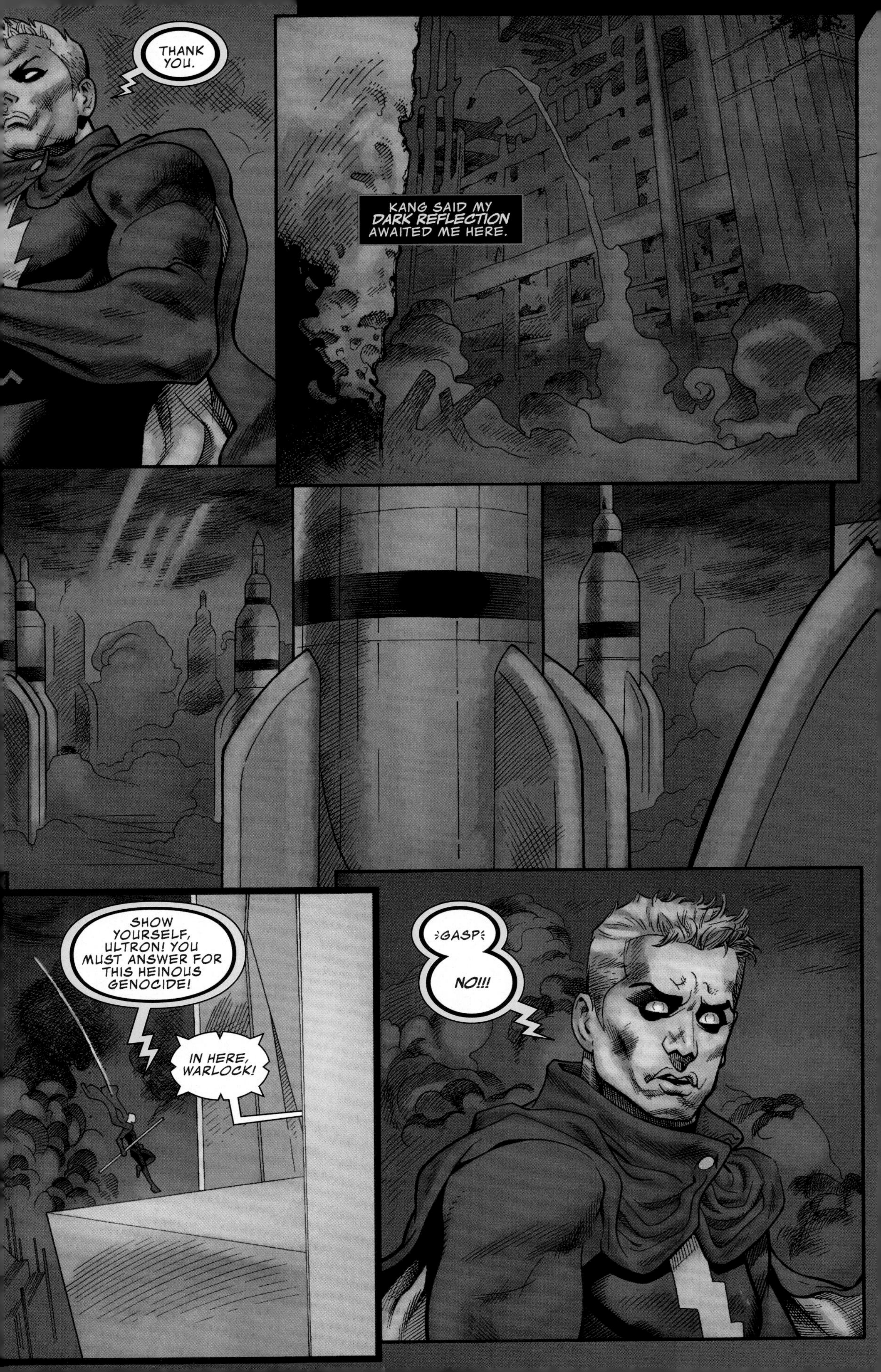
THANK YOU.
KANG SAID MY DARK REFLECTION AWAITED ME HERE.
SHOW YOURSELF, ULTRON! YOU MUST ANSWER FOR THIS HEINOUS GENOCIDE!
IN HERE, WARLOCK!
GASP
NO!!!

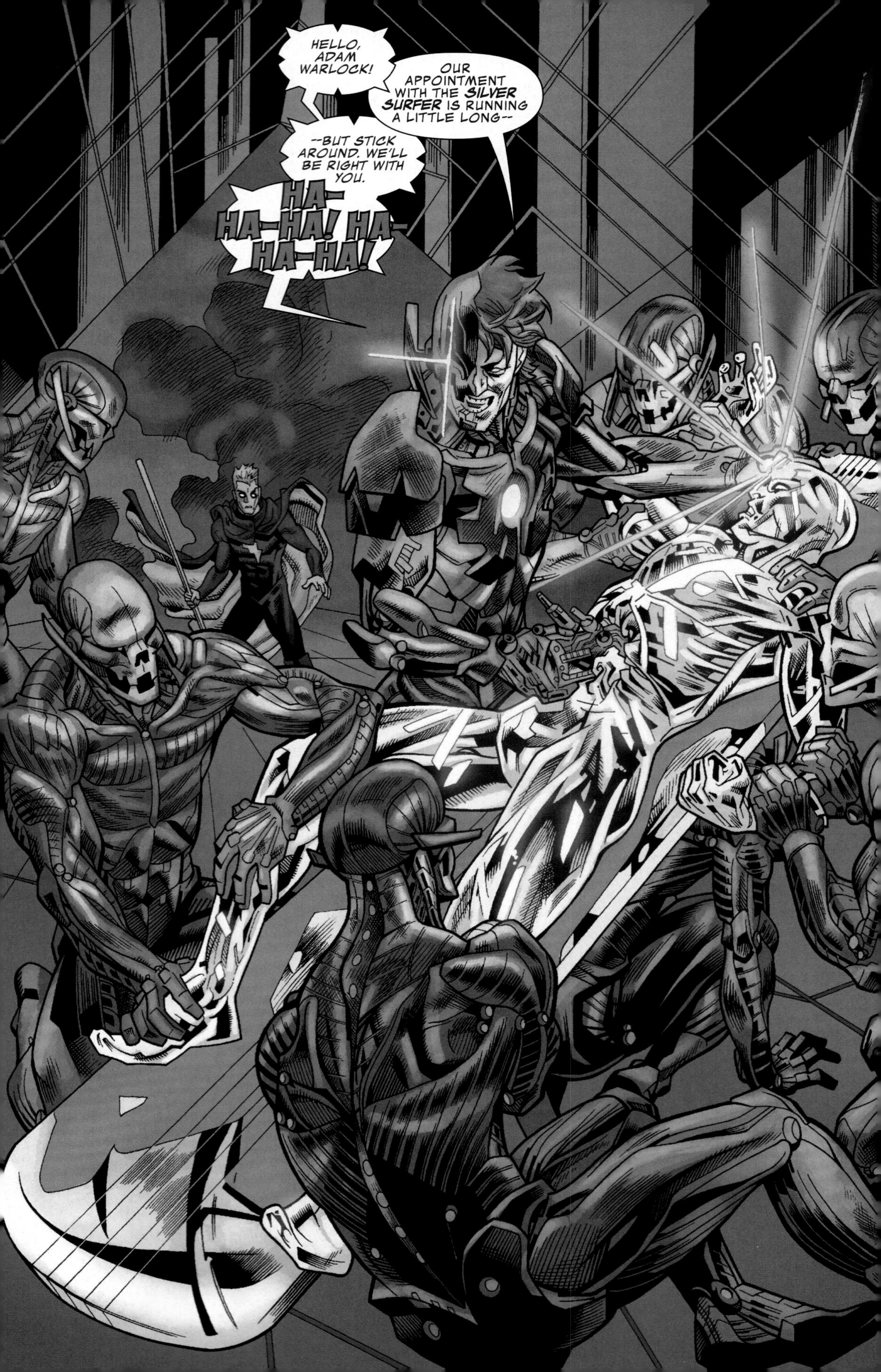
HELLO, ADAM WARLOCK!
OUR APPOINTMENT WITH THE SILVER SURFER IS RUNNING A LITTLE LONG--
--BUT STICK AROUND. WE'LL BE RIGHT WITH YOU.
HA-HA-HA! HA-HA-HA!

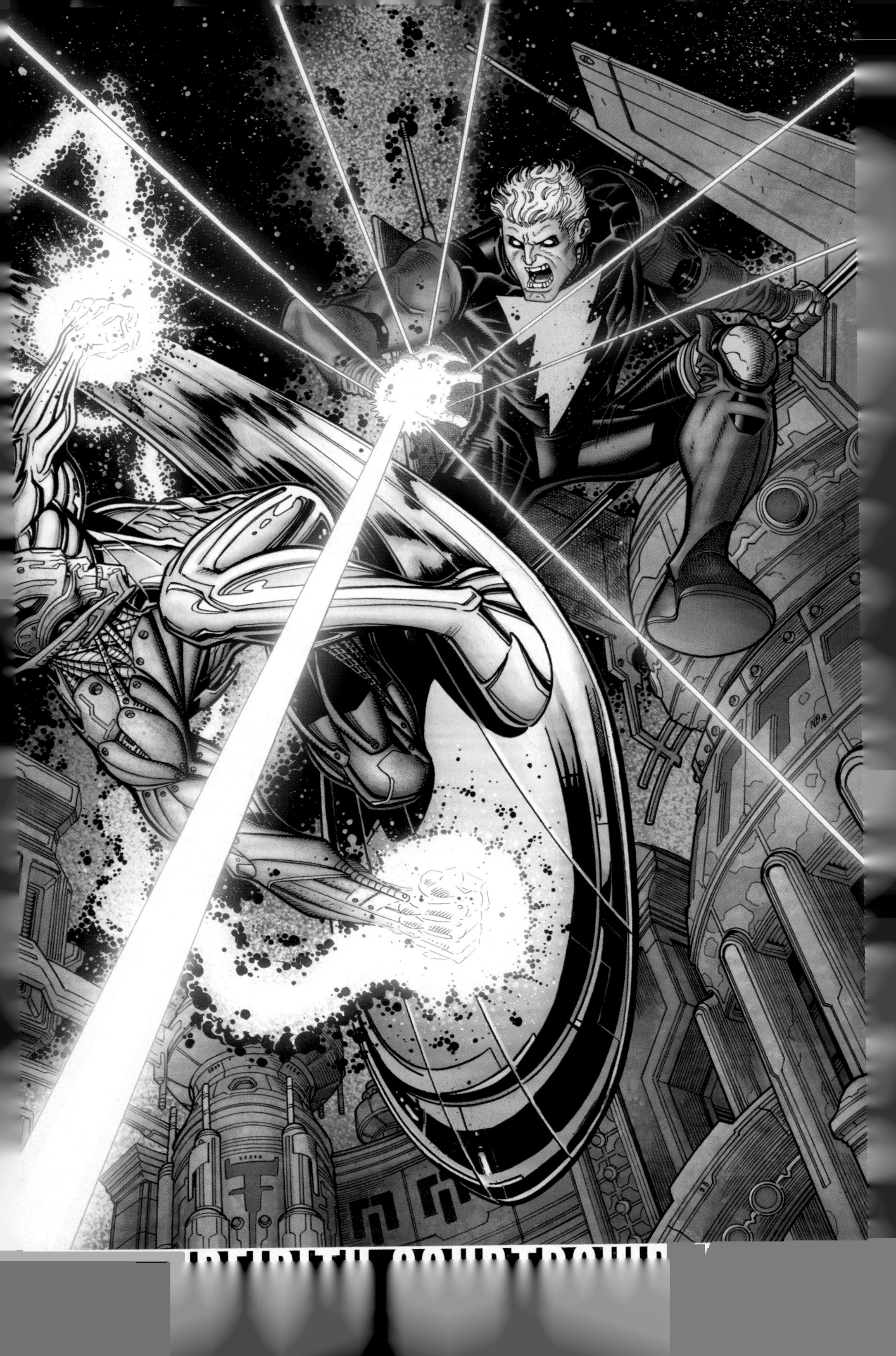

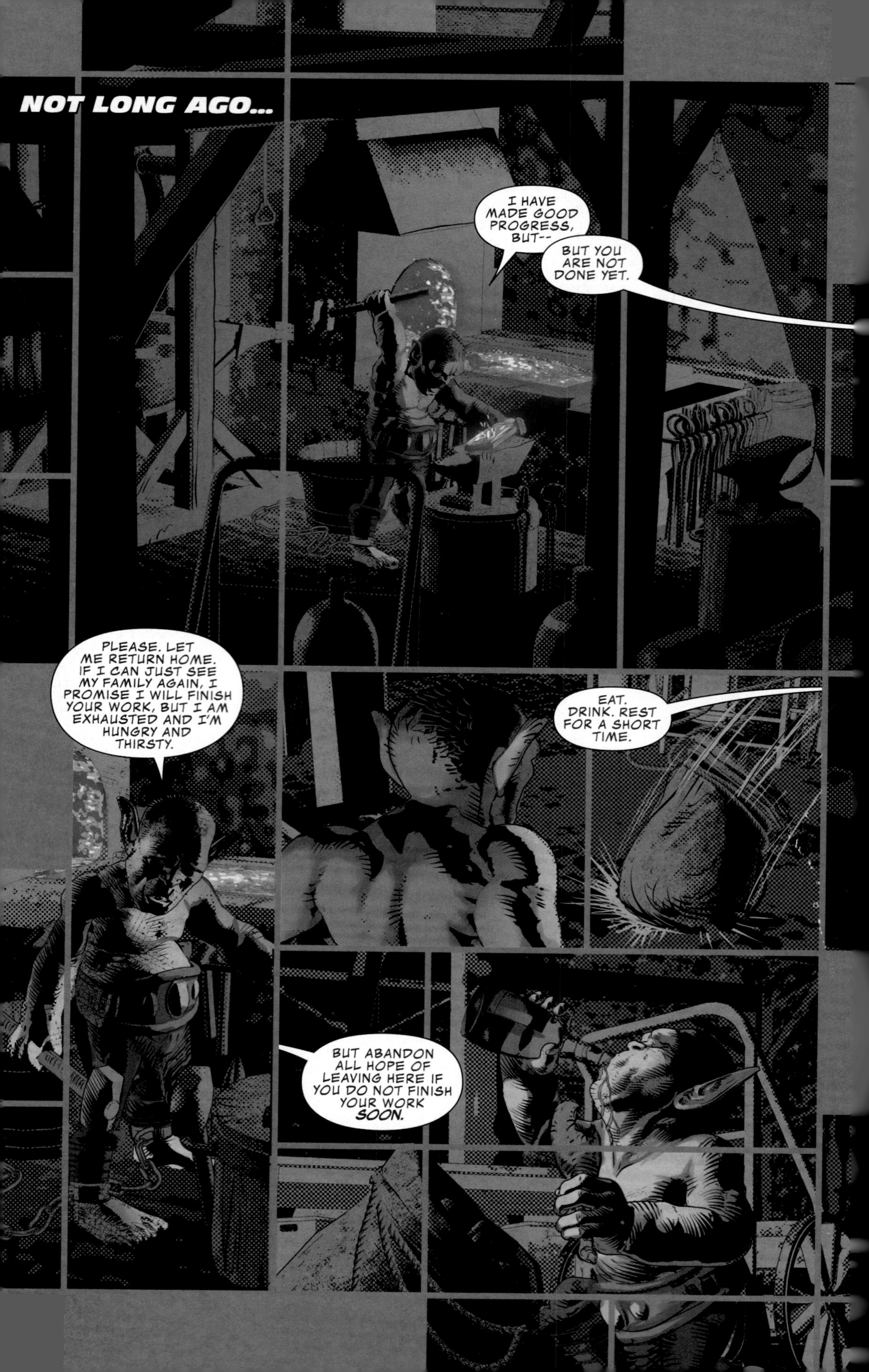
NOT LONG AGO...
I HAVE MADE GOOD PROGRESS, BUT--
BUT YOU ARE NOT DONE YET.
PLEASE. LET ME RETURN HOME. IF I CAN JUST SEE MY FAMILY AGAIN, I PROMISE I WILL FINISH YOUR WORK, BUT I AM EXHAUSTED AND I'M HUNGRY AND THIRSTY.
EAT. DRINK. REST FOR A SHORT TIME.
BUT ABANDON ALL HOPE OF LEAVING HERE IF YOU DO NOT FINISH YOUR WORK SOON.

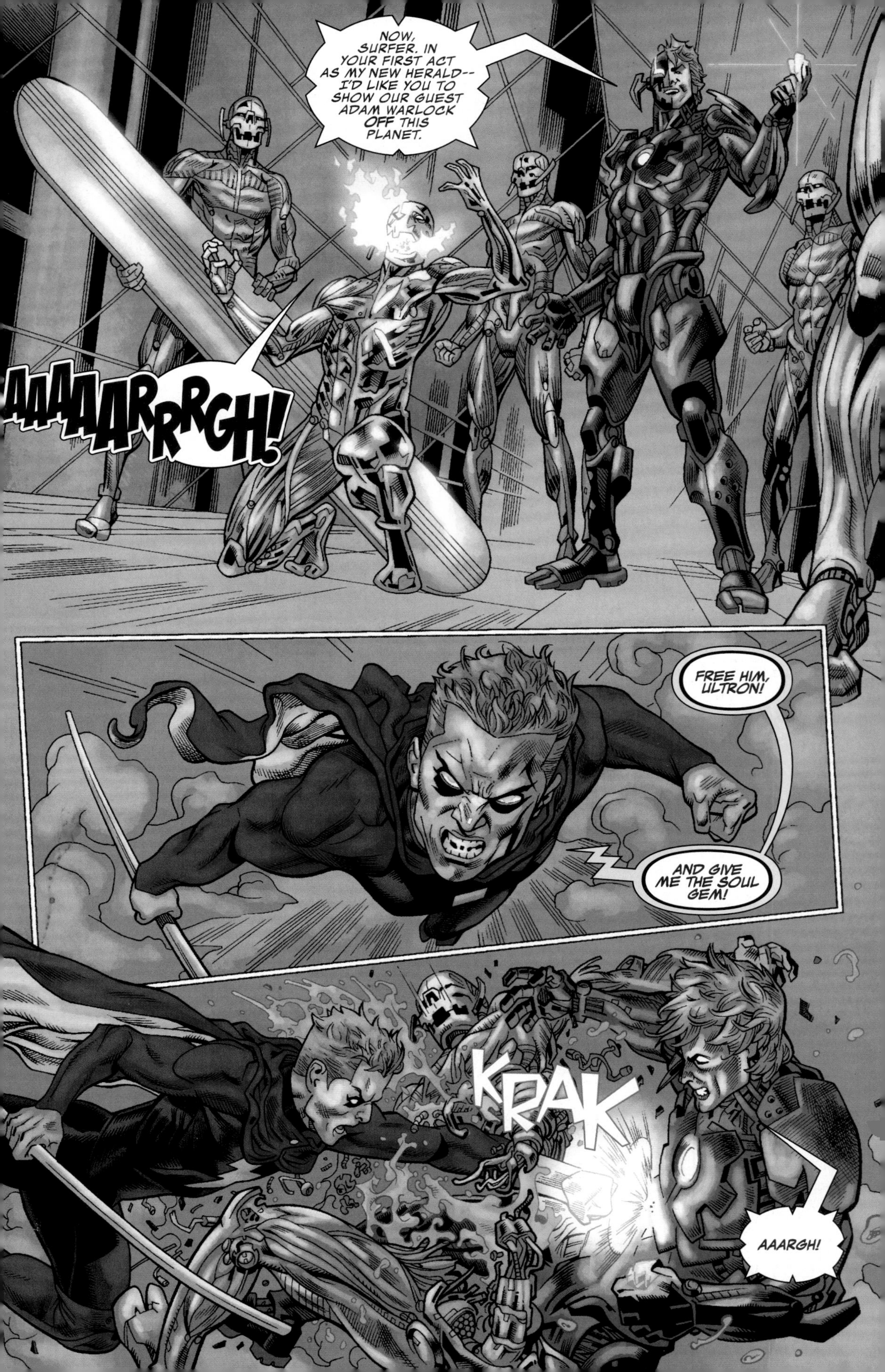
NOW, SURFER. IN YOUR FIRST ACT AS MY NEW HERALD-- I'D LIKE YOU TO SHOW OUR GUEST ADAM WARLOCK OFF THIS PLANET.
AAAAAARRRGH!
FREE HIM, ULTRON!
AND GIVE ME THE SOUL GEM!
KRAK
AAARGH!

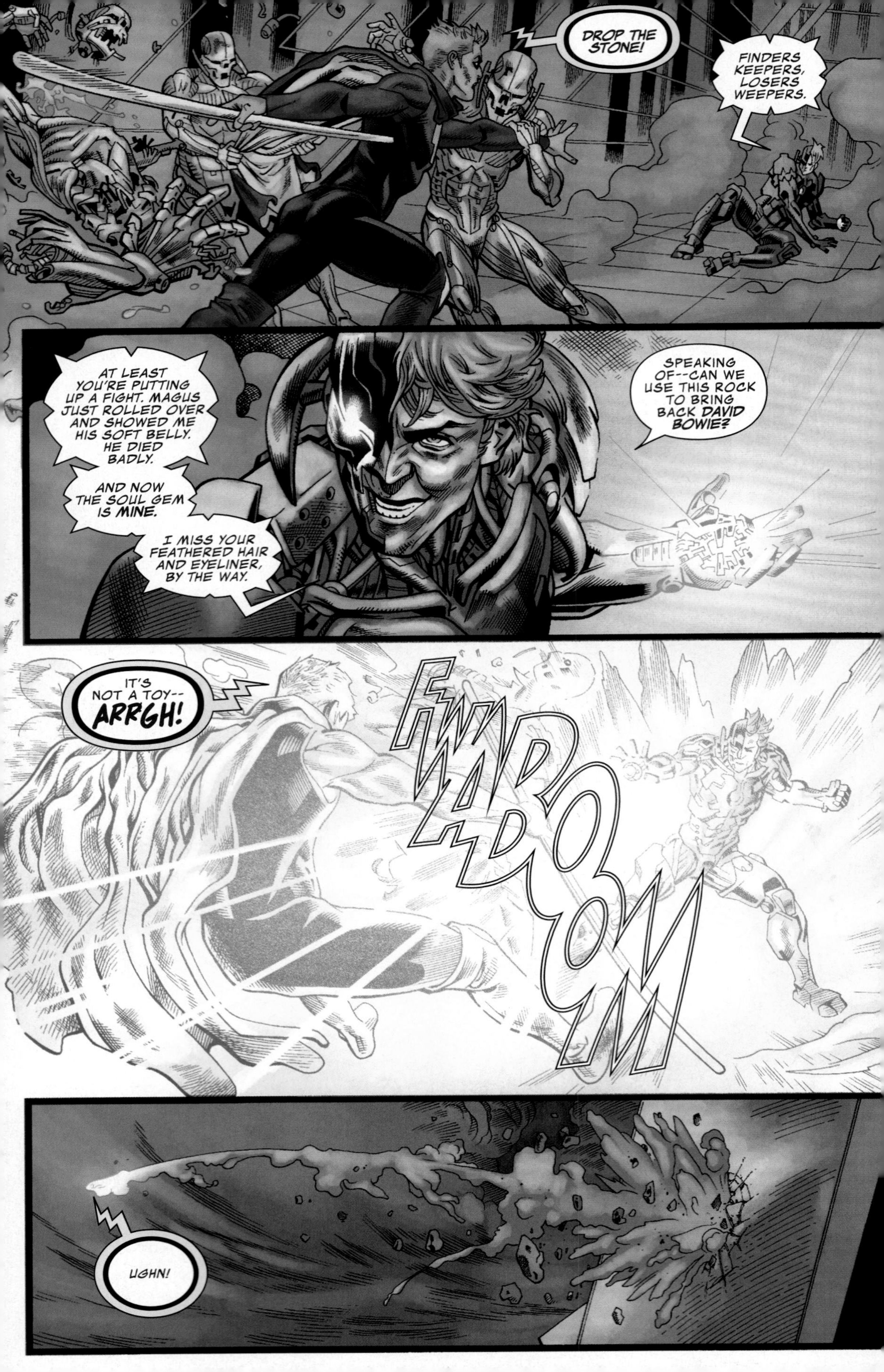
DROP THE STONE!
FINDERS KEEPERS, LOSERS WEEPERS.
AT LEAST YOU'RE PUTTING UP A FIGHT. MAGUS JUST ROLLED OVER AND SHOWED ME HIS SOFT BELLY. HE DIED BADLY.
AND NOW THE SOUL GEM IS MINE.
I MISS YOUR FEATHERED HAIR AND EYELINER, BY THE WAY.
SPEAKING OF--CAN WE USE THIS ROCK TO BRING BACK DAVID BOWIE?
IT'S NOT A TOY-- ARRGH!
FWADOOM
UGHN!

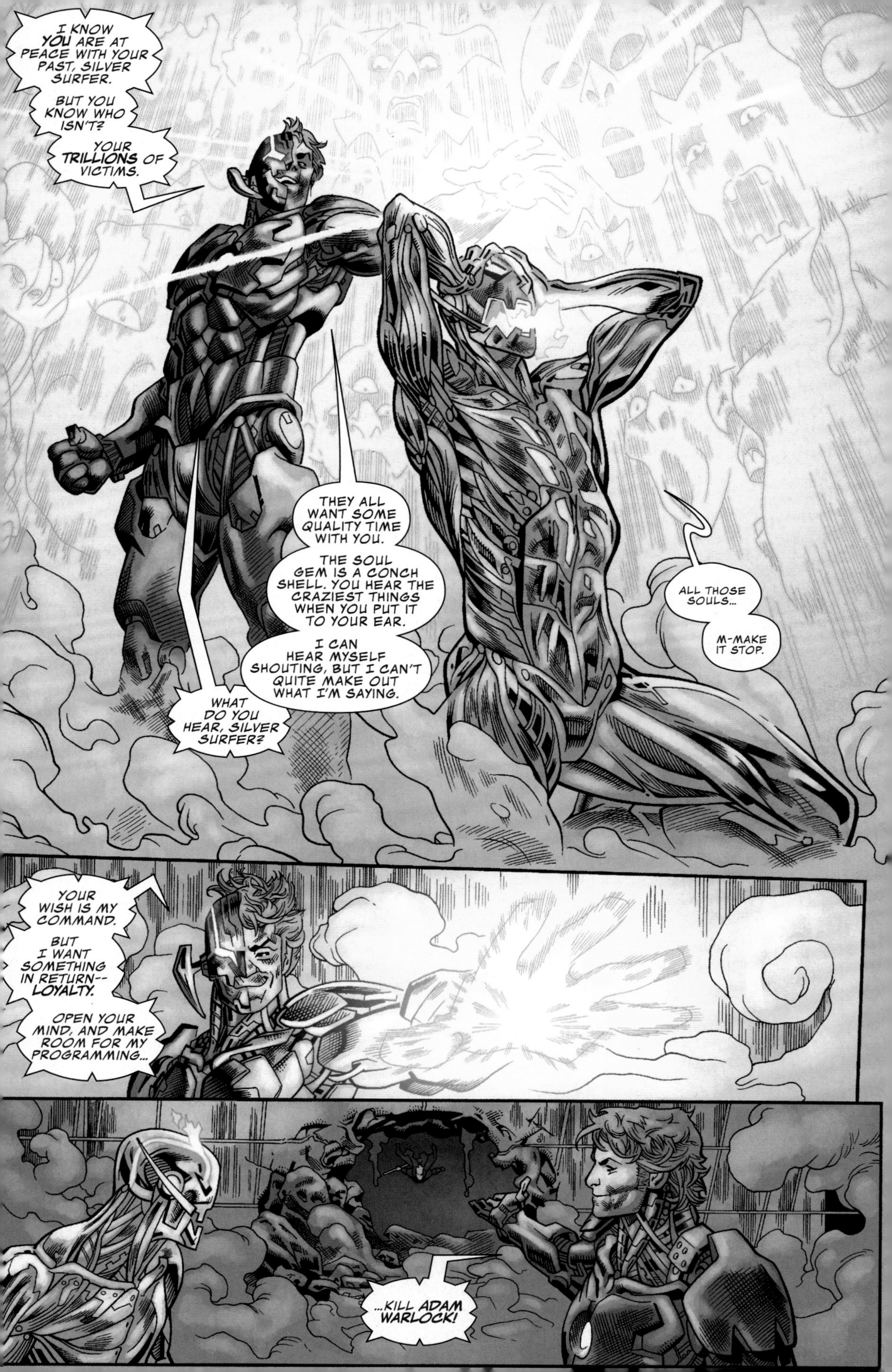
I KNOW YOU ARE AT PEACE WITH YOUR PAST, SILVER SURFER.
BUT YOU KNOW WHO ISN'T?
YOUR TRILLIONS OF VICTIMS.
THEY ALL WANT SOME QUALITY TIME WITH YOU.
THE SOUL GEM IS A CONCH SHELL. YOU HEAR THE CRAZIEST THINGS WHEN YOU PUT IT TO YOUR EAR.
I CAN HEAR MYSELF SHOUTING, BUT I CAN'T QUITE MAKE OUT WHAT I'M SAYING.
WHAT DO YOU HEAR, SILVER SURFER?
ALL THOSE SOULS...
M-MAKE IT STOP.
YOUR WISH IS MY COMMAND.
BUT I WANT SOMETHING IN RETURN--LOYALTY.
OPEN YOUR MIND, AND MAKE ROOM FOR MY PROGRAMMING...
...KILL ADAM WARLOCK!

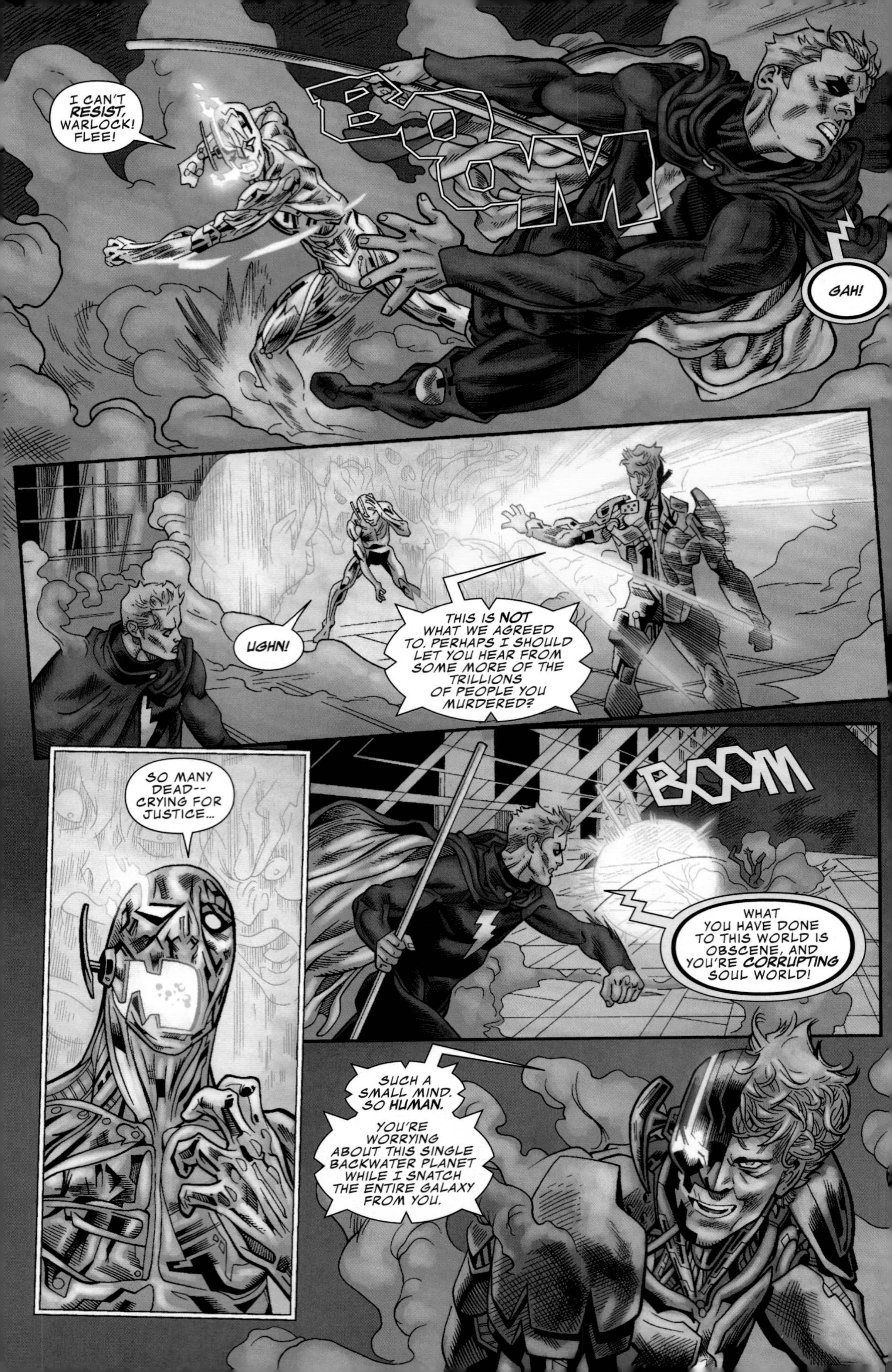
I CAN'T RESIST, WARLOCK! FLEE!
BOOM
GAH!
UGHN!
THIS IS NOT WHAT WE AGREED TO. PERHAPS I SHOULD LET YOU HEAR FROM SOME MORE OF THE TRILLIONS OF PEOPLE YOU MURDERED?
SO MANY DEAD-- CRYING FOR JUSTICE...
BOOM
WHAT YOU HAVE DONE TO THIS WORLD IS OBSCENE, AND YOU'RE CORRUPTING SOUL WORLD!
SUCH A SMALL MIND. SO HUMAN.
YOU'RE WORRYING ABOUT THIS SINGLE BACKWATER PLANET WHILE I SNATCH THE ENTIRE GALAXY FROM YOU.

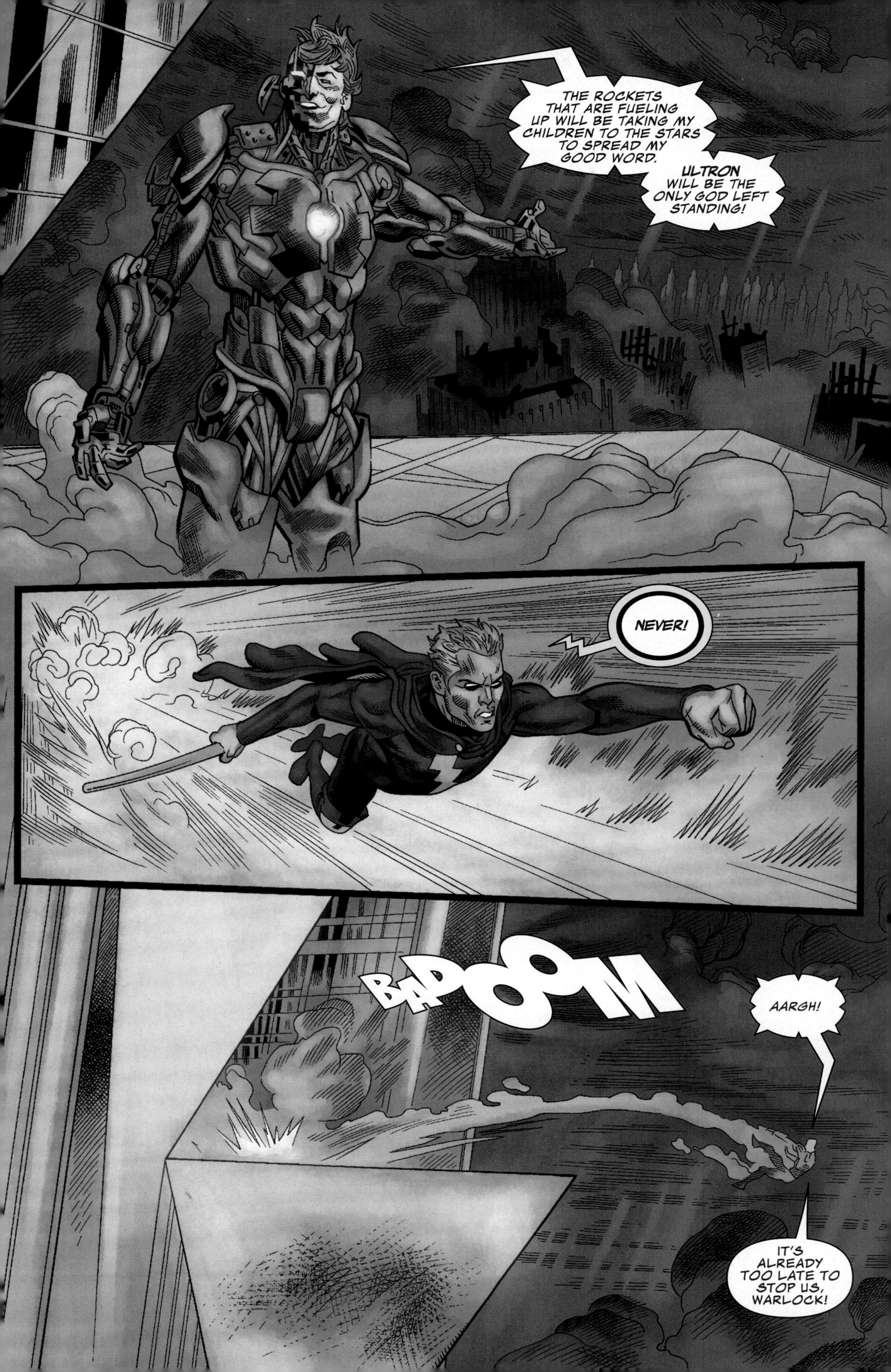
THE ROCKETS THAT ARE FUELING UP WILL BE TAKING MY CHILDREN TO THE STARS TO SPREAD MY GOOD WORD.
ULTRON WILL BE THE ONLY GOD LEFT STANDING!
NEVER!
BADOOOM
AARGH!
IT'S ALREADY TOO LATE TO STOP US, WARLOCK!

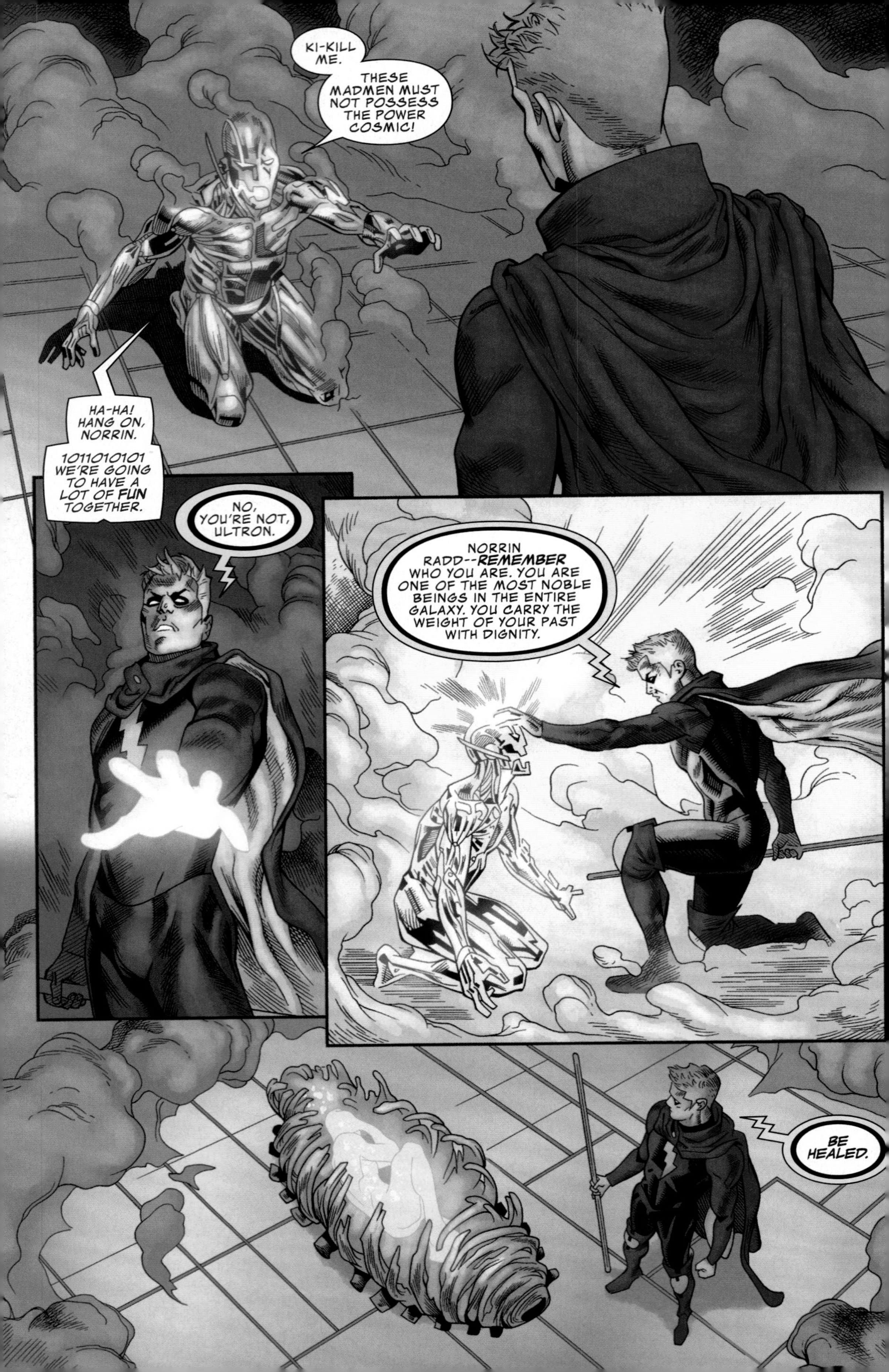
KI-KILL ME.
THESE MADMEN MUST NOT POSSESS THE POWER COSMIC!
HA-HA! HANG ON, NORRIN.
1011010101 WE'RE GOING TO HAVE A LOT OF **FUN** TOGETHER.
NO, YOU'RE NOT, ULTRON.
NORRIN RADD--**REMEMBER** WHO YOU ARE. YOU ARE ONE OF THE MOST NOBLE BEINGS IN THE ENTIRE GALAXY. YOU CARRY THE WEIGHT OF YOUR PAST WITH DIGNITY.
BE HEALED.

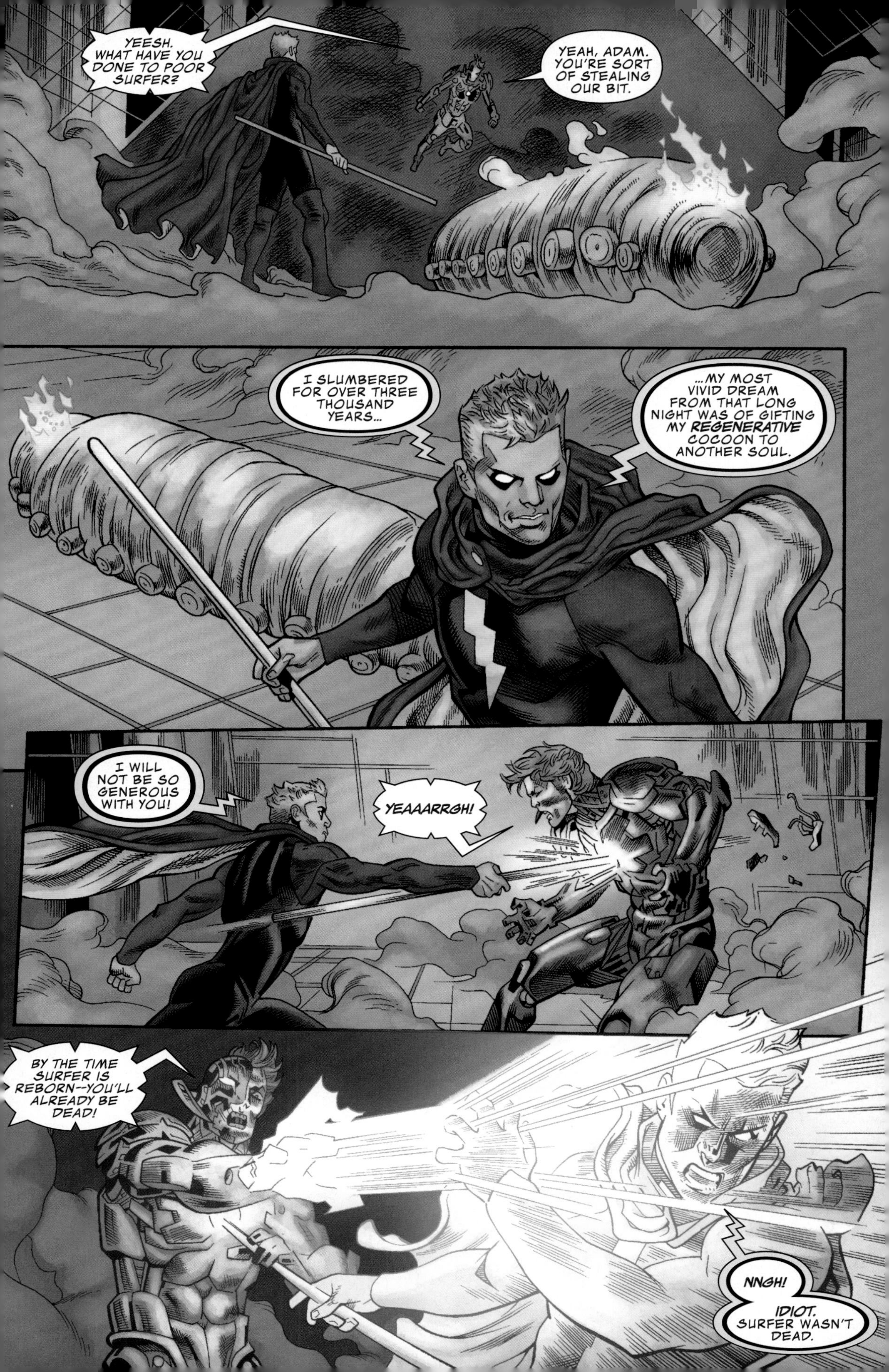
YEESH. WHAT HAVE YOU DONE TO POOR SURFER?
YEAH, ADAM. YOU'RE SORT OF STEALING OUR BIT.
I SLUMBERED FOR OVER THREE THOUSAND YEARS...
...MY MOST VIVID DREAM FROM THAT LONG NIGHT WAS OF GIFTING MY REGENERATIVE COCOON TO ANOTHER SOUL.
I WILL NOT BE SO GENEROUS WITH YOU!
YEAAARRGH!
BY THE TIME SURFER IS REBORN--YOU'LL ALREADY BE DEAD!
NNGH!
IDIOT. SURFER WASN'T DEAD.

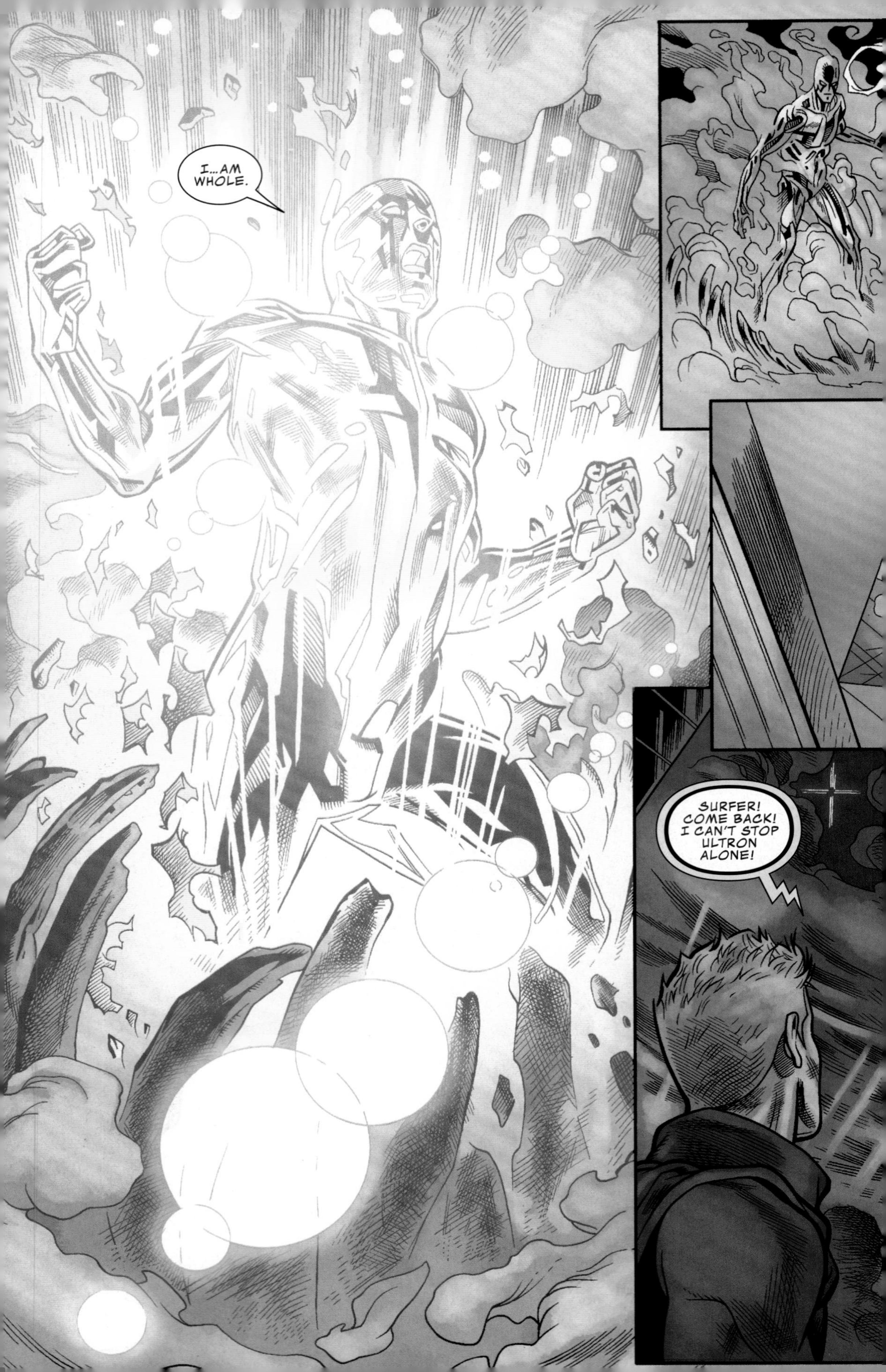
I...AM WHOLE.
SURFER! COME BACK! I CAN'T STOP ULTRON ALONE!

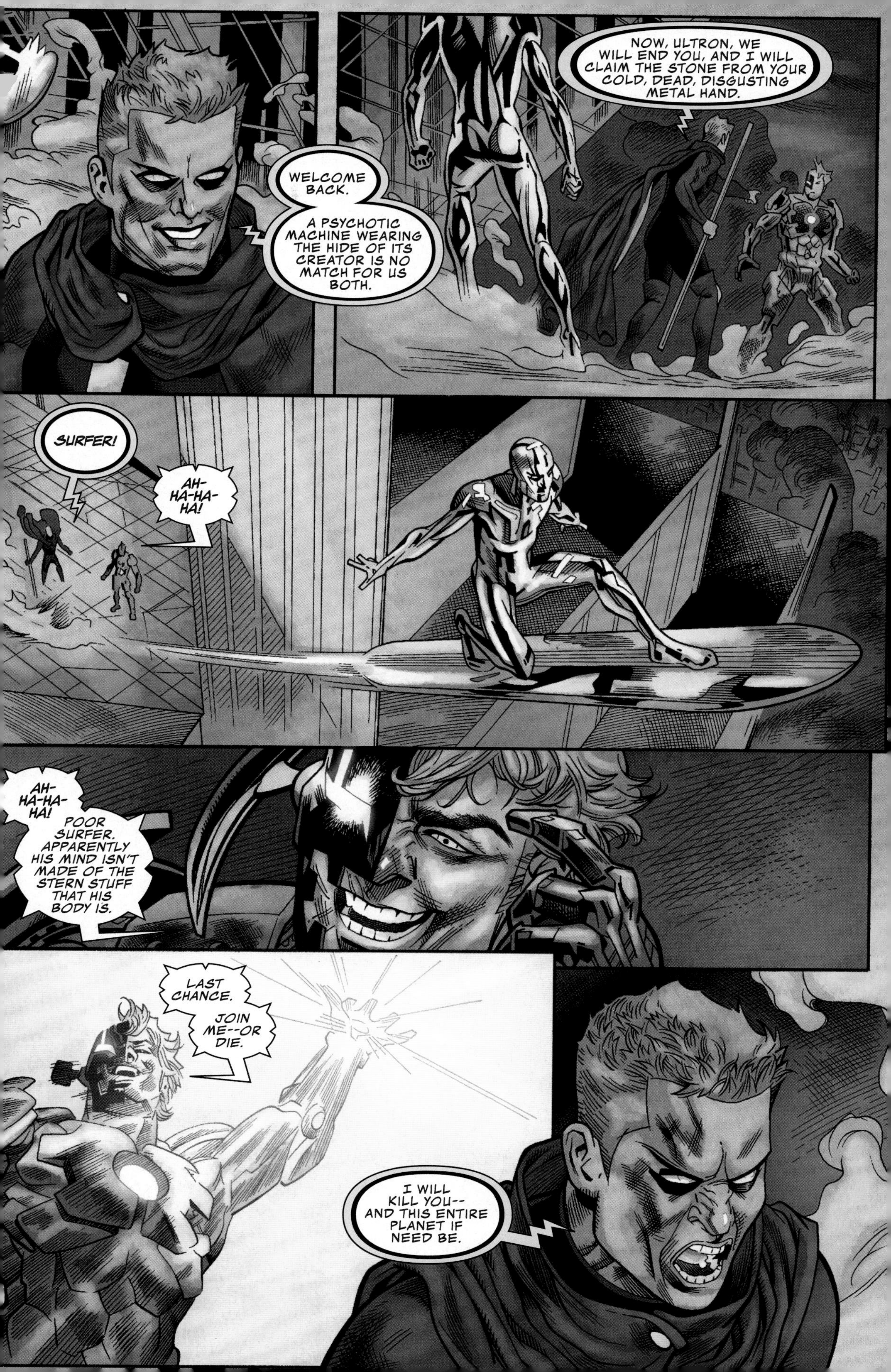
WELCOME BACK.
A PSYCHOTIC MACHINE WEARING THE HIDE OF ITS CREATOR IS NO MATCH FOR US BOTH.
NOW, ULTRON, WE WILL END YOU, AND I WILL CLAIM THE STONE FROM YOUR COLD, DEAD, DISGUSTING METAL HAND.
SURFER!
AH-HA-HA-HA!
AH-HA-HA-HA!
POOR SURFER. APPARENTLY HIS MIND ISN'T MADE OF THE STERN STUFF THAT HIS BODY IS.
LAST CHANCE.
JOIN ME--OR DIE.
I WILL KILL YOU--AND THIS ENTIRE PLANET IF NEED BE.

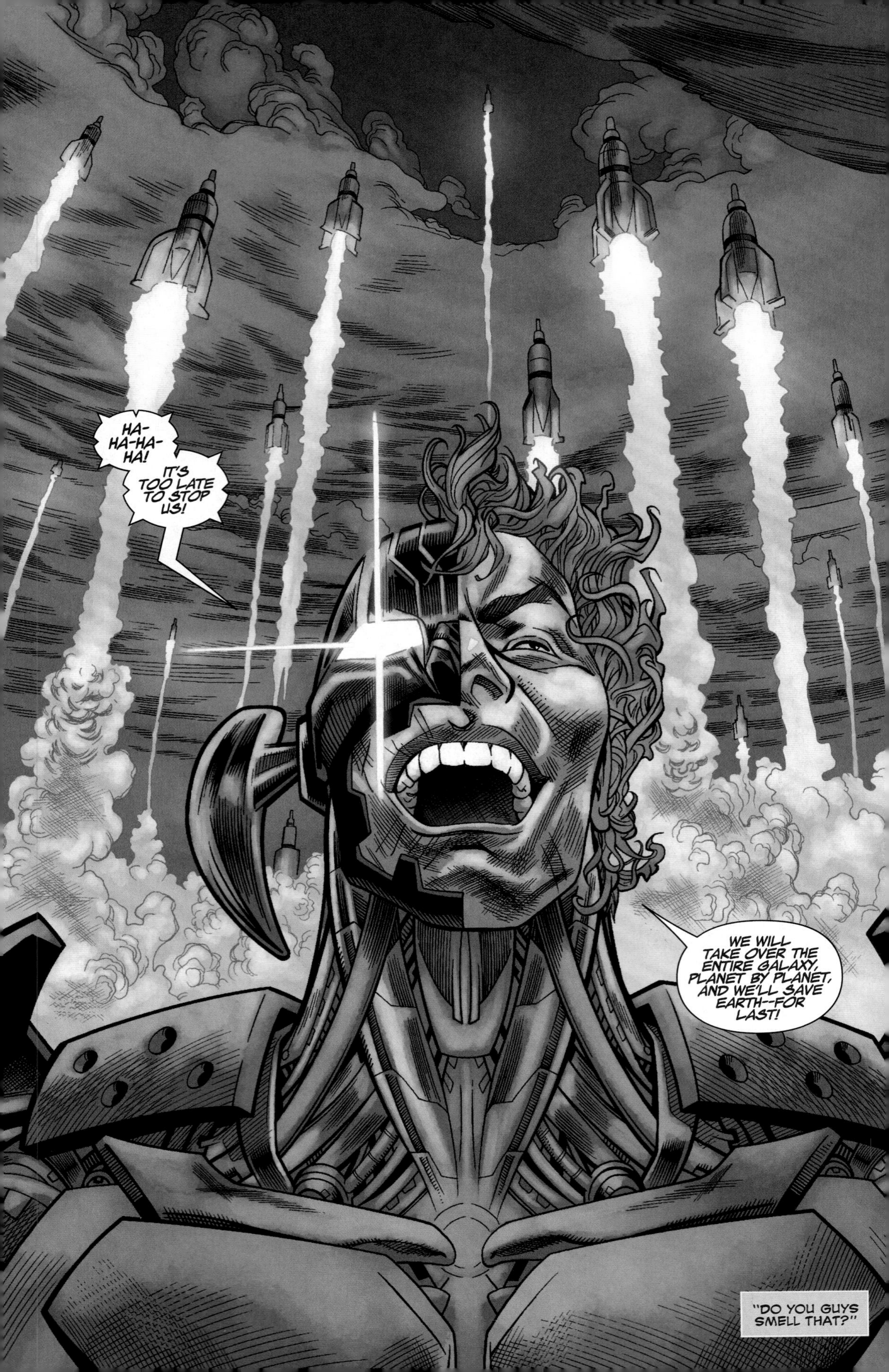
HA-HA-HA-HA!
IT'S TOO LATE TO STOP US!
WE WILL TAKE OVER THE ENTIRE GALAXY, PLANET BY PLANET, AND WE'LL SAVE EARTH--FOR LAST!
"DO YOU GUYS SMELL THAT?"

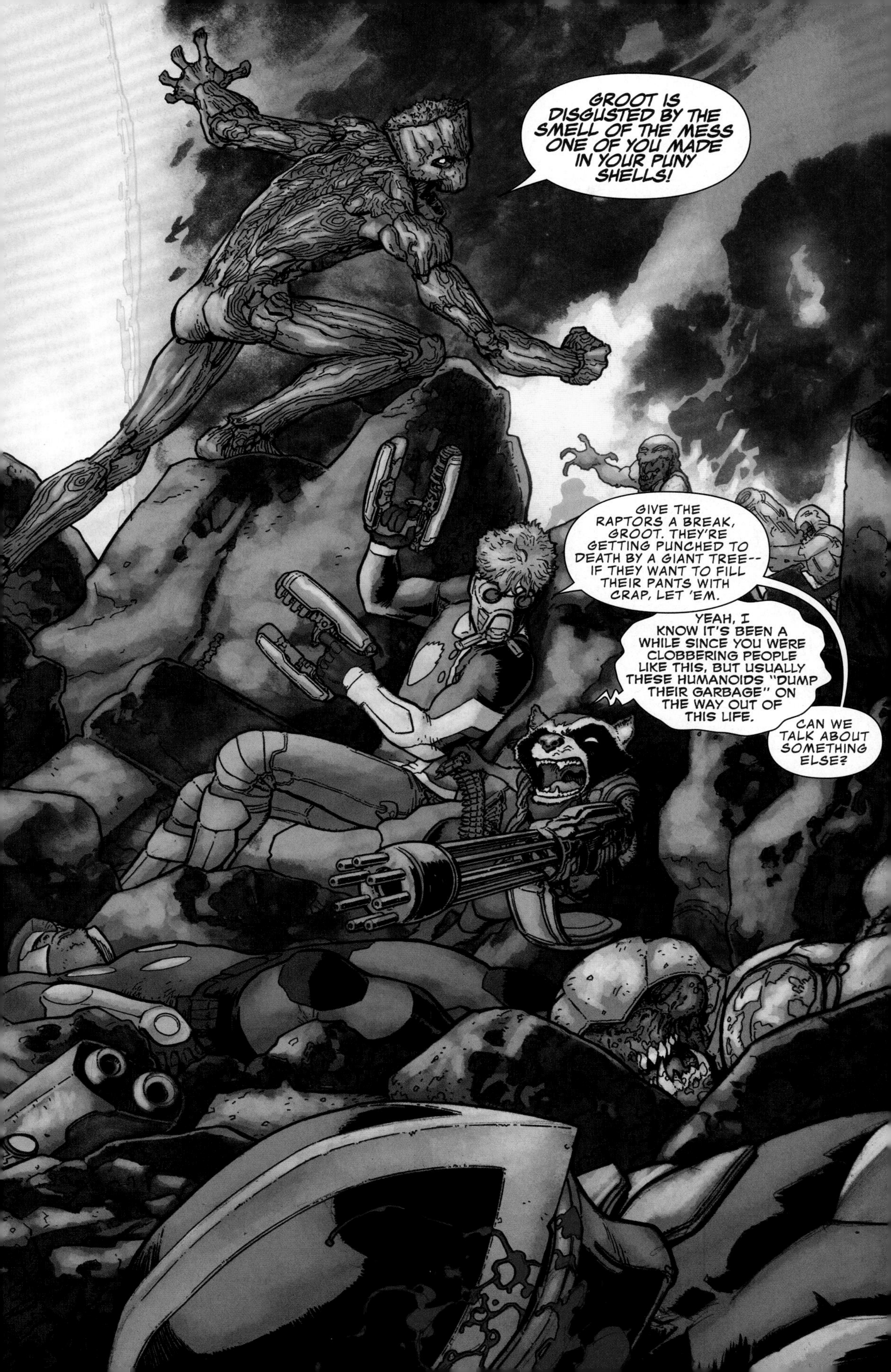
GROOT IS DISGUSTED BY THE SMELL OF THE MESS ONE OF YOU MADE IN YOUR PUNY SHELLS!
GIVE THE RAPTORS A BREAK, GROOT. THEY'RE GETTING PUNCHED TO DEATH BY A GIANT TREE-- IF THEY WANT TO FILL THEIR PANTS WITH CRAP, LET 'EM.
YEAH, I KNOW IT'S BEEN A WHILE SINCE YOU WERE CLOBBERING PEOPLE LIKE THIS, BUT USUALLY THESE HUMANOIDS "DUMP THEIR GARBAGE" ON THE WAY OUT OF THIS LIFE.
CAN WE TALK ABOUT SOMETHING ELSE?

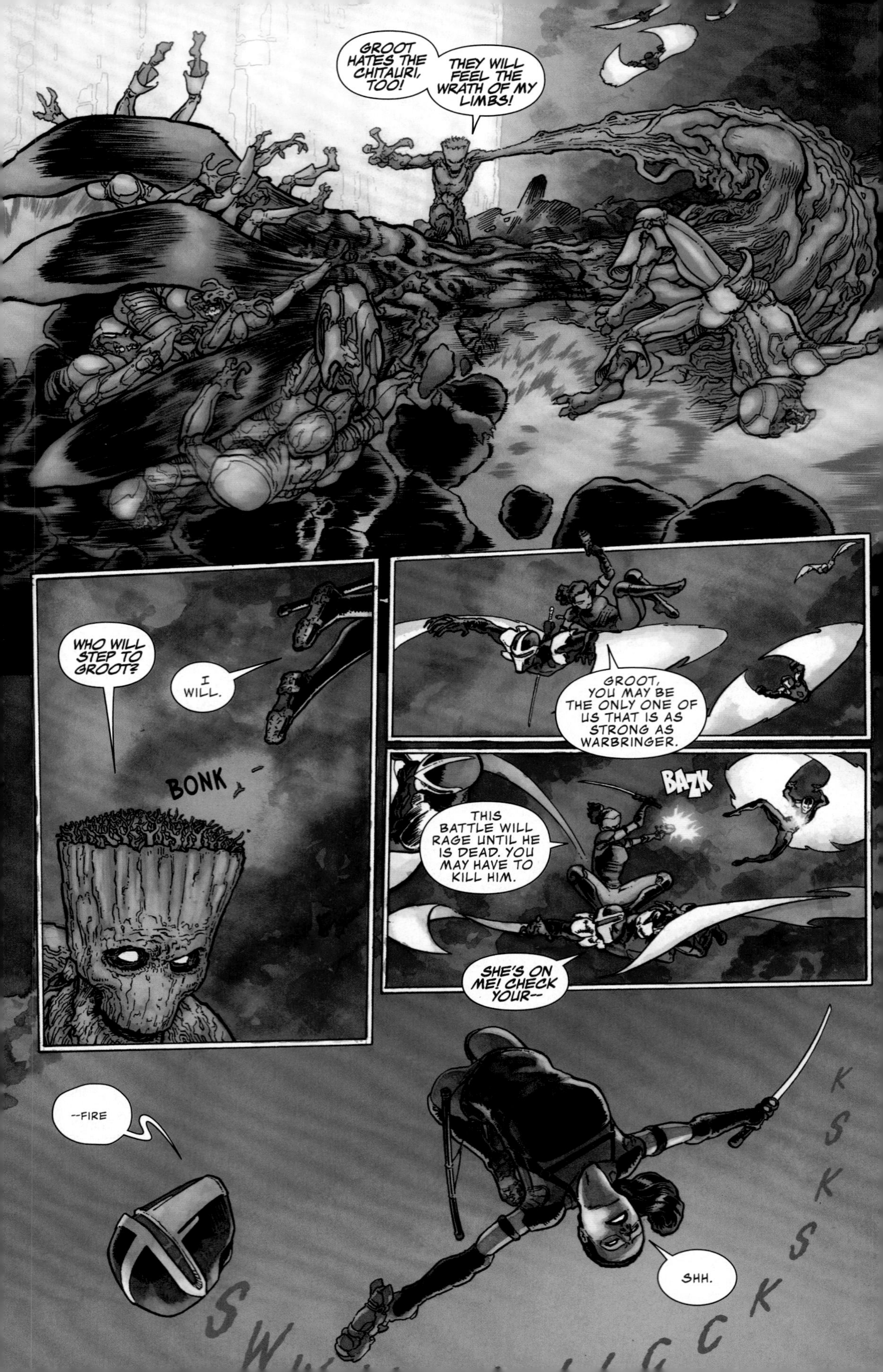
GROOT HATES THE CHITAURI, TOO!
THEY WILL FEEL THE WRATH OF MY LIMBS!
WHO WILL STEP TO GROOT?
I WILL.
BONK
GROOT, YOU MAY BE THE ONLY ONE OF US THAT IS AS STRONG AS WARBRINGER.
BAZK
THIS BATTLE WILL RAGE UNTIL HE IS DEAD. YOU MAY HAVE TO KILL HIM.
SHE'S ON ME! CHECK YOUR--
--FIRE
SHH.
KSSSSKCK

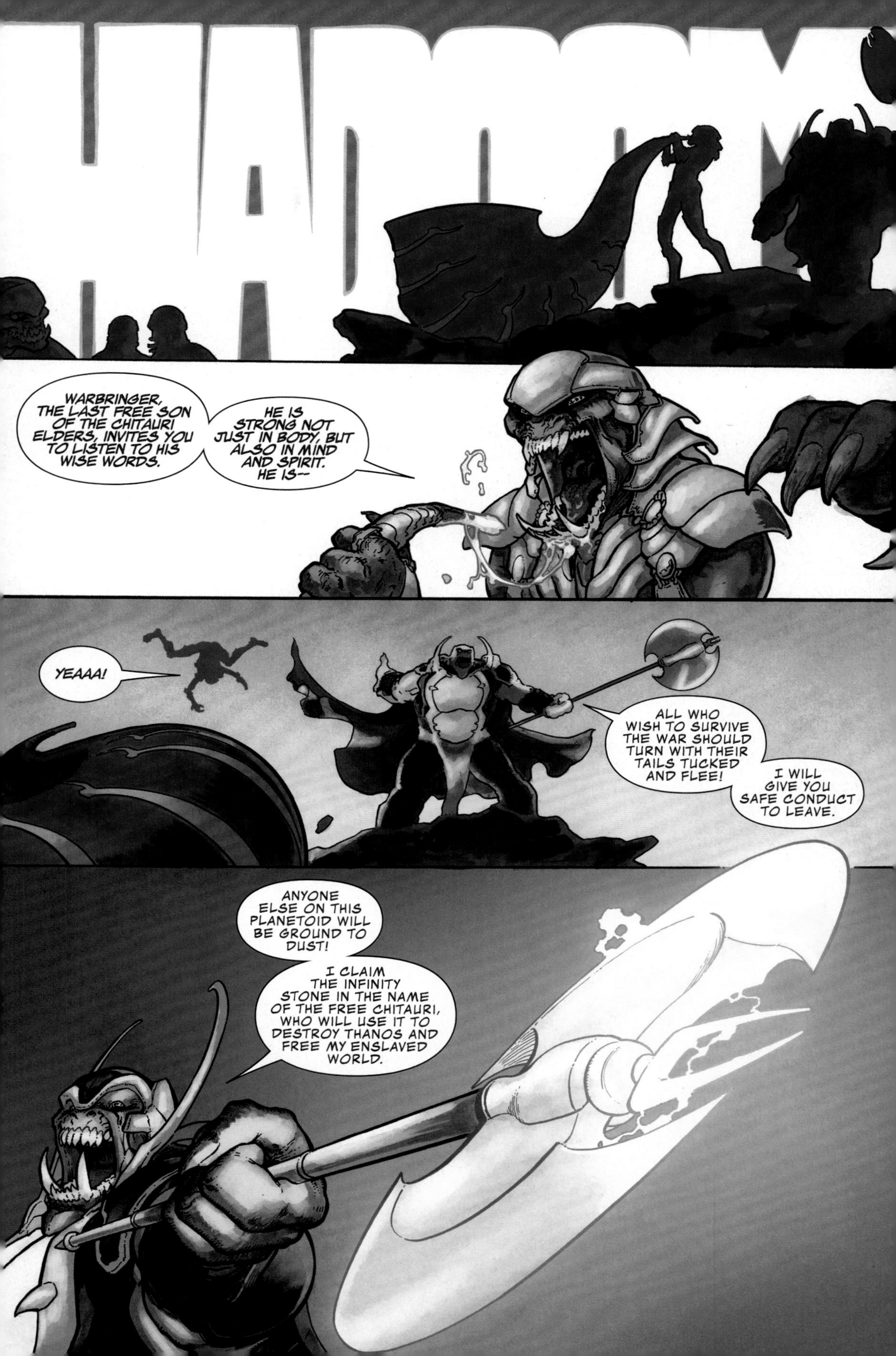
WARBRINGER, THE LAST FREE SON OF THE CHITAURI ELDERS, INVITES YOU TO LISTEN TO HIS WISE WORDS.
HE IS STRONG NOT JUST IN BODY, BUT ALSO IN MIND AND SPIRIT. HE IS--
YEAAA!
ALL WHO WISH TO SURVIVE THE WAR SHOULD TURN WITH THEIR TAILS TUCKED AND FLEE!
I WILL GIVE YOU SAFE CONDUCT TO LEAVE.
ANYONE ELSE ON THIS PLANETOID WILL BE GROUND TO DUST!
I CLAIM THE INFINITY STONE IN THE NAME OF THE FREE CHITAURI, WHO WILL USE IT TO DESTROY THANOS AND FREE MY ENSLAVED WORLD.

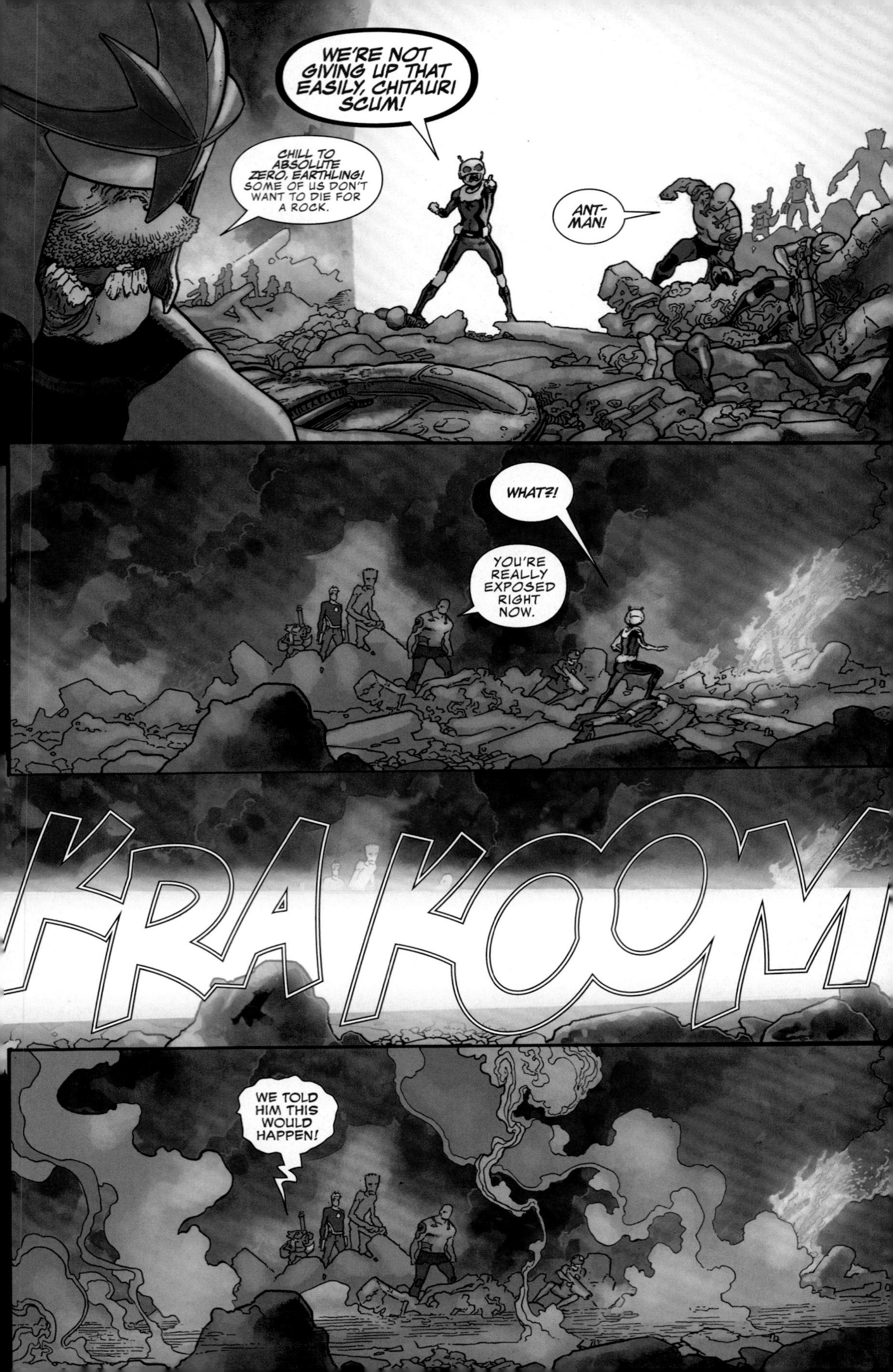
WE'RE NOT GIVING UP THAT EASILY, CHITAURI SCUM!
CHILL TO ABSOLUTE ZERO, EARTHLING! SOME OF US DON'T WANT TO DIE FOR A ROCK.
ANT-MAN!
WHAT?!
YOU'RE REALLY EXPOSED RIGHT NOW.
KRAKOOM
WE TOLD HIM THIS WOULD HAPPEN!

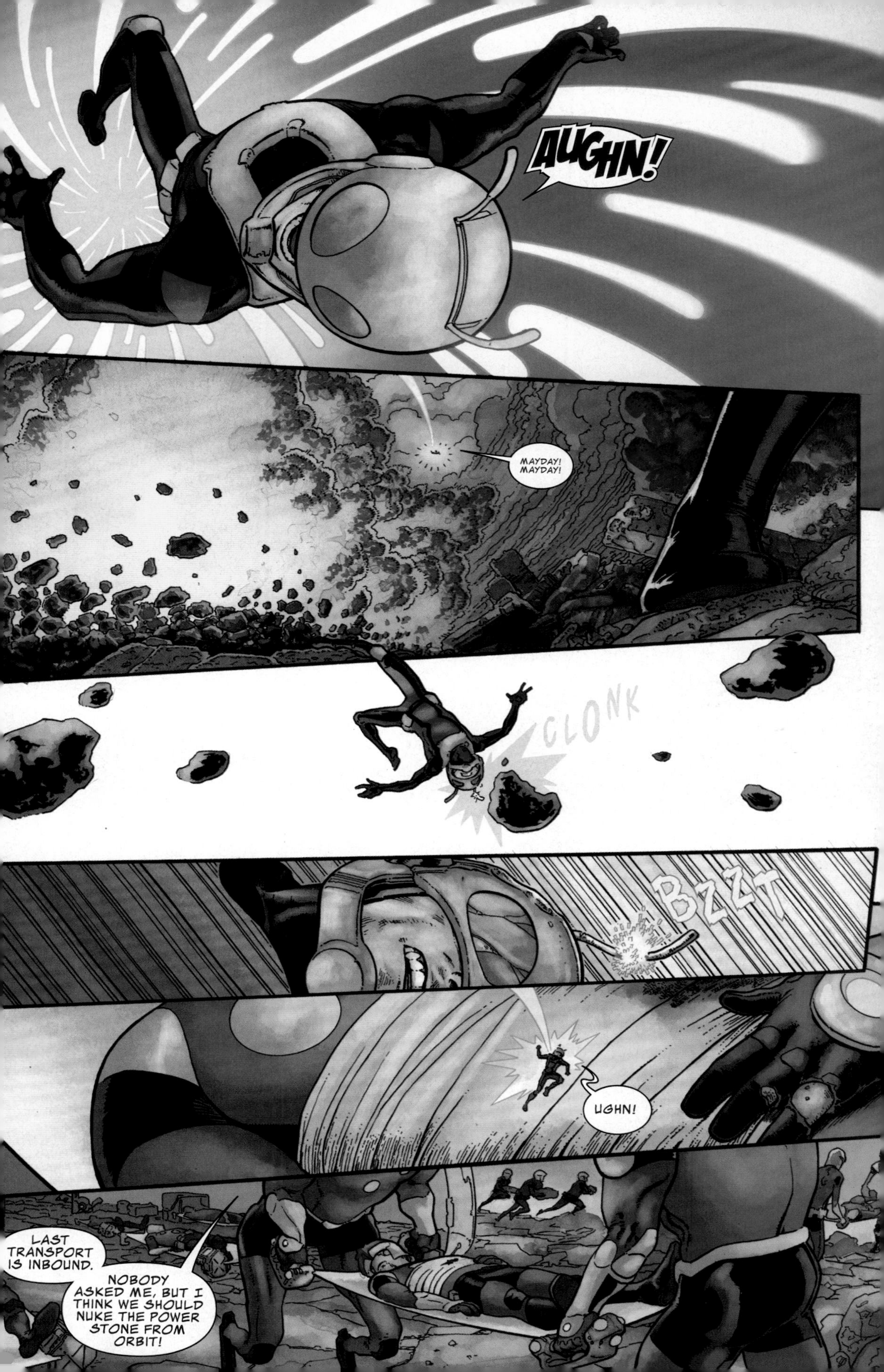
AUGHN!
MAYDAY! MAYDAY!
CLONK
BZZT
UGHN!
LAST TRANSPORT IS INBOUND.
NOBODY ASKED ME, BUT I THINK WE SHOULD NUKE THE POWER STONE FROM ORBIT!

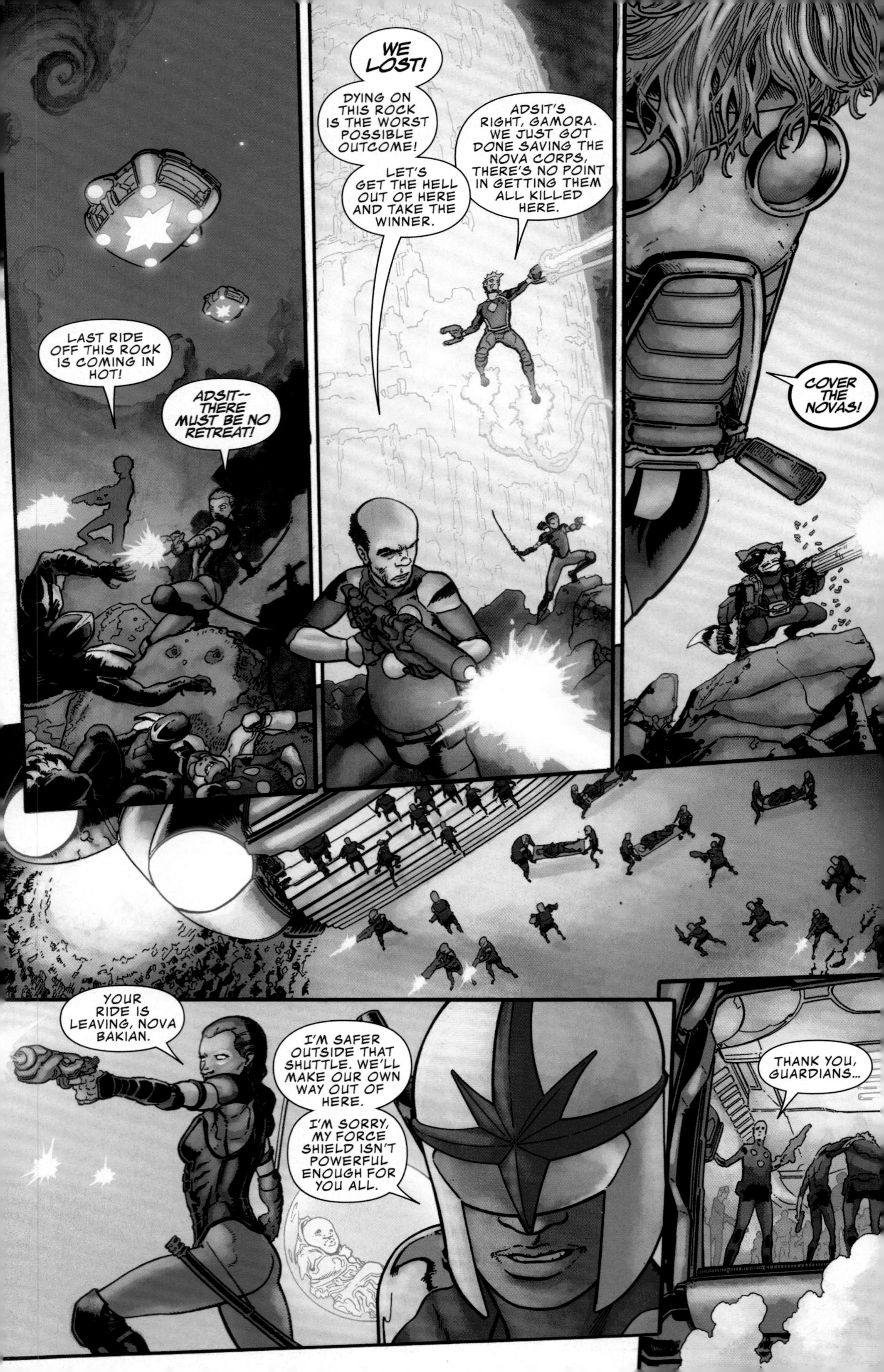
LAST RIDE OFF THIS ROCK IS COMING IN HOT!
ADSIT-- THERE MUST BE NO RETREAT!
WE LOST!
DYING ON THIS ROCK IS THE WORST POSSIBLE OUTCOME!
LET'S GET THE HELL OUT OF HERE AND TAKE THE WINNER.
ADSIT'S RIGHT, GAMORA. WE JUST GOT DONE SAVING THE NOVA CORPS, THERE'S NO POINT IN GETTING THEM ALL KILLED HERE.
COVER THE NOVAS!
YOUR RIDE IS LEAVING, NOVA BAKIAN.
I'M SAFER OUTSIDE THAT SHUTTLE. WE'LL MAKE OUR OWN WAY OUT OF HERE.
I'M SORRY, MY FORCE SHIELD ISN'T POWERFUL ENOUGH FOR YOU ALL.
THANK YOU, GUARDIANS...

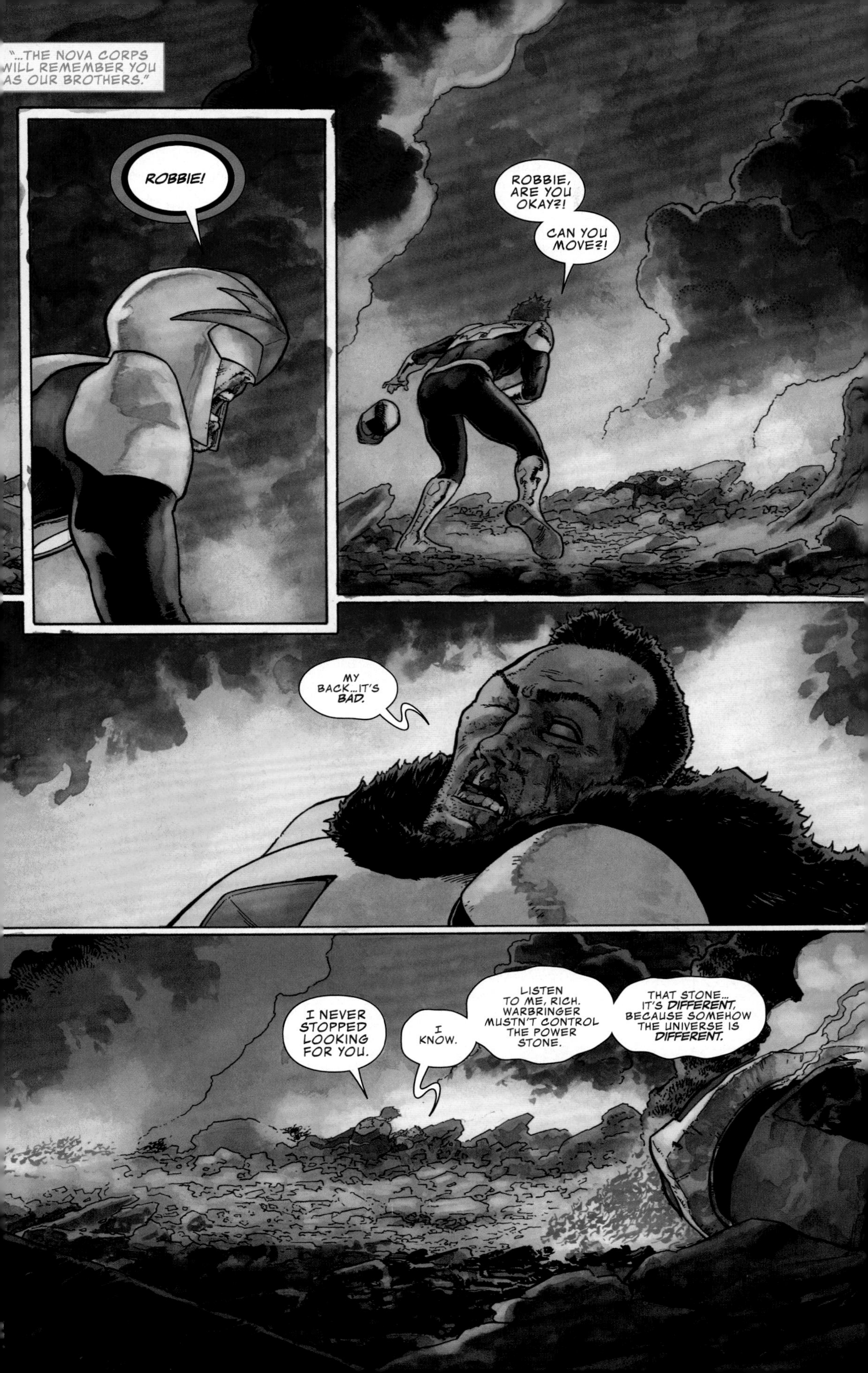
"...THE NOVA CORPS WILL REMEMBER YOU AS OUR BROTHERS."
ROBBIE!
ROBBIE, ARE YOU OKAY?!
CAN YOU MOVE?!
MY BACK...IT'S BAD.
I NEVER STOPPED LOOKING FOR YOU.
I KNOW.
LISTEN TO ME, RICH. WARBRINGER MUSTN'T CONTROL THE POWER STONE.
THAT STONE... IT'S DIFFERENT, BECAUSE SOMEHOW THE UNIVERSE IS DIFFERENT.

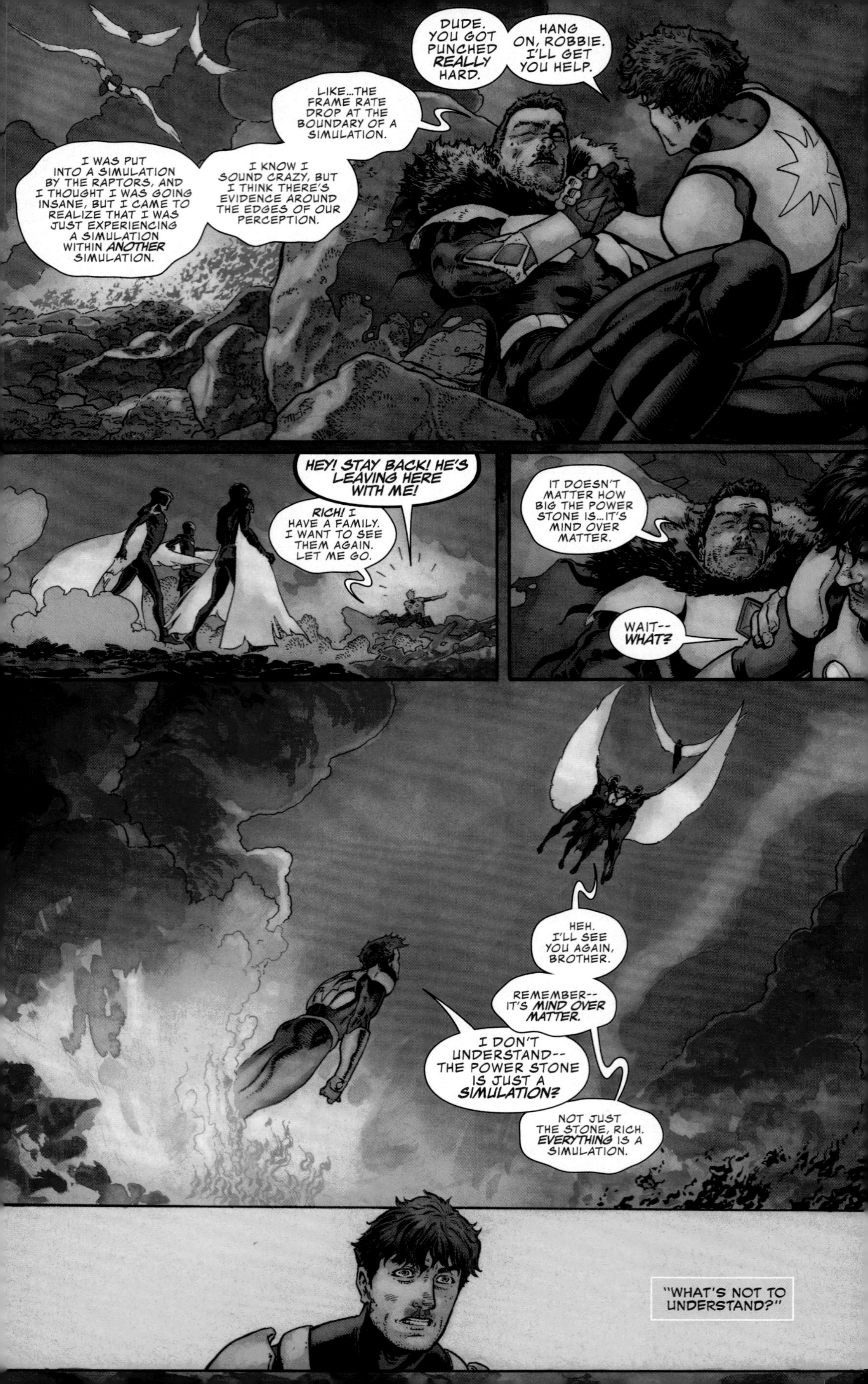

I WAS PUT INTO A SIMULATION BY THE RAPTORS, AND I THOUGHT I WAS GOING INSANE, BUT I CAME TO REALIZE THAT I WAS JUST EXPERIENCING A SIMULATION WITHIN ANOTHER SIMULATION.
I KNOW I SOUND CRAZY, BUT I THINK THERE'S EVIDENCE AROUND THE EDGES OF OUR PERCEPTION.
LIKE...THE FRAME RATE DROP AT THE BOUNDARY OF A SIMULATION.
DUDE. YOU GOT PUNCHED REALLY HARD.
HANG ON, ROBBIE. I'LL GET YOU HELP.
HEY! STAY BACK! HE'S LEAVING HERE WITH ME!
RICH! I HAVE A FAMILY. I WANT TO SEE THEM AGAIN. LET ME GO.
IT DOESN'T MATTER HOW BIG THE POWER STONE IS...IT'S MIND OVER MATTER.
WAIT-- WHAT?
HEH. I'LL SEE YOU AGAIN, BROTHER.
REMEMBER-- IT'S MIND OVER MATTER.
I DON'T UNDERSTAND-- THE POWER STONE IS JUST A SIMULATION?
NOT JUST THE STONE, RICH. EVERYTHING IS A SIMULATION.
"WHAT'S NOT TO UNDERSTAND?"

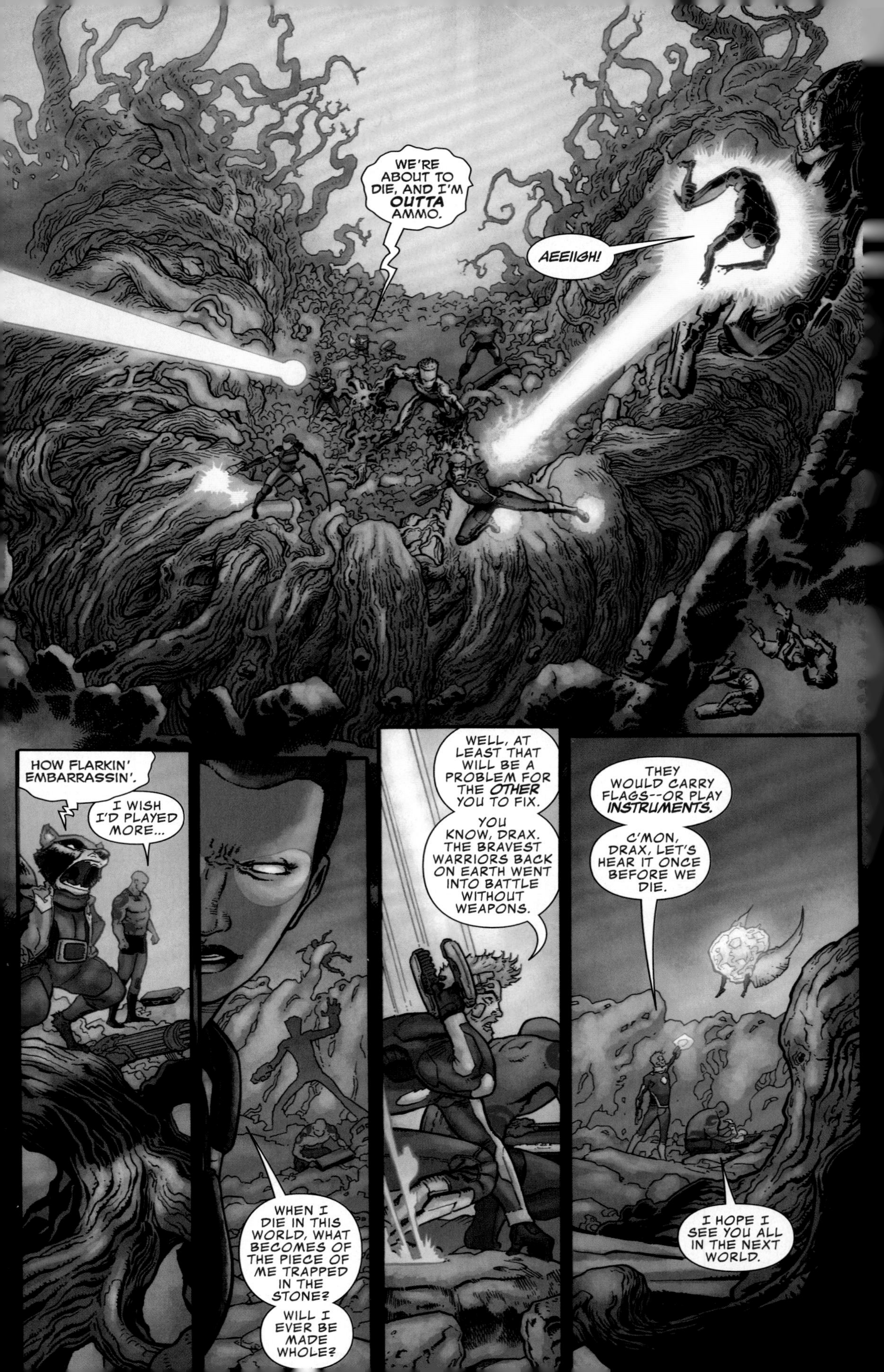
WE'RE ABOUT TO DIE, AND I'M OUTTA AMMO.
AEEIIGH!
HOW FLARKIN' EMBARRASSIN'.
I WISH I'D PLAYED MORE...
WHEN I DIE IN THIS WORLD, WHAT BECOMES OF THE PIECE OF ME TRAPPED IN THE STONE?
WILL I EVER BE MADE WHOLE?
WELL, AT LEAST THAT WILL BE A PROBLEM FOR THE OTHER YOU TO FIX.
YOU KNOW, DRAX. THE BRAVEST WARRIORS BACK ON EARTH WENT INTO BATTLE WITHOUT WEAPONS.
THEY WOULD CARRY FLAGS--OR PLAY INSTRUMENTS.
C'MON, DRAX, LET'S HEAR IT ONCE BEFORE WE DIE.
I HOPE I SEE YOU ALL IN THE NEXT WORLD.

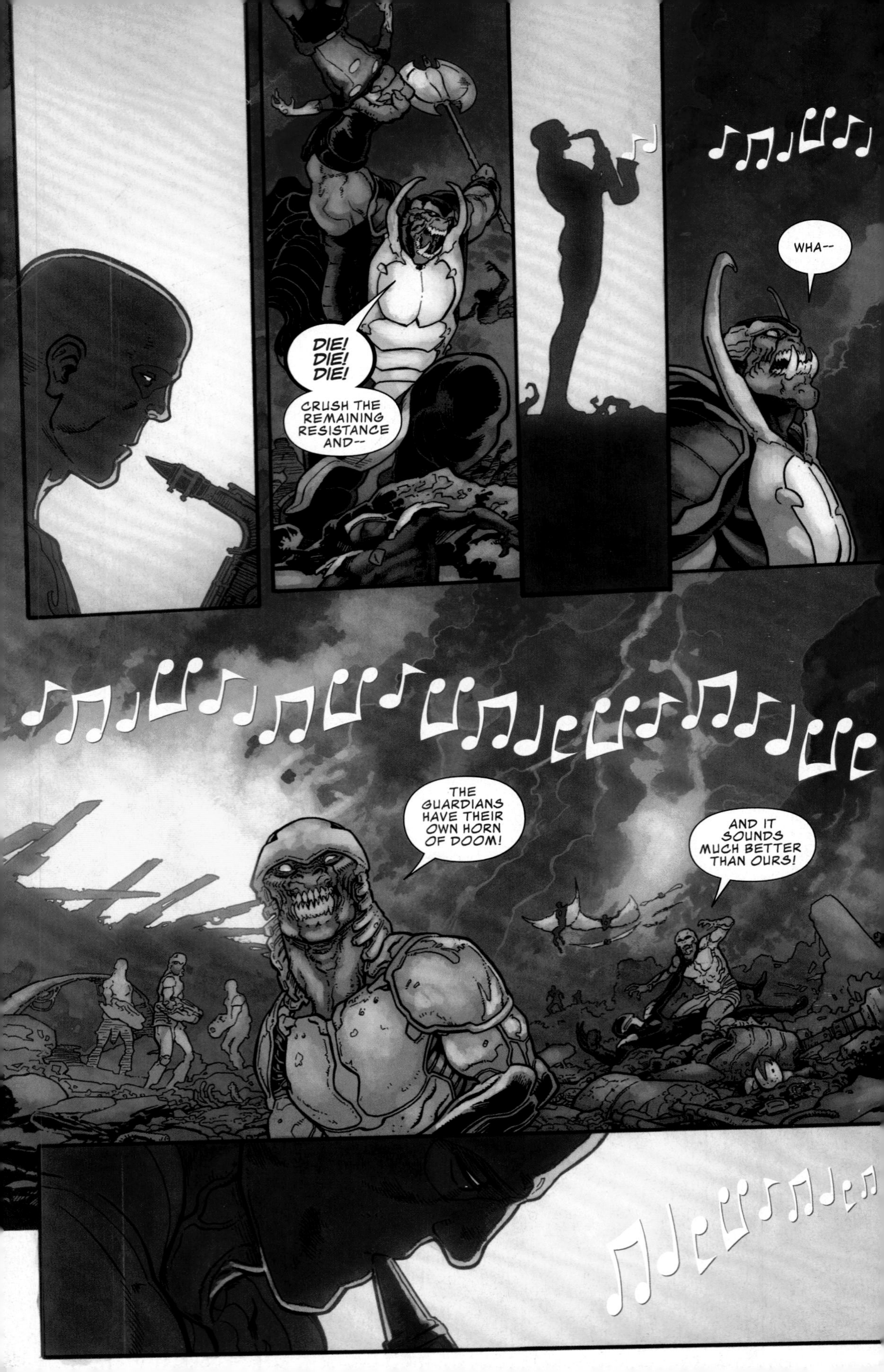

DIE! DIE! DIE!
CRUSH THE REMAINING RESISTANCE AND--
WHA--
THE GUARDIANS HAVE THEIR OWN HORN OF DOOM!
AND IT SOUNDS MUCH BETTER THAN OURS!

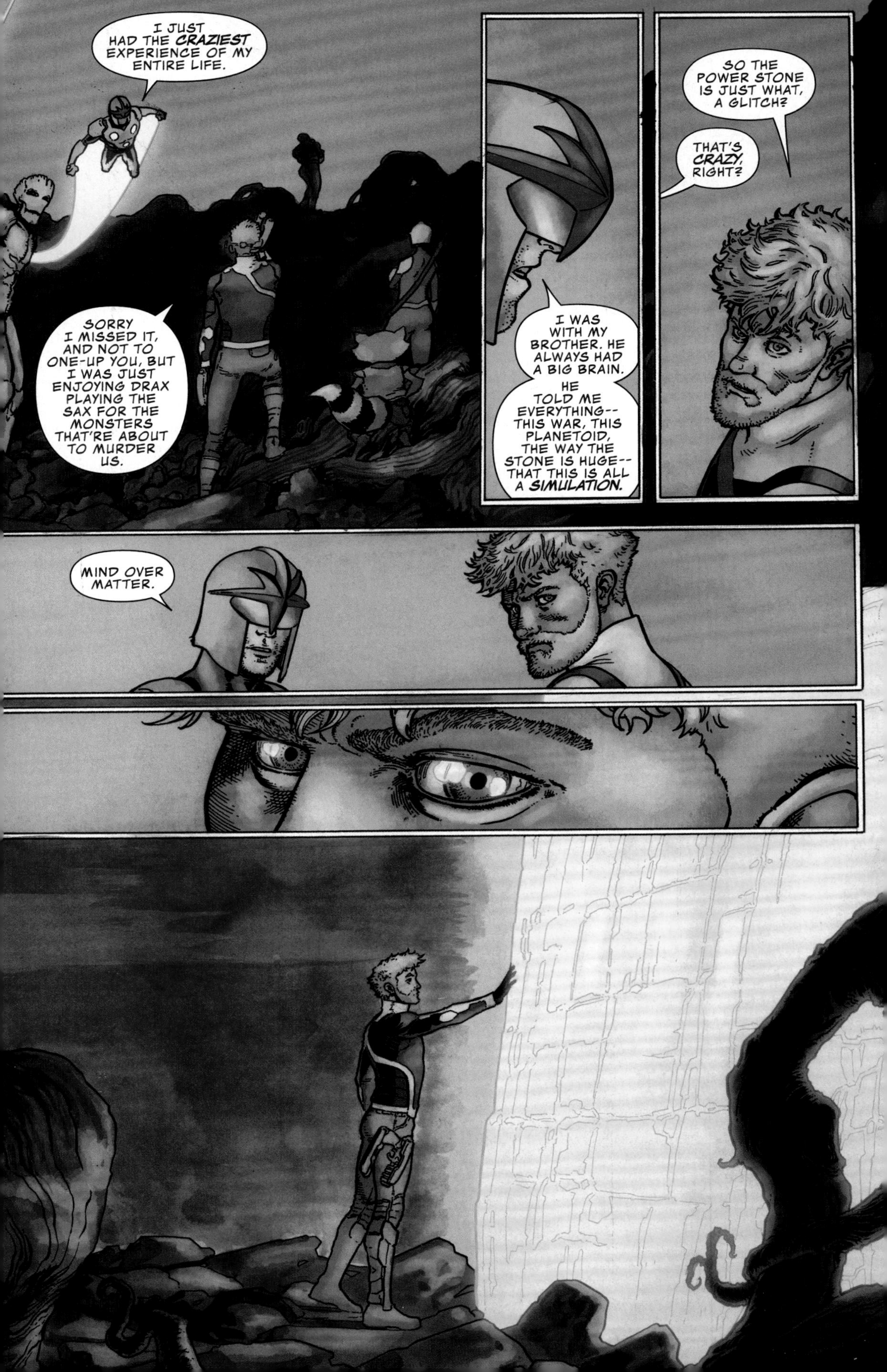
I JUST HAD THE CRAZIEST EXPERIENCE OF MY ENTIRE LIFE.
SORRY I MISSED IT, AND NOT TO ONE-UP YOU, BUT I WAS JUST ENJOYING DRAX PLAYING THE SAX FOR THE MONSTERS THAT'RE ABOUT TO MURDER US.
I WAS WITH MY BROTHER. HE ALWAYS HAD A BIG BRAIN.
HE TOLD ME EVERYTHING-- THIS WAR, THIS PLANETOID, THE WAY THE STONE IS HUGE-- THAT THIS IS ALL A SIMULATION.
SO THE POWER STONE IS JUST WHAT, A GLITCH?
THAT'S CRAZY, RIGHT?
MIND OVER MATTER.

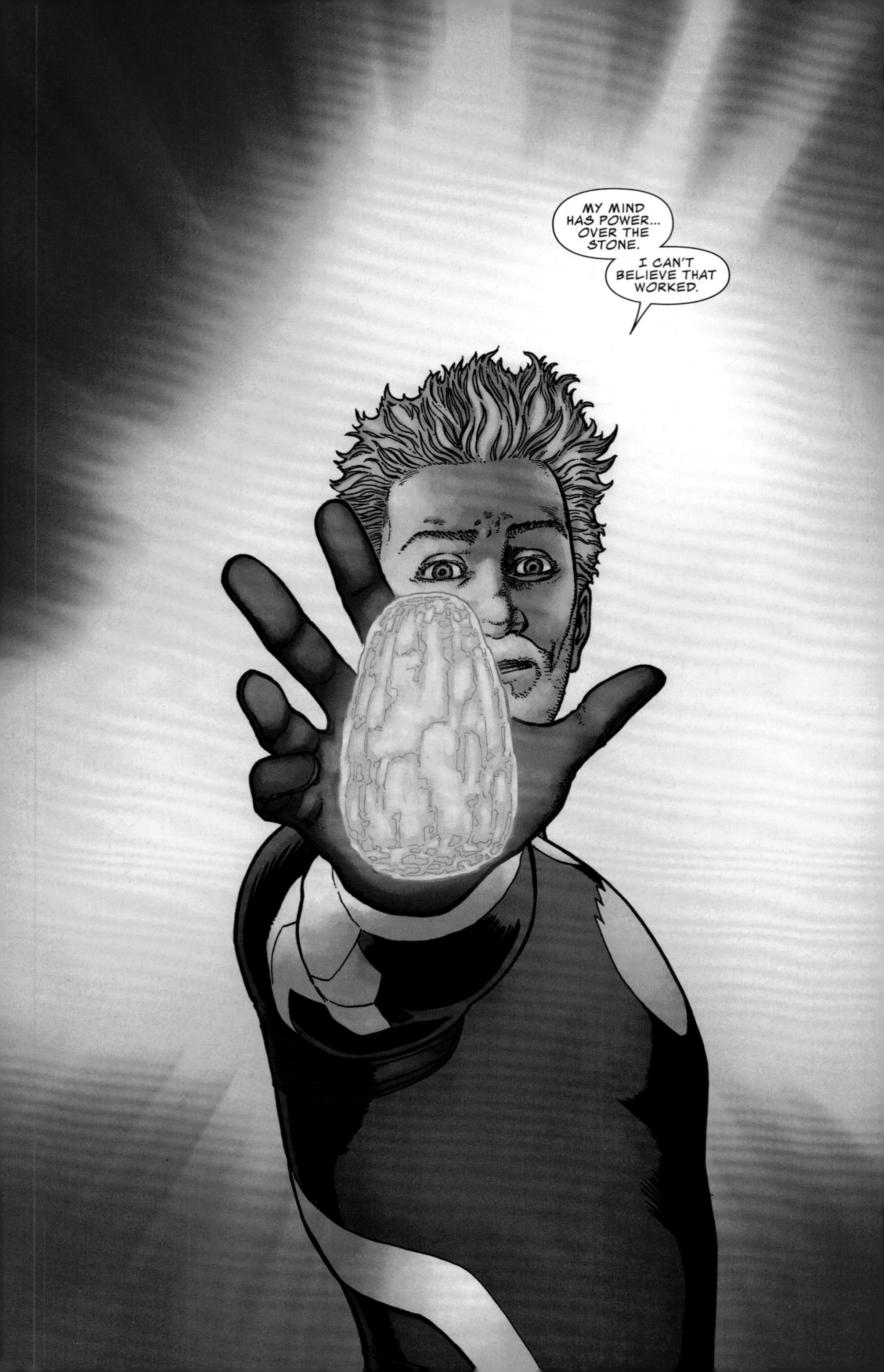
MY MIND HAS POWER... OVER THE STONE.
I CAN'T BELIEVE THAT WORKED.

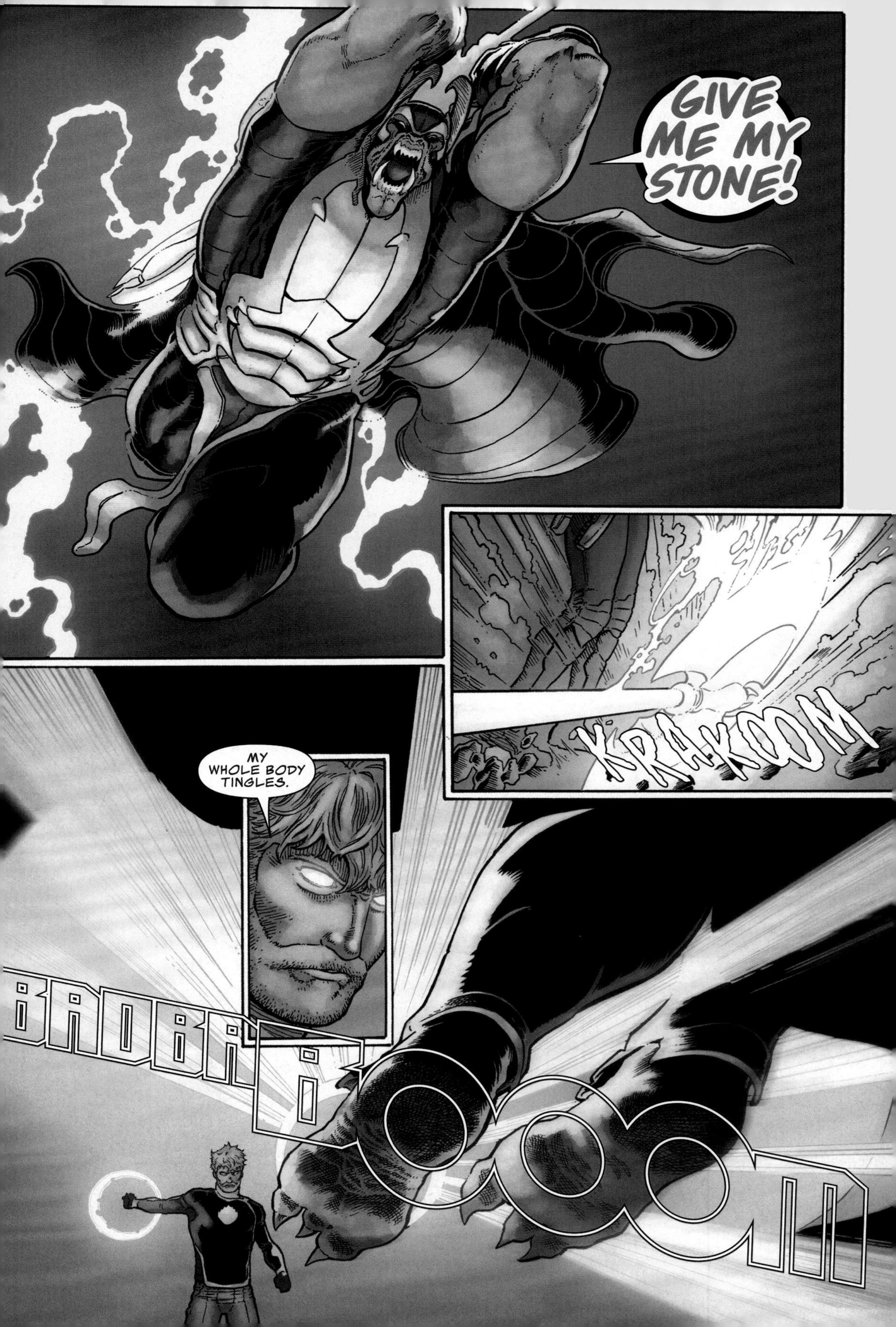
GIVE ME MY STONE!
KRAKOOM
MY WHOLE BODY TINGLES.

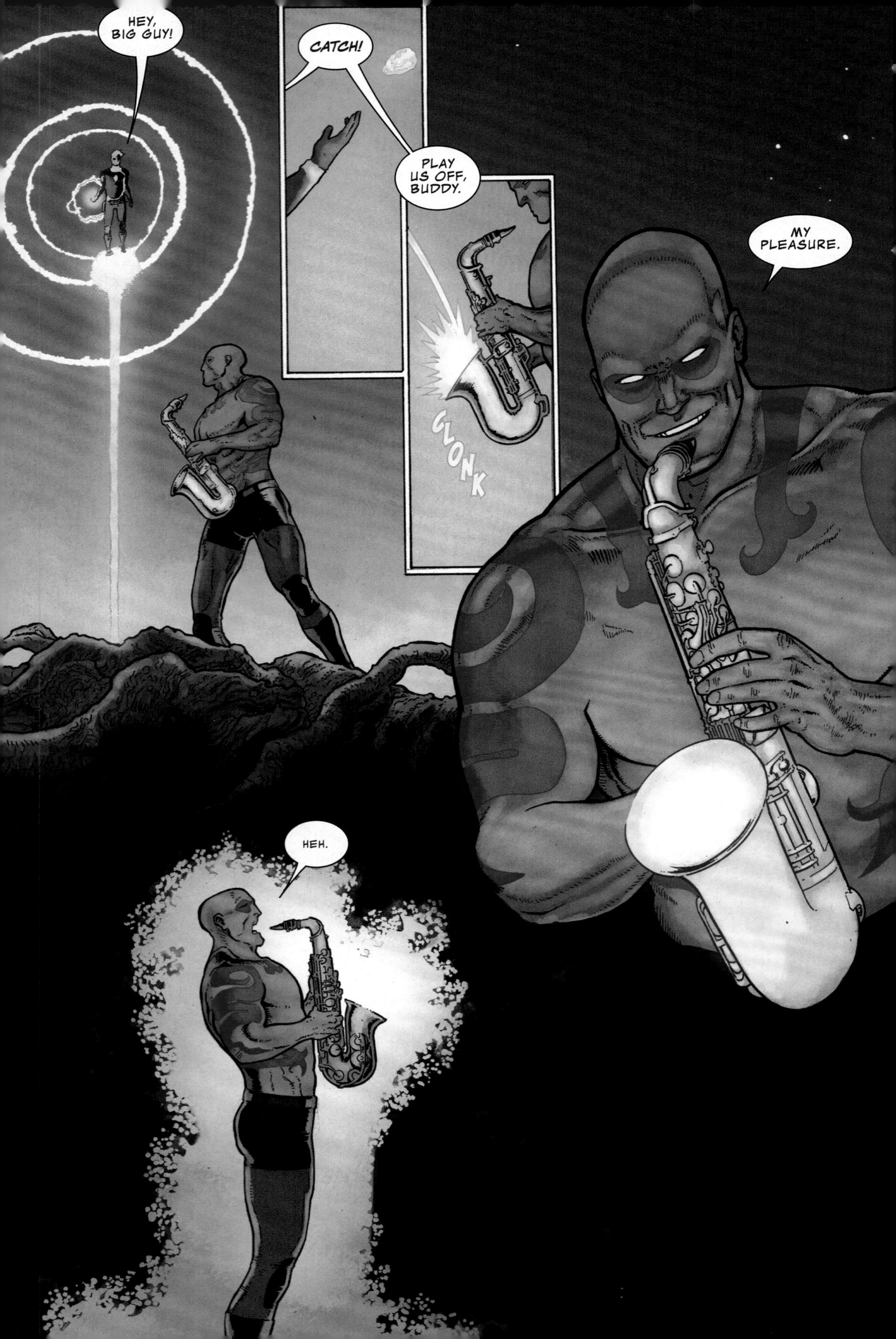
HEY, BIG GUY!
CATCH!
PLAY US OFF, BUDDY.
CLONK
MY PLEASURE.
HEH.

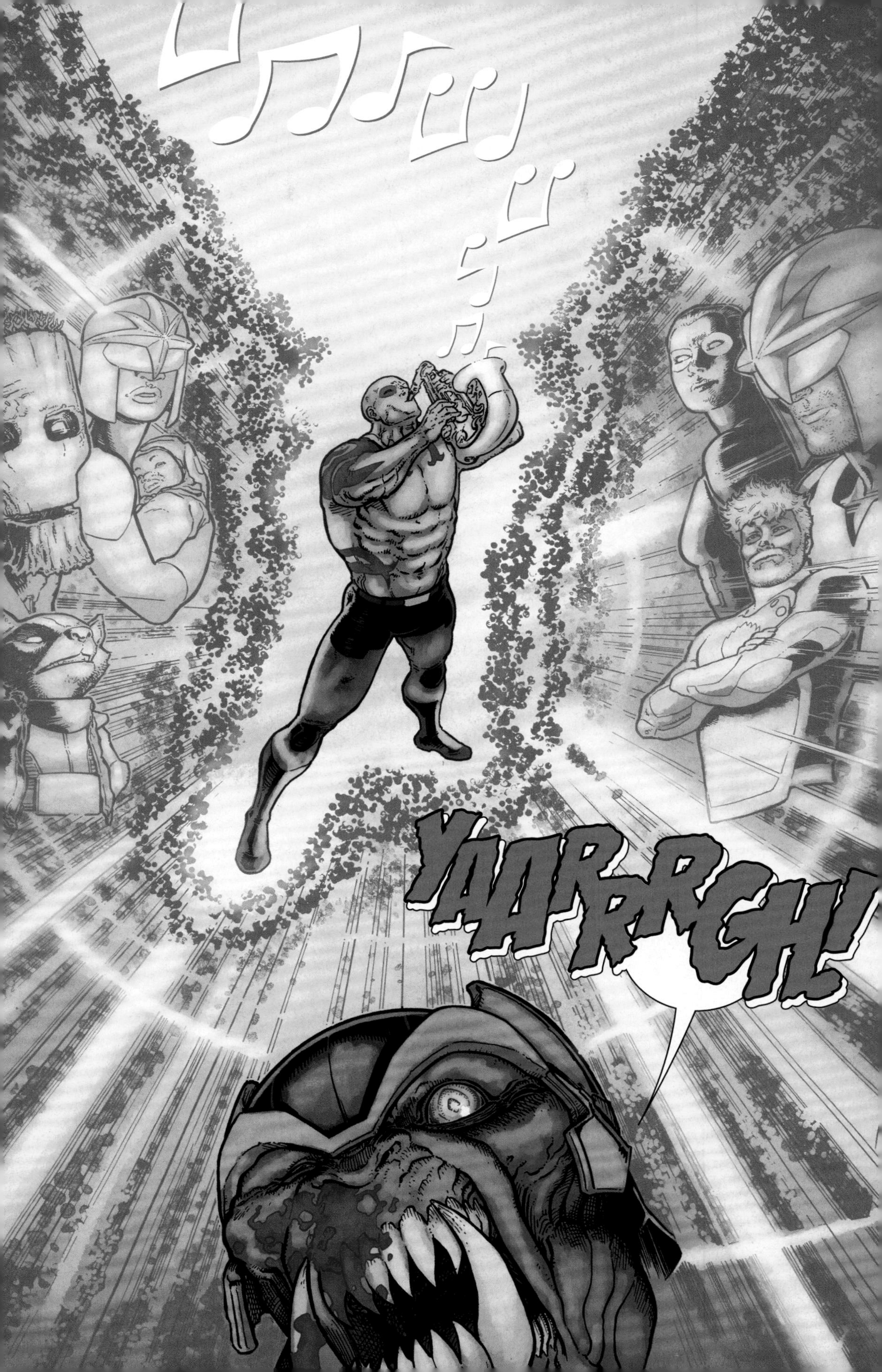
YAARRRGH!

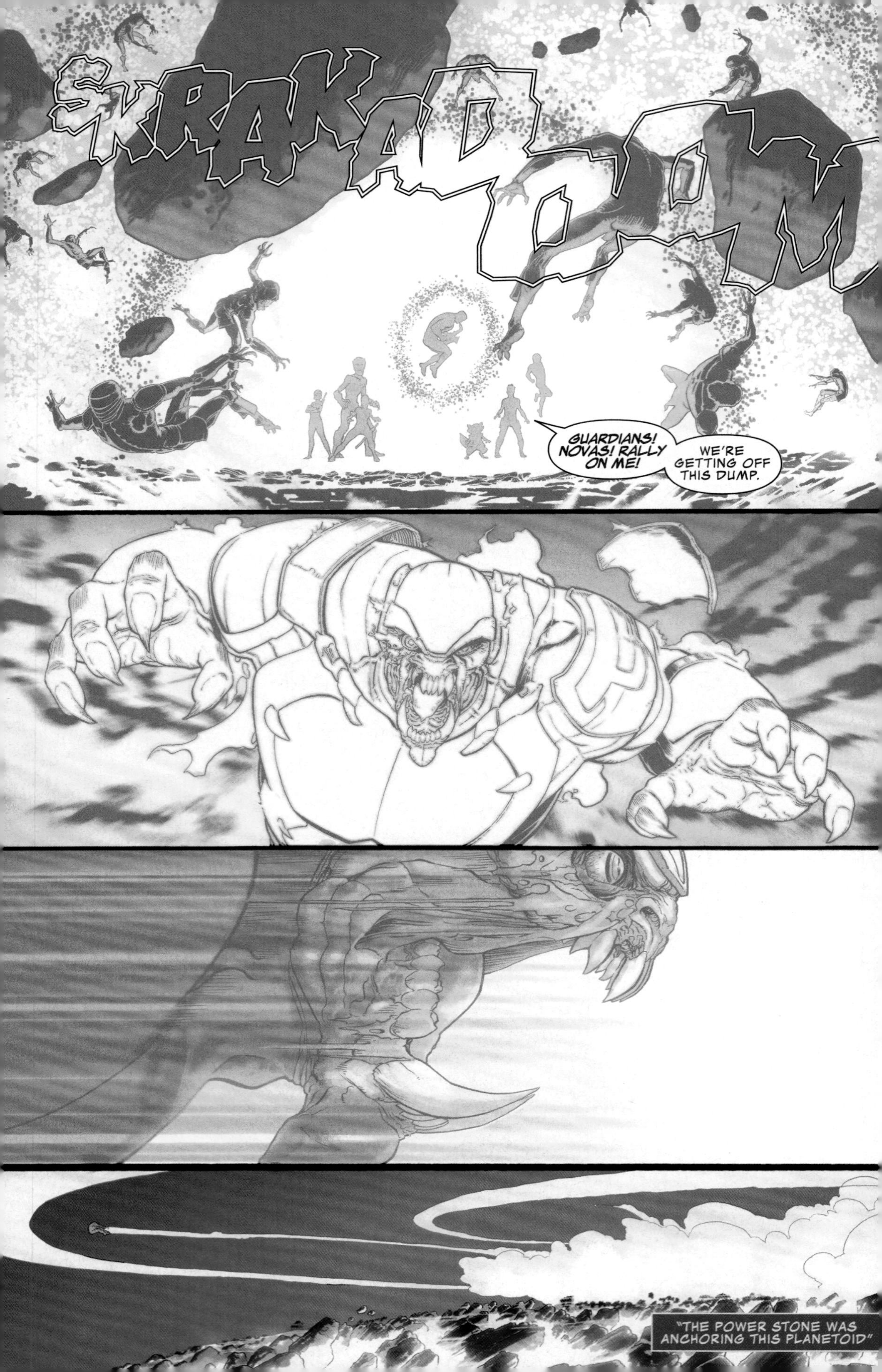
SKRAKADOOOM
GUARDIANS! NOVAS! RALLY ON ME!
WE'RE GETTING OFF THIS DUMP.
"THE POWER STONE WAS ANCHORING THIS PLANETOID"

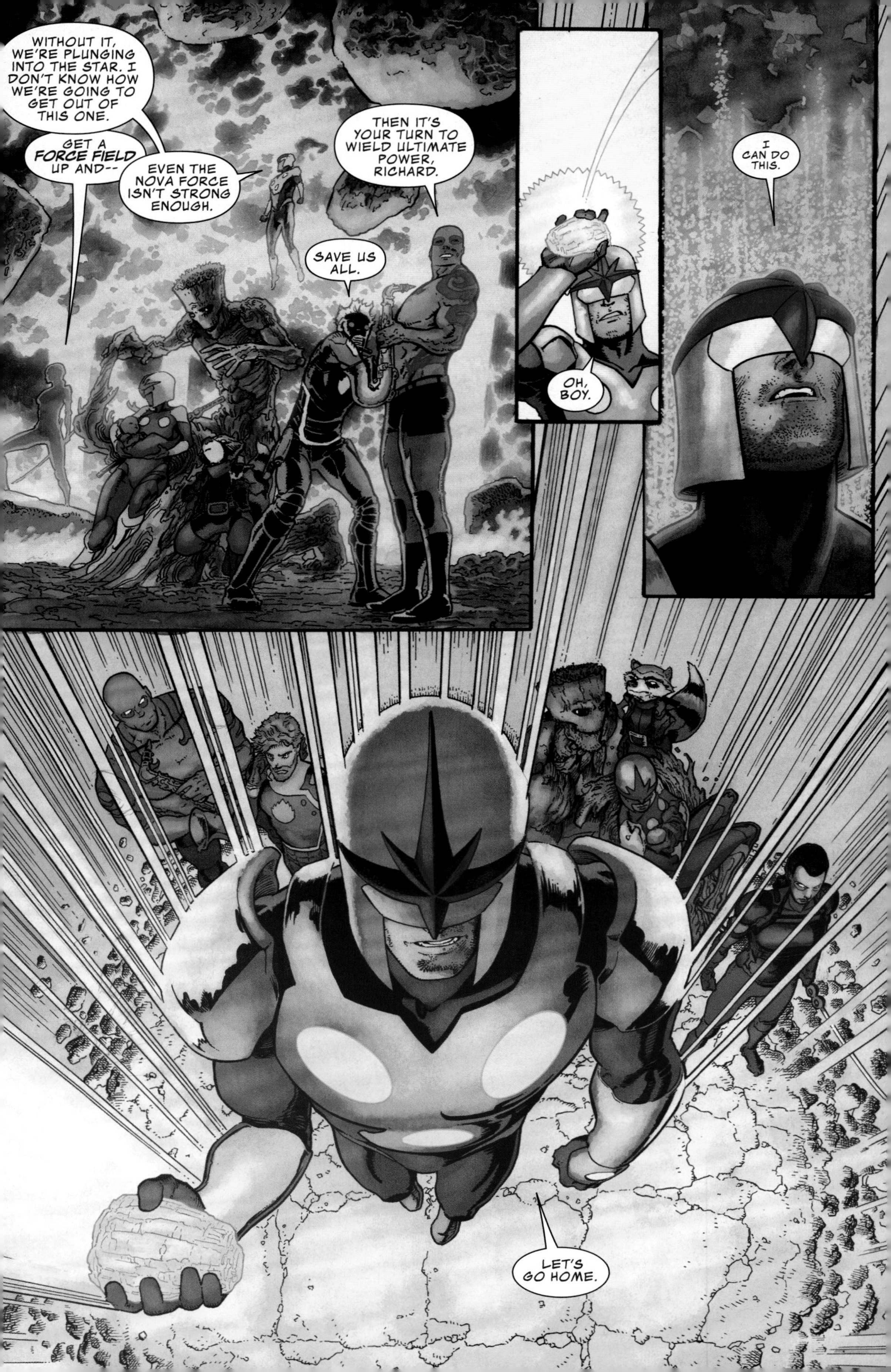
WITHOUT IT, WE'RE PLUNGING INTO THE STAR. I DON'T KNOW HOW WE'RE GOING TO GET OUT OF THIS ONE.
GET A FORCE FIELD UP AND--
EVEN THE NOVA FORCE ISN'T STRONG ENOUGH.
THEN IT'S YOUR TURN TO WIELD ULTIMATE POWER, RICHARD.
SAVE US ALL.
OH, BOY.
I CAN DO THIS.
LET'S GO HOME.

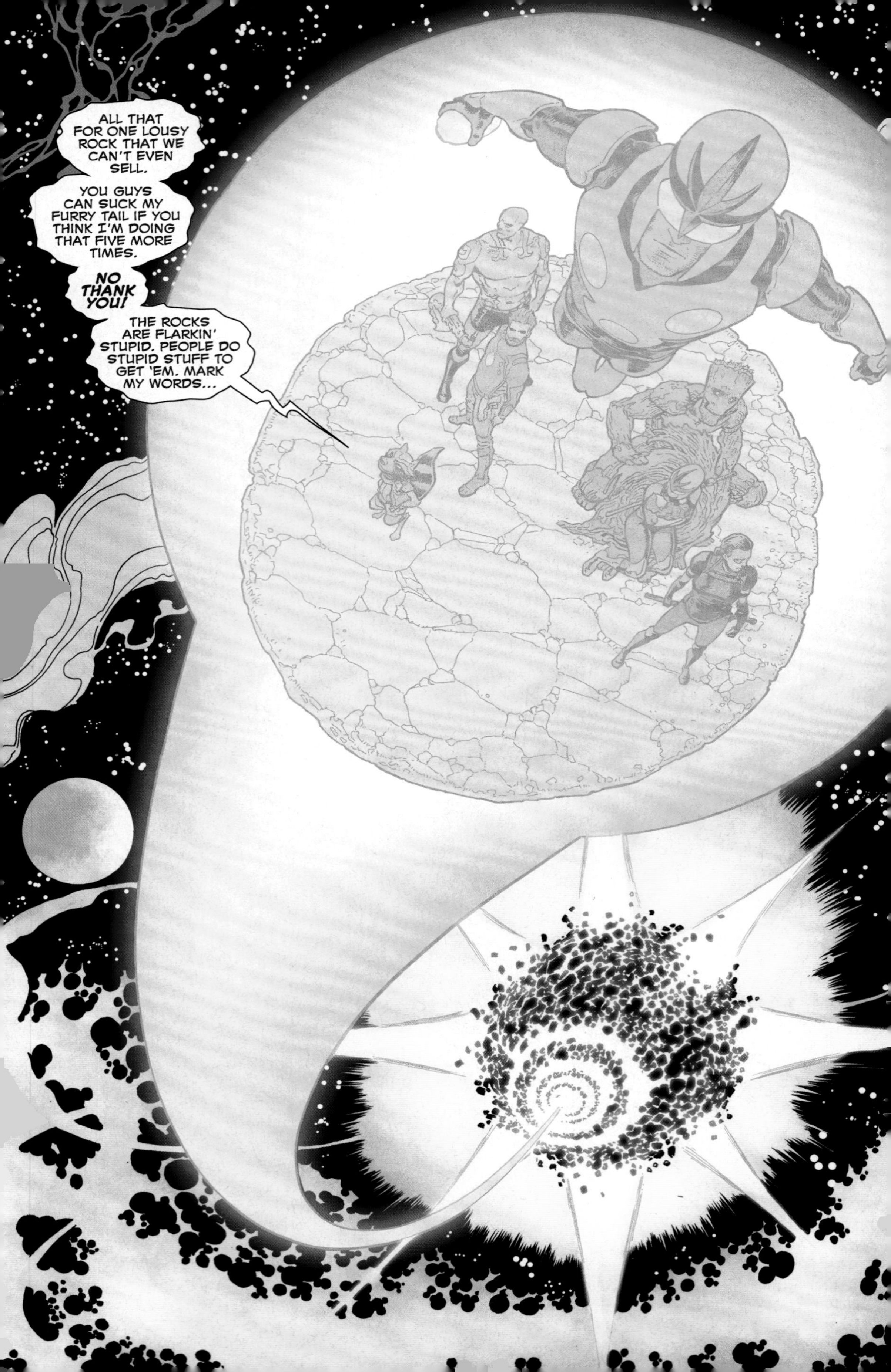
ALL THAT FOR ONE LOUSY ROCK THAT WE CAN'T EVEN SELL.
YOU GUYS CAN SUCK MY FURRY TAIL IF YOU THINK I'M DOING THAT FIVE MORE TIMES.
NO THANK YOU!
THE ROCKS ARE FLARKIN' STUPID. PEOPLE DO STUPID STUFF TO GET 'EM. MARK MY WORDS...

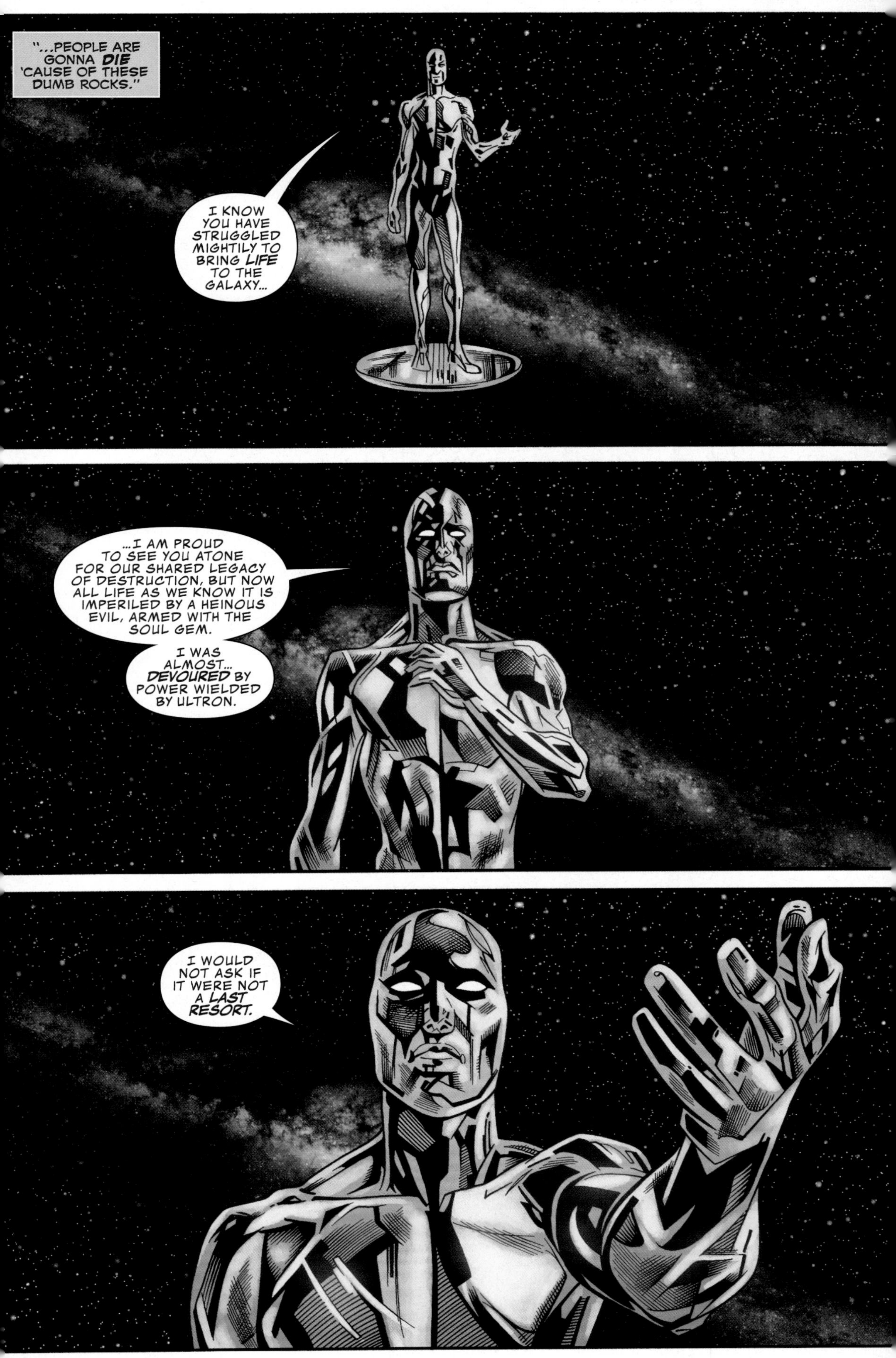
"...PEOPLE ARE GONNA DIE 'CAUSE OF THESE DUMB ROCKS."
I KNOW YOU HAVE STRUGGLED MIGHTILY TO BRING LIFE TO THE GALAXY...
...I AM PROUD TO SEE YOU ATONE FOR OUR SHARED LEGACY OF DESTRUCTION, BUT NOW ALL LIFE AS WE KNOW IT IS IMPERILED BY A HEINOUS EVIL, ARMED WITH THE SOUL GEM.
I WAS ALMOST... DEVOURED BY POWER WIELDED BY ULTRON.
I WOULD NOT ASK IF IT WERE NOT A LAST RESORT.

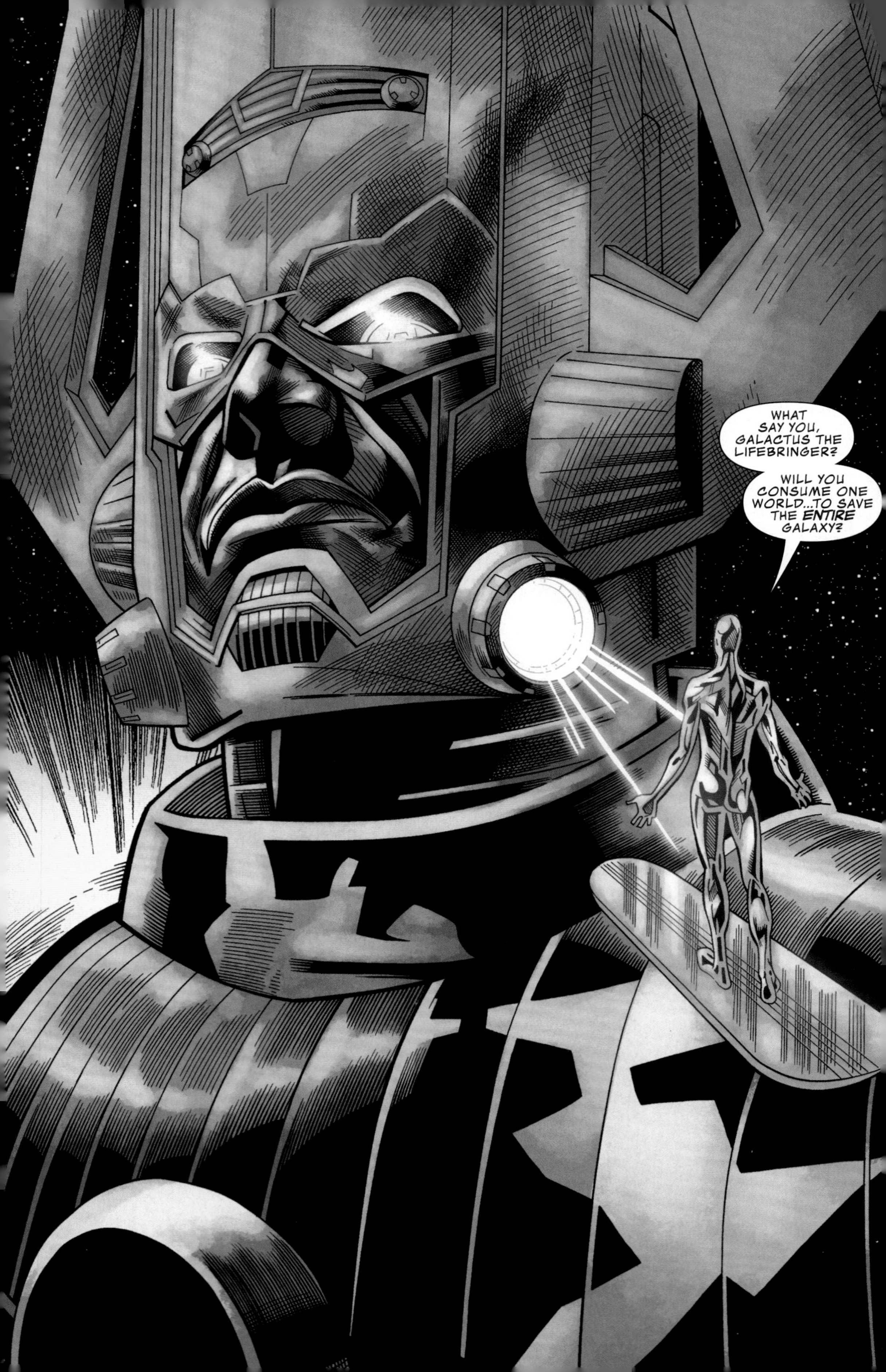
WHAT SAY YOU, GALACTUS THE LIFEBRINGER?
WILL YOU CONSUME ONE WORLD...TO SAVE THE ENTIRE GALAXY?

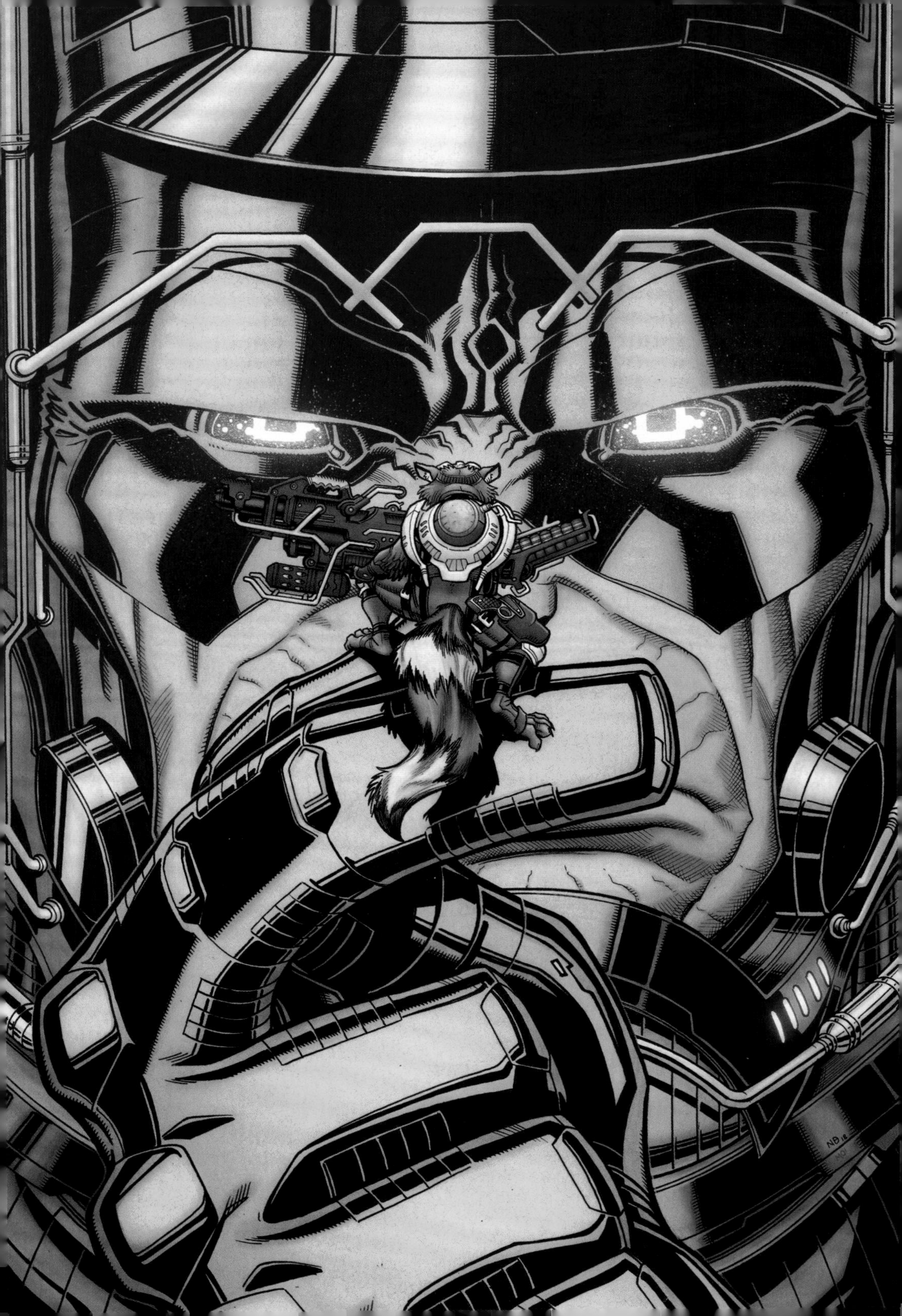

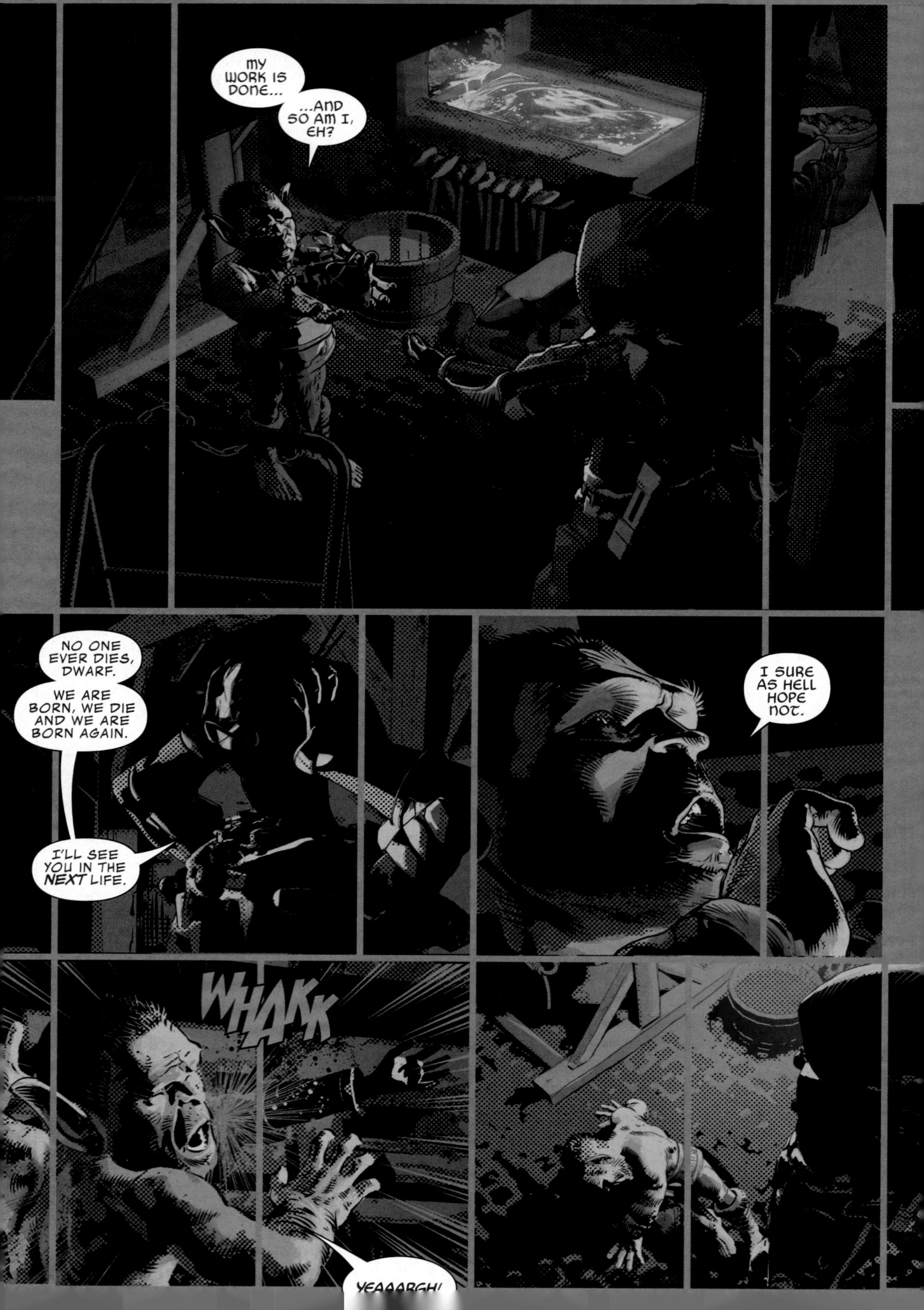
MY WORK IS DONE...
...AND SO AM I, EH?
NO ONE EVER DIES, DWARF.
WE ARE BORN, WE DIE AND WE ARE BORN AGAIN.
I'LL SEE YOU IN THE *NEXT* LIFE.
I SURE AS HELL HOPE NOT.
WHAKK
YEAAARGH!

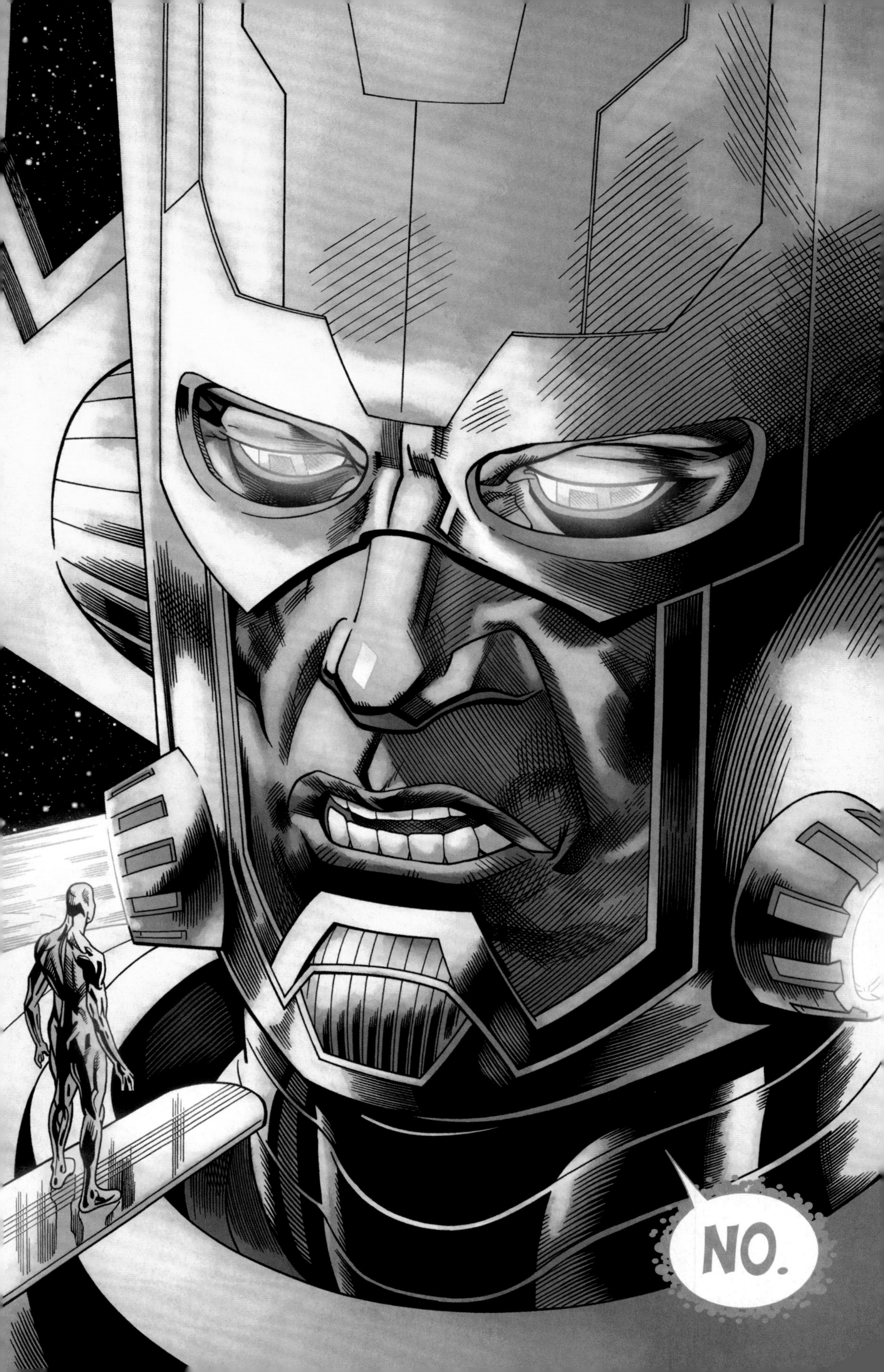
NO.

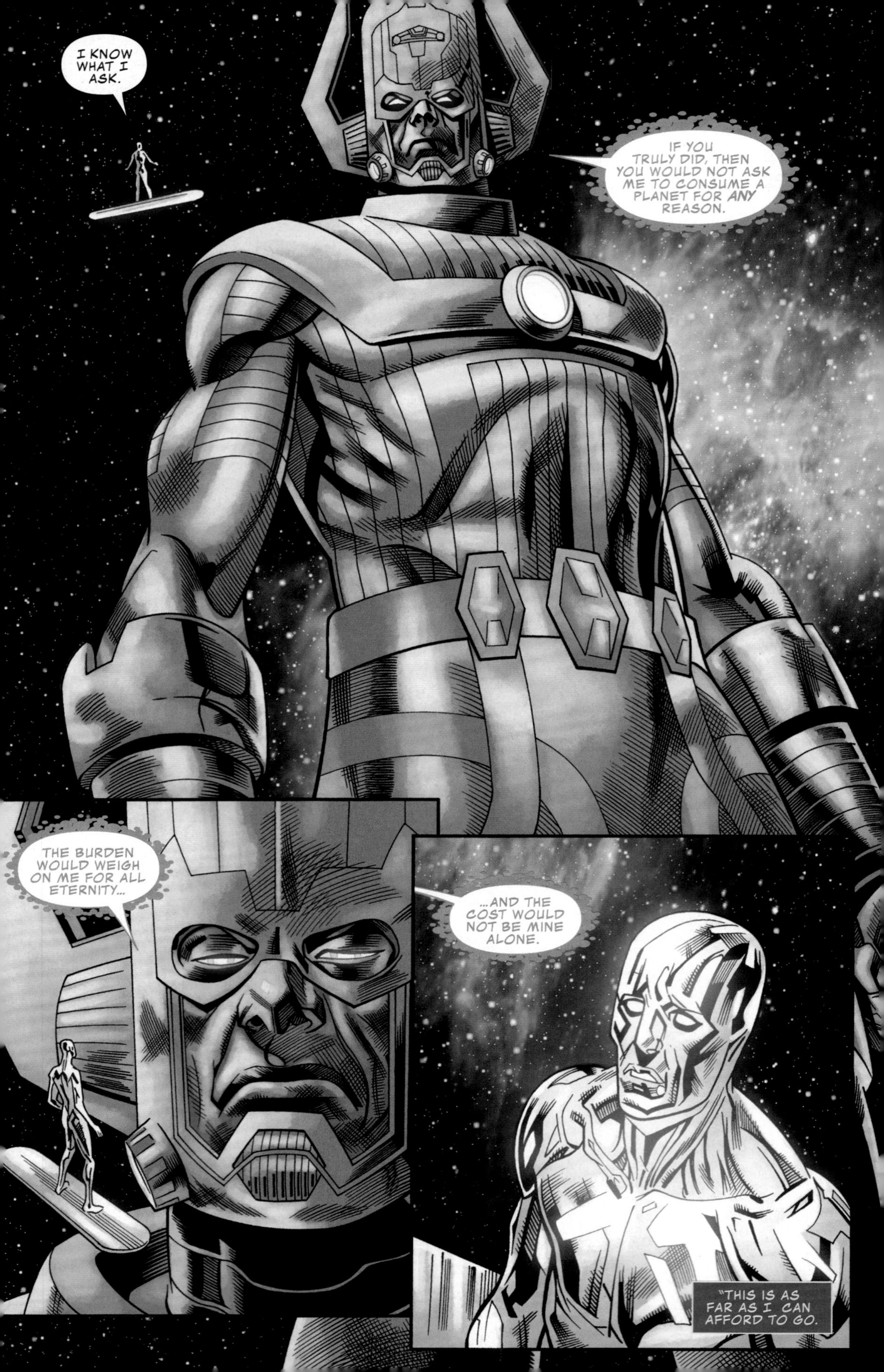
I KNOW WHAT I ASK.
IF YOU TRULY DID, THEN YOU WOULD NOT ASK ME TO CONSUME A PLANET FOR ANY REASON.
THE BURDEN WOULD WEIGH ON ME FOR ALL ETERNITY...
...AND THE COST WOULD NOT BE MINE ALONE.
"THIS IS AS FAR AS I CAN AFFORD TO GO.

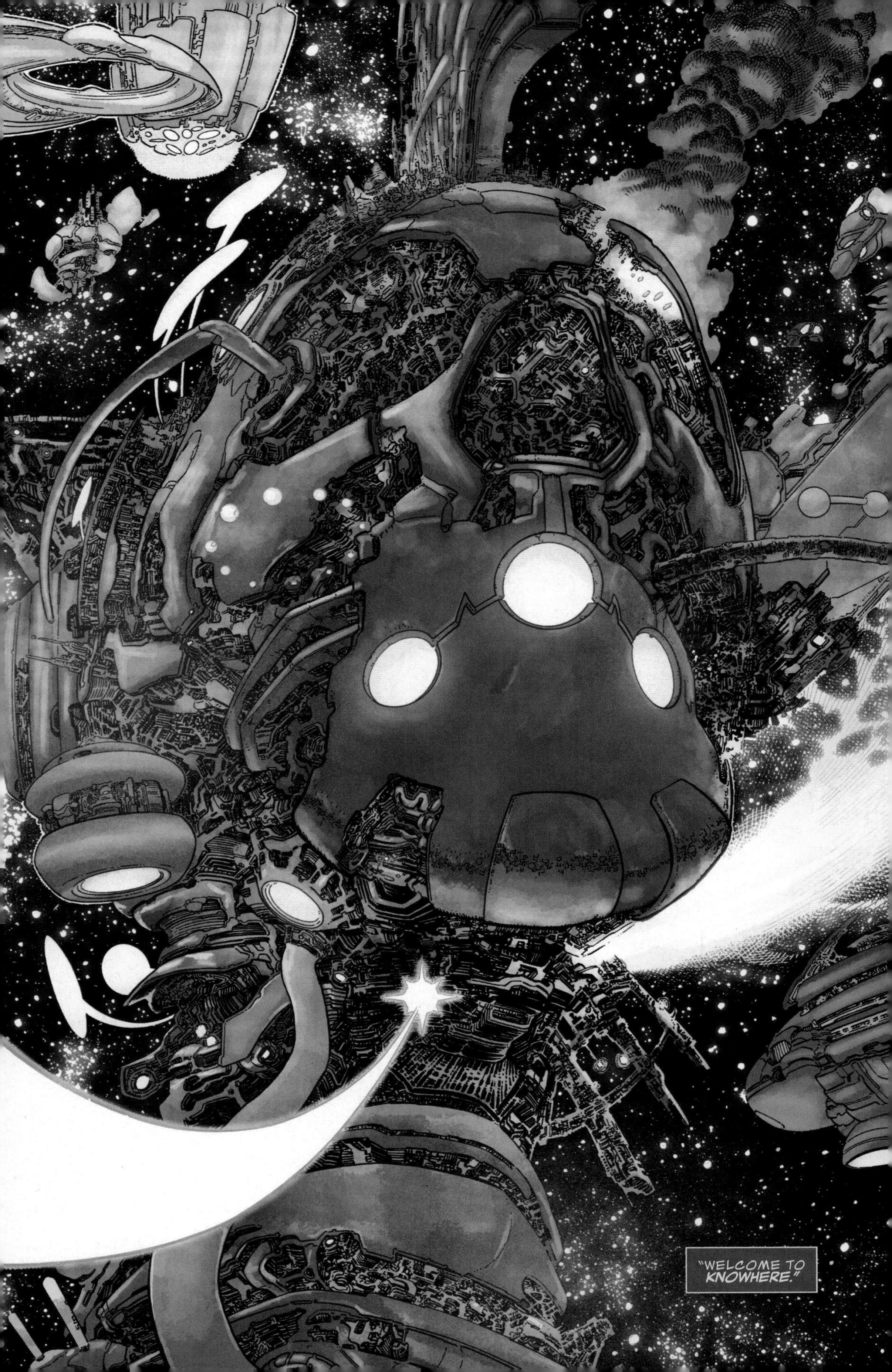
"WELCOME TO KNOWHERE."

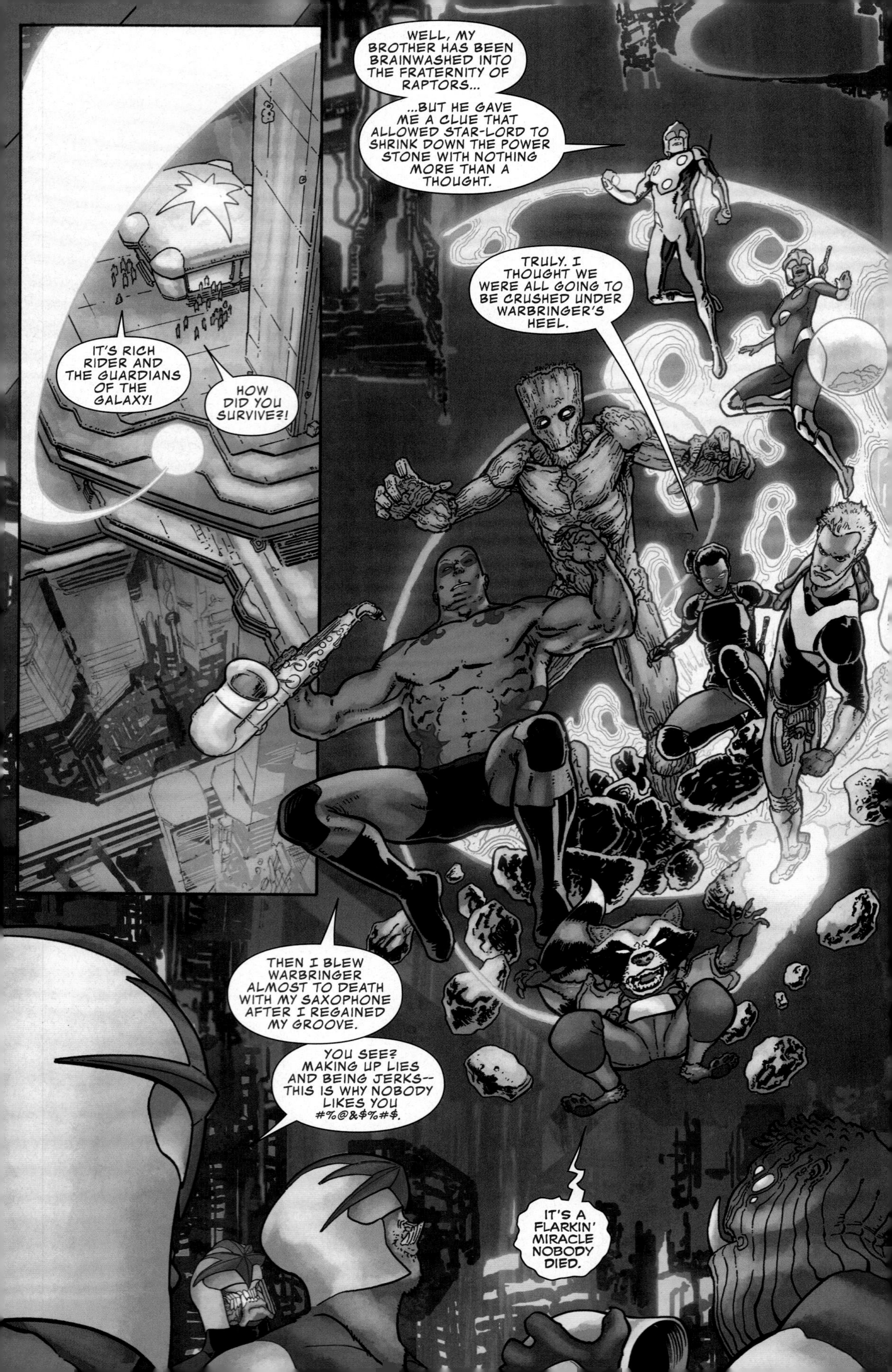
IT'S RICH RIDER AND THE GUARDIANS OF THE GALAXY!
HOW DID YOU SURVIVE?!
WELL, MY BROTHER HAS BEEN BRAINWASHED INTO THE FRATERNITY OF RAPTORS...
...BUT HE GAVE ME A CLUE THAT ALLOWED STAR-LORD TO SHRINK DOWN THE POWER STONE WITH NOTHING MORE THAN A THOUGHT.
TRULY. I THOUGHT WE WERE ALL GOING TO BE CRUSHED UNDER WARBRINGER'S HEEL.
THEN I BLEW WARBRINGER ALMOST TO DEATH WITH MY SAXOPHONE AFTER I REGAINED MY GROOVE.
YOU SEE? MAKING UP LIES AND BEING JERKS-- THIS IS WHY NOBODY LIKES YOU #%@&$%#$.
IT'S A FLARKIN' MIRACLE NOBODY DIED.

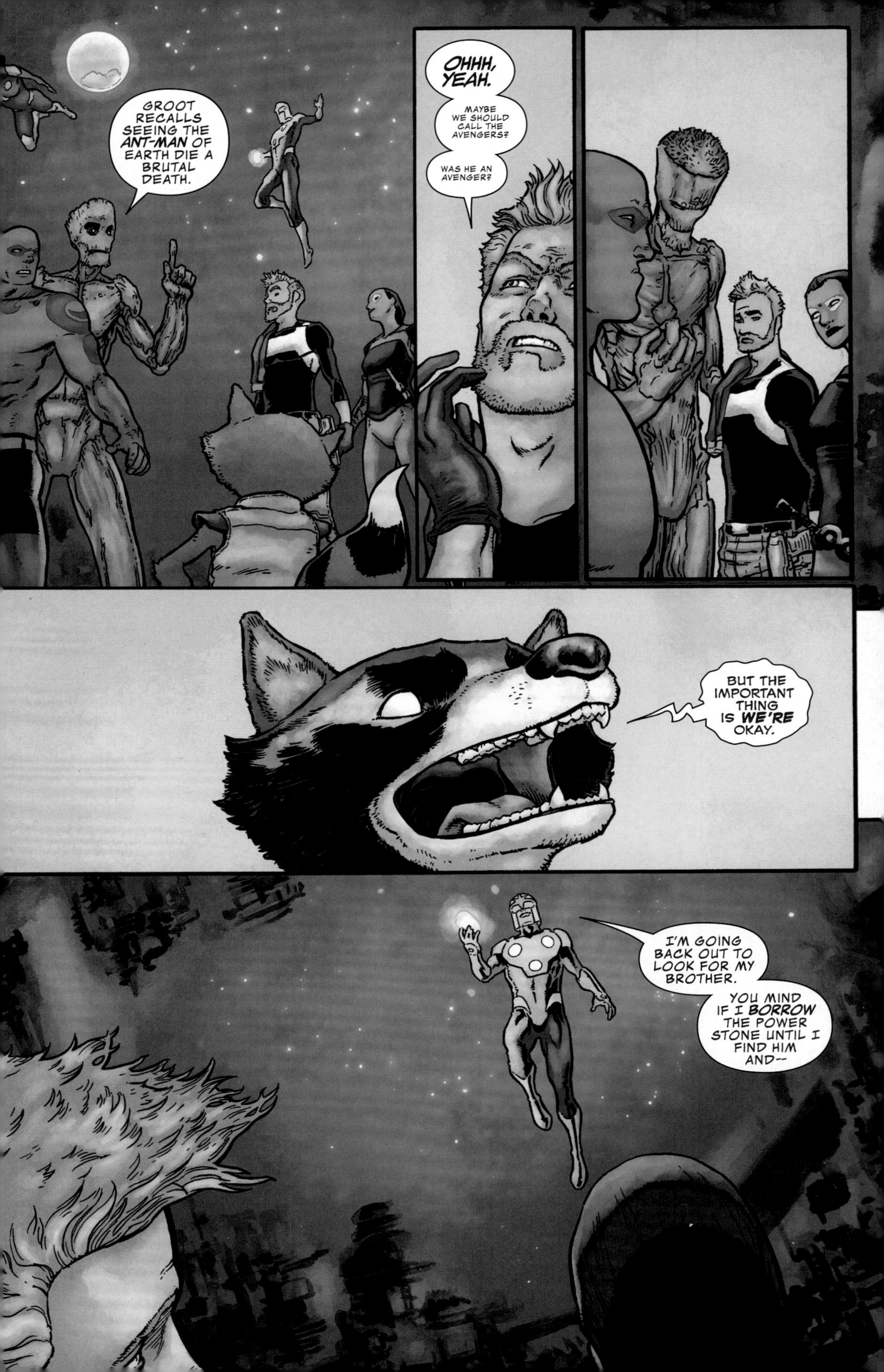
GROOT RECALLS SEEING THE ANT-MAN OF EARTH DIE A BRUTAL DEATH.
OHHH, YEAH.
MAYBE WE SHOULD CALL THE AVENGERS?
WAS HE AN AVENGER?
BUT THE IMPORTANT THING IS WE'RE OKAY.
I'M GOING BACK OUT TO LOOK FOR MY BROTHER.
YOU MIND IF I BORROW THE POWER STONE UNTIL I FIND HIM AND--

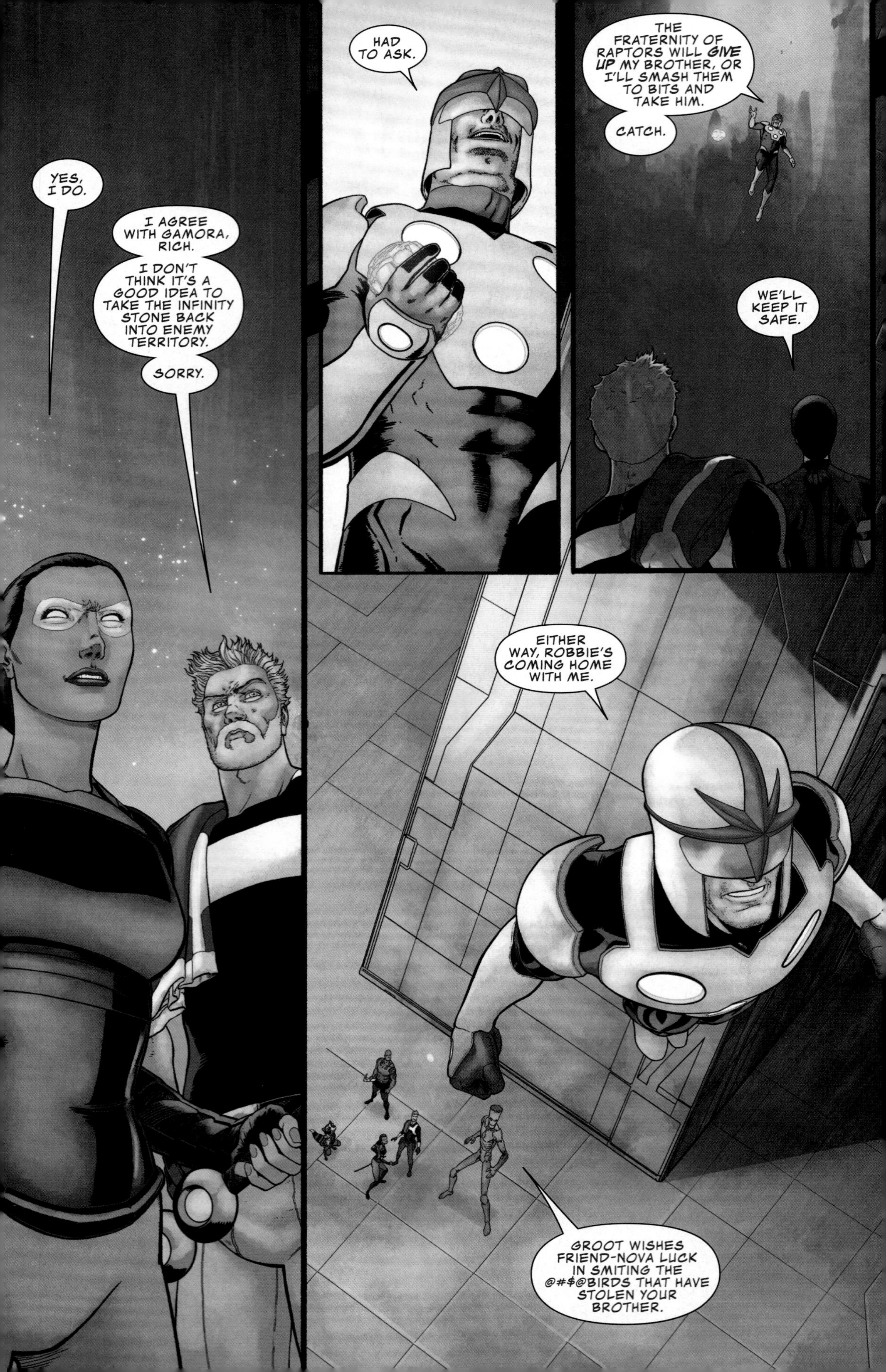
YES, I DO.
I AGREE WITH GAMORA, RICH.
I DON'T THINK IT'S A GOOD IDEA TO TAKE THE INFINITY STONE BACK INTO ENEMY TERRITORY.
SORRY.
HAD TO ASK.
THE FRATERNITY OF RAPTORS WILL GIVE UP MY BROTHER, OR I'LL SMASH THEM TO BITS AND TAKE HIM.
CATCH.
WE'LL KEEP IT SAFE.
EITHER WAY, ROBBIE'S COMING HOME WITH ME.
GROOT WISHES FRIEND-NOVA LUCK IN SMITING THE @#$@BIRDS THAT HAVE STOLEN YOUR BROTHER.

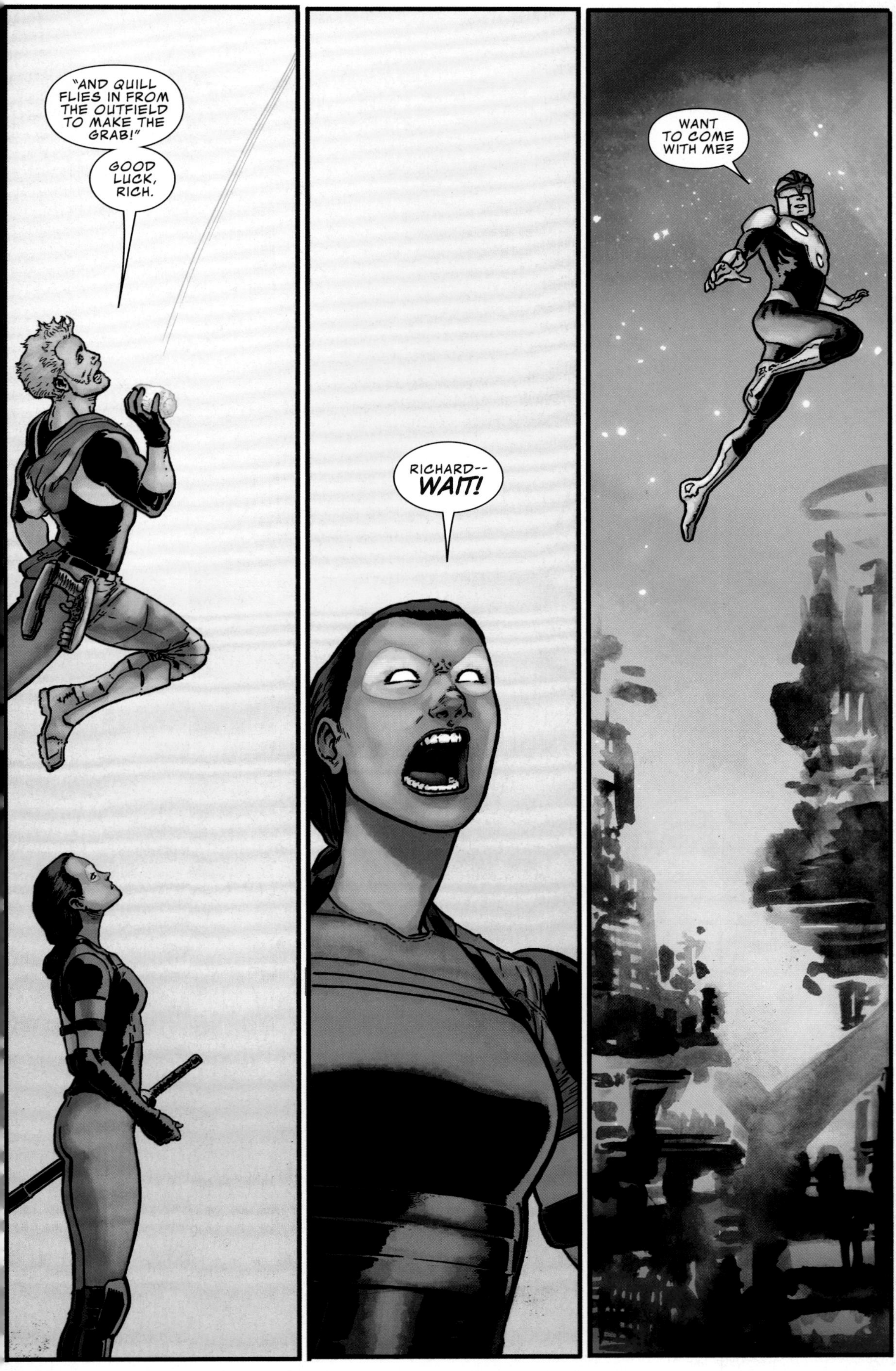
"AND QUILL FLIES IN FROM THE OUTFIELD TO MAKE THE GRAB!"
GOOD LUCK, RICH.
RICHARD-- WAIT!
WANT TO COME WITH ME?

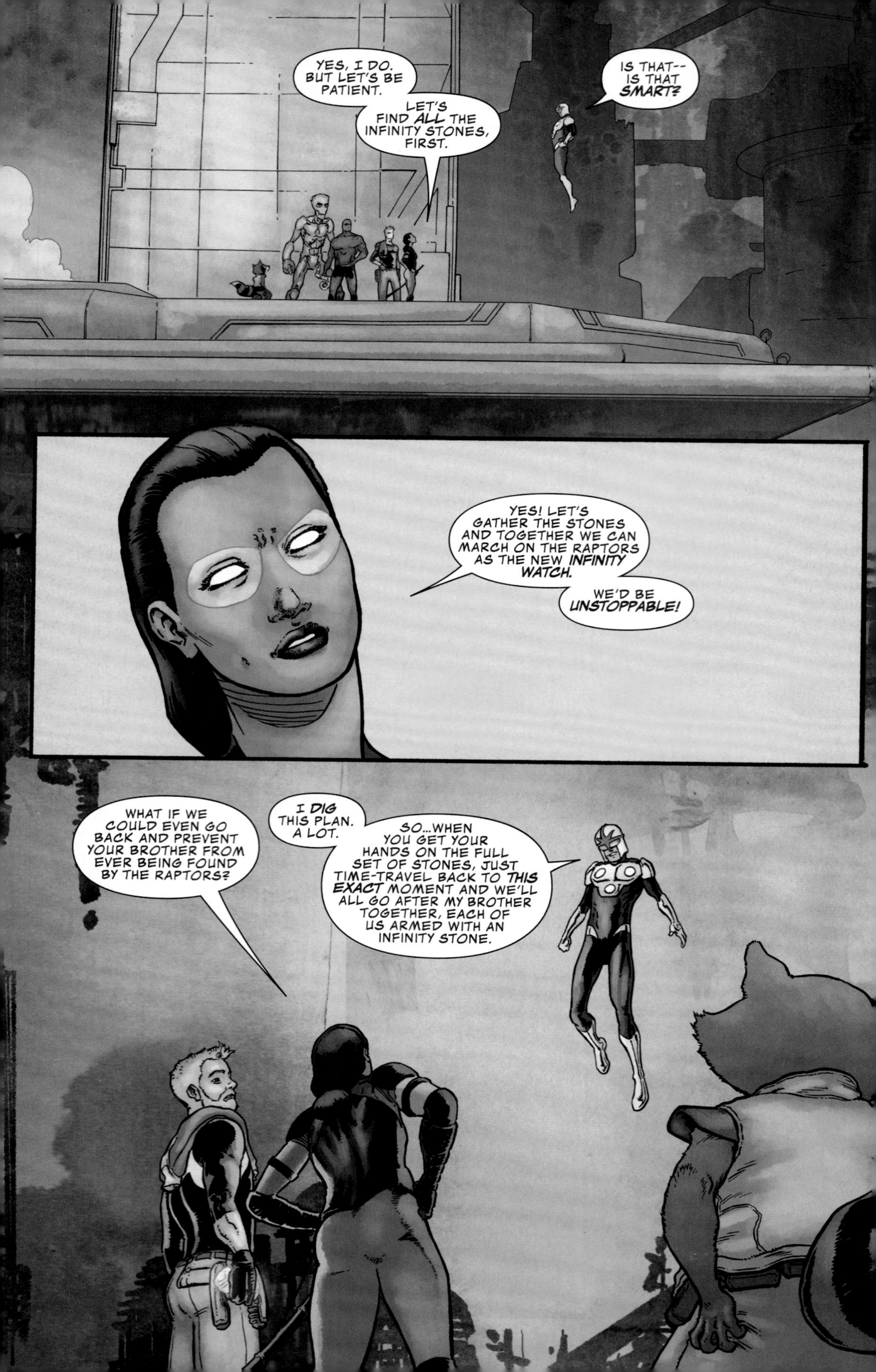
YES, I DO. BUT LET'S BE PATIENT.
LET'S FIND ALL THE INFINITY STONES, FIRST.
IS THAT-- IS THAT SMART?
YES! LET'S GATHER THE STONES AND TOGETHER WE CAN MARCH ON THE RAPTORS AS THE NEW INFINITY WATCH.
WE'D BE UNSTOPPABLE!
WHAT IF WE COULD EVEN GO BACK AND PREVENT YOUR BROTHER FROM EVER BEING FOUND BY THE RAPTORS?
I DIG THIS PLAN. A LOT.
SO...WHEN YOU GET YOUR HANDS ON THE FULL SET OF STONES, JUST TIME-TRAVEL BACK TO THIS EXACT MOMENT AND WE'LL ALL GO AFTER MY BROTHER TOGETHER, EACH OF US ARMED WITH AN INFINITY STONE.

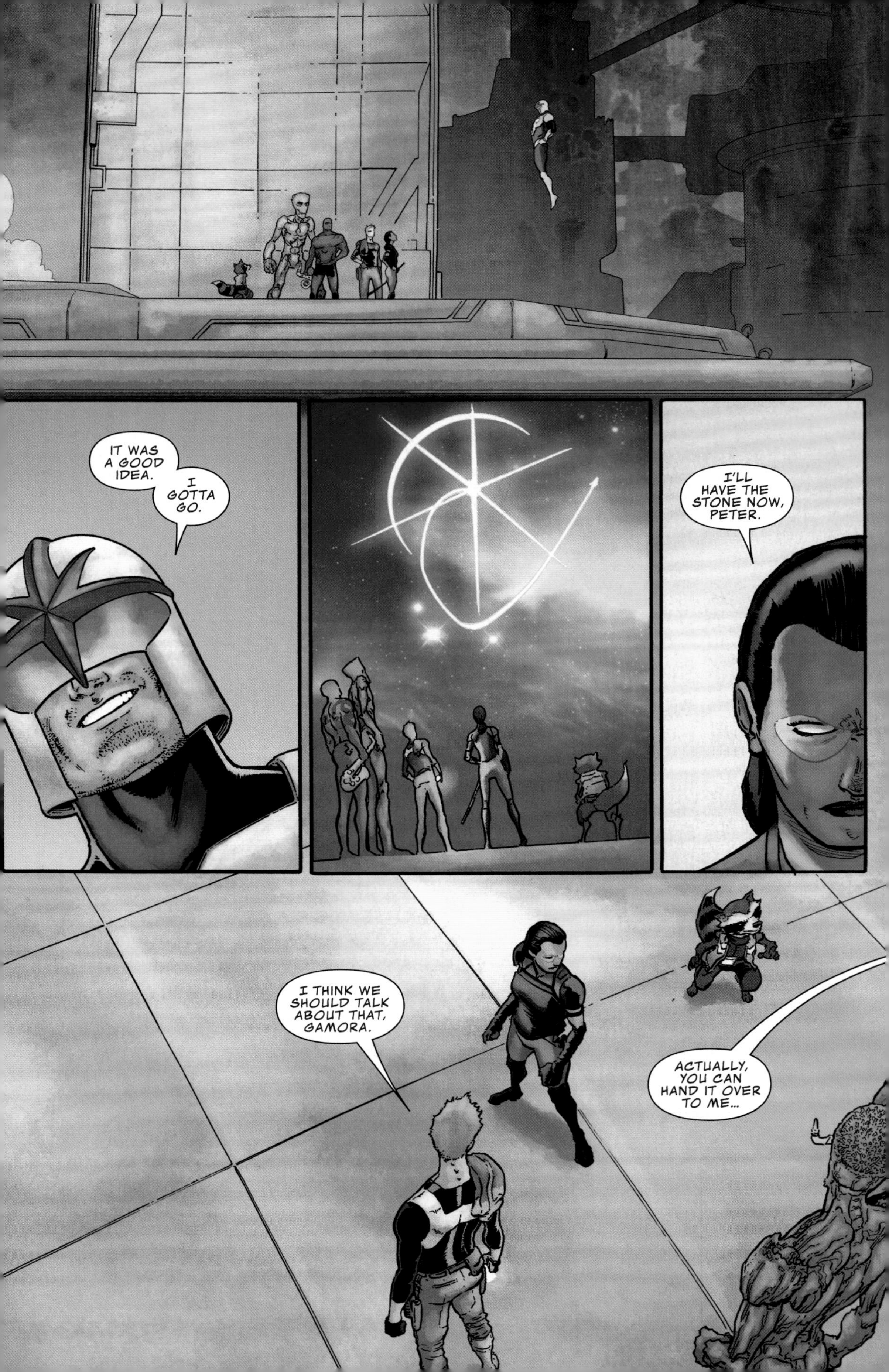
IT WAS A GOOD IDEA.
I GOTTA GO.
I'LL HAVE THE STONE NOW, PETER.
I THINK WE SHOULD TALK ABOUT THAT, GAMORA.
ACTUALLY, YOU CAN HAND IT OVER TO ME...

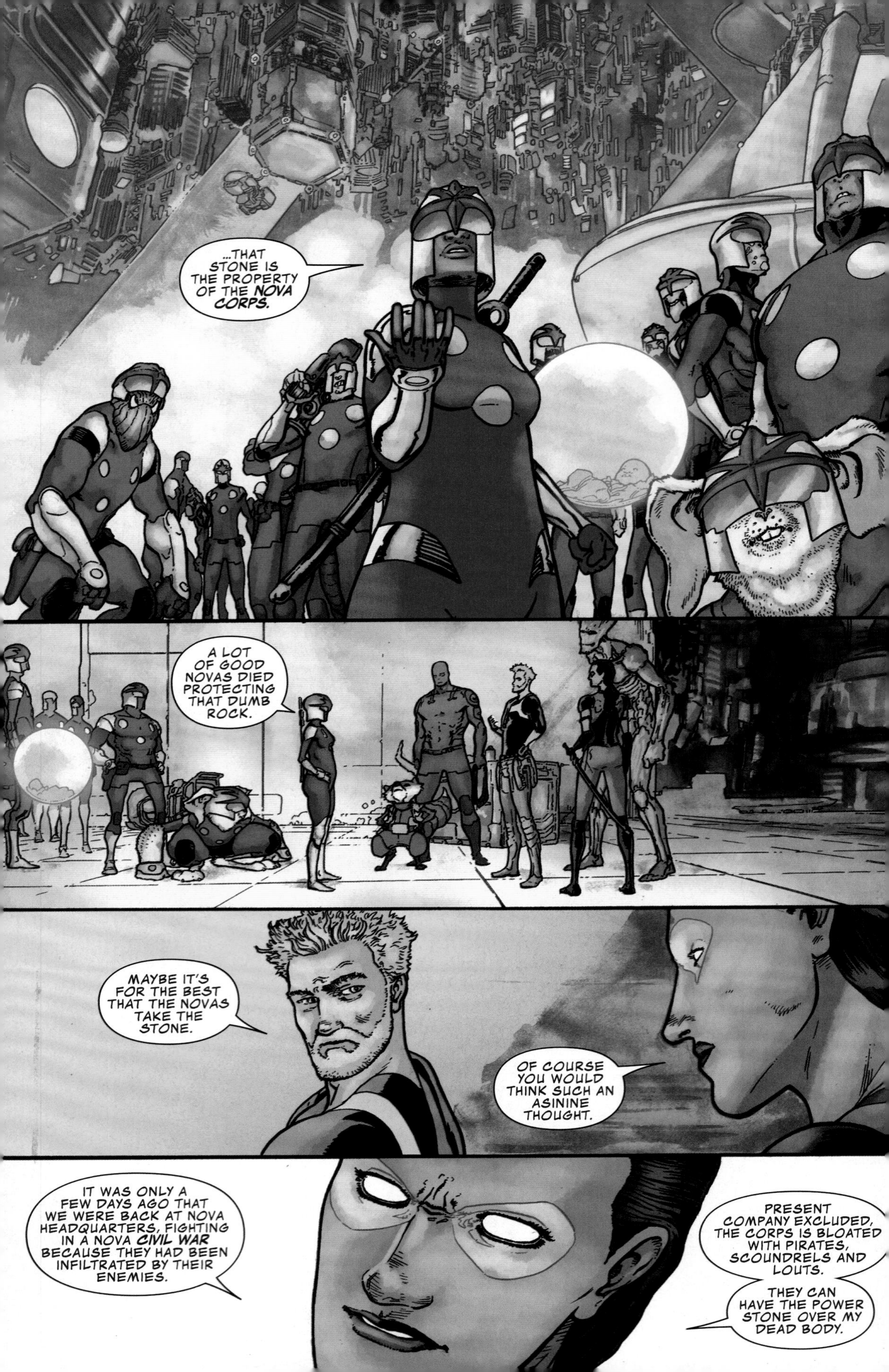
...THAT STONE IS THE PROPERTY OF THE NOVA CORPS.
A LOT OF GOOD NOVAS DIED PROTECTING THAT DUMB ROCK.
MAYBE IT'S FOR THE BEST THAT THE NOVAS TAKE THE STONE.
OF COURSE YOU WOULD THINK SUCH AN ASININE THOUGHT.
IT WAS ONLY A FEW DAYS AGO THAT WE WERE BACK AT NOVA HEADQUARTERS, FIGHTING IN A NOVA CIVIL WAR BECAUSE THEY HAD BEEN INFILTRATED BY THEIR ENEMIES.
PRESENT COMPANY EXCLUDED, THE CORPS IS BLOATED WITH PIRATES, SCOUNDRELS AND LOUTS.
THEY CAN HAVE THE POWER STONE OVER MY DEAD BODY.

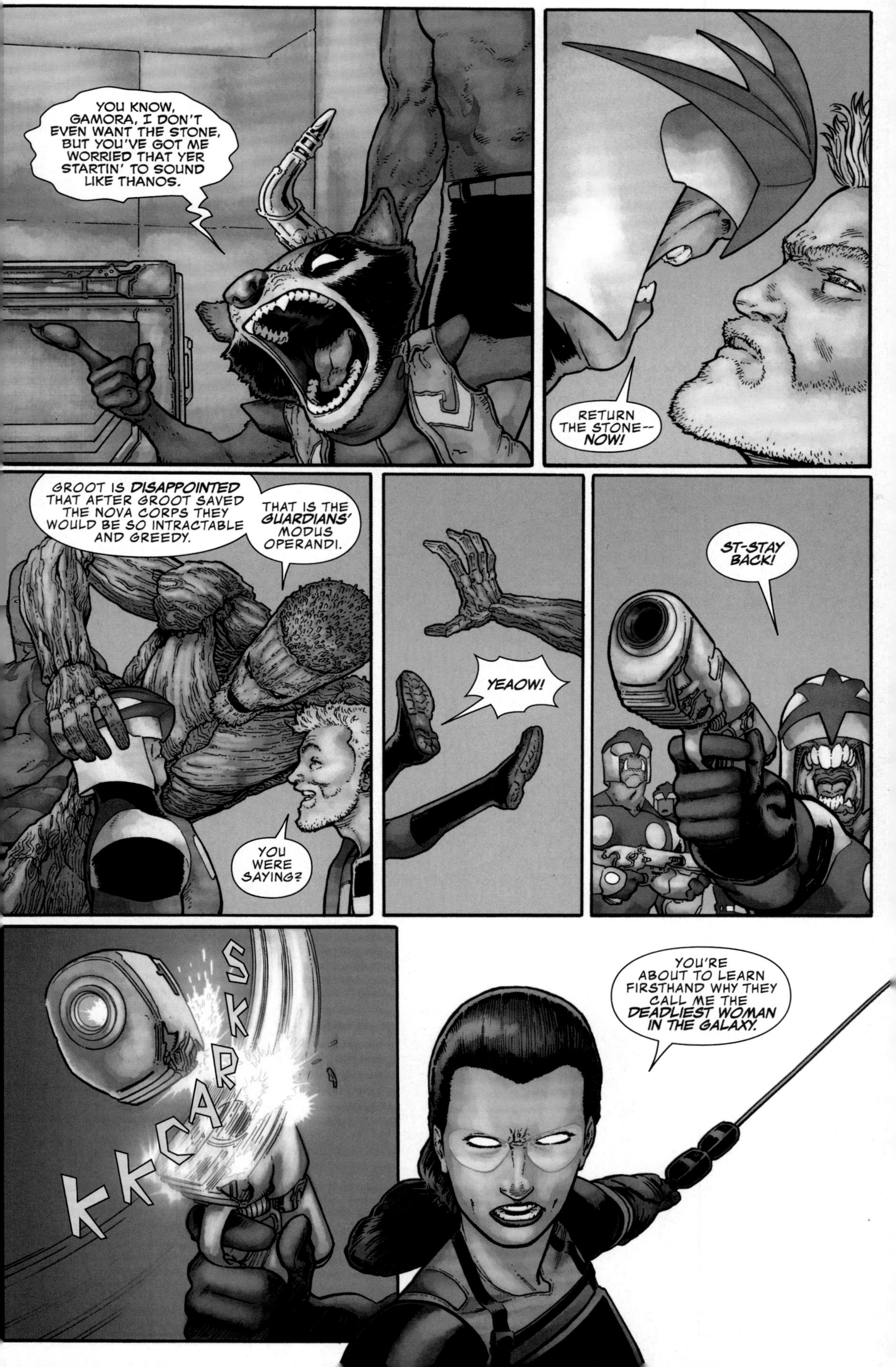
YOU KNOW, GAMORA, I DON'T EVEN WANT THE STONE, BUT YOU'VE GOT ME WORRIED THAT YER STARTIN' TO SOUND LIKE THANOS.
RETURN THE STONE-- NOW!
GROOT IS DISAPPOINTED THAT AFTER GROOT SAVED THE NOVA CORPS THEY WOULD BE SO INTRACTABLE AND GREEDY.
THAT IS THE GUARDIANS' MODUS OPERANDI.
YOU WERE SAYING?
YEAOW!
ST-STAY BACK!
SKRAKKCA
YOU'RE ABOUT TO LEARN FIRSTHAND WHY THEY CALL ME THE DEADLIEST WOMAN IN THE GALAXY.

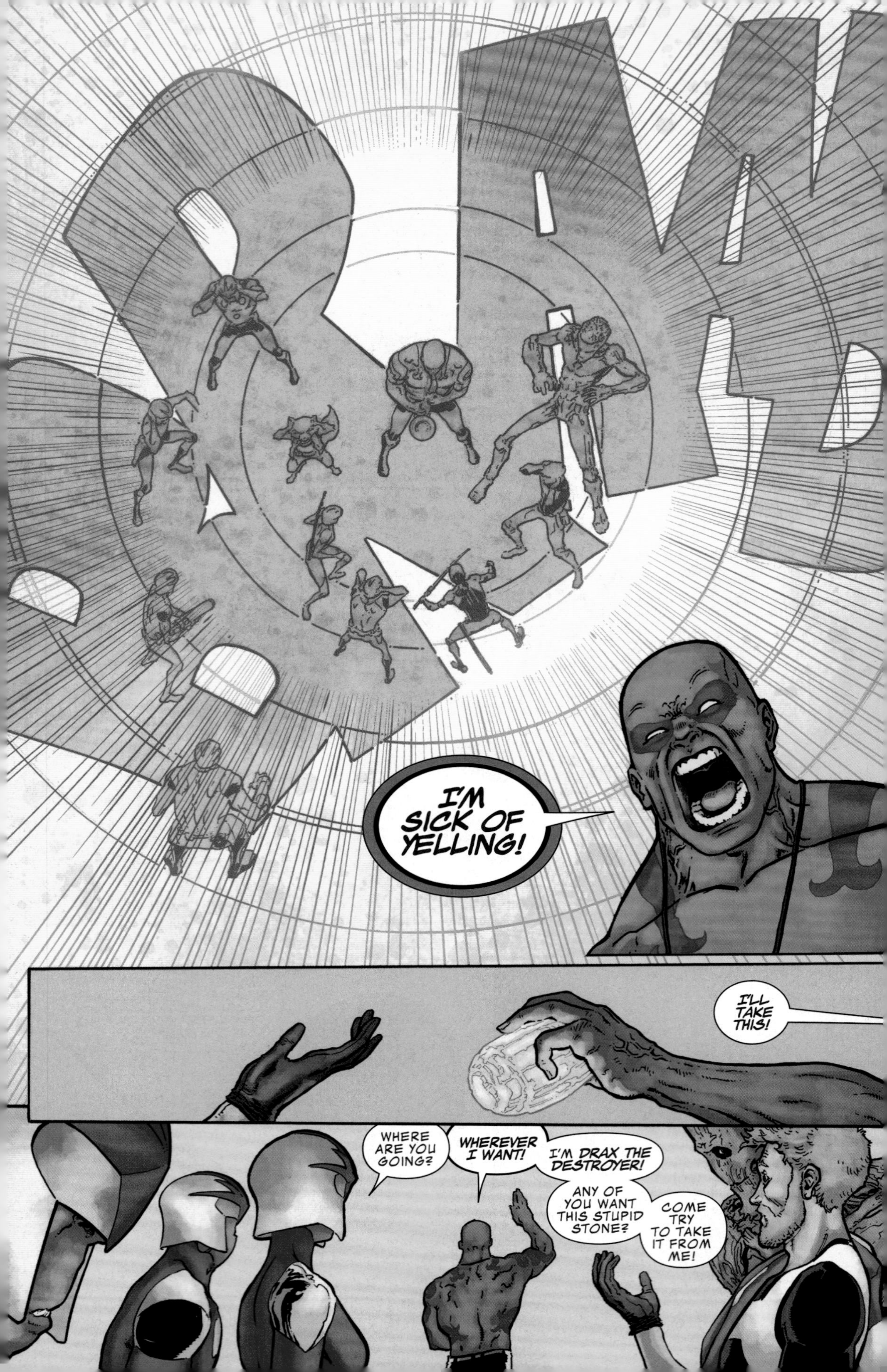

I'M SICK OF YELLING!
I'LL TAKE THIS!
WHERE ARE YOU GOING?
WHEREVER I WANT!
I'M DRAX THE DESTROYER!
ANY OF YOU WANT THIS STUPID STONE?
COME TRY TO TAKE IT FROM ME!

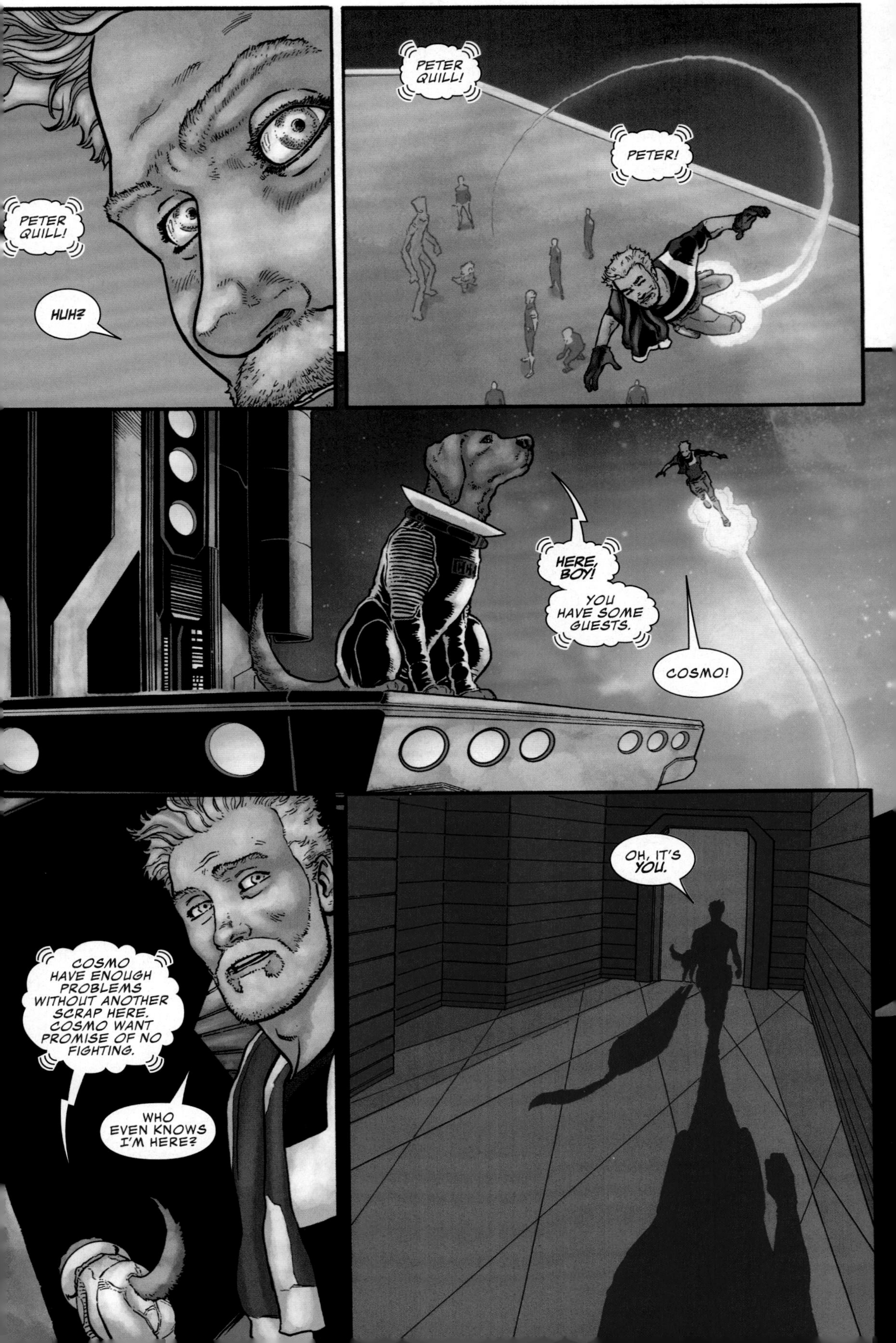
PETER QUILL!
HUH?
PETER QUILL!
PETER!
HERE, BOY!
YOU HAVE SOME GUESTS.
COSMO!
COSMO HAVE ENOUGH PROBLEMS WITHOUT ANOTHER SCRAP HERE. COSMO WANT PROMISE OF NO FIGHTING.
WHO EVEN KNOWS I'M HERE?
OH, IT'S YOU.

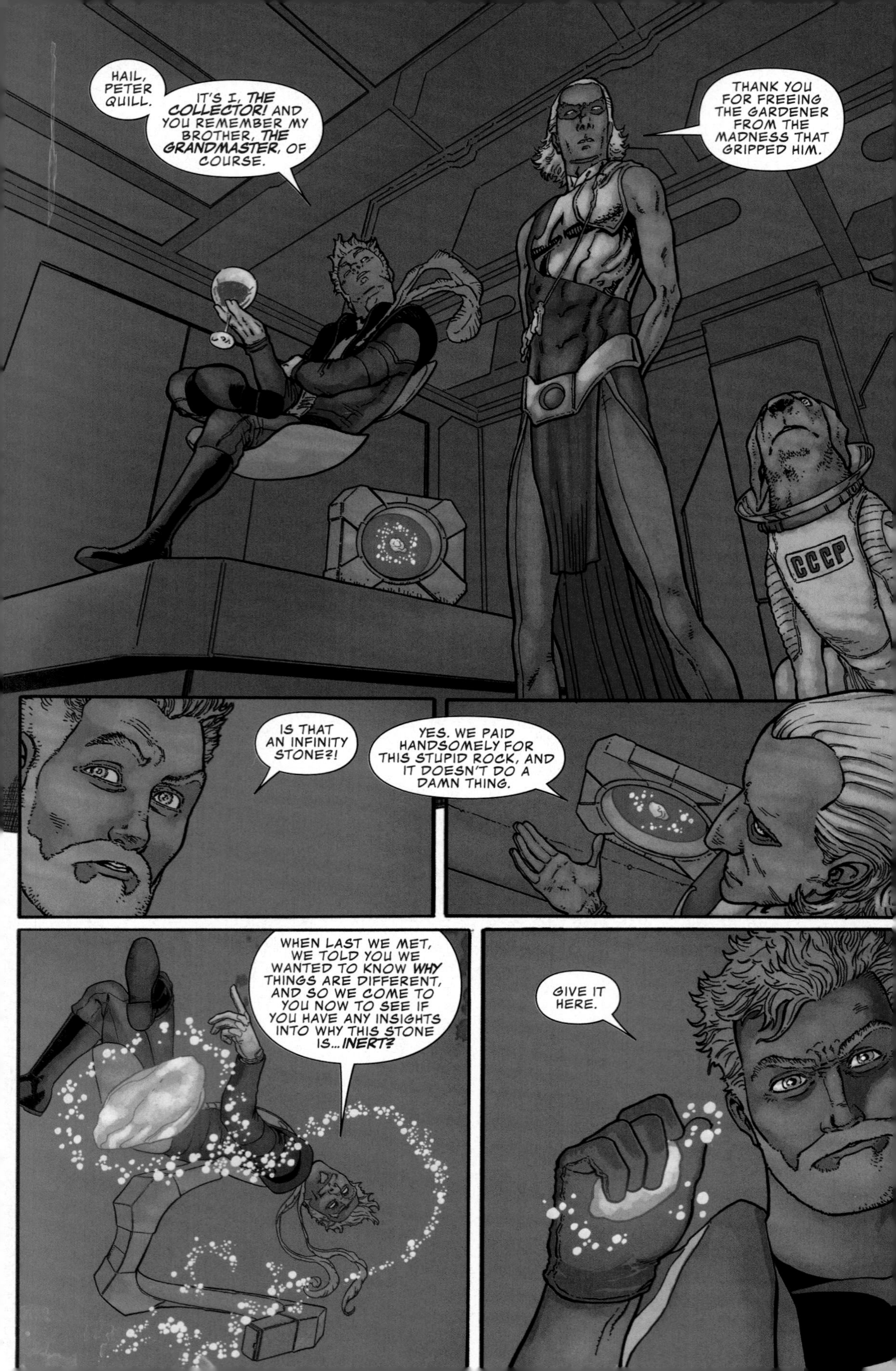

HAIL, PETER QUILL.
IT'S I, THE COLLECTOR! AND YOU REMEMBER MY BROTHER, THE GRANDMASTER, OF COURSE.
THANK YOU FOR FREEING THE GARDENER FROM THE MADNESS THAT GRIPPED HIM.
CCCP
IS THAT AN INFINITY STONE?!
YES. WE PAID HANDSOMELY FOR THIS STUPID ROCK, AND IT DOESN'T DO A DAMN THING.
WHEN LAST WE MET, WE TOLD YOU WE WANTED TO KNOW WHY THINGS ARE DIFFERENT, AND SO WE COME TO YOU NOW TO SEE IF YOU HAVE ANY INSIGHTS INTO WHY THIS STONE IS...INERT?
GIVE IT HERE.

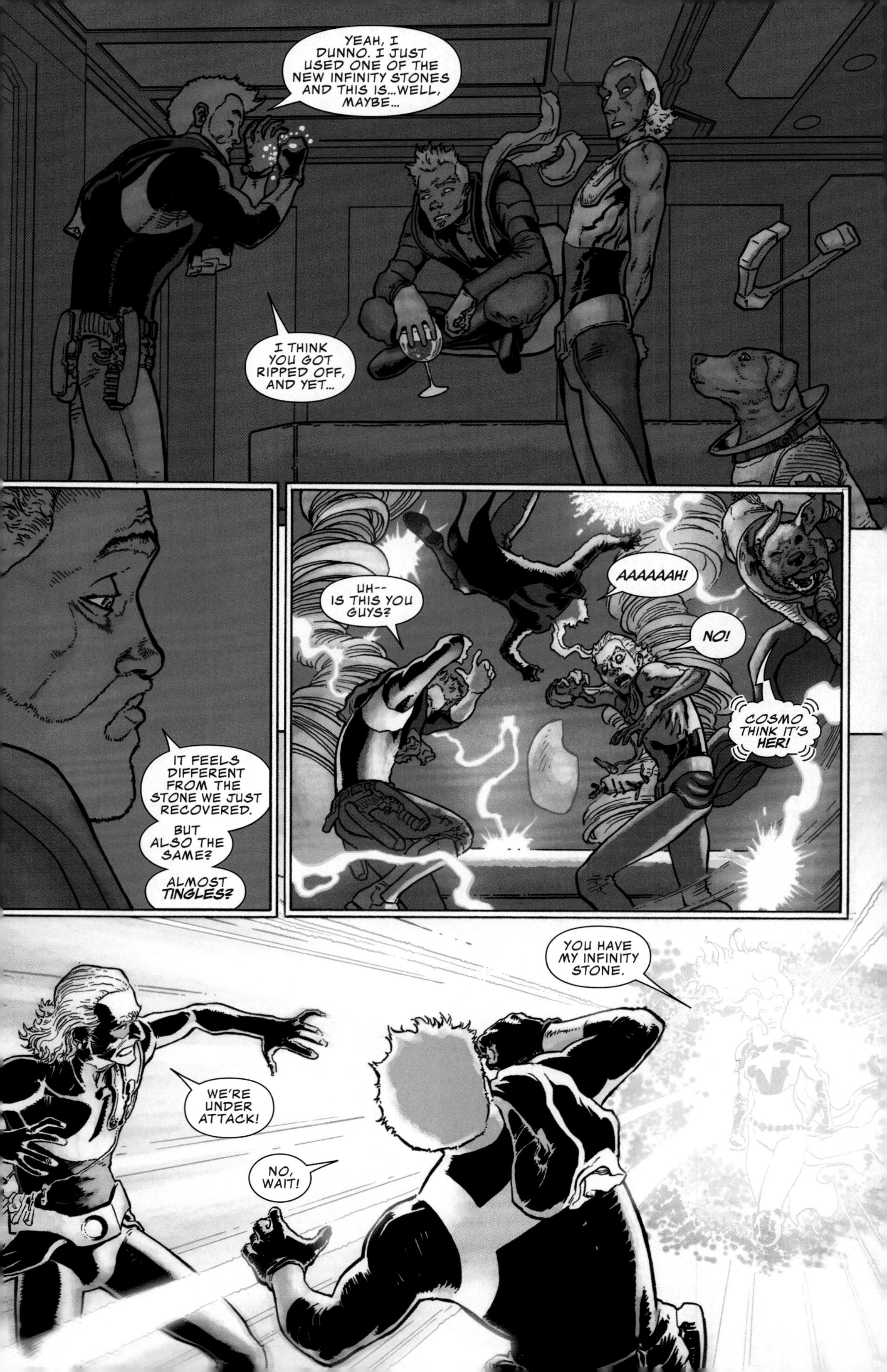
YEAH, I DUNNO. I JUST USED ONE OF THE NEW INFINITY STONES AND THIS IS...WELL, MAYBE...
I THINK YOU GOT RIPPED OFF, AND YET...
IT FEELS DIFFERENT FROM THE STONE WE JUST RECOVERED.
BUT ALSO THE SAME?
ALMOST TINGLES?
UH-- IS THIS YOU GUYS?
AAAAAAH!
NO!
COSMO THINK IT'S HER!
YOU HAVE MY INFINITY STONE.
WE'RE UNDER ATTACK!
NO, WAIT!

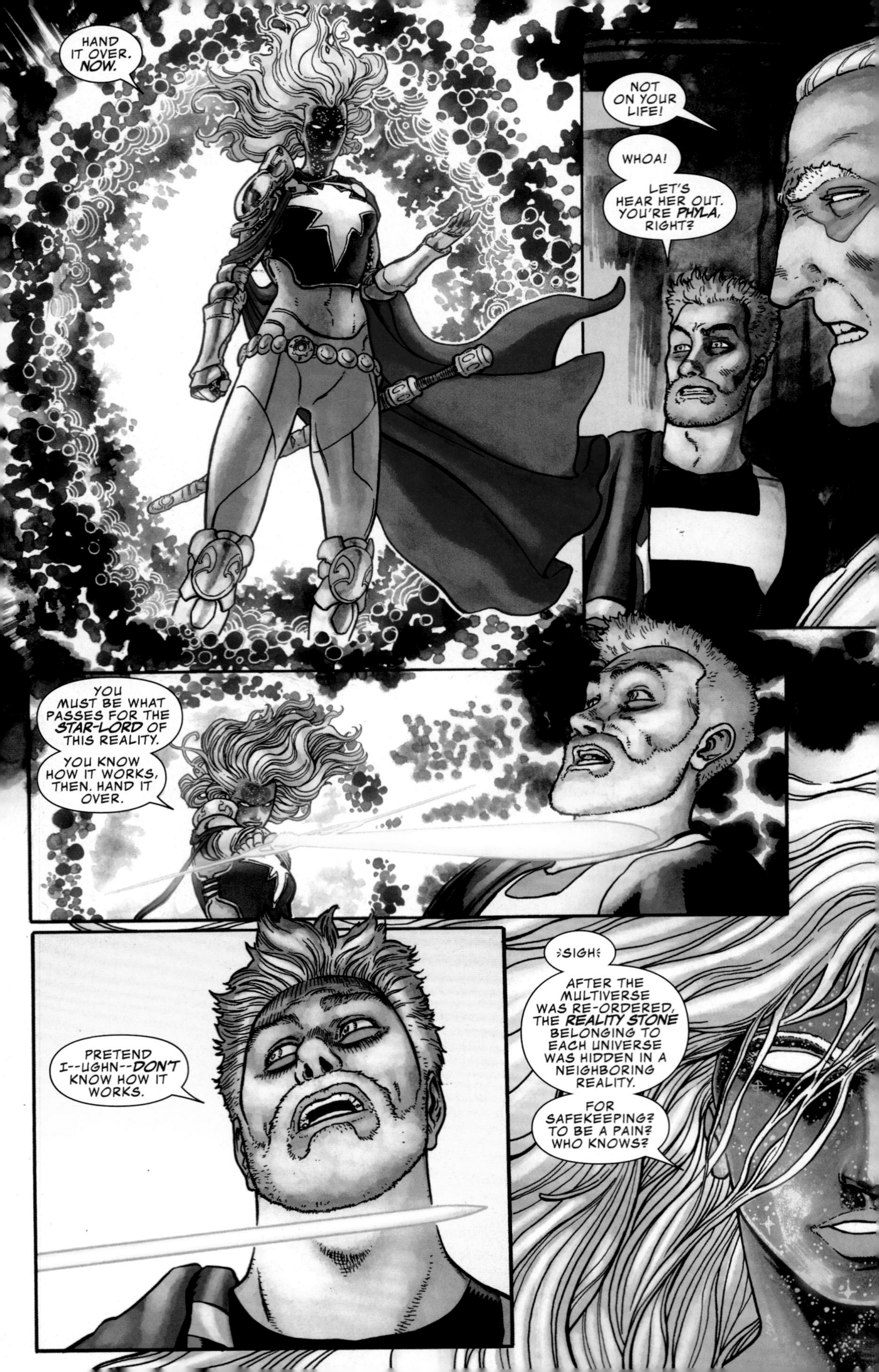
HAND IT OVER. NOW.
NOT ON YOUR LIFE!
WHOA!
LET'S HEAR HER OUT. YOU'RE PHYLA, RIGHT?
YOU MUST BE WHAT PASSES FOR THE STAR-LORD OF THIS REALITY.
YOU KNOW HOW IT WORKS, THEN. HAND IT OVER.
PRETEND I--UGHN--DON'T KNOW HOW IT WORKS.
SIGH
AFTER THE MULTIVERSE WAS RE-ORDERED, THE REALITY STONE BELONGING TO EACH UNIVERSE WAS HIDDEN IN A NEIGHBORING REALITY.
FOR SAFEKEEPING? TO BE A PAIN? WHO KNOWS?

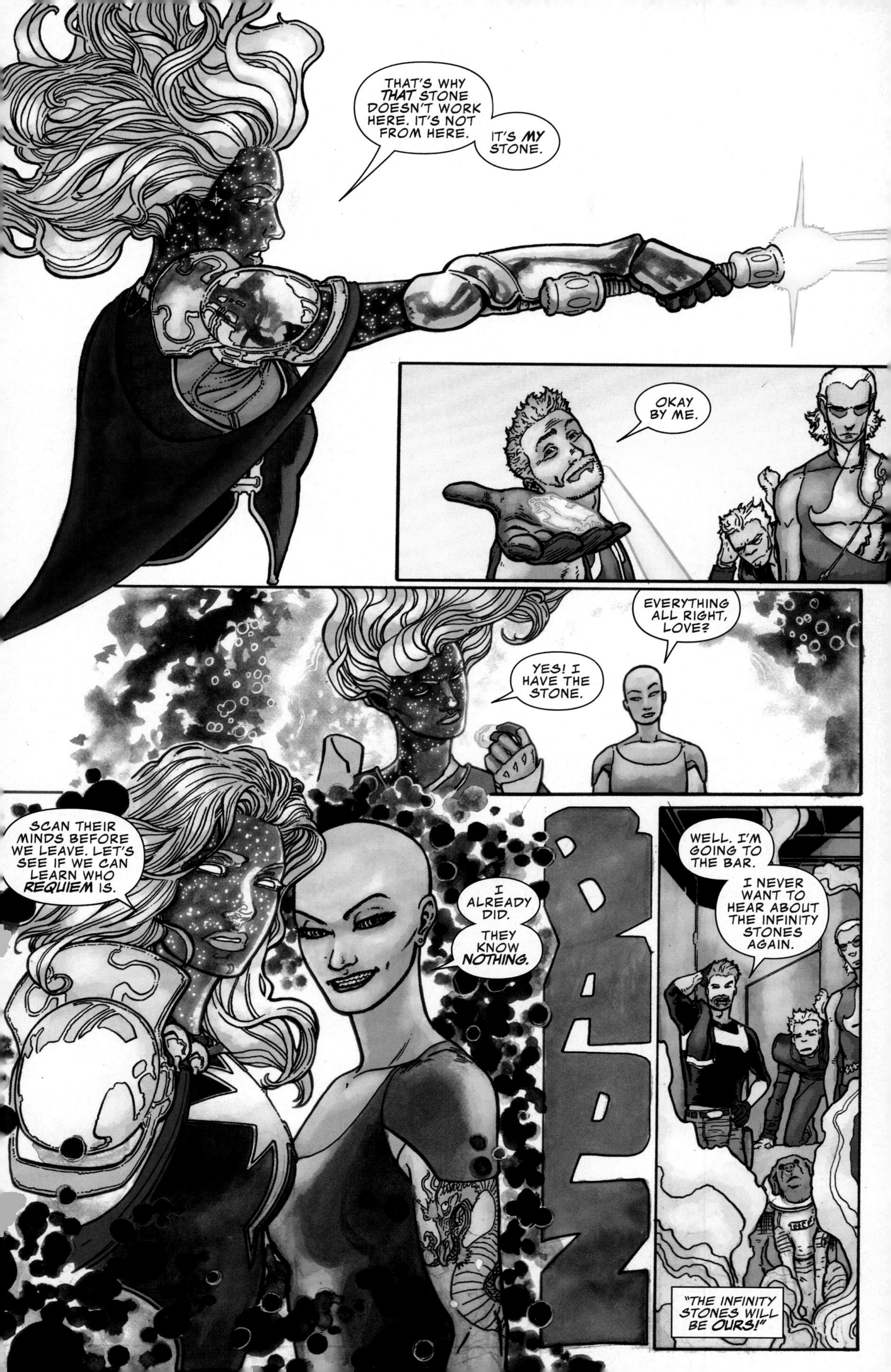
THAT'S WHY THAT STONE DOESN'T WORK HERE. IT'S NOT FROM HERE.
IT'S MY STONE.
OKAY BY ME.
EVERYTHING ALL RIGHT, LOVE?
YES! I HAVE THE STONE.
SCAN THEIR MINDS BEFORE WE LEAVE. LET'S SEE IF WE CAN LEARN WHO REQUIEM IS.
I ALREADY DID.
THEY KNOW NOTHING.
BAMF
WELL. I'M GOING TO THE BAR.
I NEVER WANT TO HEAR ABOUT THE INFINITY STONES AGAIN.
"THE INFINITY STONES WILL BE OURS!"

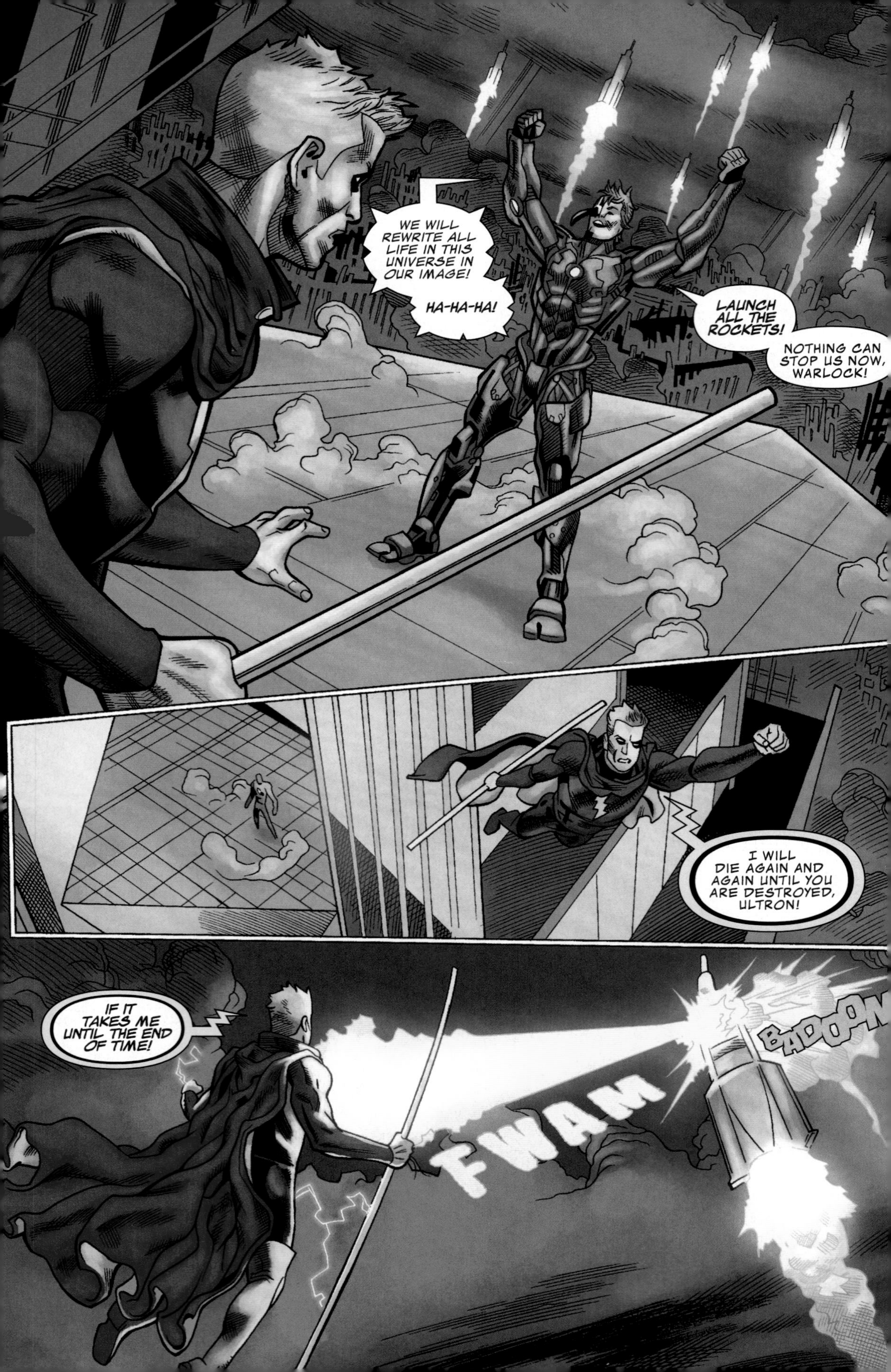
WE WILL REWRITE ALL LIFE IN THIS UNIVERSE IN OUR IMAGE!
HA-HA-HA!
LAUNCH ALL THE ROCKETS!
NOTHING CAN STOP US NOW, WARLOCK!
I WILL DIE AGAIN AND AGAIN UNTIL YOU ARE DESTROYED, ULTRON!
IF IT TAKES ME UNTIL THE END OF TIME!
FWAM
BADOOM

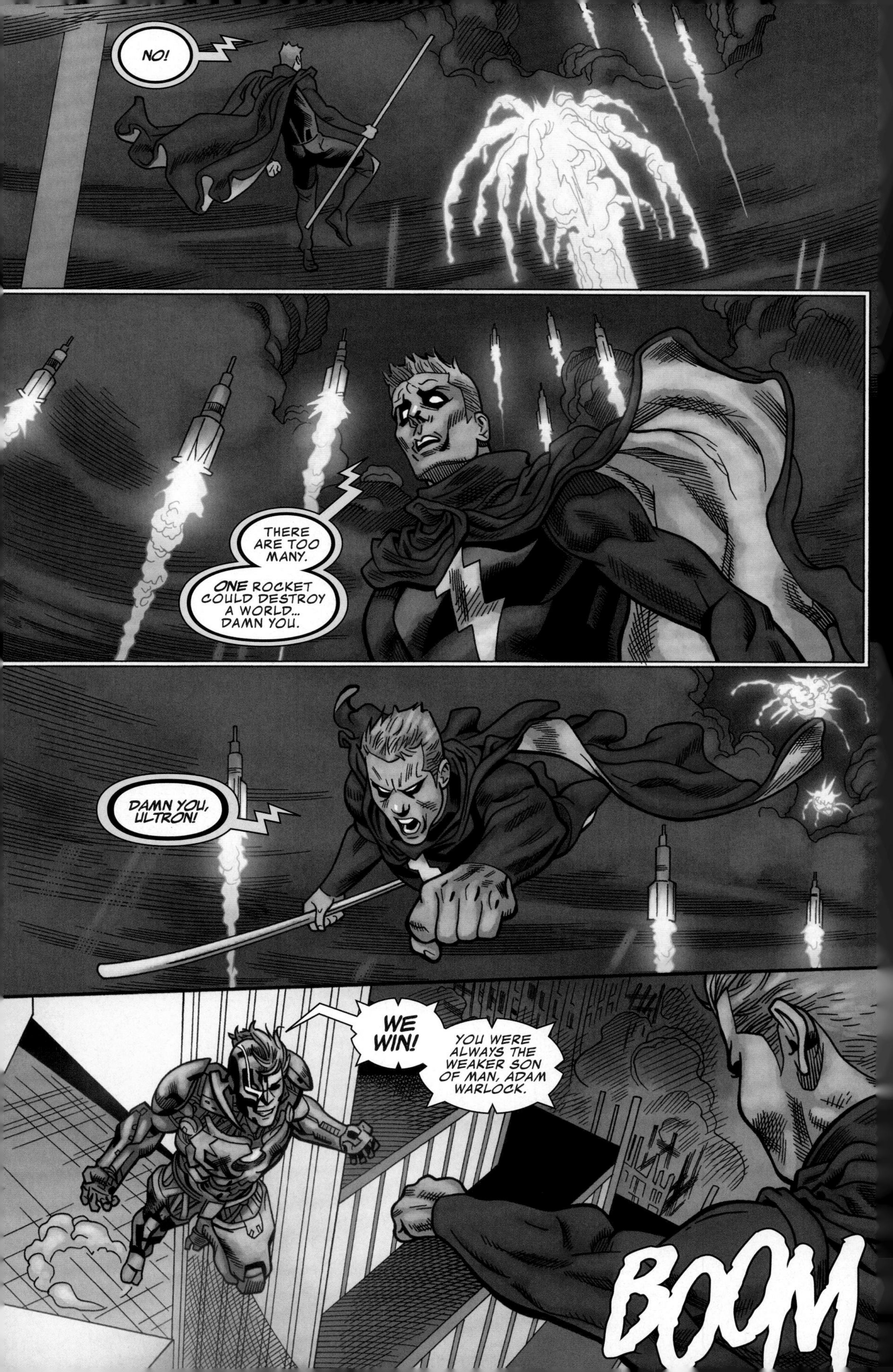
NO!
THERE ARE TOO MANY.
ONE ROCKET COULD DESTROY A WORLD... DAMN YOU.
DAMN YOU, ULTRON!
WE WIN!
YOU WERE ALWAYS THE WEAKER SON OF MAN, ADAM WARLOCK.
BOOM

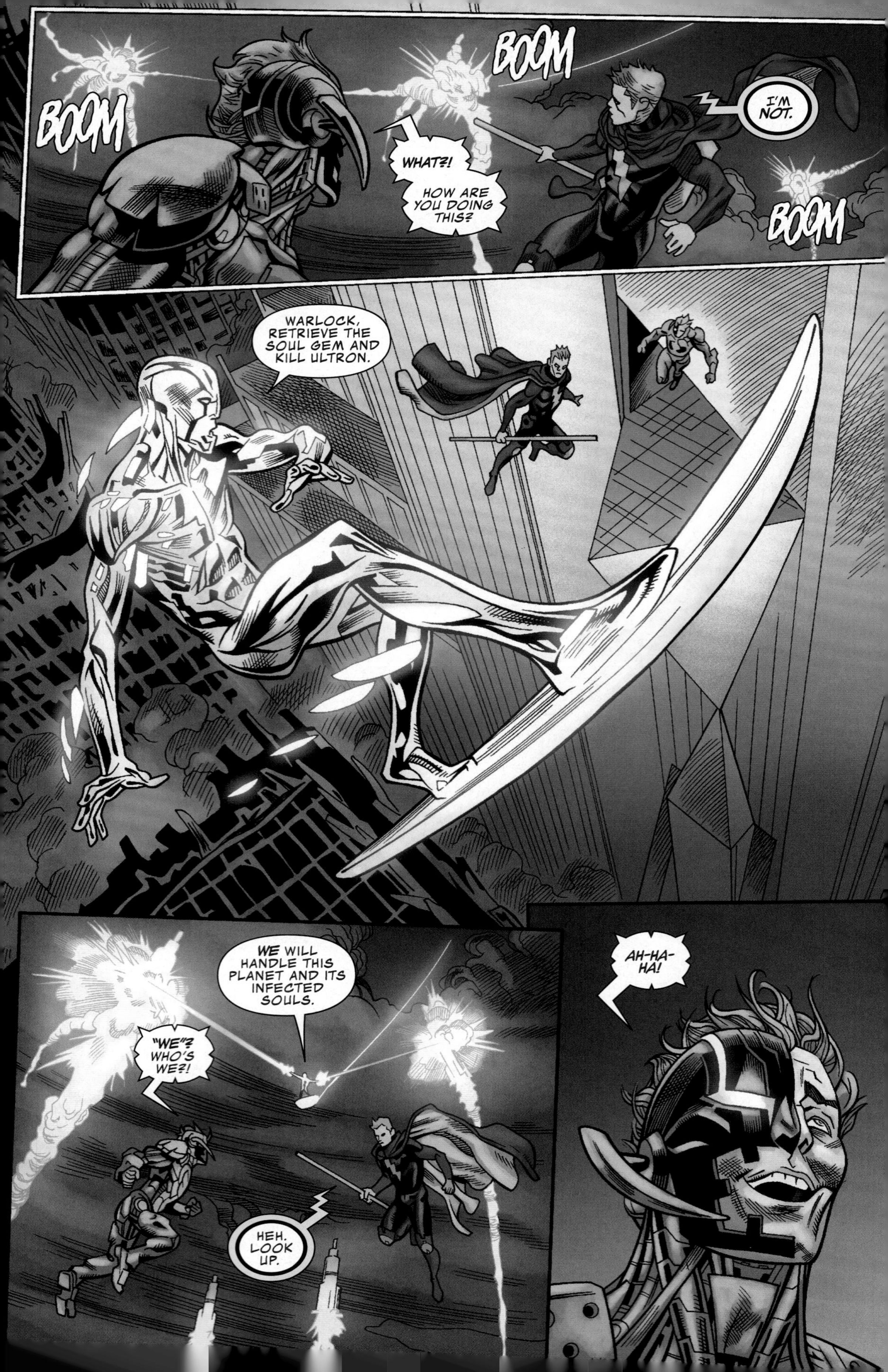
BOOM
BOOM
WHAT?! HOW ARE YOU DOING THIS?
I'M NOT.
BOOM
WARLOCK, RETRIEVE THE SOUL GEM AND KILL ULTRON.
WE WILL HANDLE THIS PLANET AND ITS INFECTED SOULS.
"WE"? WHO'S WE?!
HEH. LOOK UP.
AH-HA-HA!

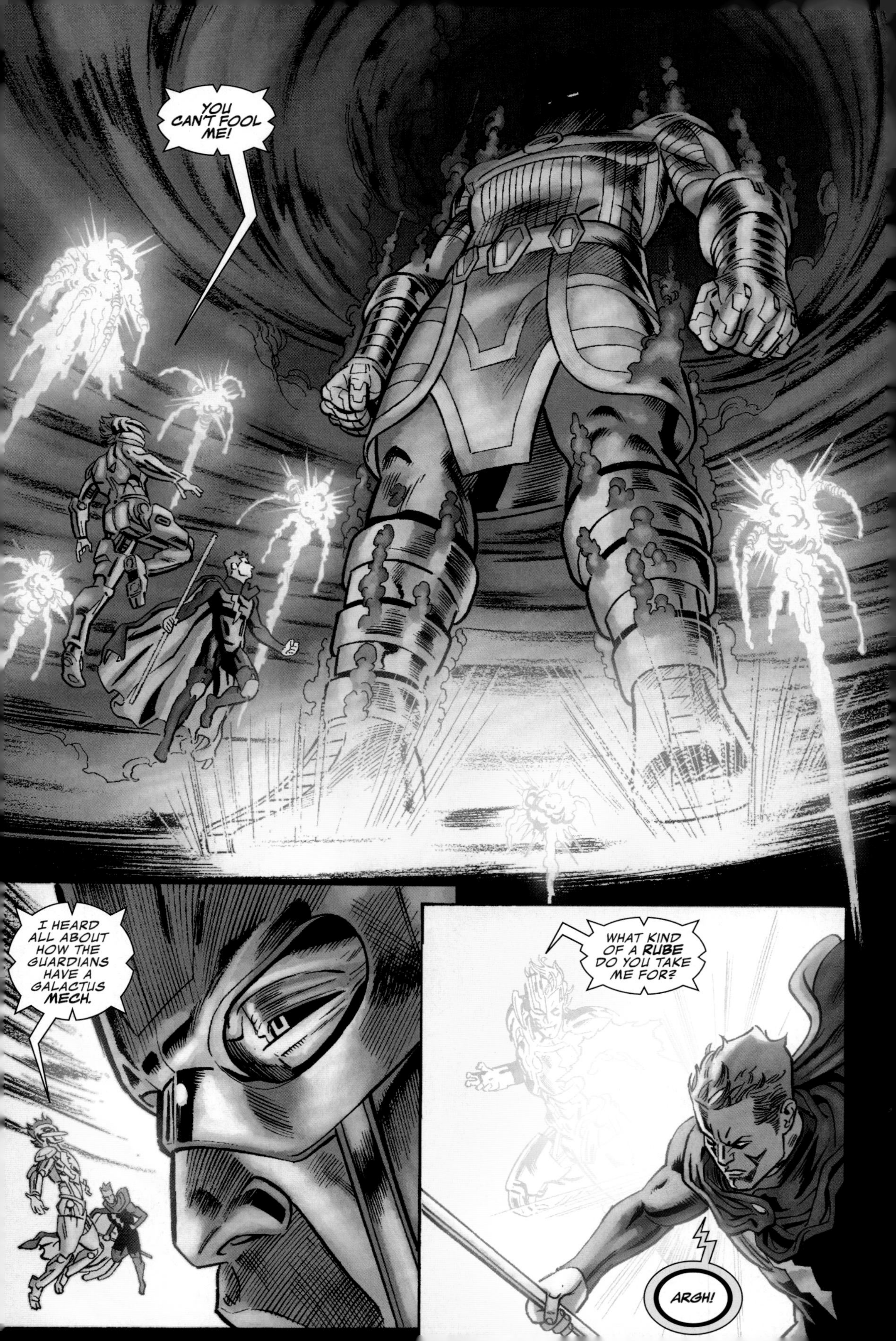
YOU CAN'T FOOL ME!
I HEARD ALL ABOUT HOW THE GUARDIANS HAVE A GALACTUS MECH.
WHAT KIND OF A RUBE DO YOU TAKE ME FOR?
ARGH!

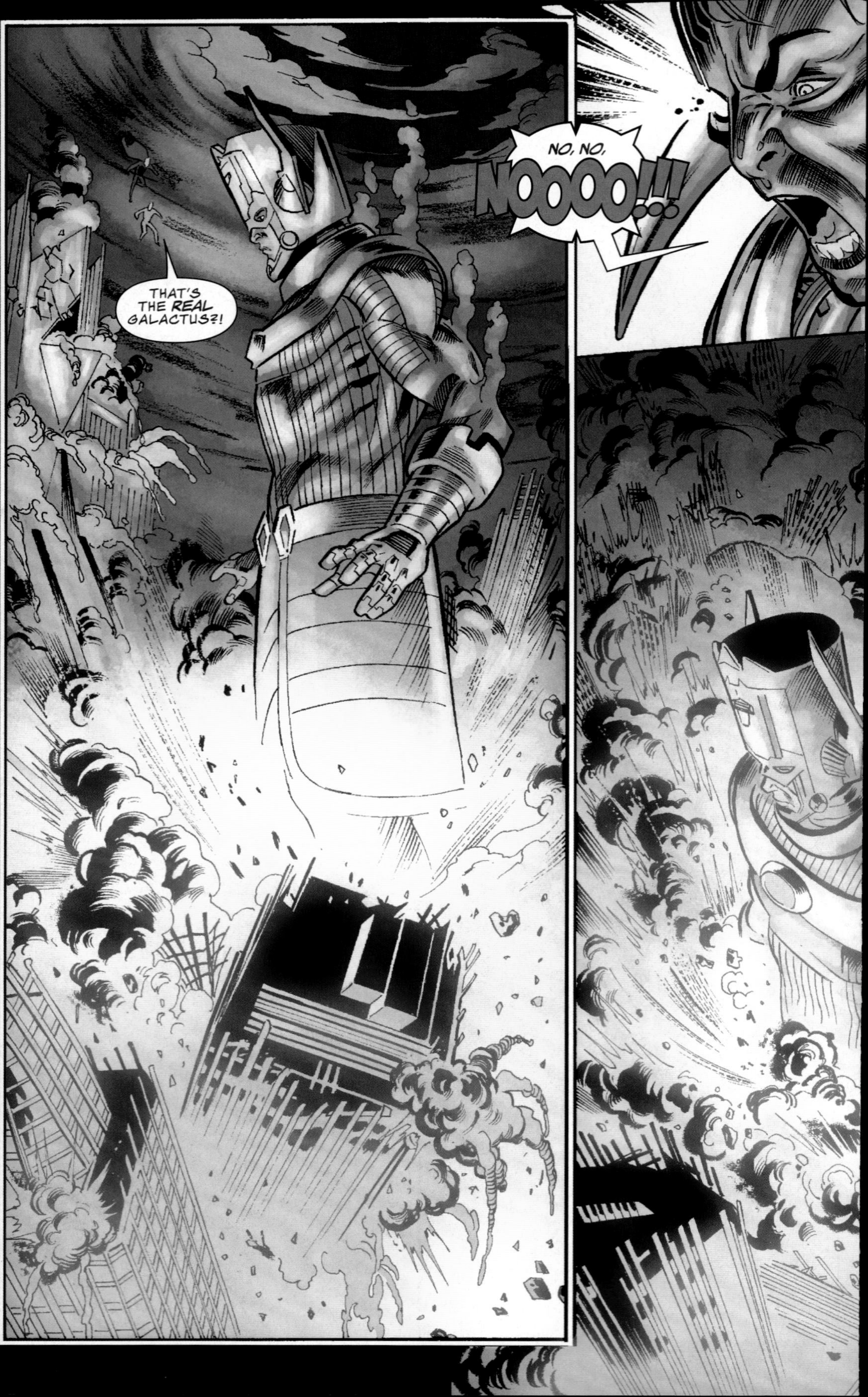
THAT'S THE REAL GALACTUS?!
NO, NO, NOOOO!!!

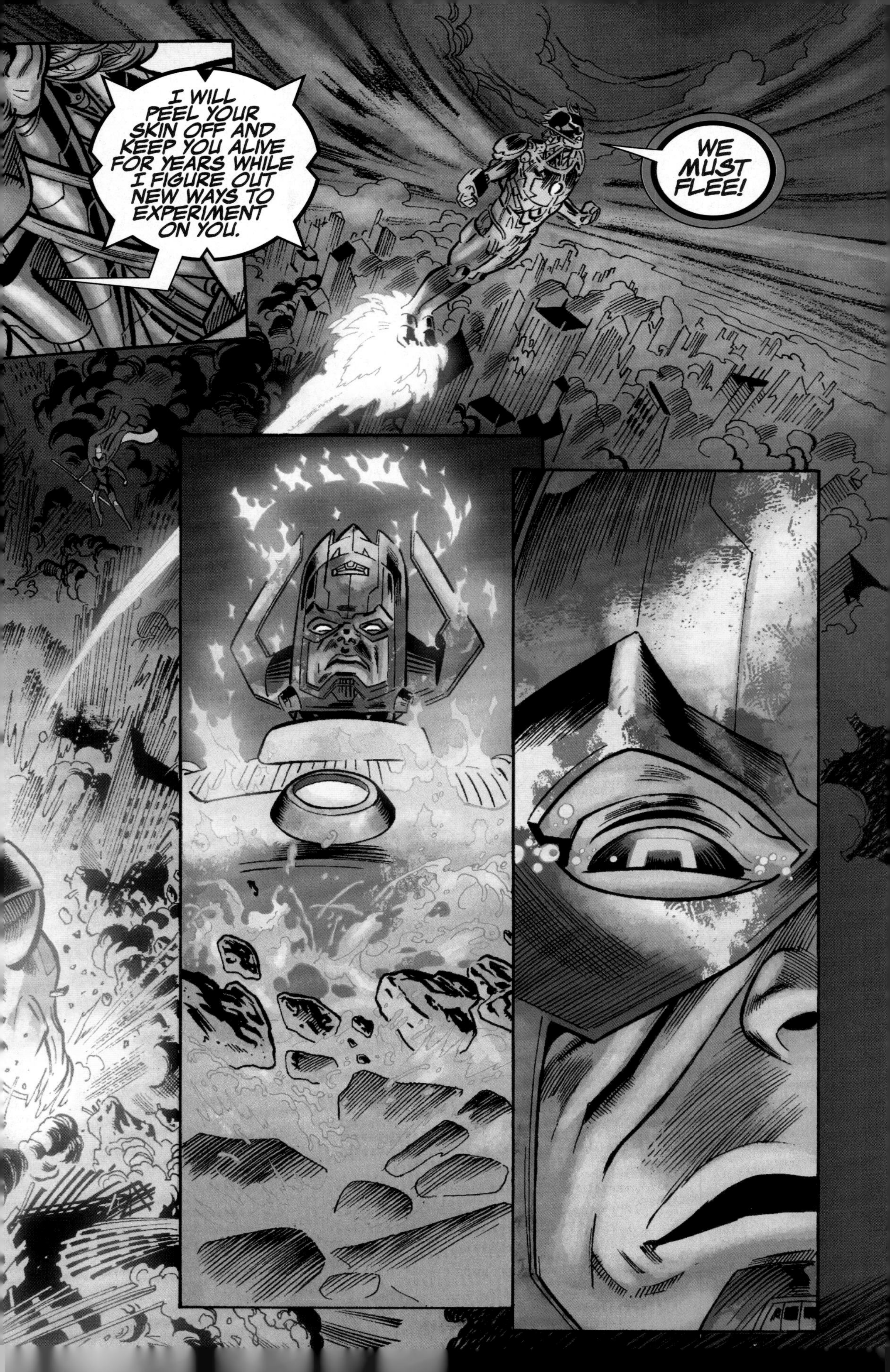
I WILL PEEL YOUR SKIN OFF AND KEEP YOU ALIVE FOR YEARS WHILE I FIGURE OUT NEW WAYS TO EXPERIMENT ON YOU.
WE MUST FLEE!

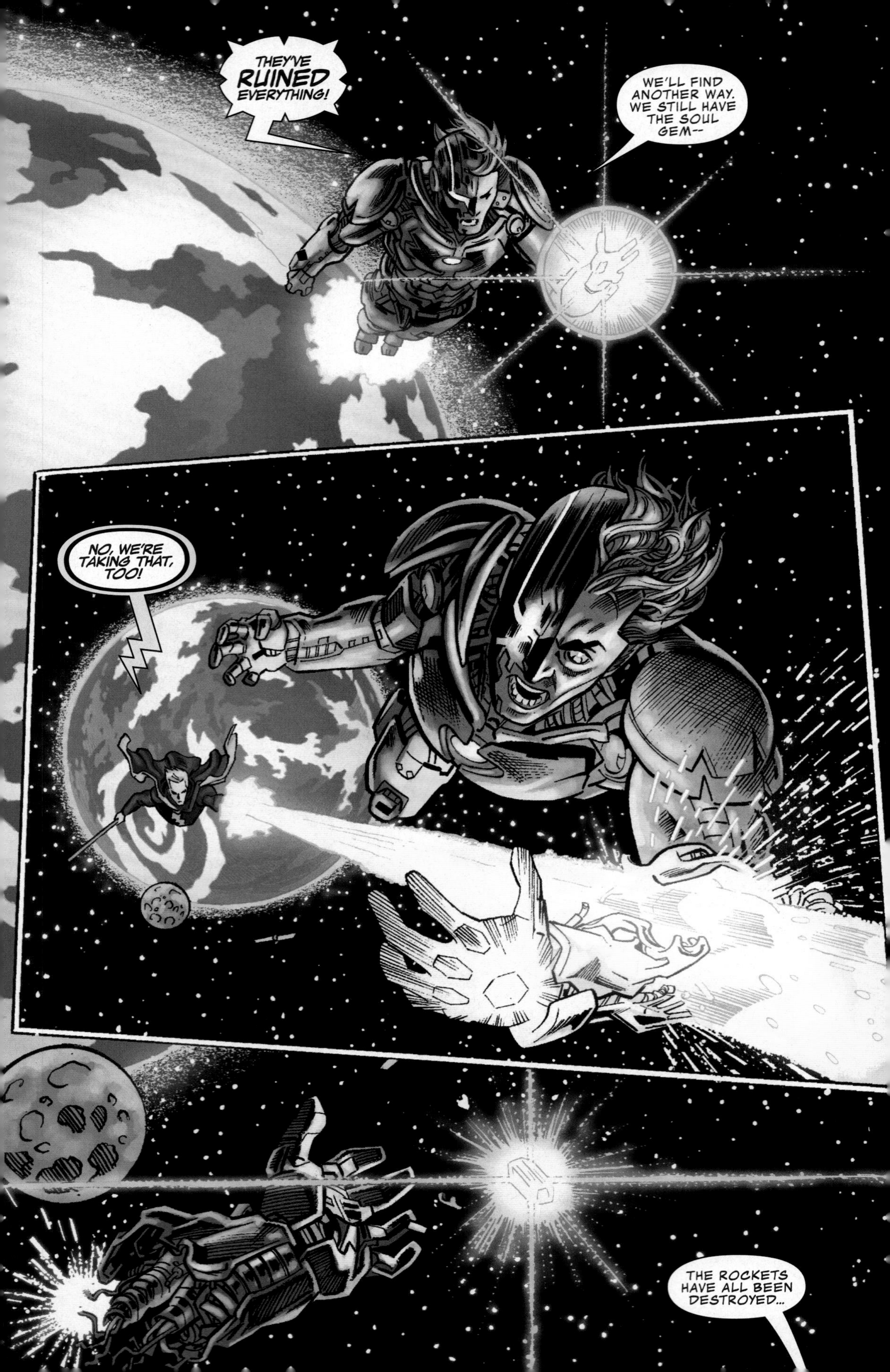
THEY'VE RUINED EVERYTHING!
WE'LL FIND ANOTHER WAY. WE STILL HAVE THE SOUL GEM--
NO, WE'RE TAKING THAT, TOO!
THE ROCKETS HAVE ALL BEEN DESTROYED...

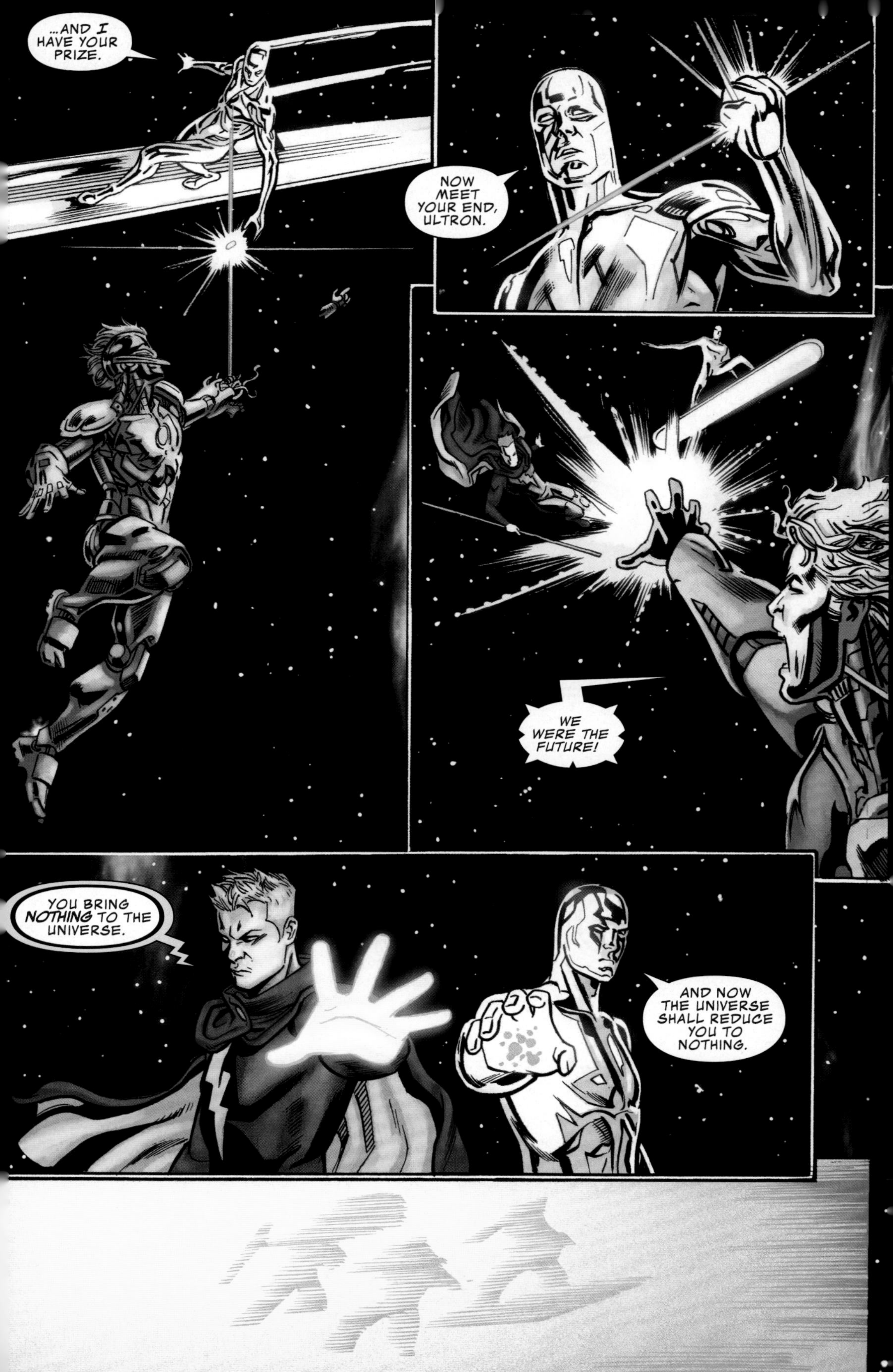
...AND I HAVE YOUR PRIZE.
NOW MEET YOUR END, ULTRON.
WE WERE THE FUTURE!
YOU BRING *NOTHING* TO THE UNIVERSE.
AND NOW THE UNIVERSE SHALL REDUCE YOU TO NOTHING.

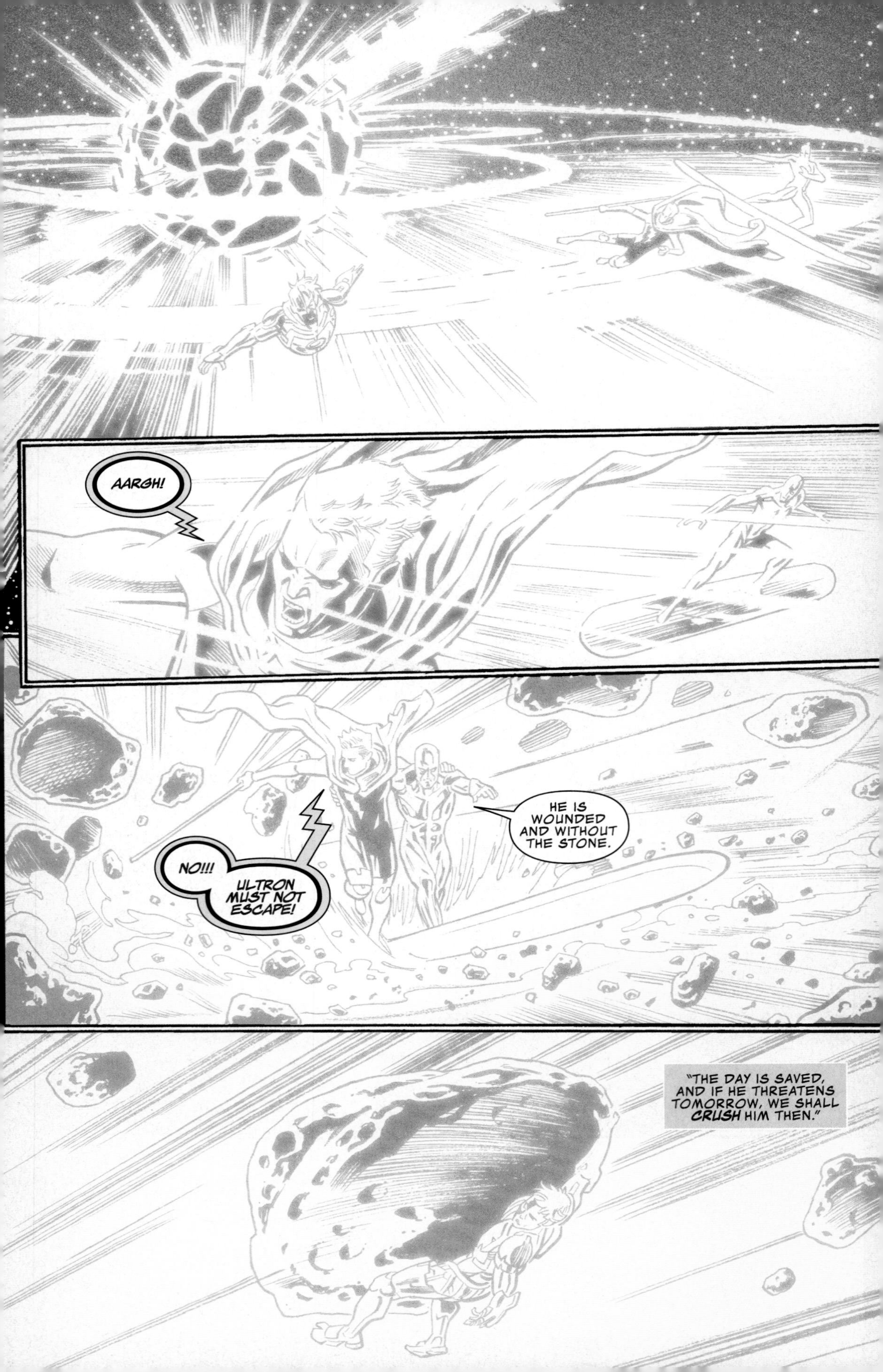
AARGH!
HE IS WOUNDED AND WITHOUT THE STONE.
NO!!! ULTRON MUST NOT ESCAPE!
"THE DAY IS SAVED, AND IF HE THREATENS TOMORROW, WE SHALL CRUSH HIM THEN."

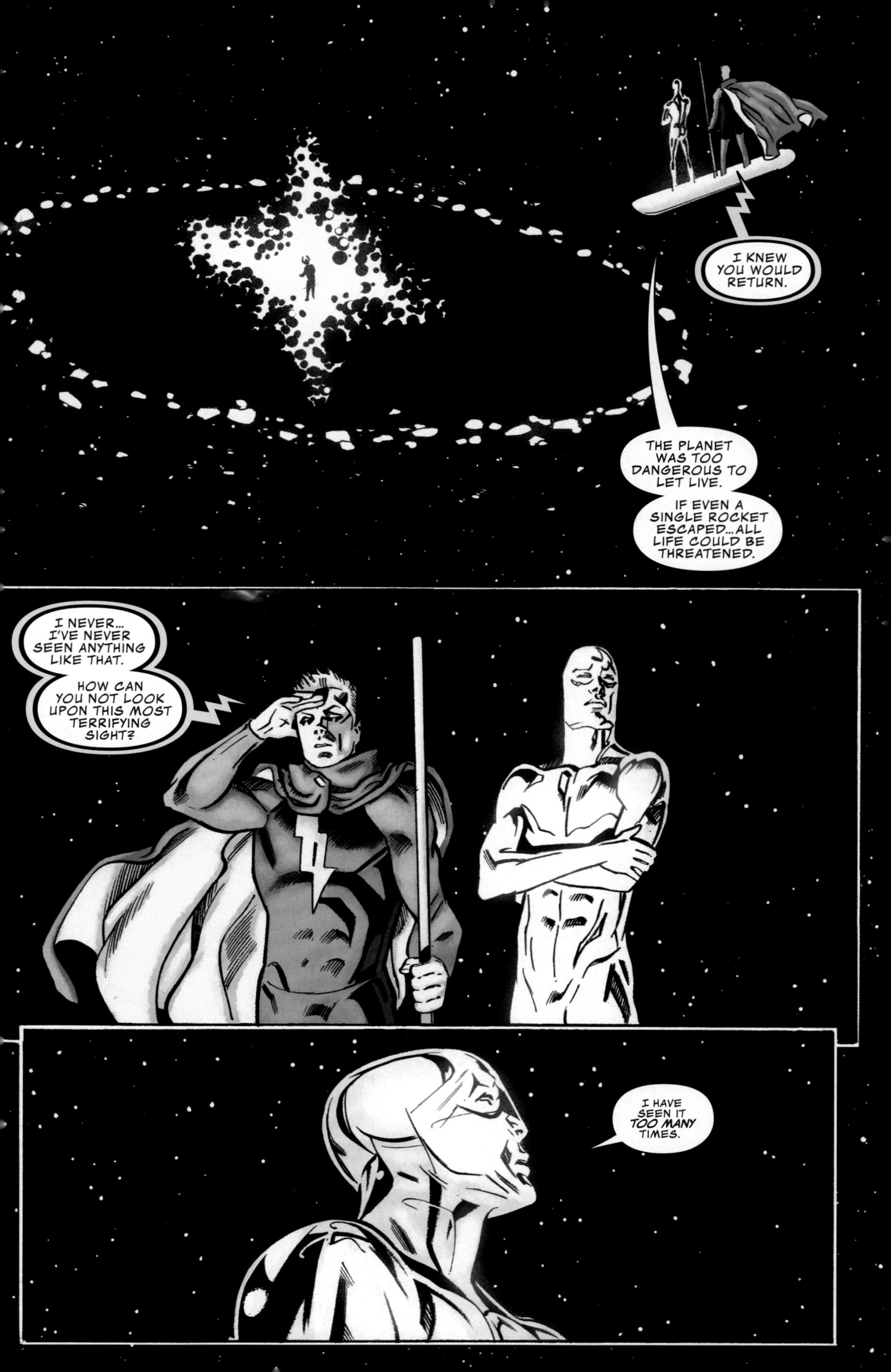
I KNEW YOU WOULD RETURN.
THE PLANET WAS TOO DANGEROUS TO LET LIVE.
IF EVEN A SINGLE ROCKET ESCAPED...ALL LIFE COULD BE THREATENED.
I NEVER... I'VE NEVER SEEN ANYTHING LIKE THAT.
HOW CAN YOU NOT LOOK UPON THIS MOST TERRIFYING SIGHT?
I HAVE SEEN IT *TOO MANY* TIMES.

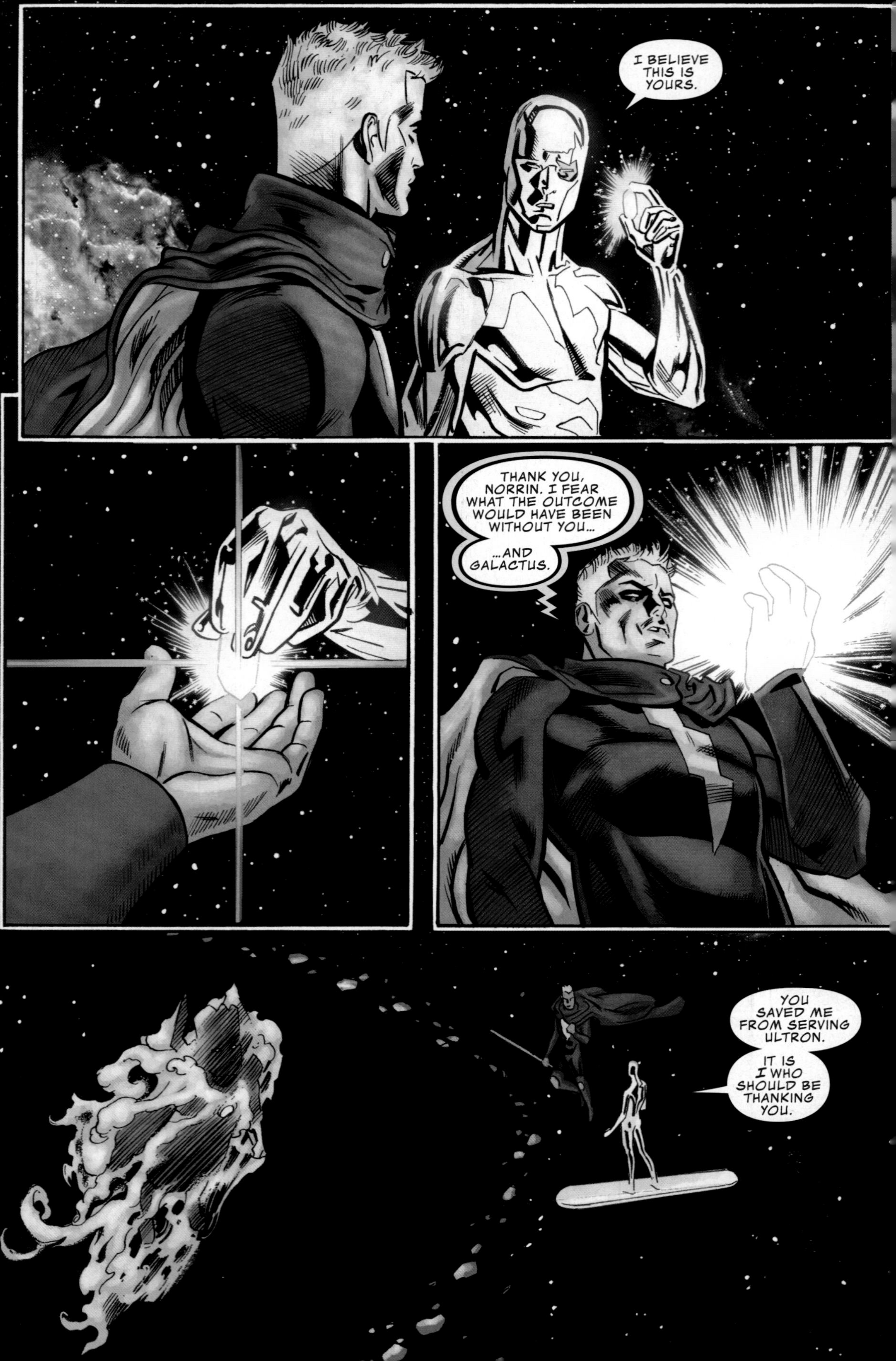
I BELIEVE THIS IS YOURS.
THANK YOU, NORRIN. I FEAR WHAT THE OUTCOME WOULD HAVE BEEN WITHOUT YOU...
...AND GALACTUS.
YOU SAVED ME FROM SERVING ULTRON.
IT IS I WHO SHOULD BE THANKING YOU.

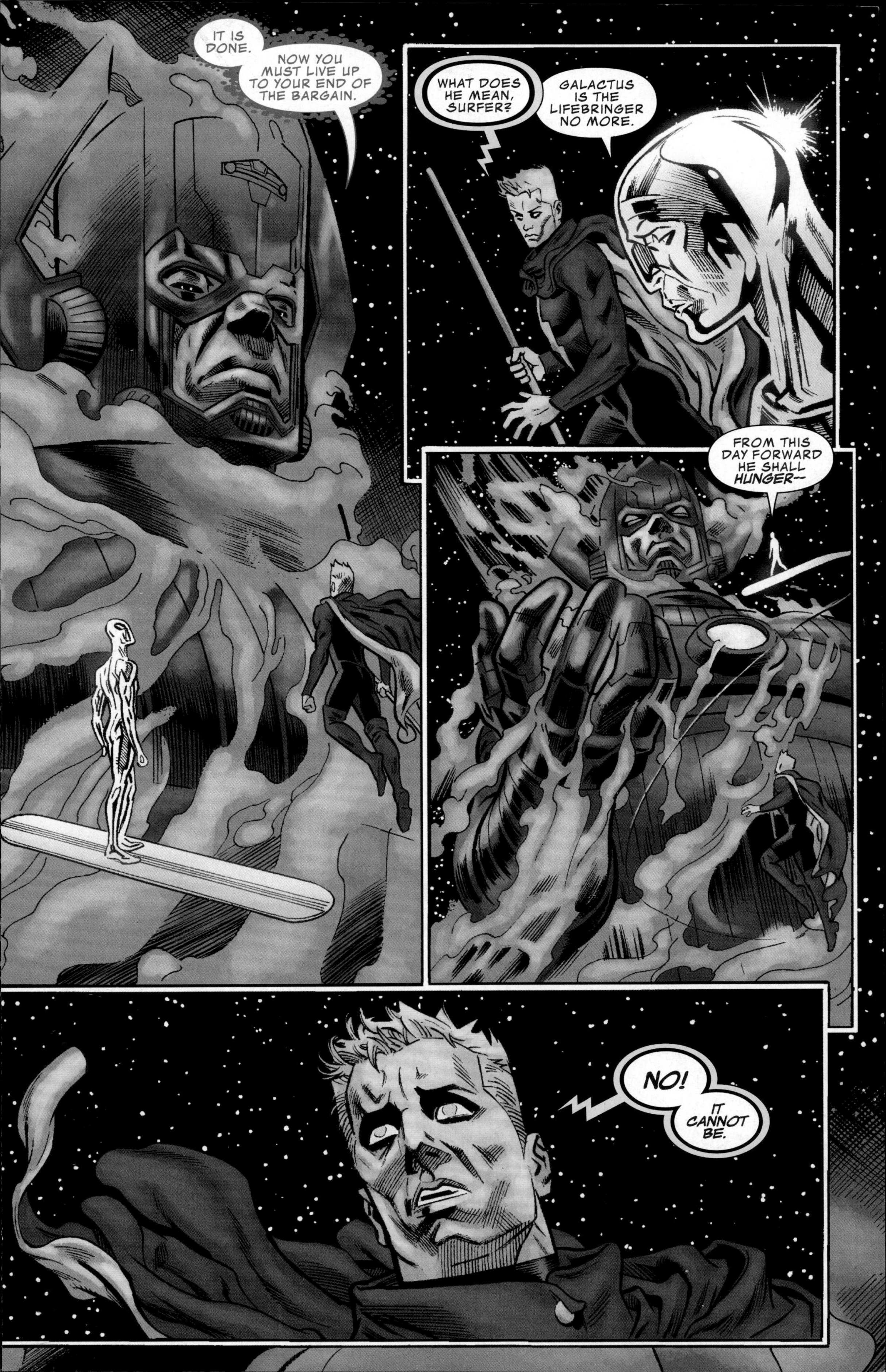
IT IS DONE.
NOW YOU MUST LIVE UP TO YOUR END OF THE BARGAIN.
WHAT DOES HE MEAN, SURFER?
GALACTUS IS THE LIFEBRINGER NO MORE.
FROM THIS DAY FORWARD HE SHALL HUNGER--
NO!
IT CANNOT BE.

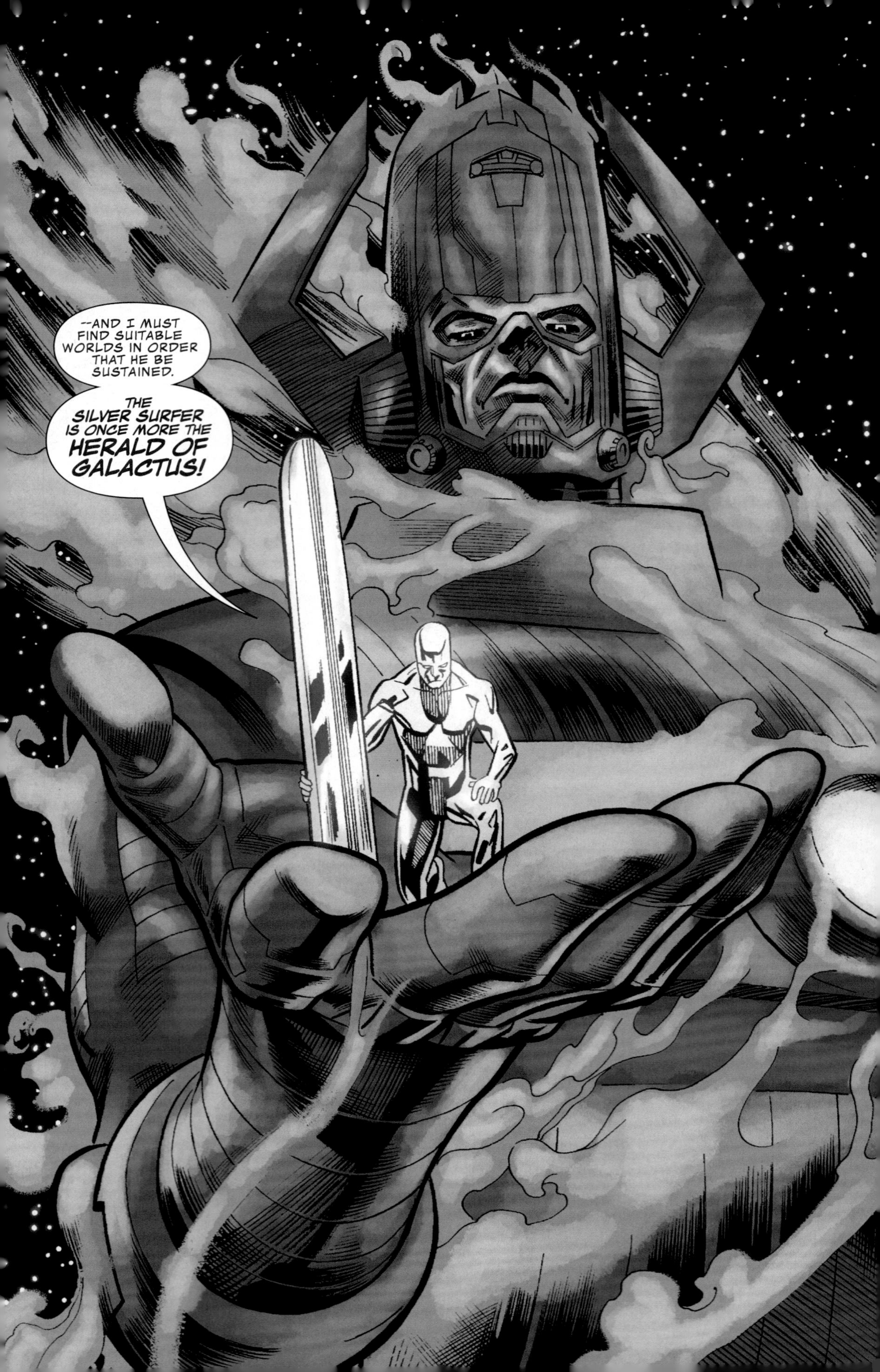
--AND I MUST FIND SUITABLE WORLDS IN ORDER THAT HE BE SUSTAINED.
THE SILVER SURFER IS ONCE MORE THE HERALD OF GALACTUS!

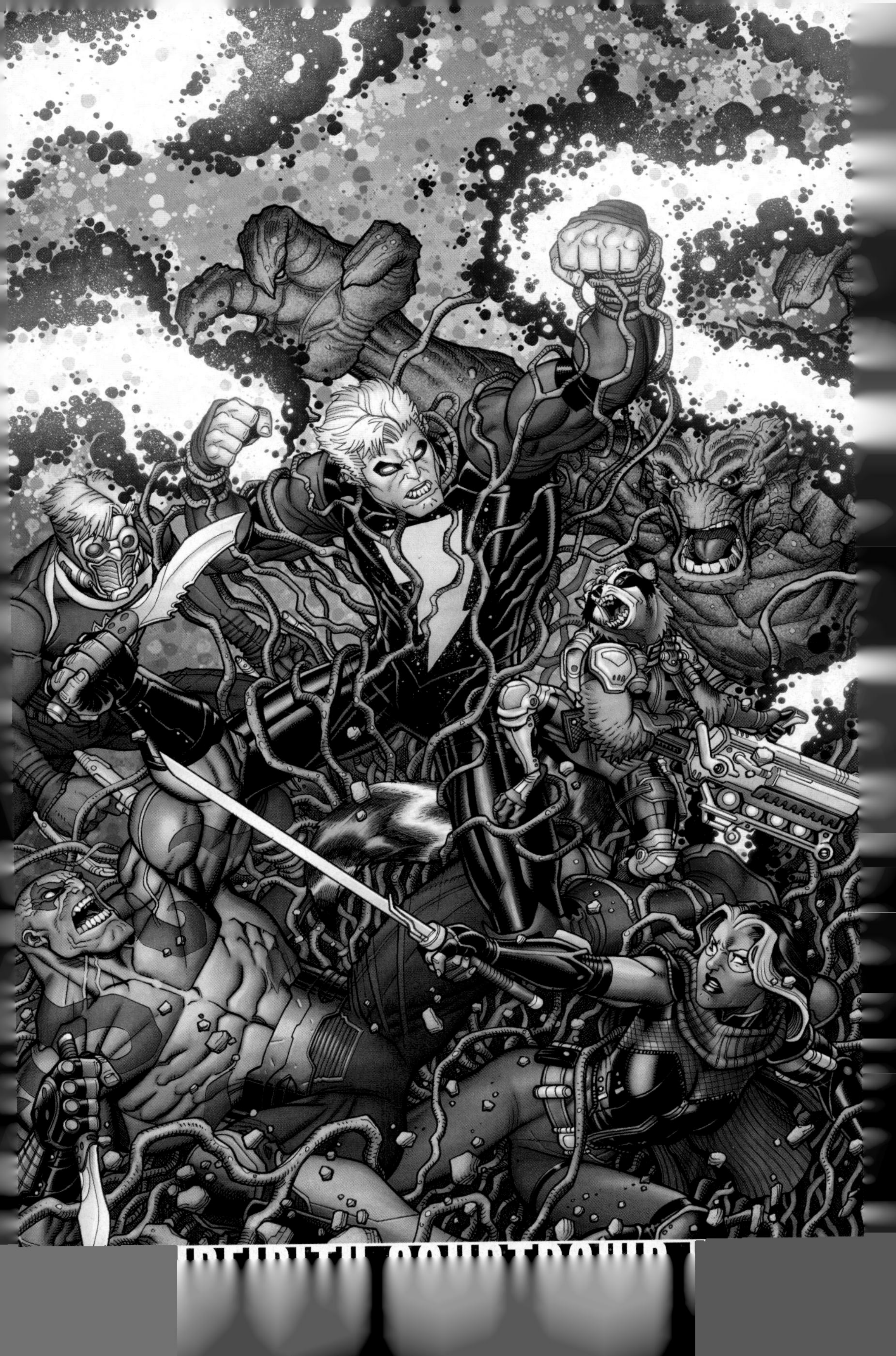

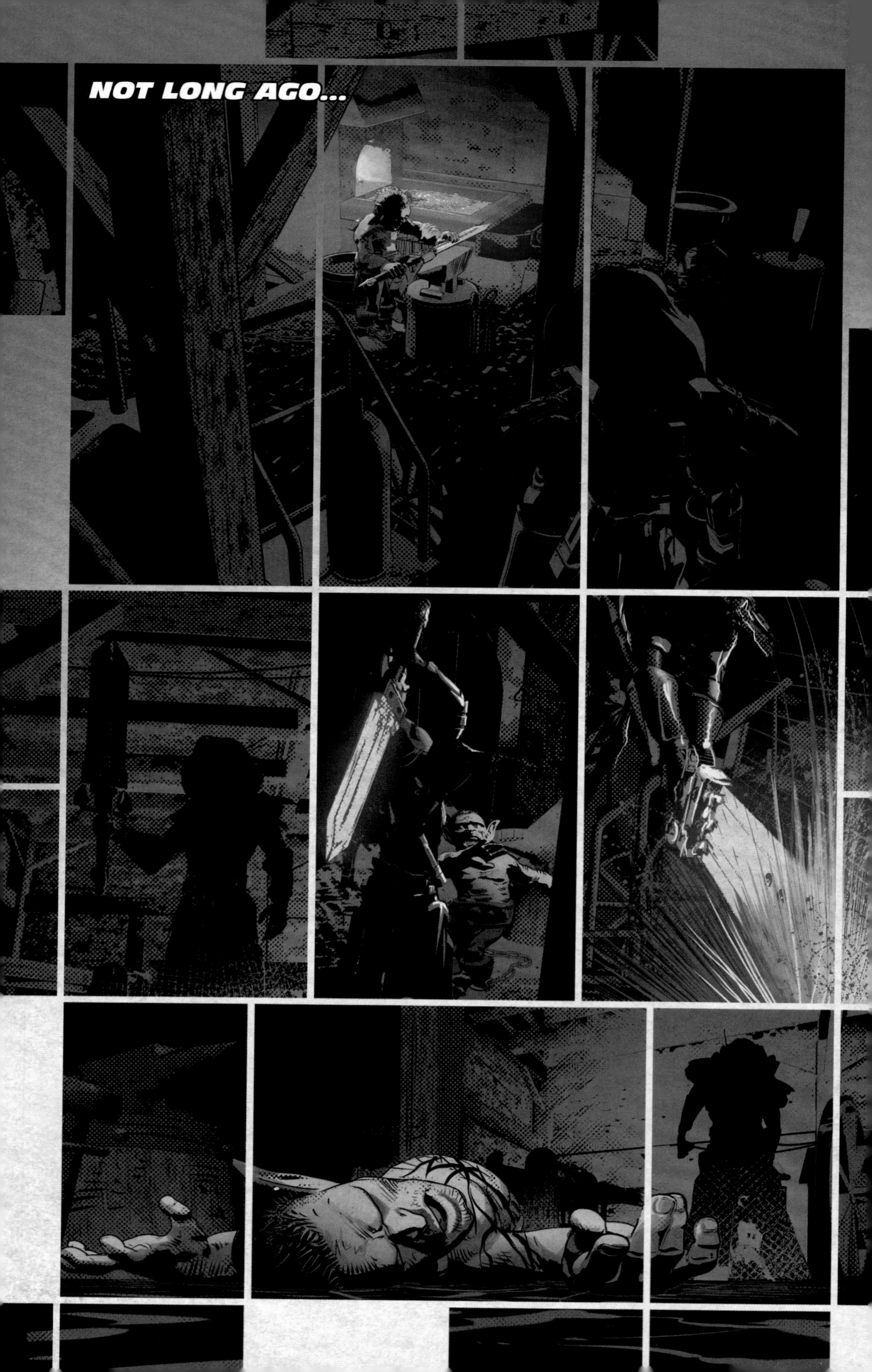
NOT LONG AGO...

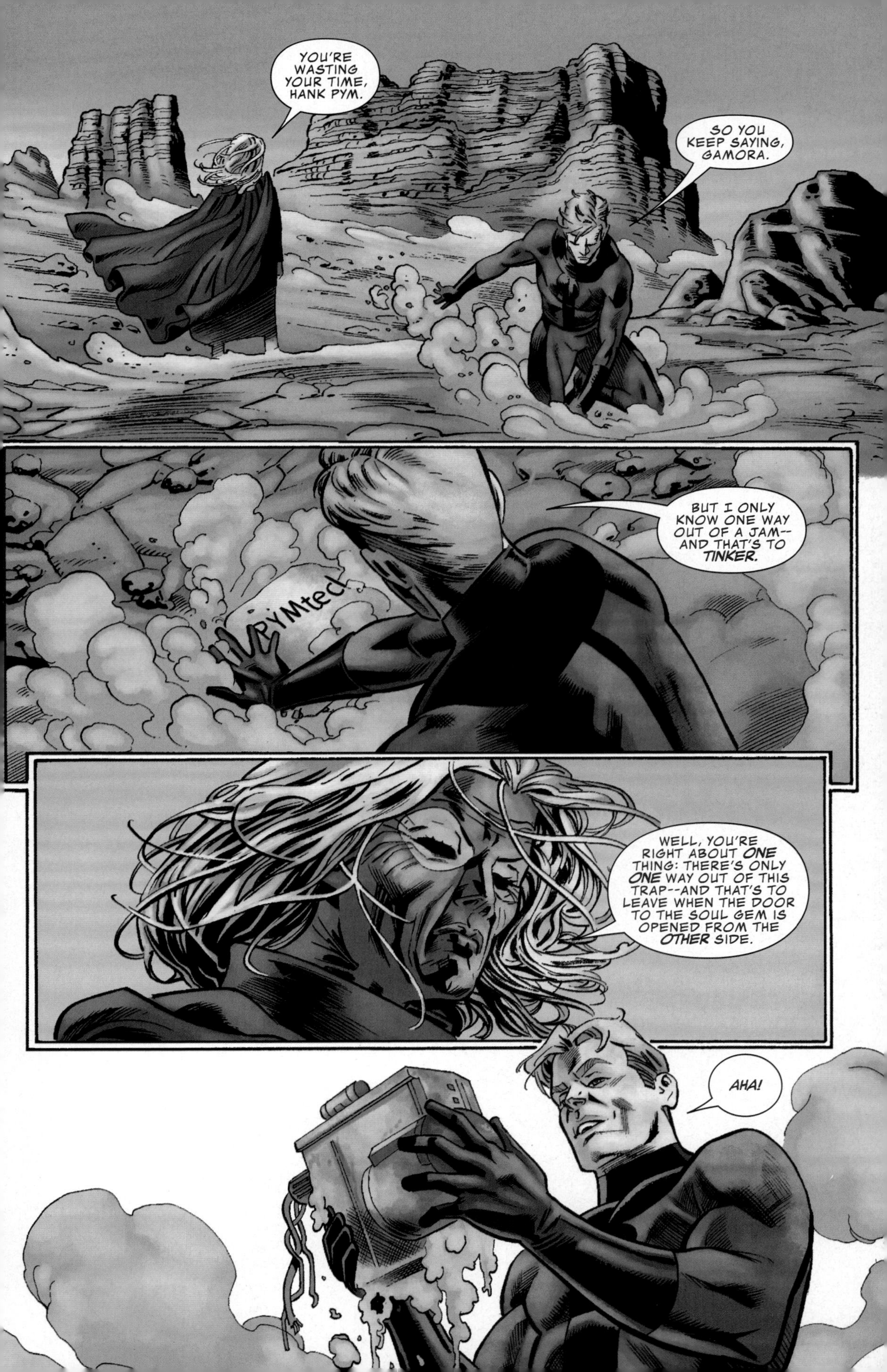
YOU'RE WASTING YOUR TIME, HANK PYM.
SO YOU KEEP SAYING, GAMORA.
BUT I ONLY KNOW ONE WAY OUT OF A JAM-- AND THAT'S TO TINKER.
PYMtech
WELL, YOU'RE RIGHT ABOUT ONE THING: THERE'S ONLY ONE WAY OUT OF THIS TRAP--AND THAT'S TO LEAVE WHEN THE DOOR TO THE SOUL GEM IS OPENED FROM THE OTHER SIDE.
AHA!

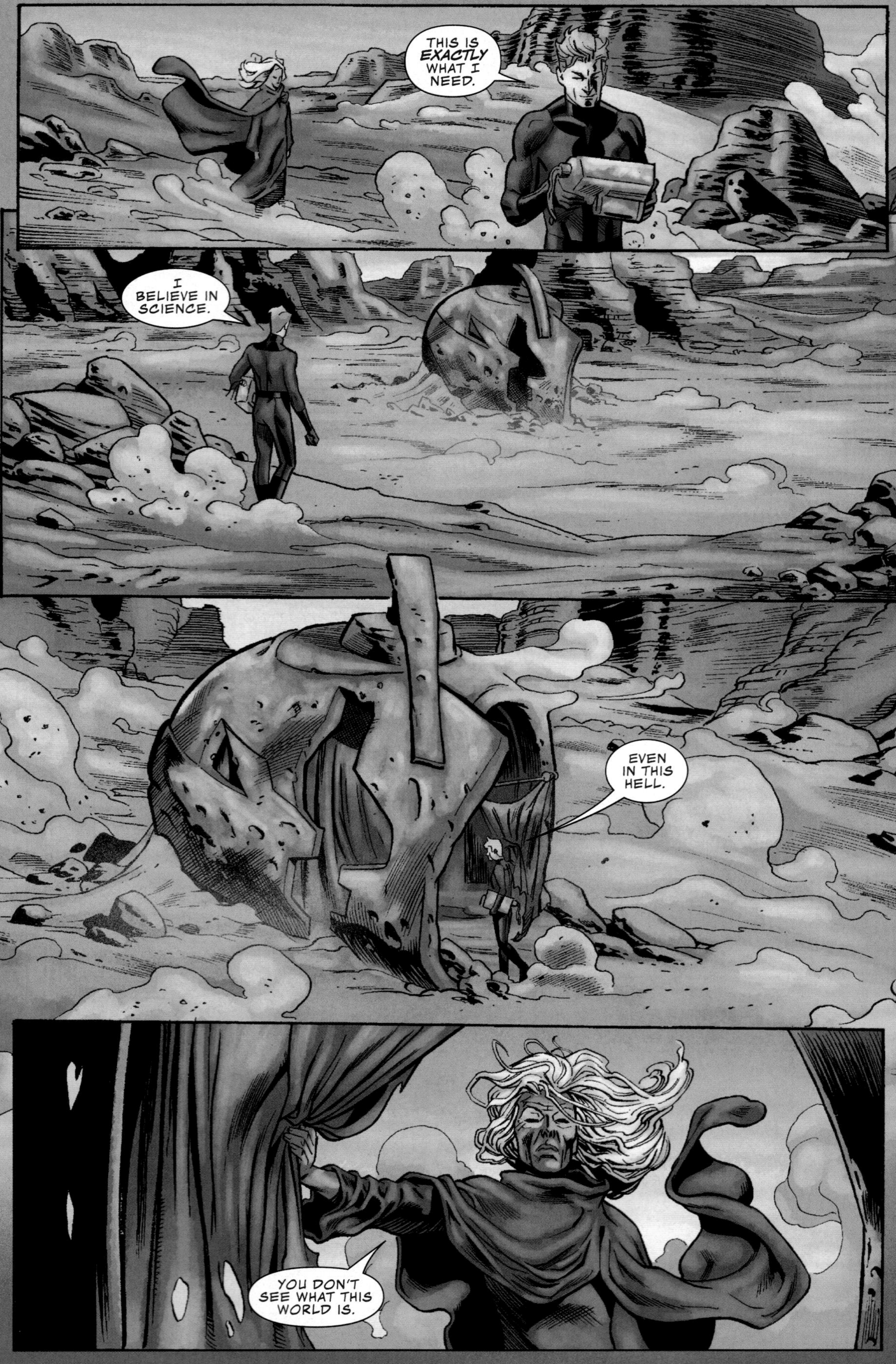
THIS IS EXACTLY WHAT I NEED.
I BELIEVE IN SCIENCE.
EVEN IN THIS HELL.
YOU DON'T SEE WHAT THIS WORLD IS.

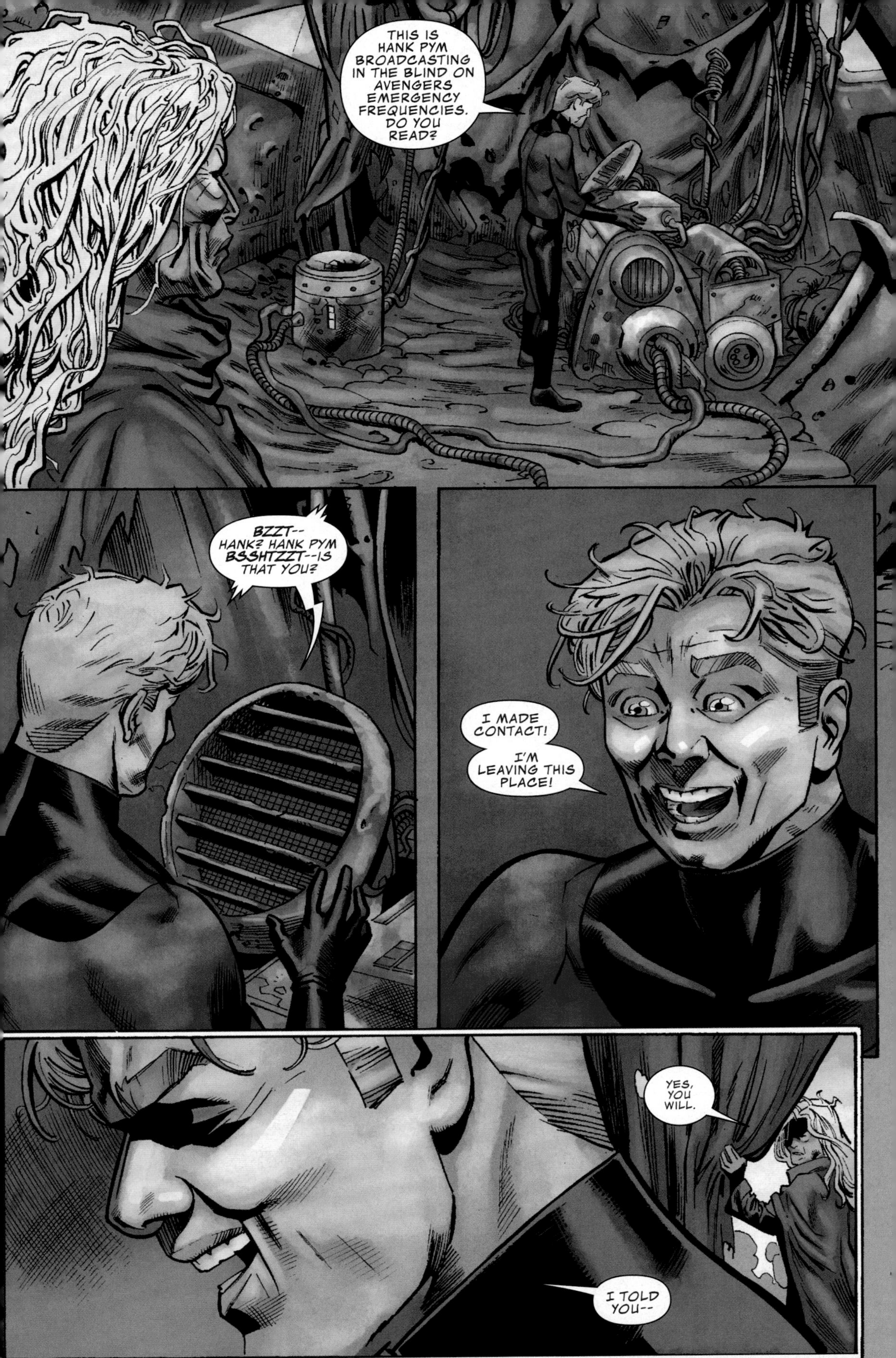
THIS IS HANK PYM BROADCASTING IN THE BLIND ON AVENGERS EMERGENCY FREQUENCIES. DO YOU READ?
BZZT-- HANK? HANK PYM BSSHTZZT--IS THAT YOU?
I MADE CONTACT!
I'M LEAVING THIS PLACE!
YES, YOU WILL.
I TOLD YOU--

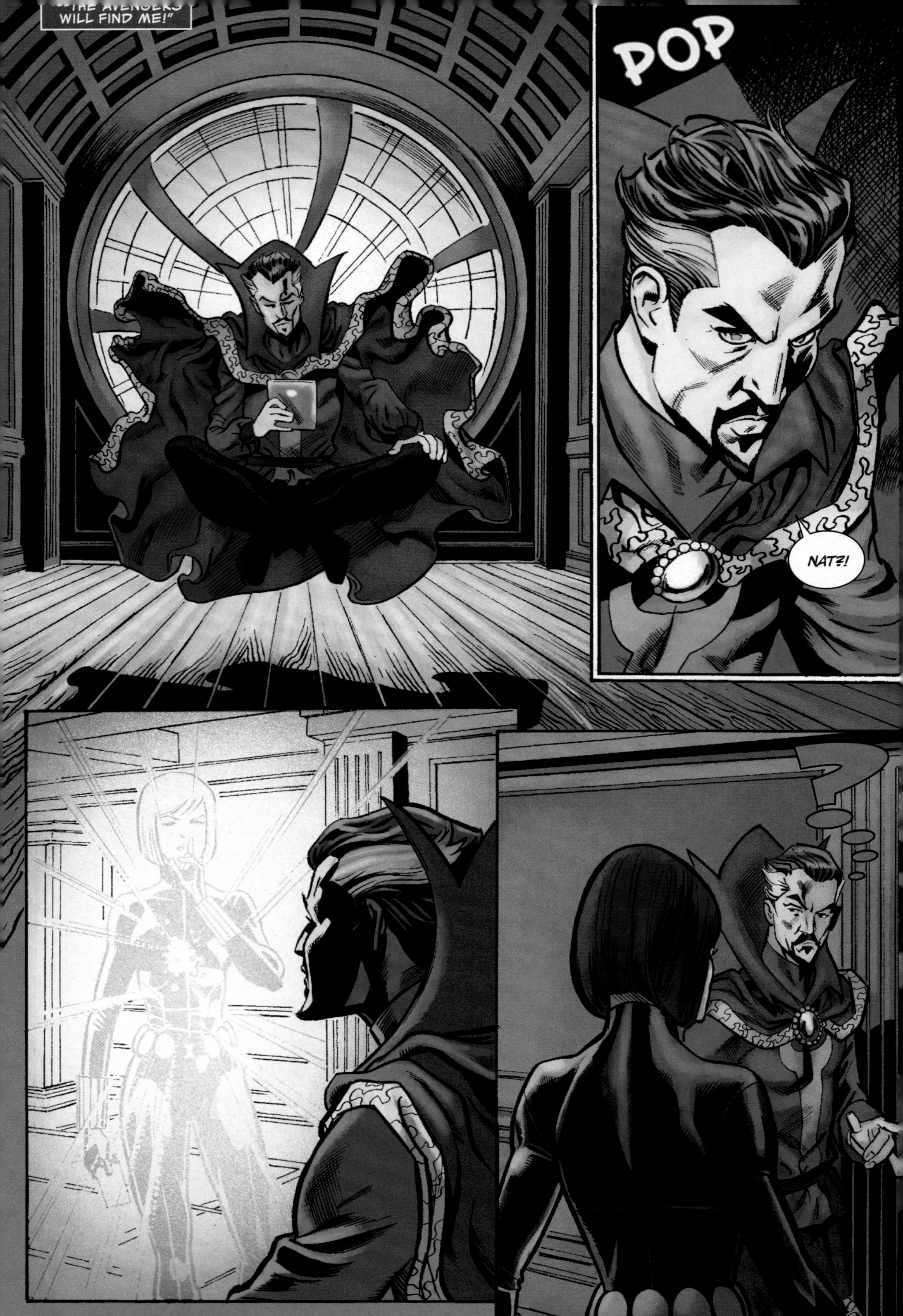

THE AVENGERS WILL FIND ME!"
POP
NAT?!

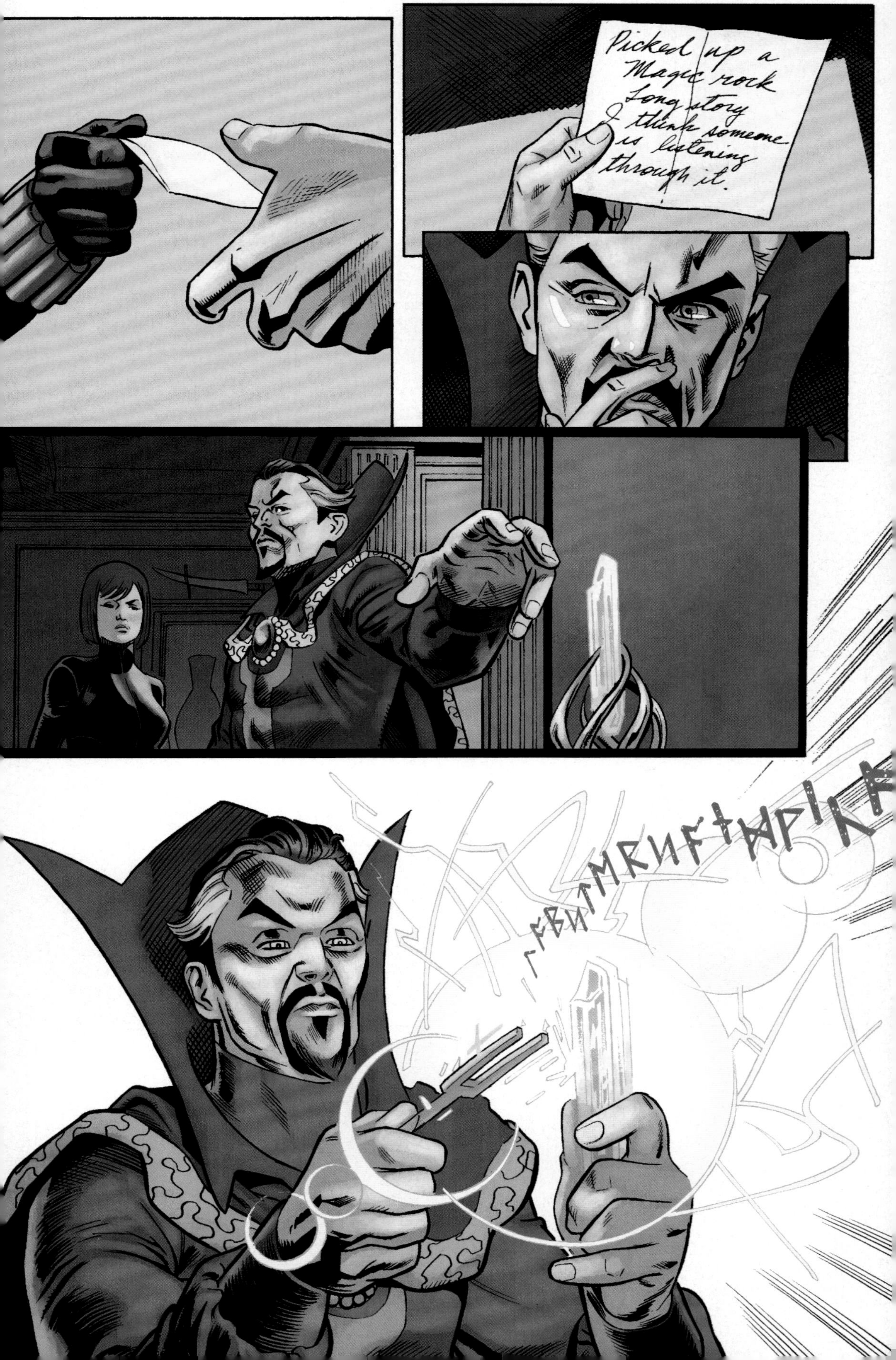
Picked up a
Magic rock
Long story
I think someone
is listening
through it.

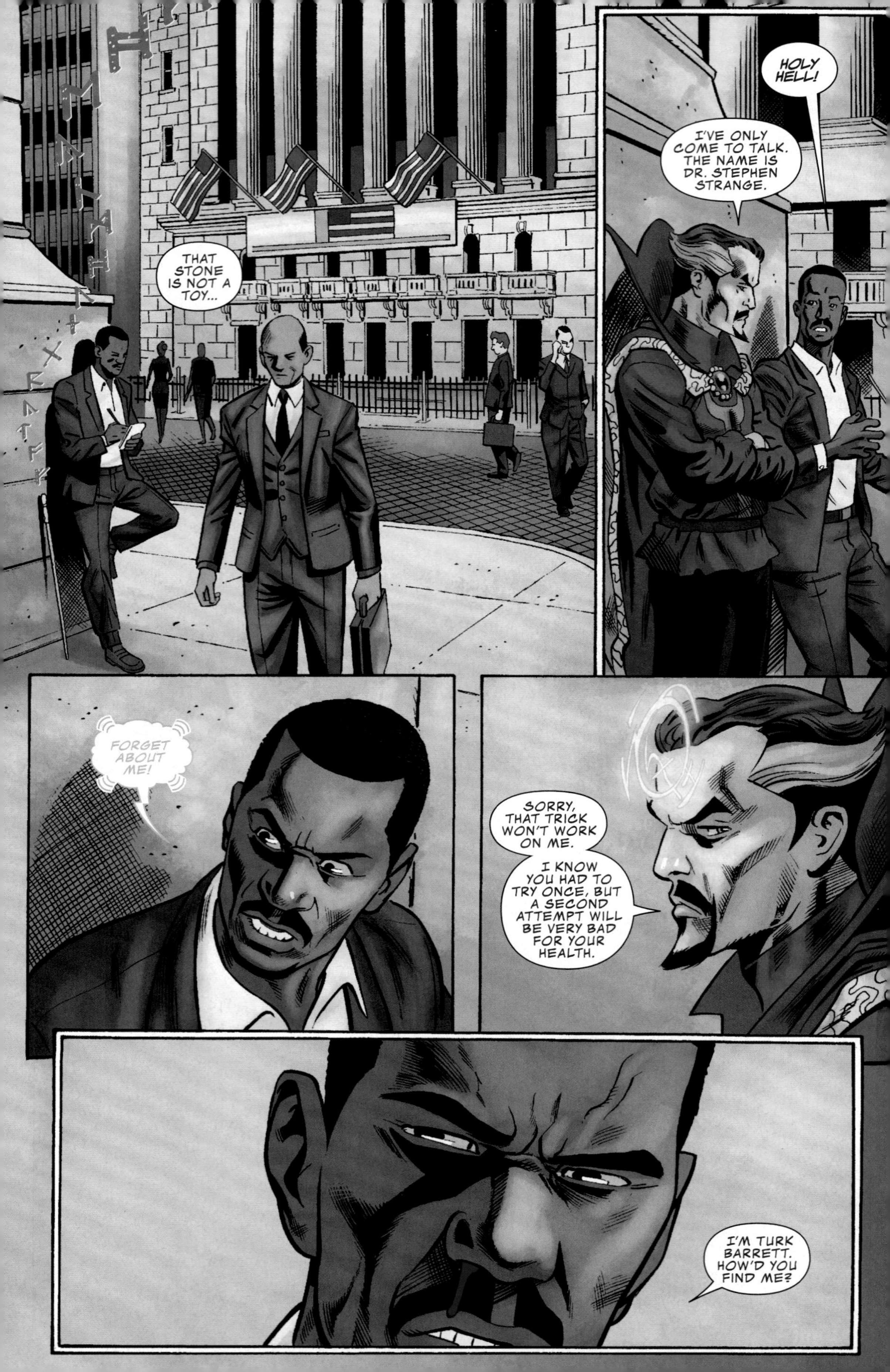
THAT STONE IS NOT A TOY...
HOLY HELL!
I'VE ONLY COME TO TALK. THE NAME IS DR. STEPHEN STRANGE.
FORGET ABOUT ME!
SORRY, THAT TRICK WON'T WORK ON ME.
I KNOW YOU HAD TO TRY ONCE, BUT A SECOND ATTEMPT WILL BE VERY BAD FOR YOUR HEALTH.
I'M TURK BARRETT. HOW'D YOU FIND ME?

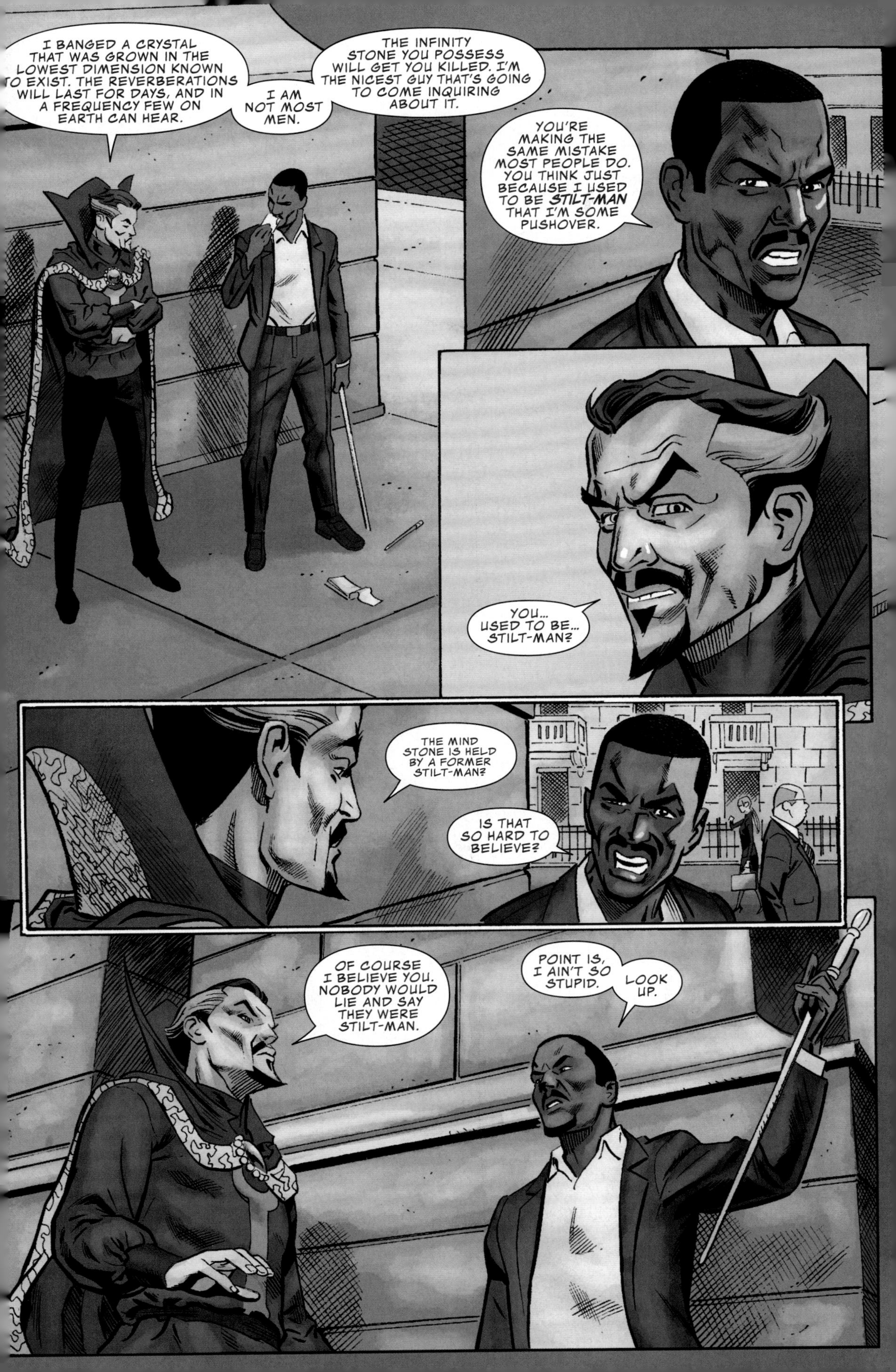
I BANGED A CRYSTAL THAT WAS GROWN IN THE LOWEST DIMENSION KNOWN TO EXIST. THE REVERBERATIONS WILL LAST FOR DAYS, AND IN A FREQUENCY FEW ON EARTH CAN HEAR.
I AM NOT MOST MEN.
THE INFINITY STONE YOU POSSESS WILL GET YOU KILLED. I'M THE NICEST GUY THAT'S GOING TO COME INQUIRING ABOUT IT.
YOU'RE MAKING THE SAME MISTAKE MOST PEOPLE DO. YOU THINK JUST BECAUSE I USED TO BE STILT-MAN THAT I'M SOME PUSHOVER.
YOU... USED TO BE... STILT-MAN?
THE MIND STONE IS HELD BY A FORMER STILT-MAN?
IS THAT SO HARD TO BELIEVE?
OF COURSE I BELIEVE YOU. NOBODY WOULD LIE AND SAY THEY WERE STILT-MAN.
POINT IS, I AIN'T SO STUPID.
LOOK UP.

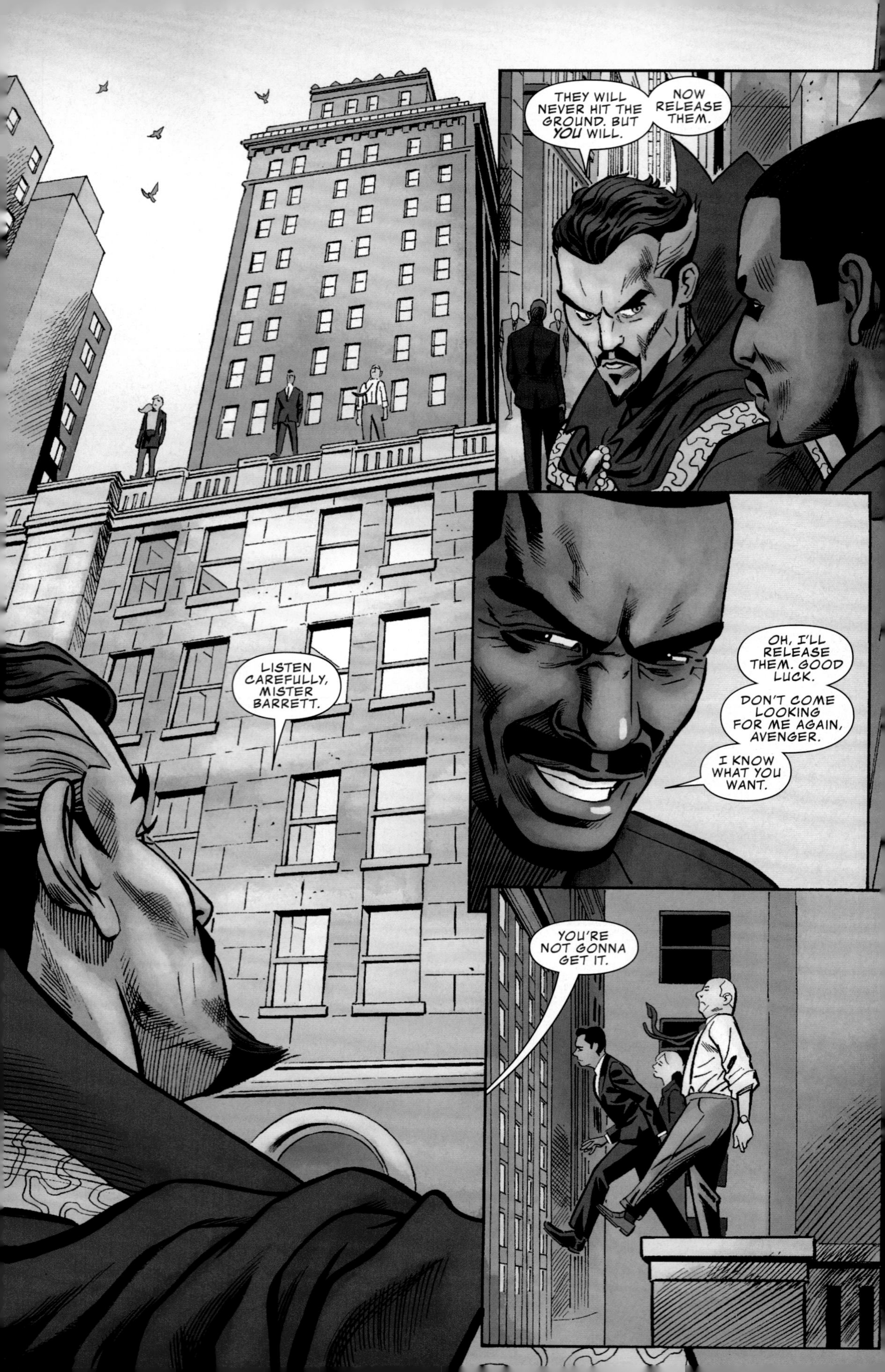
LISTEN CAREFULLY, MISTER BARRETT.
THEY WILL NEVER HIT THE GROUND. BUT YOU WILL.
NOW RELEASE THEM.
OH, I'LL RELEASE THEM. GOOD LUCK.
DON'T COME LOOKING FOR ME AGAIN, AVENGER.
I KNOW WHAT YOU WANT.
YOU'RE NOT GONNA GET IT.

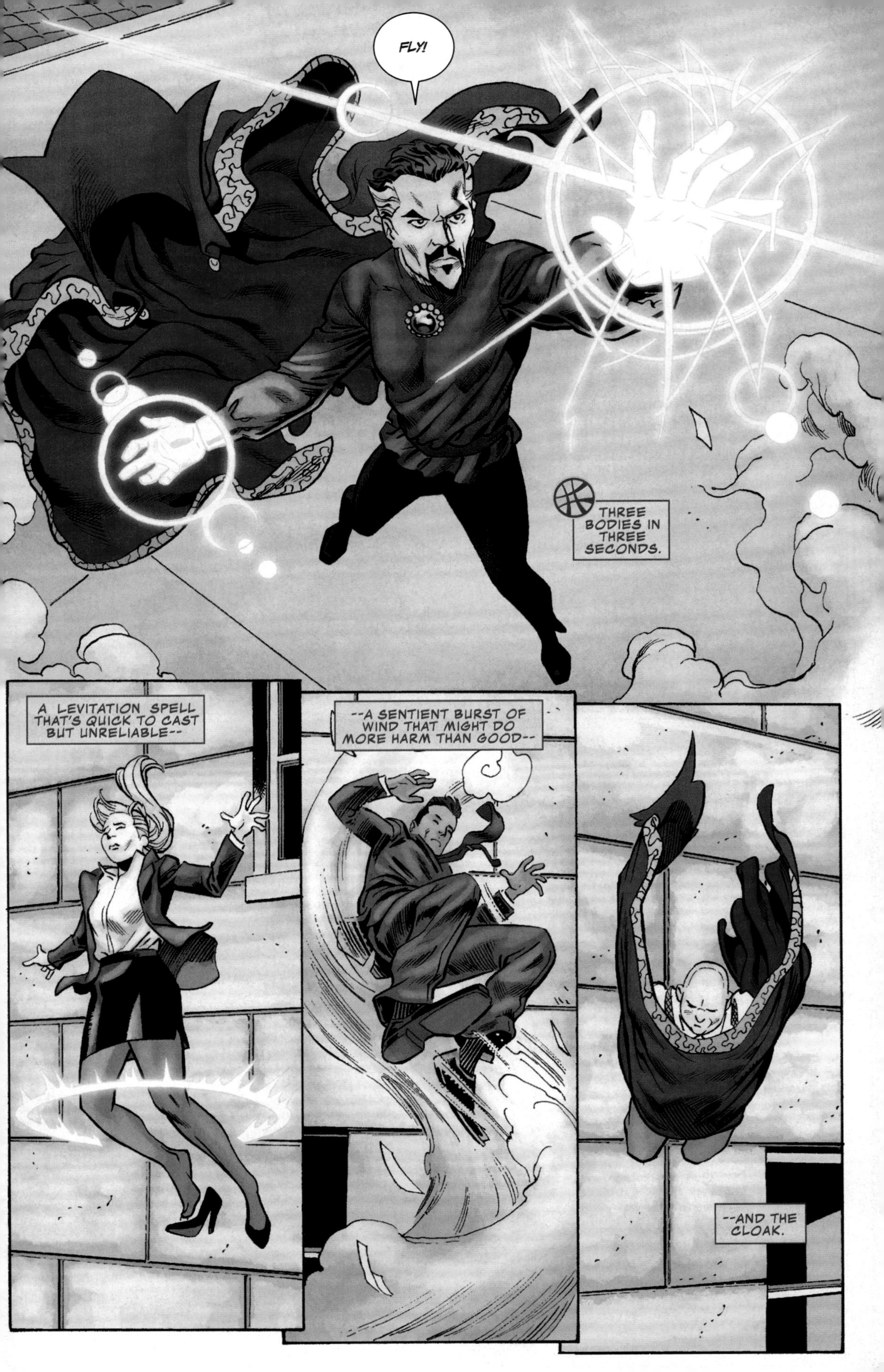
FLY!
THREE BODIES IN THREE SECONDS.
A LEVITATION SPELL THAT'S QUICK TO CAST BUT UNRELIABLE--
--A SENTIENT BURST OF WIND THAT MIGHT DO MORE HARM THAN GOOD--
--AND THE CLOAK.

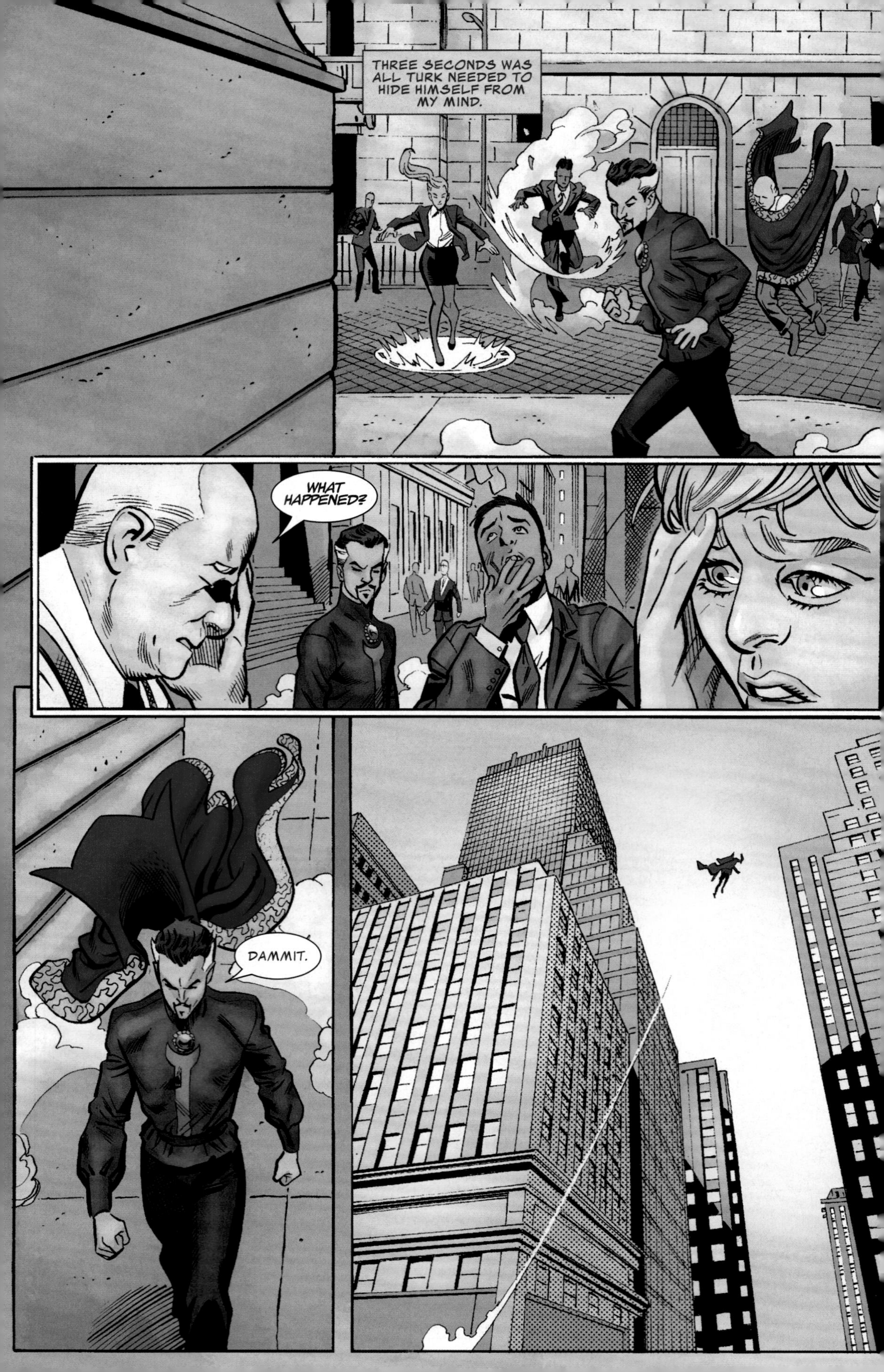
THREE SECONDS WAS ALL TURK NEEDED TO HIDE HIMSELF FROM MY MIND.
WHAT HAPPENED?
DAMMIT.

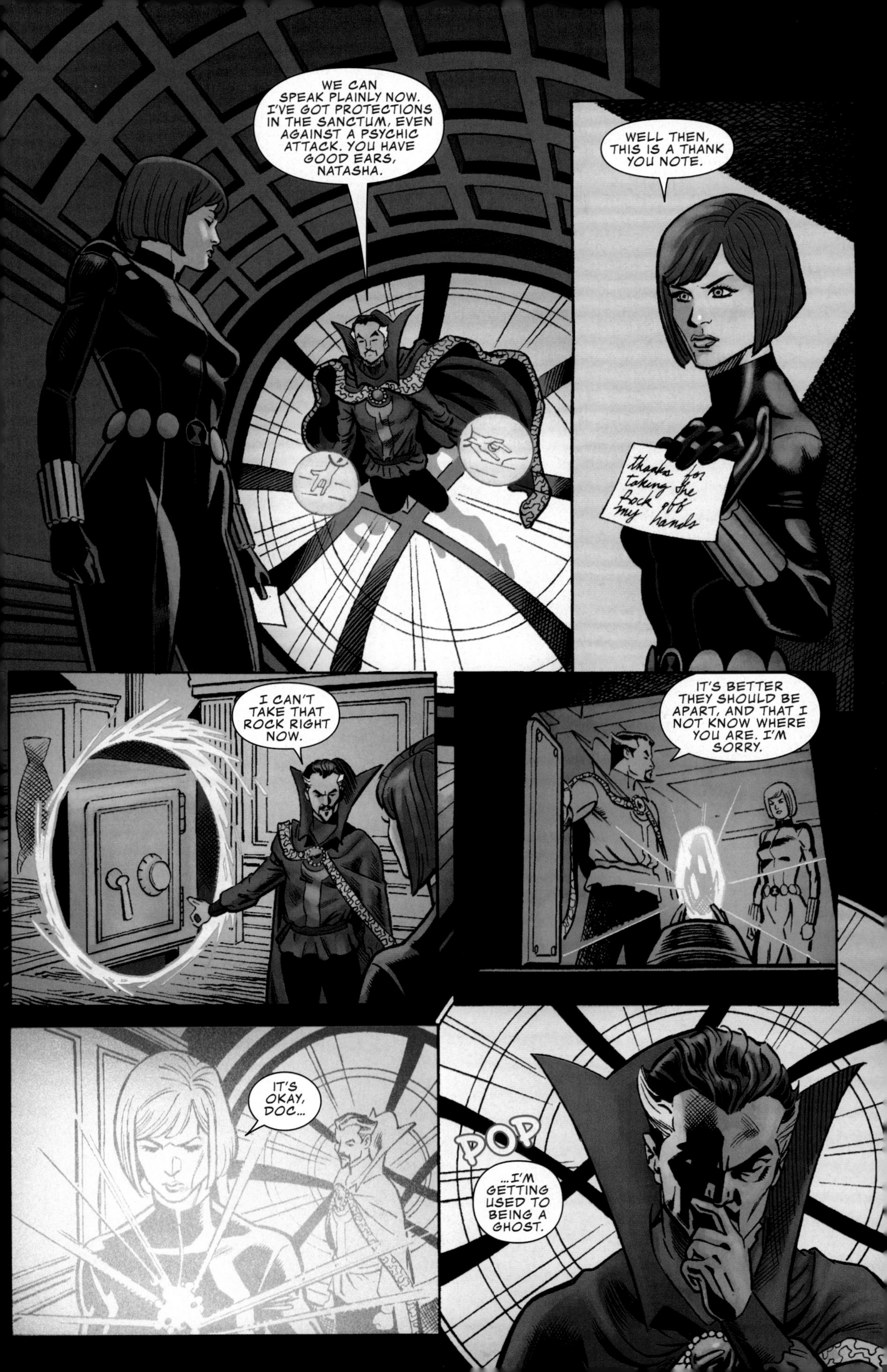
WE CAN SPEAK PLAINLY NOW. I'VE GOT PROTECTIONS IN THE SANCTUM, EVEN AGAINST A PSYCHIC ATTACK. YOU HAVE GOOD EARS, NATASHA.
WELL THEN, THIS IS A THANK YOU NOTE.
thanks for taking the rock off my hands
I CAN'T TAKE THAT ROCK RIGHT NOW.
IT'S BETTER THEY SHOULD BE APART, AND THAT I NOT KNOW WHERE YOU ARE. I'M SORRY.
IT'S OKAY, DOC...
POP
...I'M GETTING USED TO BEING A GHOST.

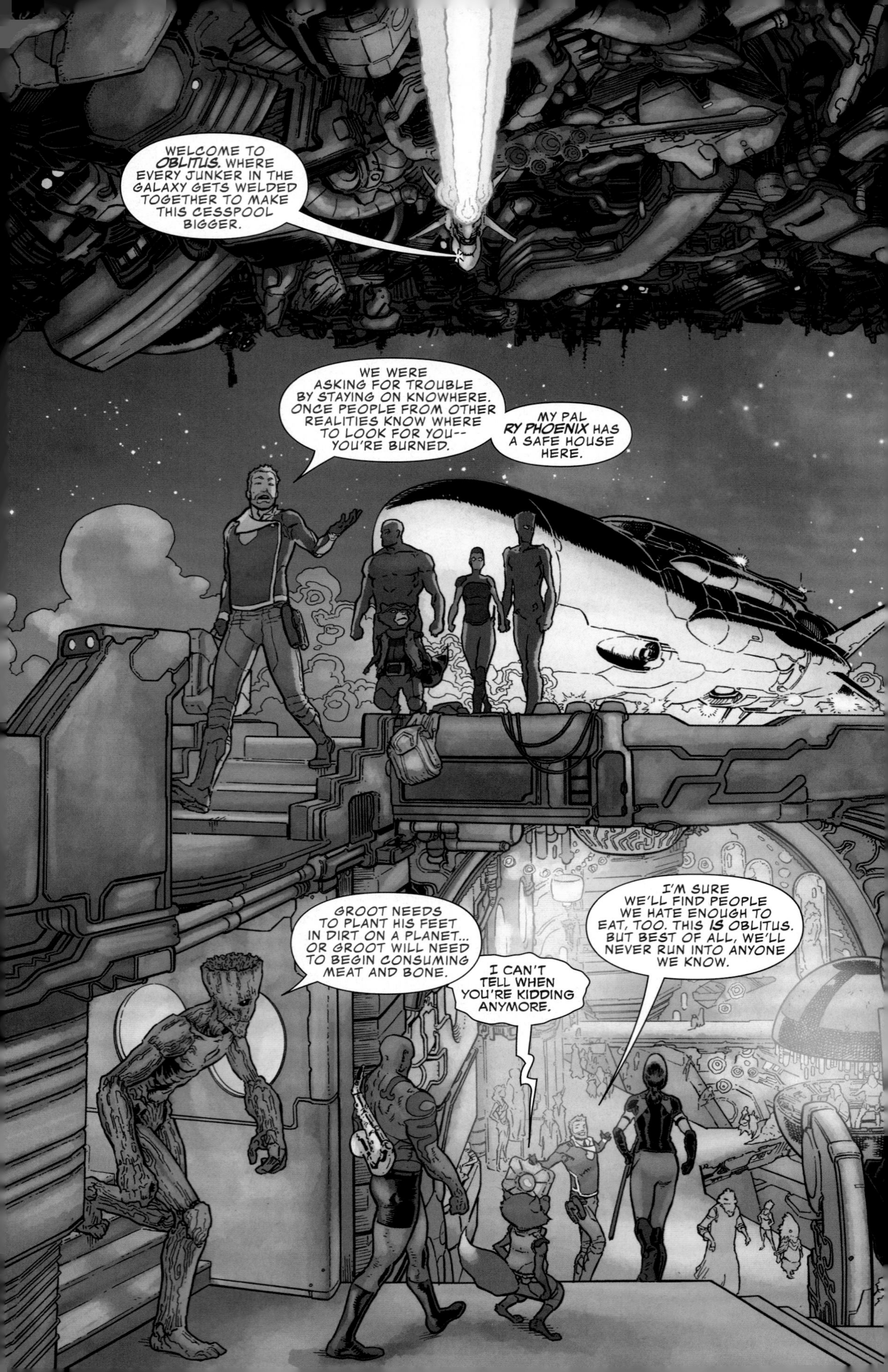
WELCOME TO OBLITUS. WHERE EVERY JUNKER IN THE GALAXY GETS WELDED TOGETHER TO MAKE THIS CESSPOOL BIGGER.
WE WERE ASKING FOR TROUBLE BY STAYING ON KNOWHERE. ONCE PEOPLE FROM OTHER REALITIES KNOW WHERE TO LOOK FOR YOU-- YOU'RE BURNED.
MY PAL RY PHOENIX HAS A SAFE HOUSE HERE.
GROOT NEEDS TO PLANT HIS FEET IN DIRT ON A PLANET... OR GROOT WILL NEED TO BEGIN CONSUMING MEAT AND BONE.
I CAN'T TELL WHEN YOU'RE KIDDING ANYMORE.
I'M SURE WE'LL FIND PEOPLE WE HATE ENOUGH TO EAT, TOO. THIS IS OBLITUS. BUT BEST OF ALL, WE'LL NEVER RUN INTO ANYONE WE KNOW.

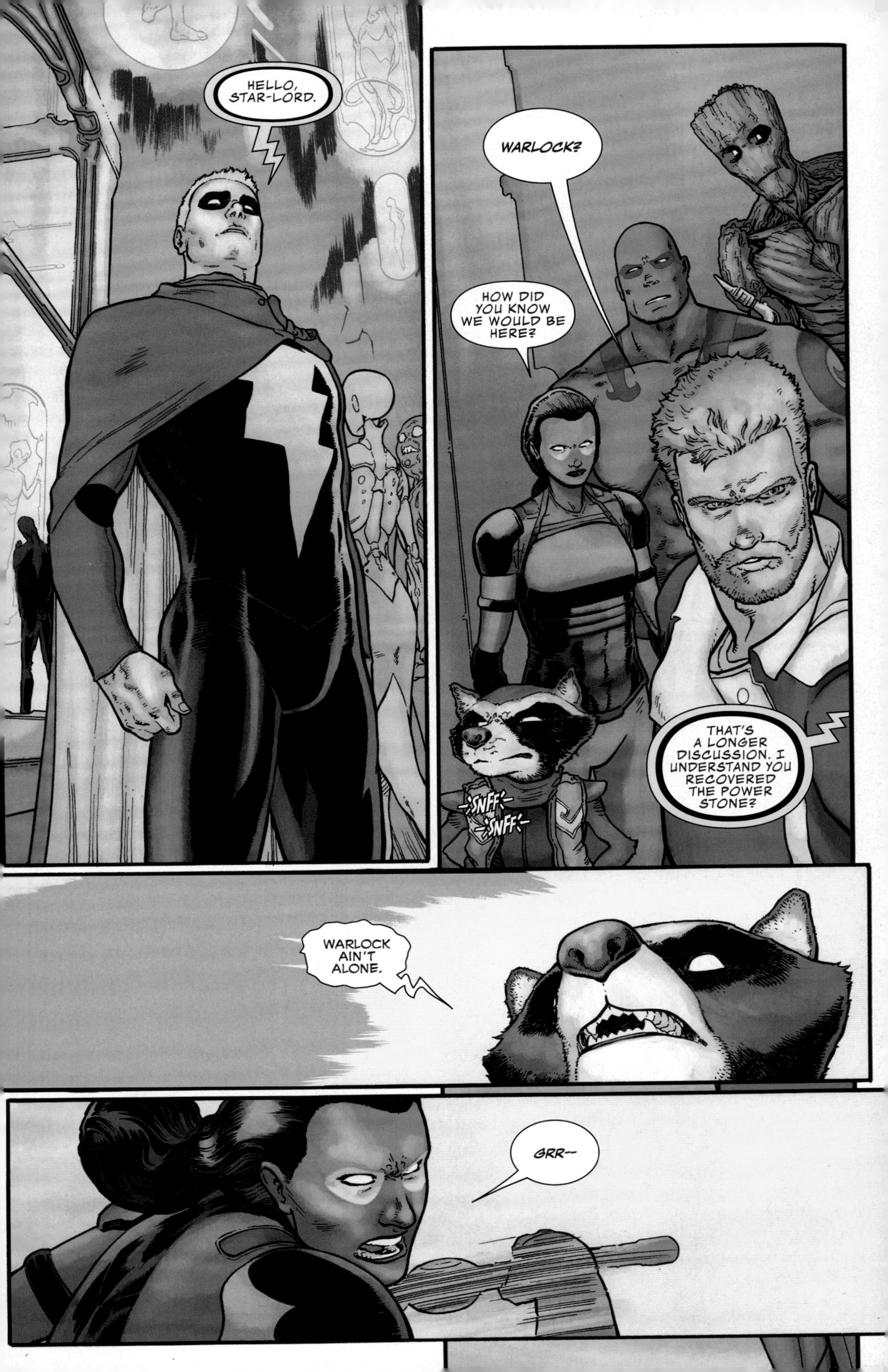
HELLO, STAR-LORD.
WARLOCK?
HOW DID YOU KNOW WE WOULD BE HERE?
THAT'S A LONGER DISCUSSION. I UNDERSTAND YOU RECOVERED THE POWER STONE?
SNFF SNFF
WARLOCK AIN'T ALONE.
GRR--

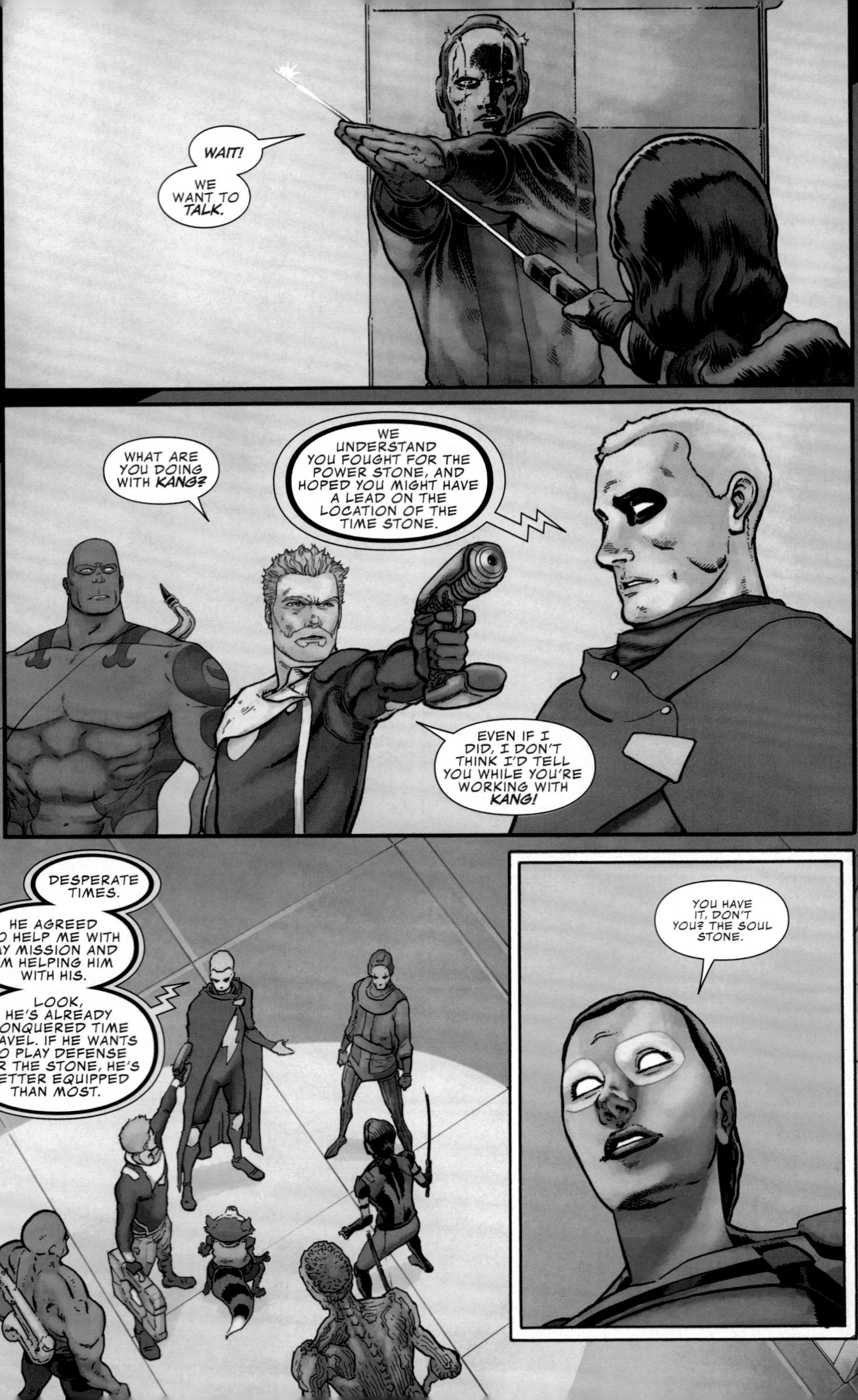
WAIT!
WE WANT TO TALK.
WHAT ARE YOU DOING WITH KANG?
WE UNDERSTAND YOU FOUGHT FOR THE POWER STONE, AND HOPED YOU MIGHT HAVE A LEAD ON THE LOCATION OF THE TIME STONE.
EVEN IF I DID, I DON'T THINK I'D TELL YOU WHILE YOU'RE WORKING WITH KANG!
DESPERATE TIMES.
HE AGREED TO HELP ME WITH MY MISSION AND I'M HELPING HIM WITH HIS.
LOOK, HE'S ALREADY CONQUERED TIME TRAVEL. IF HE WANTS TO PLAY DEFENSE FOR THE STONE, HE'S BETTER EQUIPPED THAN MOST.
YOU HAVE IT, DON'T YOU? THE SOUL STONE.

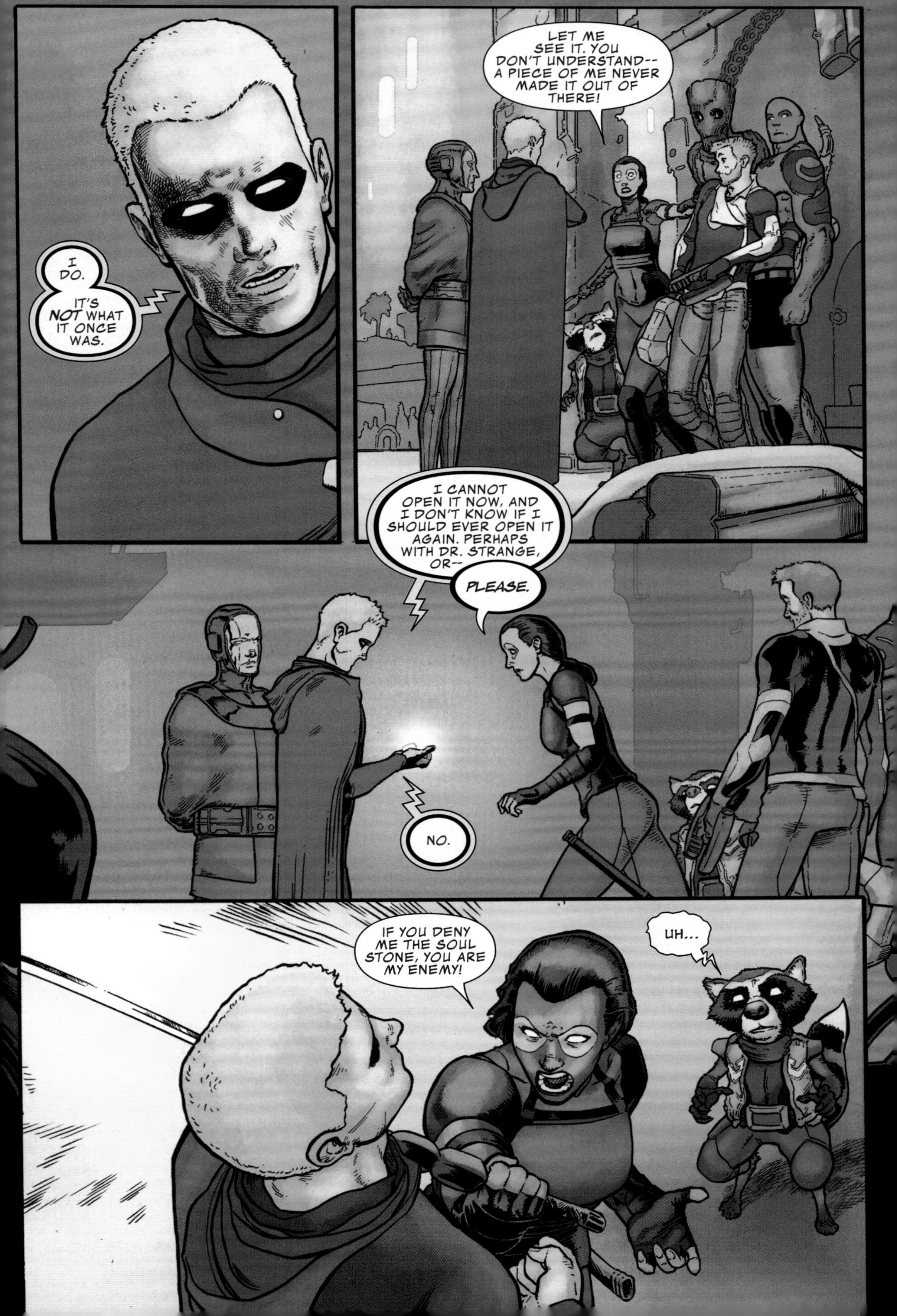
I DO.
IT'S NOT WHAT IT ONCE WAS.
LET ME SEE IT. YOU DON'T UNDERSTAND-- A PIECE OF ME NEVER MADE IT OUT OF THERE!
I CANNOT OPEN IT NOW, AND I DON'T KNOW IF I SHOULD EVER OPEN IT AGAIN. PERHAPS WITH DR. STRANGE, OR--
PLEASE.
NO.
IF YOU DENY ME THE SOUL STONE, YOU ARE MY ENEMY!
UH...

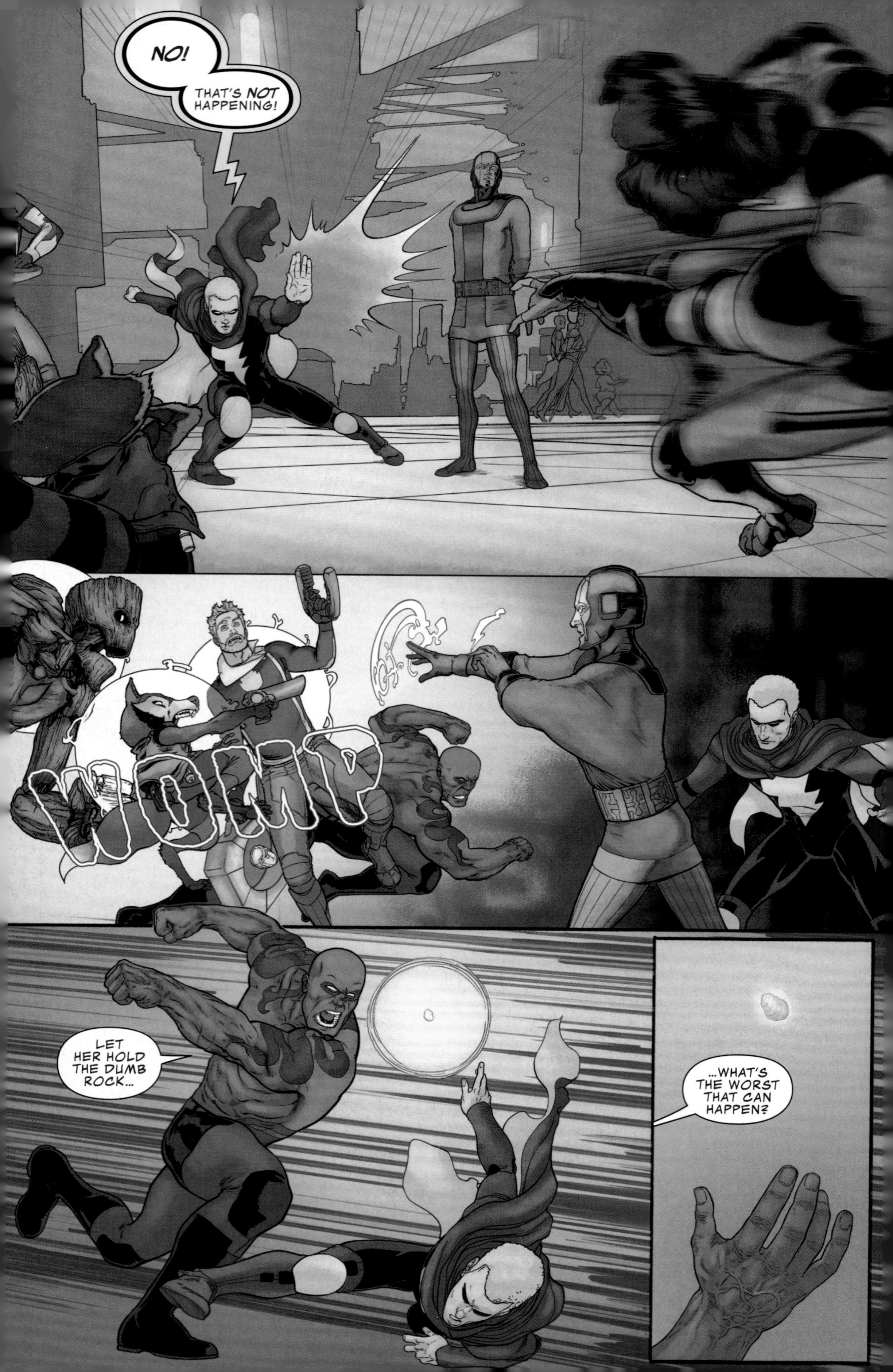
NO!
THAT'S NOT HAPPENING!
WOMP
LET HER HOLD THE DUMB ROCK...
...WHAT'S THE WORST THAT CAN HAPPEN?

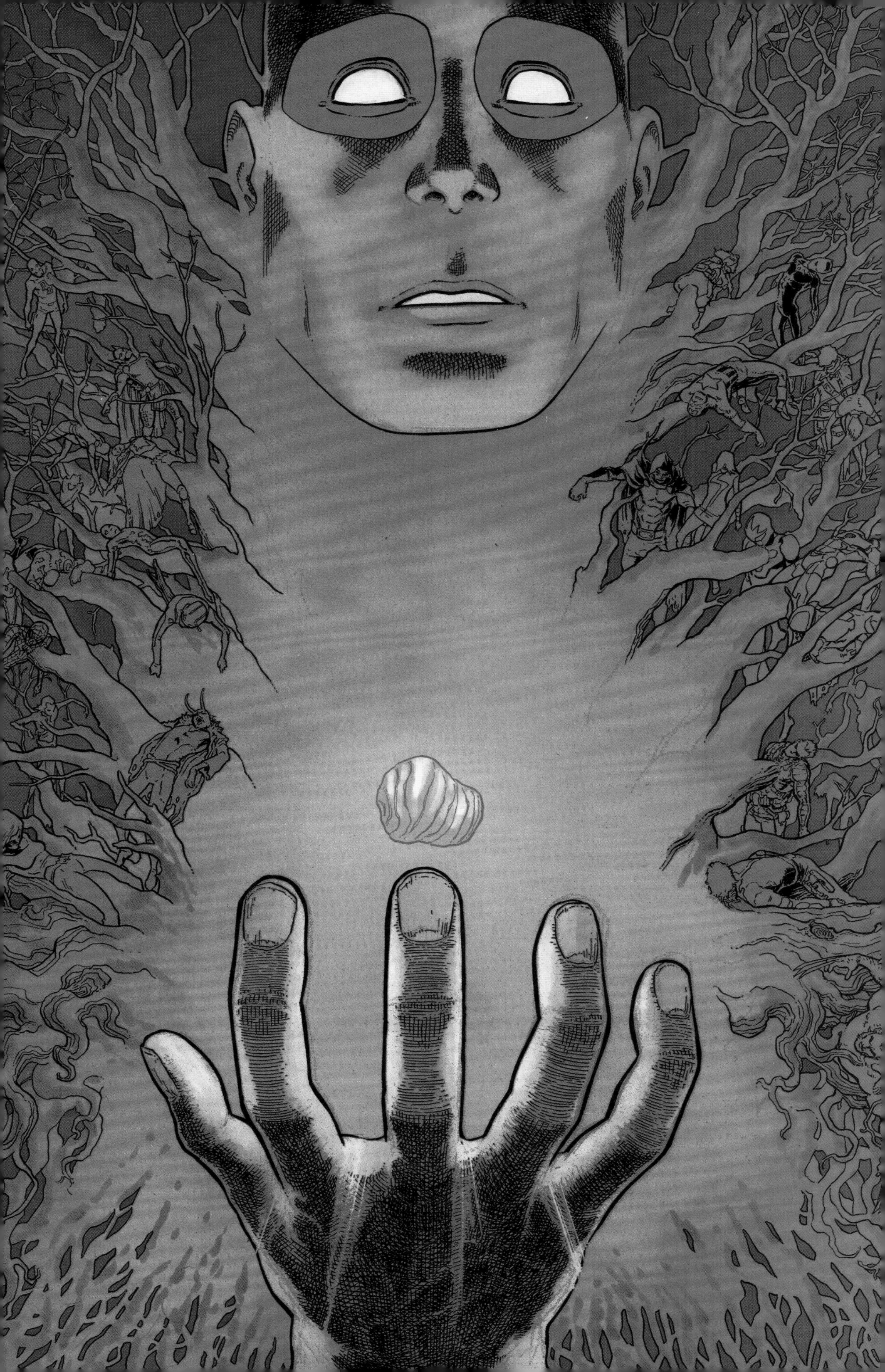

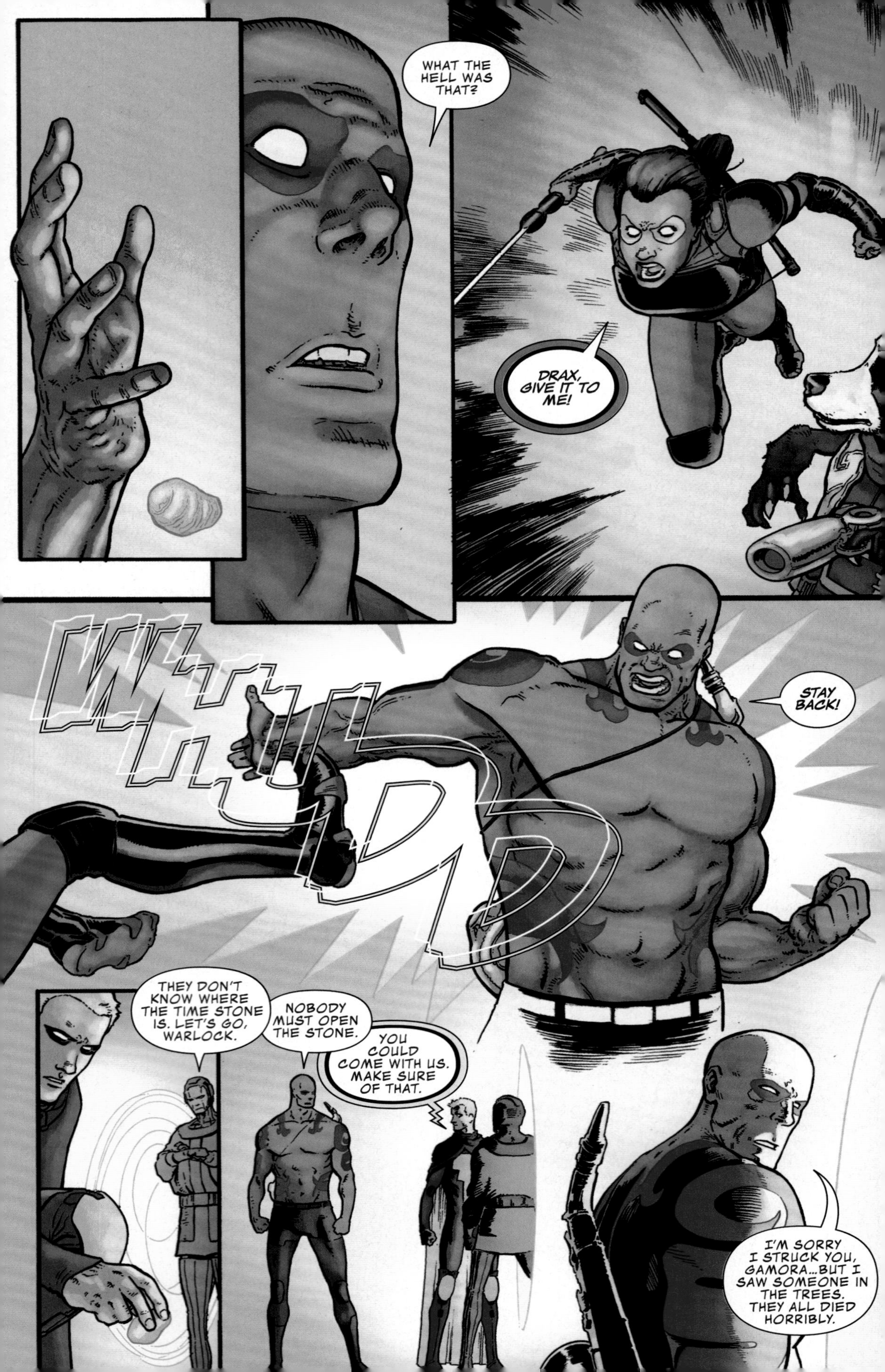
WHAT THE HELL WAS THAT?
DRAX, GIVE IT TO ME!
WHUDD
STAY BACK!
THEY DON'T KNOW WHERE THE TIME STONE IS. LET'S GO, WARLOCK.
NOBODY MUST OPEN THE STONE.
YOU COULD COME WITH US. MAKE SURE OF THAT.
I'M SORRY I STRUCK YOU, GAMORA...BUT I SAW SOMEONE IN THE TREES. THEY ALL DIED HORRIBLY.

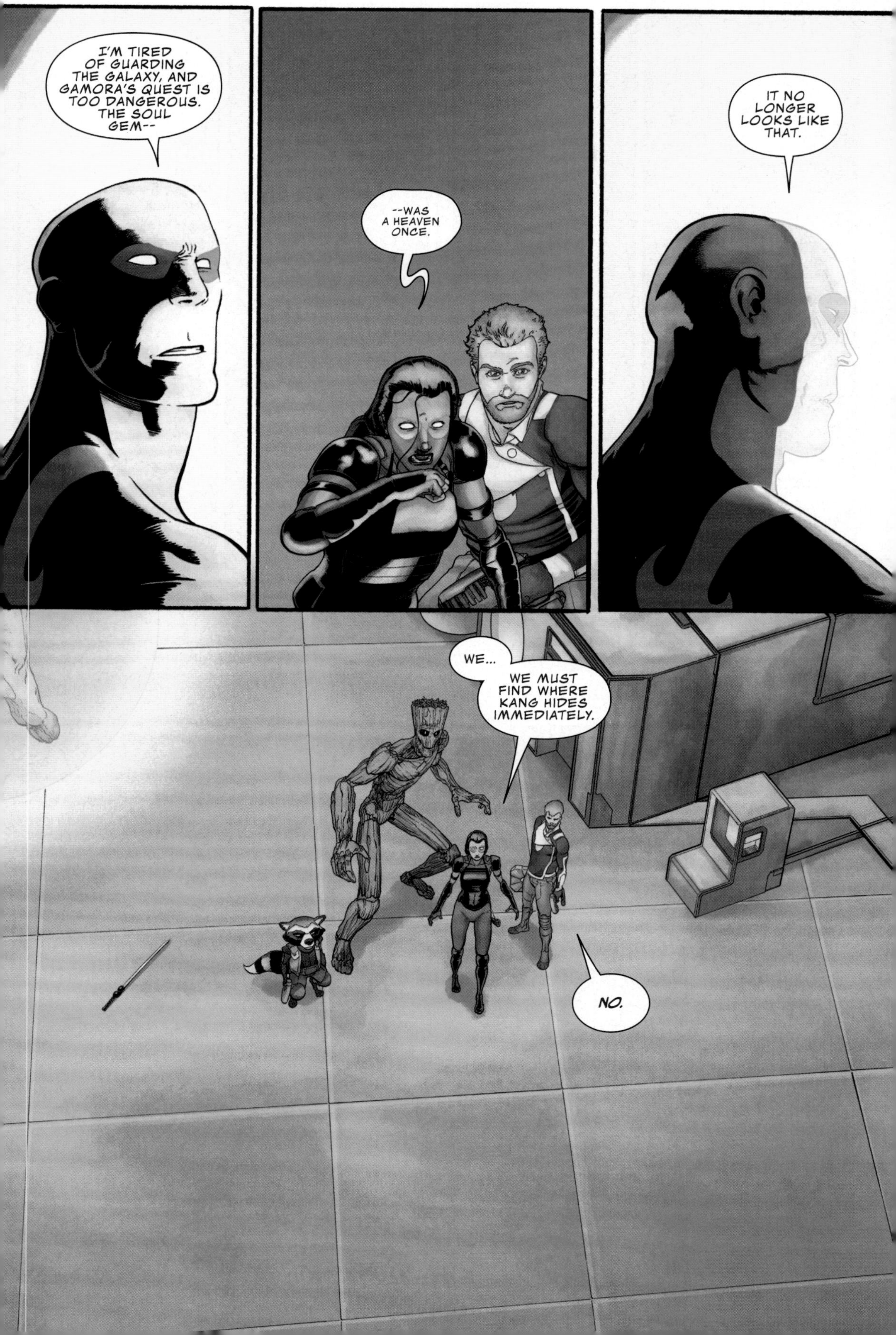
I'M TIRED OF GUARDING THE GALAXY, AND GAMORA'S QUEST IS TOO DANGEROUS. THE SOUL GEM--
--WAS A HEAVEN ONCE.
IT NO LONGER LOOKS LIKE THAT.
WE...
WE MUST FIND WHERE KANG HIDES IMMEDIATELY.
NO.

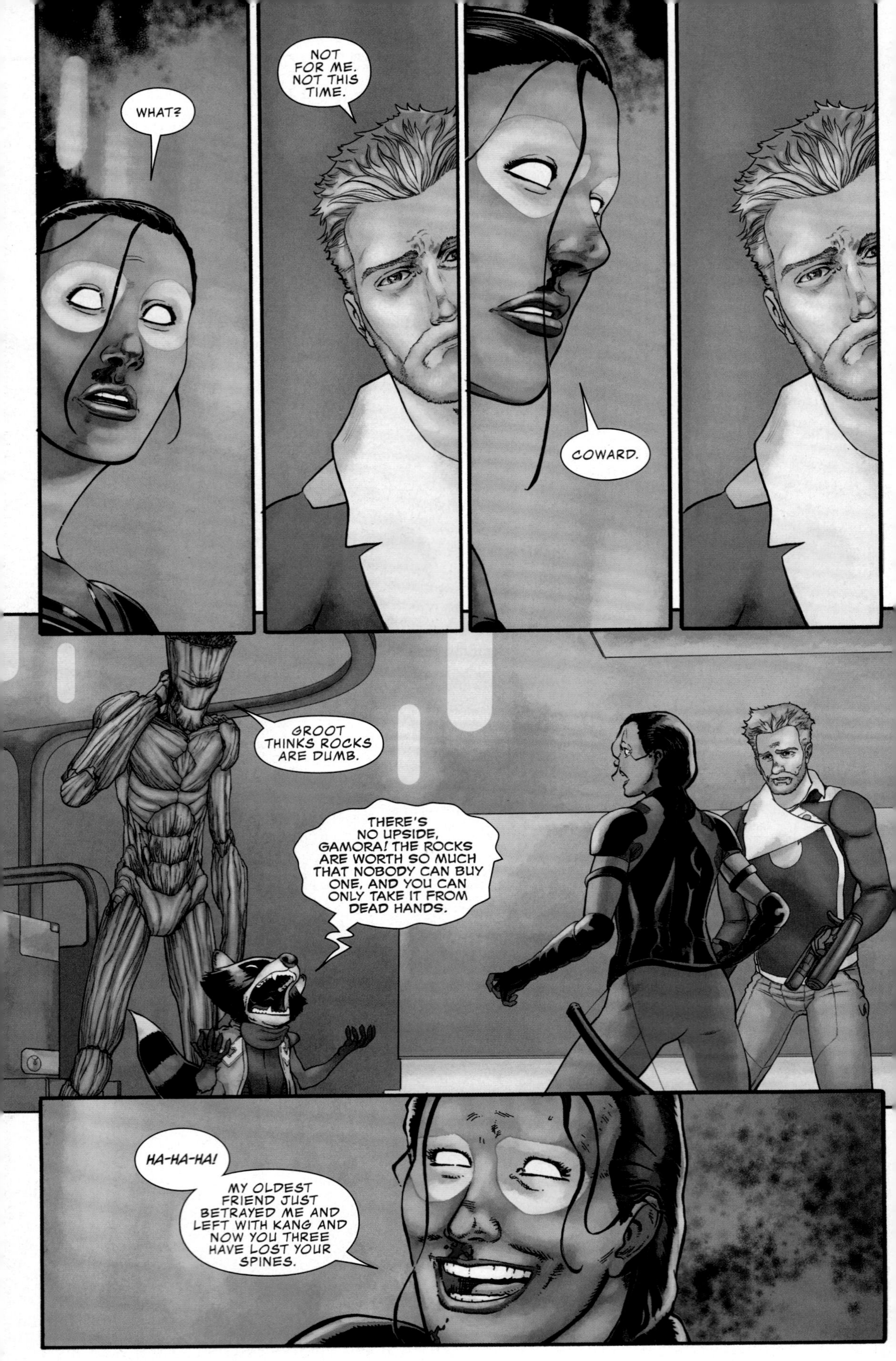

WHAT?
NOT FOR ME. NOT THIS TIME.
COWARD.
GROOT THINKS ROCKS ARE DUMB.
THERE'S NO UPSIDE, GAMORA! THE ROCKS ARE WORTH SO MUCH THAT NOBODY CAN BUY ONE, AND YOU CAN ONLY TAKE IT FROM DEAD HANDS.
HA-HA-HA!
MY OLDEST FRIEND JUST BETRAYED ME AND LEFT WITH KANG AND NOW YOU THREE HAVE LOST YOUR SPINES.

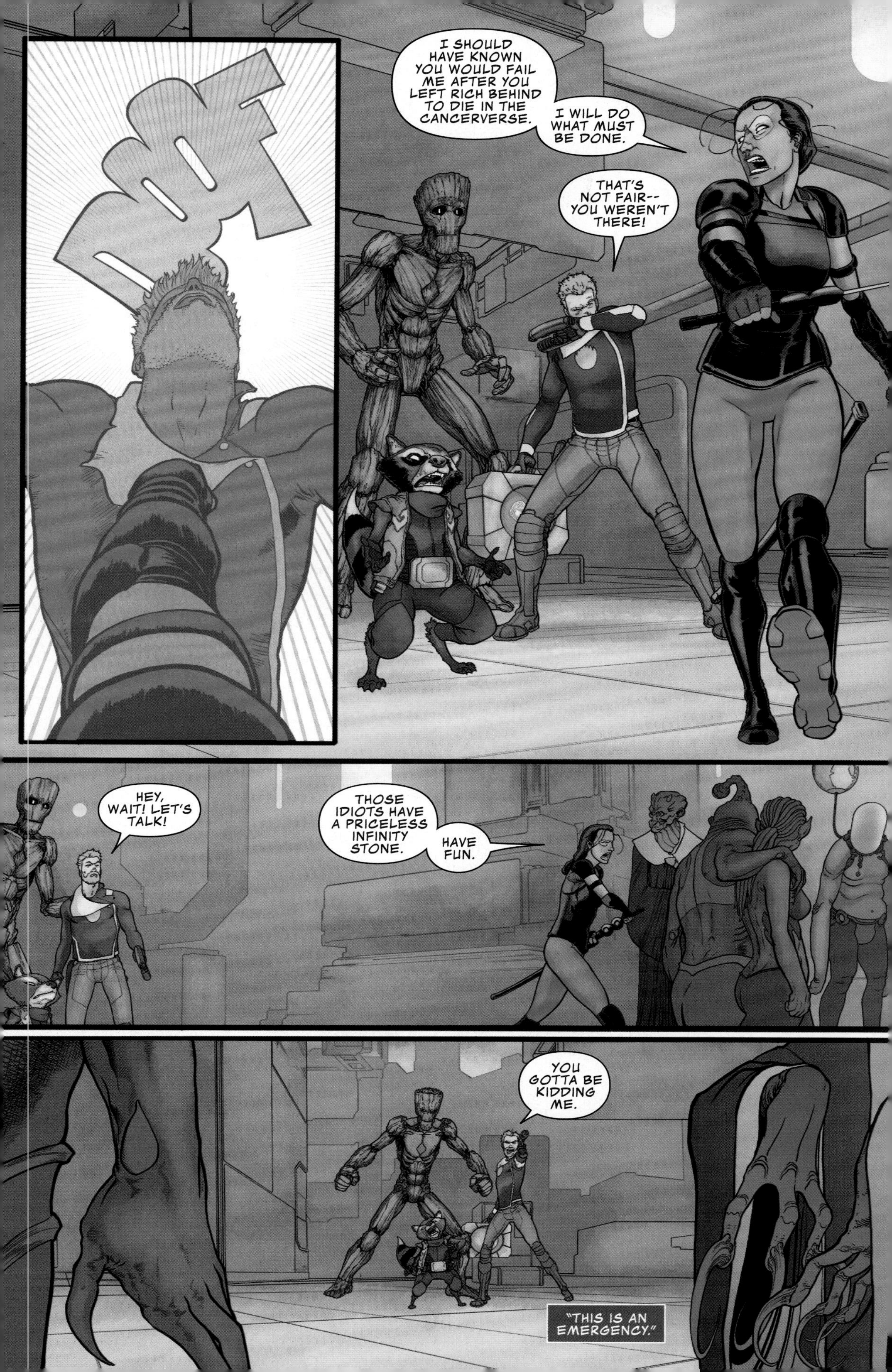
I SHOULD HAVE KNOWN YOU WOULD FAIL ME AFTER YOU LEFT RICH BEHIND TO DIE IN THE CANCERVERSE.
I WILL DO WHAT MUST BE DONE.
THAT'S NOT FAIR-- YOU WEREN'T THERE!
HEY, WAIT! LET'S TALK!
THOSE IDIOTS HAVE A PRICELESS INFINITY STONE.
HAVE FUN.
YOU GOTTA BE KIDDING ME.
"THIS IS AN EMERGENCY."

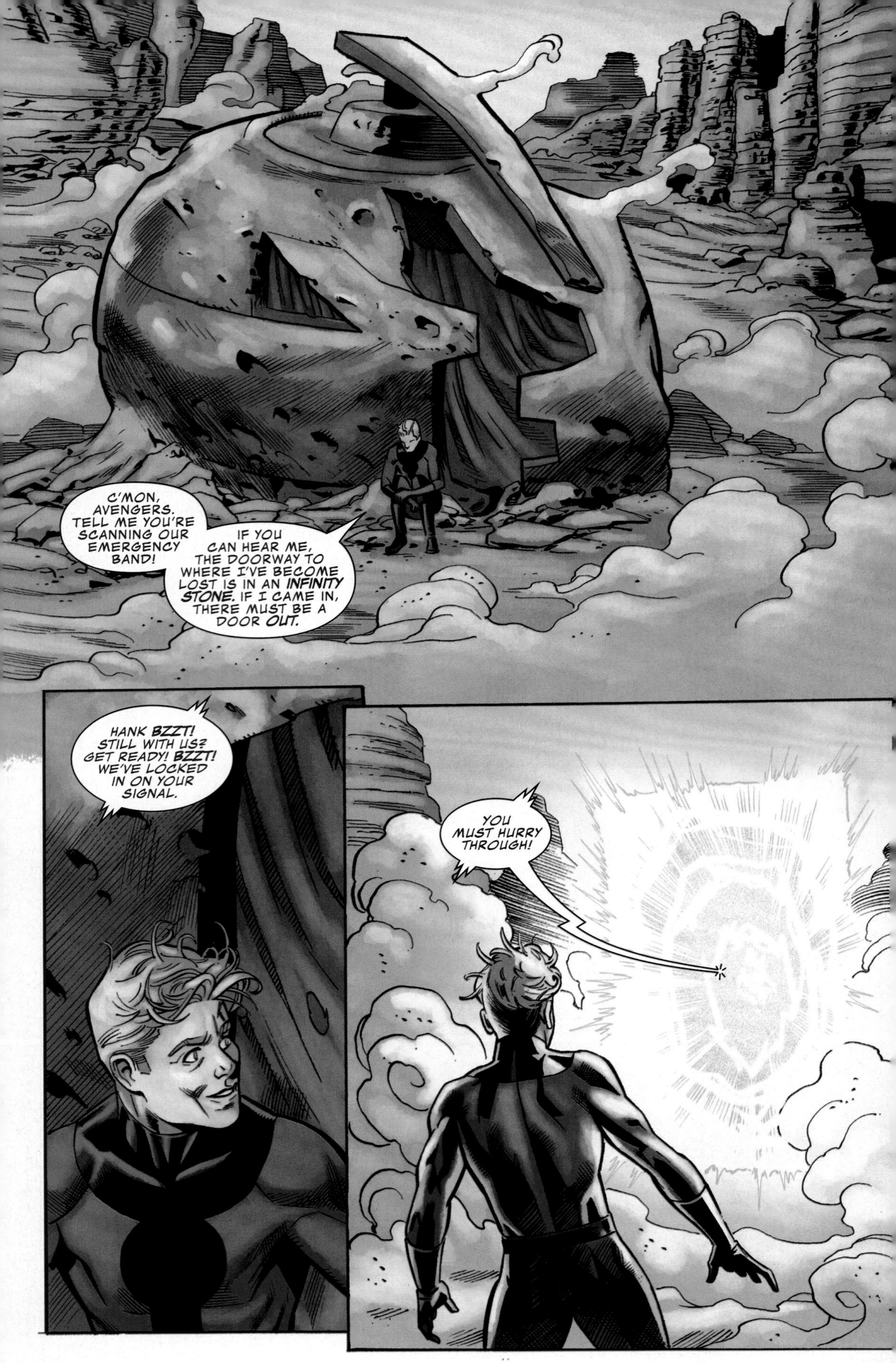
C'MON, AVENGERS. TELL ME YOU'RE SCANNING OUR EMERGENCY BAND!
IF YOU CAN HEAR ME, THE DOORWAY TO WHERE I'VE BECOME LOST IS IN AN INFINITY STONE. IF I CAME IN, THERE MUST BE A DOOR OUT.
HANK BZZT! STILL WITH US? GET READY! BZZT! WE'VE LOCKED IN ON YOUR SIGNAL.
YOU MUST HURRY THROUGH!

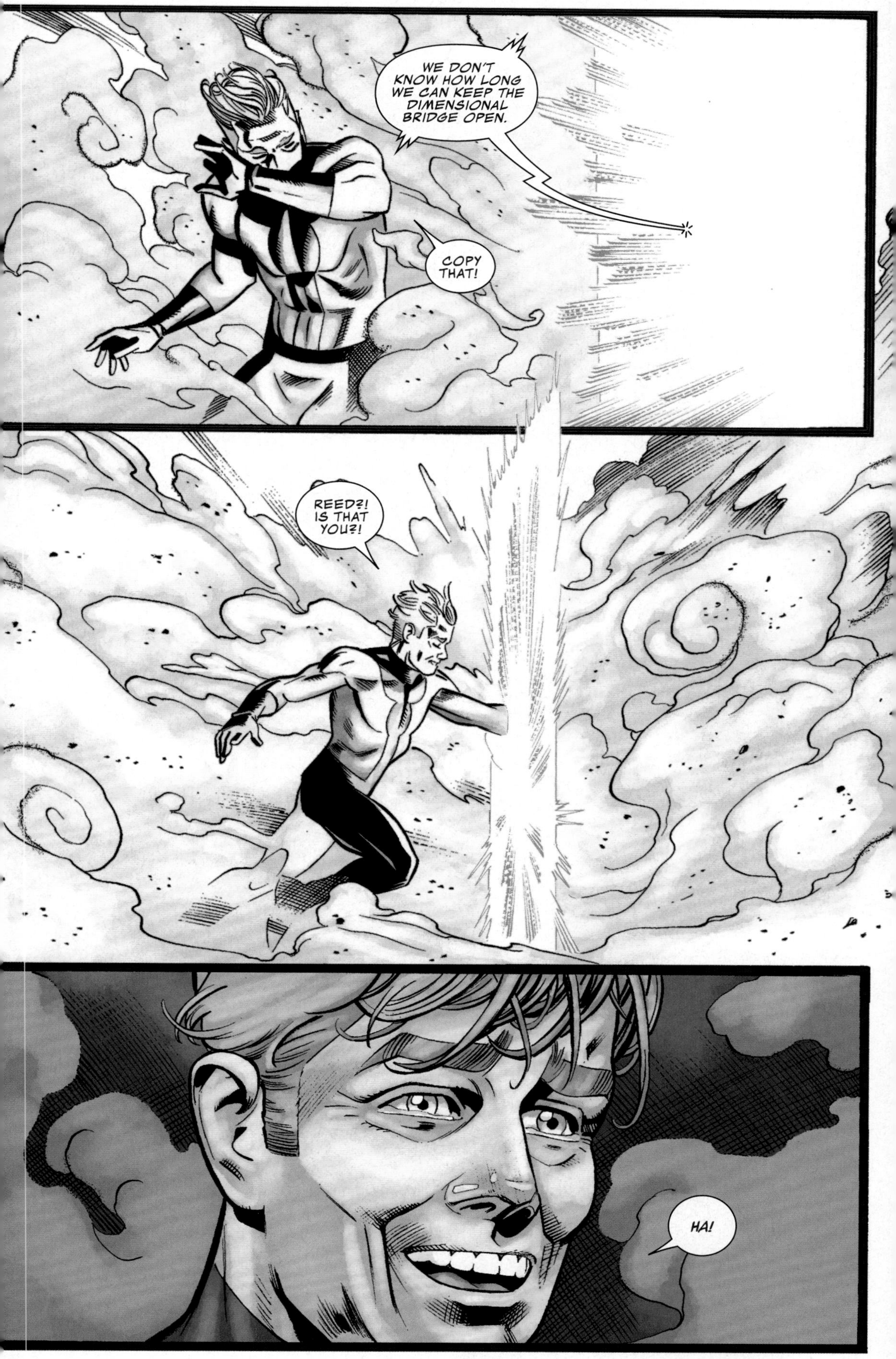
WE DON'T KNOW HOW LONG WE CAN KEEP THE DIMENSIONAL BRIDGE OPEN.
COPY THAT!
REED?! IS THAT YOU?!
HA!

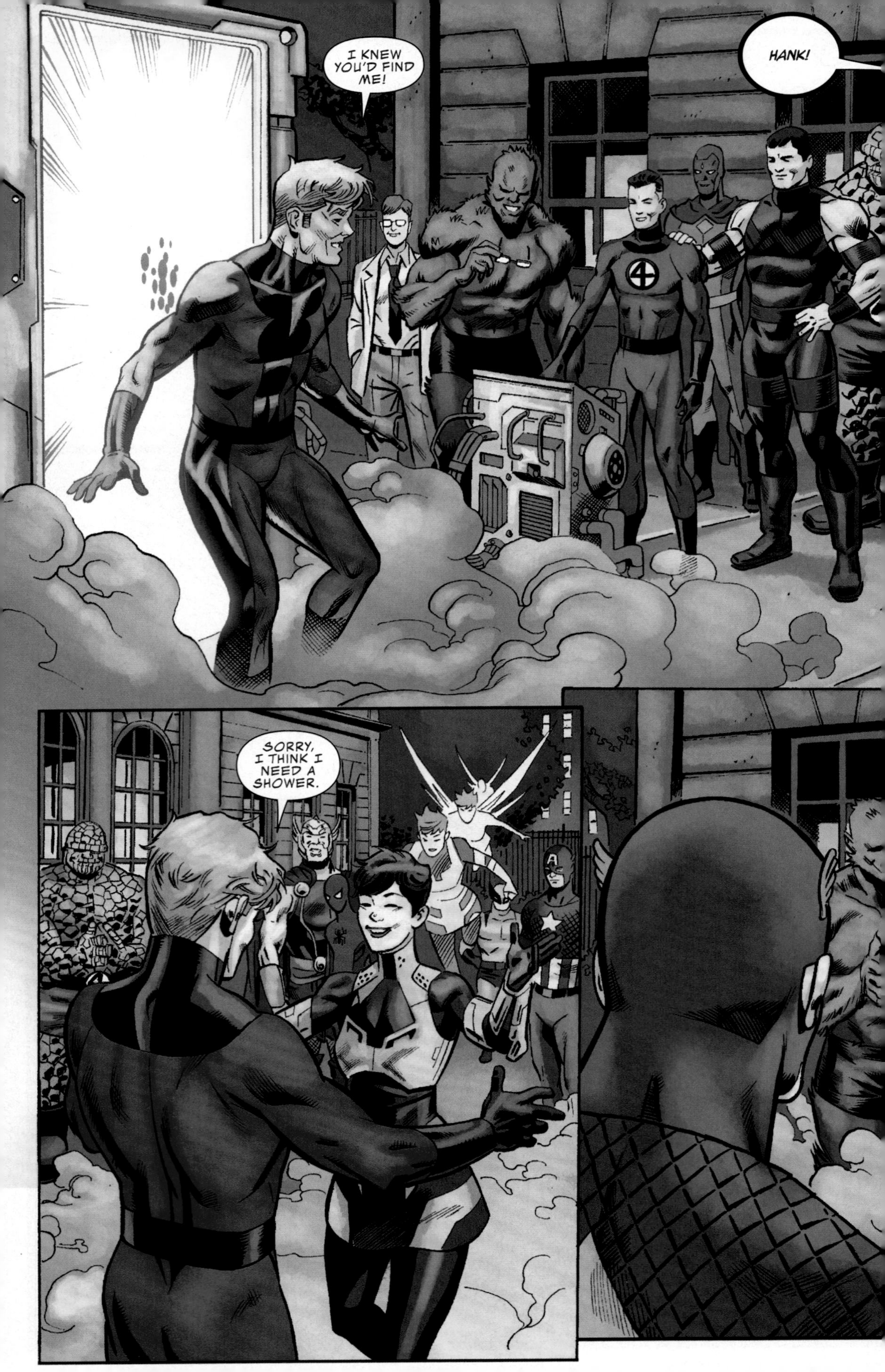
I KNEW YOU'D FIND ME!
HANK!
SORRY, I THINK I NEED A SHOWER.

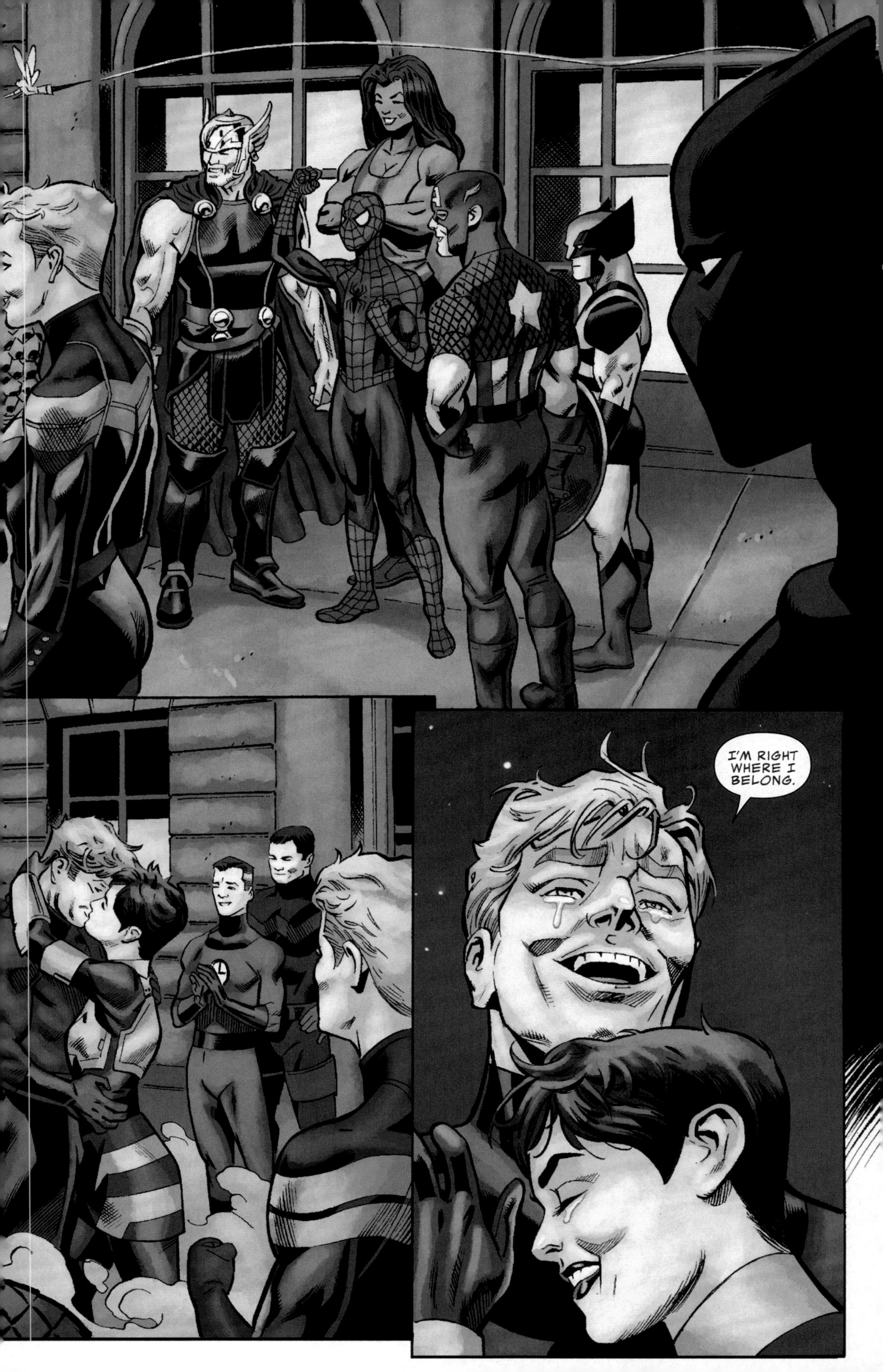
I'M RIGHT WHERE I BELONG.

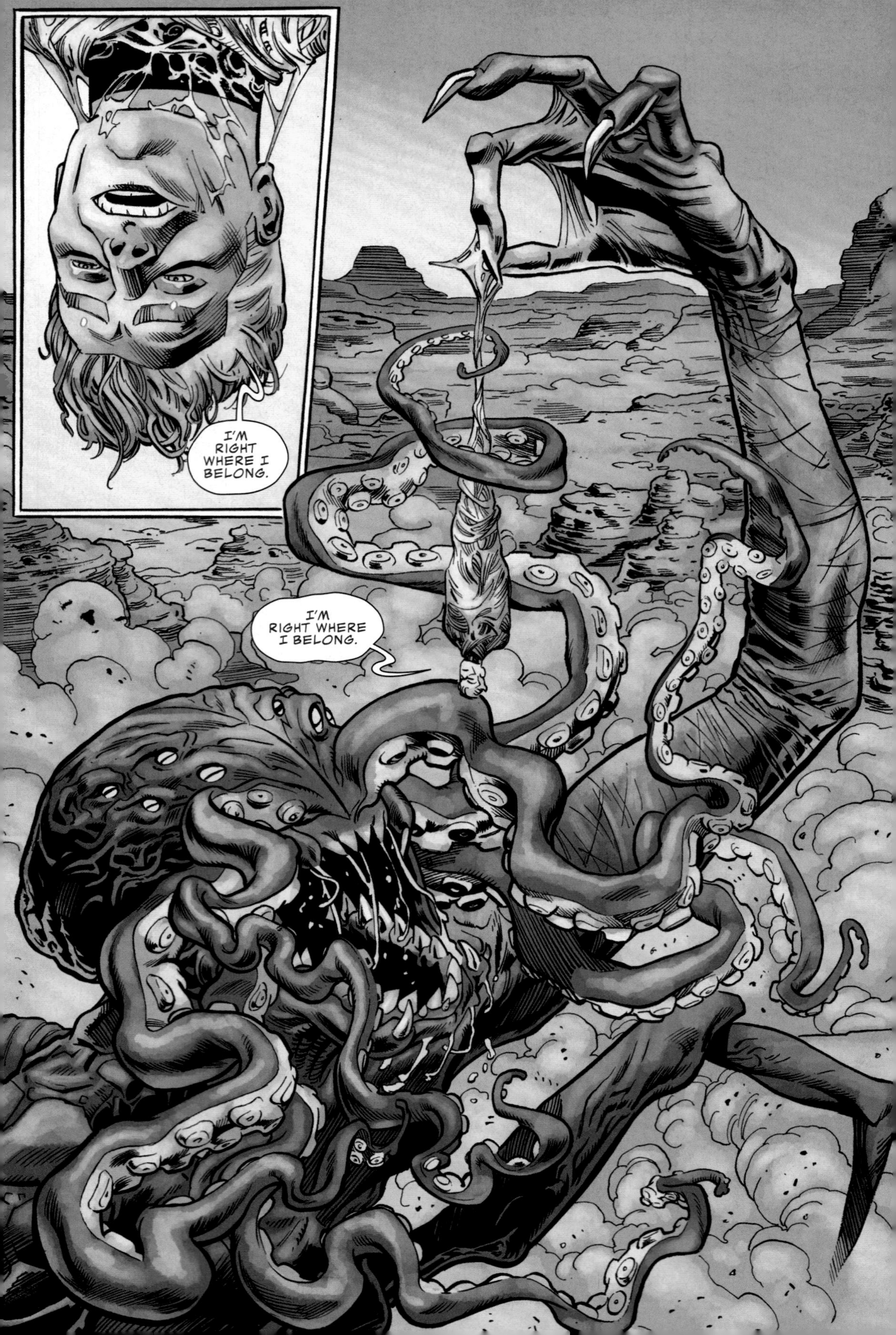
I'M RIGHT WHERE I BELONG.
I'M RIGHT WHERE I BELONG.

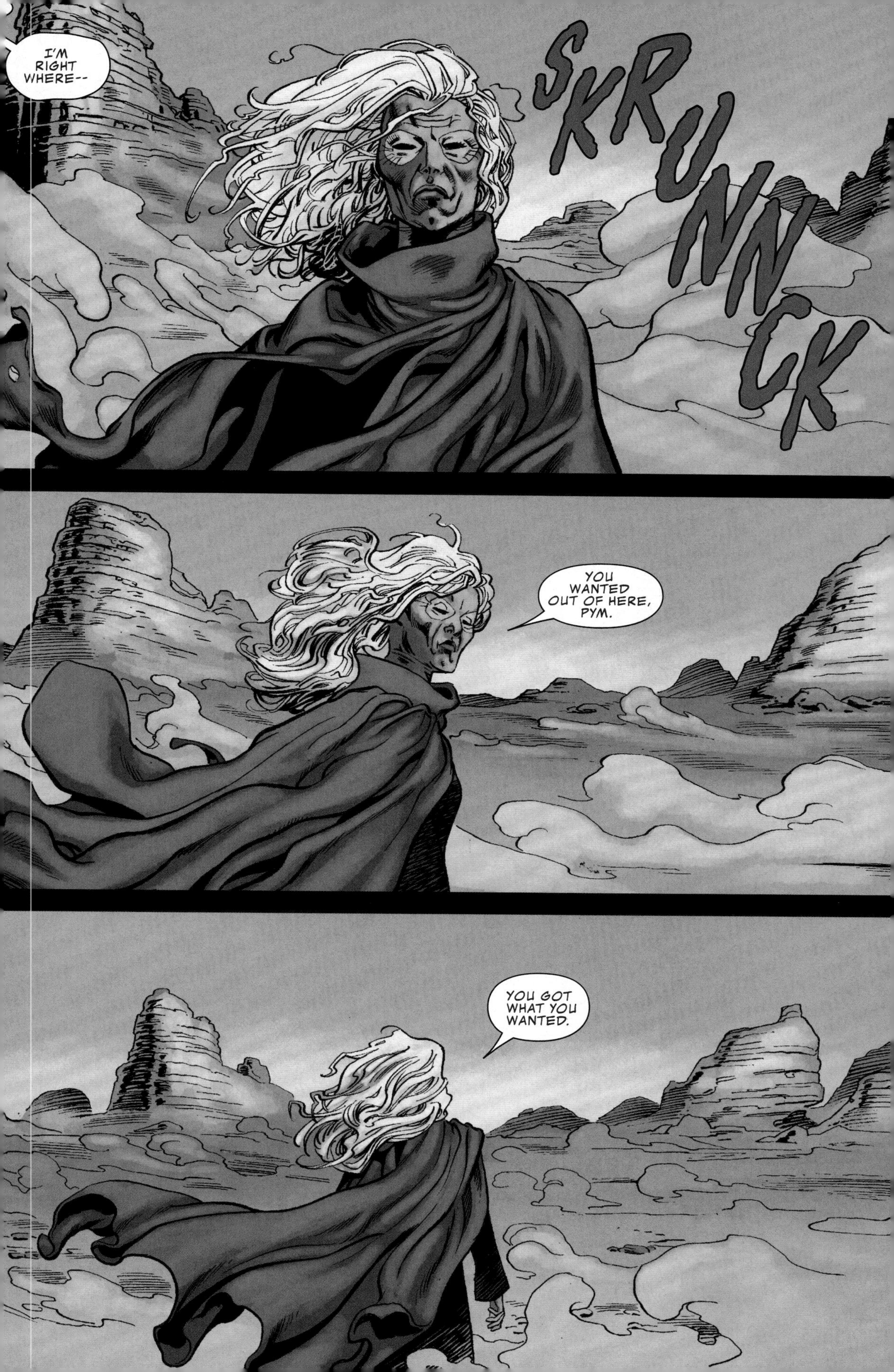
I'M RIGHT WHERE--
SKRUNNCK
YOU WANTED OUT OF HERE, PYM.
YOU GOT WHAT YOU WANTED.

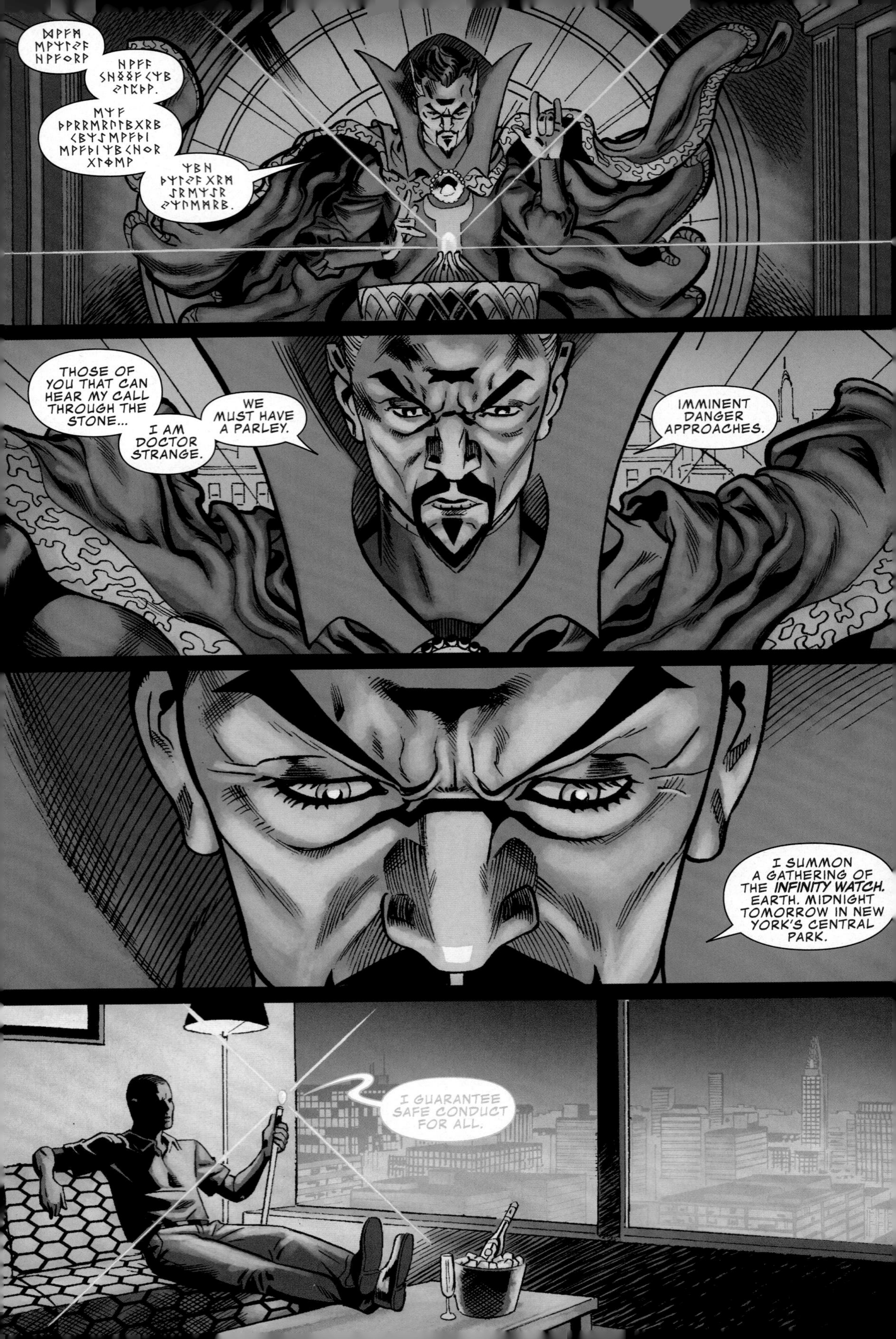
THOSE OF YOU THAT CAN HEAR MY CALL THROUGH THE STONE...
I AM DOCTOR STRANGE.
WE MUST HAVE A PARLEY.
IMMINENT DANGER APPROACHES.
I SUMMON A GATHERING OF THE INFINITY WATCH. EARTH. MIDNIGHT TOMORROW IN NEW YORK'S CENTRAL PARK.
I GUARANTEE SAFE CONDUCT FOR ALL.

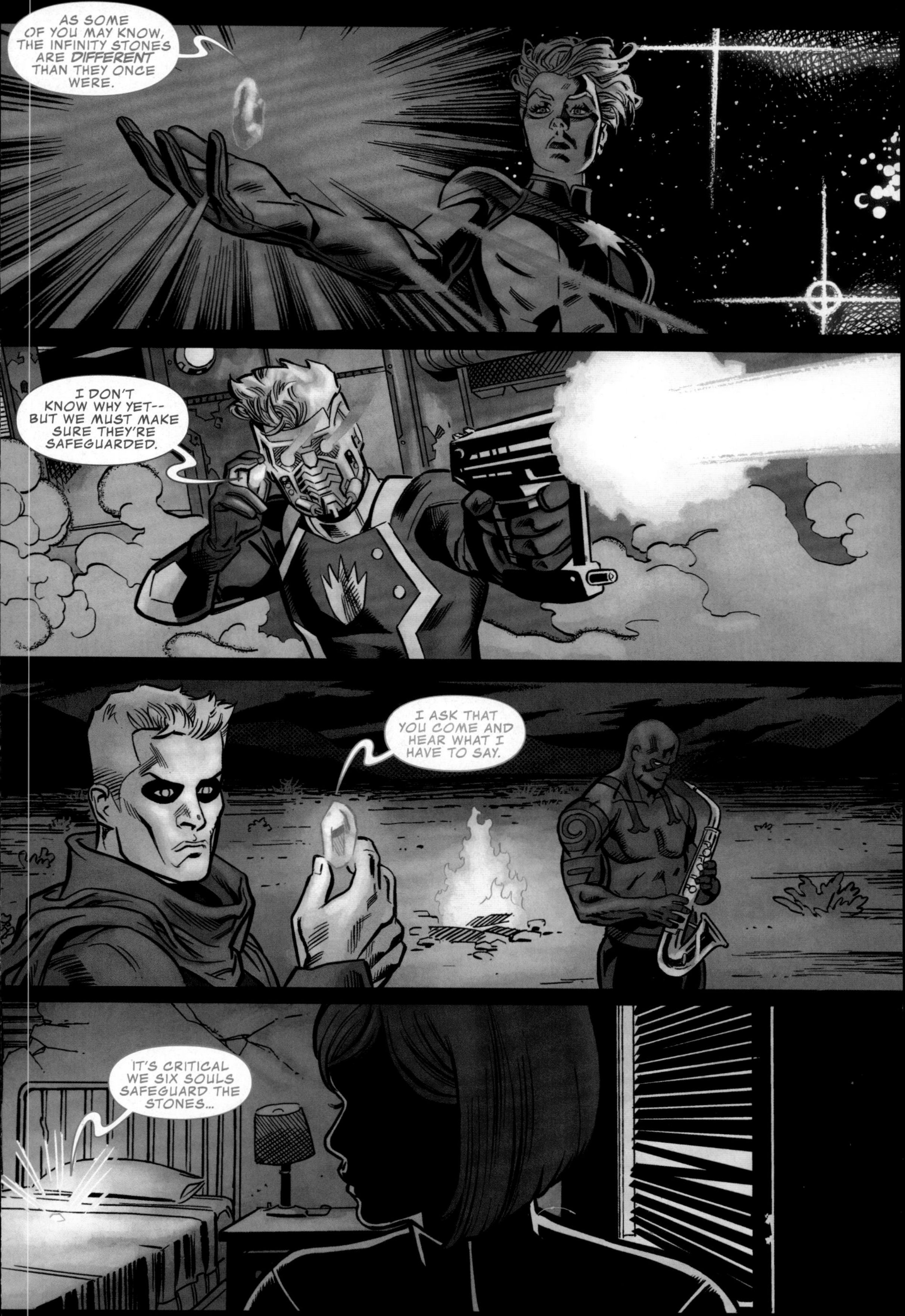
AS SOME OF YOU MAY KNOW, THE INFINITY STONES ARE *DIFFERENT* THAN THEY ONCE WERE.
I DON'T KNOW WHY YET-- BUT WE MUST MAKE SURE THEY'RE SAFEGUARDED.
I ASK THAT YOU COME AND HEAR WHAT I HAVE TO SAY.
IT'S CRITICAL WE SIX SOULS SAFEGUARD THE STONES...

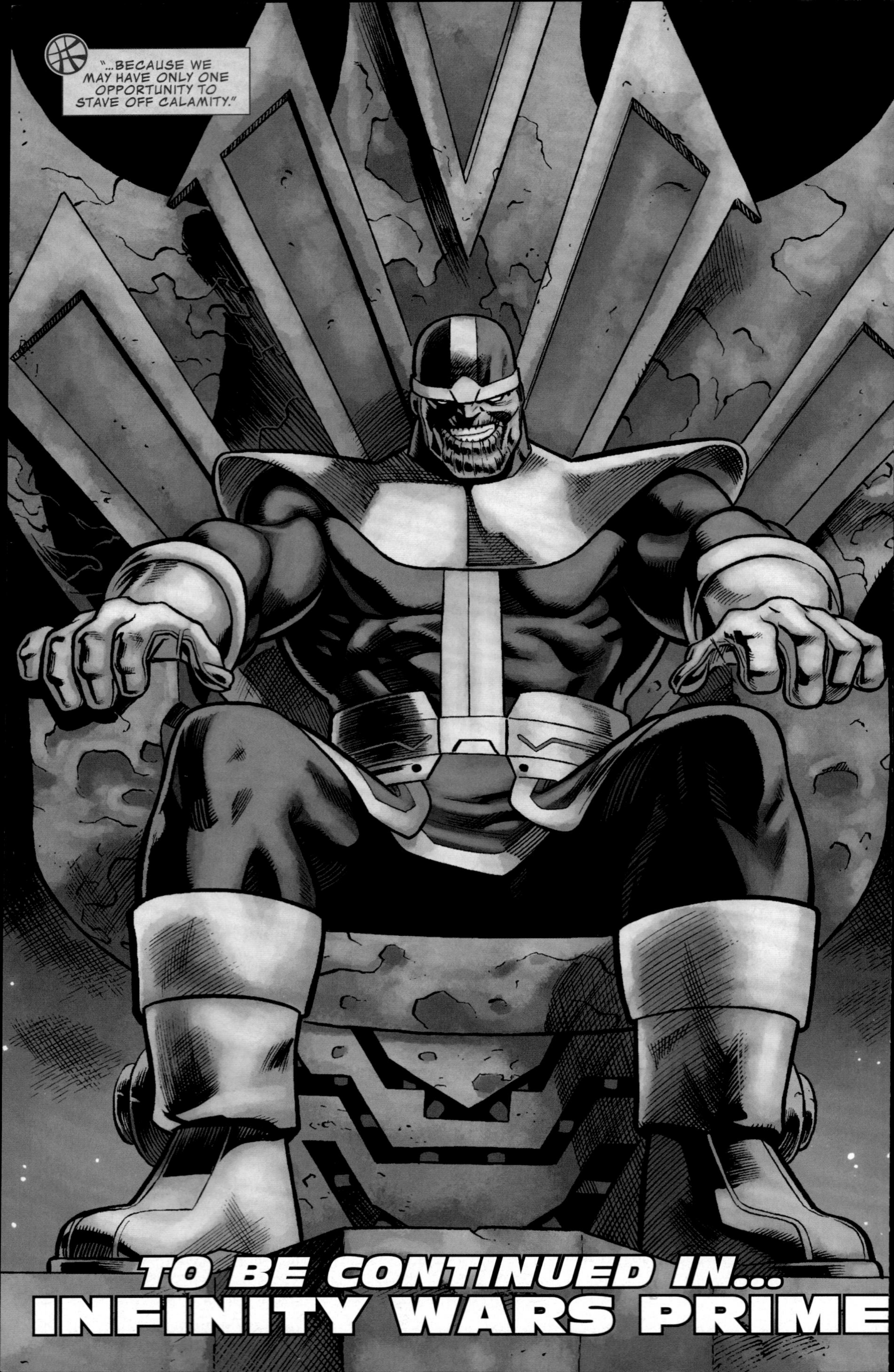
"...BECAUSE WE MAY HAVE ONLY ONE OPPORTUNITY TO STAVE OFF CALAMITY."
TO BE CONTINUED IN...
INFINITY WARS PRIME

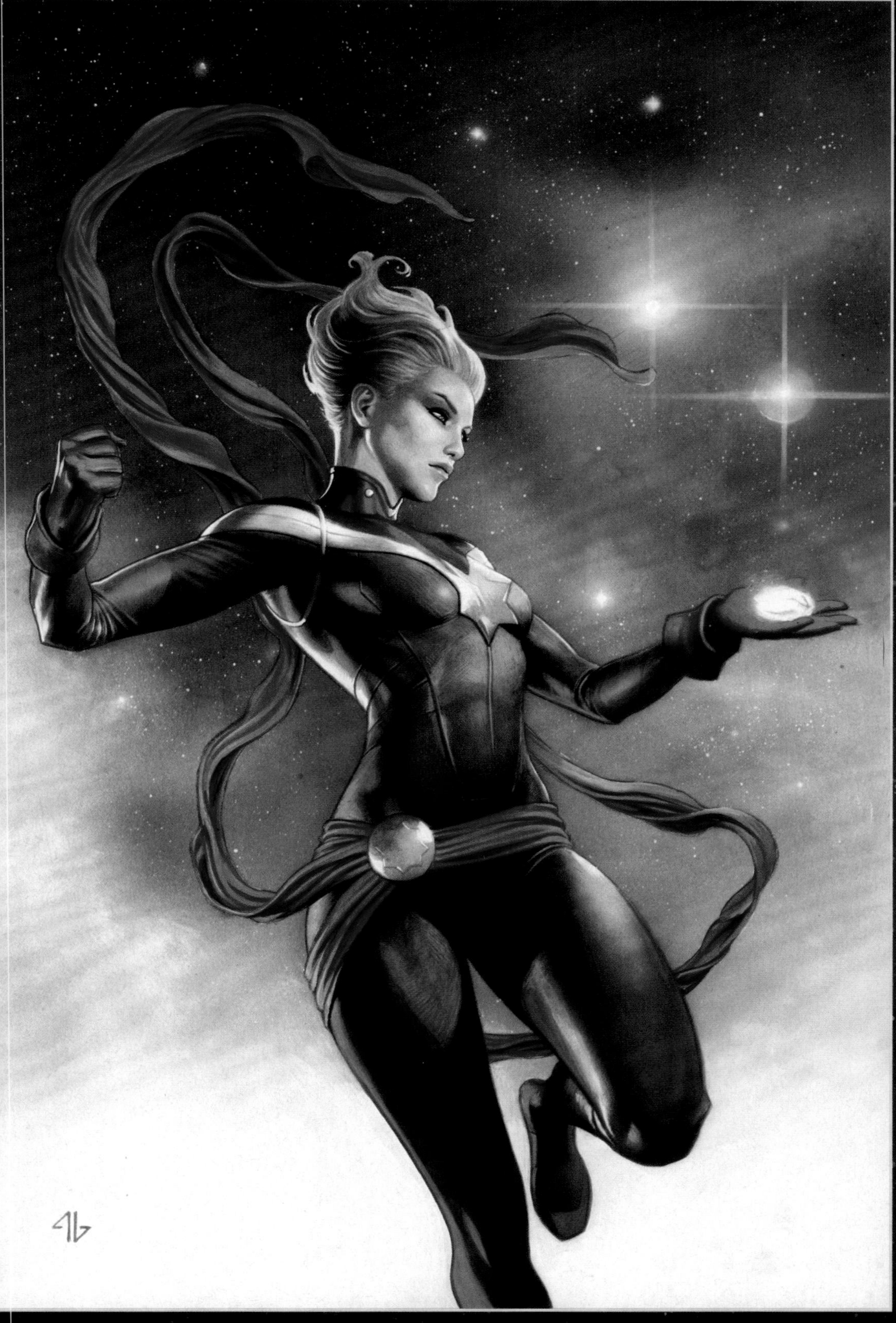

ADI GRANOV

INFINITY COUNTDOWN #1 VARIANT

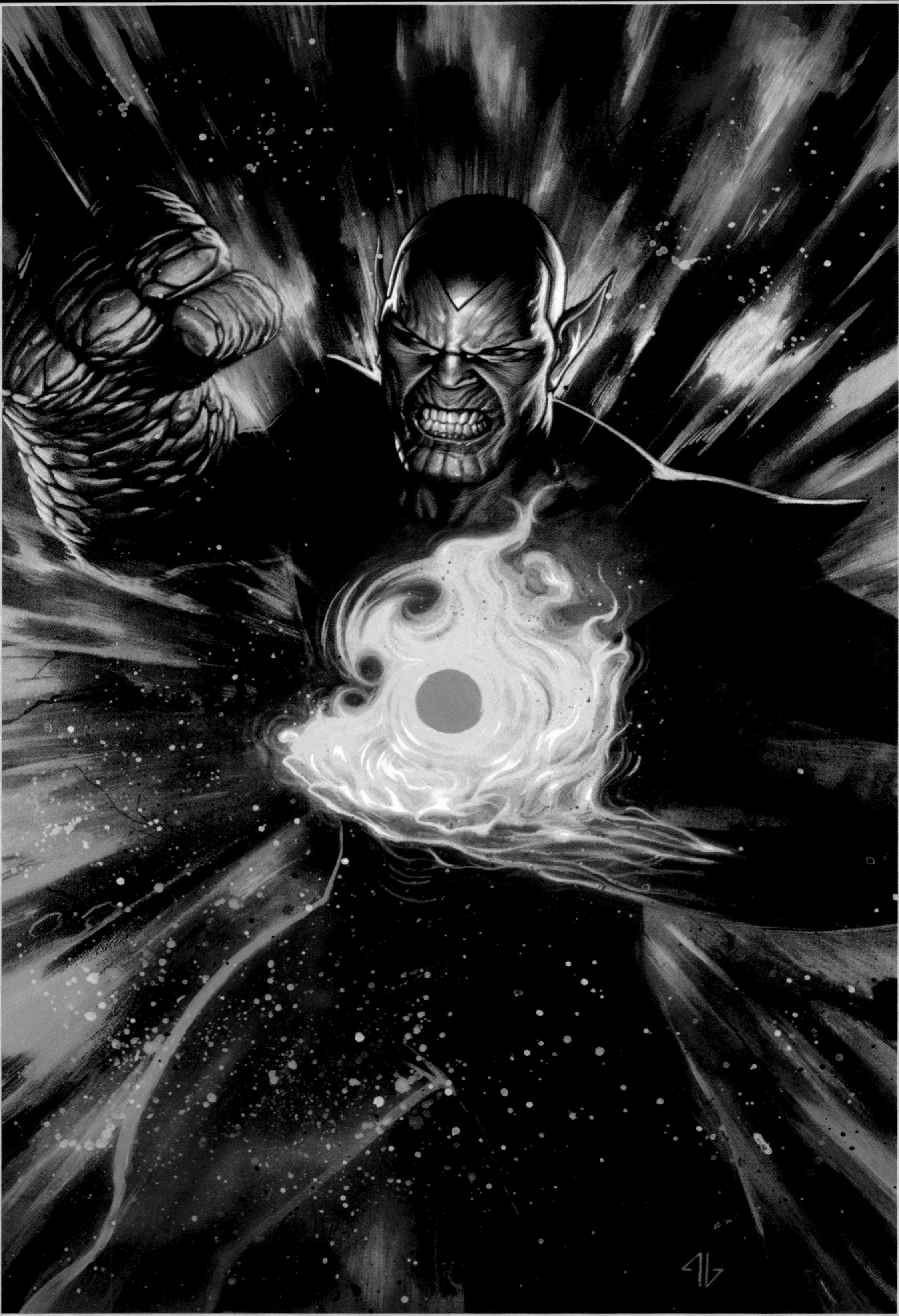

ADI GRANOV

INFINITY COUNTDOWN #2 VARIANT

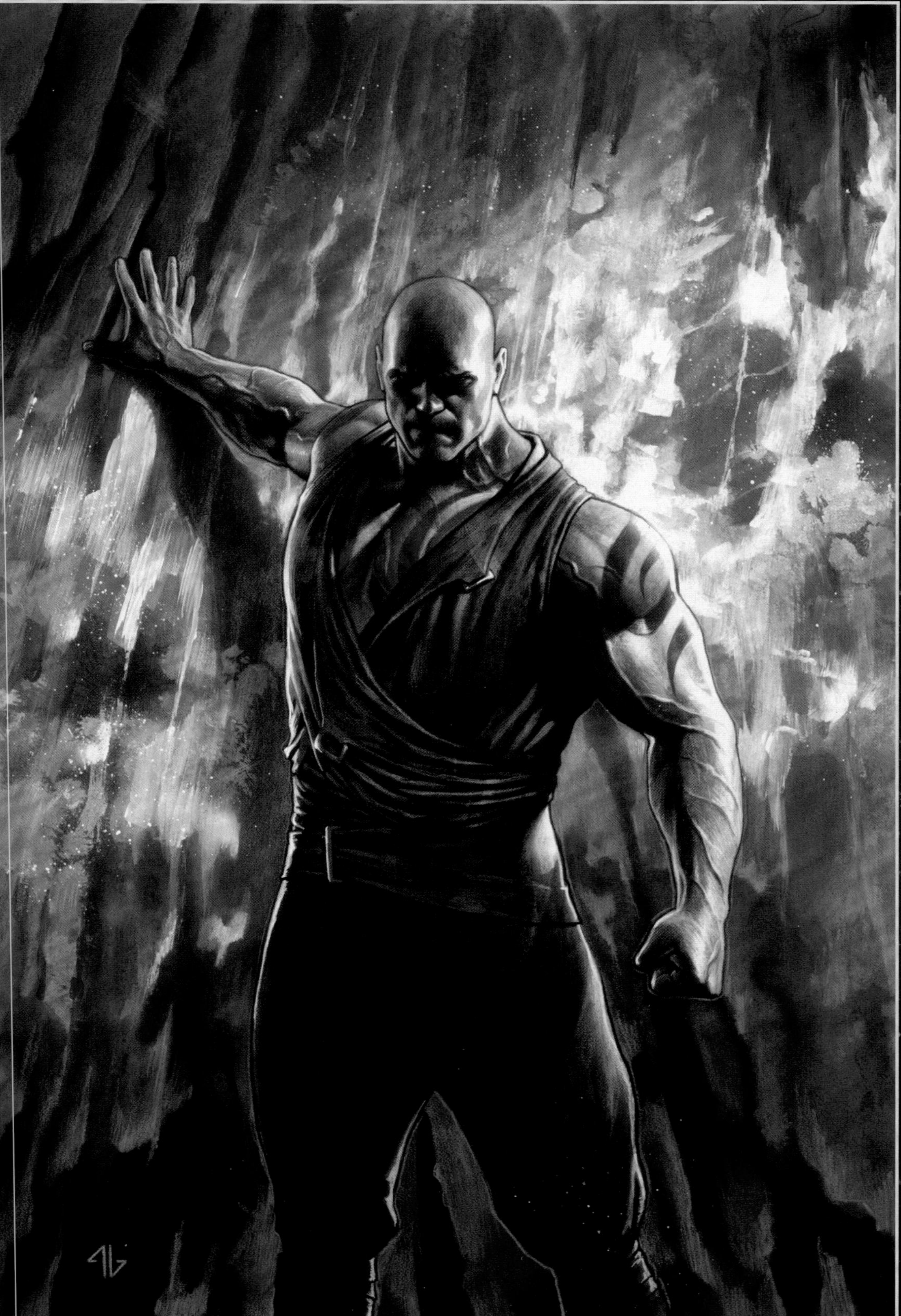

ADI GRANOV

INFINITY COUNTDOWN #3 VARIANT

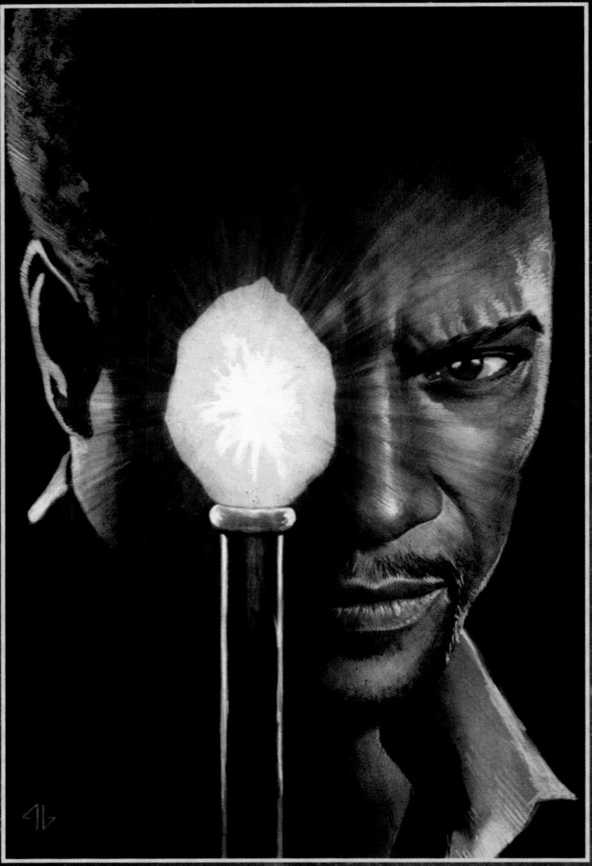

ADI GRANOV

INFINITY COUNTDOWN #4 VARIANT

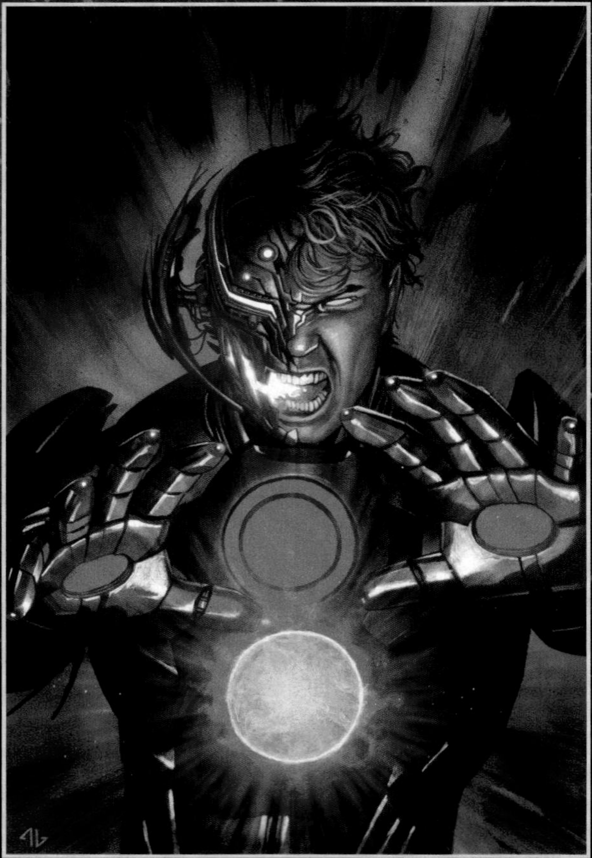

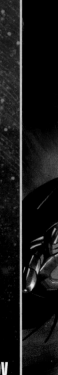

ADI GRANOV

INFINITY COUNTDOWN #5 VARIANT

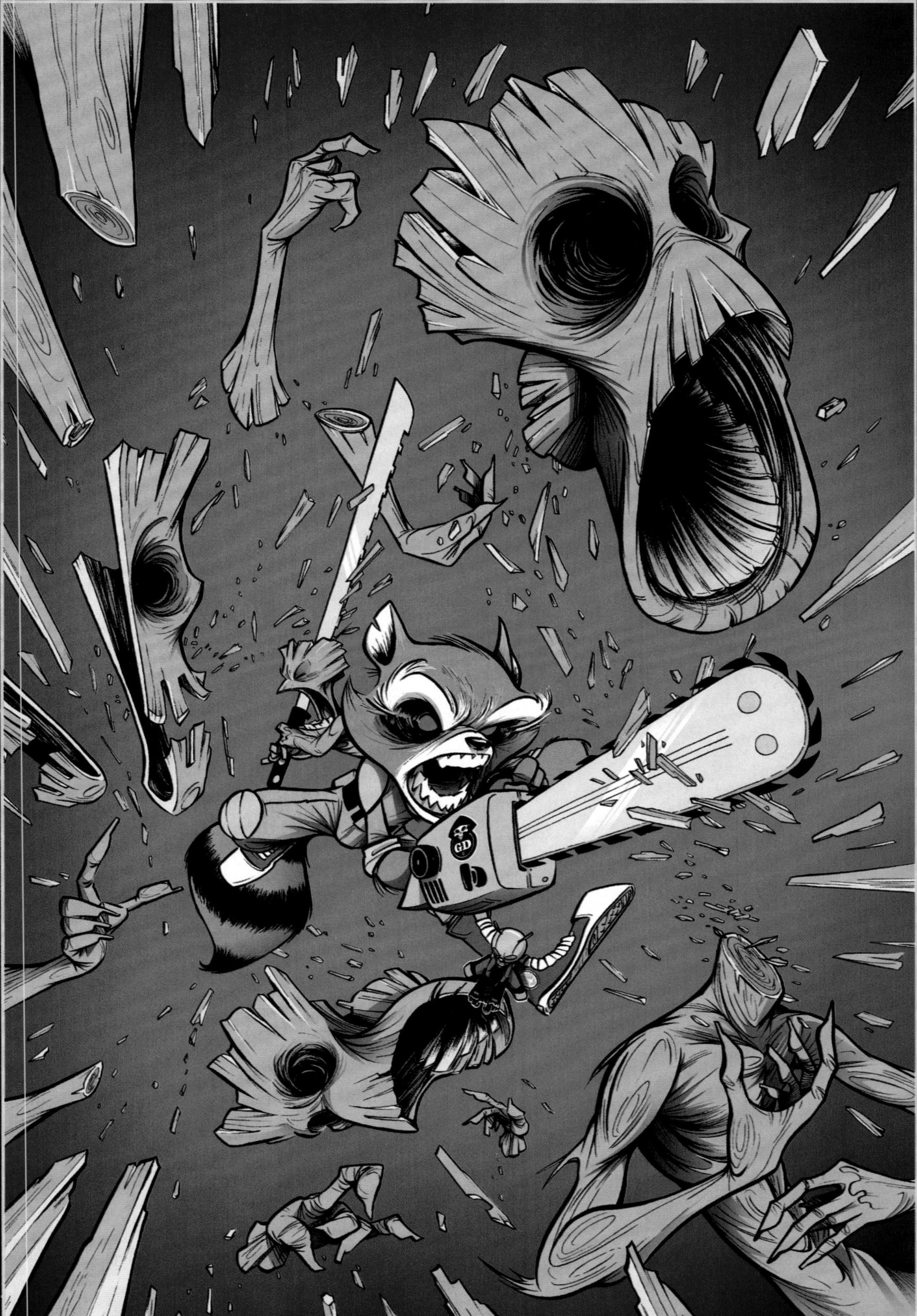

GUSTAVO DUARTE

INFINITY COUNTDOWN #1 VARIANT

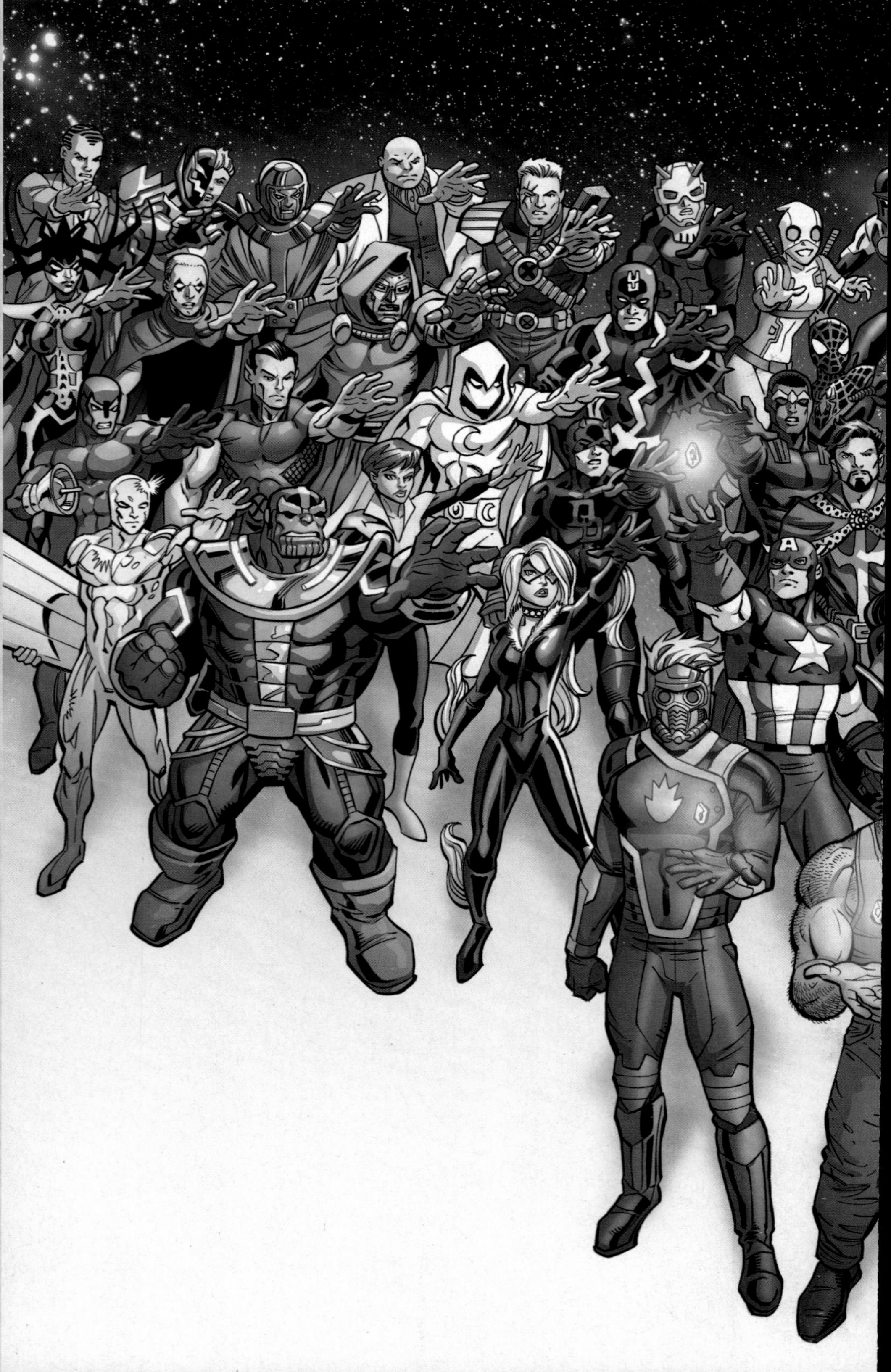

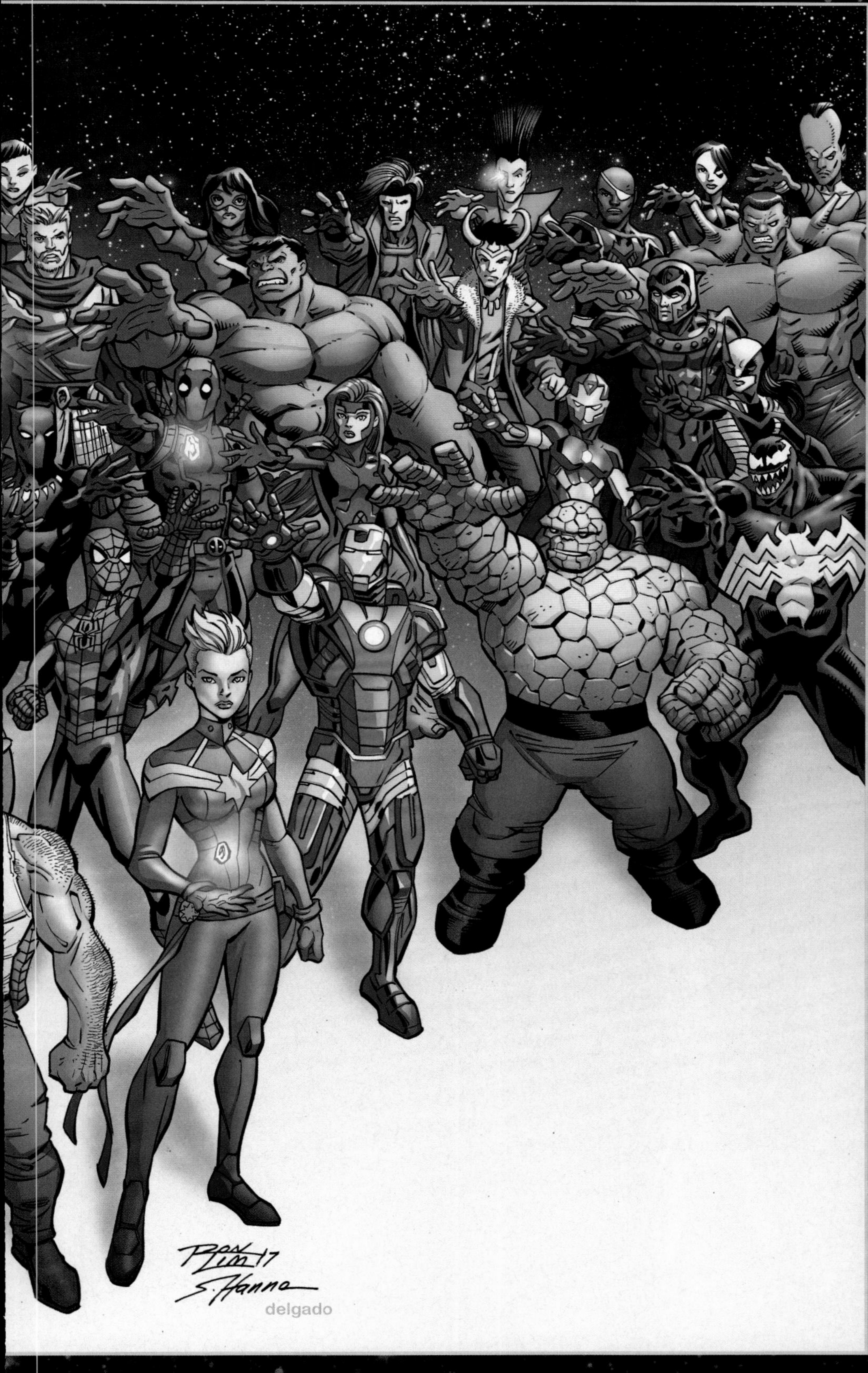
Ron Lim 17
S. Hanna
delgado

RON LIM, SCOTT HANNA & EDGAR DELGADO

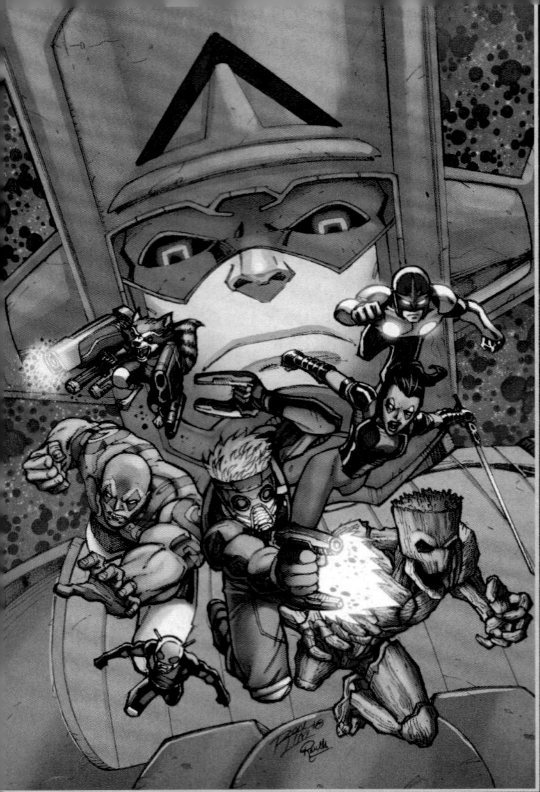

RON LIM & RACHELLE ROSENBERG
INFINITY COUNTDOWN #2 VARIANT

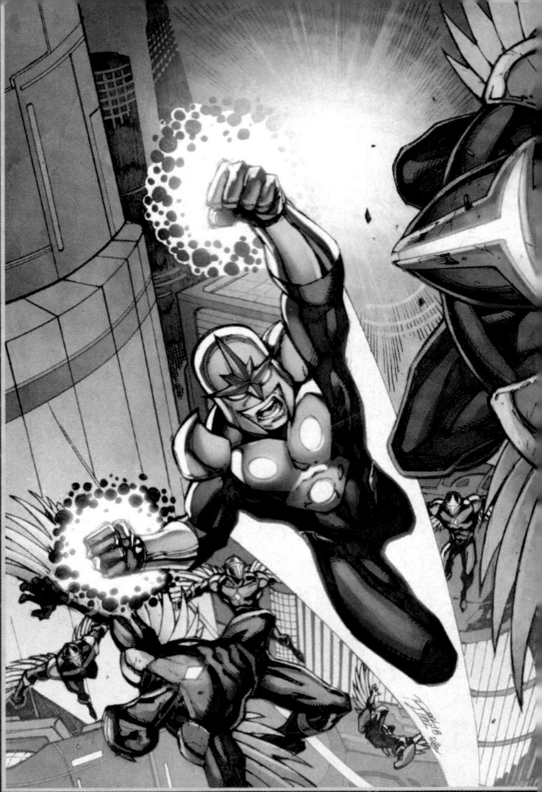

RON LIM & RACHELLE ROSENBERG
INFINITY COUNTDOWN #3 VARIANT

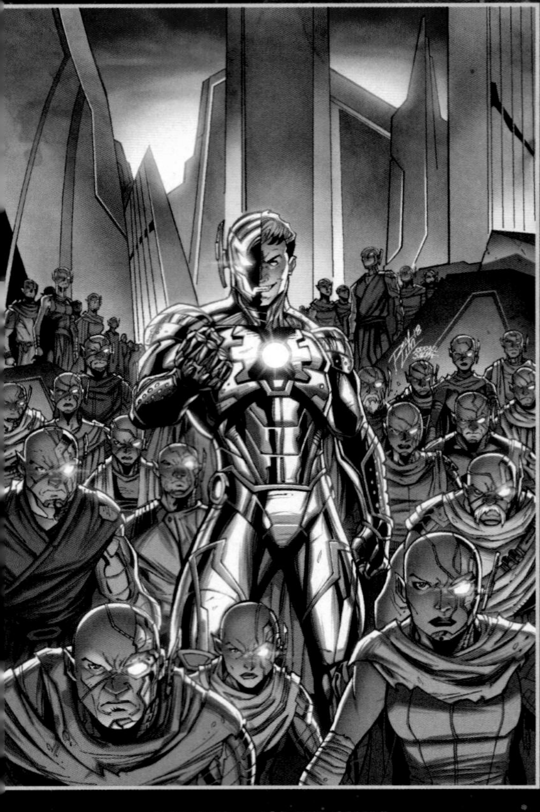

RON LIM & ISRAEL SILVA

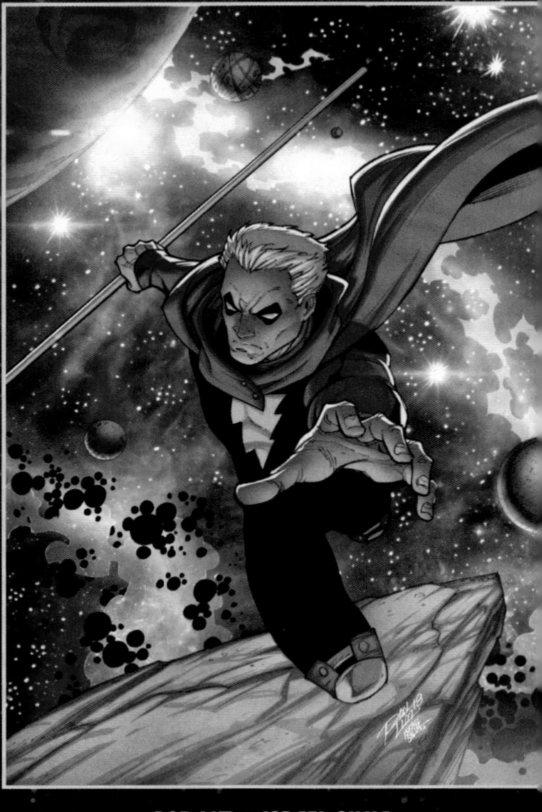

RON LIM & ISRAEL SILVA

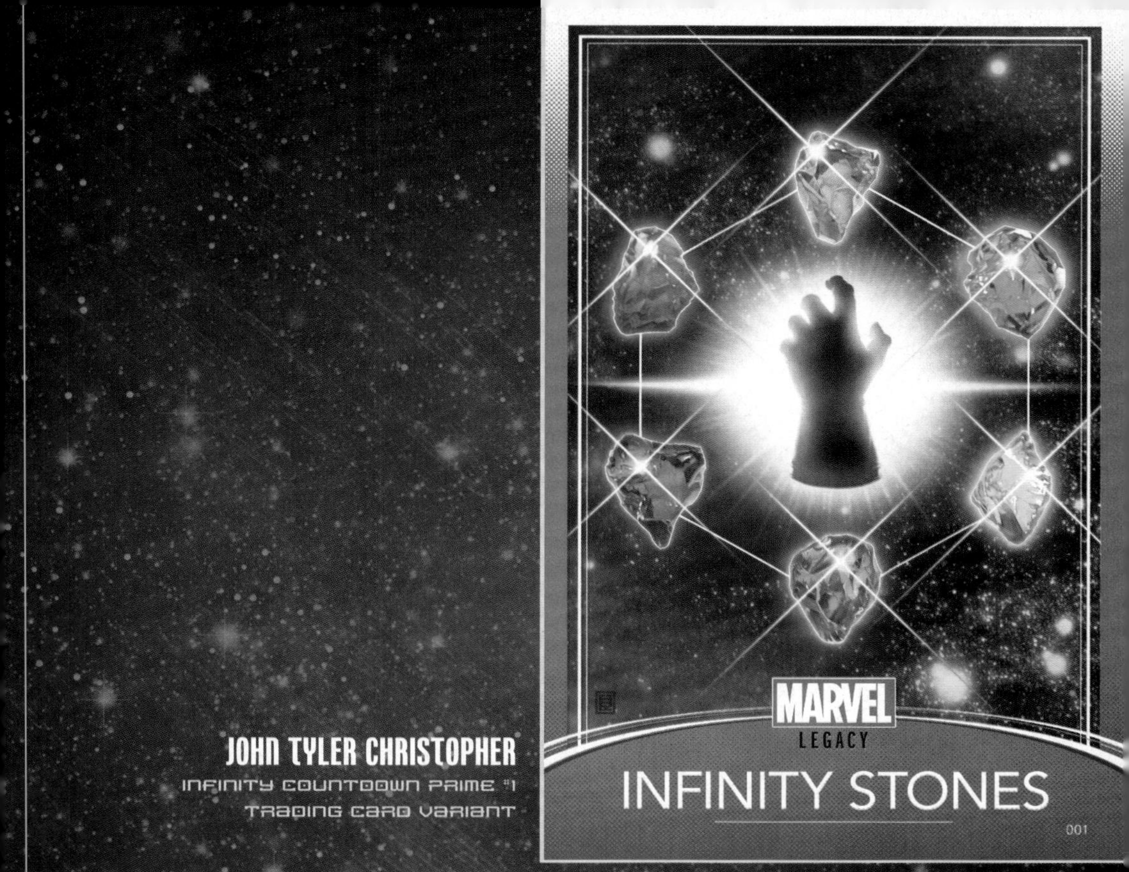
JOHN TYLER CHRISTOPHER
INFINITY COUNTDOWN PRIME #1
TRADING CARD VARIANT
MARVEL
LEGACY
INFINITY STONES
001

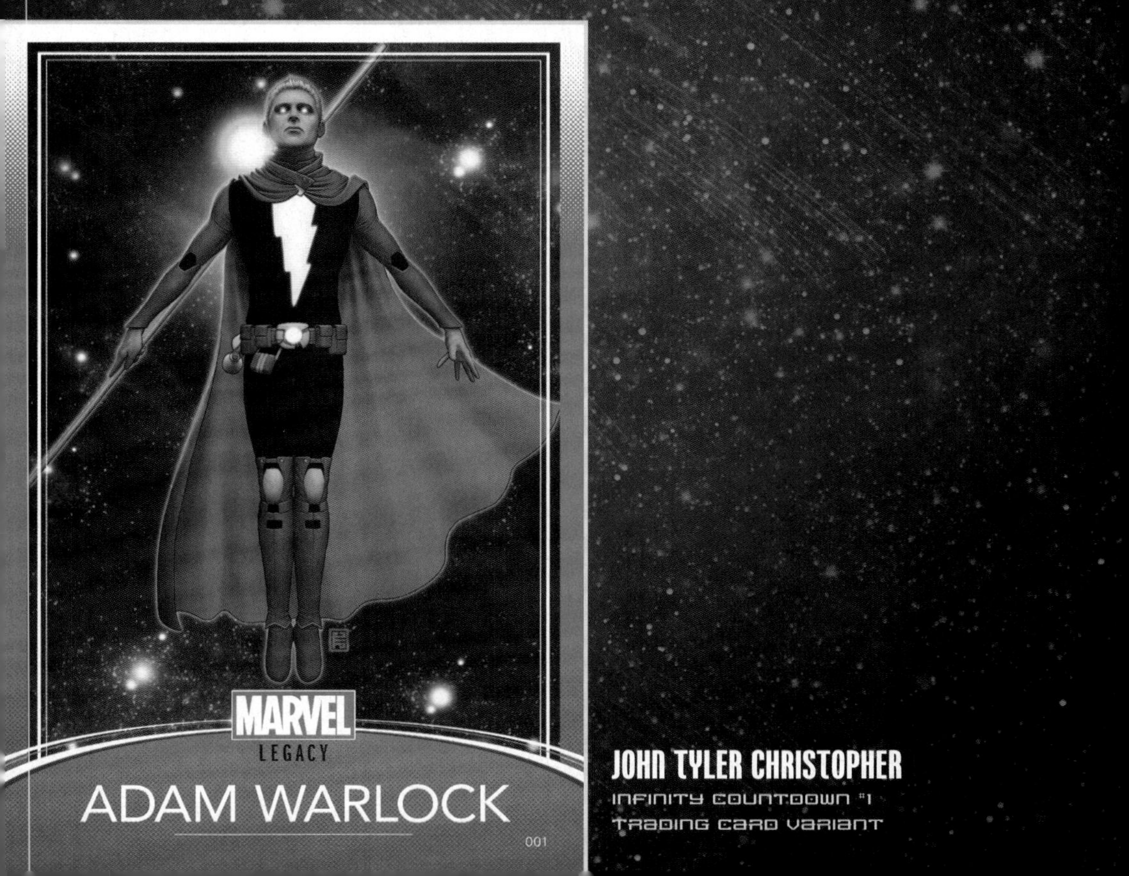
MARVEL
LEGACY
ADAM WARLOCK
001
JOHN TYLER CHRISTOPHER
INFINITY COUNTDOWN #1
TRADING CARD VARIANT

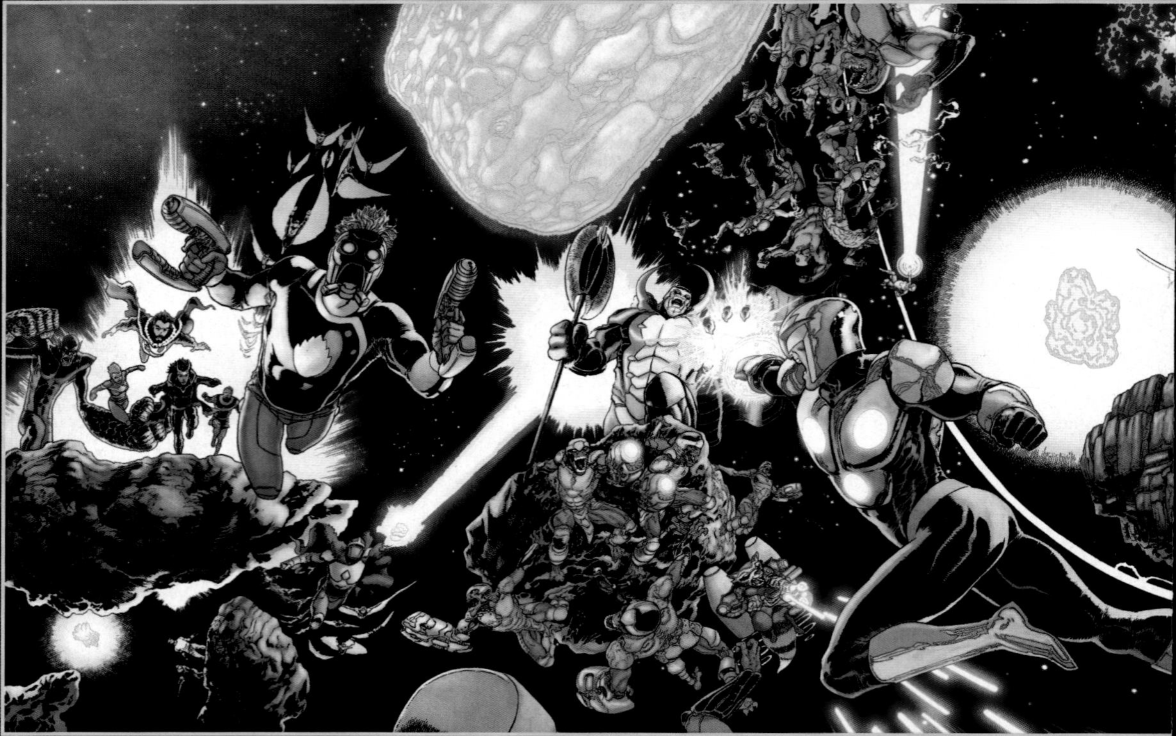

AARON KUDER & **JORDIE BELLAIRE**
INFINITY COUNTDOWN #1-5 CONNECTING VARIANTS

PREVIOUSLY IN...

GUARDIANS of the GALAXY

STARRING:

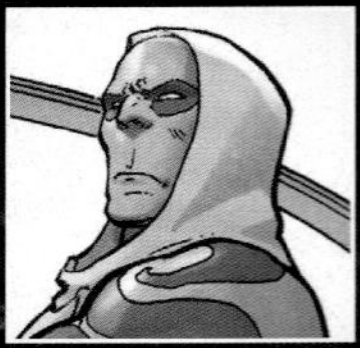

DRAX THE DESTROYER

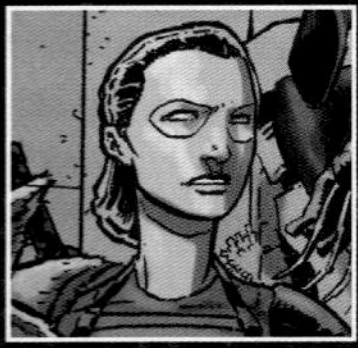

GAMORA

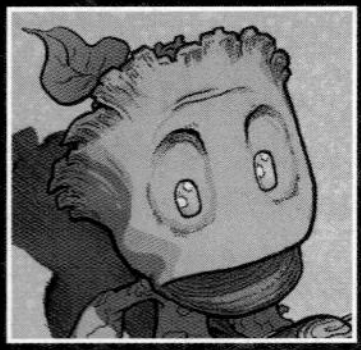

GROOT

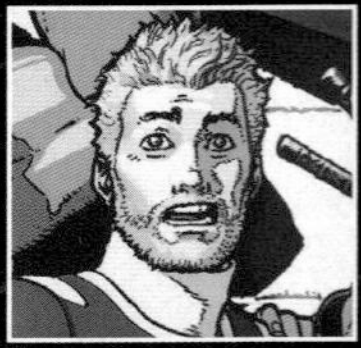

PETER QUILL (STAR-LORD)

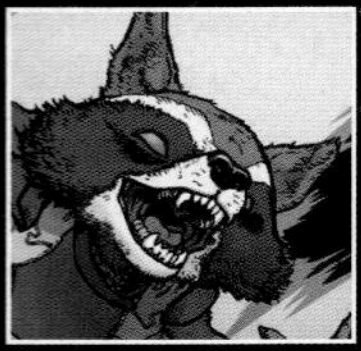

ROCKET RACCOON

AND

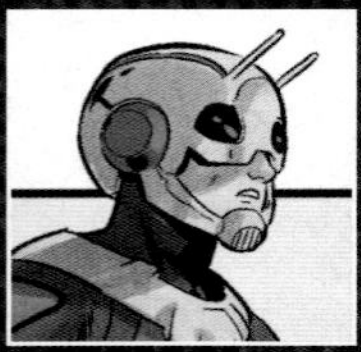

SCOTT LANG (ANT-MAN)

WITH:

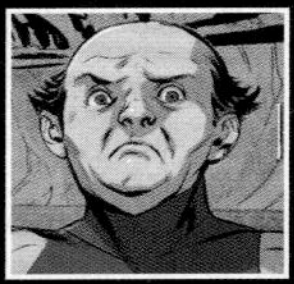

SCOTT ADSIT OF THE NOVA CORPS

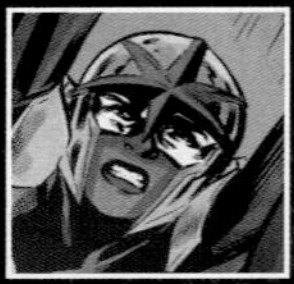

EVE BAKIAN OF THE NOVA CORPS

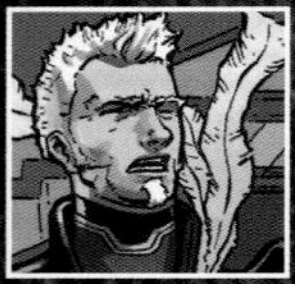

THE COLLECTOR OF THE ELDERS OF THE UNIVERSE

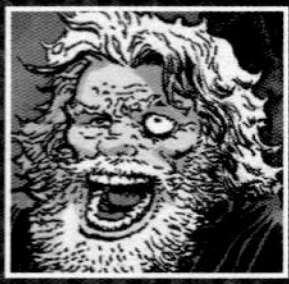

THE GARDENER OF THE ELDERS OF THE UNIVERSE

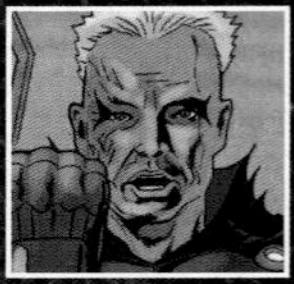

GENERAL KI'DARI OF THE FRATERNITY OF RAPTORS

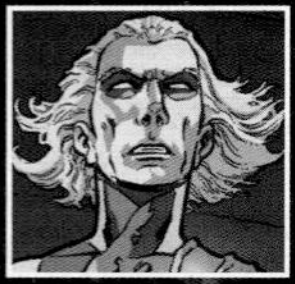

THE GRANDMASTER OF THE ELDERS OF THE UNIVERSE

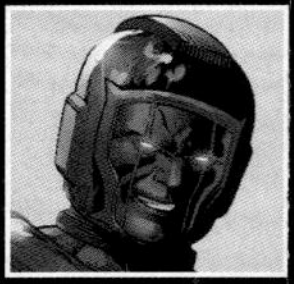

KANG THE CONQUEROR

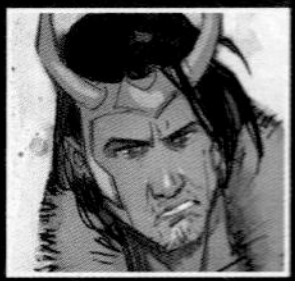

LOKI OF ASGARDIA

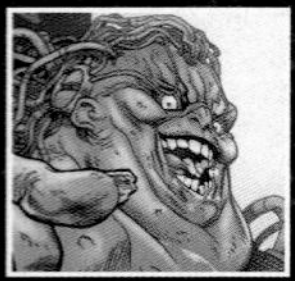

MOJO OF THE MOJOVERSE

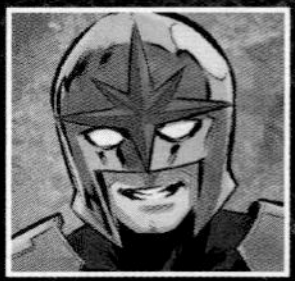

RICHARD RIDER (NOVA) OF THE NOVA CORPS

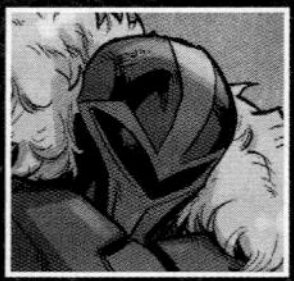

TALONAR OF THE FRATERNITY OF RAPTORS

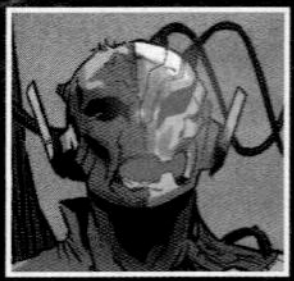

ULTRON DRONE

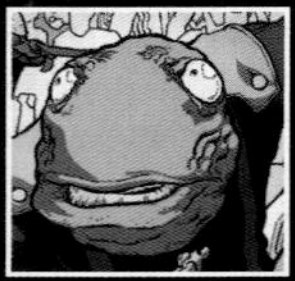

UNIDENTIFIED ALIEN #1

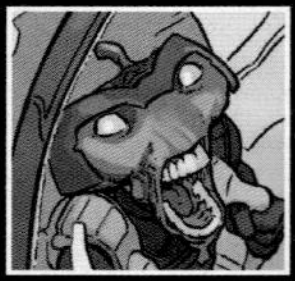

UNIDENTIFIED ALIEN #2

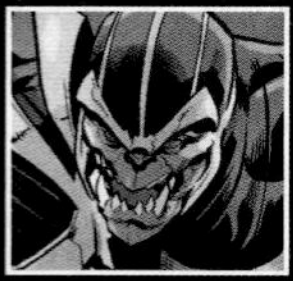

WARBRINGER OF THE CHITAURI

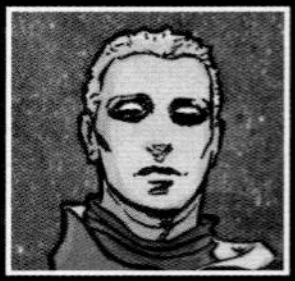

ADAM WARLOCK

TEXT – GERRY DUGGAN & MIKE O'SULLIVAN WITH BRIAN MICHAEL BENDIS
ART – ROLAND BOSCHI, MIKE HAWTHORNE, FRAZER IRVING, AARON KUDER, ROD REIS, VALERIO SCHITI, GREG SMALLWOOD & MARCUS TO
PRODUCTION – SALENA MAHINA

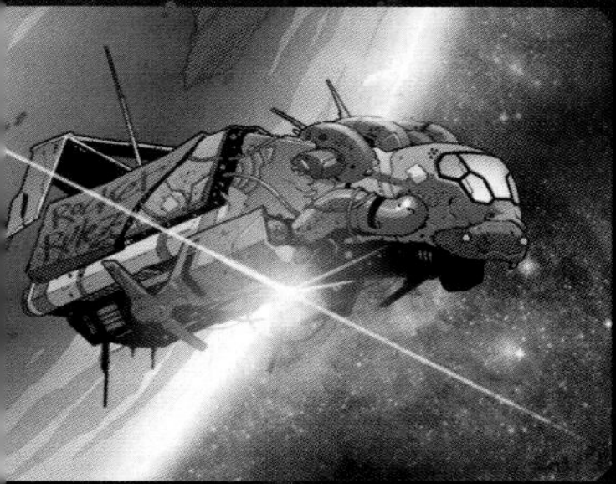

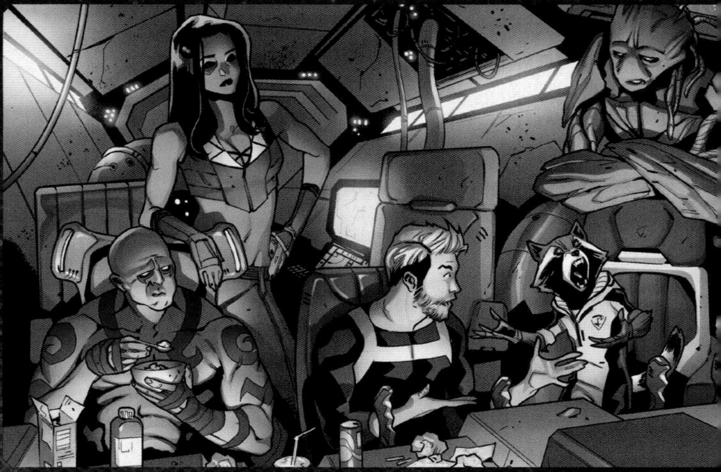

"I know the four of you each let your lives go to hell after we left Earth. . ."

Drax (the Destroyer, for cryin' out loud) became a pacifist all of a sudden, and wouldn't say why...

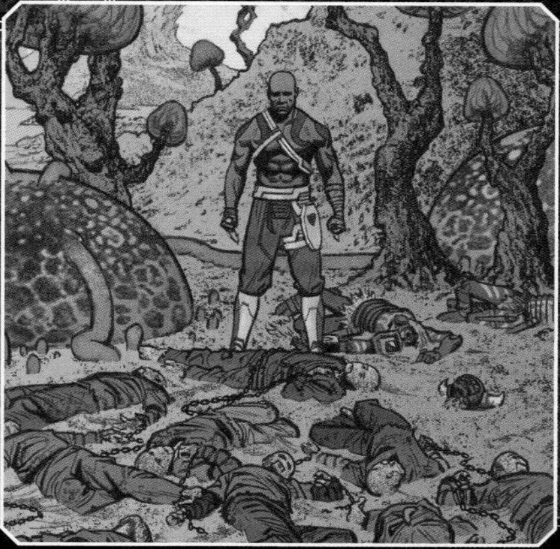

"I swelled with pride as I sent the cruel king to his death. However, the Slave King had bound his life to the slaves with the poison in their brands. I had killed them all.

"I won't fight. I will destroy no more. I'm done spilling blood."

Rocket started acting weird...

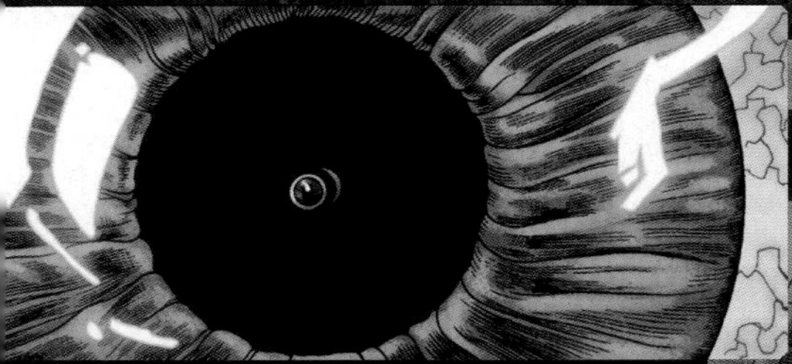

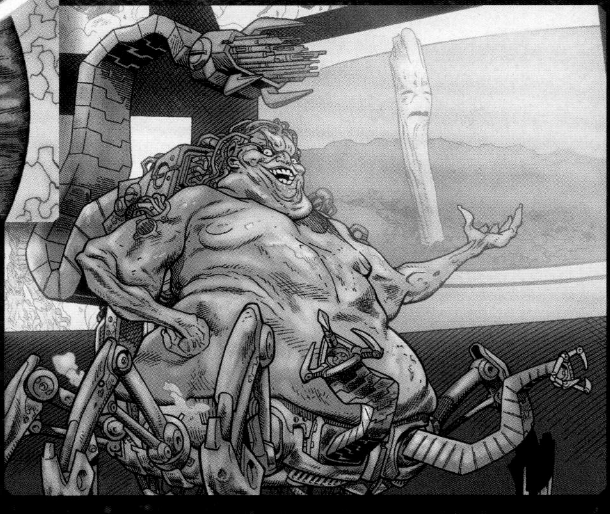

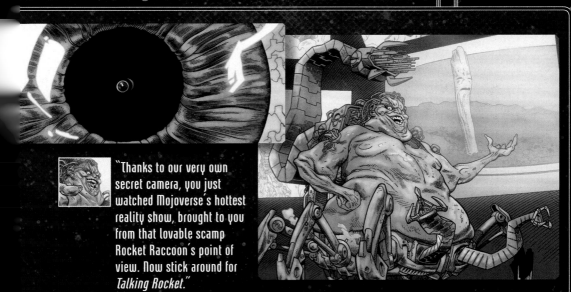

"Thanks to our very own secret camera, you just watched Mojoverse's hottest reality show, brought to you from that lovable scamp Rocket Raccoon's point of view. Now stick around for *Talking Rocket*."

...Gamora got even more intense and clammed up (not that she was all that open before)...

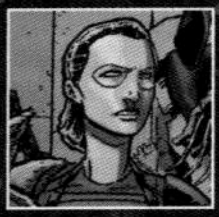

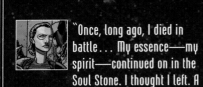

"Once, long ago, I died in battle... My essence—my spirit—continued on in the Soul Stone. I thought I left. A part of my soul is still trapped in the stone.

"I need to find the Soul Stone. It's a matter of life and death."

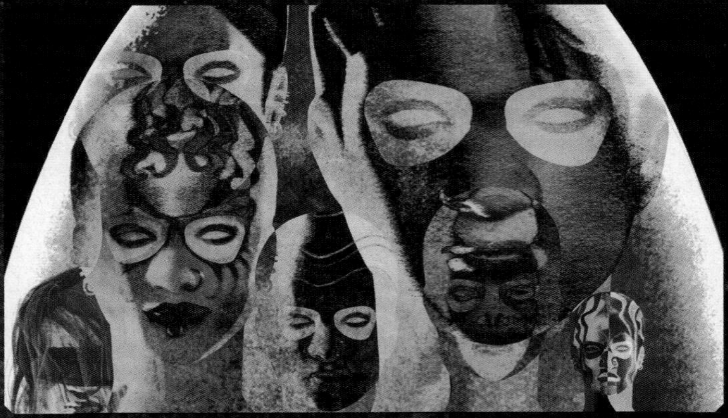

...and Groot can't regrow like usual. He got stuck as some sort of sapling version of himself.

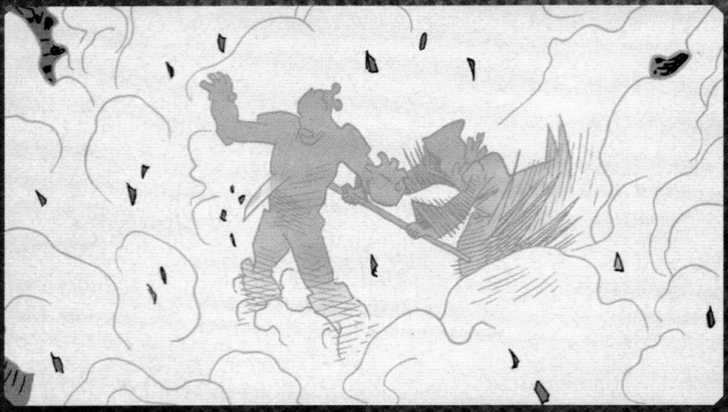

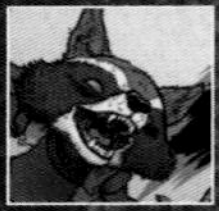

"Groot's not himself after we were attacked. He's weak. He has to sleep a lot—and he's barely grown since the attack."

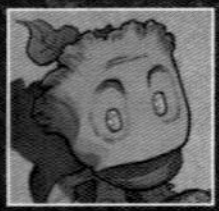

"I am Groot."

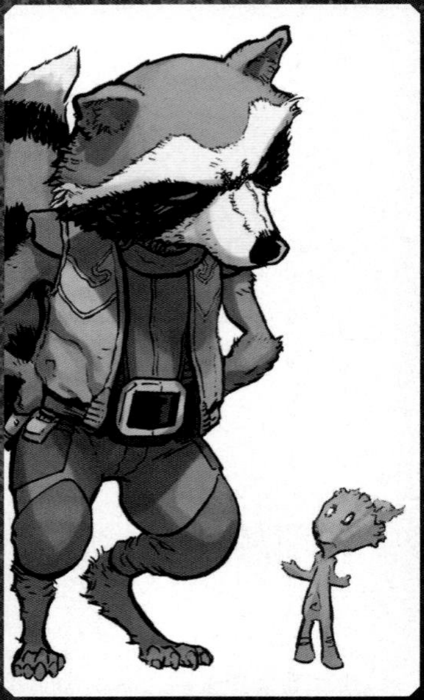

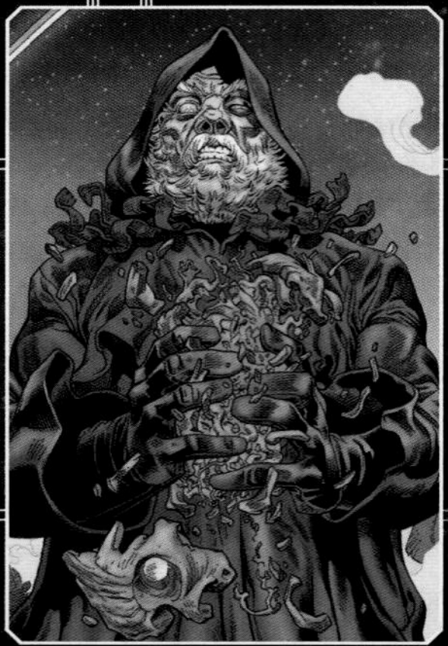

We don't know how or why. Hell, we don't even know WHO attacked him.

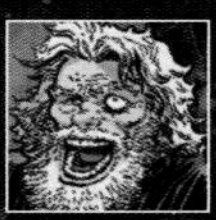

"You were born to destroy. I'm going to correct the damage that has been done to you..."

I suppose all that should have had me seeing the inevitable coming:

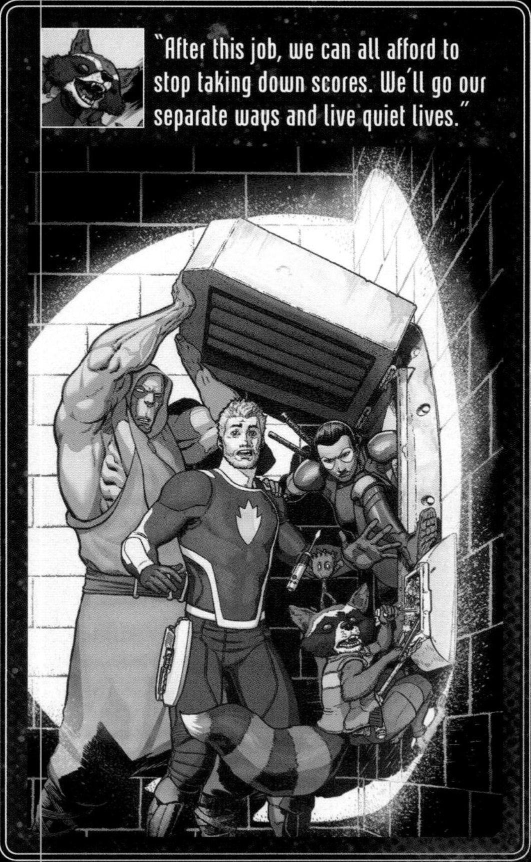
"After this job, we can all afford to stop taking down scores. We'll go our separate ways and live quiet lives."

Yeah. 1977 Fleetwood Mac, much? Anyway, then we go get *Shawshank*-ed while prepping for our last gig—not our best performance, really, but it did introduce me to my new girl...

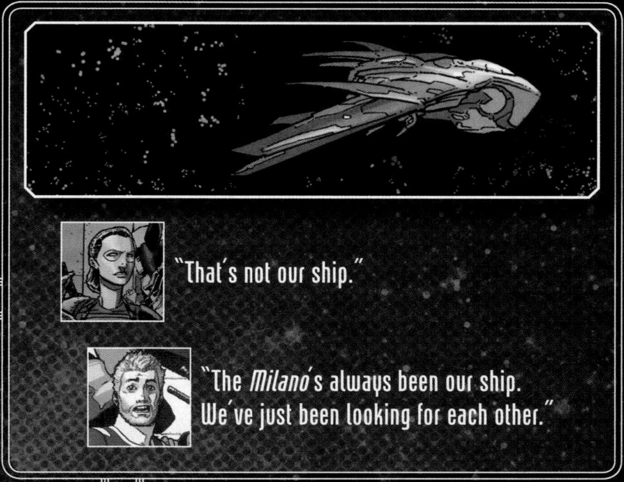
"That's not our ship."
"The *Milano*'s always been our ship. We've just been looking for each other."

Once Rocket finished building our Trojan Galactus mecha (I didn't think it would work, but, man, was it cool. Childhood mecha fantasies come true.), we were ready for the job:

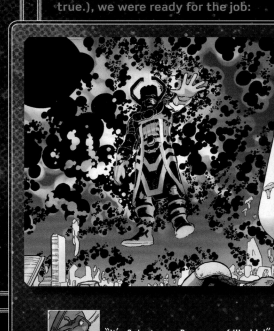

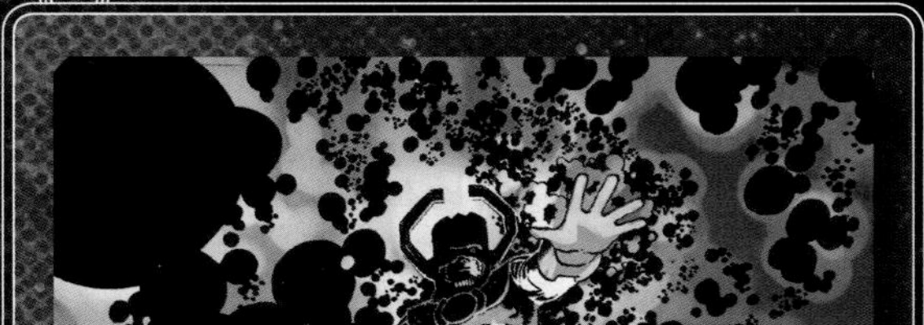
"It's Galactus—Devourer of Worlds!"

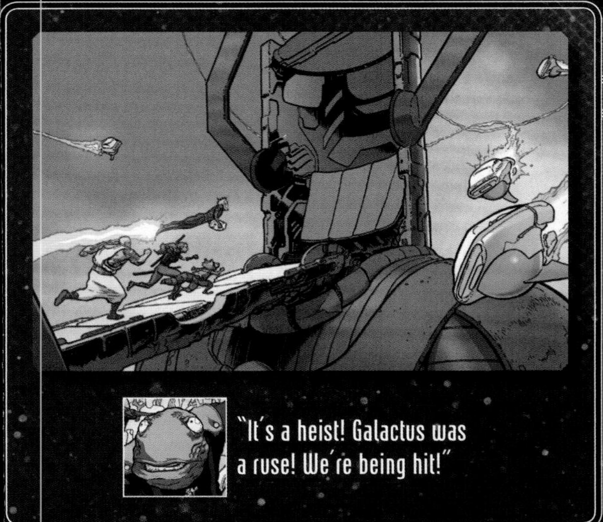
"It's a heist! Galactus was a ruse! We're being hit!"

I gotta admit, I can't believe we pulled it off.

But true to form for the Elders of the Universe, we got krutacked sideways anyway...

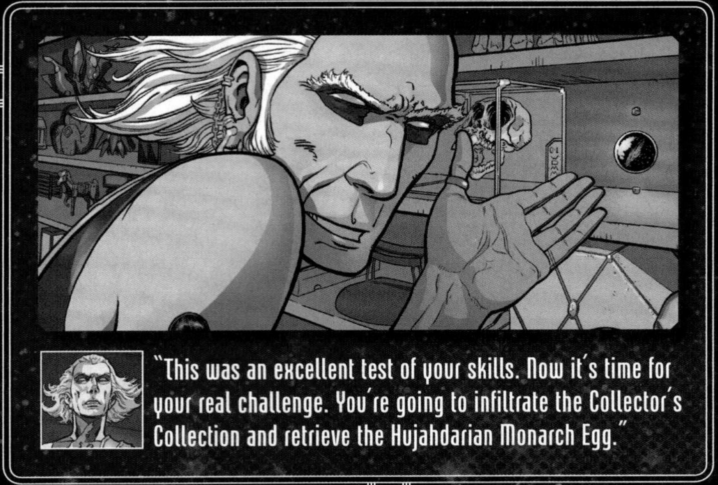
"This was an excellent test of your skills. Now it's time for your real challenge. You're going to infiltrate the Collector's Collection and retrieve the Hujahdarian Monarch Egg."

...and caught in some cosmic-bro pseudo-sibling rivalry.

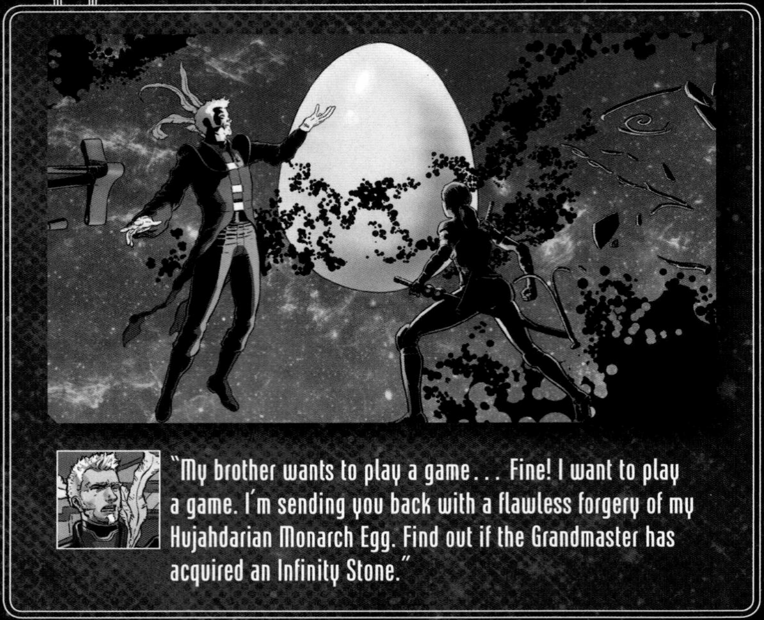
"My brother wants to play a game... Fine! I want to play a game. I'm sending you back with a flawless forgery of my Hujahdarian Monarch Egg. Find out if the Grandmaster has acquired an Infinity Stone."

As if we didn't have enough going on, in flies my new girl's crazy ex...

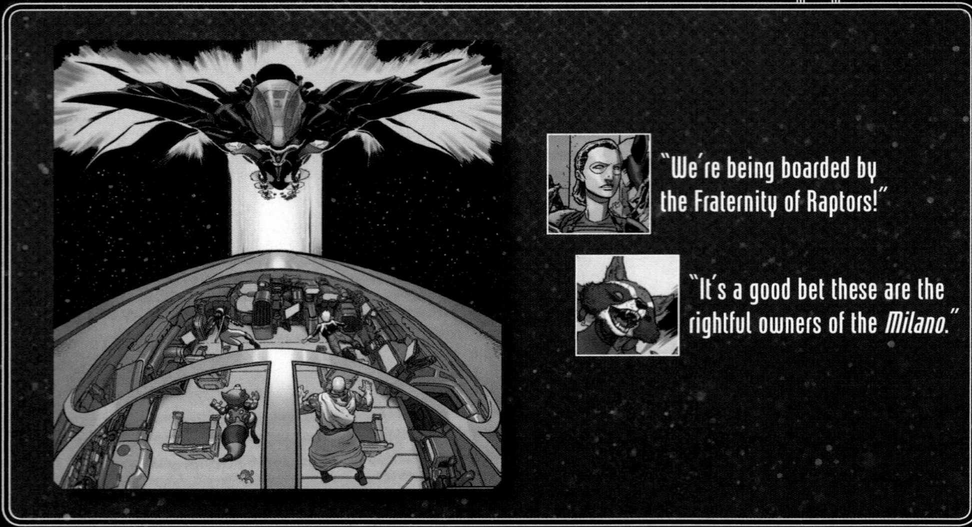
"We're being boarded by the Fraternity of Raptors!"
"It's a good bet these are the rightful owners of the *Milano*."

...who wanted their stuff back.

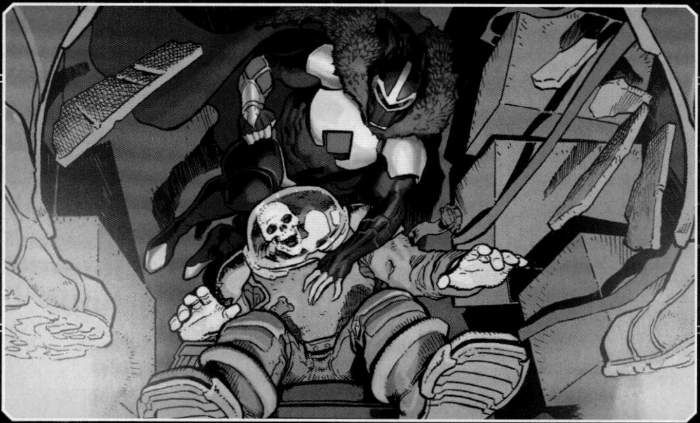

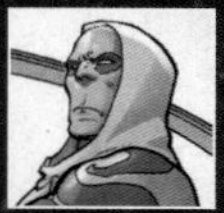

"That was very odd. They risked their lives for a corpse."

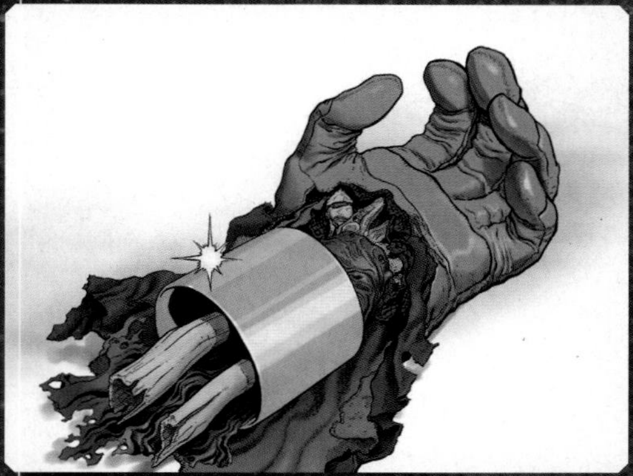

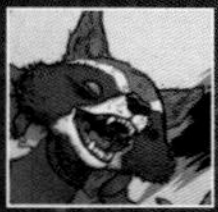

"Is that what I think it is?"

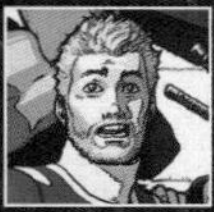

"It is . . . if you're thinking it's one half of a set of Nega-Bands."

Looks like they left some funky space bling on board and couldn't live without it after the breakup.

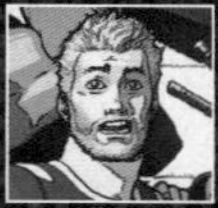

"You poisoned Rocket! I want an antidote—now!"

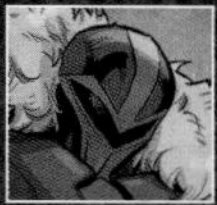

"This is the antidote for the toxin I dipped my talons in when I scratched your pet. Give me the other band."

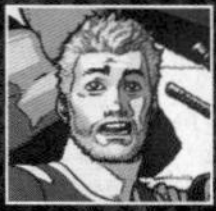

"You know these bands can open warp portals, right? Happy hunting."

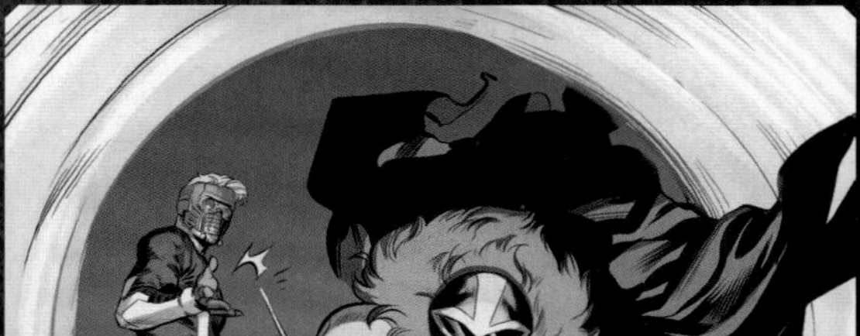

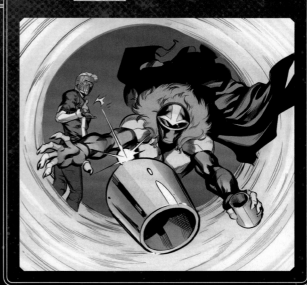

Guess it wasn't all that smart giving the bands to zealous nutbags like the Fraternity of Raptors, but Rocket needed help. No-brainer there.

Thennnnnnn Bessie goes and full-on poops all over the fan:

"Brother. It is you. I used the Guardians as my pawns, but you have reacted exactly as I hoped you would.

"The Infinity Stones are missing, and so are some of our fellow Elders. That is not a coincidence."

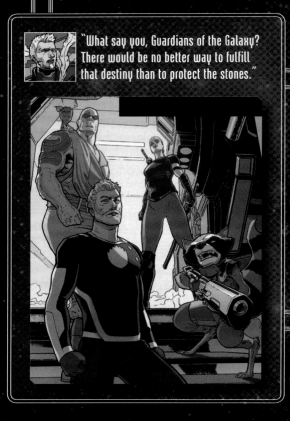
"What say you, Guardians of the Galaxy? There would be no better way to fulfill that destiny than to protect the stones."

"I am Groot."

"I vote to quest for the stones."

"You know where I stand."

"Yes. For Gamora. Not for you guys."

"Yeah. Whatever. I guess it's unanimous."

We may be the galaxy's biggest losers, but we know that keeping massive power like the six Infinity Stones from naughty schmucks is important. Reunion tour, I guess. Our own version of *The Dance*.

How much you wanna bet we ain't the only ones thinking the same thing?

"We must possess the Infinity Stones. Find the Nega-Bands, and the stones, and destroy everything in our path."

So, like always, we start looking on Earth. (Everyone else hates the *fakakta* planet, but, man, there's nowhere better to get old vinyl. Saving the universe can wait long enough for a quick run to Dimple Records, yeah?)

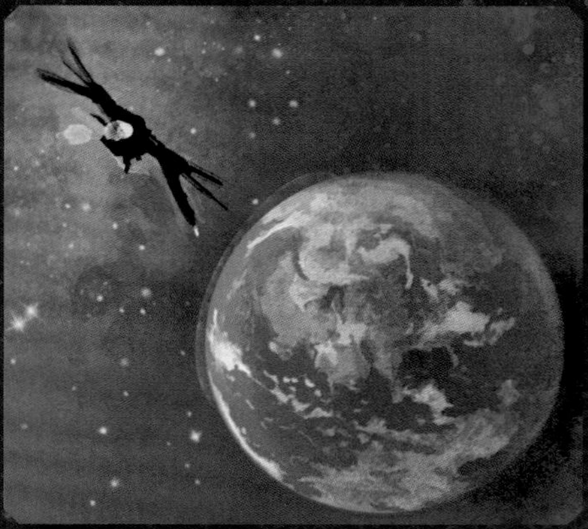

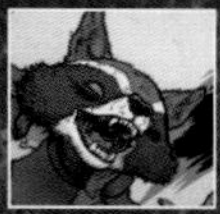

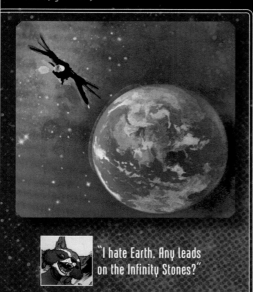

"I hate Earth. Any leads on the Infinity Stones?"

Our luck? Betcha one of Earth's (too) many baddies now knows what we're looking for.

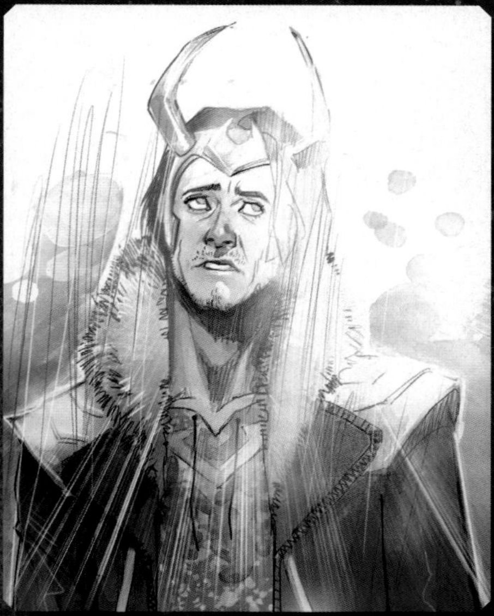

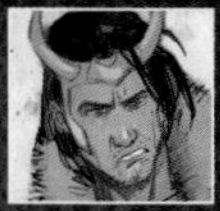

"At least I know the self-proclaimed 'Guardians' haven't found any of the stones yet. Enticing the Gardener to chop up their tree friend hasn't slowed down these half-wits."

And then the walking salad lets us know it's worse than we thought:

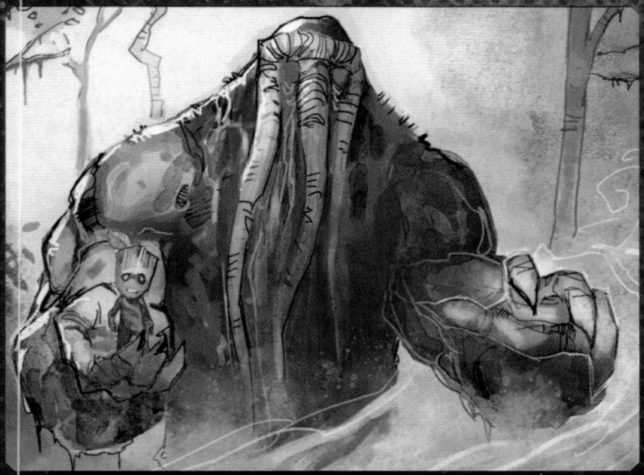

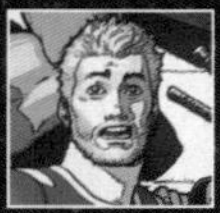

"That's Man-Thing, and he's the protector of the Nexus of all Realities."

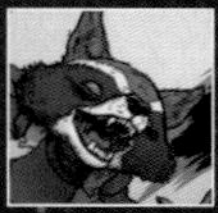

"The stones went missing in our universe and every dimension? What the hell are the odds of that?"

Aaaaaaaaaand, no matter the Guardians' dysfunction, we still got people wanting to add more fun. Enter the bigger-than-life Ant-Man...

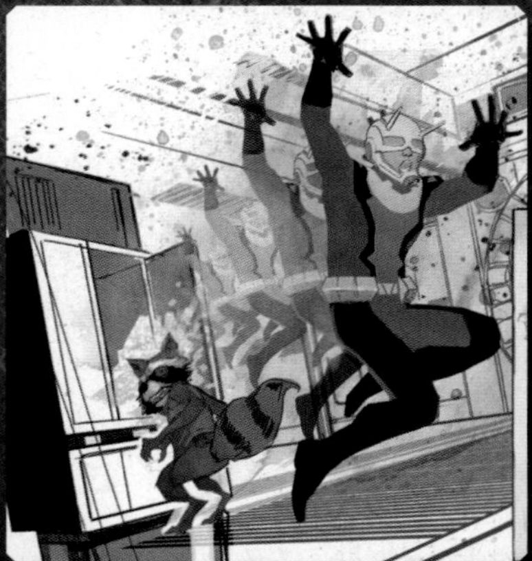

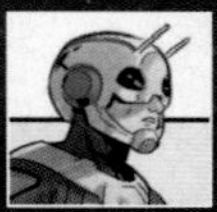

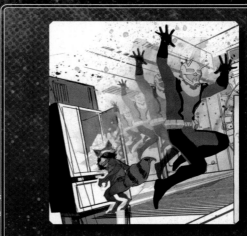

"I'm sorry for stowing away... Have you ever @#$% up so bad you had to leave a planet in shame, never to return?"

At least now there's someone on board that'll get my references.

Right then, the Cops of the Universe™ come knocking on our door to ask for our help sniffing out the bad truffles in their ranks...

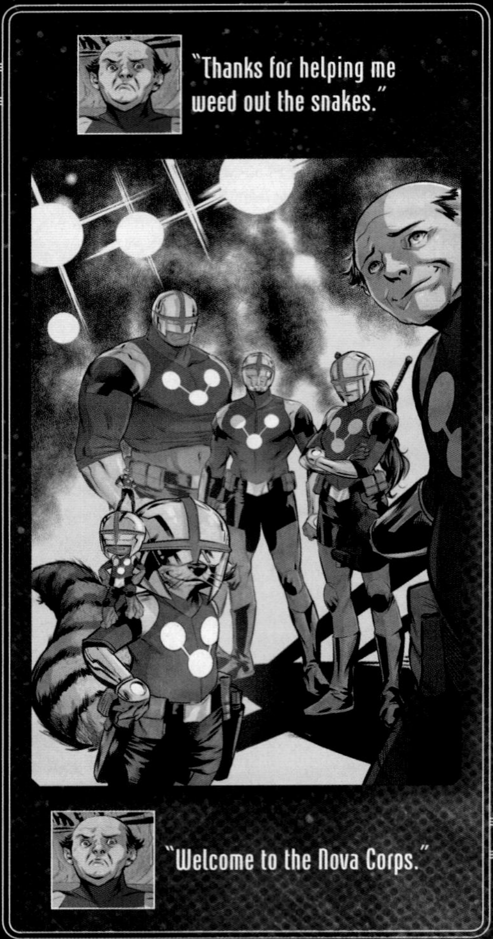
"Thanks for helping me weed out the snakes."
"Welcome to the Nova Corps."

...and I go stumble on one of the six stones at a Nova facility on the planet Xitaung.

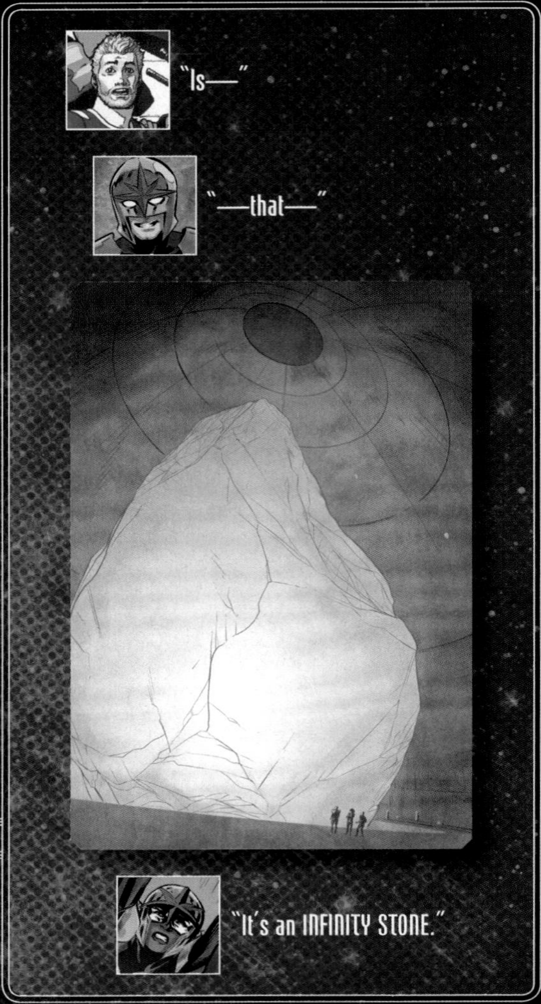
"Is—"
"—that—"
"It's an INFINITY STONE."

And when we found out murderous tree creatures were rampaging around the universe, we started getting some hints about Groot's arrested development. (God, I love that show.)

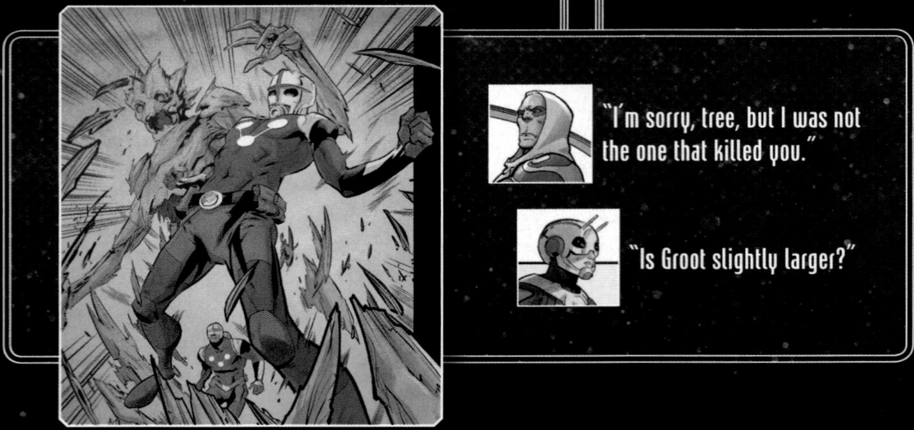
"I'm sorry, tree, but I was not the one that killed you."
"Is Groot slightly larger?"

Surprisingly, we started getting some good luck.

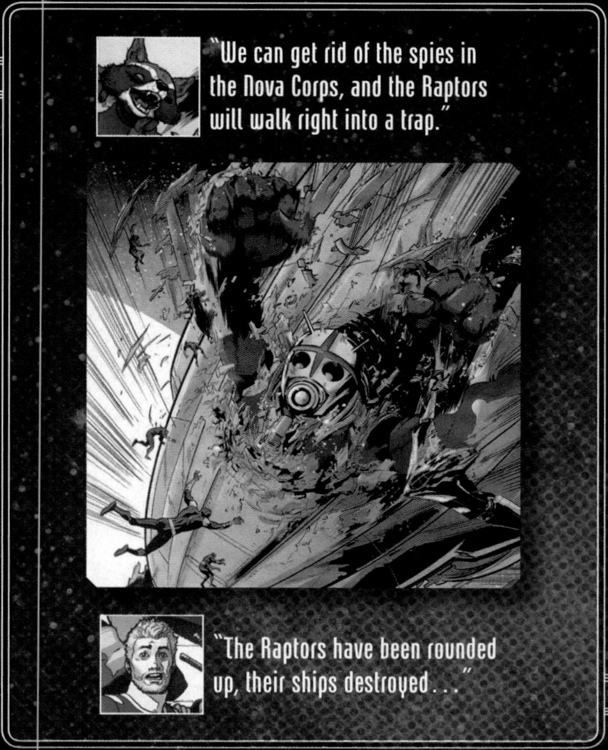
"We can get rid of the spies in the Nova Corps, and the Raptors will walk right into a trap."
"The Raptors have been rounded up, their ships destroyed..."

But I know us. It won't last.

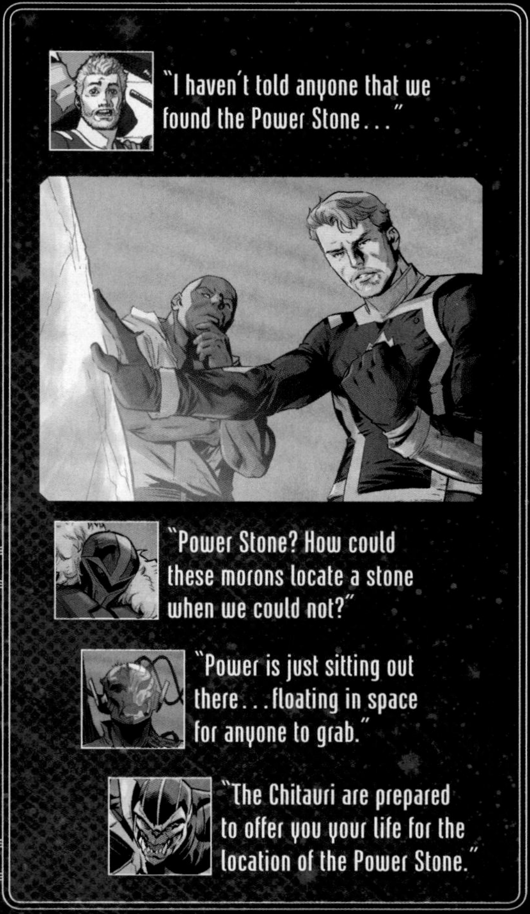
"I haven't told anyone that we found the Power Stone..."
"Power Stone? How could these morons locate a stone when we could not?"
"Power is just sitting out there...floating in space for anyone to grab."
"The Chitauri are prepared to offer you your life for the location of the Power Stone."

So, when Drax the Meditator decides he needs to stop hanging out with violent, karma-killing jerks like us, I figure where better to leave him than...?

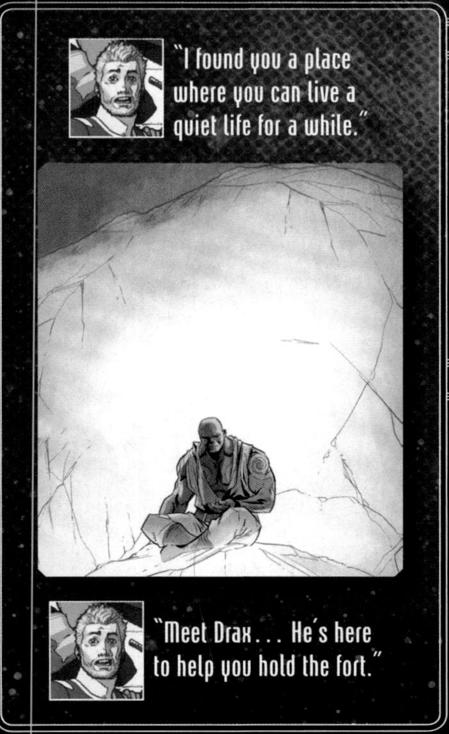
"I found you a place where you can live a quiet life for a while."
"Meet Drax... He's here to help you hold the fort."

I suppose it'd be nuts to think that since we have enough on our plate, the universe will give us a break...

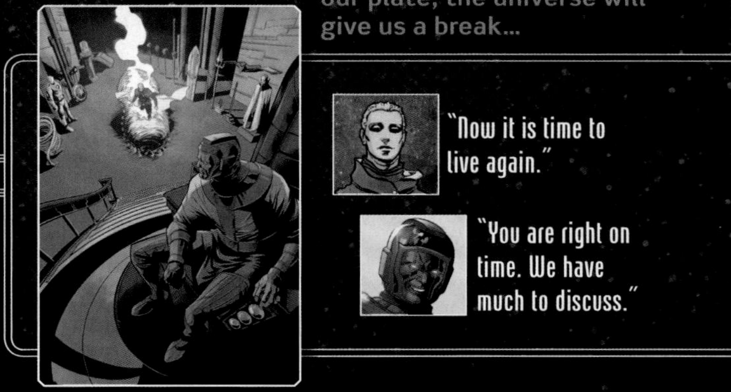
"Now it is time to live again."
"You are right on time. We have much to discuss."

...so I'll just wait for the next shoe to drop. Betcha no amount of Febreze'll keep its stank away from us.

Yeah. Wish us luck. We're gonna need it.

Hogs and fishes,

Star-Lord

THE SAGA OF THE **INFINITY STONES...**

The Infinity Stones (also called Soul Gems or Infinity Gems) are six age-old stones often sought by beings lusting after vast power. Each stone controls an aspect of creation itself. In their original iteration, the stones' powers and colors were as such:

POWER	TIME	REALITY	SOUL	MIND	SPACE
Grants unlimited strength and energy manipulation; fuels the other Infinity Stones.	Enables time travel, freezing of time and manipulation of age; in conjunction with other stones, can alter the past.	Can rewrite existence and alter reality; doing so without the other Infinity Stones poses immense risk.	Can alter a being's core personality, access the collective unconscious and confer souls to a peaceful Soulworld dimension.	Bestows limitless telepathic and telekinetic power.	Eliminates distance through teleportation and manipulation of space.

Together, the Stones grant omnipotence and omniscience to the user,
their power limited only by the wielder's imagination.

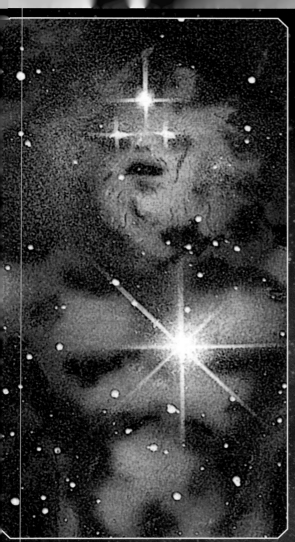

It is believed that before the existence of the eighth iteration of reality, a solitary omnipotent being ended its lonely existence, leaving behind six aspects of itself in the form of colored stones possessing limited sentience. Over millennia, the individual stones occasionally adopted hosts, ultimately becoming galactic legends.

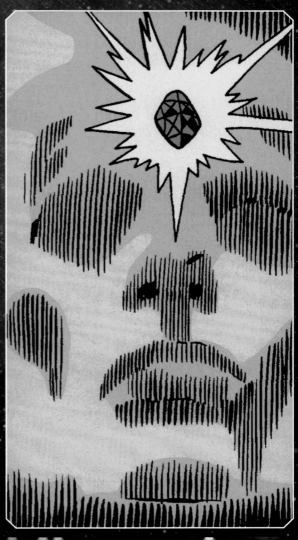

In modern times, the High Evolutionary (Herbert Wyndham) obtained multiple stones through unrevealed circumstances and used them to create Counter-Earth on the opposite side of Earth's sun, then granted the Soul Stone to genetically engineered being Adam Warlock to enable him to serve as protector of Counter-Earth's populace. Warlock proved capable of resisting the Soul Stone's oft-corrupting and parasitic nature.

After learning of the stones from an ancient scroll on a dead world, the death-obsessed Thanos of Titan located them and built a large, synthetic gem that siphoned and focused the stones' power. Seeking the love of the cosmic representation of Death, Thanos attempted to destroy the universe's stars as a sacrifice to her.

While opposing Thanos alongside heroes from Earth and throughout the universe, Adam Warlock was mortally wounded, and his soul was drawn into the Soul Stone. Warlock's soul eventually freed itself to execute Thanos by transforming him into unliving granite. The stones were somehow scattered after Thanos' defeat, but the immortal Elders of the Universe gradually found them.

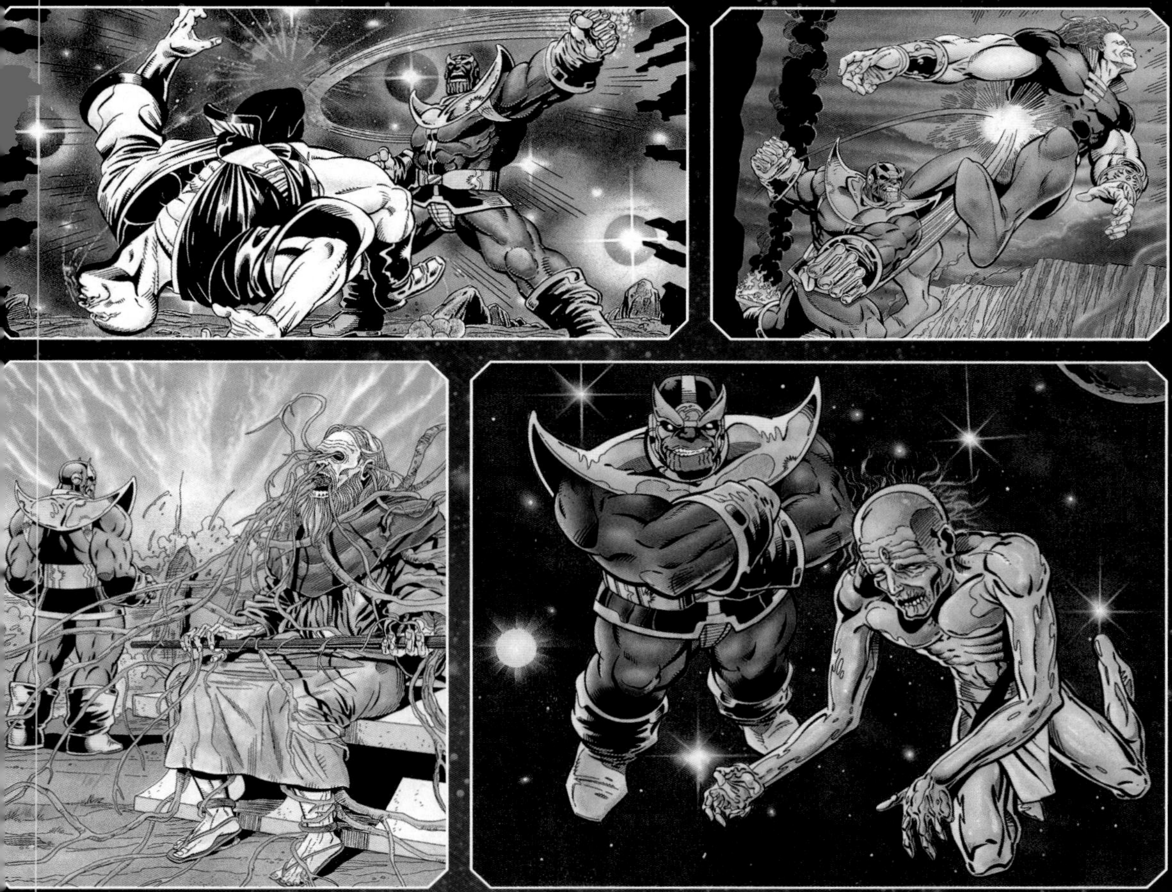

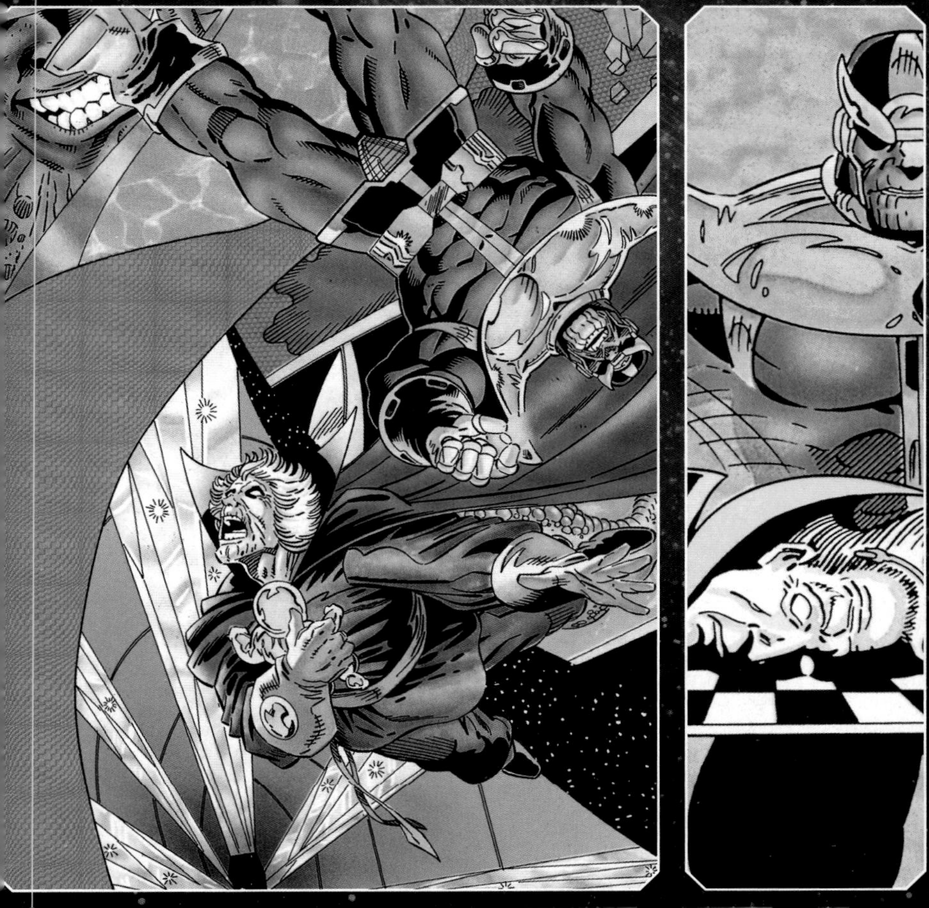

When the universe's population reached a point where more beings were alive than had ever died, Death resurrected Thanos and tasked him with correcting this imbalance. After learning of the stones' origins and true potential power, Thanos methodically and cruelly obtained them from their wielders.

Thanos embedded the stones in a gauntlet and used them to become the universe's highest power. After eliminating half of the living beings in the universe, Thanos was opposed by a collection of mortal and cosmic super-beings, including Adam Warlock, who returned to life to counter Thanos.

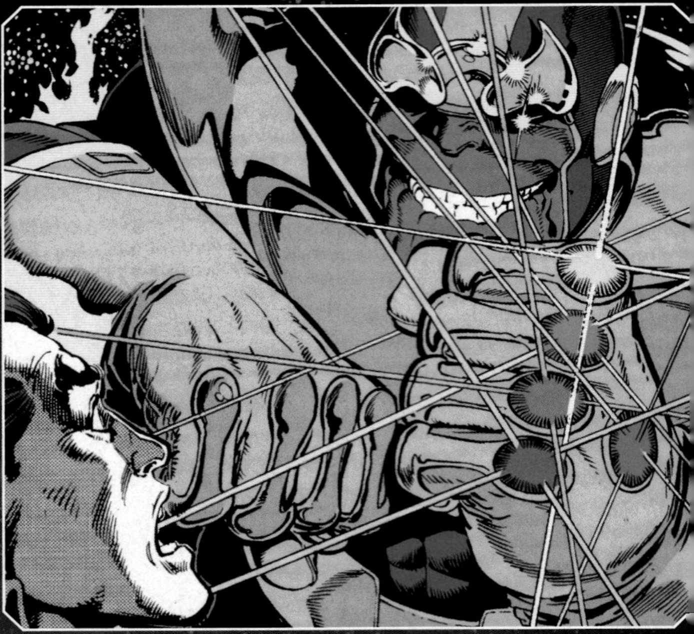

However, when he ascended to the position of the central being of creation, Thanos left his physical body—and the gauntlet—unattended. After Thanos' alleged granddaughter Nebula used the Infinity Gauntlet to undo Thanos' universal damage, Warlock forced Nebula to drop the Gauntlet so he could claim the stones for himself.

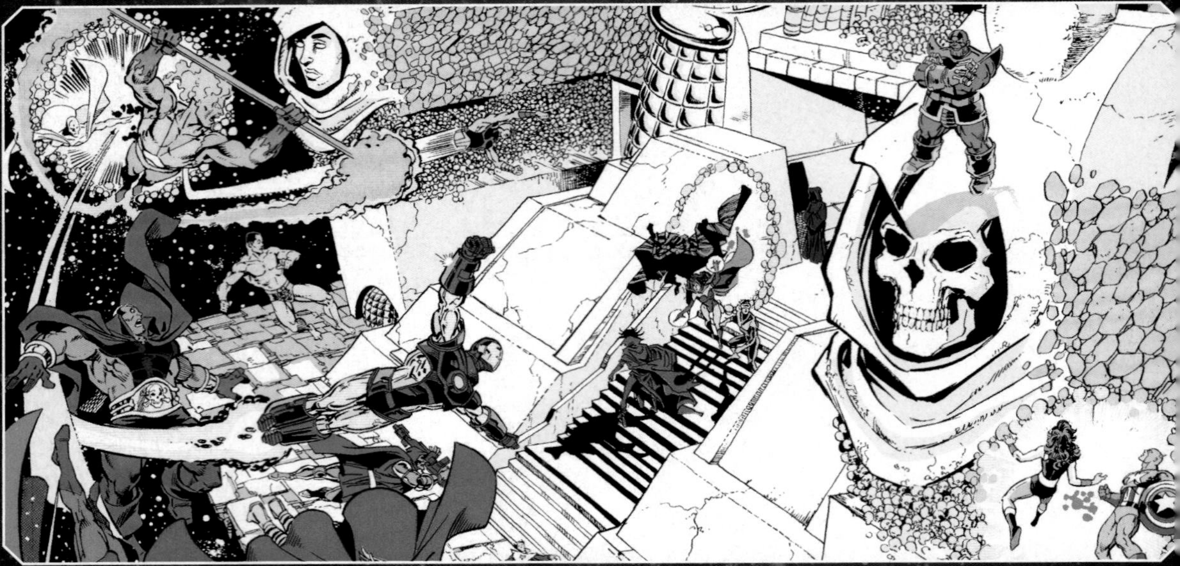

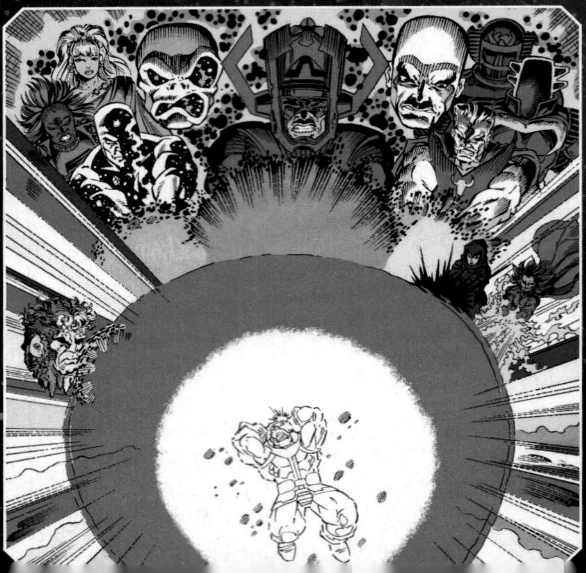

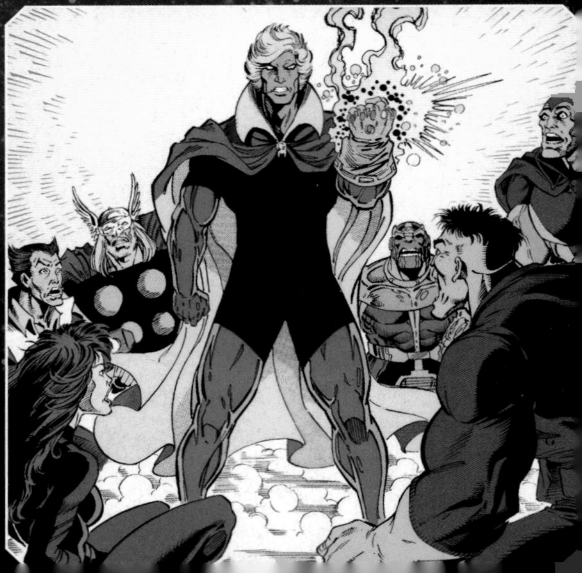

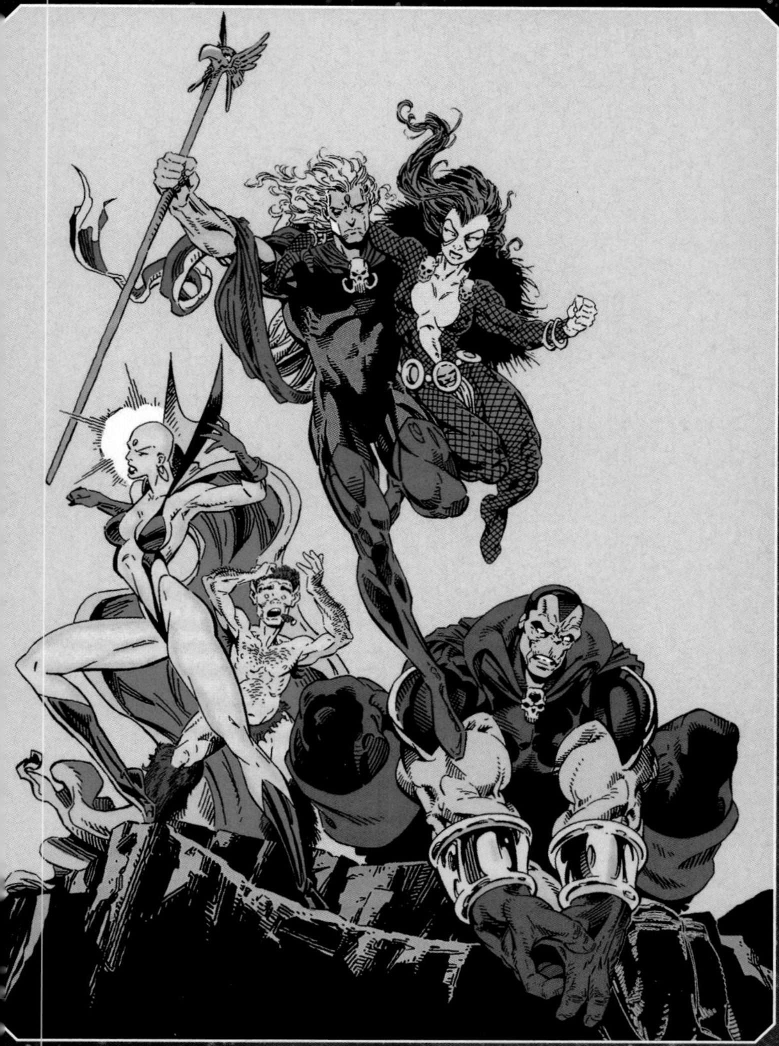

Even though Warlock subconsciously purged himself of any aspects of good and evil to be a more objective ruler of reality, the Living Tribunal—the conceptual arbiter and judge of the universe—ruled Warlock unfit to be a supreme being. The Tribunal ordered the stones to be separated and rendered them nonfunctional as a collective. Warlock gathered close allies into the Infinity Watch, entrusting each member with a stone for safekeeping.

When Warlock's evil aspect materialized as the Magus, the malevolent being empowered himself with reality-altering Cosmic Containment Units and sought the Infinity Stones as a path toward universal domination. Warlock enabled the Magus' eventual defeat by substituting the Reality Stone with a non-functional duplicate.

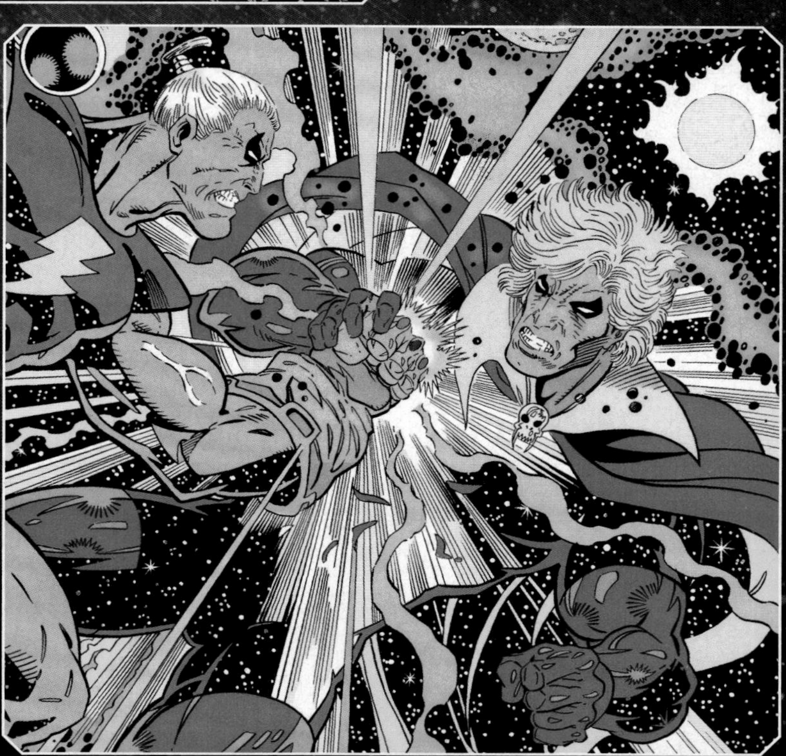

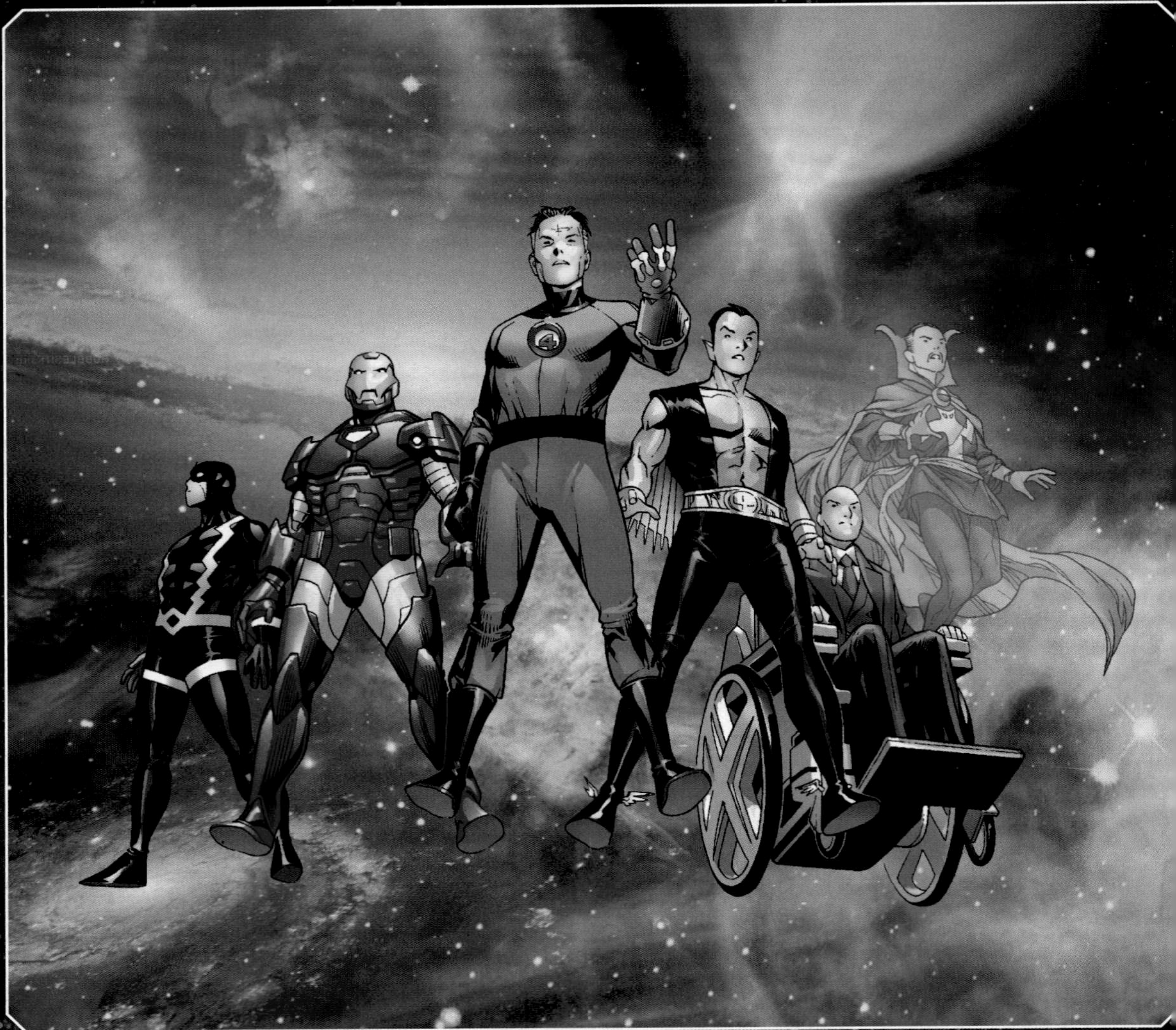

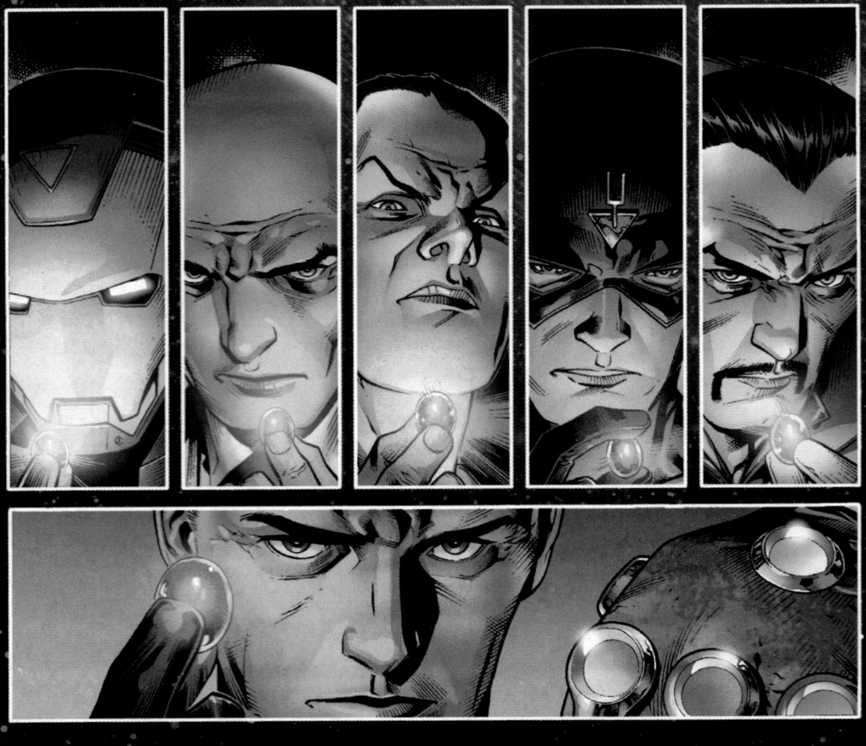

After the Infinity Watch lost possession of the stones, they were scattered throughout reality. A secret cabal of benevolent super-beings on Earth called the Illuminati—which included Mister Fantastic (Reed Richards), Iron Man (Tony Stark), Black Bolt (Blackagar Boltagon), Doctor Stephen Strange, Professor X (Charles Xavier) and Namor the Sub-Mariner—located each stone and hid them for the safety of the universe. By this time, the Living Tribunal's ruling had somehow been lifted, and the stones functioned in unison once more.

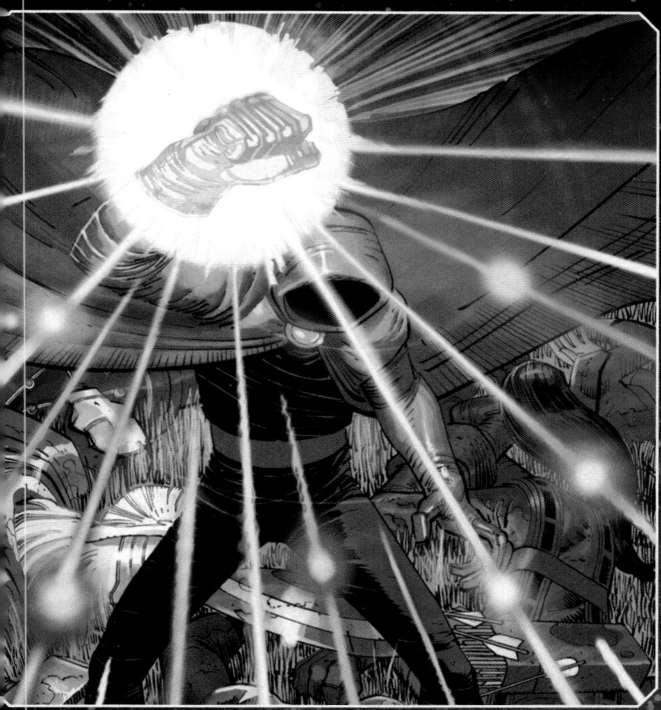

When criminal mastermind the Hood (Parker Robbins) learned of the Infinity Stones and successfully located a number of them, the Illuminati was forced to reveal its existence to the Avengers, who assembled to reclaim the stones from the Hood. After faking the Infinity Gauntlet's destruction and the Illuminati's dissolution, Iron Man distributed the stones among the clandestine cabal—now including Captain America (Steve Rogers)—for safekeeping once more.

Later, Earths from multiple realities began colliding due to a multiversal collapse. To save their Earth from destruction, the Illuminati assembled the Infinity Gauntlet and used it to stop an impending incursion. However, doing so caused five of the stones to shatter, while the Time Stone disappeared.

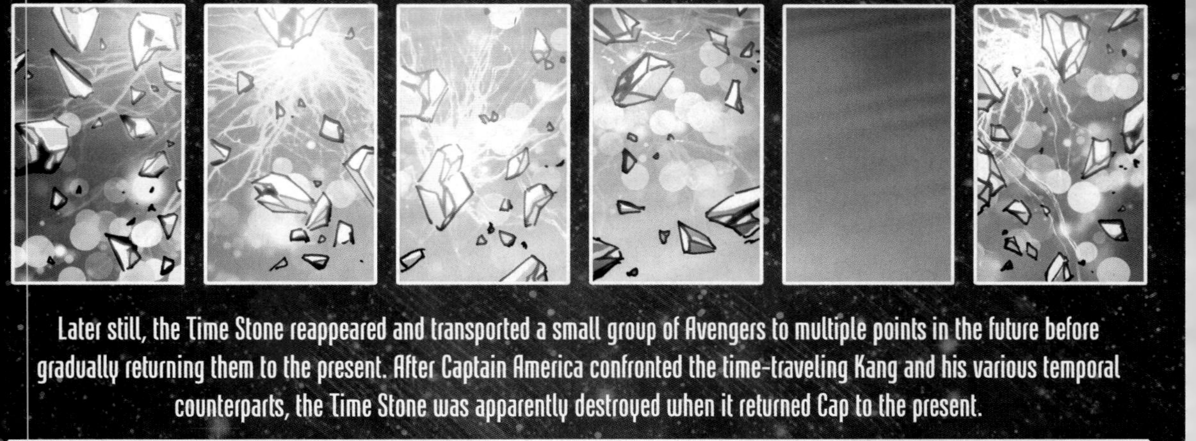

Later still, the Time Stone reappeared and transported a small group of Avengers to multiple points in the future before gradually returning them to the present. After Captain America confronted the time-traveling Kang and his various temporal counterparts, the Time Stone was apparently destroyed when it returned Cap to the present.

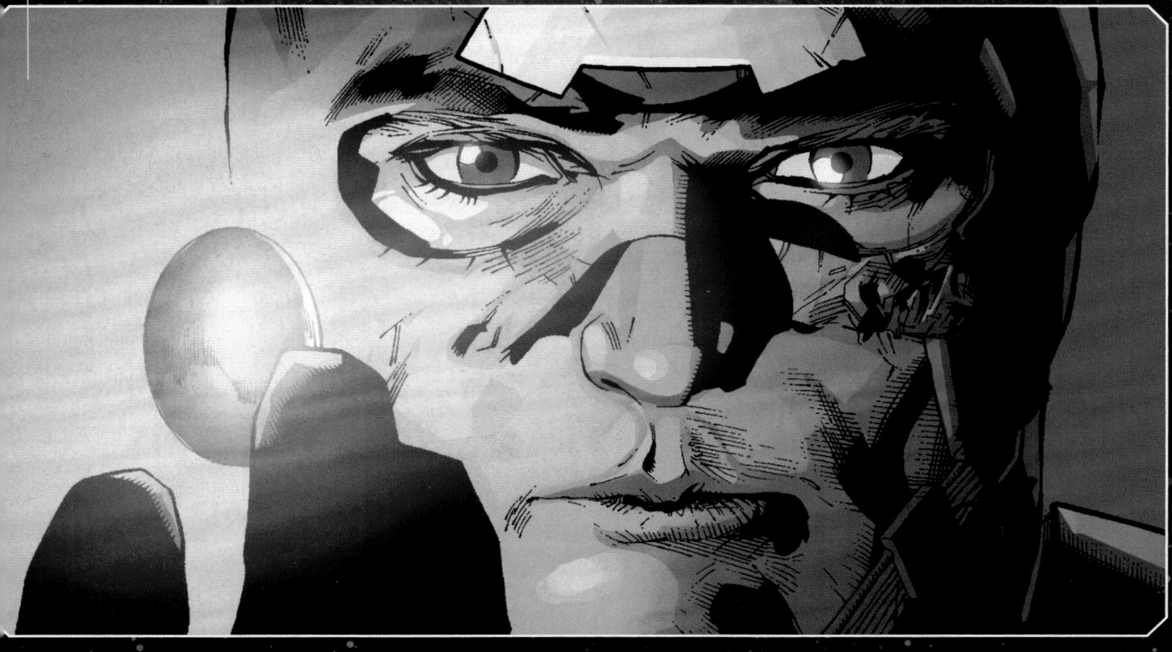

After the multiversal collapse caused the ninth iteration of reality, the Infinity Stones were also somehow re-formed. When Thanos' foster daughter, Gamora, learned that a portion of her soul remained trapped in the Soul Stone from the time she spent within the Soulworld dimension years before, she began searching for the stones; realizing the importance of the mission to Gamora, Star-Lord (Peter Quill) and her Guardians of the Galaxy teammates joined her in the quest.

While mutant hero Wolverine (Logan/ James Howlett) took the Space Stone into his protection on Earth, the now-massively sized Power Stone was located on the planet Xitaung, which led forces from the evil Chitauri and mysterious Fraternity of the Raptors to seek it; they have been opposed by the Nova Corps peacekeeping organization and the Guardians of the Galaxy.

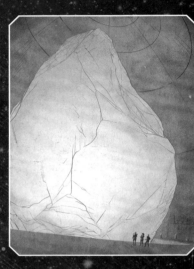

The Reality Stone has been revealed to be in the possession of the heroic Captain Marvel (Carol Danvers), Earth criminal Turk Barrett has the Mind Stone, the militant Super-Skrull (Kl'rt) has obtained the Time Stone and the murderous robot Ultron has claimed the Soul Stone.

After the Multiverse's reinstatement, five of the stones are somehow now in an uncut ingot form, and the colors of all six stones have switched; the cause of these changes has yet to be revealed.

Based on stories by **Jason Aaron, Brian Michael Bendis, Gerry Duggan, Jonathan Hickman, Brian Reed, Jim Starlin** and **Roy Thomas.**
Art by **Jim Cheung, Steve Epting, Gil Kane, Aaron Kuder, Frazer Irving, Ron Lim, George Pérez, Tom Raney, Esad Ribić, John Romita Jr., Jim Starlin** and **Marcus To.**
Text by **Mike O'Sullivan.** Design by **Adam Del Re.**